A Concise History of Russia

Accessible to students, tourists, and general readers alike, this book provides a broad overview of Russian history since the ninth century. Paul Bushkovitch emphasizes the enormous changes in the understanding of Russian history resulting from the end of the Soviet Union in 1991. Since then, new material has come to light on the history of the Soviet era, providing new conceptions of Russia's pre-revolutionary past. The book traces not only the political history of Russia, but also developments in its literature, art, and science. Bushkovitch describes well-known cultural figures, such as Chekhov, Tolstoy, and Mendeleev in their institutional and historical contexts. Though the 1917 revolution, the resulting Soviet system, and the Cold War were a crucial part of Russian and world history, Bushkovitch presents earlier developments as more than just a prelude to Bolshevik power.

Paul Bushkovitch is a professor of history at Yale University, where he has taught for the past 36 years. He is the author of *Peter the Great: The Struggle for Power, 1671–1725* (Cambridge 2001); *Religion and Society in Russia: The Sixteenth and Seventeenth Centuries* (1991); and *The Merchants of Moscow, 1580–1650* (Cambridge 1980). His articles have appeared in *Slavic Review, Russian Review, Jahrbücher für Geschichte Osteruopas*, and *Kritika*. He is a member of the editorial board for the *Cahiers du Monde Russe*.

"For any student trying to get a grasp of the essentials of Russian history this book is the place to start. To cover everything from the origins of the Russian people to the collapse of the Soviet Union in one short book requires great skill, but Paul Bushkovitch is one of the leading experts on Russian history in the world and he manages this task with great insight and panache."

– Dominic Lieven, Trinity College, Cambridge University

"This is a lively and readable account, covering more than a thousand years of Russian history in an authoritative narrative. The author deals perceptively not only with political developments, but also with those aspects of modern Russian culture and science that have had an international impact."

– Maureen Perrie, University of Birmingham

"If you want to understand Russia, and the story of the Russians, you can do no better than Paul Bushkovitch's *A Concise History of Russia*. Bushkovitch has performed a minor miracle: he's told the remarkably complicated, convoluted, and controversial tale of Russian history simply, directly, and even-handedly. He doesn't get mired in the details, lost in the twists and turns, or sidetracked by axe grinding. He tells you what happened and why, full stop. So if you want to know what happened and why in Russian history, you'd be advised to begin with Bushkovitch's masterful introduction."

– Marshall Poe, University of Iowa

"Both learned and accessible, this short history of Russia's troubled passage to the present tells a story of a state and a people who created an empire that much of the world saw as a threat. Whether as the 'Gendarme of Europe' or the 'Red Menace,' Russia and its Soviet successor (even Putin's Russia today!) have been as much misunderstood as they have been feared. Paul Bushkovitch brings us a sober reading of Russia's difficult rises and falls, expansions and contractions, reforms and revolutions. Rather than seeing the preceding millennium as a prelude to the seventy years of the Soviet Union, he gives us a rounded portrait of a country hobbled and humbled by its own geography, institutions like autocracy and serfdom, and grandiose plans to create utopia. Judicious in its judgments, this gracefully written work ranges from high politics to music and literature to open a window through which a reader might begin or renew an acquaintance with the enigmas that were Russia."

– Ronald Grigor Suny, University of Michigan

CAMBRIDGE CONCISE HISTORIES

This is a new series of illustrated "concise histories" of selected individual countries, intended both as university and college textbooks and as general historical introductions for general readers, travelers, and members of the business community.

Other titles in the series:

A Concise History of Australia, 3rd Edition
STUART MACINTYRE

A Concise History of Austria
STEVEN BELLER

A Concise History of Bolivia, 2nd Edition
HERBERT S. KLEIN

A Concise History of Brazil
BORIS FAUSTO, TRANSLATED BY ARTHUR BRAKEL

A Concise History of Britain, 1707–1975
W. A. SPECK

A Concise History of Bulgaria, 2nd Edition
R. J. CRAMPTON

A Concise History of the Caribbean
B. W. HIGMAN

A Concise History of Finland
DAVID KIRBY

A Concise History of France, 2nd Edition
ROGER PRICE

A Concise History of Germany, 2nd Edition
MARY FULBROOK

Series list continues following the Index.

A Concise History
of Russia

PAUL BUSHKOVITCH

Yale University

CAMBRIDGE UNIVERSITY PRESS
Cambridge, New York, Melbourne, Madrid, Cape Town,
Singapore, São Paulo, Delhi, Tokyo, Mexico City

Cambridge University Press
32 Avenue of the Americas, New York, NY 10013-2473, USA

www.cambridge.org
Information on this title: www.cambridge.org/9780521543231

First published 2012

Printed in the United States of America

A catalog record for this publication is available from the British Library.

Library of Congress Cataloging in Publication data
Bushkovitch, Paul.
A concise history of Russia / Paul Bushkovitch.
p. cm. – (Cambridge concise histories)
Includes bibliographical references and index.
ISBN 978-0-521-83562-6 (hardback : alk. paper) – ISBN 978-0-521-54323-1
(pbk. : alk. paper)
1. Russia – History. 2. Soviet Union – History. 3. Russia (Federation) –
History. I. Title.
DK37.B86 2011
947–dc23 2011026272

ISBN 978-0-521-83562-6 Hardback
ISBN 978-0-521-54323-1 Paperback

CONTENTS

List of Figures   *page* ix

Abbreviations   xi

Acknowledgments   xiii

Prologue   xv

1. RUSSIA BEFORE RUSSIA   1

2. MOSCOW, NOVGOROD, LITHUANIA,
   AND THE MONGOLS   19

3. THE EMERGENCE OF RUSSIA   37

4. CONSOLIDATION AND REVOLT   59

5. PETER THE GREAT   79

6. TWO EMPRESSES   101

7. CATHERINE THE GREAT   117

8. RUSSIA IN THE AGE OF REVOLUTION   138

9. THE PINNACLE OF AUTOCRACY   155

10. CULTURE AND AUTOCRACY   172

11. THE ERA OF THE GREAT REFORMS   186

12. FROM SERFDOM TO NASCENT CAPITALISM   208

13. THE GOLDEN AGE OF RUSSIAN CULTURE   228

14. RUSSIA AS AN EMPIRE   249

15. AUTOCRACY IN DECLINE   272

16. WAR AND REVOLUTION   293

17. COMPROMISE AND PREPARATION   318

18. REVOLUTIONS IN RUSSIAN CULTURE   334

19. BUILDING UTOPIA   351

20. WAR   371

21. GROWTH, CONSOLIDATION, AND STAGNATION   393

22. SOVIET CULTURE   413

23. THE COLD WAR   429

Epilogue: The End of the USSR   447

Further Reading   461

Index   473

LIST OF FIGURES

1. Vladimir Cathedral of the Dormition (Twelfth Century) *page* 14
2. Birchbark Document 210 25
3. Kirillov Monastery (15–16 centuries) 30
4. "Kremlenagrad" 44
5. Peter the Great 89
6. Bashkirs 124
7. Catherine the Great 127
8. St. Petersburg c. 1800 144
9. Village Council 158
10. Alexander II 190
11. Russian Peasant Girls 217
12. *Ilya Muromets* 221
13. Tchaikovsky 235
14. Repin/Tolstoy 246
15. Nomadic Kirghiz 268
16. Witte 277
17. Nicholas II 278
18. Lenin and Colleagues 307
19. Stalin and Others at Gorky's funeral 364
20. Ilyushin II 384

ABBREVIATIONS

BRBML   Beinecke Rare Book and Manuscript Library
LOC   Library of Congress
LOC PG   Library of Congress, Prokudin-Gorsky Collection
NASM   Smithsonian National Air and Space Museum
NYPL   New York Public Library
YCBA   Yale Center for British Art

ACKNOWLEDGMENTS

The first chapters of this book were written at the University of Aberdeen, Scotland, during a semester of residence with the support of the Carnegie Trust for the Universities of Scotland. Without the Carnegie Trust and Aberdeen University the beginning would have been much more difficult. I owe a particular debt of gratitude to Paul Dukes, Robert Frost, Karin Friedrich, Jane Ohlmeyer, and Duncan Rice, in their different ways my hosts for an eventful time. Over the years my colleagues have kindly read and commented on many of the chapters, letting me know when I was on the right track and when I was not. For reading as well as discussion and bibliographical help, I thank Nikolaos Chrissidis, Laura Engelstein, Hilary Fink, Daniel Kevles, John MacKay, Edgar Melton, Bruce Menning, and Samuel Ramer. Many years of conversation about Russian culture with Vladimir Alexandrov, Katerina Clark, Nikolai Firtich, Harvey Goldblatt, Vladimir Golshtein, Andrea Graziosi, Charles Halperin, Moshe Lewin, Alexander Schenker, and Elizabeth Valkenier made many chapters much richer than I could have made them alone. Valerie Hansen and Frank Turner provided more help than they ever realized. As ever, Tatjana Lorkovic was invaluable.

I would also like to thank Tom Morehouse of the New England Air Museum, Kate Igoe of the Smithsonian National Air and Space Museum, Maria Zapata of the Haas Art Library of Yale University, David Thompson and Maria Singer of the Yale Center for British Art, and Kathryn James and E. C. Schroeder of the Beinecke Rare

Book and Manuscript Library of Yale University. Their courtesy and professionalism were invaluable in the search for suitable images.

Maija Jansson suffered through the long gestation and birth pains of the book, putting up with a distracted and often crabby author. She read the whole manuscript, some of it several times, and kept reminding me that it would come to an end, and so it did. To her I dedicate the result.

PROLOGUE

Russia is not an idea. It is a specific country, with a particular place on the globe, a majority language and culture, and a very concrete history. Yet for most of the twentieth century, outside of its boundaries, it has been an idea, not a place – an idea about socialism. Tremendous debates have raged over its politics, economics, and culture, most of them conducted by and for people who did not know the language, never went there, and knew very little about the country and its history. Even the better informed wrote and spoke starting from presuppositions about the desirability or undesirability of a socialist order. Some were crude propagandists, but even the more conscientious, those who learned the language and tried to understand the country, began by posing questions that came from their assumptions about socialism. The result was a narrow agenda of debate: was a planned economy effective or not? How many political prisoners were there? How could the Soviets put a man in space? Should the system be called socialism, communism, or totalitarianism? Was "communism" a result of Russian history? Did the Russian intelligentsia prepare the way for communism, unintentionally or not? Did the gradual modernization of Russia make 1917 inevitable? In all these debates the history of Russia up to the moment of the revolution was just a preface.

In Russia the collapse of the Soviet Union brought to light a flood of historical publications. These publications include numerous monographs on a great variety of topics, many biographies, and a massive quantity of publications of the various records of the

Soviet regime, including the deliberations of its leaders. The aim of these publications was to illuminate the areas previously closed to investigation, and naturally the first post-Soviet writings were devoted to the most controversial or mysterious issues. Books on the Ribbentrop-Molotov pact of 1939, collectivization, and famine; publications of Stalin's private correspondence; and other issues were first on the agenda. Western historians participated in these publications, which gave a whole new understanding of the contentious issues of Soviet history. Yet the result is far from perfect. As the document publications and monographs continue to pour out in Russia and abroad, they pose more and more questions that historians used to the politicized debates of the Cold War era never thought about. Paradoxically, it seems harder rather than easier to understand the story of the Soviet era of Russian history. The present work reflects this difficulty, and the reader will find many questions left unresolved.

The collapse of the Soviet Union, paradoxically, has had as much or more effect on the writing about Russia's history before 1917. Now the earlier history is not just a preface but a millennium of time that no longer ends in the Soviet experience, however important that may be. The flood of new publications, in this case mainly from historians in Russia, includes virtually every period and aspect of Russian history before 1917. There are now not just biographies of tsars and empresses, but also of major and minor political figures and fairly ordinary people. Local history has come into being, providing the kind of concrete knowledge of the variety of the country's history that has been routine in other countries for a long time.

Russia in its history and in its present is a mix of many different elements. Until the fifteenth century the people called themselves and their land "Rus," not Russia ("Rossiia"), and it included many territories not now within Russian boundaries. From its inception it contained peoples who were not Russian or even Slavic, but whom Russians understood as integral parts of their society. By 1917 the tsars and millions of Russian settlers in the steppe and Siberia had acquired a territory far beyond the original medieval boundaries, and the Soviet state conserved most of that area. Consequently its history has to extend beyond the boundaries of today's Russian

Federation and incorporate the various incarnations of Russia as well as its diversity.

A society economically backward until the twentieth century, Russia shared many traits with nearly all pre-industrial societies – primitive agriculture, small and few cities, mass illiteracy. Russia's historical fate was to become the largest contiguous political unit in the world and eventually expand over the whole of northern Asia. It was a realm equally distant from Western Europe and from the Mediterranean world. It covered huge areas but was extremely thinly populated until the end of the seventeenth century. For the first seven hundred years its peripheral status was strengthened by its adherence to Europe's minority Christian faith, Orthodoxy, rather than any of the Western European churches. Then, with Peter the Great, Russia entered European culture within a single generation and participated in all phases of European cultural life onwards, starting with and including the Enlightenment. Cultural evolution was easier and faster than social and political change, creating a society with a modern culture and an archaic social and political structure. The rapid industrialization of Russia after 1860 in turn created tensions that led to the spread of Western ideas that were not necessarily the dominant ones in the West. Thus for most of the twentieth century Marxism, an ideology born in the Rhineland out of the philosophy of G. W. F. Hegel combined with British economics and French utopian socialism, reordered Russian society while remaining marginal in the lands of its birth.

In the West itself, Russia was simply remote. For the English poet John Milton it was "the most northern Region of Europe reputed civil." Milton's view reflected the way Europeans perceived Russia from the Renaissance onward, as part of Europe and as "northern" rather than "eastern." It is only in the nineteenth century that Russia became "eastern" to Europeans, and to many Russians as well. In nineteenth-century Western Europe, "eastern" was not a compliment: it implied that Russia, like the lands the West was then colonizing, was barbaric, despotic, and dirty, and the people probably were inferior in some way. Europeans did not learn Russian, and they did not study the country, and neither did Americans, until the beginning of the Cold War. Even when Tolstoy and Tchaikovsky had become part of the Western pantheon, the country as a whole was still a mystery, as Winston Churchill insisted. The uniqueness of the Soviet order only increased that element of mystery. In contrast, when the French Revolution occurred, it took place in the center of Western Europe among a people whose language had become the principle language of international communication. The Russian Revolution took place in a far country, and few outside Russia knew the language or had any understanding of the country and its history. Even though the Bolsheviks created a new society following a Western ideology, it necessarily remained an enigma in the West.

Had the Russian Revolution found no followers abroad, perhaps Soviet society would have remained a peculiar system studied only by a few devoted scholars. Its impact however, was enormous, and remains so to this day. China, the world's most populous country is still ruled by a Communist Party that shows no signs of sharing power, whatever its economic policies. Communism was the central issue of world politics for two generations of the twentieth century. The inevitable consequence was that commentators in the West, journalists or scholars, even ordinary tourists looked at an idea, the Soviet version of socialism, not at a specific country with a specific history. With the end of the Soviet Union, Russian history no longer has to be the story of the unfolding of one or another idea. It has become the continuous history of a particular people in a particular place. The present book is an attempt to reflect that change. It seeks above all to tell the story and explain it where possible. In many cases explanations are hard to come by, but it is the hope that the reader will find food for reflection in a history that is nothing if not dramatic.

Map 1. Kievan Rus' in the Eleventh Century.

Map 2. Russia in the First Half of the Sixteenth Century.

Map 3. Russia at the Time of Peter the Great.

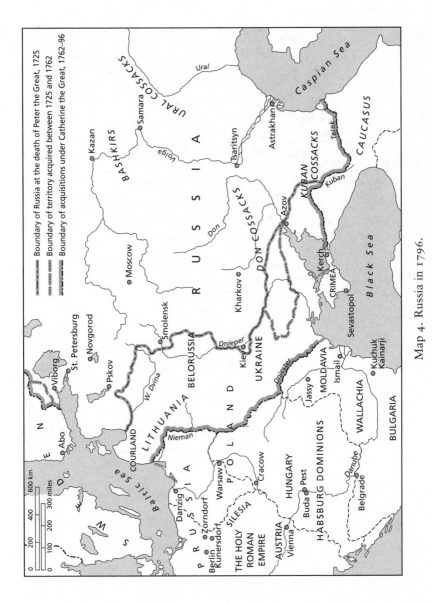

Map 4. Russia in 1796.

Boundary of Russia at the death of Peter the Great, 1725
Boundary of territory acquired between 1725 and 1762
Boundary of acquisitions under Catherine the Great, 1762–96

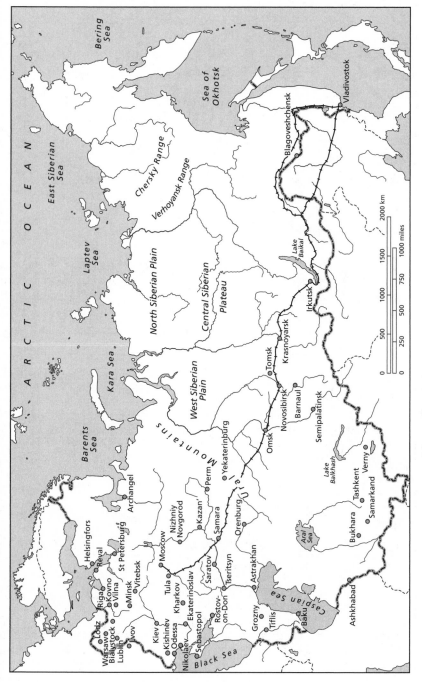

Map 5. Russia in 1913.

Scale:
0   200   400   600   800 km
0   100   200   300   400   500 miles

Farthest limit of German advance

Soviet Union boundary, 1941

Murmansk

Kandalaksha

Archangel

N. Dvina

Kotlas

Kirov

SWEDEN

FINLAND (War with Russia, 1939–40)

KARELIA

Helsinki

Leningrad ⊙ Tikhvin

Vologda

ESTONIA

Baltic Sea

Riga
LATVIA

LITHUANIA

Danzig

EAST PRUSSIA ⊙ Vilna ⊙ Smolensk

Kalinin

Volga

Kazan

Gorkii

Mozhaisk ⊙ Moscow

Oka

Tula

Kuibyshev

Minsk

BELORUSSIA
⊙ Bialystock
Brest

Warsaw ⊙

Orel ⊙

POLAND

U K R A I N E

Kursk ⊙

Voronezh

Volga

Kiev

Kharkov ⊙

Don

Stalingrad

SLOVAKIA

Lvov

Dnepropetrovsk

⊙ Budapest
HUNGARY

BESSARABIA

Rostov-on-Don

R O M A N I A

Belgrade

Dnieper

Kerch

Kuban

YUGOSLAVIA

Bucharest ⊙

Sevastopol ⊙ Yalta

Novorossiisk

Mozdok

Terek

⊙ Sofia
BULGARIA

Black Sea

CAUCASUS

Batum

Istanbul

T U R K E Y

Erivan

Map 6. Soviet Union in the Second World War, 1941–5.

I

Russia before Russia

Russian history begins with the polity that scholars have come to call Kiev Rus, the ancestor of modern Russia. Rus was the name that the inhabitants gave to themselves and their land, and Kiev was its capital. In modern terms, it embraced all of Belarus, the northern half of the Ukraine, and the center and northwest of European Russia. The peoples of these three modern states are the Eastern Slavs, who all speak closely related languages derived from the East Slavic language of Kiev Rus. In the west its neighbors were roughly the same as the neighbors of those three states today: Hungary, Poland, the Baltic peoples, and Finland. In the north Kiev Rus stretched toward the Arctic Ocean, with Slavic farmers only beginning to move into the far north.

Beyond the Slavs to the east was Volga Bulgaria, a small Turkic Islamic state that came into being in about AD 950 where modern Tatarstan stands today. Beyond Volga Bulgaria were the Urals and Siberia, vast forests and plains inhabited by small tribes who lived by hunting and gathering food. The core of Kiev Rus was along the route that ran from northern Novgorod south to Kiev along the main rivers. There in the area of richest soil lay the capital, Kiev. Even farther to the south of Kiev began the steppe.

The lands of Kiev Rus lay in the forest zone of the great East European plain. There are no mountains or even large ranges of hills to break this plain between Poland and the Urals. The forest zone is deciduous in the south around Kiev – oak, beech, chestnut, and poplar trees, while farther north the predominant forests were and are composed of the northern coniferous trees: pine, fir, and birch. The best soil, dark and moist, was in the south, where fields opened out among the trees closer to the steppe. In the northern part of the forest zone the soil was sandy and marshes were frequent, thus agriculture was rarer and concentrated around lakes and along the great rivers. The great rivers were the arteries of life. The Dniepr, Western Dvina, Volga, Oka, and the smaller rivers around Novgorod (the Volkhov and others) provided routes to the south and east via Lake Ladoga to the Baltic Sea. Along them princes and warriors, merchants and peasant farmers could move freely, at least in the summer months when the rivers were not frozen.

In the west and east of Kiev Rus the boundaries were those of political control and ethnicity. In the south the ethnic and political boundary was at its basis an ecological boundary. South of the Kievan lands to the Black and Caspian Seas lay the great steppe – flat grasslands with few trees and the "black earth" – dry but not arid. The long grass concealed enormous numbers of animals, including antelopes, wild horses, and even panthers, while the rivers supported myriad ducks and wild geese as well as sturgeon and other fish. Centuries later, the Russian writer Gogol wrote of the steppe: "The farther along in the steppe the more beautiful it became... The plow had never touched the infinite waves of wild growth. Only the horses that hid in the grass as in a forest had stamped it down. Nothing in nature could have been better. The whole surface of the earth was like a green and gold ocean, on which millions of various flowers splashed" (*Taras Bulba*). This steppe was actually the western extension of the great Eurasian steppe that extended all the way to Manchuria, which covers today's Mongolia, northern China, Xinjiang, and Kazakstan. From time immemorial it was the land of the nomads and the great nomadic empires – first the Iranian Scythians and Sarmatians of classical antiquity, who were then later replaced by the fearsome Huns and then wave after wave of Turkic peoples. These nomads did not wander aimlessly over the landscape, but instead they followed a regular annual migration over a greater or lesser area. They kept close to the valleys of the great rivers – the Danube, Dniepr, Don, and Volga – where they found winter and summer pastures for their animals. The nomads did not try to settle in the forests, but they used them as a source of booty and slaves, and when they could, they also laid tribute on the settled peoples. For centuries this had been the relationship of nomad and farmer throughout northern Asia and beyond. The steppe and its nomads were to form a crucial element in the history of Kiev Rus, and later Russia, into the eighteenth century.

Archeology tells us a great deal about the settlement and life of the early Eastern Slavs. They were certainly the predominant group along the central axis of Rus from Kiev to Novgorod by at least AD 800, and were still moving north and east, settling new lands. They had built many villages and fortifications of earth with wooden palisades, and they buried their dead with the tools and weapons necessary for life in the next world. From other sources we have some idea of their gods: Perun, the god of thunder and the sky, was apparently the chief god, but there was also Veles, the god of cattle; Stribog, the wind god; and the more shadowy fertility gods, Rod and Rozhanitsa. Around Kiev there were round spaces formed of stones that seem to have been sites of the cult, but Slavic paganism never had any written texts (or none that survived) to give us a glimpse of their actual beliefs.

Reconstructing the political history of the early Slavs is equally complicated. Legend says that the Viking Rurik came from over the sea with two brothers to rule Novgorod in AD 862. This is a classic foundation legend found in many cultures and as such was crucial to the self-consciousness of the subsequent ruling dynasty. The text, the Kievan *Primary Chronicle* of 1116, which recounts the legend, is vague about the establishment of Rurik's descendants in Kiev. Supposedly the Viking Oleg went down the rivers and took the city in 882, but his relationship to Rurik was not specified. Did either of them even exist? Prince Igor, allegedly Rurik's son, was a real person who did rule from Kiev (913–945), until a rebellious tribe killed him. The clan ancestor remained Rurik, who thus gave his name to the ruling dynasty, the Rurikovichi.

The Rurikovich dynasty was originally Scandinavian, as legend and the early names suggest: Oleg from Norse Helge and Igor from Ingvar. Our unique written source, the *Primary Chronicle*, called them Varangians, one of the names for Scandinavians used in Byzantium. In other places it said they were called Rus, not Varangians. Further on, the text localized Rus in the Kiev area, but most it often called the whole state and people Rus. The author was serving his rulers, identifying princes and people, and leaving the historian with a muddle virtually impossible to sort out. In any case the first Rurikovichi were undoubtedly Scandinavian and their appearance in Rus was part of the expansion of the Scandinavian peoples in the Viking age. Unfortunately the archeological evidence does not fit the legends in the *Primary Chronicle* very well. Viking finds are concentrated for these early centuries around the southern rim of Lake Ladoga and in the town of Old Ladoga. The chronicle stories tried to place them in Novgorod, but Novgorod did not even come into existence until about AD 950, after the dynasty of Rurik was already established in Kiev. And in Scandinavia itself there were no sagas of Viking triumphs and wars in Russia to match those recounting the conquest of Iceland and the British Isles. In the lands that were once part of Kiev Rus, there are no runestones memorializing the great warriors and their deaths, such as those that cover Scandinavia and the western islands where the Vikings roamed. All we can say for sure is that a group of warriors whose base was probably Ladoga, with its Scando-Slavic-Finnish community, came to Kiev around AD 900 and began to rule that area, quickly establishing their authority over the whole vast area of Kiev Rus.

The world of AD 950 looked very different from how we might imagine it today. Western Europe was an impoverished collection of weak petty kingdoms and local dynasties. The great Carolingian Empire was now a century in the past and the classic feudal society of medieval Europe was just coming into being. In France the great regional lords and barons owed only the most theoretical obedience to their king. The greatest power in the north for the moment was Denmark, as the Danish kings controlled much of England and the Vikings had small kingdoms in Ireland and Scotland. The Emperor still reigned in Germany, and in Italy the papacy was still under his thumb, while the regional rulers of Germany and Italy grew more and more independent. Most of the Iberian Peninsula was under Arab rule, with a few tiny Christian principalities hanging on in the north.

The great powers and centers of civilization were the Arab Caliphate and the Byzantine Empire. Only a few centuries earlier the Arabs had taken Islam to the far corners of western Eurasia, to Central Asia and Spain, and the Abbasid Caliphate in Baghdad was now the center of that world. These were the great centuries of medieval Arab culture – the time of the translations of Aristotle and other works of Greek learning and of the Islamic commentary and development of Greek ideas and Greek science. The Caliphate was immensely rich, and the many coin hoards found on the Rus lands testify to its trade with northern neighbors. Even more important to Kiev Rus was Byzantium. The Greeks had recovered from the immense shock of the Arab conquests of the seventh and eighth centuries, and by AD 900, a revived Byzantium was master of Anatolia and the southern Balkans. Theirs was a complex civilization, a Christian society with a rich monastic culture and at the same time the heir of classical antiquity. While monks spent their days in liturgy and contemplation, their relatives and patrons were reading Homer and Thucydides, Plato and Demosthenes. Laymen wrote the empire's history not as monkish chronicles in simplified language like those of Western Europe, but in pure Attic Greek following the models of the ancients. The Byzantine Empire was also a bureaucratic state on the late Roman model, dependent on written Roman law and paper documentation. Boys were set to learn all this material from a young age, following the sequence of subjects and texts already laid down in Roman times. For the Byzantines did not call themselves Greeks but Romans, *Rhomaioi*, and their country was to them still Rome.

The Byzantines were not the immediate neighbors of Kiev Rus and communication was difficult. The most intimate contact was with the Turkic nomads of the great steppe. From about AD 750, the steppe was ruled by the Khazars, a nomadic people whose center was on the lower Volga and who laid tribute on the southern Rus tribes. The Khazars were a unique people, for their rulers, their kagans, had converted from Turkic paganism to Judaism and had copies of the Hebrew Bible. Nomadic empires were short-lived, and in the middle of the tenth century the Turkic Pechenegs replaced the Khazars, only to be supplanted about a century later by another Turkic people, the Kipchaks – or Polovtsy, as the Rus called them. In the steppe the Kipchaks lived in a series of large groups, each on one of the main rivers, the most important to Rus being those on the Dniepr, Northern Donets, and Don. Their annual migration between winter and summer pastures involved great herds of horses, cattle, sheep, and even camels, with the Kipchaks following them in felt tents mounted on carts. Their religion was the ancient Turkic paganism centered on the sky and the ancestors. Farther east the Kipchaks spread to the lower Volga and the Caucasus and traded with the Byzantine cities in the Crimea. For long periods the Rus and the Kipchaks raided one another's lands almost annually, each group seizing animals, slaves, and hostages from the other. Relations were not only hostile, for the Rus princes took wives among the daughters of the Kipchak chiefs, who in turn took an active part in the internal feuds of the Rurikovich dynasty. Some of the Kipchaks eventually adopted Christianity, apparently from Rus or the Greeks.

WARRIORS AND CHRISTIANS

In the tenth century, Kiev Rus was hardly a state at all. Rather it was an assembly of tribes – Poliane/Rus around Kiev, Slovene in Novgorod, Krivichi and Viatichi in between, and several others – ruled from Kiev by a prince of the dynasty of Rurik and his warrior band or *druzhina*. The tribes paid tribute to the Kiev princes, who visited them occasionally for that purpose. Otherwise the vast majority of the people were peasant farmers scattered in the clearings of the forests and owning no master but the princes of Kiev. This was still a pagan world, as the legend of the death of Prince Oleg suggests. The story was that a wizard predicted that his horse would cause the prince's death. Oleg put the horse out to pasture and forgot the prophecy, but years later he heard that the horse was dead and remembered it. Oleg went out to see the skeleton of the horse as it lay in a field. As he placed his foot on the skull to lament, a poisonous snake crawled out and bit him. Thus the prophecy was fulfilled.

These Kiev princes spent their time on wars that were essentially raiding expeditions against the Khazars, their successors the Pechenegs, and the richest prize of all, the Byzantines. In log boats they could follow the coast to Constantinople itself, and they raided it several times before they made treaties with the emperor regulating their status as traders. Princess Olga, the widow of Prince Igor, became a Christian about this time, perhaps after a journey to Constantinople. She ruled the land until about AD 962, but her son did not follow her beliefs. Sviatoslav, the son of Igor, was the last pure warrior chieftain in Rus; he spent his time fighting the Greeks and other rivals on the Danube and in the steppe. On his campaigns he slept on the ground with his saddle for a pillow and cut strips of raw horsemeat to roast for his food. He met his death in the steppe coming home from a raid on Byzantium, and the Pechenegs made a drinking cup of his skull.

His son Vladimir (AD 972–1015) at first followed in his father's path. He too was a great warrior, and he maintained control over the Kiev lands by placing his many sons to rule over distant territories. He tried to organize their pagan beliefs and set up a temple in Kiev to Perun, the god of thunder, and other deities. Soon, however, he turned to the religion of his grandmother Olga, the Christianity of Constantinople. The chronicle records several stories of his conversion, probably none of them true, but they remain a part of Russian conceptions of the past to this day. One story was that the decision grew out of a raid on the Byzantine town of Chersonesus in the Crimea. The raid ended in a compromise, according to which the Greeks kept their town but Vladimir married a Byzantine princess and became a Christian. Another story was that his neighbors proposed that he adopt their religion. First a Muslim came from Volga Bulgaria and seemed very persuasive until Vladimir learned of the prohibition on alcoholic drinks. "The joy of Rus is drinking," he told the Bulgarian, and sent him away. Then Vladimir turned to Rome, and the rituals and fasts seemed attractive but the objection was that the ancestors of the Rus had rejected Latin Christianity. Then a Khazar Jew came, but Judaism failed because of the exile of the Jews, clearly a sign of God's wrath. Then a Greek "philosopher" came and explained Christianity, giving a brief account of the Old and New Testaments, emphasizing the fall and redemption of man. He was very convincing, but the prince wanted final proof and sent a delegation to Bulgaria, Rome, and Constantinople. The services of the Muslims and Latins failed to win approval, for they lacked beauty. Then the Rus went to Constantinople and attended the liturgy in Saint Sophia, the great cathedral built by Justinian, and reported that they were so impressed that they did not know if they were on earth or in heaven. The choice was for Christianity as understood in Byzantium, and it determined the place of Kiev Rus, and later of Russia, in European culture for centuries.

Vladimir ordered the people of Kiev to be baptized in the river Dniepr, but the new religion caught on slowly outside the major centers. Vladimir himself put away his concubines and married the Byzantine princess, but in many of his values he remained part of the pagan world of the warrior prince. Once, several years after the conversion (AD 996), his warriors began to complain to him that at banquets they had to eat with wooden spoons, not with silver. The prince replied, "it is not for me to get warriors with silver and gold, I shall get silver and gold with my warriors, as my father and his father did" – hardly a sentiment for a Christian ruler. In and around the greater towns, however, Christianity gradually made its way. The Greek clergy in Constantinople supplied the heads of the new church, the metropolitans of Kiev, but other bishops were mostly natives. The founding of the Kiev Monastery of the Caves in the 1050s, dedicated to the Dormition of the Virgin, provided Rus with its first monastery, the key institution for Byzantine Christianity. The monastery produced not only its own saints in its founders Antonii and Feodosii but also the bishops for the eparchies outside of Kiev. The Caves Monastery and the others that soon arose around Kiev and Novgorod also provided the libraries and writing skills that produced the *Primary Chronicle* and other records, but of course their main role was spiritual. It was the monks who provided the charisma to spread a new religion.

The new religion had to be made to fit a society very different from the sophisticated urban world of Byzantium. The introduction of Christianity did not bring with it other aspects of Byzantine civilization, for the tradition of the eastern churches was one of a vernacular liturgy. In Kiev Rus the mass was not in Greek but in a ninth-century Bulgarian dialect scholars call Old or Church Slavic. At that time the Slavic languages were all very similar to one another, so this was a readily comprehensible language in Kiev. The use of Church Slavic implied that the liturgy, the scriptures, and other holy books had to be translated into Slavic, an arduous task but one that removed the need to learn Greek for all but a few learned monks. Much Christian literature and all of the secular literature of Byzantium remained unknown in Kiev Rus and later societies. The Russians would discover Greek antiquity in the eighteenth century from the West.

The relations of Rome and Constantinople in these early centuries were complicated. The famous mutual anathema of the Pope and the Patriarch of Constantinople of 1054 was not the decisive break that it seemed to later historians, and the people of Rus were barely aware of it. One of Kiev's Greek metropolitans did write a short tract denouncing the Latins, but native writers did not join him and the *Primary Chronicle* is silent on the events. It was only with the Fourth Crusade, the destruction and conquest of the Byzantine Empire by the crusading armies from Western Europe in 1204, that the people of Rus took notice of the division and where their loyalties lay. The Rus chroniclers covered this event in extensive and bloody detail – the massacre of the people and the desecration of the churches. The Rus people were not just Christians, they were Orthodox Christians.

Orthodox Christianity would determine the character of Russian culture until the eighteenth century and in some ways beyond it. For the Western observer, it has always presented a problem, seeming familiar, but actually not. Most Westerners know more about Buddhism than about Orthodoxy, as the latter forms no part of daily experience nor is it encountered in the course of a normal education. Analogies do not help much. Orthodoxy is not Catholicism with married priests.

The differences between Orthodoxy and the Western Catholic church that emerged during the Middle Ages were of a different order than those that later divided the western church at the time of the Reformation. Theological issues were not central, and were to some extent exaggerated to provide more convincing explanations for the hostilities. The difference over how the doctrine of the Trinity should be expressed in the Nicene Creed, that is, the Catholic addition of the words *filioque* ("and the son") to the mention of the "Holy Ghost, which proceedeth from the father" does not signify any important difference in the actual understanding of the Trinity. The main issue in 1054 was one of church governance. The eleventh century was the time of the gradual emancipation of the papacy from the power of the Holy Roman emperors, and the path chosen was the centralization of ecclesiastical power in the person of the pope. The traditions of the eastern patriarchs were those of a conciliar church. Only the assembled patriarchs and the rest of the higher clergy could determine doctrine or matters of church government. The Patriarch of Constantinople was not a pope. The papacy also managed to assert its independence from the emperors and other rulers in matters of church government and certainly in doctrine, whereas the Eastern Church operated with the more nebulous notions of "symphony" of emperor and patriarch. Lesser matters, like the celibacy of the parish clergy in the west, flowed from these basic decisions. A celibate clergy was free of the entanglements of secular powers; a married priest was part of his local society.

Many differences between the eastern and western churches arose in matters that are hard to pin down and included differences of culture and attitudes rather than dogma and basic belief. The notion of the church building and the liturgy as the meeting points of the divine and human worlds, of spirit and matter, was and is central to Orthodox life and devotion. Preaching and the minute examination of behavior in sermons and in the confessional were not central, even if practiced to some extent. Orthodox monasticism was much less organized, as the monasteries did not form orders with a recognized head and the rules were much less detailed and specific. At the same time, Orthodox monasticism had a prestige and charisma in the east that even the most revered Catholic orders did not approach. For most of the history of Rus until the sixteenth century, we know far more about monasteries than bishops, many of whom are only names to us. By contrast, the western medieval church's annals are filled with saintly and powerful bishops. Finally, the Eastern Church had a rather different attitude toward learning. For the Catholic church of the Middle Ages, the great intellectual enterprise was the interpretation of Aristotle's corpus of writings in the light of revelation and the teachings of the church. The Orthodox, save a few late Byzantine imitators of the West, did not bother with philosophy or Aristotelian science. These were exterior knowledge, not bad in itself but not the final truth. The truth was in Christianity, best studied by monks in isolation from the world, not only from its temptations but also from its secular writings. This attitude fit well into Byzantine society, with its flourishing secular culture, but less so in Rus. In Rus, and later in Russia, there was no secular culture of the Byzantine type, so it was only the Christian monastic culture that flourished.

DRUZHINAS AND PRINCES

Vladimir's son Iaroslav "the Wise" ruled Kiev Rus from 1016 until his death in 1054 after a contentious and violent beginning in which two of his brothers, princes Boris and Gleb, perished at the hand of their elder brother, Iaroslav's rival. They became the first Russian saints. Iaroslav's state was no longer the primitive band of warriors of the previous century ruling over distant tribes. Kiev had become a substantial town with a princely palace and Iaroslav ruled over the land with his retinue, the *druzhina* and various "distinguished men," his boyars. All of them lived in Kiev, though they seem to have had lands around it and elsewhere. The *druzhina*, the old warrior band, seems to have become more organized and settled down and behaved more like an army and a group of advisors than simple warriors. They were not alone on the political landscape, for the people of Kiev occasionally played a part as well, assembling on the town's main square to form a *veche*, or popular assembly.

We know a certain amount about the society and legal system of Kiev Rus because shortly after Iaroslav's death his sons put together a list of laws and regulations called "Rus Justice," a brief but illuminating document. Most of the provisions seem to have reflected existing traditions, but in the first articles Iaroslav's sons began with an innovation: they banned blood revenge in cases of murder. Instead they substituted an elaborate system of payments. The murderer was to pay a certain amount if he killed a boyar or man of distinction, less for a member of the *druzhina*, still less for an ordinary person or a peasant, and least of all for a slave. Generally, for killing a woman the criminal had to pay half of the fine for killing a man of the same status. The laws gave much space to listing the payments for insults of all kind, ranging from slandering a woman's virtue to harming a man's beard. The judges of these and other cases were to be the administrators of the princely estates who thus took on a much larger role than that of simple economic administrators. The "Rus Justice" must have been written for them, as much of it was taken up with complex rules for debt-slavery, various forms of temporary or limited bondage, and relations with the village community. This was a law code entirely appropriate for Rus society, one that, needless to say, bore no relationship whatsoever to Byzantine law. Nor did the Kievan state establish a hierarchy of administrators relying on written documents in imitation of Byzantium. In Rus the basic laws might be written down, but administration was in the hands of a tiny group of servants of the prince's household relying on oral communications, tradition, and only a very few written texts like the "Rus Justice."

Iaroslav's reign represented a high point of stability in Rus. Norwegian princes took refuge with him from civil wars in their homeland, and one of his daughters married the king of France. In the 1030s he inflicted a decisive defeat on the Pechenegs that kept the steppe frontier quiet for a generation. He was patron of the building of the Saint Sophia cathedral and the Caves Monastery, as well as other foundations. His sons and nephews ruled distant territories without much contention. Relations with the Greeks were regular, if occasionally unharmonious. The first (and last for a long time) native metropolitan of Kiev, Ilarion (1051–1054), praised him as a new Constantine and a new David. The apparently idyllic calm would not last for long.

After Iaroslav's death more disputes arose, but unity was soon restored and persisted throughout the reign of Iaroslav's grandson Vladimir Monomakh (1113–1125) and his son Mstislav (1125–1132). In the middle of the twelfth century several centers of power began to emerge, although Kiev itself and the land around it were in decline. The city and title of Grand Prince of Kiev became the prize for contending regional powers. In the northeast, the core of the later Russia, the principality of Vladimir emerged as the main power, and in 1169 its ruler prince, Andrei Bogoliubsky, sacked Kiev and took the title of Grand Prince of Kiev. He fell victim to a conspiracy of his own boyars in 1174. Through Andrei's brother Vsevolod (1176–1212) the Vladimir dynasty would rule the northeast for the next several centuries. For the time being, their attention was elsewhere, for the Vladimir princes had rivals in the west and south, especially in Galich near the Polish border. The territories of Kiev Rus were growing apart.

The increasing vitality of local centers also produced a town unique in Russian medieval history, Novgorod. Novgorod had been the second center of Kiev Rus, legendarily the first stop of the Viking dynasty. It was an important city that traded in the Baltic in the eleventh century, and its wealth was reflected in the Novgorod cathedral of Saint Sophia, built around 1050. Early Novgorod was a typical princely city, and the Kiev princes often sent their eldest sons to rule in their names. In the twelfth century, however, Novgorod set out on its own path. The Novgorodians expelled their prince in 1136 and chose another. From that moment on, they treated the prince as an elected general rather than a ruler. Before 1136 the princes had appointed a deputy with the title of *posadnik,* and now the popular assembly, the *veche,* elected the *posadnik* from among the boyars of the town. In 1156 the people even elected the archbishop, choosing from among three candidates proposed by the local clergy. This practice was contrary to Byzantine canon law, but the metropolitan of Kiev never challenged it.

Thus Novgorod developed into a unique polity among the princely states of medieval Rus. Novgorod was not a commercial republic, such as medieval Florence or the Flemish cities, for it was not merchants, bankers, and cloth manufacturers who sat in the city's council. Merchants and artisans in Novgorod remained humble folk, present in the *veche* but with little real influence. The city's elite consisted of boyars, rich landholders with large houses in the town and extensive possessions in the surrounding countryside. Many of the richest also controlled the northern forests, for it was the forests that were the real source of Novgorod's wealth. After 1200 the Novgorodians ceased to travel west with their goods, as the league of north German trading cities, the Hansa, had come to dominate the trade of all countries around the Baltic Sea. The Germans journeyed to Novgorod to buy furs, beeswax for candles, and other forest products. The furs ranged from simple squirrel skins to the sables of the northern forests that fetched high prices in the west. In return, the Novgorodians bought Flemish and English cloth and a host of smaller items from the western towns.

By 1200 Kiev Rus was a single state in name only; the ruler of Kiev itself was either an outsider or a minor princeling. Other than Novgorod, each territory had a local princely dynasty springing from the old Kiev dynasty of the Rurikovichi. Because Kiev Rus did not know primogeniture, each of a prince's sons had to be provided for, and in any case the eldest uncle could also be considered the rightful ruler. Thus, innumerable small principalities

Figure 1. The Twelfth Century Dormition Cathedral in Vladimir (c. 1900).

emerged, though at the same time several regional centers of power – Vladimir, Smolensk, Chernigov, and Galich – maintained control over lesser princes. These were agrarian societies, each with a small boyar elite that ruled the peasants and advised the prince, though some of the towns, especially Smolensk, had wider commercial ties. The towns were becoming wealthier, for in the regional centers like Vladimir, magnificent stone churches arose and monasteries with stone churches and walls were also founded near the towns. Builders and icon painters came from Byzantium, and the Rus people began to learn their skills.

Byzantine contacts were easy, for the one single institution remaining was the church. As Metropolitan of Kiev, a Greek usually headed the church that oversaw the whole breadth of the land. The Greek clergy and the priests and monks of the Rus had their hands full with the Christianization of the people and the creation of a new culture that went with the new religion. The Christianization of the people went slowly, and outside of the towns there were few churches. While Kiev rapidly became a major center of the new faith, provincial towns still celebrated burials in which warriors were put to rest with their weapons, horses, slaves, and food for their journeys to the other world. In 1071 there was a wave of incidents of revolt and resistance led by pagan priests in Novgorod and in some of the towns of the northeast. In these circumstances the clergy concentrated on very basic issues. From a series of questions put to the mid-twelfth century bishop Nifont of Novgorod, we know some of these concerns. The clergy tried to enforce the rules of Christian marriage (that dictated which cousins could be married to each other) and rules governing sexual behavior. Many of these questions were about timing, that is, if intercourse between man and wife was proper during Lent or when it was proper for priests. Ritual purity for both clergy and laity figured more largely than sex itself. Which animals were "clean" and which not and the prohibition on eating the meat of strangled animals were prominent issues in these questions. For all of the various sins, the punishments were denial of communion and penance for greater or longer periods. The exposition of Christian doctrine to the laity remained on a very elementary level.

Even Christian works in this situation retained pre-Christian elements. The *Primary Chronicle*, the work of Christian monks, denounced the pagan customs of the early people of Rus but in the same pages glorified its pre-Christian rulers, recounting stories like the death of Oleg without comments. The princes of the ruling dynasty were generally known by their pagan names until about 1200. For most princes we do not even know the baptismal names. At the very end of the Kievan period, the *Igor Tale*, a brief story of an unsuccessful raid on the Kipchaks, called the Rus the children of Dazhbog, the sun god, but ends with praise of the princes and warriors who fought for the Christians against the pagans. The old ways had power almost to the end of Kiev Rus.

The new culture that came with Christianity brought with it writing and various types of Byzantine devotional literature. The most widely disseminated, and anchored in the liturgy (and thus open to the illiterate) were the lives of the saints. Alongside the lives of the Byzantine saints, Rus itself very quickly began to glorify its own holy men, and these works more than any other give some insight into the religious world of Kiev Rus.

The first saints were Princes Boris and Gleb, younger sons of Vladimir murdered in 1015 by their brother Sviatopolk "the Cursed" during the succession struggle after the death of Vladimir. By the end of the eleventh century, the two brothers were the objects of reverence and their bodies moved to a shrine near Kiev. Commemoration of the brothers began to appear in the liturgy, and the monk Nestor of the Caves Monastery wrote an account of their lives and death. Boris and Gleb were unlikely Christian saints. Though they led a blameless life and died young, it was their death that made them saints, but they were not martyrs for the faith. Sviatopolk was not challenging Christianity, merely eliminating potential rivals in a political struggle. The message of Nestor's text is the humility and meekness of the two boys, the wickedness of their murderer, and by implication, the need for harmony and virtue in the ruling dynasty.

More conventionally Christian were the accounts of the lives of the founders of the Kiev Monastery of the Caves, Saints Antonii and Feodosii. Antonii's life was that of a hermit seeking salvation and nearness to God by prayer, tears, and fasting. Feodosii's portrait was that of the abbot, hegumen in the Eastern Church, who also fled the temptations of the world but built a great institution to make this path possible for others. It was he who sought out a rule of liturgical observance and monastic life from the great monastery of the Studiou in Constantinople and it was he who built the church, the monastery walls and buildings, and supervised the monks until his death. The Caves Monastery, like its prototype in Constantinople, was not physically remote from the city of Kiev: today it is well within the city boundaries and Feodosii's monks withdrew from the world, in part, to serve it better. In later accounts the monks perform acts of heroic asceticism, but also demonstrate to the people of Kiev the superiority of Orthodox Christianity by predicting the future and healing the sick, often in direct competition with representatives of the Latin faith, Armenian Christianity, and Judaism, as well as pagan sorcerers. In Nestor's account of Feodosii's life the hegumen was not shy in condemning acts of the Kiev princes that he thought to be unjust. In 1073 Princes Sviatoslav and Vsevolod expelled the rightful ruler, their elder brother Iziaslav. The usurpers sent for Feodosii to join them at a feast to celebrate their victory, but the holy monk replied, "I will not come to the table of Beelzebub and eat food soaked with blood and murder."

In Kiev, Vladimiir's son Iaroslav built the cathedral of the Holy Wisdom, Saint Sophia, in 1037. The dedication was in imitation of the great church of Constantinople, the sixth century cathedral of the Emperor Justinian. Later rebuilding conceals the original look of the exterior, which probably followed the Greek norms of the time. The basic plan was a nave and transept of equal length (the "Greek cross"), which gave the building a squarish look, and the roof surmounted with round drums supporting the domes. These would have been the Byzantine hemispherical domes, not the characteristic onion shape of later Russian churches. The Kievan Saint Sophia was also a much more modest creation than its grand prototype and followed middle Byzantine style in using several smaller domes instead of the enormous central dome created by Justinian's architects.

The Kievan Saint Sophia was also connected with the prince's palace by galleries, with a special place reserved for the prince and his family – a Byzantine touch later abandoned in Rus. The magnificent mosaics and frescoes, still extant today, also followed the Greek prototype, with inscriptions everywhere in Greek. At the top was (presumably) Christ as Pantocrator, the ruler of the universe, below him the extant images of the apostles, the Mother of God, and then the Eucharist. On the walls were the life of Christ and his Mother, prophets, and saints. This order put Christ in heaven, then symbolically depicted his movement down from the world of the spirit to the earth. The path lay through his Mother, his apostles, and the Eucharist, three ways in which the spirit of Christ reached the material world and thus to all men. The physical structure of the church signified the presence of Christ in the world in consequence of the Incarnation.

The Kievan Saint Sophia, like Greek and other Rus churches of the time, presumably had a row of icons along the altar rail. This row was not yet the high icon screen of later Russian churches, and thus the cathedral may have contained only a dozen or so images. Few icons exist today that can be surely dated to Kievan times, and none can be placed with any certitude in Kiev's cathedral. The twelfth century is richer in surviving icons, the most famous example being the image of the Vladimir Mother of God, a Greek (probably Constantinople) icon that found its way to Vladimir in the northeast, where it rested in the Cathedral of the Dormition of the Mother of God in that city. It is a typical work of the period, with Mary in fine dress holding the infant Christ in her arms, again the visible image of the Incarnation and the presence of Christ in the world that is the center of the Orthodox understanding of his role. The physical image itself was crucial to belief in Christ's presence. As the Byzantine monk Saint Theodore of the Studiou monastery put it: "If reverence toward the image of Christ is subverted, then Christ's incarnation is also subverted".

As the peasants cleared the land and tended their crops, and the princes built churches and warred on one another, a cloud was gathering on the horizon. In 1223 a new and strange people appeared on the southern steppes, and the Kipchaks hastened to assemble allies from among the Rus princes. The combined army went out to meet the newcomers and found them on the River Kalka, just north of the Sea of Azov. The strangers were the Mongols, who utterly destroyed the Kipchak/Rus army and went on to raid the area of Kiev. "They returned from the river Dniepr and we know not whence they came or whither they went. Only God knows whence they came against us for our sins," said the Novgorod chronicler. They would come again.

2

Moscow, Novgorod, Lithuania, and the Mongols

After the gradual disintegration of Kiev Rus, the regional powers that supplanted it began to grow apart. In these centuries the territories of Novgorod and the old northeast began to form a distinct language and culture that we can call Russian. Though the older term *Rus* persisted until replaced by Russia (*Rossiia*) in the fifteenth century, for this period we may begin to call the area *Russia* and the people *Russian*. In these centuries, Russia, like the other territories of Kiev Rus that would fall to Lithuania, experienced a cataclysm in the form of the Mongol invasion, one that shaped its history for the next three centuries.

The Mongol Empire was the last and largest of the nomadic empires formed on the Eurasian steppe. It was largely the work of Temuchin, a Mongolian chieftain who united the Mongolian tribes in 1206 and took the name of Genghis Khan. In his mind, the Eternal Blue Heaven had granted him rule over all people who lived in felt tents, and he was thus the legitimate ruler of all inner Asian nomads. The steppe was not enough. In 1211 Genghis Khan moved south over the Great Wall and overran northern China. His armies then swept west, and by his death in 1227, they had added all of Inner and Central Asia to their domains.

The astonishing success of the Mongols came from their ability to balance the advantages of nomadic society with the benefits of sedentary civilizations. The basic unit of Mongol society was the clan, and in each clan the women tended to the animals and the men learned the arts of war. Genghis Khan mobilized the whole of his people for war, and the Mongols were superb horsemen, disciplined and skilled warriors, and ruthless conquerors. They could not take cities with cavalry, however, and thus the Mongols recruited men from China and Central Asia who knew how to make and use siege engines. This combination was unbeatable. Rich cities like Khwarezm in Central Asia that tried to resist were exterminated. Spreading terror before them, the Mongol armies overwhelmed Iran and Iraq and took the rest of China. A typhoon prevented them from taking Japan, but only in Viet Nam was human resistance strong enough to defeat them.

The battle on the Kalka had been part of a reconnaissance. In 1236 the full force of the Mongol army moved west under the command of the grandson of Genghis Khan, Batu, son of Jochi. With perhaps a hundred thousand warriors at his disposal, Batu first subdued Volga Bulgaria and the Kipchaks, and then during the years of 1237 through 1240, in a series of campaigns, he smashed Vladimir and the other northeastern towns. He razed Kiev to the ground, wiping out the people or selling them into slavery. The old center of Kiev Rus was gone, and would not recover for a century and a half. Batu continued on to the west, defeating a hastily gathered army in eastern Germany, and then turning south to Hungary, a suitable terrain for a nomadic host. There Batu's army wintered over and Europe was in panic. Suddenly in the spring of 1242 the supreme Khan Ogedei died, and the army returned home to Mongolia to participate in the succession, never to return.

The great Mongol empire soon split into four large domains (or ulus): China, Central Asia, Iran with Iraq, and the western steppe. The last was the ulus of Jochi in Mongol terminology, the heritage of Jochi's son the conqueror Batu. The Persians and later scholars would call it the Golden Horde, while the Russians just referred to it as the Horde (or *Orda*, a military camp, in Mongol). The Golden Horde was a nomadic state whose center lay on the lower Volga, in the city of Sarai, near the later Stalingrad. As a nomadic state, its people followed the annual migration, wintering near the mouths of the rivers and moving north with the melting snows. This had been the pattern of the Kipchaks and the Khazars before them, but the Golden Horde was on a much grander scale. It stretched from

Rumania in the west to the eastern parts of Kazakstan and included Khwarezm in Central Asia, the latter a bone of contention with the Central Asian ulus of Chagatai. Like most nomadic states, the Golden Horde included agricultural lands along the borders. One of these was Khwarezm, others were the land of the Volga Bulgarians, the Crimea, and the Rus principalities, both in the southwest and the northeast. In the Rus principalities the khans experimented with their own tax collectors, but eventually they simply required the Grand Prince of Vladimir, the nominal supreme ruler of the northeast, to send the annual tribute to Sarai. The Horde demanded tribute and obedience, nothing else. The center of attention of the Khans of the Golden Horde was not on the Rus lands but on the south, and on the contested borderlands with Central Asia (Khwarezm) and Persia (Azerbaidzhan). These were rich territories that also included important trade routes. By comparison, the northern pine forests of Rus, with their sparse population, were not much of a prize.

Thus the Rus principalities, and especially those of the northeast and Novgorod, were included on the fringes of a vast Eurasian empire. Historians often speak of this period as one of "Mongol rule," but the term is misleading, for the actual population of the Golden Horde included almost no actual Mongols outside of the khan's household. Batu had incorporated the Kipchaks and other Turkic peoples into his army and soon all that remained of the Mongols was the name *Tatar*, the name of one of the leading Mongol clans. In Russian it came to signify the nomads of the Horde and the peoples who descended from them. The language of the Horde was not Mongolian but Kipchak Turkic, the lingua franca of the steppe and of the Horde's winter capital at Sarai. Sarai was a great city, with much of it made of felt tents and considered an important waystation on the trade route from Europe to Inner Asia and China. The population of the city included all sorts of people: Tatars, Greeks, Latins, Armenians, Persians, and many of the Muslims of Central Asia. There was even an Orthodox bishop of Sarai, which became an eparchy of the metropolitanate of Kiev. The Mongols had been tolerant of various faiths, and the Horde continued this policy even after its conversion to Islam under Khan Uzbek in the 1330s.

During the succeeding centuries, life continued much as before for the people of the former Kiev Rus. The princes feuded with one another over land and power, the cities slowly came back and the churches were rebuilt. The tribute to the Horde must have been a burden, but not enough to prevent the recovery of the devastated areas. In the northeast, the main prize of political contest was the Grand Principality of Vladimir, which not only gave control of that town and its lands but a theoretical overlordship of the whole area and even of Novgorod. The Grand Principality of Vladimir was now in the gift of the khan in Sarai. Thus, Alexander Nevsky, who ruled in Vladimir (1252–1263), came to the throne after more than a decade as Novgorod's elected prince. He went to Sarai to the khan for confirmation of his title and power. From 1304, however, Vladimir ceased to be an independent center of power, and like Kiev earlier, it became the prize in the struggle for power among the northeastern princes of Tver and Moscow. Ultimately the Moscow dynasty would secure the Vladimir land and title for itself, forming in the process the Russian state. Medieval political rivalries make dull reading for the modern reader, for they were an endless chain of petty conflicts, military and diplomatic; appeals to higher authorities; and short-lived and quickly reversed alliances.

Moscow first appears in written sources in 1147 as a small fortress, but it seems to have been Daniil, Prince of Moscow (circa 1280–1303) and grandson of Alexander Nevsky who consolidated the small territory along the Moscow River. His son Iurii Danilovich expanded that territory, but his power was limited by Prince Michael of Tver's acquisition of the Vladimir throne in 1305. From that moment Moscow and Tver were locked in a bitter struggle for that throne that included the Moscow-inspired execution of Michael of Tver in 1318. Eventually Michael became a saint, honored most of all in Moscow. The murders and denunciations to the Horde continued until Iurii's son Ivan ("Kalita," the Moneybag) finally secured the Vladimir throne from Khan Uzbek in 1328 and held it until his death in 1340. His success guaranteed Moscow the leading position among the northeastern princes, and with time his descendants came to be the Grand Princes of Moscow *and* Vladimir. The new town had eclipsed Vladimir and Ivan proceeded to fortify Moscow with the first wooden Kremlin.

It was not only the Vladimir title and suzerainty over the Russian princes of the northeast that came to rest in Moscow. The Mongol conquest and destruction of Kiev had left the Metropolitan of Kiev, the head of the church, without a home until Metropolitan Maximos, a Greek, moved his residence to Vladimir in 1299. His successor was Peter (1306–1326), not a Greek but a nobleman from southwest Rus, who identified himself with Moscow and on his death was buried in the Kremlin's Dormition Cathedral. Ivan Kalita convinced his successor, the Greek Theognostos, to remain in Moscow as well. The Moscow princes now had at their sides the Metropolitans of Kiev and All Rus.

By the middle of the fourteenth century Moscow was in a secure enough position to dominate the politics of the area. It had incorporated a number of lesser principalities and exerted hegemony over almost all others. Only Novgorod had real freedom of action. The limit to the power of the Moscow princes came not from their neighbors but from the Khans of the Golden Horde; however, here as well the situation was changing, if only gradually, and it was changing in Moscow's favor. Dmitrii Ivanovich, the grandson of Ivan Kalita, inherited these advantages when he came to the Moscow and Vladimir throne in 1359. His early years were spent building a new white-stone Kremlin in Moscow and on rivalries with other Rus princes and Lithuania. Then in 1378 he defeated a raiding party from the Horde. At that moment the Horde had its own internal problems – for the Emir Mamai, commander of the western wing of the Horde, had come to overshadow the khan himself. Mamai set out against Dmitrii to restore his own and the Horde's prestige and power over their unruly vassal. Instead, the battle on Kulikovo field, near the upper Don River, in 1380 was a resounding victory for Dmitrii, who was ever after known as Dmitrii Donskoi.

Later writers greatly inflated the significance of this battle, for it did not liberate Russia from the Horde, even if it was the first important victory over the Tatars since 1240. Mamai's defeat led to his elimination from the politics of the Horde, and in 1382 the new Khan Tokhtamysh led a massive army toward the north. This time Dmitrii chose to retreat, and Tokhtamysh took Moscow and burned it to the ground. Dmitrii did not live long enough to see the outcome, for he died in 1389. Two years later the great conqueror Tamerlane, already master of Central Asia, turned against the Golden Horde and defeated Tokhtamysh. This was a mortal blow, coming at a time of increasing dissension among the various chiefs and tribal groupings within the Horde. Raids and even major campaigns by the Tatars continued, but without great success. In the 1430s the Horde began to break up, although the theoretical supremacy of the senior khanate over Russia lasted until 1480.

The principalities of northeastern Rus which ultimately came under the rule of the Moscow princes were not the only components that formed the Russian state. The other was Novgorod, which had already begun to form its own style of government in the twelfth century. Its distinctive economy, founded on the forests of the north and the commercial tie to the German Hansa, gave it a wealth that its neighbors must have envied. In addition, its location meant that subordination to the Golden Horde remained very theoretical. During most of the thirteenth century the Novgorodians chose to recognize the sovereignty of the Grand Prince of Vladimir, who sent a viceroy to lead the city-state's army, but they now made a formal treaty with their sovereign. In the 1290s Novgorod's people further altered the balance of power. From then on they elected their *posadnik,* their mayor, for a term of one year from the "Council of Lords," which was formed of representatives of each of the five "ends" of the town. As the same man could be reelected, the new system made the city's government even more oligarchic but also more independent of the prince or his deputies.

The political history of Novgorod is recorded in its chronicles and those of its neighbors, but the daily life of the city is also known to us as that of no other medieval Russian town. Starting in the 1930s Soviet archeologists made it into one of the most extensive medieval sites ever excavated, unintentionally aided by the German Wehrmacht, which destroyed most of the modern city in World War II. Dozens of medieval houses and workshops, barns, and midden heaps have given a remarkable picture of the life of medieval Novgorod. The water-logged soil of the site preserves organic material, including the log-paved roads that crisscrossed the town. Leather shoes, wooden vessels and tools, as well as objects of stone, glass, and metal have come to light. The log roads also provide the

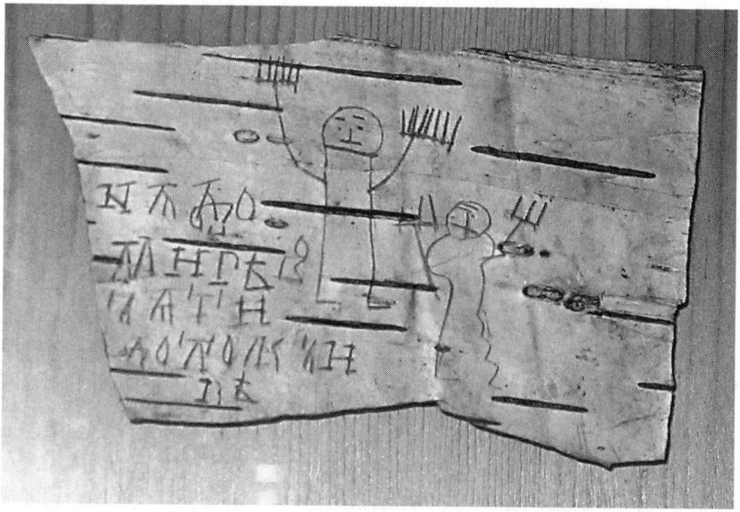

Figure 2. A Child's Writing Exercise from Medieval Novgorod (Birch Bark Document 210).

archeologist with an invaluable tool: a sequence of logs that form a database for dendrochronology (dating by tree-rings). As such, finds can be dated in Novgorod with a great degree of accuracy. Perhaps the most remarkable and wholly unexpected find came in 1951, when a student working on the site found a round cylinder of birchbark encased in mud. Her presence of mind led to the discovery that the bark, when unrolled, had writing on it, which was incised with a sharp pointed stylus. This was the first of the birch bark letters, of which thousands now exist from Novgorod and hundreds from other medieval Russian sites. These were not literary compositions but simply letters, orders to servants, reminders from wives to their husbands, labels for baskets (such as "rye" or "barley"), and records of debts.

All of these finds show us a thickly populated town. Houses were built in yards enclosed by wooden fences with a larger house for the master and often several smaller huts of servants or artisans. Each house had barns and storage sheds for animals, fodder, and the tools of the household. Houses of great boyars and their dependents were jumbled together with humble homesteads with a workshop to sustain a smith or carpenter. Children's toys and the ever-present spindles record the occupations of children and the spinning and weaving of the households' women. Some of the birch bark documents are more exotic, depicting the exercises of children learning to write and occasional prayers and letters between nuns. They reveal a society with a certain basic literacy, where men and women could write simple letters, even if most could not copy or read complex religious texts in Church Slavic.

Novgorod was a major cultural center, and the considerable manuscript production of its cathedral clergy and monasteries remain to this day as testimony of their activity. Church building reflected Novgorod's wealth as did its patronage of icon painters from faraway Byzantium, like Theophanes the Greek (circa 1350–1410). Theophanes is responsible for some of the more remarkable frescoes from medieval Novgorod, as far as we can judge from what has escaped the ravages of time, warfare, and politics. His images create a sense of mystic light around his subjects, perhaps the influence of the mystical teaching among Byzantine monks known as hesychasm.

Novgorod's location put it in a different international context from Vladimir and Moscow. A generation before the Mongol invasion, Novgorod was confronted with enemies as fierce and perhaps ultimately more dangerous than the nomads of Inner Asia, the Christian Crusaders of western Europe. They came in two groups. The larger, but perhaps the less dangerous to Novgorod, were the German crusading orders, the Teutonic Knights, and the Swordbearers. These were monastic orders of celibate warriors, formed into a community to fight against the opponents of Christianity. At the end of the twelfth century, pushed out of Palestine by the victorious Muslims, they turned their attention to the east shore of the Baltic Sea, where several of the native peoples of the area, the Old Prussians, Lithuanians, Latvians, Estonians, and Finns remained pagans, untouched by Christianity in either western or eastern form. There the Teutonic Knights received land on the border of the Prussian lands from a sympathetic Polish duke and built their first castles. Systematically they subdued and exterminated the Prussians in the name of Christ, bringing German peasants to settle in their place. Within two generations Prussia, the East Prussia of twentieth century politics, was a German territory ruled by the order.

Prussia would eventually develop into a problem for Poland, but for Novgorod it was their allies that were the threat. Around 1200 German knights landed near Riga and began to subdue the lands of today's Latvia and Estonia, turning the natives into their tenants and eventually serfs. All power rested in the hands of the archbishop of Riga and the order of the Swordbearers. The Swordbearers joined the Teutonic Knights in 1237 as the subordinate Livonian order, cementing German rule. The resultant social and ethnic hierarchy lasted through various political changes into the twentieth century.

For the moment the Novgorodians found a new and dynamic neighbor in place of the weak Estonian tribes of earlier centuries. To makes things worse, another crusade was afoot. Sweden was also moving east, gradually conquering the Finnish tribes. As they moved east along the coast of Finland, the Swedes began to threaten Novgorod's vital trade route to the Hansa that ran through the Gulf of Finland and the Neva river. In 1240 the Swedish Earl Birger, a man more powerful than the King of Sweden himself, landed an army in Novgorod's territory on the south bank of the Neva. The local Finnish tribe, the Ingrians, sent south to Novgorod for help, and the city's newly elected prince, Alexander of Vladimir, came out to fight. The Swedes were driven into the sea, and Alexander for ever after was known as Alexander of the Neva, or Alexander Nevsky. Two years later he defeated the Livonian knights on the ice of Lake Chud, on the Estonian border, in a battle that was of little significance at the time, but eventually made great twentieth century cinema: Sergei Eisenstein's 1938 epic with Sergei Prokofiev's music. The medieval Novgorodians, however, knew what was important. Prince Alexander's epithet remained Nevsky, in memory of the truly crucial defense of Novgorod's trade, while his defeat of the knights was relegated to a few lines in the chronicle. The Livonian knights had other concerns, which distracted their attention away from the rich and powerful Novgorod. This concern was Lithuania, the main enemy of the knights in both Prussia and Livonia.

Of the peoples of the eastern Baltic, Lithuania alone managed to retain its independence. As the Teutonic Knights moved inexorably over their new territories, the Lithuanian tribes came together under one prince. Grand Prince Gediminas (1316–1341) transformed

Lithuania into a major power. He established his capital in Wilno, closer to his new territories, lands that today comprise the whole of Belarus. His even more successful son Algirdas (1341–1377) added Volhynia, Kiev, Chernigov, and parts of the Smolensk lands to his domain. Lithuania had become in extent, if not by population, the largest country in Europe. The Lithuanian princes of the house of Gediminas now ruled more than half of the former lands of Kiev Rus, excepting only Novgorod and the northeast under the Vladimir princes, and Galicia in the southwest, which the kings of Poland had recently taken.

The Lithuanian polity was an unusual amalgam of cultures, languages, and religions. The Lithuanian language had as yet no alphabet and was neither written down nor used by the new state for recordkeeping. Instead, the Lithuanian chanceries used a variant of the East Slavic language of Kiev Rus. In religion the Lithuanian rulers and people remained pagans, though the conquest of the Orthodox lands to the south introduced a new element. The Lithuanian princes placed their kinsmen and other Lithuanian nobles in charge of the new lands and many of them converted to Orthdoxy. These new Orthodox Lithuanian princelings and nobles formed a new elite on the territory of the old Kiev Rus, with the old boyars falling to the status of local squires. Yet the Grand Duke of Lithuania himself remained pagan, and as such the object of the crusading zeal of the Teutonic Knights.

The Knights were a threat not just to Lithuania, but also to Poland, newly reunited by the efforts of Casimir the Great (1333–1370). In 1385 the Poles faced a dual dilemma: increasing pressure from the Knights and the succession to the throne. Poland's ruler Jadwiga, styled "King" of Poland, as yet had no husband, and the nobles then chose Jogailo (Jagiełło), the Grand Duke of Lithuania to be her husband and their king. Jogailo would provide invaluable aid against the Teutonic Order, but he first had to become a Catholic Christian. The conversion and marriage, accompanied by an agreement of union in 1385–6, produced a new polity, the Polish-Lithuanian Commonwealth, that would dominate the politics of Eastern Europe until the seventeenth century. It was a personal union of the two states, each preserving its own institutions and administration under the same monarch. The more immediate impact of Jogailo's election as king of Poland was to create a state capable of defeating the Teutonic Order. Poland and Lithuania's victory came at the battle of Grunewald (Tannenberg) in 1410. This was the turning point in the long struggle, and by the middle of the fifteenth century the Teutonic Order was reduced to a minor vassal of the Polish crown.

Jogailo's marriage fundamentally reordered Lithuania. A bishop was appointed to Wilno and the conversion of the Lithuanian people to Catholicism began. The vast majority of the Slavic population remained Orthodox, and Orthodox nobles and princes retained their positions for the ensuing decades. The religious division within the Lithuanian state would have far-reaching consequences in the coming centuries, but for the moment, the main result was to encourage the formation of the Belorussian and Ukrainian nationalities, like the Russians born out of the earlier Kiev Rus. With the growing strength of Lithuania, the lands around Kiev revived and once again began to form a center of Orthodox culture. The city of Kiev and the Kiev Monastery of the Caves came back to life. The Ukrainian monks of Kiev and other centers recovered their traditions by sending to Moscow and Vladimir for copies of the old Kievan texts, the *Primary Chronicle*, and the stories of the Cave Monastery. Thus a new religious and cultural center came into being, one that eventually would have a profound impact on Russia.

The political and military struggle with its many rivals was not the only concern of the Moscow dynasty. From 1354 to 1378 the see of the Metropolitan of Kiev and All Rus was in the hands of Saint Aleksei, born to a boyar family in Moscow as Fyodor Biakont. Aleksei's long metropolitanate coincided with a movement of monastic revival that enjoyed his patronage as well as that of the Moscow princes.

Kiev Rus had supported many monasteries, for almost every major town had several – as did some minor towns. In 1337 the monk Sergii of Radonezh decided to establish a hermitage in imitation of the desert fathers of late antiquity and the monks of Byzantine Mount Athos. He found a forest some thirty miles north of Moscow and soon other hermits joined him. Eventually they

Figure 3. Monastery of the Dormition of the Mother of God (Kirillo-Belozerskii) around 1900.

founded a monastery dedicated to the Holy Trinity with Sergii as its leader. The new monastery stressed the importance of the common life of the monks: common prayer and attendance at liturgy, common meals, and common work. All gifts to the monastery went to the community, which was supervised by a hegumen (an abbot in Western terminology), who directed the community with firmness and humility. This revived form of monasticism with strong Byzantine inspiration spread rapidly throughout the northeast of Russia. By the time of Sergii's death in 1392 he had inspired many followers, and they went on to found numerous new communities such as the monastery of Saint Kirill (Sergii's pupil) in northern Belozero. Later in the fifteenth century Saints Zosima and Savvatii traveled all the way to the Solovki islands in the White Sea to build Russia's third great monastery.

Russia was now beginning to acquire its own saints, for in addition to the Saints Boris and Gleb came the holy metropolitans Peter and Aleksei, and especially Saint Sergii of Radonezh. The relics of the two metropolitans in the Kremlin's Dormition cathedral and those of Saint Sergii in the Trinity Monastery were already the object of pilgrimage and the subjects of stories of miraculous events. Soon all three entered the liturgy as saints and Moscow now had its own saints to rival those of Kiev and Vladimir. The three saints raised Moscow's prestige, particularly the rather political cults of the metropolitans. The sainthood of Sergii, Kirill of Belozero, and other monastic saints represented a less political piety, centered on the monasteries and the relics of their saints. The monasteries were the charismatic center of Orthodox piety and for the next two hundred years, almost all new Russian saints were holy monks or metropolitans.

The monastic ideal even permeated writings about laymen. The fifteenth century *Oration on the Life and Death of Prince Dmitrii Donskoi* praised him not so much for his great victory over the Tatars but for his exemplary Christian life, his abstinence from sexual intercourse after his children were born, his fasts, and his all-night vigils in church. These were monastic, not princely, virtues, and the text is a far cry from the earlier lives of saintly princes, such as Boris and Gleb, Michael of Tver, or especially Alexander Nevskii. Yet the *Oration on Dmitrii* was the example for all later accounts of virtuous princes to the end of the sixteenth century.

The greatest achievement of the monastic revival, and perhaps the only one to arouse enthusiasm in modern times, was the impulse it gave to architecture and icon painting. The monastery churches were at first rather modest, with a square plan and a roof supported by four interior columns. The design was ubiquitous, and it combined necessary simplicity with economy of resources. It also easily provided for the high icon screen, which came into practice at this time in Russia's monastery churches. The high icon screen soon became universal, running up from the floor of the church nearly to the ceiling and cutting off the altar from the congregation. In the middle were doors, or "royal gates" (*tsarskie vrata*), through which the priest came after the consecration of the bread and wine for the Eucharist. The order of the icons was not random. On the lowest tier, at or just below eye level, were the "local" icons, to the right of the doors stood the image of the saint or feast to which the church was dedicated. Thus, a church of Saint Nicholas would have an image of that saint, and a church of the Resurrection would have a depiction of the resurrection of Christ. The next – above eye level, and thus most visible to a standing congregation – was the "deesis tier," the centerpiece of the whole screen. In the middle over the doors, the usual image was Christ in Majesty, which depicts Christ seated on a throne surrounded by symbols of glory. By his sides were John the Baptist and Mary; the three together formed an image of the Incarnation, as well as of the ensuing intercession of Christ for sinful humanity. Mary and John slightly bow before Christ as a gesture of appeal to his mercy. On either side of this central composition were the four apostles. Above these large icons was the "festival tier," which depicted the main festivals of the Christian year, starting with the Annunciation in March (not with Christmas, as might be expected). Above these, again, in larger format were the Old Testament prophets and patriarchs, sometimes forming two tiers. At the center was usually another icon of the Mother of God, flanked by David and Solomon, and the prophets. The basic idea of these images was the presence of Christ in the world and his incarnation to save mankind. The icon screen, like the church around it, was the meeting point of the world of the spirit and the visible world. This was not a new idea in Orthodoxy, but the monastic movement had found a way to express it with even more depth and clarity.

Thus icons became both more numerous and, if possible, more important. Theophanes the Greek came to Moscow from Novgorod in the 1390s and worked with local painters. The most important of these was the monk Andrei Rublev (circa 1370–1430), whose work hung on the icon screens of many monasteries around Moscow and eventually even in the Kremlin's Annunciation Cathedral. Rublev's icons display less of the hieratic stiffness of the older schools and portray a certain warmth in the face of Christ and in the faces of saints that seems to accord well with the inwardness of the newer monastic piety. Like other forms of that piety, Rublev's icons provided an example for his pupils and imitators, and the new style spread far beyond the monasteries. The work of Rublev and his contemporaries was a new departure that laid the basis of the Russian icon of the succeeding centuries.

During the fourteenth century Moscow had established hegemony over the northeast – but only hegemony. At the death of Vasilii I (1389–1425), Tver remained a thorn in its side. Novgorod pursued its own policies and a number of the principalities of the northeast remained effectively independent. Lithuania continued to play an important role and often a hostile one, in spite of Vasilii's marriage to a Lithuanian princess. Nevertheless, Vasilii held on to power and even expanded the territory directly subject to Moscow. The mechanism of expansion was simple: when Moscow annexed a territory the local elite, the local boyars and landholders were co-opted into Moscow's army and administration, and their landholdings were confirmed. If resistance was unusually strong, land was confiscated or the local elite moved elsewhere and were given new land, but such extreme measures were unusual. Moscow could usually count on the loyalty of the new recruits, who exchanged local autonomy for a share in the rewards of serving a growing and successful power.

Moscow's success and the loyalty of its boyar elite were tested to the limits in the stormy and bloody events of the reign of Vasilii II (1425–1462). Vasilii II was only ten years old at the time of his father's death and his right to rule was immediately challenged by his uncle Iurii in northern Galich. Iurii's challenge set off a civil war that quickly brought him victory and rule in Moscow. The victorious Iurii ordered the young Vasilii exiled to Kostroma on the Volga river. Then the Moscow boyars showed their hand. Many moved to Kostroma with their retinues, while others just abandoned Iurii. Isolated in the Kremlin, Iurii fled back north and died in 1434. His eldest son Vasilii Iur'evich "the Squint-eyed" took up the cause, proclaiming himself the rightful heir to the throne. After much marching and counter marching, Grand Prince Vasilii defeated his cousin Vasilii Iur'evich in 1436 and had him blinded as well. This act of cruelty was not the end, for Iurii's second son, Dmitrii Shemiaka, replaced his brother as leader of the rebels. An unexpected defeat of Grand Prince Vasilii at the hands of a Tatar raiding party in 1445 gave Shemiaka a chance, and he took Moscow and blinded Vasiliii in revenge for his brother. Again the Moscow boyars, initially friendly, switched their allegiance back to Vasilii and Shemiaka fled north. He made a last stand in 1450, lost again, and then fled to Novgorod. There he died in 1453, according to the chronicle story, from a poisoned chicken fed to him by an agent of the Grand Prince.

These dark and confused struggles could take place in comparative isolation because great changes were taking place in the Horde. Fatally weakened by Tamerlane's campaigns, the Horde began to disintegrate. In 1430 Crimea broke off and in 1436 Kazan' formed an independent khanate on the middle Volga. Like the earlier Volga Bulgaria, it was an agricultural society with a nomadic fringe on the south and a Muslim culture with religious ties to Central Asia. Of the Golden Horde remained only the "Great Horde," a small group of nomadic tribes that raided Russian and Lithuanian territory, but was no longer capable of ruling Moscow. Vasilii II even established his own dependent khanate at Kasimov on the Oka river southeast of Moscow, whose Tatar warriors served the Moscow dynasty for the next two hundred years.

The rule of the Mongols, or more properly the Golden Horde, over Russia had lasted a little over two centuries. Initially the conquest had been extremely destructive, but its later economic effects were largely confined to the payment of tribute. The inclusion of Russia in the Horde's domain may have even strengthened Russia's trade with the east, judging from archeological evidence, the coins and pottery of the Horde and its eastern and southern neighbors found in Russian towns. The Mongol episode also provided material for endless speculation in modern times on the imagined effect of the "Mongols" on Russia. For racial theorists in Germany and elsewhere it made Russia "Asiatic." In fact, the Horde had little traceable effect on Russian society. Religion provided a cultural barrier on both sides, and the two societies were incompatible: Russia a rather simple sedentary society and the Horde a state with relatively complex institutions specific to nomadic society. In China, Central Asia, and Persia, the Mongols moved in among the sedentary peoples and were assimilated into them, but not in Russia. Russia's geography prevented that outcome. Some modern historians have made much of the "oriental" character of the Russian state, again an alleged legacy of the Mongols. The problem with such theories is that they lack empirical foundation. The words and institutions that may have entered Russian from Mongolian via Turkic (such as *tamga*, for a sort of sales tax and *yam*, for the messenger system that relied on villages with special status to provide the riders and their horses) were marginal institutions. These were only extra bits in a state formed by the prince's household ruling an agricultural society. Finally, the notion of Mongol influence at the basis relies on the notion of innate Asiatic slavishness and despotism, and it is neither an accurate description of the Mongol polity nor, as we shall see, of the Russian state that emerged after 1480.

The events in the Orthodox church were as momentous as the fall of the Horde. After the death of metropolitan Aleksei, the Greek church chose the Bulgarian Kiprian to succeed him. Kiprian's mission was to keep together under his jurisdiction the Orthodox lands of Lithuania, Moscow, and Novgorod, as they had been in Kievan times. This was not an easy task, for both Lithuania and Moscow wanted control but Kiprian was a powerful figure in the church as well as in politics, and it was a cultural force, to boot. On his death in 1406 the Greek Photios received the see and largely identified his interests with Moscow. Photios died in 1431, right at the start of Moscow's dynastic turmoil. His death deprived Grand Prince Vasilii of a crucial ally at the worst possible moment. Unfortunately his replacement was another Greek – Isidoros – who arrived in Moscow in 1434. Exactly at that time the Byzantine Empire was in its last agony, reduced to the city of Constantinople and a few islands. In a vain effort to secure aid from Western Europe, Emperor Constantine XI agreed to discuss church union with Rome. Isidoros quickly left Moscow for Italy to join the Greek prelates in discussion. In reality, Rome proposed simple surrender, and at the council of Florence in 1439 the Greek bishops, including Isidoros, gave in under pressure from the Emperor. They accepted the supremacy of the pope and the Latin position on the *filioque*. Among the Greeks, the news provoked a firestorm of opposition, especially in the monasteries, since the fourteenth century renewed centers of Orthodox piety. The surrender at Florence divided and weakened Byzantium rather than strengthened it, and in any case Western aid

never came in sufficient quantity. In 1453 the army of Mehmed the
Conqueror breached the walls and gates of Constantinople and put
an end to a millennium of Byzantine civilization. In its place the
Sultans built Istanbul into the great capital of an Islamic empire.
Justinian's church of Saint Sophia became a mosque.

When the news of the fall of Constantinople reached Moscow,
the affairs of the Russian church were long settled. Isidoros had
traveled back to Moscow with the news of Florence, and in 1443
the Russian bishops met with him to consider the situation. They
unanimously rejected subjection to Rome, deposed Isidoros, and
elected in his place, Bishop Iona of Riazan at the direction of Grand
Prince Vasilii. The Orthodox church in Russia was now separated
from the Greeks, for it had elected a leader without reference to
Constantinople, which was now in the hands of unionists. Russia's
autocephaly, as its ecclesiastical independence is called, was not
planned. It was the result of necessity, the only solution to the
dilemma presented by the apostasy of the Greeks at Florence. In
his testament Iona specified that when Orthodoxy was restored
in Constantinople, even if under the Turks, Russia would return
to obedience to the Greek bishops. This was a pious hope that
remained unfulfilled, for the Russian church continued to choose
its own metropolitan. For the Moscow princes this was a great
opportunity, as it meant that they would be the only secular rulers
with a voice in the affairs of the church in Russia.

Grand Prince Vasilii II died at the age of forty-seven in 1462. He
had emerged the victor in a ruthless struggle with his own uncle
and cousins and maintained the hegemony of Moscow. He had
encouraged the church to assert its orthodoxy and its independence
from the Greeks. His eldest son Ivan was already twenty-two, old
enough to rule in his own right. As the future would soon reveal,
the young prince was ready to seize the opportunity that his father
had left him.

3

The Emergence of Russia

At the end of the fifteenth century, Russia came into being as a state – no longer just a group of related principalities. Precisely at this time in written usage the modern term *Rossia* (a literary expression borrowed from Greek) began to edge out the traditional and vernacular *Rus*. If we must choose a moment for the birth of Russia out of the Moscow principality, it is the final annexation of Novgorod by Grand Prince Ivan III (1462–1505) of Moscow in 1478. By this act, Ivan united the two principal political and ecclesiastical centers of medieval Russia under one ruler, and in the next generation he and his son Vasilii III (1505–1533) added the remaining territories. In the west and north, the boundaries they established are roughly those of Russia today, while in the south and east the frontier for most of its length remained the ecological boundary between forest and steppe. In spite of later expansion, this territory formed the core of Russia until the middle of the eighteenth century, and it contained most of the population and the centers of state and church. The Russians were still a people scattered along the rivers between great forests.

In the south and east, mostly beyond the forests and out in the steppe, Russia's neighbors remained the Tatar khanates that emerged in the 1430s from the breakup of the Golden Horde: Kazan, Crimea in the Crimean peninsula, and the Great Horde ruling the steppe. The Great Horde in turn broke up around 1500 to form the khanate of Astrakhan on the lower Volga and farther east the Nogai Horde. Farther east the khanate of Siberia held sway over the tiny population of the vast plain of the Ob' and Irtysh rivers. These states were complex social organisms. Kazan' was the only one to occupy part of the forest zone, and its people settled along the rivers and farmed the land like the Russians but with a nomadic appendage where the steppe began to the southeast. The Nogais were pure nomads. Crimea and Astrakhan' were somewhere in between, their population made up of mostly steppe dwellers, but Astrakhan' was a town and Crimea had towns and garden agriculture. Its location meant that it had a lively trade and close political ties with its great neighbor to the south, the Ottoman Empire.

At this moment the Ottomans were at the peak of their power, for in 1453 Mehmed the Conqueror, already master of most of Anatolia and the Balkans, took Constantinople, the ancient capital of Byzantium. In 1516 the Turks moved south, quickly capturing the Levant and Egypt, north Africa and Mesopotamia. Thus the last great empire of western Eurasia was born, and it soon turned its attention to central Europe. In 1524 the defeat of Hungary at the battle of Mohacs laid open the road into Germany and in 1529 the Ottomans laid siege to Vienna itself. For the moment, the Ottoman Turks paid little attention to Russia. Their great opponents were Iran and the Holy Roman Empire, and in any case the Crimeans, from 1475 Ottoman vassals, stood between Russia and the Turks. The Sultans in Istanbul wanted the Crimean cavalry for the Turkish wars in Hungary and Iran and did not want to waste them in raids against a minor state far in the north. At the same time the Sultans gave their Crimean vassals considerable freedom of action, and Ivan III was able to establish an understanding with the Crimeans that lasted into the sixteenth century. Russia continued to play a major role in the politics of the steppe, sending and receiving envoys back and involving itself in the endless feuds and rivalries among the ruling dynasties and clans.

To the west Russia had only one major rival, Lithuania, now united with Poland. The resultant Polish-Lithuanian state was the hegemonic power of Eastern Europe, more populous than Russia and more powerful than any of its neighbors. Poland, having vanquished the Teutonic Knights and fended off the Tatars and Turks to the south, had only Russia as a rival left. Poland's power came not only from the weakness of most neighbors, but also from its political structure, for the growing role of the diet provided a major role for the magnates and nobility. The diet gave its elites an important stake in the prosperity of the state but a strong king still guaranteed basic order and direction. That constitution would lead to ruin later, but in 1500 it was more durable than that of its neighbors', and Poland's armies could dominate the field against most enemies.

Russia's other neighbors to the west were of little account. The Livonian Order was too small and too decentralized to matter much in political affairs, and Sweden (including Finland) was part of the united kingdom of Denmark, Norway, and Sweden until 1520. The center of gravity of the three kingdoms was in Denmark, which was too far to the west to pay much attention to the remote border of Finland and Russia. Trade continued through both Livonia and Finland, and even increased in importance, but with little overall political effect.

The situation of its neighbors allowed Russia to emerge onto the stage of European politics at an exceptionally favorable moment. The Tatar khanates were preoccupied with one another and the Ottomans, while Livonia and Sweden for very different reasons scarcely impinged on Russia's consciousness. Russia had only one important rival, Poland-Lithuania, the primary focus of its foreign policy. That rival was powerful enough to provide a challenge to the new state of Ivan III, a challenge which he handled with great skill.

The new Russian state that emerged at the end of the fifteenth century was much larger and more complex than the medieval Moscow principality even in its later phases. A new state required new institutions and terminology. The Grand Prince began to style himself "Sovereign of All Rus" or even "autocrat," the latter to signify his new independence from the Horde and any other claimants. Ivan III did not rule alone, any more than did his predecessors. Russia's ruling elite now included princelings and boyars from the newly acquired territories, Iaroslavl' and Rostov princes, and Lithuanian Gediminovichi – all of whom formed an expanded ruling elite around the prince of Moscow. This new elite was small for the time being, for in Ivan III's time it comprised only eighteen or so families, growing to about forty-five by 1550. Most of the senior men from these clans made up the duma, or council of the Grand Prince, and held the rank of boyar, or that of a sort of junior boyar with the untranslatable title "*okol'nichii*."[1] Just barely a formal institution, the duma met with the prince in the palace and discussed the major issues of law and administration, war and peace. The men of these ruling clans attained the rank of boyar and other ranks and offices by tradition and a complex system of precedence (Russian "*mestnichestvo*") that regulated their place in the court, military, and government hierarchy. The precedence system mandated that no man should serve the prince at a lesser rank and office than had his ancestors.

The Grand Prince had some leeway with the precedence system, for it did not dictate exactly who in each clan should receive what rank. The system required only that some of the men from each of the great families should receive certain ranks, and that the greatest should sit in the duma and receive the rank of boyar. In theory the princes could appoint anyone to the duma, but in practice they chose members of the same families year after year, adding new ones only occasionally. These men were not just servants of the prince, but also immensely wealthy aristocrats with great landholdings – the pinnacle of a much larger landholding class. The Russian nobleman's primary duty was service in the army, mainly on the frontier, for the administration of the state was in the hand of a tiny group of officials and princely servants.

Some of these officials were great boyars, like the treasurers, usually chosen from the Greek Khovrin clan, or the major domo and the equerry, who managed the Kremlin palace and the prince's household. To assist these aristocrats there were also secretaries, men of lesser status from the prince's household who were sometimes of Tatar origin. Most of them served in the Treasury, where a dozen or so clerks and copyists kept the records of foreign policy and the charters and testaments of the princes, carefully preserved with the furs, jewels, tax receipts in silver, and other treasures in the basement under the palace church of the Kremlin, the Cathedral of the Annunciation. In the time of Ivan III there were only a few

---

[1] From *okolo* (around, about); that is, someone "around" the person of the prince.

dozen such secretaries, and the state was still essentially the prince's household, its offices being rooms in his palace.

For all their dominant role in Russian politics, the Kremlin and its elite were not the whole of Russia. Several million of peasants, almost all of them still free and most of them tenants only of the crown, made up the great mass of its population. They grew the food, raised cows and chickens, and supplemented their meager fare from the berries, mushrooms, and wild game of the great forests. Their status as tenants of the crown, however, was rapidly coming to an end as the great monasteries and the boyars encroached on their lands. The Grand Princes needed to reward loyal supporters, especially in newly annexed territories, and to maintain a cavalry army as well. The army had to live off its own, from the private lands of the cavalrymen. The princes so far lacked cash to pay them, and thus it was not merely to curry favor that the princes granted lands. The only restriction that they could put on such grants was to give them with the proviso that the estate could not be sold or willed without the knowledge of the prince. This type of grant was called *pomest'e*, and great boyars as well as humble provincials received such lands. The landholding class of cavalrymen fell into two broad groups: the "Sovereign's court" who served in Moscow (at least in theory) immediately below the boyars, and the "town gentry" of the provinces. The "town gentry" normally held their lands mainly in one local area and served together in the cavalry. The elite of the army was the Sovereign's court. The growth of the state and its army meant constant tinkering with the organization of the landholding gentry, but the basic outlines that began to form late in the fifteenth century remained until the end of the sixteenth. Then the *pomest'e* system spread to the southern borders, considerably enlarging the landholding class at the expense of the peasant freeholders. This new situation contributed greatly to the upheavals of the ensuing decades.

The gentry resided mainly in the towns, most of which were small, and the boyars lived in Moscow. A few centers, Moscow, Novgorod, and Pskov were real cities that supported merchants who traded with Western Europe or the Near East. Though a largely agrarian economy, Russia was not bereft of crafts or commerce, nor was it a land of subsistence peasants cut off from any markets.

The sheer size of the country and the sparse population dictated exchange among regions: almost all salt, for example, came from saline springs in the northern taiga belt until late in the seventeenth century. The men who boiled down the water to make salt and ship it south made great fortunes. Most notable were the Stroganovs, who amassed a fortune large enough to finance the first steps in the conquest of Siberia. Novgorod and its neighbor Pskov remained important centers of trade with northern Europe through the Baltic Sea, but their capacity was limited by the small rivers and absence of large harbors at the east end of the Gulf of Finland. Then in 1553 the English sea captain and explorer Richard Chancellor made his way around Norway into the White Sea, landing at the mouth of the Northern Dvina River. With this voyage a direct path for large ships opened to Western Europe, and Tsar Ivan the Terrible encouraged the English Muscovy Company to bring their ships every summer to the northern port. The Dvina and other rivers made possible the long journey from Moscow to the new port of Archangel, and the English were soon joined by the even more enterprising Dutch. Moscow itself was the hub of all Russian trade, and the city grew rapidly throughout the 1500s. Commerce with Russia was not minor for the Dutch and English, for by 1600 the Dutchmen engaged in the Archangel trade had made so much money that they could form a new company, the Dutch East India Company, which then set out to conquer what is today Indonesia. The Russian trade partly financed Holland's greatest commercial adventure.

Against this background of social change and economic evolution the rulers of Russia and their court did not remain idle. For the whole of his life Ivan III conducted a relentless struggle to expand the power and territory of the grand princes of Moscow. The annexation of Novgorod was his greatest victory, but not the only one. He exploited the dissatisfaction of the regional princelings of Lithuania along his western border so as to encourage several of them to accept his sovereignty, and he rounded out and confirmed these acquisitions by war. He absorbed Moscow's ancient rival Tver' in 1485 and established his influence over the last two independent territories of Riazan' and Pskov so that his son could later annex them without effort. Equally important, he put an end to the two and a half centuries of Russian dependency on the Tatar Hordes.

In 1480 the Khan of the Great Horde sent its army north toward Moscow. Ivan and many of his boyars hesitated, unsure whether they should meet the Tatars or just flee north. With some encouragement from the church, he went out to meet them at the Ugra river, a small tributary of the upper Don. After a few days of watching one another, the two armies departed for home. This event, the "standing on the Ugra," was ever after seen in Russia as the end of Tatar overlordship. Ivan moved aggressively into the space left by the fragmentation of the Horde, involving himself in Kazan's dynastic politics. With time, Ivan's intrigues with the Tatars would have great consequences.

Ivan III of Moscow began to call himself the ruler of "All Rus," but his new larger state demanded a better defended and more adequate capital. For this Ivan turned to Italy, the center of European architecture as well as engineering and fortification. He had already been in contact with Italy from the time of his marriage in 1473 to Zoe Paleologue, the daughter of the last Byzantine ruler of the Peloponnesus, for Zoe had taken refuge from the Turks at the papal court. There were other Greeks in Moscow as well, who had extensive contacts with their compatriots and relatives in Italy, and through them Ivan sent for architects and engineers to rebuild the Moscow Kremlin and its churches. The result was that the Kremlin, the quintessentially Russian place to the modern eye, with its ancient churches and pointed towers in dark red brick, was not the work of Russians at all, but with few exceptions the product of Italian masters.

The earlier Kremlin of the fourteenth century had had white stone walls in the usual native style of Russian fortresses, and within the walls were wooden dwellings for princes and boyars as well as stone churches. Ivan did not want to modify the basic form of the churches. That form had a spiritual meaning that a Western plan could not have. Aristotele Fioravanti of Bologna solved the problem by building a new and larger Dormition Cathedral in the Kremlin with Italian technique but Russian form. Then he and others, Marco Ruffo and Pietro Antonio Solari from Milan, Aloisio da Caresano, and others went to work on the walls. One of the builders wrote back to a brother in Milan that the prince of Moscow wanted a castle "like that of Milan" (referring to the Sforza castle), and that

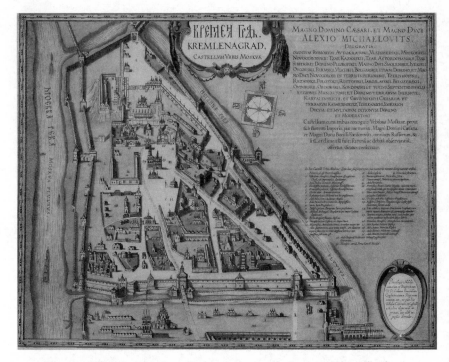

Figure 4. The Moscow Kremlin in a Seventeenth Century Atlas. The drawing shows the towers with low roofs after the example of the Sforza Castle. The high-pointed roofs on the towers that are so familiar today were added in the 1670s.

is more or less what the prince got. They also began a new palace in the north Italian style, parts of which still survive. Only the churches were built in the traditional Russian style, albeit by Italian builders, with the sole exception of the Annunciation Cathedral, the palace chapel. Today the Italian work is visible only in the walls and the "House of Facets," one of the main audience chambers. The other fragments of the old palace and the Renaissance elements in the churches were heavily "russified" by later repairs. The seventeenth-century addition of pointed roofs to the towers along the wall effectively concealed the Milanese model, but in 1520 the palace and the walls must have looked very Italian indeed.

The new Russia with its Italianate Kremlin may have taken its architecture, if only for a generation, from Italy, but it remained

Orthodox in religion and its culture remained firmly religious. The context of Orthodoxy, however, had altered, for the emergence of the new state had come rapidly on the heels of a major change in the status of the Orthodox church, the establishment of autocephaly in 1448. The new situation of the church and of Russia required a new conception of Russia's place in the divine plan of salvation, and as early as Ivan III's "standing on the Ugra" of 1480 the church found the answer. Russia was to be understood as a "new Israel," and the Russians were a new chosen people with their capital in Moscow, the new Jerusalem. Like the ancient Israelites, the Russians were the one people on earth chosen by God to receive the correct faith. Like ancient Israel, Russia was beset on all sides by unbelieving enemies, the Catholic Swedes and Poles to the west and the Muslim Tatars to the south and east. Critical to their survival, as for ancient Israel, were firm adherence to the correct faith in God and punctilious obedience to God's commandments. Such faith and behavior would guarantee survival, for God would deliver their enemies into their hand, as he had done for King David. If they could remain faithful, they would avoid the fate of ancient Israel until Christ came again to earth.

Holding to the correct faith in last years of the reign of Ivan III had become, however, a serious problem. For the first time since the conversion of Saint Vladimir in 988, the Russian church found itself confronting opponents from within and was beset by internal disputes over the system of belief. In Novgorod a small group of clergy began to question the Orthodox formulation of the notion of the divinity of Christ, the common forms of devotion involving icons, and monasticism as well. As they seem to have questioned the Christian notions of the Trinity, their opponents, mainly Saint Joseph of Volokolamsk, labeled them Judaizers, exaggerating their dissent and slandering them as enemies of Christianity. The group acquired some followers in Moscow, even among the officials of the Kremlin offices, before it was suppressed in 1503, and the leaders were burnt as heretics. These were the first such executions for heresy in Russian history. The church could find no defense of such actions in its traditions, and had to turn to the West, to a description of the Spanish inquisition taken from the words of the Imperial ambassador, to justify the executions.

More widespread was the controversy over monastic life that arose at the same time and lasted for a generation. This dispute was far from an arcane debate among monks, for monasticism was still central to Orthodoxy as it emerged from the medieval period. The Kremlin itself included the monastery of the Miracle of Saint Michael the Archangel and the Convent of the Ascension, the activities of both of which formed integral parts of the life of the court. The city of Moscow had dozens of small monasteries within its walls, and several great ones just beyond them. Only a day's journey north, Saint Sergii's Trinity Monastery was the annual site of the pilgrimage of the whole court for the saint's festival in September. Every Russian town of any consequence boasted one or two monasteries in or around it. For much of the first half of the sixteenth century Russian monks discussed the proper type of monastic life, some stressing individual asceticism and common life. Both styles were part of Orthodox tradition, exemplified in the work and teaching of Saint Joseph of Volokolamsk and Nil Sorskii. Eventually some of Nil's posthumous followers came to question the very idea of monastic landholding as an obstacle to a holy life.

This controversy was purely Russian, but the church was not entirely isolated from the world. Orthodox brethren still made up most of the population of the Balkans under Turkish rule, and the great monasteries on Mount Athos provided spiritual leadership. The most prolific writer on religious topics in early sixteenth-century Russia was actually a Greek named Michael Trivolis (1470–1556), in monastic life he took the name Maximos. Maksim the Greek, as he was known in Russia, had spent his youth in Venice and Florence, but ultimately came to reject the Renaissance secular culture for Orthodox monasticism. In this decision he imitated Savonarola, with whose teaching he was acquainted. In Russia he provided an encyclopedic collection of tracts and essays on topics from the errors of Islam to the correct stance on monastic landholding. His mild critique of that practice and other deviations from the then dominant notions among the higher clergy led to his condemnation and exile in the 1530s, but even in exile he remained a major figure in the church and ultimately the young Ivan IV ordered him released.

His writings were widely copied and remained authoritative on many subjects for the ensuing century.

Ivan III's successor, Vasilii III (1505–1533), came to the throne not as the eldest son but as the result of Ivan's decision to give it to him. He was the son of Ivan's second wife, the Greek Sophia Paleologue, and Ivan chose him, after some hesitation, over his grandson by his first wife (his son by the first wife had died). Much of Vasilii's effort was to go to maintaining and expanding Russia's position in the world. The territorial rivalry with Poland-Lithuania ended in a war that was successful for Russia with the capture of Smolensk in 1514. Smolensk was the last ethnographically Russian land outside the rule of Moscow, and in addition its conquest provided the state with a major fortress far to the west of Moscow. Though the war ended only in a truce, it fixed the Russo-Polish boundary for a century. Relations with the Tatar khanates, in contrast, involved a bewildering chain of intrigue and counter-intrigue as well as endless Tatar raids for slaves and booty on the southern frontier. About this time Vasilii adopted the practice of mobilizing the army on that southern frontier every summer, whether a formal state of war existed or not, for there was no other way to prevent the annual raids that formed an important part of the nomadic economy.

Vasilii's greatest challenge, however, came not from the Tatars or Poland but from his own dynastic problems. For his first wife he had taken Solomoniia Saburova, not a foreign princess like his mother but the daughter of a prominent boyar. The marriage was successful in all but one crucial respect: no children were born. After much controversy and consultation with the church, he pressured Solomoniia into entering a convent and finally dissolved the marriage in 1525. Vasilii then married princess Elena Glinskaia, the daughter of a Lithuanian prince whose clan had taken refuge in Moscow after it had failed to successfully challenge its own sovereign. The Glinskiis had remained a powerful family in Russian exile, and claimed descent from the Tatar emir Yedigei, a great warrior who had fought Tamerlane himself in the early fifteenth century. In 1530 Elena gave birth to a son Ivan, who would be known to history as Ivan the Terrible.

IVAN THE TERRIBLE

Like so many such epithets "Terrible (*grozny*)" was a product of later romanticism, not of the sixteenth century. Even Ivan's most determined Russian opponents never used it, and indeed in the language of the time the Russian word *grozny* would have meant "awe-inspiring" (the English is a traditional mistranslation) and so it had mildly positive connotations. Be that as it may, Vasilii's untimely death in 1533 put the child Ivan on the throne of the Grand Prince of Moscow and all Rus, a situation that required a regency consisting of his mother and several prominent boyars to run the country. The great boyar clans, the Glinskiis and Shuiskiis, Bel'skiis and Obolenskiis, competed for power at the court and did not hesitate to exile and execute the losers. The death of Ivan's mother in 1538 spurred on the intrigues, and only the marriage and majority of the young prince imposed a certain calm on the political waters.

Shortly after his marriage to Anastasiia, the daughter of the boyar Iurii Romanov-Koshkin, Ivan was crowned by Makarii, the head of the church as Metropolitan of Moscow, in 1547 in the Kremlin's Dormition cathedral. Makarii crowned him not just Grand Prince, like his father, but also Tsar, a title derived ultimately from the name of Caesar. Tsar was the popular name among the Slavs for the Roman and Byzantine emperors, and thus conveyed a proclamation of equality in rank with those rulers as well as the Holy Roman Emperor in the West. Tsar was also the Russian word for title of the Khan of the Golden Horde and his successors in Kazan' and Crimea as well as of the Ottoman Sultan. Most important, it was the title of David and Solomon in the Slavic Old Testament. In case anyone missed the point, Ivan had the walls of the audience chambers of the Kremlin palace decorated with Old Testament scenes. There the Old Testament kings ("tsars" to the Russians) surrounded Joshua's conquest of the land of Canaan. Henceforth Russia's rulers were tsars, the equals of the Western Emperor, the Sultan, and the Old Testament kings.

Thus began a reign of unprecedented activity that lasted thirty-five years, full of drama and victory, bloodshed, and defeat. Untiring in pursuit of his goals, Ivan left his mark on generations to come.

Within a short time of his coronation, he set out on the first of his great enterprises. In the years of the regency, Moscow's influence in Kazan' had slipped, permitting Kazan' once again to fall to hostile khans. Ivan set off to end the threat by installing a pro-Moscow khan, but after repeated failures to take the city, he simply annexed it when it fell to the Russian army in 1552. Ivan was only twenty-two years old, and he did not stop there. His armies went on down the Volga to Astrakhan' and seized it and its territory as well. These conquests presented the Russians with a new situation, for never before had any substantial non-Christian population existed within their borders. On the capture of Kazan, Ivan ordered the Tatars remaining in the city to move out beyond the fortress walls, subsequently building a cathedral and settling Russians in their place in the city. Some of the Tatar elite entered Russian service, most of whom eventually converted to Orthodoxy, but many more fled to Crimea. The tsar enrolled thousands of Tatars in his army with the status of military servants. Other lesser landholders, townspeople, and peasants as well as the other nationalities of the khanate, the Chuvash, Mari, and Udmurt peasants, now acquired a special status. In place of the usual Russian taxes they paid *yasak*, a sort of tribute, to the tsar. Beyond these measures, the Russians did nothing to further subjugate the Tatars and other Volga peoples. There was no attempt at mass conversion. Virtually all Tatars and Bashkirs remained Muslims, visiting their mosques for Friday prayers, sending young men to Samarkand and other Central Asian towns to acquire the knowledge to become imams, and reading the Koran and other religious literature as before. There was no equivalent to the expulsion of the Moors from Spain after the end of the Reconquista.

With Astrakhan' came control of the whole of the Volga basin and surrounding lands. By the 1560s the Russians had a fort on the Terek river at the foot of the Caucasus, looking up at the high mountains. Ivan established relations with the Circassian mountaineers of the Caucasus and the Circassians' lesser dependents, the Chechens and other peoples. The conquest of the Volga, a response primarily to the local situation on the border with Kazan', put Russia into a new geopolitical situation. Its control of the Volga for the first time in history cut off the western part of the Eurasian steppe from the main body to the east. Nomadic peoples continued to cross the Volga back and forth until the eighteenth century, but now they crossed under Russian control.

In the course of the 1550s Ivan acquired experience and maturity. In 1553, to be sure, he suffered a grave illness and some of the boyars were unwilling to accept his son as the rightful heir. This crisis, however, passed and peace returned to the court. Ivan governed with the boyars and apparently under the influence of his spiritual father Silvestr, the priest of the palace church, the Annunciation Cathedral, and his favorite Aleksei Adashev, a man of low rank in the landholding class but capable and able to work with the great boyar clans. The tsar and his government seem to have worked together fairly harmoniously. Together they expanded the state apparatus in Moscow and the provinces and reorganized the army. Peace did not last long: in 1558 tsar Ivan began a war with the aim of the annexation of Livonia, a war that would continue after his death and have profound effects on Russia. Livonia in 1558 was a country in crisis, which was brought on by the Reformation and the end of the Livonian Order that had ruled since the thirteenth century. As the state dissolved, various groups of knights began to turn to neighboring powers for support: the first group turned to Poland. Ivan had long advanced claims to the area based on spurious dynastic arguments, and indeed he claimed Livonia as the territory of his ancestors, which it had never been. In the winter of 1558, he decided on a preemptive strike to counter possible Polish involvement. The Russian army moved into Livonia and quickly captured Dorpat (Tartu) and the important port of Narva just across the Russian border. These two towns, and particularly Narva, seem to have been Ivan's primary goals. At the lowest ebb of his military fortunes in coming years, he offered to give up everything else if he could keep Narva.

In the beginning, fortune favored the Russian armies, but their very success inevitably aroused the opposition of Poland-Lithuania. While the Russians were successful and English merchant ships began to come to Narva, Ivan cultivated the friendship of Queen Elizabeth of England, even proposing various marriage schemes. As the years wore on, however, Russia proved unable to sustain the necessary military effort. The Polish army defeated the Russians at several important battles, and to complicate matters, the nobles of northern Estonia turned to Sweden for help. The Swedish forces landed in Reval in 1561, turning the war into a three-way contest. In this situation the political harmony at the Russian court began to evaporate. It seems that Adashev and Silvestr had always harbored doubts about the Livonian enterprise, and with Russian defeats some of the boyars, the most important being Prince Andrei Kurbskii, went over to Poland. Ivan's wife, Anastasiia, died in 1560, and Ivan chose for his second wife the daughter of the Circassian prince Temriuk, the new tsaritsa taking the name Maria in baptism. Metropolitan Makarii's death in 1563 removed the last restraining influence over the tsar. Ivan grew suspicious of many of the great boyars, whom he suspected of disloyalty to his policies and perhaps even his person. He had several of them executed or exiled. Many of them, he would claim, had been reluctant to support his young son as heir to the throne during his illness in 1553. In December 1564, Ivan suddenly left the Kremlin, taking with him only his family, his immediate and trusted servants, and the treasury. First he went south to one of the small suburban palaces and then turned northeast, circling around the city and coming to stay at Aleksandrovo, a small town some hundred miles to the northeast of Moscow. There he stayed several weeks, remaining out of all communication with the capital. He then sent a messenger to Moscow with an announcement that must have come to the population like a thunderbolt. The Tsar of all Russia announced that he was angry at the treason and misdeeds of the boyars and he abdicated the throne. Only the populace of Moscow was exempted from his suspicions: toward them he had no anger. After a few days, the people and the boyars, led by the church, sent a delegation out to Aleksandrovo, begging him to change his mind. Ivan consented and returned to Moscow.

The winter journey to Aleksandrovo and back was the beginning of five years of bloodshed and upheaval, the period that marked Ivan for later generations as "the Terrible." Sergei Eisenstein's famous film of of 1944 about Ivan ended its first part precisely at this moment, the petition of the people at Alexandrovo. Eisenstein's portrait was notably ambiguous and historians have never ceased to debate Ivan's policies and personality. Some have even argued that he was paranoid, but there is too little evidence to analyze his personality. We know only what he did, not his inner thoughts and feelings.

On his return from Alexandrovo, Ivan divided the country and the state into two parts, reserving the income and administration of the north, Novgorod, and much of central Russia to himself, as the "Oprichnina."[2] The Oprichnina was a separate realm within the state, with a separate boyar duma and Oprichnina army. The remainder of the country he left to the boyars and the old boyar duma. Partly a military measure, the Oprichnina served Ivan as a political base from which to strike at the boyars whom he considered unreliable. Executions followed gruesome torture, and whole communities, like the landholders of the Novgorod area, were sent into exile on the Volga frontier. Protestations from the church were to no avail, and in 1568 Ivan had Metropolitan Filipp deposed and soon afterwards killed. Compliant churchmen were appointed in his place and the places of his supporters. Eventually some of the leaders of the Oprichnina were themselves killed, and finally in 1570 Ivan executed nearly two thousand people in Novgorod, including nobles and townspeople. Then, as suddenly as he had begun, he terminated the whole policy in 1572, prohibiting even the use of the name Oprichnina.

After the end of the Oprichnina, Russia's internal politics were relatively quiet, broken only by bizarre episodes like Ivan's temporary abdication in 1575 in favor of Semen Bekbulatovich, a scion of the Astrakhan' khans who had converted to Orthodoxy, or the death of Ivan's heir, Ivan Ivanovich, in 1581. The story, perhaps true, was that Tsar Ivan struck his son in a rage and the heir died on the spot. Toward the end of his life Ivan compiled long lists of his victims and sent large gifts to the great monasteries with orders to pray for the souls of those who had perished at his orders. The war in Livonia stagnated, but by 1580, Stefan Bathory, the newly elected king of Poland managed to expel the Russians and divide Livonia with Sweden. The only success for Ivan was Bathory's subsequent failure to take Pskov after a long siege.

In 1584 Ivan died while playing chess in the Kremlin palace. He had nothing to show for the Livonian war but a country ruined

---

[2] From old Russian *oprich'*, meaning "separate" or "apart from."

by overtaxation to support a failed war. His earlier successes were overshadowed by the disorder and bloodshed of the Oprichnina years, though his conquests on the Volga remained as a permanent and crucial acquisition. In the very last years of Ivan's life another rather different expedition enlarged Russia even further. In 1582–1583 the Cossack Yermak, perhaps sponsored by the Stroganovs rather than Ivan himself, crossed the Urals into western Siberia, following the rivers to the capital of the Tatar khanate of Siberia. There a few thousand Tatars ruled other native peoples of the Urals and subarctic regions. Yermak took the city, established a Russian fort nearby to be called Tobol'sk, and proclaimed Russian rule in the name of the tsar. Ivan and his successors quickly moved to send a small garrison and a governor, and the western third of Siberia was theirs. Russia now extended east to the longitude of modern Karachi, and by the 1640s further exploration and conquest brought Russia to the Pacific Ocean. The true importance of all this was far in the future, but for the time it meant a seemingly inexhaustible supply of sable and other furs to sell to the Dutch and English – all to the great profit of the northern Russian merchants and the tsar's treasury.

THE TIME OF TROUBLES

On Ivan's death the country was slowly recovering from the disasters of the last twenty-five years of his reign. He had two surviving sons, the eldest Fyodor from Anastasiia and Dmitrii (born 1582) from his fourth wife, Mariia Nagaia. Fyodor, who appears to have been limited in both abilities and health, was married to Irina Godunov, the sister of Boris Godunov, a boyar who had risen from modest origins in the landholding class through the Oprichnina. With the accession of his brother-in-law to the throne, Boris was now in a position to become the dominant personality around the tsar. First, however, he had to get rid of powerful boyar rivals who saw their chance to restore their power at the court. Indeed at the beginning of Fyodor's reign virtually every boyar clan that had suffered under Ivan returned to the duma if they had not already done so. Boris lost no time in marginalizing them one by one and forcing some into exile. His second problem was the presence of the tsarevich Dmitrii, for Fyodor and Irina had only a daughter who died in infancy. Boris imported doctors from the Netherlands to examine Irina, but to no avail. Thus after Fyodor's death the throne would presumably pass to Dmitrii, but in 1591 he perished, supposedly because he accidentally stabbed himself with a toy sword while playing. This was the conclusion of the official investigation. Naturally the rumor persisted that Boris had secretly ordered him killed, and the mystery has remained unsolved to the present. Certainly Dmitrii's death made possible all that came later.

In 1598 Tsar Fyodor died. His reign had been one of modest success under the guidance of Godunov. A short war with Sweden recovered the originally Russian territory on the Gulf of Finland lost in the Livonian war. This outcome produced no gains in Livonia itself, but at least Russia was back to the pre-1558 status quo. Godunov's government also reinforced the standing of the church by convincing the Greek Orthodox patriarchs not only to recognize the autocephaly of the Russian church but also to give the Metropolitan of Moscow the title of Patriarch in 1588–9. In the long run, far more important, and indeed fateful, were the changes in Russian rural society. In spite of the opening of new lands in the south and a booming trade, Russia acquired a new and ominous institution, the serfdom of the peasantry. Virtually all peasants in central and northwestern Russia lost their personal freedom at the end of the sixteenth century and became the bondsmen of the landholding class, boyars and lesser gentry, as well as of the church. The details of the serf's status were never defined in Russian law, other than by the provision that their owners might recover them if they fled. At first this right of the owner could be exercised only for a few years, but from 1649 it became perpetual. Other relations between master and serf were in the realm of custom. Peasants paid rent as they had before, in kind or in cash, but labor services also became for a time nearly universal. Fortunately for the peasants most landlords were far away, in the towns or even in Moscow itself, and only the great boyars could afford numerous stewards of their estates. The absence of resident masters left the village community to manage payments and services itself, as well as most other affairs. Nevertheless the serfs came under the thumb of the landlord whenever he chose to exercise his power. In the north and on the eastern and southern borders where there were few or no landholders, the peasants – some twenty-five percent of the Russian peasantry – remained free, but even there they were fearful of the future. With Fyodor dead Boris was determined to take full power. The death of all the heirs of Ivan had extinguished the dynasty that had ruled since the time of Prince Vladimir of Kiev. There were other princes of the line of Rurik, but rather than work out the genealogy and find an heir, the Russian elite chose to elect a new tsar. The Patriarch called an Assembly of the Land that included the boyars, the senior clergy, and representatives from the provincial gentry, and the Moscow merchants. There were several possible candidates among the boyars, including the Romanov clan, prominent boyars for two centuries and the relatives of Ivan the Terrible's first wife Anastasiia and Tsar Fyodor. Instead, Boris managed to garner enough support in the duma, the church, and other circles to support his own candidacy, and soon the Assembly of the Land proclaimed Boris Godunov the tsar of all Russia.

This was to prove a hollow victory. Among the first acts of Tsar Boris was to exile the Romanovs and their allies. He ordred Fyodor Nikitich, the senior Romanov, to take monastic vows, removing him from politics, and he also forced Fyodor's wife to enter a convent. The duma soon consisted only of Boris's relatives and clients and a few others too timid or cowed to resist. Perhaps Boris could have waited out the palace intrigues and eventually restored a more harmonious court, but he did not have the chance. In the early 1600s famine struck the land, which created hardship and unrest, and the free peasants and Cossacks of the southern border began to grow restive. Then a new element arrived with the person of Grishka Otrep'ev, a defrocked monk from a minor landholding family who claimed that he was the tsarevich Dmitrii miraculously preserved from death and had hidden since 1591. Otrep'ev had gone to Poland some years before and told his story there, convincing the powerful magnate Jerzy Mniszech of his prospects and receiving Mniszech's daughter Marina in marriage. Otrep'ev collected an army of Polish nobles discontented with their own king and ready for adventure as they crossed into Russia at the end of 1604. At first he made little progress, other than inspiring some of the local peasantry and Cossacks to join him. Boris sent out an army to capture the pretender, but early in 1605 the commanders of the army went over to the False Dmitrii, as he was known thereafter. Boris still had plenty of resources on which to draw, but his sudden death changed everything. The way to Moscow was open, and Grishka Otrep'ev entered the Kremlin in June 1605, as Tsar Dmitrii with an entourage of Poles and the support of many of the Russian boyars as well as the Cossacks. The story of Boris would later inspire Pushkin and Mussorgsky to great artistic heights, but for contemporaries his reign inaugurated a decade and a half of upheaval and war – the Time of Troubles.

The Time of Troubles (*smuta*, or "confusion" in Russian) was the result of the acceleration and unusual violence of the factional battles at the tsar's court after Ivan IV's death combined with the rebellions of the Cossacks and peasants. These agrarian revolts centered along the southern border since the new settlers came primarily from villages in the interior where the peasantry had recently been enserfed. In the south the peasantry and Cossacks were still free but had reason to fear that serfdom would soon catch up with them. To make matters worse, many of the new gentry landholders in the south, settled there to provide cavalry on the border, were equally discontented, fearful of falling into the peasantry and convinced that state policy favored the boyars over them. These two conflicts at the top and bottom of Russian society were not the whole story of the Troubles, for the result of the initial events was a general collapse of order in Russian society. The central government lost control of the situation, and the provinces were left to themselves, some choosing to obey the governors sent from Moscow, some not. The governors soon found that even with some local support they were on their own, improvising matters as best they could. Large numbers of armed bands began to roam the country, including some Poles and Ukrainians who had come to Russia with Dmitrii and some Russian Cossacks, many of them just local bandits. The various short-lived governments in Moscow tried to put together a viable army to control the situation, but to no avail.

The reign of "Tsar Dmitrii" was short. Within a year the populace of Moscow rebelled and stormed the Kremlin, tearing the pretender to pieces and killing many of his followers. They burned his body and shot the remains out of a cannon pointed at Poland.

Marina saved her life by hiding under the skirts of one of her ladies in waiting, but she was soon captured. Prince Vasilii Shuiskii and other boyars were behind the riot, and Vasilii himself ascended the throne in May 1606. Vasilii Shuiskii's seizure of the crown with the support of only a small group of boyars only worsened the chaos, for in opposition a vast peasant rebellion enveloped the south of the country and new pretenders arose. After Vasilii managed to defeat the peasants the next year, the "thief of Tushino," another pretender, took up residence in the village of that name west of Moscow and besieged the capital. Marina Mniszech and her father turned up in the Tushino camp and pretended to recognize him as the true Tsar Dmitrii once again having been miraculously saved from death. The thief of Tushino was no longer just a peasant rebel, for he had the support of several Polish regiments and had attracted a number of Russian boyars to his camp. The elite had split once again, and to make matters worse King Sigismund of Poland appeared before Smolensk with a great army. In desperation Tsar Vasilii Shuiskii turned to Sweden, making a treaty in 1609 that gave him the mercenary army he wanted although under Swedish command, but ceded the Russian territory on the Gulf of Finland to his new ally. The Poles defeated the Russians and the Swedish mercenary army, which then went over to Sigismund. Shuiskii's regime collapsed in 1610 and seven of the boyars formed an interim government in Moscow. At this point many of the boyars and the gentry, realizing Poland's strength, decided to support the candidacy of Sigismund's son Wladyslaw for the Russian throne. Negotiations with the King of Poland grew increasingly difficult for the Russian boyars and some began to resist his conditions. Sigismund responded by throwing them in prison. The Polish army occupied Moscow, while the surrounding anarchy reached its nadir. The King's army only added its forces to the already numerous Polish bands of soldiers who roamed the countryside, competing for booty with ever more Russian Cossacks, peasant rebels, and simple bandits. For the population it was difficult to tell these bands apart, as their aims and methods were essentially the same. In many areas the inhabitants fled to the forests or farther away looking for safety.

Some areas of the country resisted the Polish-sponsored regime. The Trinity Monastery endured months of siege rather than recognize the new order in Moscow. The Volga and the North began to rally with the encouragement of the church. In Nizhnii Novgorod and elsewhere the merchant Kuzma Minin and the local gentry formed a volunteer army and provisional government. By the summer of 1612 the army, under the command of Prince Dmitrii Pozharskii, was strong enough to move toward Moscow and in October they defeated the Poles before the city wall. Soon they were able to enter the Kremlin, and while war and anarchy still raged, the leaders of the army, the remaining boyars and higher clergy called an Assembly of the Land to choose a new tsar. Once again they rejected the dynastic principle in favor of the consensus of the elite and the population as a whole. The Cossacks were particularly vocal, and the choice fell on the sixteen-year-old Michael Romanov, the son of Boris Godunov's erstwhile enemy Fyodor Romanov, who had become the monk Filaret. Tsar Michael was crowned in July of 1613. As his father Filaret was in prison in Poland, the leadership of the new government fell to Michael's mother, the nun Marfa, and her relatives, favorites, and the boyars who had finally come to support Minin and Pozharskii. Five more years were necessary to defeat the Poles and expel the Swedes from Novgorod and the northwest. In the south rebellion only slowly receded. The first false Dmitrii's wife, Marina, took up with the Cossack chieftain Ivan Zarutskii and the two terrorized the lower Volga region for years until the new tsar's army finally defeated them and executed Zarutskii. Marina soon died in prison. Russian society had been smashed, Smolensk lost to Poland, and the Russian coast of the Gulf of Finland ceded to Sweden at Stolbovo in 1617. Huge areas were devastated and depopulated. The Troubles, however, were over, and a new era began.

4

Consolidation and Revolt

The end of the Time of Troubles brought peace to Russia and a new dynasty of tsars, one that would remain on the throne until 1917. The decades that followed the Troubles saw the restoration of the social and political order that had existed before, so that Russia looked very much the same as it had on the day that the Assembly of the Land elected Boris Godunov tsar. Yet under the surface of restored customs and institutions, earlier trends gathered speed and new developments appeared. Serfdom provided a rigid framework that determined the life of most Russians and slowed, but did not preclude, economic changes and growth. At the other end of Russian society, at the court and among the higher clergy, shifts in religious sentiment and cultural changes were taking place that would have far-reaching effects.

Rapid population growth meant greater prosperity and also made it possible for Russia to absorb and preserve the new acquisitions in Siberia and on the southern steppes. Growing integration into the burgeoning European markets meant wealth for merchants and townsmen. The rebuilding of the government was not limited to the restoration of the old system and old institutions. The creaky apparatus of the Moscow offices of state managed more or less to maintain control over a huge area and an unruly population. Control, in the Russian context, was always a relative matter, for this was also the "rebellious" century of Russian history: with not just the Troubles but urban riots in Moscow and elsewhere, the first great Cossack and peasant revolt of the legendary Stenka Razin, and the politically crucial revolts of the musketeers at the end of the century. Each time, however, the authorities eventually restored order and, after 1613, the state did not collapse.

In the long run, more important even than economic growth or political success were the cultural changes. These are difficult to describe, for they lack the drama of the later transformation under Peter, and they were all still within the limits of a predominantly Orthodox culture. These changes within Orthodoxy were a response to Russian religious, social, and political needs, but they came by way of close interaction with the Orthodox church of Kiev, with mainly Ukrainian monks and clergy and the books and new ideas they brought to Moscow. For half a century, from the 1630s to the 1690s, Kiev was a major center of influence on Russian thought and life. At the same time, political events in Poland – the revolt of the Ukrainian Cossacks – brought Russia into war with Poland and ultimately changed the political balance in Eastern Europe in Russia's favor. For most of the seventeenth century the politics and culture of Poland and its peoples were crucial to Russian affairs.

None of these developments were visible in the years immediately after 1613 at the court of the first Romanov, Tsar Michael (1613–1645). Michael resumed appointments to the duma and other offices following the precedence system, as did his predecessors. The court was not quite the same, for the experience of the Time of Troubles seems to have taught the boyars the need for consensus, and for sixty years the court intrigues lost the desperate and murderous quality that had marked the previous century. Michael's father Filaret returned from Polish captivity in 1619 and was immediately named Patriarch of the church. Within a few years he was the de facto regent of Russia, co-sovereign with his son. Patriarch Filaret's main goal was to exact revenge on Poland, a goal that the boyars did not share. At his urging in 1632 Russia tried to retake Smolensk by relying on mercenary regiments hired in Western Europe. The war was a disaster and in 1633 Filaret died, allowing the tsar and the boyars to end the war. Tsar Michael, now ruling without his father's supervision, turned to other matters.

The restoration of order and peace allowed the countryside to recover, and by Michael's death, most of the damage from the Troubles had been repaired. The great accomplishment of the reign was the construction of several lines of forts at the main river fords and on the hills along the southern frontier. In the woods between the forts, workmen felled trees and left them in a tangle to keep out the Tatar cavalry. The defenses were a huge undertaking running over a thousand miles from the Polish border to the Urals. The purpose was to keep out the Tatar raiders, and it worked well enough to allow the peasantry and gentry to move south, for the first time farming the rich black earth of the steppe in large numbers. The tsar gave land to the settler-soldiers to maintain the line of fortifications. A whole society of petty gentry and peasant-soldiers grew up along the line of forts, and beyond the new line, out in the steppe facing the Tatars, were the Cossacks along the southern rivers, the Don, the Volga, and the Iaik farther east. A hundred years after Ivan the Terrible's conquests, the southern steppe finally began to add to Russia's wealth and power.

The seventeenth century was also the first full century of serfdom, yet Russia's agriculture and population rapidly recovered from the Troubles and trade boomed. The resettlement of areas devastated by the Troubles brought agriculture back to feed an expanding population, and over the century, in spite of a general European rise in prices and growing demand, food prices in Russia remained virtually static. We know little about the life of the Russian peasant in this century beyond these larger facts, but it seems that the village community known from later times had taken final form by the end of the century. The peasants held the land from their lords as a village, and themselves managed the distribution of land among households. Craft production grew and spread, not only in the towns but even in the villages, and at the end of the century men who were peasant serfs in legal status began to enter the ranks of the merchants and entrepreneurs. Siberia came under as effective Russian control as it ever would, and its border with China was defined by treaty in 1689 to run along the Amur river. Every year a caravan of Chinese goods that was modest in extent came to Moscow, but over the years the annual trade brought profit to merchants and tsars alike.

The growth of population, commerce, and the state meant that Moscow swiftly became a major city. By the middle of the seventeenth century it contained within its walls perhaps one hundred thousand inhabitants. Half of these Muscovites were part of the army or the palace complex: the soldiers of the elite regiments of musketeers (some 10,000 to 15,000 of them) and their families, and the servants and dependents of the tsar's household. These palace servants formed whole neighborhoods that supplied the tsar with cloth and silverware, took care of his hundreds of horses, and cooked the food for his giant banquets. Several thousand Muscovites were the bond servants of the great aristocrats, the richest of whom by 1650 had several hundred in their Moscow houses. The other half of the city's population were the true urban population, the great merchants and innumerable artisans of all types, along with clergy, wage laborers, beggars, and all the variety of folk that peopled a great city. All of them lived on narrow winding streets lined with wooden houses that made the city vulnerable to frequent fires. Only the more important churches were stone, and only boyars and a few great officials or merchants built houses of stone or brick. These larger houses were set deep in courtyards surrounded by high wooden fences and jammed with stables and storehouses filled with food and drink brought from the country by the master's serfs. Boyars built their houses according to traditional Russian form, not European architectural norms, and divided them into separate women's and men's quarters.

Outside the city walls to the northeast was a whole settlement of foreigners, the "German suburb" that was composed of merchants, mercenary officers, and the many others who supplied their needs. Established in 1652 on the initiative of the church, which feared foreign corruption, the German suburb was a small replica of northern Europe, with a brick Lutheran church with a pointed spire and regular streets with brick houses, taverns, and a school. The "Germans" (who included also Dutchmen, Englishmen, and Scots) were the most numerous of the foreigners, ultimately to be the most important, but Moscow was a rather cosmopolitan city. Ukrainian monks and priests found homes in Moscow's churches and monasteries, bringing a new variant of Orthodoxy to Russia. The Greeks also had their own monastery, and Greek merchants mixed with Armenians and Georgians from the Caucasus. More exotic peoples came from the southern borders and farther east: Circassians serving the tsar, Kalmuks and Bashkirs bringing huge masses of horses every year to sell, Tatars of all sorts, and even "Tadzhiks," the merchants from Khiva and Bukhara in far-off Central Asia.

Economic prosperity went hand in hand with the recovery and development of the state. By the end of the century several hundred clerks now staffed dozens of offices that tried to administer the vast Russian land. They had developed complex procedures and practices, keeping records of the tsar's decrees that defined their actions and recording their own decisions on innumerable rolls of paper housed in their archives. Like most early modern states, Russian administration concentrated on the collection of taxes, the administration of justice, and (when needed) on military recruitment. In Russian conditions these were daunting tasks. In order to collect taxes from the peasants, Moscow attempted to discover and record how much land each peasant household had and how good it was. The central authorities had the resources to survey the population for tax purposes every fifteen or twenty years at best, and then not in the most efficient of ways. Given the paucity of local administrators, Moscow sent its officials to a few district centers and relied on the gentry and village elders to provide them with information about each village and household. Obviously everyone, landholder and peasant alike, had an interest in underreporting assets, and the officials could check on them only in the most obvious cases of evasion. Again it was the village elders who actually brought in the taxes, many of which were still paid in kind. The only sure source of revenue was the sales tax and the tsar's monopoly on the sale of vodka and other alcoholic drinks, sure because it was collected in towns and markets and was often farmed out to merchants and other entrepreneurs.

The attempts to administer justice were no easier. Russia before Peter was not a lawless land of arbitrary rule as later liberals often portrayed it. Indeed the officials of the Moscow offices who administered justice erred as much or more by legal pedantry than arbitrariness. They followed the Law Code of 1649, and indeed the Code circulated in the provinces as well, among officials and gentry alike. The greatest problem was that the Moscow offices (and then the tsar) were the only real courts for most cases, with provincial governors and officials often acting more as investigators than judges. The life of these governors was not easy, and in the investigation of criminal cases they and their few subordinates relied largely on polling the neighbors of the accused and the victim, in order to find evidence. Provincial governors were required to rule areas the size of small European countries with a handful of assistants and no effective armed force. Only on the distant borders did Moscow send out enough men and soldiers to run things effectively and maintain order. Local governors and central offices tried to provide a court of first instance for disputes over land ownership and decisions regarding major crimes, but the lack of officials outside of Moscow and a few provincial capitals on the borders forced the government to rely on the cooperation of local inhabitants, which lead to mixed results. Even with extra manpower, the far borders were still difficult to control, often with disastrous consequences.

At Michael's death in 1645 the boyars and clergy quickly acclaimed his eldest son Aleksei as his successor. Again the tsar was young, only sixteen years old, as he was born in 1629. The constellation of boyars around him at court determined the course of events for the first decade or so. Tsar Aleksei soon married Mariia, the daughter of Ilya Miloslavskii, an ally of the young tsar's tutor, the powerful boyar Boris Morozov. Morozov in turn married Mariia's sister, consolidating his position at court and his influence over the young tsar. Morozov's taxation schemes, which involved substituting a high tax on salt for the usual sales taxes, soon created a crisis. In July 1648, the Muscovites rioted, killed several prominent boyars and officials, and demanded Morozov's head. Aleksei was able to save him, and the unrest subsided. Part of the resulting compromise was a new Assembly of the Land – this one to confirm a new law code, and in 1649 the printing presses issued Russia's first compilation of laws, the Conciliar Code of 1649. Morozov returned to the court, but it was Ilya Miloslavskii, Aleksei's father-in-law, a man whom the tsar feared rather than loved, who held sway. Soon Miloslavskii had a rival in Patriarch Nikon, who ascended the patriarchal throne in 1652. Nikon would set in motion changes in the church that ultimately led to a schism, but his political role outside of the church was no less important. For Russia was already faced with a new crisis, and this time it was a foreign crisis.

Russia was not alone in defending its southern frontier with bands of Cossacks. Poland-Lithuania as well maintained such a force of irregular troops on the Dniepr river facing the Crimeans. The Cossacks settled beyond the frontier in the islands below the rapids (Zaporozh'e). These Cossacks were largely Ukrainian peasants in origin and thus Orthodox in religion. They had come to the border much like Russian Cossacks fleeing serfdom at home, but in this case they fled religious oppression as well, for the usually tolerant Poland did not extend this favor to the Orthodox. The surrender of the Orthodox hierarchy in Poland-Lithuania to Rome in 1596 formed a new Catholic Uniate church on the basis of the previous Orthodox church. The king declared Orthodoxy illegal, confiscated Orthodox church buildings and property, and handed them over to the Uniates. In 1632 a new King of Poland partially reversed his father's policy and declared a compromise, allowing an Orthodox metropolitanate in Kiev and Orthodox worship in some areas. The compromise was not enough, for the enserfed Ukrainian peasants saw religious as well as social oppressors in their mainly Polish masters. Then in the winter of 1648 the Ukrainian Cossacks elected a new hetman, or commander, without the king's approval. The new hetman, a minor nobleman named Bohdan Khmel'nyts'kyi, and his Cossack host began to move northwest out of Zaporozh'e, proclaiming relief from religious and other oppression. The hastily gathered Polish army was utterly annihilated and the Ukrainian lands exploded in revolt; peasants and Cossacks alike murdered and expelled the Polish gentry, the Uniates, and the Jews.

Khmel'nyts'kyi could defeat the king's army in the field, but he knew that soon he would need allies. At first he allied with Crimea, but this alliance was difficult to maintain as the interests of the two parties differed greatly. The hetman turned to Tsar Aleksei, begging him to support his Orthodox brethren. This message was not welcome news in Moscow. The Ukrainian Cossack emissaries arrived soon after the 1648 riot in Moscow, and neither Aleksei nor the boyars had any desire to support peasant rebels in neighboring countries. Besides, Tsar Michael (in his last years) and his son Aleksei had been trying to come to an agreement with Poland to form an alliance against the Crimeans. Aleksei hesitated for five years, offering vague promises to the Cossacks and sending peace feelers to the king of Poland. In the spring of 1653, the hetman sent yet another embassy to Moscow and offered Aleksei overlordship of the Ukrainian Cossack host. This time the tsar agreed, apparently at the prompting of Patriarch Nikon. Shortly afterward in January 1654, an embassy from the tsar signed an agreement at Pereiaslav in the Ukraine with the hetman to take the Cossacks and their land "under his high hand" while affirming their newly-won autonomy, now within Russia. The agreement also committed Russia to war with Poland, a war that fundamentally reshaped the balance of power in Eastern Europe.

The war was to last for thirteen years, until 1667. Aleksei had a new army, for he had hired western officers to form regiments of Russian soldiers on European lines. In the first years of the war the Russian army quickly recaptured Smolensk and went all the way to Wilno. After considerable back-and-forth, and Khmel'nyts'kyi's death in 1656, Russia and Poland signed a treaty in 1667. Poland regained most of its territory, but the treaty was nevertheless a distinct Russian victory: Smolensk remained Russian and the Ukraine east of the Dniepr with the city of Kiev continued to form an autonomous hetmanate under the tsar. Though even the Russians did not yet realize this, Poland's time as the great power of Eastern Europe was over, for the Cossack revolt and the war had done too much damage to the social and political fabric of the Polish-Lithuanian state. Its economy and population stagnated for the next hundred years, leaving the field to Russia.

Russia had not escaped entirely unscathed. The war had led to an adulteration of the silver currency with copper coins that moved the people of Moscow to riot in the "copper revolt" of 1662. The tsar had to call out the new-style infantry regiments officered by foreign mercenaries to restore order. Far more serious was the ferment on the Don that broke out as the great Cossack revolt of Stenka Razin in 1670. Similar in some respects to the Ukrainian revolt, the Russian events lacked the religious and ethnic element; indeed, many of the native peoples of the southern border joined Razin. The Russian Cossacks were also more plebeian than the Ukrainian, who included minor gentry among their leaders. They struck terror into the tsar's court, capturing Astrakhan' and other Volga towns with the slaughter of nobles and officials alike. Tsar Aleksei's armies finally defeated and captured Razin in 1671 and brought him to Moscow, where he was executed. As the revolt showed, expansion into the southern steppe added enormously to Russia's territory, its agricultural potential, its population, and its power, but it also added to the tensions in Russian society.

The southern steppe and its peoples were only one part of the larger complex of territories and peoples that made Russia an increasingly multi-national society. The territory lost to Sweden in 1619 meant the loss of some smaller Finnish groups, the Ingrians and part of the Karelians who had inhabited part of the Novgorod lands from the beginning of recorded history. Swedish attempts to force the Orthodox Karelians into the Lutheran faith and the arrival of Swedish landlords in villages of free peasants brought a sizeable migration across the Russian border into the lands around Lake Onega and even south towards Tver'. Lesser Finno-Ugrian peoples continued to populate parts of the Russian north, but until 1654 the largest of the non-Russian peoples included the Tatars, Bashkirs, Chuvash and other Volga peoples brought under Russian rule in the sixteenth century. They continued to live under a separate status as payers of *yasak* rather than the usual Russian taxes. This separate status continued after the establishment of serfdom, with the para-doxical result that the Tatar peasantry was not enserfed. The Rus-sian authorities continued to accept but not encourage Islam, and they staged no organized attempts at conversion. Conflicts were over land, as Russian peasants settled more and more among them, pri-marily among the Bashkirs, who mounted several small rebellions. Farther south the arrival in the 1630s of the Kalmuks, a Mongolian Buddhist people fleeing internal strife in their homeland, disrupted the relations among the nomads just beyond Russia's border. As Buddhists the new arrivals had poor relations with the Crimean and other Muslim peoples in the area. The Kalmuks formed important allies for the Russian tsar, accepting his general overlordship and providing him troops in foreign wars and internal disturbances. The Circassians were loyal as well, siding with the tsar against Razin's rebels.

The Pereiaslav treaty of 1654 brought into the Russian state a new element in the form of the Ukrainian Hetmanate. The originally democratic Cossack host quickly turned into a society ruled by a hereditary elite of Cossack officers. Under the Pereiaslav agreement the Cossacks continued to elect the hetman who in turn appointed the officers, administered justice (according to the old Polish laws), managed his own treasury, and commanded the Cossack army, all this without consulting the tsar. The tsar maintained garrisons in Kiev and other principal towns, whose commanders also exercised control over the towns, though those retained their elected urban governments. The Ukrainian church was more complicated, as the Metropolitan of Kiev was not under the jurisdiction of Moscow but rather of the Greek patriarchate of Constantinople, which accepted the Moscow Patriarch as its head only in 1687.

The inclusion of the Ukrainian hetmanate in Russia had such profound effects because it strengthened the ties between Kiev and Moscow at a time when changes were taking place in the Russian Orthodox church. These changes led the elite of the Russian clergy to turn to Ukrainian models of piety, but also sparked a religious upheaval that ultimately led to schism. Even in the time of Tsar Michael there had been symptoms of renewal in the church. Voices arose among the clergy complaining that Russian priests did not do enough to bring Orthodox teaching to their congregations. No one challenged the centrality of the liturgy, but the reformers called for more systematic preaching and that meant a more learned clergy and a more varied religious literature. By the accession of Tsar Aleksei to the throne, the leader of the new trend was his spiritual father Stefan Vonifat'ev, and the group included Nikon, the Metropolitan of Novgorod, and Avvakum, a village priest from the Volga area who had risen to become archpriest in one of the main Moscow churches. They had the favor of the tsar, but until 1652 they made little headway.

Increased contract with the Orthodox in the Ukrainian lands had given the Russians new ideas, as the Ukrainians were engaged in a continuous battle to defend Orthodoxy by reinforcing it in the minds and hearts of the believers. In the Kiev Academy the Ukrainian clergy had a new type of education, unknown in Russia, derived from Jesuit models. It emphasized language and rhetoric, the arts of persuasion, as well as philosophy. The Kiev Academy taught its pupils not just Slavonic but also Latin, which was still the language of scholarship in both Catholic and Protestant Europe. In 1649 Tsar Aleksei brought the first group of Ukrainian monks to Moscow to teach and also to help with the editing and publication of liturgical and devotional texts. Then Patriarch Iosif died in 1652, and with prompting from the tsar, the clergy elected Nikon to be his replacement. Patriarch Nikon took with particular fervor to the examination of the service books, and in 1653 he began to issue service books with corrected texts. These corrections were made so as to bring the Russian texts in line with the Greek (and Ukrainian) versions, which he considered more authoritative. The new versions also mandated a few changes in daily devotional practices, such as the manner of making the sign of the cross. For some centuries Russians had done this holding straight the index and middle finger (symbolizing the dual nature of Christ) and folding the other three, while the Greeks held folded together the first two fingers and the thumb (for the Trinity). Nikon, however, commanded the Greek practice, arguing that the Russian version slighted the Trinity. As the Russian (and older Greek) tradition asserted that the entire liturgy and all associated practices recreated the sacrifice of Christ rather than merely reminding one of it, these small actions were of critical importance. Some of Nikon's former allies in the reform movement under the leadership of the archpriest Avvakum, however, refused to conform. Avvakum recounted later that he heard of the changes during Easter week in 1653 and "we saw that winter was on the way – hearts froze and legs began to shake". Since Avvakum persisted in his refusal to conform and began to preach against the new books, Nikon and the tsar sent him and his followers into exile, as far away as possible into Siberia to the east of Lake Baikal.

The exile in 1655 of Avvakum and his few followers among the clergy seemed to put an end to the controversy. Nikon's reforms of the liturgy and his sponsorship of the Ukrainian teachers and scholars in Moscow continued. Nikon was a powerful figure and a personality who brooked no opposition or perceived slight. In 1658 one of the tsar's favorites insulted Nikon's servant at a reception for a visiting Georgian prince, and Nikon announced that he was leaving the patriarchal throne. Perhaps he expected an apology from the tsar and the boyar in question, but they were not forthcoming. Nikon retired to his newly founded Monastery of the New Jerusalem to the west of Moscow and remained there. His actions produced a crisis, for he had not abdicated the office of patriarch, he had merely left its duties. Tsar Aleksei sent emissaries to persuade him to return, but he refused.

While Nikon sulked, the remaining church authorities continued to produce new versions of the texts with the help of the Ukrainians. They published new translations of the Greek fathers of the church, this time working from Western printed editions of the Greek texts rather than Byzantine manuscripts. The Ukrainians preached at major court occasions and the principal holidays of the Orthodox calendar, and taught a few Russian clergy their skills. All of this innovative activity took place in and around the court, while at the opposite end of Russian society a storm was brewing. In the provinces the new books began to produce discontent, and local priests and monks remembered Avvakum and his protest. The dissidents began to pick up wider support among the groups of ascetics that had arisen since the 1640s in the upper Volga towns and villages. Aleksei and the bishops were forced to take action. In 1666–1667, just as the Polish war was coming to a close, they called a council of the Russian church, which two of the Greek Orthodox patriarchs and other Greek clergy also attended. The council formally deposed Nikon and selected a successor, though Nikon refused to acknowledge its its authority. The Greek patriarchs also tried to convince Avvakum of his errors, reminding him that in the whole world the Orthodox crossed themselves with three fingers. This argument had no effect, for Avvakum replied that the faith of the other Orthodox peoples was impure: only the Russians had kept the true faith. The council condemned him and approved the changes in the texts. Nikon went into exile in the northern Ferapontov Monastery, but his cause of reform had triumphed. The new books became the standard texts, and most Russians adopted the new rituals. That is, most people – those among the bishops, the clergy, and the population of central Russia – but the dissidents did not disappear. Avvakum went into exile to Pustozersk, a small fort north of the Arctic Circle, but he did not stop writing until his execution in 1680. His teaching began to spread in the northern villages, in the Urals and Siberia as well as the Don and the southern frontier. Tsar Aleksei and his successors sent soldiers to try to force them back to Orthodoxy, and in 1678 in remotest Siberia some of the Old Believers, as they came to be known, tried a new tactic. When the soldiers approached, the entire community assembled in a wooden church and set it on fire, burning themselves to death. This tactic made persecution extremely difficult, for church and state could declare victory only if the Old Believers came back to Orthodoxy. Their deaths, while still unreconciled, signified failure. The result was a standstill, and the Old Belief continued to spread. Its followers already numbered in the tens of thousands and the movement continued to find new adherents. As they grew in numbers they also disagreed among themselves on many issues, some condemning the mass suicides, others not. The more radical groups formed entire dissident churches with no priests or bishops and held simple services led only by an "instructor." Some Old Believer communities resembled Orthodox monasteries; others were indistinguishable in all but ritual from their Orthodox neighbors. All the Old Believers rejected the authority of church and state, some proclaiming that the Romanov dynasty was the visible Antichrist. Pacific rather than rebellious, the Old Belief nevertheless struck fear into the hearts of tsars and bishops alike for the next two hundred years. An undeniably native tradition of dissent and resistance had been born.

The council of 1666–1667 had restored order in the church everywhere but in the remote wilderness where the Old Believers took refuge. At the court in Moscow the changes in religious practice deepened and spread, bringing with them new cultural forms. In 1664 a new figure appeared at court, the Kiev-trained Belorussian monk Simeon Polotskii. Simeon very quickly won the favor of the tsar and many boyars, and Aleksei appointed him tutor to the heir to the throne, Tsarevich Aleksei. When the boy died in 1669 Simeon remained an important figure, preaching in and around the court, writing celebratory verse for court occasions as well as panegyrics and consolatory verse for great boyars. He ran a school where the children of clergy and officials studied Latin and Church Slavic and learned to write and preach by the rules of classical rhetoric. Simeon's work was symptomatic of the cultural shift in the Russian elite. Starting in the 1660s or 1670s a few boyars began to have their sons taught Polish and Latin and books no longer exclusively religious, began to circulate among the small court elite, the officials, and a few of the Moscow clergy. Books of physical and political geography, sacred history as understood in the West, and other tracts brought new vocabulary and new concepts to Russia, even if they lacked the intellectual apparatus that brought them forth in Europe. The readers of these texts among the clergy cultivated the styles of writing that were fashionable in Warsaw and Kiev – panegyric and religious verse, sermons, and other forms. The sermons, especially the printed sermons of Simeon Polotskii, began to find an audience outside of Moscow and the court elite. In the last years of the reign of Tsar Aleksei, the tsar and his favorite and foreign minister, Artamon Matveev, sponsored a court theater which presented examples of Baroque drama in Russian. The playwright was the Lutheran pastor Johann Gregory from the German Suburb and the boy actors were only the pupils from his school, but the texts were in Russian and the performances even included ballet interludes. Tsar Aleksei's interests extended beyond theater, for he asked the Danish ambassador for a telescope, or as the tsar put it, "a tube of the invention of Tycho Brahe." The theater ceased after Tsar Aleksei's death, but his son and successor Fyodor (1676–1682) provided Simeon Polotskii with ample support, even allowing him to set up his own printing press where he printed his sermons and his rhymed Psalter.

By the 1680s the new cultural forms were well ensconced. Patriarch Ioakim (1675–1690) sponsored in 1685 the establishment of the Slavo-Greco-Latin Academy, the first more or less European school in Russia. Ioakim had very definite views of the West, as he was a firm opponent of Catholicism and the Protestant churches. Part of his reason for supporting the school was to combat what he saw as Catholic tendencies among the Russian and Ukrainian followers of Simeon Polotskii in Moscow. To teach and manage the school he appointed two Greeks, the brothers Sophronios and Ioannikios Likhudes, who taught what they had learned in Italy and the Greek schools of the Ottoman lands – that is to say, the European Jesuit curriculum founded on philology and the explication of Aristotle. The Greeks brought Western culture to Russia as much as did the Ukrainians.

All these innovations in culture and religion were the work of the court and ecclesiastical elite, and only slowly spread to the rest of the population and the provinces. The new culture does not seem to have been the work of any one faction or group, rather it was common to the elite as a whole, though more prominent in the lives of some individuals than others. Religion and culture failed to produce discord in the court, but other factors made it the scene of great political drama. The relative harmony of the decades after the Time of Troubles began to come apart by 1671.

In the early years of the reign of Tsar Aleksei the dominant figures at court were his erstwhile tutor and brother-in-law Boris Morozov, his father-in-law Ilya Miloslavskii, and in 1652–1658 Patriarch Nikon. Morozov's death in 1661 left Miloslavskii the single dominant figure, but as Aleksei grew and matured he relied less on his father-in-law, whose behavior was often abrasive. Miloslavskii died in 1668, after Aleksei had signed the peace with Poland against the wishes of many of the boyars. He appointed the architect of that peace, Afanasii Ordin-Nashchokin, to head the Ambassadorial Office. Ordin-Nashchokin, a provincial nobleman who knew foreign languages and had the tsar's favor, received boyar rank. He and the tsar both shared the aim of turning the peace with Poland into real cooperation against the Ottomans. Some such alliance was all the more necessary since the establishment of Russian overlordship in the Ukraine and the Russian garrison in Kiev put Russia in a new position in Eastern Europe, now facing Crimea across the steppe. The country faced the full might of the Turks, and the tsar and his minister wanted Polish allies, something upon which the boyars looked with suspicion. Unfortunately Ordin-Nashchokin's arrogant manner of implementation of the policy of reconciliation with Poland in the Ukraine led to rebellions and Ordin-Nashchokin fell from favor. In 1670 Tsar Aleksei found a new head for the Ambassadorial Office who understood the need for alliances against the Turks but who also got along well with the Ukrainians. He chose the musketeer Colonel Artamon Matveev, several times a successful emissary to the Cossacks and now the tsar's new favorite.

The need for a new man to direct foreign policy came at the same time that a major dynastic issue arose. In 1669 the heir to the throne, Tsarevich Aleksei Alekseevich, died, an event followed swiftly by the death of his mother Mariia. The second son was Fyodor (born 1661), a capable and intelligent boy but extremely sickly. The third surviving son Ivan (born 1666) was both physically and (it seems) mentally handicapped. In addition, Aleksei had already lost several children, mostly boys, and without a new wife he could not be sure of the succession. The new wife, whom Aleksei married in 1671, was to be Natalia Naryshkina, the daughter of a colonel of one of the musketeer regiments. The Naryshkins were clients of Aleksei's new favorite, Artamon Matveev, with whom they had served in Moscow and other places. Natalia bore the tsar a son on May 30, 1672, and baptized him Peter. Peter was a healthy boy, and Matveev had now another reason to enjoy the tsar's favor and maintain allies in the tsaritsa's family.

Matveev was not only in favor through his connections with the Naryshkins. He managed the complicated relations with the Ukrainian Cossacks, Poland, and Russia's other neighbors, and appointed his clients to almost all the major offices of the Russian state. He faithfully executed the tsar's wishes, if disagreeing with him on occasion, and arguing his and the tsar's views in the duma. Aleksei did not give him a monopoly of power: the palace administration and the tsar's household remained under the aegis of Bogdan Khitrovo, the tsar's other major favorite in his later years, though Khitrovo seems to have avoided major political issues. In the words of the Danish ambassador, Matveev was Russia's "kinglet." Such a rise to power could not fail to provoke the jealousy of the boyars, but as long as the tsar lived, Matveev remained supreme. Then, in January 1676, Tsar Aleksei died suddenly at the age of forty-seven.

The accession of Tsar Fyodor, only fifteen years old and sickly, put power back into the hands of the senior boyars. Within weeks they ousted Matveev's clients from the main offices and engineered the exile of Matveev himself. Prince Dolgorukii and Ivan Miloslavskii, the cousin of the tsar on his mother's side, were the most influential, and behind the scenes Tsarevna Irina, the young tsar's aunt, was the most powerful of all. As Matveev slowly moved toward Siberian exile, his enemies lodged a charge of sorcery against him. The accusation was a wild combination of dramatic charges from former servants that came down to his reading of a book borrowed from the Apothecary's Office, probably containing chapters on medicinal astrology. Then some of Tsaritsa Natalia's Naryshkin brothers were accused of attempting to kill the tsar several years before during a session of archery practice. Gruesome torture of the Naryshkin servants and clients yielded extensive testimony but confirmed nothing substantial. At the widowed Tsaritsa Natalia's intervention Tsarevna Irina put a halt to the proceedings. Matveev went back to an even more remote exile and several of the Naryshkins were exiled to their estates. For the next few years Matveev's enemies at court reigned supreme, forming a sort of boyar regency over the young tsar. Tsaritsa Natalia remained in the background, raising her son and looking to the future.

Fyodor was physically weak but surprisingly strong-willed. On Irina's death in 1680 he married for the first time and began to emancipate himself from the tutelage of the boyars. His new wife even appeared in Polish dress, and Fyodor's health seemed to revive. When she died during childbirth a year later, all seemed to be lost, but instead Fyodor moved on, reforming court dress and then at the end of 1681 moving to reform the army and abolish the precedence system that in theory had ruled the court, administration, and army for two centuries. He had his own favorites and relied in his military reforms on Prince V. V. Golitsyn, one of Russia's greatest aristocrats. Fyodor allowed Matveev to return to his estates near Moscow and lifted the exile of the Naryshkins. In February he married Marfa Apraksina, a young girl from provincial gentry, a marriage that brought to the court her younger borothers Petr and Fyodor, still boys now on the way to greater things. The tsar's health worsened and on April 2, 1682, he died, plunging Russia into a crisis.

The crisis again arose from the problem of succession. Fyodor had no children, and his eldest brother, Ivan, was fifteen years old, but weak and unhealthy. None of the boyars seem to have considered him fit to rule, nor did Patriarch Ioakim. The alternative was Peter, then nine years old. The choice of Peter would mean that the Miloslavskii clan, the maternal relatives of Ivan, would lose their chance for power, for Peter's mother was a Naryshkin and an ally of Matveev, who had recently returned from bitter exile.

The death of Tsar Fyodor coincided with murmurs of discontent among the musketeers – the soldiers who guarded the Kremlin and had provided the core of the infantry army before the advent of European style regiments. Their discontent was aimed at the oppressive practices of their colonels, but someone convinced them that their real enemy was the Naryshkins and Matveev. The musketeers stormed into the Kremlin and demanded that their enemies be turned over to them. Terrified, the boyars advised surrender, and Matveev was hurled from the stairs onto the upturned pikes of the musketeers. Several of the Naryshkins were hunted down and killed, though Natalia was able to save her father and eldest brother. The soldiers rampaged through the city, killing two of the Princes Dolgorukii and others who were suspected of favoring Peter and his family. After a few days the clergy and boyars met together and proclaimed Ivan and Peter co-tsars. The disturbances ceased, but two new stars had risen on the horizon, Prince Ivan Khovanskii and Tsarevna Sofia.

Khovanskii made himself the darling of the soldiers, and for a tense summer he seemed to be poised to assert supreme power behind the façade of the two boy tsars. Khovanskii, however, was outmaneuvered, and it was Sofia, Ivan's sister and Peter's half-sister, who assumed power. In September, when the musketeers had quieted down, she had Khovanskii arrested and executed, and for the next seven years she ruled as regent of Russia. Her favorite and, effectively, her prime minister was Prince V. V. Golitsyn, who had recently come to prominence under Tsar Fyodor.

From the very beginning Sofia presided over a court riven by faction. Early on she managed to sideline her Miloslavskii relatives and rule with Golitsyn alone, though in the mind of Peter, then and later, it was the Miloslavskii clan that was his and his mother's enemy. For Natalia did not cease to aspire to claim full power for her son. As he grew up, she acquired allies among the boyars, Prince Boris Golitsyn (the cousin of V. V. Golitsyn) and the more exotic Prince Mikhail Alegukovich Cherkasskii, a boyar but by origin a Circassian from the north Caucasus serving the Russian tsars. Relations were tense, and Cherkasskii even brought out a knife during a dispute with V. V. Golitsyn – in the yard of the Trinity Monastery no less.

Peter was still too young to participate in the intrigues and the arguments, and he spent these years outside of Moscow at Preobrazhenskoe, a village to the east of Moscow where his father had built a small wooden house for the summer. There Peter began to "play" soldiers, forming his servants and courtiers into European style infantry regiments and having them drilled by European officers. Peter was fascinated by artillery and he learned how to use it in these years as well. Soon he had a trained force of several hundred men, his own personal regiment. Even more significant was his encounter with boats.

He told the story himself, many years later. In an old barn Peter happened to notice a small boat, one that was constructed differently from Russian boats. Peter was already studying mathematics, probably for military purposes, with Frans Timmerman, a Dutch merchant and amateur astronomer, and he asked Timmerman why the boat did not look like typical Russian boats. The answer was that it was built to sail against the wind. Peter was amazed by the answer, and Timmerman found a Dutch sailor who put the boat in order and showed the young tsar how to tack into the wind. Peter was captivated immediately, and took the boat to a nearby lake to practice. He also asked the young Prince Iakov Dolgorukii, who was about to leave for France on a diplomatic mission, to bring him back navigational instruments. Dolgorukii returned in 1688 with an astrolabe, and thus began Peter's love affair with boats and navigation – an affair that would last his whole life.

In the mean time Sofia had committed Russia to a new foreign policy. She wanted to continue the policy of confronting the Ottomans, in this respect following Matveev, but unlike him she decided to do it in close alliance with Poland. The opportunity had come with the foundation of the Holy League in 1682 by Austria, the Papacy, Venice, and Poland, with the aim of a united struggle against the Turks. After long and tiresome negotiations, Sofia joined the League in 1685–6 and entered into military collaboration with Jan III Sobieski, the King of Poland and the victor at the great siege of Vienna of 1683. Russia's part in the coalition was to defeat Crimea. Thus, in 1687 Golitsyn took a large Russian army south from the Ukrainian hetmanate across the steppe to Crimea. The Tatars burned the waterless steppe, depriving his horses of fodder and he had to retreat. His only accomplishment was to replace Hetman Samoilovych, a Naryshkin ally and an opponent of the war, with the compliant Ivan Mazepa, a name that would return.

A repeat of the campaign in 1689 brought the same result, and rumors even circulated that Golitsyn had made a secret deal with the enemy. On his return, Sofia tried to portray the campaign as a success, rewarding the troops and ordering triumphal liturgies, but Peter would have none of it.

Peter was now seventeen, and he stayed away from the Kremlin in Preobrazhenskoe. Suddenly on August 7, 1689, one of his chamberlains was arrested in Moscow and the rumor swept the city that Sofia was going to have Peter killed. One of the musketeers rode out to warn Peter, who got out of bed in his shirt and jumped on a horse. With his closest servants and courtiers he rode through the night to the Trinity Monastery, soon to be joined by his mother and her boyar allies. The next weeks were a standoff, but by the end of the month it was clear that most of the boyars, Tsar Ivan's household, the patriarch, and the foreign mercenary officers were on Peter's side. Even the musketeers would not back Sofia. Peter returned to Moscow in triumph and sent Sofia to the Novodevichii Convent on the southwest side of Moscow. Peter, with his Naryshkin relatives, was now securely in power, for Ivan presented no challenge and died in 1696. No one could have then predicted it, but Russia was poised for a fundamental transformation.

5

Peter the Great

The reign of Peter the Great saw the greatest transformation in
Russia until the revolution of 1917. Unlike the Soviet revolution,
Peter's transformation of Russia had little impact on the social
order, for serfdom remained and the nobility remained their masters. What Peter changed was the structure and form of the state,
turning the traditional Russian tsardom into a variant of European
monarchy. At the same time he profoundly transformed Russian
culture, a contribution that along with his new capital of St. Petersburg has lasted to the present day.

The first few years of Peter's rule gave little indication that such
great events were coming. The removal of Sofia in 1689 gave control to Peter's mother and her Naryshkin relatives and their allies,
who seem to have gotten along poorly with one another once in
power. A son Aleksei was born in 1692 to Peter's wife Evdokiia, so
the succession seemed assured. Peter himself remained in the background training his soldiers, drinking with the foreign officers in the
German suburbs, and sailing his boats. Peter had many eccentricities, and they appeared early. He was nearly seven feet tall, but
was thin-boned with narrow shoulders and rather fine features.
He shaved his beard early but left a thin moustache. His capacity
for alcohol was gigantic and this perhaps had some relationship
to the endless "colics" and other stomach disorders that plagued
him all his life. He sometimes flew into tremendous hysterical rages

that only his wife (his second, Catherine) was able to calm. His relations with women were surprisingly restrained. His greatest recreation was anything that involved boats, leading him to go north to Archangel in 1693 to see the ocean for the first time. His mother Natalia sent him a letter ordering him not to go out to the dangerous open sea and he obeyed. Then in February 1694, she died. Right away Peter ceased to appear at any of the Kremlin ceremonies, and the whole ritual of the Russian court, now over two centuries old, came to an end. Then Peter went to Archangel again, and this time he went out to sea on a Dutch ship.

During these years Peter made two acquaintances in the German suburb who were to shape his policy for the next few years. One was Patrick Gordon, then in his fifties, a Catholic Scot who had served in the Russian army since 1661, primarily as a specialist in fortification and artillery. Gordon was a firm proponent of the Turkish war and played a crucial role in training the new European style regiments of the army. The other was Francois LeFort, a Geneva Swiss who was also a mercenary officer, but whose relationship with Peter was more personal than Gordon's. LeFort was the ringleader of many of the drunken parties, and it was LeFort who introduced Peter to Anna Mons, the daughter of a German tavern keeper. These relations were not just friendships, as Gordon and LeFort were the young tsar's favorites and informal political advisors, and Anna cemented the influence of LeFort.

When Peter returned to Moscow from his first brief sea voyage in the fall of 1694, he decided to renew Russia's efforts against the Turks, largely in abeyance since he came to power. The boyars were not happy with this decision, but he simply ignored them, and moved an army south down the Volga and Don rivers to Azov, the Turkish fort at the mouth of the Don on the Sea of Azov. The siege was unsuccessful, largely because the Turks could resupply the fort from the sea; so Peter built a navy. He built it at Voronezh on the Don, far inland, with Dutch carpenters and ship builders. He brought officers from the Netherlands, Venice, and France, and in the spring of 1696 his fleet sailed down the Don and with its help he took the fort, which was his first victory. He celebrated his victory not just with the traditional prayers, but also with a triumphal procession into Moscow in full Baroque style, with arches bearing images of Hercules and one with Julius Caesar's "I came, I saw, I conquered" in Church Slavic. So that the public would understand these strange gods, he had a pamphlet printed to explain it all.

Peter then prepared for an action far more strange than his Baroque triumph – a journey to Western Europe. He quickly settled the affairs of the new territories and the navy and appointed a small committee of boyars to govern in his absence, only to find that there was a conspiracy to replace him afoot among other aristocrats. The conspirators were few in number but Peter saw them as growing from the seed of the old factions that had opposed his mother in the 1680s. The conspirators were mainly concerned about their own positions in the hierarchy of offices, but some were also shocked at his trip abroad and even more at his plans to send young boyars to Holland and Venice to learn foreign languages and the art of navigation. The conspirators were executed, and Peter left Moscow, stopping at Riga and Berlin before he arrived in Amsterdam, which was his chief goal.

Peter traveled incognito as a member of the Russian embassy headed by the boyar Fyodor Golovin and Lefort, an embassy with the charge of strengthening the coalition against the Ottomans. While Golovin and LeFort negotiated, Peter took instruction in carpentry and ship building in the shipyards of Zaandam. There the Dutch told him that in England they built ships differently, relying on mathematics and not just their eyes to shape the hull. Peter quickly set off for London, where he visited the shipyards but also spoke to astronomers at the Greenwich observatory, attended a Quaker meeting, inspected the Royal mint, and talked to Anglican clergymen. Then he began the journey home, reaching Vienna by spring. As he rode through Central Europe, however, the political horizon was changing rapidly. Austria had reconquered huge parts of Hungary and was low on resources, as were the other allies. They wanted peace, and Peter learned this in Vienna. He had to now extricate Russia from the war with the Ottomans, and he eventually succeeded after two years of hard negotiation. Peter was disappointed, but the end of the war was actually a relief, for more pressing concerns had arisen.

In the summer of 1698 he had news from Moscow that the musketeers had revolted once again, demanding better conditions, and
apparently they were in some sort of contact with the imprisoned
Sofia. Peter rushed home, only to find that the boyars had already
executed the leaders over the advice of the generals. Peter was furious, and ordered a relentless and gruesome interrogation of the
prisoners under torture. Hundreds were eventually executed with
the participation of the tsar and the boyars. Peter never got to the
bottom of the musketeers' motives, and he suspected the boyars,
even those to whom he had entrusted the government, of conceal-
ing evidence or worse. As the interrogation drew to a close, Peter
decided that he could no longer work with the boyars because they
were too quarrelsome among themselves and unreliable. Henceforth
he would rely on his favorites.

Peter had returned from Europe with two new favorites, Golovin
and a junior officer of bombardiers, Alexander Menshikov. Gordon
and LeFort wanted Peter to maintain his alliance with Austria
and prepare for another Turkish war, but he had other plans,
and in any case both Gordon and LeFort died about this time.
Golovin came from an old boyar family and was well educated.
He had negotiated the treaty of Nerchinsk that delimited their
mutual border with China, and had succeeded in part because he
could speak to the Jesuits at the Chinese court in Latin. Menshikov
was the exact opposite, the son of a falconer at the court who
had served in Peter's play regiments, which became his guards.
Menshikov had little education, though he had acquired enough
"soldier's German" to speak to foreigners who lacked Russian.
Menshikov was also LeFort's replacement at the drinking parties
and Peter's close personal friend. They also both supported Peter's
divorce from his wife Evdokiia, the mother of his son Aleksei. Most
important, they both supported Peter's new project, the war with
Sweden.

The war with Sweden would occupy most of the rest of Peter's
reign. On its eve Peter decreed the first of his reforms, mandating
that men of the upper classes must shave their beards, and that both
sexes of the gentry must henceforth wear Western clothing in place
of traditional Russian dress. He also ordered the year to be dated
from the birth of Christ, not the creation of the world so that Russia

would be in keeping with the educated world as he saw it. These decrees aroused a certain amount of discontent, especially the new dress. Boyar women in particular did not like the new clothing, as it meant that their hair was not covered (and thus their new dress was immodest) and they could not manage the stockings and high heels. Many of them wore the new clothes only at court, switching back to traditional dress at home.

Peter also began to reorder the state. The collecting of taxes from townspeople was taken from the provincial governors and put in the hands of the urban elites, and he imposed a stamp duty on official papers. These were experiments, eventually abandoned, but a more basic change was silent. Peter ceased to create boyars and call the boyar duma. Similarly, when the patriarch of the church died in 1701, Peter allowed no new patriarch to be chosen and appointed the Ukrainian abbot Stefan Iavorskii as "conservator of the patriarchal throne." Thus the traditional and canonical head of the Orthodox church in Russia simply disappeared. To make matters worse, Peter also took control of the revenues of the monastic estates, keeping most of them and doling out a stipend for the use of the monks. Peter wanted to ensure revenue for his war, and did not want any interference from the aristocracy or the church.

The war with Sweden was a response to Peter's disappointment in the outcome of the Azov campaigns. He had taken the fort to be sure, and gained an outlet to the Black Sea, more or less, but the Turks would not permit the Russians to trade on the Black Sea much less pass the Bosporus into the Mediterranean. Russia had reentered the war too late to derive much benefit from its victory. As Peter was returning from Vienna in 1698 to deal with the musketeer revolt, he had a long meeting with the new king of Poland, Augustus of Saxony. Augustus had large ambitions and considered himself a great military commander. He wanted to seize Sweden's Baltic provinces, an old demand of the Polish nobility, but he also wanted to use them to strengthen his very shaky position in Poland. His natural allies against Sweden, the hegemonic power of northern Europe, were Denmark and Russia, and he was able to recruit Peter to his cause.

As is so often the case in war, all the initial calculations were wrong. Augustus' small army tried to take Riga in 1700, but failed ignominiously. The young king of Sweden Charles XII, a born battlefield commander, knocked Denmark out of the war in a matter of weeks, and then shipped his army to the Baltic provinces. Peter had moved his newly trained European-style army to besiege the town of Narva in Swedish Estonia. Charles marched swiftly to the attack, landed on the unprepared Russians in the middle of a snowstorm and routed them. Only Peter's guards regiments were able to withdraw in order, and most of the foreign and Russian officers were captured. Peter had to begin all over again. Fortunately, Charles had other plans. Contemptuous of Russian capabilities, he turned his attention to Poland, spending the next eight years dethroning Augustus and setting up a Swedish puppet in his place. Peter had a breathing space and he used it well.

What was Peter trying to accomplish in going to war against Sweden, a power that everyone thought virtually invincible? Officially he announced that he was recovering the territory lost at the end of the Time of Troubles, that is, the eastern part of the Gulf of Finland where St. Petersburg now stands. This was ancient Russian territory (that was true) and thus his patrimony. At the same time Peter wanted a port for Russia more convenient for trade and communication than distant Archangel. Azov had not worked out, and the only other option was the Baltic shore. Indeed Narva had been the object of Ivan the Terrible's wars a century and a half earlier. Peter had no way of knowing that the war would turn into an epic duel that would change the face of northern and eastern Europe, and it seems that his initial aims were modest. Again like so many wars, the conflict acquired a logic of its own and ended in ways that no one could have imagined.

For the time being, the war absorbed all his energies and those of the state. Administration was concentrated in the hands of Peter's favorites Golovin and Menshikov, but this arrangement meant that government was essentially improvised. During this period Peter had no court, for he spent most of his time with the army or in his small houses around Moscow, especially the residence in Preobrazhenskoe. His style of life at this time and ever after was unique for a Russian or European monarch. He went about the country and the army with no guards and no suite, but he took his lathe and woodworking tools with him everywhere. The absence of a court suited him perfectly, as he hated any sort of ceremonial and the court amusements that were usual in most of Europe. His idea of a good time was to arrange a great drunken celebration with his officers or Dutch sea captains and end the evening with fireworks. The scene of these amusements, and of the government as well, was increasingly in his new city, St. Petersburg. The city was the result of his persistence after the defeat at Narva. Peter rebuilt his army and sent it into the Baltic provinces, in effect training it under fire in many small engagements with the enemy. In 1702 he felt confident enough to move against a larger objective, the Swedish fort on the Neva River, Nöteborg. He took it after a short siege and renamed it, ignoring the previous Russian name and calling it Schlüsselburg, in German the "Key Castle." The next year he moved down the Neva and quickly seized the small Swedish town at its mouth, where he immediately began to build a new fortress, the fortress of St. Peter and Paul, to defend the area from sea and land. Around the fortress he began to build a new city as a naval base and a potential commercial port for Russia on the Baltic. He was not waiting for the war to end, and through the years to come in the darkest moments of the war, it was St. Petersburg that was his one unshakeable demand.

There were plenty of dark moments. By 1706 Charles had managed to force Augustus to abdicate the Polish throne and in the next two years the Swedish king gradually moved east through Poland to expel Augustus's remaining supporters and the Russian army. Charles was fresh from a long series of victories and hailed in Europe as one of the world's great commanders, so it is not surprising that he had far-reaching plans to rely on boyar and popular dissent to overthrow Peter and establish a weak and compliant government in Moscow. His assumption was that Peter's army could not effectively oppose him. As the Swedes moved toward the Russian border, however, their situation rapidly deteriorated. The Russians had stripped most of the land of food and fodder and Charles's army was low on supplies. To make things worse, each encounter with the Russian army revealed that Peter's officers were learning their profession, and Swedish successes came harder each time. Then Charles reached the Russian border and stopped to rest, hoping that his manifestos had caused discontent to boil over among the Russian boyars and people, but nothing happened. Russia was quiet, and winter was coming on. Charles decided to turn south into the Ukrainian Hetmanate, but first he hoped to join up with a Swedish relief army coming from Riga that had fresh supplies. At Lesnaia Peter struck. Moving his dragoons rapidly through the forest he fell on the relief army, driving it from the field and seizing its supplies. Charles now had more men but no fresh supplies.

For the moment his hope was in the Ukrainians. He had long been in secret correspondence with the Ukrainian Hetman Ivan Mazepa, who promised to rebel against the Russian tsar and bring over the whole Ukrainian Cossack host. When Charles arrived in the Ukraine, however, only some of the Cossack generals and a few thousand men joined him. The rank and file Cossacks would not follow and remained loyal to the tsar. Thus the Swedes settled down for the winter, finding adequate food but no military supplies. When spring came, the Swedish king moved northeast toward Moscow, but stopped to besiege the fortified town of Poltava so as not to leave enemy troops in his rear.

Peter decided to make his move. He marched his army toward the town but instead of attacking, he constructed a fortified camp on the outskirts and waited. Charles would have to attack him soon, for clouds of Cossacks made foraging impossible. On the morning of June 27, 1709, the invincible Swedish army marched through the morning mist toward the Russian camp and turned right, ready to attack. Peter brought his artillery out to meet them, and about ten o'clock the Swedes moved forward in frontal attack, a maneuver that had so often brought them victory. This time it failed. Peter's guns cut them to pieces, and the Swedish line stuck fast in close combat with the Russians, and then broke. By noon Charles's army was a mass of refugees heading west for the Dniepr River, and Russia had become a great power.

The victory at Poltava was the turning point of Peter's reign, for it ensured that eventually he would emerge the victor and keep St. Petersburg. It also radically changed his and Russia's position in Europe. Charles had already given the final blow to Polish power and prestige, and now Peter had done the same to Sweden. He was free to concentrate on securing his conquests, and in 1710 he wrapped up the Baltic provinces and took the Finnish town of Viborg, thereby ensuring his new city, soon to be his new capital, of a protective belt of territory as well as several new ports for his empire.

The war with Sweden dragged on until 1721, for Charles was much too courageous and too stubborn to give up, even when he had lost all of Sweden's possessions in Germany, the Baltic provinces, and Finland. To defeat him Peter had to maintain his army and use it and create a navy in the Baltic Sea, based in St. Petersburg. The navy in particular was extremely expensive, though vital to pressure Sweden to make peace. When peace came at last, Peter returned Finland to Sweden, minus Viborg, but kept the Baltic provinces. St. Petersburg was secure.

The strain of the war very soon required Peter to think more carefully about the structure of his state. Golovin's untimely death in 1706 made change urgent. In 1708 he formally replaced both the traditional central offices as well as the improvised chancelleries of his favorites with the governors of eight huge provinces that took over most of the business of taxation, recruitment, and the courts. The new arrangement was not just a change in formal structure, for Peter appointed men from old aristocratic families (such as the Golitsyns and Streshnev) as well as his in-laws (the Apraksins), and, of course, "Aleksashka" Menshikov to run St. Petersburg and the huge province around it. The resulting decentralization left a gap in the center, so in 1711 he established the Senate as a coordinating body, particularly to work when he was away. Prince Iakov Dolgorukii, fresh from a daring escape from Swedish captivity, was its president, and aristocrats and their clients were prominent among its members. Peter had created a new balance in the government, combining great aristocrats with his favorite Menshikov. The balance was further enhanced by the appearance of a new favorite and Menshikov's rival, Prince Vasilii Dolgorukii (Prince Iakov's cousin). The prince held no major office, but was always present at court and employed in a series of delicate and confidential matters.

Peter now had the beginnings of a court again in St. Petersburg. He also ordered the government offices to the new city, and required the aristocracy and many merchants to move there and build houses.

This was not a popular idea, for the new capital was expensive, damp, subject to flooding, and far from the Russian heartland. The merchants could not trade easily as long as the war continued, and the aristocracy was particularly unhappy with the need to leave their warm and comfortable Moscow mansions for the banks of the Neva. Peter himself built no great palace in his new city, no Russian Versailles. His Winter and Summer "Palaces" in St. Petersburg were essentially six-room houses suitable for a modest country gentleman. Peter's new court was small and unostentatious, in keeping with his residences. Moreover the physical center of the new city was not the tsar's palace but the Admiralty, the administrative center of the navy and its principal site for shipbuilding. The main avenue of the new city, Nevsky Prospect, began at the Admiralty, not the palace, and the radial avenues laid out after Peter's death began at the same place. In Peter's final plan, the government would have its seat on Vasil'ev Island on the north side of the river, across the water from the Winter Palace and the Admiralty. The island would also serve as the main center for commerce. The main harbor was still at Kronstadt, as the waters were too shallow near the city. The country villas of the tsar and elite stretching along the Gulf of Finland to the southwest were an integral part of the new city. These were modest houses with extensive gardens, modeled on the Dutch villas along the Vecht River near Utrecht. Among the villas stood the ancestor of the now magnificent Peterhof, then a modest country house for the tsar notable only for the fountains and gardens. Menshikov's palace at Oranienbaum farther along the coast was much larger and grander. Peter's plan was in fact too modest, and the government gradually moved south to be near the tsar in the Winter Palace. The architecture of the city after his death quickly grew very much grander. The city that would become a great imperial capital with Roman arches and classical architecture and ornament started its existence as a modest port and royal residence in north European style.

Peter built his new city and court with a new wife at his side. This was Catherine, and her story was perhaps the strangest of the whole era. When the Russian armies began to move into the Baltic provinces, one of the local Lutheran pastors had a maid named Marta, and she with the rest of the family was taken off to Moscow

Figure 5. Peter the Great. Engraving after the equestrian statue of Peter by Etienne-Maurice Falconet erected at the order of Catherine the Great in 1782.

as part of the policy of harrying the area. There her master set up a school. Marta came to the attention of Peter around 1704, and she became his mistress in place of Anna Mons. When Marta accepted Orthodoxy and took the name Catherine, Peter married her in 1712. By this time they already had several children, all girls, one of them, born in 1709, who would be the future empress Elizabeth. Catherine was a strong and important figure in the court, generally allied with Menshikov but also working to keep harmony when crises threatened, and to moderate Peter's anger when it overflowed.

In this new city Peter set about once more to reorder the structure of church and state. In 1715 he sent one Heinrich Fick, a German jurist, as a spy to Sweden, whose mission was to study the Swedish administrative system. Fick returned with detailed knowledge, and on this basis Peter began the process of recreating a central government to be headed by Colleges, each run by a committee consisting of Russian officials and foreign experts. Peter was also increasingly discontented with Stefan Iavorskii, who had strong notions of episcopal power and believed that Russia needed to exterminate heretics. Iavorskii came into conflict with both the tsar and the Senate over the case of an obscure religious dissident in Moscow, and though Peter partially conceded to Iavorskii's demands for executions, he decided to place the church under a new system. Another Ukrainian bishop, Feofan Prokopovich, recently arrived in Petersburg, had the task of finding a suitable arrangement.

These were major changes and they took time to elaborate, especially with the continuing war with Sweden. Other concerns were equally prominent in the tsar's mind. In the autumn of 1714 Peter discovered the extent of corruption on the part of Menshikov and many other major officials. The building of St. Petersburg was a particular gold mine for corruption, as thousands of peasants were conscripted every year to work; feeding and paying them was an obvious area for padding the work rolls and underpaying the workmen. The guilty officials were whipped and sent into exile, and Menshikov was sentenced to return literally millions of rubles to the treasury. He kept his position as governor of St. Petersburg, but lost the tsar's favor. At court the Dolgorukiis and their allies were triumphant. Menshikov was not the only problem. Peter's son by his first wife, Aleksei Petrovich, was now in his twenties, and had proved a serious disappointment to his father. Peter had given him a Western education, had him taught German and French, history and geography, but he did not take to it very well. A German wife (sister to the Emperor Karl VI's wife) did not help either, as Aleksei treated her with coldness and contempt and found a mistress among his servants. Aleksei was lazy, uninterested in learning, politics, or warfare and preferred drinking with his circle of servants and clergy. Stefan Iavorskii began to see him as a future advocate of church interests, perhaps wrongly, but he let his views be known.

Relations between father and son worsened, and the existence of Peter's second wife Catherine meant that other heirs to the throne might be born. Finally, in 1715, both Catherine and Aleksei's wife gave birth to sons almost simultaneously. There were now two possible heirs if Peter chose to bypass his eldest son. The tsar wrote to Aleksei chiding him for his indifference to the qualities needed for a future ruler, and Aleksei responded by offering to enter a monastery. Peter gave him another warning, and then went off to Western Europe to look after the continuing war and to do more traveling, this time to France.

While Peter was away a crisis arose in the supply of the Russian army in Finland, and the Senate, with its aristocratic supporters, dragged their feet. Peter was furious and sent order after order, but nothing happened. Menshikov stepped in to commandeer ships and send the supplies, thus instantly restoring himself to favor. His crimes were forgiven. A few weeks later, Aleksei Petrovich, the heir to the Russian throne, disappeared from Petersburg. For several weeks, no one knew where he was. Finally Peter's emissaries found him in Vienna, where he had gone to take refuge with Emperor Karl, Aleksei's brother-in-law, a man seriously unhappy with Peter's rise to power and his potential influence in Germany. The Emperor gave him shelter, and Aleksei proposed to Karl's ministers that he be given an army to overthrow his father. This was a tall order, and the Austrians feared Peter's reaction, so they hid the tsarevich, first in the Tirol and then in Naples. There Peter sent one of his diplomats, Peter Tolstoi, to bring him back, and Tolstoi succeeded, in the process laying the foundation of the fortunes of the Tolstoi family for two centuries.

Aleksei returned to Moscow in January 1718. Thus began a long interrogation during which the extent of Aleksei's support among the aristocracy and church became evident, not least because the tsarevich himself informed on them all. His sympathizers included the other favorite, Prince Vasilii Dolgorukii, Stefan Iavorskii, and many great aristocrats. As far as Peter could tell, they had not planned anything specific, but they also had known of Aleksei's flight to Vienna. Peter faced a dilemma: either he could punish them all in imitation of Ivan the Terrible, or he could minimize the whole affair by punishing a few and thus cover it up. With some persuasion from his wife, he chose the second alternative. A dozen or so persons of low rank were executed. Prince Vasilii Dolgorukii and others were exiled, and Aleksei brought before the assembled Senate, ministers, generals, and high clergy for trial. The laymen voted for the death penalty, with dozens of men named by Aleksei as his supporters signing the document. Before Peter made a final decision about execution, the tsarevich died, probably from the aftereffects of judicial torture, but no information that is reliable exists about the cause of death.

Be that as it may, Peter's problem was solved. He decreed that henceforth the tsar could choose his successor at will. He then proceeded to implement the new form of government, the Colleges, and to place over the church a new institution, the Holy Synod, a committee of clergy and laymen with a lay "Ober-procuror" as its head. This structure came from Prokopovich's reading of Swedish legislation for the Lutheran church, and was a sharp break with Orthodox tradition. In the new arrangement the tsar became the "protector" of the church, and in practice he appointed the members of the Synod. The church would no longer be able to play a role in politics and oppose his reforms.

The seven years from the death of Aleksei to the death of Peter himself in January 1725 saw the culmination of Peter's reordering of government, culture, and his foreign policy. The end of the Swedish war was a great relief, but he did not rest on his laurels. He immediately set off to use the momentary political confusion in Iran to seize some of its northern provinces, a scheme abandoned after his death but revealing of Peter's thinking. The motivations here were purely commercial: control of the silk-producing areas of Iran, greater access to the Iranian market, and further on to the markets of the Near East and India. Utterly impractical, the plans show the extent to which Peter wanted to graft commercial appendages onto his agrarian empire.

With the restoration of central government, Peter established a Table of Ranks to replace the old court and military ranks he had allowed to lapse. It established an equivalency of civilian and military ranks, and provided for ennoblement of plebeians whose talents allowed them to advance. As a framework for the Russian state administration it lasted until 1917. In the same years Peter also tried to reorganize Russian provincial administration, redrawing the large provinces into fifty small ones, with subdivisions and a separation of administration and the judiciary all based on a Swedish model. Russia, however, lacked the resources for such a system, and after Peter's death the number of provinces was reduced to fourteen, with another crucial administrative layer below the provincial governors. All this tinkering did not solve the problem of ruling a vast state with limited resources.

Peter's victories added a new element to the Russian state in the form of the Baltic provinces of Estland and Livonia. For the first time Russia had territories with a powerful local elite that was not Orthodox. The loss of their privileges and lands to Swedish absolutism had led many of the German nobility of the area to support Peter and when he finally pushed out the Swedes in 1710 he granted the nobility their old privileges, including local courts, diets, and control of the Lutheran church on their estates. Elected town government was restored in the hands of the urban German merchants. In the Ukrainian Hetmanate, Peter took a stronger hand, for he engineered the election of Ivan Skoropadskii to replace the pro-Swedish Mazepa in 1708, and then, on Skoropadskii's death in 1722, abolished the office of hetman altogether. He left, however, the rest of the Hetmanate's political and legal structure intact and it survived until the 1780s. Thus Russia had not only new territories and peoples, but distinct legal and local political systems in Livonia and the Ukrainian Hetmanate, both differing from the Russian structure. In both places traditional privileges and a system of local elections kept power and wealth in the hands of the local nobility, while the tsar appointed governors to exercise general supervision.

Peter's intervention in the border provinces was limited. In the inner Russian provinces he proceeded with more new and reformed institutions. After 1718 he replaced the old Russian tax system and his own innumerable financial improvisations with a single tax, the "soul tax," to be paid by all non-nobles, which also structured finance and social relations until the 1860s. Some of these measures lasted and some did not, but all of them meant that the Russian state now had its basic institutions, their powers and duties, spelled out in law for the first time. The laws were published and provided with elaborate prefaces giving out the rationale for each measure.

The new system of government now looked formally more or less the same as that of the rest of Europe's monarchies.

Along with the new form of government came a new culture. Peter did not suppress the old religious culture, he merely began to import a new one – the secular culture of contemporary Europe. He sent hundreds of young noblemen abroad, encouraged and sometimes directed the translation and printing of European books – not great classics but the textbooks of history, architecture, mathematics, geography, and other subjects. In the last years of his life he sent his personal librarian abroad to recruit scientists for an academy of sciences to be established in St. Petersburg, instructing the librarian to particularly look for mathematicians and physical scientists. The project was on the point of realization when he died, but his wife and successor formally established the academy in his memory. The result was the Russian Academy of Sciences, founded in 1725. Peter was not only interested in science and art, but he also wanted to Europeanize Russia's social habits. In the european thought of the time, a cultivated and polished people were necessary for an orderly state. Thus in 1719, Peter decreed that the nobility was to change its forms of socializing. The all-male banquets of the old days were to end, and in their place the nobility were to hold a sort of open house (known as "assemblies") on particular days, and invite their acquaintances including those of lesser rank. Amusements were to be cultivated – music, dancing, and card-playing – and most important, the assemblies must include women. Like so many of Peter's cultural decrees, it required what had already come into fairly general practice, As the diplomats immediately realized, the assemblies were also a perfect point of exchange of information about politics and simply the news of the day.

Almost the last thing he did before he died was to order the translation of the German jurist and historian Samuel Puffendorf's book, *On the Duties of Man and the Citizen*. A widely read popular account of the nature of the state, it founded government ultimately on natural law and a contract among men in the state of nature. Puffendorf also stressed the ruler's duty to work for the general good, not just his own, and the citizen's duty of obedience without any sort of rebellion. He thought natural law was the work of God, but otherwise he strictly separated the state and its laws from divine commands. For Peter this meant that the tsar was still the sovereign, but the character of his rule was based on natural and human law, not merely tradition and the ruler's personal piety. Western political thought had entered Russia.

Peter the Great, with his personal eccentricities and the scale of his accomplishment was a ruler unique in Russian history. For most of the eighteenth century he was the great ideal of the Russian monarchy and its supporters at home and abroad. As time passed, Peter's image changed, for already in Catherine's time conservative noblemen began to complain, echoing their ancestors of Peter's time, that Peter had imported foreign ways to Russia, undermining its ancient religion and morality. In the nineteenth century a full-blown quarrel broke out about this issue, pitting liberal and radical Westernizers against Slavophile admirers of Russian tradition – that is, Peter's admirers were pitted against his detractors. This was a dispute fraught with metaphysics and national pride, but the question remains: What did Peter really accomplish?

The most obvious answer has to do with religion. The administrative subordination of the church to the tsar was only one side of the changes Peter wrought, however important. Peter was determined to put the church in its place, but he was not irreligious. He attended the liturgy at least once a week in St. Petersburg and more often during Lent and Easter week. His style of religious observance in other respects deviated from traditional Orthodoxy. After his mother's death, he never made a pilgrimage to any of the many shrines of miraculous relics and icons. In his new capital there was only one monastery, in contrast to the dozens in Moscow, and it was founded only in 1714. Peter went there on occasion, but the attraction was the sermons of the Ukrainian monks, which Peter sought out and seems to have enjoyed. The monastery was dedicated to Prince Alexander Nevskii, certainly a saint in the Orthodox Church, but one known mainly for his military victories, including that over the Swedes on the Neva. In case the significance of the choice was not clear enough, Peter ordered the celebration of the saint's feast day moved from the traditional November 30 to August 23, the day of the conclusion of the treaty of Nystad that ended his own war with Sweden. Peter knew his scripture and liturgy, and could trade biblical quotations with his correspondents, but his personal piety was the outgrowth of the cultural changes in Russian Orthodoxy of the seventeenth century, the emphasis on sermons and learning over miracles and monasticism.

The key here is the change in emphasis: Peter did not abolish monasteries or suppress the devotion to miracle-working relics. Similarly Peter was not out to eliminate religion. The consequence of his policies was to end the universal domination of religion in Russian culture, and to reduce it to the place it held in the mental life of early modern Europe after the Renaissance: a foundational belief system in a society whose high culture was already secular. Thus he accomplished in thirty-six years a change in Russian culture that took centuries in Western Europe.

The new secular culture imported into Russia in Peter's time was undoubtedly European. At the time, no one thought of it that way. Neither Russians nor Europeans used the terms "Westernization" or "Europeanization." They thought Peter had brought education and culture in place of ignorance, light in the place of darkness. Moreover, the term "European," can be misleading, as it conceals the choices Peter as well as other Russians made among the great variety of European culture. Peter's personal tastes were unusual to say the least. He had what some contemporaries called a "mathematical mind," meaning that he was interested in what was then understood to be mathematics. That meant not just a theoretical science of numbers, but also mechanics, hydraulics, fortification, surveying, astronomy, architecture, and many other sciences and techniques that employed more or less mathematics. There were no European monarchs who shared these tastes and they were unknown among Russian aristocrats at his court. He also had a passion for the Dutch, their language, their ships, their engineering and architecture, and their painting. In general his personal culture took its inspiration from Protestant northern Europe, and from there he borrowed his laws and administration, his navy, the engineering for his new capital, and much more. His architects, however, were more German or Italian, in spite of his Dutch leanings, and his sculptors were Italian. His choices were eclectic as were those of the other Russians, mostly aristocrats, whose cultural interests in Western Europe we can trace. Many of the aristocrats, and apparently all of Peter's opponents, were more attracted by the culture of Catholic southern Europe and Poland – by the Baroque grandeur of Rome and the aristocratic constitutions of Venice and Poland. Some parts of European culture had not yet arrived in Russia, jurisprudence, medicine, and the scholarly study of the classics. For the time being the result was a strange mixture of Baroque Europe and the early Enlightenment, a combination of disparate and sometimes contradictory elements derived from European thought and culture.

Part of the cultural transformation of Russia was a new conception of the state. The traditional Russian state's goals were very simple: maintenance of the power of the tsar and his government at home and abroad and the conservation of the state by the just and Christian behavior of the rulers. Peter introduced a secular goal, the good of the state (including its subjects) as well as the means to achieving that goal, that is, the establishment of good and legal order and the education of the elite in European culture. It was the latter in particular that Peter's spokesmen repeatedly stressed, proclaiming that he had brought light (learning) into darkness (ignorance), and that is also how Peter's European contemporaries saw his achievement. Equally important was the creation of explicit written and legal foundations of governmental institutions, not a constitution in the modern sense, but a sharp break with the customary, unwritten, foundations of previous Russian government. The structure he created was noticeably similar to European monarchies, and was accepted as such in the West. It shared with many European states one fundamental contradiction, that the monarch was the source of all law. That being the case, how could the legal order be preserved if the ruler chose to ignore it? Eventually this contradiction in the continental European states could only be resolved by the French Revolution and its consequences, but for the time it seemed to work.

The Russian state looked like Europe, but it had its peculiarities. Russia lacked one important institution that was universal in European states, a trained legal profession. Russia was not to get a university with a law faculty until 1755, and a trained legal profession came only in the nineteenth century. Another typically Russian problem with Peter's state was that its new features were concentrated in St. Petersburg. The tsar's reform of provincial administration had never been very effective, languished for lack of suitable personnel, and was abolished after his death. Unlike European monarchies, Russia lacked an administrative structure dense enough and well trained enough to execute the sovereign's will on provincial society. Unimpeachably enlightened measures formulated in the capital did not affect the provinces, and just to collect taxes Peter often had to rely on specially delegated military officers. To some extent the new state floated in the air over a society that was not changing with the pace of the capital or even Moscow. For the peasants, relations with the state had hardly changed.

With all these limitations, however, Peter succeeded and transformed his country forever. He did not do this without the aid of some previous changes, particularly in the culture of the church and the boyar elite in the last decades of the seventeenth century. His reordering of the state, however, had no precedent, and came out of his early improvisations and the decision to adopt Swedish models of administration. Peter did not do all of this alone. A major part of his success was his political skill in managing a reluctant aristocracy that inevitably lost part of its power in the new arrangements. The aristocrats, legends aside, were not boyars in long beards trying to restore Orthodox Russia as it was in 1650. They too were European, but with different goals and interests from the tsar, and Peter managed them by including enough of them in the new government, army, and diplomatic corps to keep them quiet if not fully satisfied. Peter also had popular discontent to contend with, and that did have an element of cultural conservatism. When this discontent turned into rebellion, he suppressed it with savage punishments, to the approval of Europe. No one supported rebels against the crown. With the aristocrats Peter worked entirely differently, pretending to ignore their sympathy for his son and keeping them in the center of government along with his favorites and Western experts until the end of his reign. Thus Peter kept the elite together and allied with him and his policies. His mastery of court politics was as important as his relentless determination and iron will.

Peter's death in January 1725, plunged Russia into a political crisis, for one of the many paradoxes of his reign is that he did not carry out the provisions of his decree permitting the tsar to nominate his heir. Therefore at his death there were several possible alternatives: his wife Catherine, crowned his empress the previous year; his ten-year-old grandson Peter by the unfortunate Aleksei; and several daughters by Catherine. The latter were too young or married abroad, and the choice came down to Catherine or Peter under a regency. The ruling elite split over the choice, but after considerable pressure from the guards regiments, the Senate opted for Catherine. For the first time the guards made their wishes felt and opted for a woman. Though Catherine had a reputation as a very strong personality ("the heart of a lion," said the French ambassador), she did not prove an effective ruler, and very soon state business went to Menshikov and a Supreme Privy Council formed to manage the state. Then Catherine died in 1727. Menshikov seemed poised for supreme power with a boy tsar, but the aristocrats proved too powerful, and the Supreme Privy Council exiled him to Siberia, where he died. The Princes Dolgorukii and Golitsyn were masters of the government and they signaled a new course, moving the capital back to Moscow. They cemented their position by marrying the young tsar to a Dolgorukii princess. Then fate intervened. Suddenly in 1730 Peter II died of smallpox. The aristocrats had to find a new monarch, and they did not choose Peter's remaining daughter Elizabeth but his niece, Anna, the daughter of his erstwhile co-tsar Ivan V. Anna ruled in Baltic Kurland as the widow of the Duke, and was quickly summoned to Moscow. At the same time the aristocrats decided to hold on to power by compiling a series of conditions that Anna would have to sign to ascend the throne, conditions giving power to the sitting members of the Supreme Privy Council, the Dolgorukiis and Golitsyns. Here they made a fatal error, for the conditions gave power not to the aristocracy as a whole, but to a clique of families. As the English ambassador reported, the Russian aristocrats "have no true notions of a limited government." When Anna came to Moscow, she quickly sized up the situation and with the support of the other aristocratic clans, the rank and file nobility, and the guards, she tore up the conditions and restored autocracy. Russia was back on the road Peter had mapped out, but with another woman on the throne who had no direct heirs, male or female. No one knew that for the next sixty-six years Russia's rulers would be women, like Anna, put on the throne by male aristocrats and guards officers.

6

Two Empresses

With the restoration of autocracy, Anna came to the throne as Empress of Russia, and after a time she sent the leaders of the Golitsyn and Dolgorukii clans into exile. The ten years of Anna's reign in the memory of the Russian nobility was a dark period of rule by Anna's German favorites – particularly her chamberlain – Ernst-Johann Bühren (Biron to the Russians), who was allegedly all-powerful and indifferent to Russian interests. That memory was a considerable exaggeration. After a brief interlude, Empress Elizabeth, Peter the Great's daughter and a capable and strong monarch succeeded her (1741–1761). Underneath all the drama at court, Russia's new culture took shape, and Russia entered the age of the Enlightenment. In these decades we can also get a glimpse of Russian society that goes beyond descriptions of legal status into the web of human relations.

Politically Anna's court was not a terribly pleasant place, though the story of "German domination" is largely a legend. Anna was personally close to Biron, who had served her well in Courland, where she had lived since the death of her husband the duke in 1711. She entrusted foreign policy to Count Andrei Ostermann and the army to Count Burkhard Christian Münnich, but the three were in no sense a clique. Indeed, they hated one another and made alliances with the more numerous Russian grandees in the court and in the government. The truth was that Anna relied on them and a few others and she did not consult with the elite as a whole. The Senate languished. Not surprisingly, Anna was terrified that there would be plots against her in favor of Elizabeth, Peter's eldest surviving daughter, or other candidates for the throne, and she used the Secret Chancellery to try to uncover them. The darkest episode of the reign was the trial and execution of her minister Artemii Volynskii in 1740 on the charge of insulting the Empress. This was an excuse: the real reason for his death was Volynskii's loss of favor with Biron and Ostermann and his own ambitious plans, which frightened Anna and many others in her entourage.

Anna's reign was by no means a failure. She restored much of Peter's work that had been rejected by the oligarchy in the time of Peter II. She returned the capital to St. Petersburg and abolished the Supreme Privy Council. She did not restore the Senate to power, ruling with a Cabinet of Ministers dominated by her favorites. Her government tried to reduce the burden on the country of the large military and naval establishment that Peter had created, but found that they could not. Instead, Russia fought a successful war in Poland to keep France from placing a king on the Polish throne who would be hostile to Russia and Austria – and then Russia went to war with Turkey. Münnich proved a highly capable commander, and Russia was able to return the fort at Azov that was lost in 1711.

Since Anna's husband had died before they could produce children, she remained childless. In accord with Peter's 1722 succession law she chose her heir, albeit on her deathbed: a two-month-old infant who was given the name Ivan VI. The baby's connection with the Russian throne was remote. He was the grandson of Anna's elder sister Catherine, who had married the Duke of Mecklenburg in 1716. Catherine's daughter, also named Anna, in turn married the Duke of Brunswick-Bevern-Lüneburg, and Ivan was their first son. In other words, the tsar of Russia was actually a minor German prince with only the most tenuous connection to the country he was supposed to rule. The baby tsar obviously had to have a regent to rule for him, a fact that brought the conflicts among the grandees into the open. At first Biron was in charge, but Münnich quickly ousted him, only to fall victim to Ostermann and the infant tsar's parents. Complicating matters was a Swedish declaration of war during the summer of 1741, an attempt by the Swedes to get revenge for their earlier defeats. Not surprisingly in this situation an elaborate plot came into being with all sorts of international ramifications (the French ambassador was one of the leaders) and in November 1741, the guards overthrew the regency and carried Elizabeth on their shoulders into the Winter Palace. Ivan VI and the Brunswick family were sent into exile in northern Russia, Ivan to perish in the Mirovich affair of 1764 and his family to be released only some twenty years later.

Elizabeth's reign brought a renewed sense of normalcy to Russia. The remaining Golitsyns, Dolgorukiis, and alleged confederates of Volynskii were returned from exile, their lands and position restored. The Senate was restored to the position that it had under Peter. The Russian army defeated the Swedes, quickly ending the war in 1743. Elizabeth was intelligent and capable, but rather lazy and self-indulgent. The number of her dresses was legendary, and in a modest way she followed her father's taste for banquets and drink. Secretly she married her lover, originally a Ukrainian choir-boy named Aleksei Razumovskii, who became a major figure at court. He was clever enough to not try to overshadow the others, and for most of the reign affairs were in the hands of the Shuvalovs, the brothers Peter and Alexander, and the chancellor (foreign minister) Aleksei Bestuzhev-Riumin. All of these men, like their rivals the Vorontsovs, came from families of ancient nobility but far from the great aristocracy, who now settled into secondary positions in government and diplomacy. Elizabeth's grandees were relatively new men who owed their positions to Peter's promotion of talented young men from outside the small circle of old aristocratic families. Bestuzhev-Riumin was an experienced diplomat, and the Shuvalovs had been part of Elizabeth's personal entourage in the 1730s. Though they owed their rise to their personal connection with the new empress, they proved energetic and intelligent. They were the first since Peter's time to systematically turn their attention to the economic development of Russia, primarily toward strengthening its commerce. In 1752 they convinced Elizabeth to abolish all internal tolls and modestly raise the tariff, so that trade would be freer but the state revenue would not suffer. Less happy was their scheme to increase revenue through the state vodka monopoly by raising the price. There were other ideas, the most important to produce a new law code, and the plan to secularize monastery lands, though neither were realized. They also introduced their young cousin Ivan Shuvalov to Elizabeth, and he became a major force in Russian culture.

Elizabeth's decision to join Austria against Prussia in the Seven Years War (1756–1763) put any reform plans on the shelf. Russia's army performed well against the supposed military genius of the age, Frederick the Great, and even briefly occupied Berlin in 1760. The death of the Empress on Christmas day 1761 in the Julian calendar, however, put an end to Russia's participation in the conflict, and simultaneously set the stage for yet another drama.

While the court alternated between routine governance, dangerous intrigue, and dramatic palace revolutions, Russia gradually integrated the cultural changes that were the result of Peter the Great's turn toward European culture. It is not the case that the Empresses and the court elite played no role in the development and deepening of Russian culture. Empress Anna was paradoxically one of the most important innovators. It was in her reign that Russia finally abandoned the simplicity of Peter's time and acquired a court like those of other European states with the usual cultural institutions. Anna was the first to establish a court theater, beginning with an Italian Commedia dell'arte troupe, and then a regular French and German theater. She also brought an opera company, with its composer-director, the Neapolitan Francesco Araya. Anna replaced Peter's tiny Winter Palace with a new one, more in keeping with the status of Russia's rulers. Anna's government was not only concerned with the court, for she also founded the Infantry Cadet Corps, using the old buildings of Menshikov's palace. The Cadet Corps later evolved into an elite military school, but in the eighteenth century it was the main institution for the education of young Russian noblemen and had a broad curriculum that was borrowed from the academies for young nobles common in central Europe. The school taught military subjects, but also stressed modern languages, history, elementary jurisprudence, and mathematics. Not just officers, but also government ministers and many writers studied at the Cadet Corps.

Elizabeth continued in this direction, and it was she who ordered Bartolomeo Rastrelli to build the magnificent Winter Palace that stands to this day. Finally St. Petersburg had a residence for the monarch that rivaled or even outshone those of other European capitals. Elizabeth loved the theater even more than Anna, and in her court there were performances of the opera and the French theater two or three times a week. Araya kept his position to the end of her reign, writing his own operas and producing the work of other then prominent composers. In 1749 for the first time her theater put on a Russian play, *Semira*, by Alexander Sumarokov (1718–1777), a recent graduate of the Cadet Corps. *Semira* was a typical classical drama in verse in five acts, following the classical unities of time and place and imitating the French theater, Racine, Corneille, and Voltaire (then considered a great playwright and poet more than a thinker). Today it seems wooden and dull, with unexciting verse and an eminently predictable plot pitting duty against love. It was good enough, however, to enchant Elizabeth and her court, performed as it was by the boys of the Cadet Corps taking both male and female roles. Russians had no objection to female actors, the problem was that the theater was so new there simply were not any available, nor was there yet a school for girls equivalent to the Cadet Corps. The appearance of a Russian play, quickly followed by many others, required Russian actors, and by the end of the 1750s Russia had its first native theaters, the court theater as well as some short-lived enterprises outside the court network. Russia also had no school to train visual artists, and in 1756 Ivan Shuvalov founded the Academy of Arts in St. Petersburg. For the next century it would be the main center for Russian painting and sculpture.

Russia, however, still lacked a university. Peter's academy of sciences had included a university, but that aspect of the academy was too small to make much impact. Again it was Elizabeth's favorite, Count Ivan Shuvalov, who set out to correct the situation. The empress decreed the foundation of a university in Moscow that opened its doors in 1755. The university was very much on the German model, with a heavily German faculty and lectures frequently in Latin the first years, but it worked. It had two gymnasia attached to it to prepare the students – one for nobles and one for pupils from humbler stations in society. The new university had faculties of law and medicine as well as arts and sciences, and the very first graduates were to make major contributions to Russian culture.

Shuvalov had the political skills to pilot the university through the government's offices, but he turned for the programmatic details

to the Academy, and particularly to Mikhail Lomonosov (1711–
1765), who had been pressing the idea in vain for some time.
Lomonosov was in many ways the last man of the era of Peter,
for he was the son of a wealthy merchant of the far north who
owned fishing boats, but who was legally a peasant. Lomonosov had
walked south to Moscow to enter the Slavo-Greco-Latin Academy
in 1731. After graduation he was sent to Germany to study mining, but eventually opted for chemistry and related sciences. He had
to leave Marburg University in a hurry, as his landlord's daughter
was pregnant, and he threw himself on the mercies of the Russian
ambassador in Holland. Fortunately the ambassador sent him back
to St. Petersburg, where he found a position in the Academy and was
able to bring his German mistress to become his wife. Lomonosov's
most important scientific achievement was an early version of the
law of conservation of matter and energy that was later formulated by Lavoisier in France, but Lomonosov was something of a
polymath. He was a major poet, producing many odes for court
occasions, an important genre at the time, for the odes were often
declaimed at court occasions before the empress herself. These were
not just flattery, for Lomonosov used them to present a program of
enlightened and powerful monarchy that reflected his priorities and
also those of Elizabeth and the court elite. He also took time off
from his chemistry to engage in disputes over Russian history, and
most important, to codify Russian grammar. This apparently simple
contribution was fraught with consequence, for the cultural changes
of Peter's time had left the Russian literary language in a quandary.
The old literary language had been formed by the Church and it
was a combination of Old Church Slavic and vernacular elements.
Peter's reign had seen the introduction of thousands of new words
and concepts and the restriction of the church language to traditional religious texts. Lomonosov's contribution was to regularize
all this, declaring the Church Slavic elements to be appropriate for
high-style literature, but not necessarily ordinary speech or writing,
and to provide a grammar for the normal written language that was
essentially the spoken vernacular. Together with his own poetry and
other writings, he laid the foundation for the literary language of
Pushkin and Tolstoy.

Russia may not have had a university, but it certainly had a church. The time of Elizabeth was the high point of the domination of the Orthodox Church by Ukrainian bishops, who were trained in Kiev and elsewhere on Western, and to a large extent, Catholic models. They brought Latin and Western devotional literature to the Russian clergy, and continued the effort to bring their teachings to the population through sermonizing and attempts to educate the clergy. What they could not do was interfere in the process of absorption of Western secular culture. The Church in Russia, under the power of the state through the Synod, lacked the ability to ban books or interfere in the educational process. Boys in the Cadet School certainly had religious instruction, but the curriculum was entirely in the hands of laymen. As the European Enlightenment flowered, this Russian peculiarity meant that works banned in France or Italy found their way to Russia without interference from the clergy.

Starting around 1750, the Enlightenment came to Russia. For men of Lomonosov's generation, formed in the earlier part of the century, the European culture they absorbed was essentially that of seventeenth-century rationalism. The predominant philosophy at the Academy in Lomonosov's youth was that of Georg Christian Wolff, a follower and systematizer of the work of Gottfried Leibniz and Peter's advisor on the Academy of Sciences. Wolff taught a deductive rationalism that depended on mathematics and logic, not sense experience, for its conclusions. Though many Lutheran theologians saw him as a threat, Wolff had no quarrel with revealed religion and was equally respectful of absolute monarchy. This was the worldview that the philosophy faculty of Moscow University propagated as well, not surprisingly, since it still held sway in German universities until the 1770s and beyond. During the middle years of the century, however, newer ideas from France and indirectly from England began to penetrate into Russian libraries and bookstores. Voltaire's plays, some performed in Russia, illustrated classic themes of the French enlightenment, religious tolerance, enlightened monarchy, and the struggle against superstition and the clergy. As the French language began to replace German at court in these years, French writers acquired a public in Russia for the first time. In 1756 the first of Voltaire's essays appeared in Russian translation and three years later his novel *Zadig*, the first major text of the mature French Enlightenment to be translated. This small stream grew into a flood in the next reign.

The political and cultural efforts of the state and the court rested on the shoulders of the Russian peasantry, seventy percent of whom were serfs. About half of all peasants were the property of the gentry, another fifteen percent were serfs of the Orthodox monasteries, and the rest relatively free. Monastery serfs had been the object of government policy since the time of Tsar Aleksei, who had already taken control of church lands to shore up state revenues. Peter had imitated him, but after his death, control of the land went back to the church. In the 1750s the Shuvalovs decided on a more radical measure: the state would confiscate the monastery lands and make the peasants into tenants of the state. In practice this would mean the end of serfdom for monastery peasants, but the war with Prussia intervened and the reform was delayed.

The fifty percent of peasants that were the property of the gentry varied in their economic position considerably. In the old Russian heartland of central Russia and the northwest, by 1750 most peasants rarely performed labor services, though the gentry could demand them at any time. Mostly the peasants paid some sort of rent and managed the affairs of the village themselves under the supervision of an often distant estate steward and an even more distant owner. The peasant economy of these regions was a complex mix of food crops, small-scale stock raising, and more specialized pursuits like market gardening for the Moscow and St. Petersburg population, both of which were growing rapidly. Some peasants also grew flax to make linen and canvas or hemp for ropes. To the northeast of Moscow and on the upper Volga in particular, there were whole villages and even districts emerging where the peasants were scarcely farmers at all. Here they made frying pans and other iron implements, wove coarse cloth, made wooden spoons and dishes, and even produced more sophisticated items, such as painted chests, toys, and even icons on wood and metal. Herein lay the origins of the Palekh icon painting of the nineteenth century, and the later production of painted lacquer boxes. In these villages the richest artisans were merchants as well, who attended all the local fairs like the great fair near Nizhnii Novgorod or who went to Moscow and St. Petersburg. Some such peasant traders even came to Archangel as early as Peter's time. Many of these were monastery villages, but some were the property of great magnates like the Sheremetevs. In later times the Sheremetev villages would grow into great industrial cities.

South of the Oka River, where the steppe began with its black earth, a different sort of serf economy emerged. These areas were still open to Crimean slave raids, but since the 1630s the Russian state had steadily strengthened its defenses in the south, so that the area was relatively secure by 1750. The seventeenth century defensive lines had relied on armed peasants, Cossacks, and local noblemen, but Peter's regular army replaced them in large part, leaving land open for normal peasant settlement. Noblemen began to move farther and farther south, buying or receiving larger and larger estates as grants from the crown. Many of them were devoted at first to sheep and cattle raising, as this was easier to manage in remote and thinly settled areas, but soon the area began to shift to grain production and the nobles began to set up estates largely worked by labor services. This system demanded the presence of a nearby steward to give orders to the peasants or even the residence of the landowner. Labor services were much more oppressive to the peasantry, and were balanced only by the greater fertility of the southern soil.

The peasantry, however, under either system was not ground down into abject and universal poverty. Eighteenth century Russian peasants probably ate as well as their counterparts in France or Germany, at least in years of normal harvest, and they owned their own animals, ploughs, and other agricultural tools as well as modest material goods. The oppressive nature of the serf system lay not in the diet or the lack of material possessions of the peasants, but rather in the nature of the social relations that defined serfdom. Serfdom was never defined in written law, though by custom the master had nearly complete power over the serf. He could demand any sort of labor services or payments, forbid marriages, reorder the land allotments of the village community, or move whole villages to different parts of the country. Short of torturing or killing the serf, he could do anything. In practice radical mistreatment was not in the master's interest, but not all masters understood that, and in any case the threat of arbitrary exactions or commands hung over the serf for the whole of his life. The only real limit to the landowner's power was the threat of revolt or personal revenge, and this was a very real possibility given the lack of effective state power in rural areas. Yet that option meant that the peasant burned his bridges and had to flee, which was not desirable for most peasants. It was better to put up with the master and hope for the best.

Fortunately not all Russian peasants were serfs. About thirty percent of the peasantry had no master and paid only taxes and an additional "rent" to the state. These were the peasants of the north, the Urals, and Siberia, as well as many on the southern frontier. All Cossacks, who increasingly farmed the land, were also free. These areas were not unimportant, and indeed from the sixteenth to the end of the eighteenth century the north was a land of great prosperity, founded on the fur trade with Siberia and the salt springs that supplied most of Russia's needs. The Stroganov family had made its fortune as early as the sixteenth century on salt, so much so that the tsar granted them a separate legal status of their own – not noble but higher than all other merchants. Their houses in the north had been a major center of not only trade, but also of book production and icon painting. At the beginning of the eighteenth century the collection of salt from surface deposits around the mouth of the Volga took the profits out of the salt trade, but the Stroganovs turned to iron manufacturing in the Urals, along with the Demidovs, a peasant-merchant family from central Russia and a few other families. From Peter's time onward the state granted them the right to use corvée labor by the peasantry to supply the iron foundries with wood for fuel, and the iron mines prospered. The Urals mines and foundries were very remote, and the iron had to be floated down the rivers on barges during the spring floods to reach the Volga where it went on to Moscow and St. Petersburg. Much of it was even exported to England and elsewhere in Western Europe. Though a technically rather primitive industry, it made enormous fortunes for the owners, and both the Stroganovs and Demidovs entered the nobility. The profitability of the iron works rested on the unpaid labor of the state peasants "assigned" to them, and their peasants fell into a sort of semi-serfdom, which in time proved highly explosive.

The Urals and the Volga River were areas with a population that included many nationalities other than the Russians. At the time of Peter the Great's death, the Volga-Urals area had about a million people, half of them Tatars, Chuvash, Bashkirs, among others. In the seventeenth century half or more of the Tatars had served in the Russian army, while the remainder, along with the other Volga peoples, continued to pay the old yasak tax. As serfdom spread, the tax defined their status as non-serfs. From Peter's time the yasak-payers and the Tatar soldiers were almost all converted to state peasants like the Russian peasants of the north. A continuous flow of Russian peasants and nobles came into the area, avoiding the agricultural Tatar and Chuvash territories but taking much land from the nomadic Bashkirs, leading to predictable revolts in 1705, 1735, and 1755. Altogether Russia was still about ninety percent Russian, the largest minority being the Ukrainians (who made up five percent), with the Volga peoples and the Baltic provinces making up the remaining five percent. The Baltic nobles retained their privileges, as did the Cossack nobility of the Ukrainian Hetmanate. There the office of hetman itself was restored in 1727, abolished again in 1734, and then subsequently restored by Elizabeth. The empress appointed Kirill Razumovskii, the brother of her Ukrainian lover Aleksei, to the post. He would be the last hetman.

If Elizabeth was happy with local autonomy in the Hetmanate and the Baltic provinces, she was not tolerant of religious variation. She had come to power with the support of the bishops of the Ortho-dox Church, most of them Ukrainians who had absorbed Catholic notions of the need for religious uniformity. Empress Elizabeth initi-ated a new wave of persecution of the Old Believers, and supported the efforts of the Bishop of Kazan' and others to convert the Mus-lims. Hundreds of mosques were destroyed and various forms of enticement and coercion were applied to the Tatars to get them to accept Orthodox Christianity. These attempts were an abject fail-ure, for only a small percentage abjured their faith, and those in large numbers returned to Islam after the death of the empress.

Russia remained an overwhelmingly agrarian society, and few exceptions aside, peasant labor and landowning were the basis of the wealth of the nobility. The growth of the population and the cultivation of virgin land in the south brought enormous prosperity to the nobility. They demonstrated it for all to see not only in mansions in Moscow and St. Petersburg, but also in their new country houses. Traditionally Russian boyars had lived in towns, maintaining only small houses on their estates for their infrequent visits. At the end of the seventeenth century they began to build more magnificent residences around Moscow – whole complexes with churches in the new semi-baroque style of the time – but these were few and near the capital. Only in the middle of the eighteenth century did the newfound prosperity of the nobility lead to the construction of country houses with Baroque and later Classical architecture, far from the cities. These were real country houses with elaborate gardens, natural and artificial ponds, sculpture and pavilions for dining, and entertainment outside. The great aristocrats like the Sheremetevs and Golitsyns had entire theaters built into their house, suitable for drama or ballet. Some of them formed theatrical troupes from their serfs, who were taught to read, play music, and dance or act in performances that replicated European models. One of the Sheremetevs even married one of his serf ballerinas. For the average noble family such luxuries were unattainable, but all over the country noblemen built one or two story wooden houses with at least one room large enough for dances and entertainment. By 1800, obligatory style included a portico with classical columns around the house's main door. These houses became one of the centers of the life and culture of the nobility in its last century, to be memorialized in countless stories and novels of the great Russian writers from Pushkin onwards: *Evgenii Onegin*, *Fathers and Sons*, and *War and Peace*.

With the noblemen serving in the army and civil service (and legally obliged to do so from 1714 to 1762), much of the management of the estates fell on the women. One of the many paradoxes of Russian society was that noblewomen had much stronger legal rights to property and much more control over it than their counterparts in almost all Western societies of the time. Their control of their dower property after marriage was virtually complete in law (if not always in fact), and widows usually retained control of their husbands' estates. The absence of primogeniture in Russia meant that among the nobility a widow was often the ruler of the family when her sons were long-time adults with important careers. These were the ancestors of the strong women found in the classic novels that were set in the country estates a century later.

Empress Elizabeth, like her predecessor Anna, had to provide for a succession to her throne, as she had no children of her own. She chose her nephew, Karl Peter Ulrich, the Duke of Holstein-Gottorp and the son of her older sister Anna Petrovna, who had married the then Duke in 1725. Elizabeth's idea was to keep the succession in her family, not in the family of Empress Anna. The Holstein connection also had diplomatic advantages in relation to Sweden and the German states, especially Prussia. Elizabeth brought the boy to Russia in 1742 with a large suite of Holsteiners and he converted to Orthodoxy with the name Peter in honor of his grandfather, Peter the Great. The young Peter was not a particularly promising boy, and Elizabeth decided that he needed a wife. She chose Sophie, the daughter of the Duke of Anhalt-Zerbst – Anhalt-Zerbst being a small German principality in the Prussian orbit. Sophie's mother was also from the Holstein family, so that Sophie and Peter were cousins and were both related to the then King of Sweden. The family also had the support of Frederick the Great of Prussia, victorious in war with Austria (1740–1748), and whom Elizabeth opposed but wished to placate. In 1744 Sophie came to Russia with her mother and there was instructed in Orthodoxy, eventually taking the name Catherine at conversion. Thus at the age of fifteen the future Catherine the Great took up her position at the Russian court as the wife of the heir to the throne. The young girl was lonely, and her mother's intrigues only increased their isolation. The one bright spot for the princess was that she got along with the Empress well on a personal level.

At first the marriage was uneventful, a tepid friendship rather than a real marriage, and no heir appeared. As the years passed both Peter and Catherine found other interests, and as Catherine matured she found her husband's childish behavior and coarseness increasingly irritating. She also began to have political worries, for Peter stuck close to his Holstein entourage and displayed little interest in the country he was to rule. Catherine was already acute enough to realize that this was a dangerous characteristic in a future tsar. Finally Catherine had her first love affair with the young aristocrat Sergei Saltykov, and in 1754 she gave birth to a son whom Empress Elizabeth had baptized Paul. Russia now had an heir, whom Catherine in her later memoirs would make clear was the son of Sergei Saltykov, not her husband Peter. Paul's presumed parentage was a well-kept secret, even in the gossipy world of the court.

As she recovered from childbirth, Catherine began to read. She had always been more of a reader than was typical in court circles. Her choices had ranged from romances to serious works like Henri Bayle's *Dictionary*, a classic of early Enlightenment thought. Now in her momentary isolation she turned to Voltaire, Tacitus, and most important for her later conception of government, Charles-Louis de Montesquieu's *Spirit of the Laws*, which was published in 1748. Not all of her reading was so heavy, for she appreciated Voltaire's wit as much as his ideas, but most of it seems to have been books she thought valuable for the wife of a future emperor of Russia. For whatever she thought of her husband, he seemed certain to inherit the throne.

Peter had his own mistress by now, and Saltykov was sent abroad. Catherine soon took up with a young Polish nobleman, Stanislaw Poniatowski, who came to Russia with the English ambassador, but politics soon removed him as well. The politics of Elizabeth's court did not just affect Catherine's private life, but her political status as well. Russia had entered the Seven Years War in 1756 under the foreign policy leadership of Bestuzhev-Riumin, who had maintained an alliance with England and Austria against France and Prussia. Unfortunately for Bestuzhev-Riumin, as well as many of his colleagues throughout Europe, the Austrian chancellor count Wenzel Anton Kaunitz engineered a major reversal of alliances in 1756. Austria allied with France in order to get revenge on Prussia. England allied with Prussia, for in London the main enemy and rival was always France – in India and the New World, as well as in Europe. Russia had to choose, and Bestuzhev-Riumin persuaded Elizabeth to remain with Austria and join it in fighting Prussia when war broke out in 1756. At the same time Russia did not declare war on England, nor did England on Russia. This tangle led to Bestuzhev-Riumin's fall in 1758, and the rise of the Vorontsov family (whose sympathies were with France, not England) to power at court. Hence they accused Bestuzhev-Riumin of lack of zeal in the war and convinced the empress to oust him. As the Seven Years' War progressed and the Russian army kept Frederick the Great on the defensive, Peter's pro-Prussian sympathies became more and more of an irritant to Elizabeth and made him unpopular in the army and much of the court. As his wife, Catherine incurred the empress's suspicions. Personal conflicts added fuel to the flames, though Catherine was able to appeal personally to the empress through several crises.

In this delicate and potentially dangerous situation Catherine encountered Grigorii Orlov in the summer of 1760. Orlov was one of five brothers, all of them officers in the guards and very popular in that milieu. This was a powerful romantic attachment, but also politically quite important, for it was the guards who had already decided three times who would rule Russia. She also found her first real woman friend, Princess Elizabeth Dashkova. Dashkova was much younger than Catherine, but was a woman of intelligence and fortitude, and moreover was the sister of Peter's mistress, one of the Vorontsovs. In spite of this family tie, Dashkova had developed an intense personal dislike of Peter and shared the general discontent with his political orientation. The tutor to Catherine's son Paul, count Nikita Panin, a shrewd and experienced diplomat, also distrusted Catherine's husband. Though Peter was still the heir, he was acquiring many enemies.

Then, just at the moment when Prussia seemed about to collapse, Empress Elizabeth died. In January 1762, the Duke of Holstein-Gottorp ascended the Russian throne as Peter III. His first act was to make peace with Prussia, negating all of Russia's efforts and sacrifices over the previous five years. To add insult to injury, he persuaded Prussia to help him to attack Denmark, a traditional Russian ally, to recover territory he believed to rightly belong to Holstein. He even ordered Prussian style uniforms for the guards, and drilled them endlessly after the Prussian fashion. No moves could be more precisely calculated to insult the Russian army and the court elite. It did not matter that peace allowed him to take up some of the old proposals of the Shuvalov group and to abolish the requirement that noblemen serve in the army or civil service (which once again made service voluntary). Peter had hopelessly ruined his relations with his most important constituency in St. Petersburg.

Catherine and the Orlovs began to plan a way to remove him and proclaim Catherine empress in her own right. Peter had suspicions that he had enemies, and one of the conspirators was arrested. Grigorii Orlov's brother Aleksei decided that the time had come and on June 28, 1762, he came at dawn to Peterhof and told Catherine they had to strike. She had no hesitation and with Dashkova rode into St. Petersburg. Orlov took them to the barracks of the Izmailov guards, and the soldiers fell on their knees, swearing loyalty to Empress Catherine II. Catherine and her party went to the two other guards regiments, who joined her, ending at the Winter Palace by ten o'clock in the morning. A manifesto was readied, officially proclaiming her the sovereign and ordering the army and people to swear the oath of allegiance.

Peter III still remained with his Holstein hussars and German advisers at Oranienbaum, the suburban palace on the Gulf of Finland west of Peterhof that Menshikov had built decades before. Catherine donned the uniform of the oldest guards regiment, the Preobrazhenskii guards, and riding like a man on a white horse, moved out of the city toward Oranienbaum with the troops to capture her husband. Peter completely collapsed in fear, and surrendered after feeble attempts at escape. Catherine had him sent to one of his nearby estates to await incarceration under the watch of Aleksei Orlov and there on July 6, he perished. The public announcement was that he died of colic, and there was a sumptuous public funeral, but Catherine privately knew that Aleksei Orlov had taken matters into his own hands. The murder may have been unplanned, for everyone at the scene, including Peter, was drunk – but whatever the case, the murder was done. Aleksei Orlov secretly wrote to Catherine begging her forgiveness, and she kept the letter locked in her desk to the end of her life. With Peter out of the way, the once obscure German princess was now – at the age of thirty-three – Catherine II, the empress of Russia.

7

Catherine the Great

Catherine's first task on ascending the throne was to secure her power and deal with the unfinished business of her husband's reign. She quickly confirmed his decree abolishing compulsory service for the nobility, but she delayed the decree confiscating monastery lands. She had proclaimed herself the defender of Russian interests and of Orthodoxy, and she knew that the church was not happy with the move. Furthermore count Panin had plans to reorganize the central government around a state council that would have some sort of power alongside the monarch. The new empress, after a delay of more than a year, and after deposing the obstreperous and very rich bishop of Rostov, decreed the secularization of church lands in 1764. Nearly a fifth of the Russian peasantry ceased to be serfs. Regarding Panin's plans she was more cautious, merely ignoring them and keeping him to head the College of Foreign Affairs and supervise the education of her son and heir Paul.

Foreign policy demanded Catherine's attention for much of the first decade of her reign, even though she had been preoccupied with notions of reform of state and society from the time of her reading of Montesquieu and others in the 1750s. Unfortunately, Catherine could not control events and in the autumn of 1763 the king of Poland died. His death created a serious problem and Catherine had to act. From the last years of the Northern War, Poland, the onetime great power of Eastern Europe, had succumbed to a declining economy and population and an anarchic constitution. It had a weak elected king, all-powerful magnates, and a diet of nobles whose main aim was the conservation of traditional law and privileges above all else. Its neighbors, Prussia, Austria, and especially Russia liked this situation, and however absolute at home, their rulers were intent on preserving the "Golden Freedom" of the Polish nobility. A weak Poland with a tiny army suited them all and their ambassadors directed the Polish state.

The death of the king in 1763 came at a time of slowly returning prosperity and calls for modest constitutional reform. Catherine decided to support some of these calls, and with the aid of Polish allies, intimidation of their opponents, and simple bribery, placed her former lover, Stanislaw Poniatowski, on the throne of Poland. Poniatowski and his allies were able to enact some of their very modest proposals, but Catherine wanted a practical guarantee of continued Russian influence, and she found it in the issue of political rights of dissidents (non-Catholics) in Poland. Poland possessed a sizable Protestant minority (who mostly spoke German) in the northwest and a more numerous Orthodox minority in the east and southeast. The Protestants included a number of noble families as well as townsmen, but were excluded from political representation and most offices. The Orthodox were mostly Ukrainian peasants, and had no spokesman but the one Orthodox bishop, a Ukrainian from the Russian side of the border. Both groups, but especially the Orthodox peasants, were subject to continuous harassment from Catholic clergy and nobles. Catherine, through her ambassador, ordered Poniatowski and his allies to enact legal toleration of the religious dissidents. The ultimate result in 1768 was a revolt of Catholic nobles against the Russians and the king, and this involved the Russian army in the internal dissensions of Poland. Catherine knew that her intervention in Poland could have dangerous consequences, but she had formed a firm alliance with Prussia and hoped for the best. Unfortunately the Ottomans, prompted by France and understandably disturbed by the specter of even greater Russian influence in Poland, declared war on Russia at the end of the year. Russia was again at war with a major power possessing a huge – if sometimes unwieldy – army; this was a war that would have to be fought across vast and largely empty steppes very far from Russia's home bases.

The war with Turkey also put an end to one of Catherine's pet projects, the Legislative Commission. For decades the government had been aware of the confused state of Russian law, based as it was on the 1649 law code, Peter's legislation, and hundreds of decrees on particular issues that often contradicted more general statutes. Catherine saw the opportunity to carry out a thorough review and revision and to establish some general principles. To this end in January 1765, she began to compile an *Instruction*, a guideline for reform. The result was a volume of several hundred pages, compiled (as she freely admitted) of passages translated from her beloved Montesquieu; the Italian law reformer Cesare Beccaria; and German writers on finance and economics, such as the now forgotten Baron J. F. von Bielfeld. In the text she began with the principle that Russia was a European state, and it was a monarchy, not a despotism. That is, its government was based on law, not the arbitrary will of the monarch. At the same time, following Montesquieu, she argued that a state the size of Russia required an absolute monarch who would have the necessary vigor and power to rule effectively. Without that, lawlessness and chaos would ensue. The *Instruction* was not a series of specific recommendations about particular issues but a description of general principles for laws regulating social status, law courts, and the encouragement of population growth, agriculture, commerce, and industry. It concluded with a series of principles for what was then called "police" in Europe. These principles were ordinances not concerned so much with crime as they were with cleanliness, communication, fire prevention, and general good order in town and country. The text was remarkable enough, but even more remarkable was the use to which she put it.

At the end of 1766 she issued a manifesto that announced that various local communities were to choose representatives to come to Moscow to discuss the reform of the law, and a few months later she published her *Instruction* and ordered it distributed throughout the country. Thus an extensive compilation of Enlightenment political thought was to be distributed openly to the population at large, and this was to be the basis for the deliberations of the Legislative Commission in Moscow.

The Commission opened on July 30, 1767, with 428 of the 564 delegates already present. The most important group comprised the 142 deputies from the nobility and the 209 deputies from the cities (many of them also noblemen). There were also 29 delegates from the free peasants and 44 Cossack deputies. From the various Volga peoples, Tatars and others came 54 deputies – 22 deputies represented the Ukrainian Cossack nobility of the Hetmanate, and the Baltic provinces had their deputies among the nobles. Even the free Finnish peasants of the Vyborg area had their representatives. Some nobles tried to challenge their presence, but Catherine upheld them on the basis of the Swedish law of this conquered territory. The only group that was not represented consisted of the serf peasants of Russia and the Baltic provinces, who together made up more than fifty percent of the population of the state.

The process of choosing representatives was hardly a modern ideal election, for in many remote areas the nobles simply failed to show up or did so in very small numbers. In the towns it was hard to achieve consensus, and the free peasants also seem to have seen the process as a chance to petition the monarch rather than to suggest law. Nevertheless, they all did show up in Moscow and with some prompting from the empress, got down to work assembling and examining existing legislation and compiling proposals that would serve as the basis of general statutes for regularizing the status of the various groups in society in judicial institutions. The delegates were not a parliament and were not there to pass laws – they had assembled to make proposals to Catherine that she could choose to follow or not. They were also supposed to follow the guidelines of her instruction, and they generally did, but not without considerable discussion. Opinions were exchanged remarkably freely, and some of the more conservative nobles rejected the implications of the *Instruction* that were favorable to peasants and townspeople. As time passed, the various subcommissions deliberated slowly and Catherine decided to move them to St. Petersburg. By the summer of 1768, the nobles were ready with a proposal, itself the object of considerable wrangling, especially over issues like the conditions for promotion of commoners to noble rank and crimes against nobles by serfs. Catherine was getting a very rapid lesson in the values and ideas of the various classes of

Russian society, and it was fairly clear that reform of state and society would meet considerable obstacles among a large part of the nobility. The Turkish declaration of war intervened before she had to make difficult decisions. Most of the noble deputies were also army officers, and now full mobilization was necessary to deal with both Turkey and the Polish situation. The Commission was dissolved. Its work, however, was not in vain, as later events would prove.

The war with Turkey was the first serious test of Catherine's government, for the Ottoman Empire was still a formidable opponent and the Russians would have to cross vast expanses of southern steppe even to engage the enemy. In the end, the Russian army proved itself capable of the task, slowly but systematically advancing into Crimea and the Balkan Peninsula. The Russian navy sailed from St. Petersburg around Europe under the command of Aleksei Orlov and the British Admiral John Elphinstone, destroying the Turkish fleet in the harbor of Chesme in 1770. In spite of the distraction of the Polish conflict, Catherine's forces made their way into Bulgaria and forced the Ottomans to make peace on her terms at the small village of Kuchuk Kainardzha in 1774.

The treaty came just two years after a seemingly permanent settlement of the Polish situation. With Russia fighting two wars at once, Frederick the Great of Prussia saw his chance and proposed to Catherine that they both solve the problem by taking Polish territory. Austria would have to be conciliated as well, and the result would be a smaller Poland that would be less threatening, should reform succeed. Catherine agreed to this proposal after some hesitation, for she still hoped to maintain influence over the whole of Poland, but eventually she gave in. The result was the partition treaty of 1772, which gave large and valuable districts to Austria and Prussia. Catherine took a large but thinly populated slice of eastern Belorussia that provided better Russian river communications with Riga. A byproduct of the new border was the inclusion of Jews in the Russian state for the first time. For Catherine the outcome was a qualified success, as Poniatowski remained king and made modest reforms that strengthened the state and Polish prosperity while ultimately remaining subservient to Russian interests.

Two years later Catherine was ecstatic with joy to learn of the peace with the Ottomans, for it came at a difficult moment. The victory itself was reason enough to celebrate, for it brought great prestige and power to Russia and to its empress, but there was more. Russia received huge territories in the south all the way to the Black Sea coast and Crimea ceased to be a Turkish dependency, instead becoming nominally independent under Russian control. Russia's ministers and Catherine herself had been aware for decades of the economic potential of the area both as a site for new commercial ports and for agricultural settlement. The treaty not only gave the area to Russia, but also granted the right to commerce in the Black Sea and to build a navy there. Russia's position on the southern border had changed radically: there were no more Tatar slave raids and a vast territory was ready for development. The legislation for the new lands, to be called Novorossia, or "New Russia," was carefully worked out to encourage settlement but discourage the spread of serf agriculture. The new lands were to be a settler colony with flourishing cities and ports, not just an extension of the backward agriculture of the serf estates of Central Russia. Catherine had not read her Enlightenment writers for nothing.

Her right arm in transforming the new lands was to be her new lover, general Grigorii Potemkin, whose instant rise to favor took place in the first months of 1774. Potemkin was the only one of Catherine's many lovers who was her mental and political equal. If less intellectual, he was well enough educated to understand her and had the political skills to work with her. It was a great partnership and lasted long after the passion had cooled, until Potemkin's death in October 1791.

For the time being both the empress and her favorite faced daunting challenges. Ever since Catherine's coup of 1762, there had been symptoms of discontent. The first had been the Mirovich affair. The former baby Tsar Ivan VI of 1740–1741 had grown up, and Elizabeth had confined him in the fortress of Schlüsselburg in the hope that he might some day enter a monastery, and if not, he would be politically harmless. Peter III had confirmed her decisions, including the secret order to kill him if an attempt to free him was made, and Catherine confirmed these orders as well, though the codicil with the order to kill bore only Panin's signature. In July 1764, a restless and probably somewhat unstable Ukrainian guards officer named Vasilii Mirovich made a mad attempt to free Ivan and proclaim him emperor, and the soldiers guarding the ex-tsar carried out their standing orders. Mirovich's execution put an end to the affair, but it was not a good sign. Over the years there were a series of incidents, all involving small numbers of officers and nobles who spoke of replacing Catherine, but they were quickly exiled and their talk came to nothing. The background to these incidents, however, was the worrisome issue of the heir to the throne, Tsarevich Paul. Paul was nineteen in 1773, and thus in principle old enough to reign, but his mother had no intention of giving up power. Part of her reason was her increasing disappointment with her son and his association with the Panin party at court, whose cautious foreign policy had not provided the expected dividends. Catherine proclaimed her son an adult and began marriage negotiations, but kept the throne. This step terminated Panin's role as the heir's tutor, and the count gradually withdrew from the court in disfavor.

The new star, Potemkin, came at just the right time, for Russia was now in the grips of the greatest popular upheaval it would experience before the twentieth century. The source of the uprising lay in the Cossack frontier of the southeast, as it had so often before. This time it did not begin on the Don but on the Iaik, the smaller river flowing from the Ural Mountains into the Caspian Sea to east of the Volga. In these decades the Russian government was trying to establish greater control over the Cossacks, restricting their privileges and particularly their custom of electing their officers. Recent measures to this end seemed successful, until Emelian Pugachev appeared in the settlements near the provincial capital of Orenburg early in 1773. He had served in the wars, deserted, and had various adventures when he arrived and told the people that he was actually Catherine's husband Peter III. He had come to restore justice to the Cossacks and protect the Old Belief. The Cossacks believed, or professed to believe him and he quickly assembled a band of several thousand men, reinforced by the neighboring Bashkirs and Tatars as well as the peasants attached to the Urals iron works. They laid siege to Orenburg and other larger forts without success, but they

Figure 6. Bashkirs, from Atkinson, *Picturesque View*.

overran the lesser stations and massacred all who refused to join them. A huge area, most of the Urals and the Volga basin, was now in rebel hands. The reaction was swift. An army came from Moscow to suppress the revolt, and by the end of the year it was largely successful, though Pugachev himself had eluded the army. Then the next year he made a comeback and even managed to seize the important town of Kazan' for a few days. This was the high point of the rebellion, for Russian regular troops reached the town after a desperate forced march and crushed the rebel army. Pugachev now turned south toward the Don, and to reach it he passed through areas of serf agriculture. Here the region exploded; the serfs with rebel help exterminated the local nobility, including women and children. Unfortunately for Pugachev, the Don Cossacks did not move, and he recrossed the Volga, escaping to his base among the Bashkirs. There the troops finally caught up with the rebels and crushed them. Some of the Bashkirs remained loyal to Pugachev to the end, but the Cossacks eventually betrayed him. The revolt was over, and in 1775 Pugachev was executed in Moscow. Peace had finally come, at home and abroad.

Catherine's reading not only gave her a series of ideas about justice and administration but also about economic development and social status. The Enlightenment writers believed that society required a civilized population to flourish, and that came from education and culture. The new empress came to the throne at a propitious time, for the efforts of the Cadet Corps, the Academy, and Moscow University were beginning to show results. The generation that came to maturity with Catherine was the first to have absorbed European culture in full, and the first to include many men and even women who had also been abroad long enough to begin to understand European society.

Catherine was determined to speed this process along. Though by birth and culture she was German, for most of her reign she was at the center of Russian culture, unlike any monarch after her and more so than even Peter himself. She was not merely a reader, but an active participant in Europe's cultural life. She corresponded with Voltaire from 1763 until his death in 1778. She also had correspondents among the French Encyclopedists, Denis Diderot, and Jean d'Alembert, as well as the German Baron Friedrich Melchior Grimm. Grimm was a sort of literary journalist reporting from Paris, and after a visit to St. Petersburg in 1773–74 he was Catherine's chief correspondent and epistolary confidant until her death. Catherine did not merely correspond with the great men of the Enlightenment. When she heard of Diderot's financial problems she bought his library, granted him the use of it for life and paid him a salary as her librarian.

Catherine's cultural projects were numerous. Behind the scenes she was the instigator of the Free Economic Society, a group of noblemen moved by reading Enlightenment literature to form a society for the discussion of economic (especially agricultural) topics. This was an association independent of state institutions although it enjoyed the favor of the empress. The society sponsored an essay contest on the issue of peasant land ownership that inevitably raised the issue of serfdom, and it awarded a prize to a Frenchman's essay that unambiguously stated that prosperity could only flow from the full property of the peasant in his land. By implication serfdom could not create prosperity. The essay was published in Russian and French for all to read. She continued to support the university, the academies, and the schools with money and encouragement. The first Russian girls' school, the Smol'nyi Institute in St. Petersburg for young noblewomen was planned by Empress Elizabeth and came into being in 1764, and the empress reorganized and expanded the Cadet Corps. These were elite schools, but with the 1775 provincial reform came a system of schools in the provinces, which was expanded again in 1786 by a decree establishing secondary schools in all provincial capitals and a network of primary schools. Progress was slow, but by 1800 there were already over 300 schools, twice the number in existence in 1786. Later Russian secondary schools had their origin in these laws.

Even the church had its role in the process of enlightenment. At Catherine's accession most of the bishops were still Ukrainians with a strong, almost Catholic, sense of the importance of the clergy. Empress Elizabeth had begun the process of replacing them with Russians, and under Catherine a whole new generation came into power in the church. Catherine also put into law the secularization of monastic lands formulated under Elizabeth in opposition to the views of the older Ukrainian bishops. The new generation, like Platon Levshin, Metropolitan of Moscow from 1775 to 1812, had been educated on Lutheran religious scholarship and with a strong orientation toward preaching. Their goal was to bring the truths of Orthodox Christianity to the people rather than cultivating an ideal asceticism. This emphasis coincided with Catherine's, for she saw religion as the foundation of good citizenship, which was another Enlightenment precept.

Catherine's court kept up the theaters founded by her predecessors, and those theaters remained at the center of the performing arts in Russia. She eased Araya into retirement and replaced him with a series of distinguished musicians starting with the Venetian Baldassare Galuppi. Sumarokov continued to direct the stage and provide plays, and Catherine and the court usually attended one of the theaters several times a week. In 1768 she founded a society for the translation of foreign books, which sponsored a whole series

Figure 7. Catherine the Great with the Goddess Athena. Engraving by Francis Bartolozzi after Michele Benedetti. From a painting by Alexander Roslin.

of important translations, learned works, and works of entertainment for the Russian public. She also published her own magazine, *Vsiakaia vsiachina (All Sorts of Things)*, in 1769. The idea was to imitate Addison and Steele's *Spectator*, something Sumarokov had tried a few years earlier with mixed success. The journal, like its prototype, was to combine entertainment with edification without heavy-handed moralizing – a type of publication wildly popular in Catherine's native Germany and other parts of Europe. Catherine kept her role secret, though it was widely known in St. Petersburg.

The most lively response to her journal came from Nikolai Novikov (1744–1818), who launched a series of journals of his own, establishing the first important private publishing enterprise in Russia. Better written and bolder than the empress's journal, Novikov's publications acquired considerable popularity but not enough to provide much of an income, and he soon turned to publishing books for Moscow University, which assured him an indirect subsidy from the state. In Moscow, Novikov also increasingly joined in with the Freemasons, a group with a wide network and considerable impact on Russian culture at the time. The Masons were not just a social club, but a movement of ideas with defined, if nebulous, aims. Most of them had been reading the European mystical literature that was increasingly popular in the later eighteenth century, and they saw themselves as committed to self-improvement, contemplation of God and his works, and most of all, active philanthropy and the encouragement of progress in the world. Unfortunately for them, the Masons aroused all sorts of suspicions. Conservative churchmen saw them as the propagators of an alternative and pernicious religion, while many enlightened nobles took them for obscurantists. Catherine herself saw them in this way and wrote several short comedies satirizing them. The Masons were also an international society with ties to foreign dynasties in Prussia and Sweden that were unfriendly to Russia, and most serious of all, the Masons had recruited the heir, Tsarevich Paul, as a patron. This last element made them deeply suspect in the mind of Catherine, for Paul was unhappy with his marginal role in court and government and increasingly hostile to his mother as the years passed.

In spite of setbacks, Catherine did not give up sponsoring Russian literature, and in 1782–1783 she appointed her old friend Princess

Dashkova to head both the Academy of Sciences and the new Academy of Letters. Dashkova, who had met Benjamin Franklin in Paris, was the first woman member of the American Philosophical Society in Philadelphia. From these positions Dashkova was able to publish another series of literary journals and other publications and organize a committee to produce the first Russian dictionary. A decree of 1783 explicitly authorized private printing and publication, subject to censorship of the chiefs of police in the capitals.

The main problem for private publishers was not censorship or the attitude of the state but the lack of a broad audience. Only the gentry and a small body of teachers and scholars had the education to be interested in books and journals, and many of the gentry either lived on remote estates or in provincial towns and preferred French literature to Russian. The writers were less affected by this situation than the publishers, for most of the important writers were noblemen employed in state service of one sort or another, and were not therefore dependent on the sales of their work for their income. Many nobles even looked down on Novikov for trying to live from the profits of literature. State service, however, involved writers in the court factions and in a complex relationship to the empress herself.

Thus the two most important writers of the time, the playwright Denis Fonvizin (1744–1792) and the poet Gavriil Derzhavin (1743–1816) were both enmeshed in a network of personal and political loyalties at the court. Fonvizin spent his early career as a client of count Panin, which meant that toward the end of his life he was part of the patronage network centered on Paul, the heir to the throne. This affiliation made him unpopular with Catherine, but it was she who ordered the first performance of his best play, *The Adolescent*, at the court theater in 1782. Nevertheless the final resignation of Panin from all offices in 1781 contributed to Fonvizin's failure to get authorization for a journal in later years.

Fonvizin and Novikov were both graduates of Moscow University, while the poet Derzhavin came from a provincial gentry family and had only finished the Gymnasium in Kazan'. Unlike so many of his contemporaries, he never properly learned French, his only foreign language being the German he learned in Kazan'. His early career was in the army, and he played a minor and somewhat inglorious role in fighting Pugachev's rebels. At that time he came to the attention of Potemkin, and remained the favorite's client as he pursued a career in civil administration, both in St. Petersburg and the provinces, living long enough to briefly occupy the post of minister of justice under Alexander I. Derzhavin's poetry made him famous in the 1780s, as he produced odes in honor of Catherine and her victories as well as satires of courtiers and their foibles, following the model of Horace and European classicism. Like Fonvizin, he had a command of language that allowed his work to survive for Russian readers in spite of the eclipse of the eighteenth century genres that he employed.

In Russian literature, drama, poetry, and prose, a public independent of the court was just barely coming into existence at the end of Catherine's reign. Other art forms remained closely tied to the patronage of court and nobility. The court musical theater and orchestra was largely the preserve of imported musicians, and the centrality of the court in cultural life meant that the nobility heard an extensive range of European music. Native traditions remained in church music, a particular specialty of Ukrainians associated with the choirs in the imperial chapels. The most successful of these Ukrainians was Dmitrii Bortnyanskii (1751–1825), Russia's first composer, who was equally comfortable with European concerti and Russian choral singing. None of the musicians were noblemen, a fact that hampered their acceptance as serious artists. A similar situation obtained in the visual arts, where the Academy of Art dominated the scene. Catherine reorganized the Academy to give it more autonomy and better financing while retaining its mainly French instructors, and she secured for the artists a more privileged social status to fit their profession. The Russian students were all of non-noble and sometimes even serf origin, who were intended to go on to provide art for the palaces of the empress and the nobility as well as the church. The Academy also provided stipends for the students to spend time in Paris and Rome, enormously broadening the training and experience of its students. In retrospect its worst defect, other than its very "official" character, was its precise copying of European models that accorded ill with Russian possibilities and traditions. As in the European art academies, the most prestigious genre was historical painting in the style of classicism. Attempts to depict Russian history in this style found praise at the time but produced pictures that to later taste were wooden at best and often comic. Ancient Russians appeared in fantastic armor more reminiscent of the Romans than medieval Russia. More attractive to later taste were the portrait painters, who ironically had little or no ties to the Academy. The first to gain a name was Ivan Argunov (1727–1802), a serf of the extremely wealthy Sheremetev family. His successors included Fyodor Rokotov, a serf of the Repnins, and two Ukrainians, Dmitrii Levitskii (Argunov's pupil), and Vladimir Borovikovskii, the only nobleman among them. Their charming portraits of noble men and women as well as of Catherine herself filled Russian palaces and country houses and were comparable in quality to many of the French and English portraits of the time, if less inventive than the latter.

Catherine's time marked the beginning of Russian classicist architecture, which transformed St. Petersburg into the city familiar today. She was firmly against the Baroque exuberance of her predecessor Elizabeth's chief architect Rastrelli. Catherine and her contemporaries built with unmistakable Roman allusions, a proper architecture for a great imperial capital and its elites. Strict symmetry, Roman columns and triumphal arches were the order of the day. The crowning achievement of the age was the monument to Peter the Great, the "Bronze Horseman" in Pushkin's immortal phrase. The work of the French sculptor Etienne Maurice Falconet and his wife, it displayed Peter in the garb of a Roman emperor on horseback standing on a giant rock with the simple inscription "Catherine the Second to Peter the First" in Latin and Russian. Unveiled in 1782 to great ceremony, the statue remains Catherine's most powerful contribution to the city of St. Petersburg.

The years after Pugachev were not just filled with artistic projects and court entertainments, for these were the years of extensive reform of Russian government and society. Finally the Legislative Commission bore fruit, albeit indirectly: Catherine knew how the nobility thought about the issues and what might prove useful while not antagonizing them. The first task was to reorder the administration of the provinces and the towns, which involved creating a new court system. Catherine's 1775 decrees broke up the large administrative units into some forty new provinces, which in turn divided into five or six smaller units. At the level of these smaller units government essentially stopped, leaving the countryside to the nobility and the peasant communities. The most powerful local figure was the provincial governor appointed by the empress. These were invariably noblemen, sometimes including great aristocrats but more often military men. In the same decree Catherine established courts for the nobility that were to combine appointed judges with local noblemen elected to assist them. These were courts for nobility only. In areas where free peasants predominated there were also to be courts with peasants elected alongside officials to provide justice. As ever, it was the village level that was weakest and where state power often existed only on paper. In the towns, Catherine also established courts, for the townspeople alone, that consisted of appointed judges and elected assessors. Thus justice was divided among special courts for each social group and combined state-appointed judges with elected assessors.

The new legislation implied greater responsibility on the part of the nobility and the elite of the townspeople, yet many basic aspects of their status and relationship to the state remained undefined. The answers to this problem were the 1785 Charters of the Nobility and of the Townspeople. The Charter of the Nobility confirmed and broadened the rights already in practice from Peter's time and added others, including the 1762 decree on freedom from obligatory state service. Nobles could not be deprived of life and property without a trial by a court that was composed of their peers. Their nobility was hereditary, and could not be terminated without a conviction in court of specified crimes like murder or treason. They were not subject to corporal punishment, and the right to own land and serfs was guaranteed to them alone. Nobles in each province were to come together to form a provincial Assembly of Nobility, electing its own marshal and determining its own membership. The marshal was to act as the leader of the local gentry, conveying its wishes to the capital and the government's orders to the nobility. The marshals had little formal power, but as the chief representatives of the local nobility, and often with powerful connections in St. Petersburg, they were formidable figures. Provincial governors, in spite of their formal power, found it wise to cultivate the marshals of the nobility. In the towns Catherine's decrees divided the town population by simple wealth, and put most of the administration, like the courts, in the hands of the town elites. The population was to elect a governing body from among the wealthier citizens to manage the business side of town life, leaving the courts and police as specified in the 1775 provincial reform. Townspeople were also not to be deprived of life and property without conviction in a court of their peers. Lesser townsfolk were subject to corporal punishment. There was also elaborate sumptuary legislation that specified limits to ostentatious display by the lower orders. Though restricted to the upper and middle classes, the Charters were the first fruit of Enlightenment thought about the rights and duties of the citizen to be enacted into Russian law.

As Catherine and her ministers were reordering Russian government they did not lose sight of the situation on the southern border. The Ottomans were reluctant to ignore Russian gains, and the "autonomy" of Crimea under Russian stewardship proved an unstable arrangement. In 1783 Catherine annexed the territory to Russia, adding it to the vast areas of New Russia under the firm hand of Potemkin. Catherine and Potemkin began to develop larger plans of conquest in the south, tempting Austria to join them with the "Greek project," a proposal for the partition of the Balkans and restoration of a Greek monarchy with Russian princes on the ruins of the Ottoman Empire. Finally in 1787 Turkey declared war. Russian troops began to advance into the Balkans, but elsewhere the situation deteriorated. The Austrian Emperor Joseph II honored his treaty with Russia and his army began to move south too, but he was rapidly defeated by the Turks. King Gustavus III of Sweden attacked Russia as well, hoping for revenge for earlier losses and to strengthen his hand at home. Catherine had hoped for Polish troops to support the Russian effort, but when Stanislaw Poniatowski called the diet to discuss the issue, it swiftly turned into a revolutionary assembly that proceeded to throw off Russian domination and elaborate a reformed constitution. To make matters worse, Prussia cynically supported the Polish effort with a view to its own future aggrandizement in Poland.

Catherine had no one to rely upon but Potemkin and her army and navy.

Catherine showed the steel nerves that had brought her to the throne thirty years before. Hearing the guns of the Swedish fleet from her palace windows, she continued to work without giving them any notice. Progress in the south was slow, especially at first, but the new Black Sea fleet (with some help from the American naval hero John Paul Jones) was victorious and the army relentlessly pushed the Turks into the Rumanian principalities. Gustav III made little progress and found himself the object of a conspiracy of Finnish officers discontented with Swedish absolutism. His resources exhausted in spite of modest success on the sea, Gustav made peace in 1790. Turkey remained in the war.

To complicate Russia's situation still further, Britain, with its own imperial ambitions rapidly growing, began to worry about Russian movement toward the Mediterranean and adopted a hostile stance. Catherine needed success, and at the end of December 1790, general Alexander Suvorov gave it to her, taking the fortress of Izmail near the mouth of the Danube. He took the fort by frontal assault with great casualties, but he took it. In the next spring the Russians moved south toward Bulgaria, and by the end of the summer the Turks capitulated. Russia's borders now extended to the Dniestr River, including the site of future city of Odessa. Catherine had played her cards with great skill, and she had won. At that moment, Potemkin died. Catherine continued to have lovers and favorites, but none of them ever had the love and trust that Potemkin had inspired.

The wars with Turkey and Sweden had required the complete attention and resources of the Russian government, but they were aware that Europe was increasingly in crisis. The French Revolution was transforming European politics daily, and closer to home the Polish diet's reformed constitution of May 3, 1791, meant that Russia would soon have a hostile and more powerful neighbor. There was little Catherine could do about France, but Poland was a different case. She intrigued with aristocratic opponents of the new constitution, and as soon as the Turkish war ended she and her Polish allies moved against Poniatowski and the new government. The small Polish army was easily swept away, and Catherine arranged with Prussia to make a new partition. This was not her preferred option, for all along she wanted a united compliant Poland, but she realized that the new order was too popular among Polish nobles to be reversed, and that she had to conciliate Prussia and Austria.

Thus a much reduced Poland acquired a conservative constitution supported by Russian bayonets, but it did not last. In 1794 Tadeusz Kosciuszko led a rebellion in southern Poland that quickly spread to Warsaw and scored a few modest successes. Catherine was convinced that French Jacobinism was behind it, and sent in Suvorov at the head of a Russian army. Suvorov took Warsaw with great slaughter, and the partitioning powers agreed to put an end to Poland's existence. Prussia and Austria carved up the areas with predominantly Polish populations, while Russia took the Western Ukraine, the rest of Belorussia, and Lithuania.

Russia now had become a truly multi-national empire. The five-and-onehalf million new subjects brought the proportion of Russians in the state from some eighty-five percent down to perhaps seventy. Catherine did not fight the war to reunite the Eastern Slavs, but she had in fact brought into her empire virtually the whole territory of the medieval Kiev Rus.

If Catherine could do little to affect the progress of the French Revolution, she was no less frightened by its increasing radicalism, and the Russian nobility shared her fears. The policy of toleration and enlightenment gradually came to an end. Especially after the proclamation of the republic and execution of Louis XVI, the importation and circulation of new French books and even long-familiar Enlightenment writers now faced serious restrictions. In 1792 Novikov was arrested after investigation but there was no trial and he was ordered to be confined in prison indefinitely. The Masons were shut down and fell under increasing suspicion as potential supporters of the French revolutionaries. In 1796, only a few weeks before her death, Catherine established the first Russian system of state censorship, no longer depending on the Academy of Sciences or the local police to do the work.

The most spectacular case of dissent and its repression, however, had already come in 1790. In that year Alexander Radishchev, a nobleman and minor civil servant, published a book called *A Journey from St. Petersburg to Moscow*. Using the then-popular genre of the fictitious journey, he described the villages and towns of Russia and interspersed his own reflections on society and politics. His portrait of serfdom was unflattering to the extreme – in his view a system that corrupted master and serf alike was morally indefensible and economically ruinous. His political ruminations were vaguer, but they clearly suggested that autocracy was not the best way to govern Russia. Catherine read the book herself and made many marginal notes, and ultimately had Radishchev arrested. Interrogated in the Secret Department of the Senate, Radishchev was convicted in the St. Petersburg criminal court of sedition and lèse majesté and was condemned to death. Catherine commuted the punishment to exile in a remote Siberian fort, and Radishchev went off, though with a substantial stipend from one of Catherine's grandees, who interceded with the empress on his behalf.

The French Revolution and Catherine's death in 1796 brought Russia's eighteenth century to a close. For a century the state, or more accurately the monarchs and their courts, had labored to transform the country along European lines and bring European culture to Russia. In this task they had largely succeeded. Russia had institutions and laws copied from European models, and Western diplomats, merchants, and travelers felt at home in St. Petersburg, if not everywhere else in Russia. The new state structure had provided the basis for the rise of Russia to the place of a great power, and helped the growth of commerce and industry, education and science. Settlement of new areas in the south contributed to an ongoing population explosion that was rapidly making Russia the largest country in Europe, even without newly annexed territory.

The cultural transformation was profound. By the end of the century educated Russians, most of them still nobles, had absorbed most of the major ideas and artistic achievements of modern Europe and they were beginning to offer their own still modest contributions. Russian political thought had the same elements and was based on the same writings as that farther west. If Russian noblemen did not admire Rousseau's democratic musings, they did absorb the teachings of Puffendorf and Montesquieu as well as those of a host of minor writers. Monarchy in Russia was understood in much the same way as in France or Prussia, Austria or Sweden.

Russian reality imposed limits to both state-building and cultural progress. Russia was still too poor to support an extensive education system and all local government suffered from chronic lack of funds and staff. Outside of the capitals, large towns, and aristocratic country estates, life remained much as it had before, a round of rural labor punctuated by Orthodox liturgy. Areas of economic progress existed in the Urals and the trading villages and towns of central Russia, but it was still an overwhelmingly agrarian society.

Moreover, it was an agrarian society, half of whose peasant farmers were serfs. This was an issue Catherine and her enlightened friends could neither change nor even confront. She disliked the system and knew it was pernicious, not least to agricultural progress, but was aware that virtually all noblemen, on whom her throne depended, saw it as the basis of their wealth and position in society, as indeed it was. Russia was not alone in the serf system at the end of the century, it persisted in Poland and Prussia, and Joseph II had only just begun to dismantle it in Austria.

Just at the moment when Russia seemed to have achieved a stable and European order, the French Revolution changed all the rules of the game. It would now have to try to respond to a whole series of new challenges, international and domestic, cultural and political. Eventually its very survival would be at stake. It was a new and dangerous era.

8

Russia in the Age of Revolution

On his mother's death Paul came to the throne, the first undisputed and male inheritance in seventy years. His first act was to rebury Peter III, whom he believed to be his father, in the church of St. Peter and Paul with the other rulers of Russia from Peter onwards. His next act was to replace most of Catherine's ministers and officials, and send a number of them into exile. Thus began the brief and often bizarre reign of Tsar Paul.

Paul's reign began just at the moment that the French revolution, having passed through its most radical phase, began to turn outward, and the new tsar had to respond to the apparent danger from his first days on the throne. Far more conservative than his mother, he made it his priority to strengthen the power and authority of the state. He recentralized the government, reestablishing some of the colleges and reviving the Council of State. He also enlarged the Senate, and saw to it that it exercised more effective supervision of law and administration. To this end he issued an enormous number of new laws, orders, and regulations. In Paul's mind, everything needed a regulation and his job was to compose one where it did not already exist.

Even greater than the changes in institutions were the changes in style. Paul took every opportunity to assert his personal authority in matters no matter how petty. From his youth he had spent much of his time drilling the troops under his personal control, living away from his mother in the suburban palace of Gatchina, which he turned into a military camp on the style of the Prussian army so beloved by his father. Thus his reassertion of authority began with the army. He ordered the Russian army to switch to uniforms on the Prussian model and adopt Prussian drill and training, to the intense irritation of officers and soldiers alike. The French revolutionary armies had already shown the old Prussian methods to be outmoded, but Paul did not see this in his pursuit of strict hierarchy and mindless obedience. His new orders went far beyond the military, for he required anyone, of any age or sex, who encountered any member of the imperial family on the street to dismount and kneel no matter what the weather. Officers were cashiered or even exiled for minor cases of neglect of duty, details of drill, or even just court etiquette. He prescribed the details of dress for court and other occasions and enforced them with pedantic thoroughness. To many noblemen and officers, his behavior was both insulting and bizarre, but to Paul the enforcement of regulation was part of the restoration of discipline and morality that he regarded as crucial after the laxities of Catherine's rule and the threat of revolution from France. With these ends in mind he revoked many of the provisions of the Charter of the Nobility and reduced and downgraded the elective element in provincial government. Part of this program of counter-reform was the restoration of the old privileges of the nobles of the Baltic provinces and the Ukraine, and an attempt to reach some reconciliation with the Polish gentry. Thus Kosciuszko and other Polish prisoners of war were released, and the legal system of the formerly Polish provinces was maintained. He did not notice the contradictions.

Perhaps the contradictions came from his obsession with reversing the actions of his mother. Though terrified of the French Revolution and convinced that "Jacobinism" was multiplying everywhere in Europe and Russia, he released Radishchev from exile and Novikov from prison. At the same time Paul prohibited the wearing of clothing in the new French style, requiring the old three-cornered hat and knee breeches for men. Enamored of European notions of medieval knighthood and chivalry, he distrusted the self-indulgent and greedy gentry that, he thought, his mother's reign had created. Thus he decreed a limit of three days per week that serfs could be required to perform labor services. It was typical of Paul's measures that it was largely useless, for in many parts of the country the new limit was actually higher than the norm. One of the actions of his mother that he did not reverse was the establishment of state censorship, which restricted Russian publications and the importation of Western books. On Paul's orders even French music fell under suspicion.

Had Paul reigned in calmer times, he might have lasted for years as an irritating and petty despot who aroused contempt more than fear. The times, however, were anything but calm, even though Russia was far from the center of the drama in Paris. Since the fall of the Jacobin dictatorship in 1794 the Directory had directed the energies of the French nation outward to the conquest of Belgium, the Rhineland, and northern Italy. Just as Paul came to the throne, Napoleon Bonaparte was winning his first victories against Austria in northern Italy and instantly became a great hero in France. His next project was the conquest of Egypt, which brought Russia into the war. It was not that St. Petersburg had any particular interest in Egypt, but for a few months the Russians thought that he was really going not to Egypt but to Constantinople, which was an obvious threat. Paul was also enraged by Napoleon's capture of the island of Malta on his way east in 1798. Malta was just as far as Egypt from Russian interests but the rulers of the island, the Knights of Malta, had just sent a mission to the tsar. They appealed to Paul's ideals of chivalry and his desire to combat the hydra of revolution, so he became the protector of the Order of Malta. With the island in French hands, some of the knights even offered to make Paul the commander of the order. Contrary to papal wishes, the Orthodox tsar now led the exiled Catholic order, but with the French army at his door the pope was in no position to object. The Malta incident and other French actions led Paul to join Austria, Britain, and other powers in a coalition against the French. General Suvorov was called out of forced retirement (Paul had rightly associated him with Potemkin and Catherine) and sent to Italy to command an Austro-Russian army. This he did with such force and energy that he chased the French out in a few months, and stood ready to invade France. Instead, defeats on other fronts and Austrian insistence on invading France from Switzerland forced Suvorov to move north and then retreat through hostile French forces in an alpine winter to safety in southern Germany. Enraged by these events and a botched

Russian-British attempt to invade the French-dominated Netherlands, Paul broke off all relations with the coalition and made overtures to France. With Napoleon's coup d'etat in November 1799, Paul felt that France had a ruler committed to order, not further revolution, and with whom he could talk. By the end of 1800, war with Britain seemed a real possibility. Events dictated otherwise. Discontent with Paul had been growing almost since he came to the throne among the court and military elite of St. Petersburg. Paul had several sons, the eldest Alexander, born in 1777, was an agreeable and well-educated young man. Furthermore, Paul had replaced Peter the Great's succession law with his own in 1797, a law that prohibited women from taking the throne and specified primogeniture in the male line. Thus in the event of Paul's removal or death, the succession was secure.

Paul himself was afraid of assassination, and he built an entire new palace – the Castle of St. Michael – on the bank of the Fontanka River and surrounded by newly dug canals to make it inaccessible except by drawbridge. The "castle" was a strange combination of classical style and elements meant to recall a medieval Western castle, a conceit that delighted the tsar. He moved in at the end of 1800. In one sense, his fears were not in vain, for removal of the tsar was exactly what several of the officers of the guards had in mind. Their leader was the Baltic German Count Peter von der Pahlen, whom Paul had earlier exiled for trivial offenses, then forgiven and appointed military governor of St. Petersburg. Paul was too self-centered to realize what others thought of him, and regularly took friends for enemies and vice versa. In this case his mistake was to be literally fatal.

Pahlen had long harbored resentment and fear of the tsar since his earlier disgrace, and he had like-minded associates, chief among them Count N. P. Panin, the nephew of Paul's old tutor. Panin was in disgrace for opposing the rapprochement with Napoleon and Pahlen was afraid not only for himself but for the rest of the imperial family. He believed that Paul was so far alienating the nobility that disorder might ensue, a frightening possibility in the unstable condition of Europe. As the plot thickened, Alexander became aware of it and did nothing to stop it. On the night of March 11, 1801, after an evening of heavy drinking, the conspirators made their way into the

Castle of St. Michael. They found Paul after he tried to hide and arrested him: a struggle ensued and one of the officers strangled the tsar. It was the last and most violent palace coup in Russian history. A public announcement asserted that Paul had died of apoplexy and Alexander was now the tsar. The rejoicing was universal throughout St. Petersburg.

Alexander I ruled Russia for the next quarter of a century, a time full of drama. His personal imprint on the age was considerable, not least because he was the last of Russia's tsars to display a personal desire to keep Russia in step with the rapidly changing political world to the west. After Alexander, Russia's rulers opposed any political change or allowed it only under extreme duress. Toward the end of his life Alexander too began to move away from his early liberalism, but until the eve of the Napoleonic invasion of 1812 Alexander pursued a distinctly reformist policy.

Much of Alexander's liberalism was a matter of attitude rather than institutional reorganization. Censorship was radically relaxed and in 1804 a new statute appeared that established relatively mild rules and gave the task of censorship over to university professors under the Ministry of Education. New publications began to appear, such as the writer Nikolai Karamzin's journal *Messenger of Europe*, which was to remain the country's leading literary and intellectual voice for several decades. A writer of sentimental novellas and an account of his travels in Europe, he used the journal to publish on a wide variety of topics, from the latest in French literature to the revolution in Haiti. It so impressed the tsar that in 1803 he appointed Karamzin the official historian of Russia, charged with composing a history of Russia that was scholarly but in readable prose. Alexander's initiatives were a major step forward for Russian higher education, for he founded new universities in Kazan' (1804), Khar'kov (1805), and St. Petersburg (1819), at the side of the older university in Moscow. In largely Polish Wilno the academy was transformed into a university and the German university in Dorpat (Estonia) was revived. The Imperial Lycée founded in Tsarskoe Selo under the eye of the tsars became one of the principal seed-grounds of Russian culture. All of these initiatives flowed from the rather nebulous liberalism taught the young tsar by his former tutor, Frederic LaHarpe of Switzerland. LaHarpe was later execrated by conservatives as the evil genius of Alexander's reign, but in fact the tutor simply provided his pupil with the standard reading and ideas of the late Enlightenment, ideas that were still championed in the heir's boyhood by his grandmother Catherine. Alexander's youth coincided with the French Revolution, but unlike his father he did not see it simply as a threat to be confronted. He took it as part of vast changes sweeping European society and also as a warning to monarchs who failed to move with the times. His response was to try to reform the Russian state in line with the new Europe but keeping the power of the monarchy intact.

Alexander's youthful friendships were with young noblemen who shared these views and they were to play a major role in the early years of the reign. He appointed five of them, Pavel Stroganov, Nikolai Novosil'tsev, the Polish Prince Adam Czartoryski, and others, to an unofficial committee to advise him on the type of reform that Russia needed. After some initial discussion of constitutions and the evils of serfdom, the talk moved more in the direction of strengthening the administration and legal order. To this end Alexander radically reshaped the Russian government, abolishing the old colleges and other structures left from the time of Catherine and Paul and putting in their place ministries. The new ministries, modeled on those of Napoleonic France, were headed by a single minister, not a committee, and were given a large staff and wide areas of administrative control, if no legislative power. With this new structure Alexander created the bureaucratic state that was to rule Russia under the tsar until 1917. His ministries were supposed to and largely did follow legal guidelines, though the power of the tsar to make law at will introduced a major element of arbitrary power that also lasted until the end of the old regime. The lack of a legal culture was a further obstacle to legal order, but the law faculties of the new universities and the private Demidov law school in Iaroslavl' were designed to remedy this defect and in time did so, to some extent. The young graduates of these institutions with professional legal education began to replace clerks that operated simply by knowledge of existing practice and the old grandees with their

Figure 8. Central St. Petersburg with the Winter Palace from *Four Panoramic Views of St. Petersburg*, by John Augustus Atkinson, London, 1802.

general cultures derived from French literature. Alexander placed the Senate over all these institutions, now that it had been transformed into a place for administrative review and a supreme court.

The reform process was significantly aided by the appointment of Michael Speranskii to the position of state secretary to the tsar. Speranskii was as a parvenu (his father was a priest, not a nobleman) who had worked his way up by sheer intelligence and hard work. His bland exterior concealed an inner fire, fed by mystical religious beliefs and devotion to the law. He came from a successful career in the new Ministry of Justice to work directly with Alexander at legal reform. In 1809 he compiled a constitution for Russia that included a limited representative legislature and some checks on the tsar's power. This project never came into existence, but he did manage to establish a Council of State (again on the Napoleonic model) to provide a central locus of power at the side of the tsar. Henceforth new laws were generally discussed in the Council of State before the tsar made a final decision. Speranskii was also instrumental in the granting of a constitution to Russia's new acquisition, Finland. As a result of fears for Petersburg and foreign policy complications, Russia annexed Finland from Sweden in 1809, in the process giving the country its own government for the first time, if only an autonomous one within the Russian empire. Thus autocratic Russia acquired a constitutional unit within the empire that lasted as such until the empire collapsed. In Finland, the Russian tsar was a constitutional ruler.

Speranskii and his innovations were not popular with the gentry, who hated him and considered him a plebeian and supporter of "French" political ideas. In fact Speranskii was not nearly as radical as his opponents believed, for he never wished to challenge the power of the tsar, only to continue the process of legalizing the power and regularizing the process of consultation. He was also rather conservative in other ways, a religious mystic who was hardly the rigorous ideologist of the Enlightenment as his critics claimed. The center of the opposition to Speranskii and Alexander's liberal course was the salon of his younger sister, Grand Duchess Ekaterina Pavlovna, where the leading mind was Nikolai Karamzin, now hard at work on his history. In 1811 he presented Alexander with a long memorandum criticizing the reforms as alien to the Russian spirit, which consisted in autocracy and loyalty to tradition. For Alexander it was unacceptable, but such ideas would have a greater following in years to come. For the moment, Karamzin was too intellectual for most of the conservative nobility, who had simpler fears that the French might free the serfs and challenge their privileges. Speranskii's fall came in the spring of 1812, as Napoleon prepared his attack on Russia and Alexander needed the support of conservatives among the gentry in the moment of supreme crisis. Ironically the more modern institutions that Alexander and Speranskii had taken over from the French example gave the state a solidity that stood up to the French onslaught.

Alexander's internal reforms took place against the background of the titanic struggle of Napoleon with the rest of Europe. At first the new tsar held back. The assassination of tsar Paul had put an end to the notion of joining France in war against England, and Alexander seized on the opportunity for neutrality – a neutrality that allowed him the space for the first reforms.

Russia's relationship to the expanding Napoleonic Empire was necessarily complex, as Russia was far away from the center of

French expansion. For almost a century Russia's own imperial ambitions had been directed to the south, toward the Ottoman Empire and Transcaucasia, areas of secondary interest to the French. At the same time Russia was intimately involved in the politics of Europe, and could not simply ignore Napoleon's conquest and reorganization of Central Europe. Thus in 1805 Russia joined Britain, Austria, and Sweden in challenging Napoleon's might. The first result was a disaster, for Napoleon quickly moved into the center of the Austrian Empire. Alexander overrode the advice of his commander Mikhail Kutuzov and, with the Austrians, gave battle at Austerlitz in December 1805. It proved one of Napoleon's greatest victories. Then Prussia joined the alliance, but Napoleon smashed the supposedly great Prussian army at Jena the next year. Prussia, which unlike Russia had not begun to reform itself, collapsed. As the Prussians retreated east, Russia was left facing the French almost alone, but it managed to defeat them at Preussisch Eylau, one of Napoleon's rare defeats in these years. He recovered and at Friedland in June 1807, inflicted enough damage on the Russian army that Alexander decided to make peace. He met the French emperor on a raft at Tilsit in East Prussia, making peace and even an alliance with France.

The alliance with France meant joining Napoleon's boycott of English goods in European harbors as well as supporting Napoleon's diplomacy. One immediate consequence was war with Sweden, since the Swedish king remained loyal to the anti-French cause, and the conquest of Finland. Russia's larger foreign policy in these years, however, was a return to imperial conquest in the south, and war with the Turks brought the annexation of Bessarabia in 1812. The earlier annexation of Georgia (1803) gave Russia a firm foot on the south side of the Caucasus range, putting her in immediate rivalry with Iran as well as Turkey.

Alexander's alliance with France was unstable from the start. The tsar paid lip service to the boycott of English goods, but American ships began to flock to St. Petersburg carrying the very English colonial wares that Napoleon was trying to keep out. The French emperor complained mightily about this violation of the agreement as well as other issues, trying to browbeat Alexander into obedience. Alexander, however, was a master at this sort of diplomacy, and answered French complaints with unfailing charm and vague promises of friendship. As the French tone grew increasingly threatening, the tsar reminded the French of the size of his army and the extent of his country. He reminded Napoleon's envoys of the Scythians, the ancient inhabitants of southern Russia who defeated the mighty Persian Empire by retreating into the steppe. They exhausted and harassed the Persians until the invaders realized that they were short of food and had to run for home. The message could not have been clearer, but Napoleon did not heed it.

Napoleon had good reason to believe that he could conquer Russia in the spring of 1812. While France itself and Russia were about equal in population (about 35–40 million each), France drew on the resources of virtually the whole of Europe: the Netherlands, Germany, and Italy had either been annexed to the French Empire or turned into client states and thus had to provide recruits for its army. Prussia was ordered to join him, and Poland provided an enthusiastic contingent as well, fresh from fighting in Spain. Even with the Spanish war unresolved, Napoleon massed some four hundred thousand men of the French imperial army and more allies on Russia's western border in June 1812. Russia could muster about the same on paper, but about only half that many in reality. France was also a prosperous country with flourishing military industries, again enhanced by its empire. Russia, as everyone knew, was an industrially backward land dominated by primitive agriculture. Napoleon and most observers were confident of French victory, even those unsympathetic to Napoleonic aggrandizement, like the first American ambassador to Russia, John Quincy Adams.

In reality the odds were not so stacked against Russia. The establishment of the Ministry of War and a General Staff meant that Russia's army had modern organization, logistics, and planning. The chief of those plans was precisely the Scythian strategy alluded to by Tsar Alexander. The minister of war Michael Barclay de Tolly and the principal generals were all aware that this plan was Russia's only chance. The most important thing was to avoid a decisive battle near the border, where the French would have predominant force. After some hesitation, Alexander stuck to the plan of retreat and also removed himself from day-to-day command of the army. As the French moved into the interior, they had to leave more and more troops behind to guard their communications back to France.

They also learned that Russia, with its low population density and poor roads, did not provide enough food along the route of the march to allow the invaders to live off the land. They were confined to a narrow corridor quickly stripped of all resources. None of this would matter if they could destroy the Russian army, but the Russians moved east ahead of them. As the Russians withdrew, Alexander began to feel the political complications of the retreat, which offended the patriotism of the people and particularly the gentry. He decided to sacrifice Barclay and appointed Kutuzov as supreme commander. Kutuzov, the man whose advice at Austerlitz Alexander had rejected to his cost, was a sixty-seven-year-old veteran of Catherine the Great's Turkish wars as well as of more recent successes against the Ottomans in Bessarabia. Kutuzov stayed with the original plan of retreat, reluctantly giving battle at Borodino on September 7 (August 26 on the Julian calendar) 1812, only a hundred miles or so west of Moscow.

The epic battle so memorably described by Tolstoy was also the bloodiest single day of combat in nineteenth-century Europe. By now Napoleon could only field some 120–135,000 troops out of the hordes he had brought with him and Kutuzov was able to put up the same. The Russians entrenched themselves behind field fortifications and let the French attack, with such resultant slaughter that some 40–50,000 men fell as casualties on each side – about 100,000 killed and wounded in one day. The French managed to capture some of the Russian fortifications and then returned to their camp. Kutuzov, whose main goal was to keep his army able to fight, decided to withdraw entirely and marched his men east toward Moscow. Napoleon, as usual, portrayed the battle as a great French victory, though in fact it ended his chances of success. He had too few troops left to control Russia if the Russians continued to resist.

Kutuzov had no intention of surrender, and neither did the population. The Muscovites began to leave the city in the tens of thousands. Napoleon waited in vain on the Sparrow Hills (where Moscow University stands today) for a Russian delegation to offer him the surrender of the city. He entered a ghost town, with no resistance but also no people to greet him or supply his army. Kutuzov in the meanwhile had marched his army through the city and turned southeast along the main road. Then, contrary to everyone's expectations, he crossed the Moscow River and moved west. He made his camp southwest of Moscow, sitting on Napoleon's lines of communication and blocking the way to the rich agricultural provinces to the south and the Russian center of arms manufacturing at Tula. The conqueror of Europe was trapped like a rat.

From that point on Napoleon had lost the initiative and could only stave off the inevitable. Fires started and Moscow burned to the ground while the French troops looted the empty palaces of the nobility. Henri Beyle, to be later known to world literature as Stendhal, stole books from the library of the Golitsyn mansion. The French emperor waited several weeks, hoping Alexander would surrender and trying to collect food from the countryside around Moscow. There was no surrender. Cossacks patrolled the countryside and the peasants massacred French soldiers sent to forage. Finally he did the only thing left to him, retreat. He tried to go farther south, realizing that the direct road to the west had been stripped of all provisions and nothing could come from France. Kutuzov stood in his way, blocking the road south, and Napoleon was canny enough to realize that he could not risk a major battle. Instead he turned directly west, with winter coming on, hoping to get away fast enough before his troops starved to death. He failed. The Russian army and bands of enraged local peasants followed the French all the way, picking off stragglers and further complicating the already catastrophic supply system. The winter came early and hard, and eventually the emperor of the French abandoned his army to its fate and escaped to Paris to try to start over. Only a few thousand men of his great army managed to get to the Polish border.

The defeat of Napoleon in Russia transformed European politics in a few months. His unwilling allies began to desert, Prussia first of all and then Austria, joining Russia and Britain against France. The Russian army moved west into Poland and Prussia, providing the largest allied contingent at the giant battle of Leipzig (October 1813) and the subsequent campaign in France. By 1814 Napoleon's empire had come to an end. The hopeless attempt at its restoration the next year only ended in disaster at Waterloo.

Alexander, along with Britain, insisted that the restored French state have a constitution with some sort of legislature, rather than a return to absolute monarchy, and the two allies prevailed. Relations with Britain were not so smooth in other areas, as the Congress of Vienna showed. There were long battles about post-war boundaries for Prussia and Poland, primarily the result of British and Austrian fears that Russia was now too powerful. In the end, Russia's ally Prussia retained large parts of Poland and received important new territories in the Rhineland. Alexander's attitude to Poland was complicated: he wanted some sort of Polish political unit with the name Poland (no "Duchy of Warsaw"), but he wanted it under Russian influence. The result was the Kingdom of Poland, with the Russian tsar as its king – it was now part of the Russian Empire but with a constitution and its own government, similar to Finland.

The Polish settlement suggested that Alexander would continue along his previous liberal path. He soon emancipated the Estonian and Latvian serfs in the Baltic provinces, albeit without land. In 1818 he even toyed with granting Russia a constitution, considering a text written by his old friend Novosil'tsev. At the same time his private views were becoming increasingly conservative. The explanation for his new found conservatism lay not only in disillusionment with liberalism or the rightward drift of European politics but also in his religious views. Alexander fell more and more under the influence of Baroness Julie von Krüdener, a Baltic German aristocrat who had evolved a mystical pietism all her own. Krüdener had believed Napoleon to be the Antichrist and Alexander the savior of the world, and she told him so. Alexander spent more and more time reading mystical tracts and talking to Krüdener and other seers. His mystical interests had a decidedly Protestant strain to them, and the tsar even sponsored the translation and circulation of the Bible, relying largely on the English Bible Society to set up a network in Russia. He merged the ministries of education, the Orthodox synod, and the administration of non-Orthodox denominations into a single ministry under Prince Alexander Golitsyn, thus concentrating wide power over religion and culture in the hands of an imperial favorite. Golitsyn required Russian universities to teach explicitly conservative doctrines, to expunge ideas of natural law from the curriculum, and to substitute the notion that law was the expression of divine will. Similarly the scientists were to teach only ideas in accord with the Bible and revelation. The professors could do little to oppose Golitsyn, but fortunately his policies also antagonized the Orthodox Church. To the church the religion that was to be taught was a mixture of Protestant evangelicalism and mysticism, not correct Orthodoxy. It was the church and secular conservatives who eventually managed to discredit Golitsyn by 1824, but not before his and Alexander's notions put an indelible stamp on the Russian culture of those years.

Even more powerful than Golitsyn was General A. A. Arakcheev, originally a favorite of Alexander's father Tsar Paul. Alexander had recalled him from exile in 1803 to head Russia's artillery, and in 1809–10 he was Minister of War. Politically very conservative, Arakcheev was an extremely competent military administrator, but with a narrow education and a powerful streak of arrogance and cruelty. In 1814 Alexander made him the head of his personal chancellery, which meant that all the ministers, generals, and courtiers had to approach the tsar through Arakcheev. He was also largely responsible for hare-brained schemes like the military-agricultural settlements. The idea was to turn some of the villages of state peasants into military units with the aim of reducing costs and encouraging discipline and better agricultural practices among the peasantry. Instead the result was discontent and rebellion among the peasants that resulted in a series of revolts, which Arakcheev suppressed with savage cruelty. There were other measures. In 1817 Alexander turned the Gendarmes, originally a military police force designed to deal only with soldiers, into a militarized police force charged with the preservation of internal order, the first such police force in Russian history. The Special Department of the Ministry of the Interior also began to look for internal dissent.

Abroad Alexander's initial liberalism in France quickly faded as he and the Austrian chancellor Metternich became the prime movers behind the Holy Alliance. The Holy Alliance included Prussia and France as well as some lesser states in an agreement with Russia and Austria to fight the hydra of revolution wherever it appeared, such as the revolutions in Spain and southern Italy in 1822–23. French and Austrian troops suppressed these attempts at constitutional order, but for Russia the greatest challenge came when the Greeks rose in revolt against their Ottoman masters in 1821. Catherine and even Paul had encouraged Greek revolts against the Turks earlier on in expectation of Russian territorial gains in the Balkans, and now the occasion presented itself to satisfy Russian aims in the area. Alexander hesitated, even though many of the Greek leaders were politically quite conservative. Metternich finally convinced him that the Turks were the legitimate rulers of the Balkans, and that the Greeks deserved no more support than the Spanish rebels who fought against their king. The Greeks were left to fight on alone, in defiance of obvious Russian interests in weakening the Turks and supporting an Orthodox people.

The conservative turn in Alexander's thinking came in the wake of the 1812 victory over Napoleon, but in other sectors of Russian society the same events had the opposite effect. Among the officers of the Russian army – young noblemen with European education – the great victory brought an enormous pride in their country and its people, and gave them tremendous confidence in themselves. As the army moved west in 1813–14, many of them saw Western Europe for the first time, and with an almost universal knowledge of French and German were able to observe and investigate unfamiliar phenomena in detail. They dined in Parisian cafes, read newspapers, attended lectures, and met their counterparts in French and German salons. They came prepared, for their education had familiarized them with the basis of European thought – Kant and Montesquieu, Goethe and Rousseau. They read the latest works of the French liberal leaders Germaine de Stael and Benjamin Constant, the conservatives Chateaubriand and de Maistre, and they learned about English experiments in popular education. Some followed the debates of the English parliament in the French press, and others looked at more exotic systems by studying the constitutions of the United States and the state of Pennsylvania.

After the heady years of victory and fuller acquaintance with Western European life and thought, the return home was a cold bath for many. They knew that serfdom had been a matter of debate and condemnation since the mid-eighteenth century and that Napoleon had abolished it in Poland and the Prussian reformers in their own land. Russia was now for the first time the only European country to have such an institution. Furthermore, their own tsar, as everyone knew, had insisted on a constitution for the French, and within his own empire for Poland and Finland. What about Russia?

From about 1816–17 groups of young officers began to form more or less secret literary and debating societies with the aim of continuing the intense dialogue and reading of the war years. The first was the Union of Salvation, with only some thirty members, utilizing rituals imitated from the Freemasons to keep their actions deeply secret. There were already serious political discussions at this stage, and soon there were even more. In 1818 they founded a larger secret society, the Union of Welfare, which even had a literary society associated with it, the Green Lamp. Reading poetry, writing theater reviews, and drinking parties were as much part of the movement among these young officers as politics, but by 1821–22 they began to move toward more concrete plans of action and to write constitutions for the future. By 1825 there were two centers of this activity. In St. Petersburg, where most of the guards regiments were stationed, several hundred officers formed the Northern Society, with the aim of overthrowing the monarchy and proclaiming a constitutional state. The majority, led by Nikita Murav'ev, a captain in the Guards General Staff, wanted a constitutional monarchy and a legislature elected on a property-based franchise. More radical was the poet and ex-guards officer Kondratii Ryleev, an official in the Russian-American company that administered Alaska, who moved toward republicanism. Farther south, a similar radicalism inspired Pavel Pestel', colonel of the Viatka Infantry regiment, and other officers of the army stationed in the Ukraine close to the Ottoman frontier. Pestel' compiled an elaborate constitution for a democratic republic along Jacobin lines. Tactically there were many disagreements as well: should the army be the basis of a revolt? How much should they tell the troops? Was it enough to just remove the tsar, or did they need to kill him? And was that right? The disagreements were never resolved because they seemed too distant. The conspirators were still actively recruiting and expected Alexander to live a long time.

The new police forces and the various repressive policies failed to detect the presence of the conspiracy until it was much too late. In the summer of 1825 the all-powerful Arakcheev was immobilized by personal disaster: his longtime housekeeper and mistress, a monster of sadism, was murdered by his serfs. The general was plunged into despair, increased by the discovery that she had been embezzling large sums of money and had convinced him that her son by one of her lovers was Arakcheev's. In the southern army an officer of English origin named Sherwood sent in a secret report naming many of the conspirators, but it was too late.

On November 19, 1825, the tsar suddenly died at the age of only forty-seven. Alexander had been on tour of the Crimea and died at Taganrog, far from the capital or any other large city and word did not reach St. Petersburg until December. The first consequence was confusion. By the succession law of 1797, the heir to the childless Alexander should have been his younger brother Konstantin, the tsar's viceroy in Warsaw. Unknown to virtually everyone, Konstantin had abdicated the throne in 1822 by agreement with Alexander and left papers to that effect with the Council of State. Thus the heir would be the next brother Nicholas, but Alexander had never bothered to tell him about it. Thus the news came as a shock to Nicholas, who insisted on hearing formally from Konstantin himself. While couriers raced back and forth between St. Petersburg and Warsaw, Nicholas ordered the troops quartered in the city to swear the oath of allegiance to Konstantin and refused to take the throne. Finally a definitive answer came from Warsaw, and Nicholas ordered a new oath for December 14.

The conspirators knew most of this, as they included in their ranks officers with frequent duty in the Winter Palace. They decided to forestall Nicholas and bring out the troops in revolt in the morning before the administration of the oath. The rebels assembled on the Senate Square, only a block from the Winter Palace, and demanded that the throne go to Konstantin, a tactic designed to give time for a seizure of power. Nicholas refused to budge now that he knew that he was legally the tsar, and he called in loyal troops. For most of the short December day the two bodies of soldiers faced one another in the falling snow, and several attempts to resolve the issue failed. Finally, as sunset approached in the afternoon, Nicholas gave the order to fire, and the artillery dispersed the rebels. The first attempt at revolution in Russian history was over. Nicholas now had to decide what to do with the rebels, and how to rule the country.

9

The Pinnacle of Autocracy

The first acts of the new reign were the capture, investigation, and trials of the Decembrists, as they were known immediately and for ever after. Several hundred officers and men of the rebel regiments, as well as a few civilians, were immediately arrested. Tsar Nicholas appointed a court of numerous officials and high officers, the most distinguished being Michael Speranskii, who had returned from exile and was now again in favor. The investigation was long and detailed, conducted in secret, and eventually ended in the execution of five of the rebels, including Pestel' and the poet Ryleev, for the crime of plotting against the life of the tsar. Thirty-one others were sentenced to death as well for the same crime, but Nicholas decided to ignore their obvious guilt and commuted the sentences to labor and exile in Siberia. All together one hundred twenty-one of the rebels made the long journey east. Another four hundred fifty were either released without punishment or demoted and transferred to line regiments in the Caucasus.

In Russian history the punishment of the Decembrists became a classic example of official cruelty, but the most striking aspect of their treatment was its lenience. The number of death sentences was about the same as in the reprisals for the Italian constitutionalist revolts of 1820–21 and far less than for similar actions in Spain. Nicholas chose to hold back, perhaps because he still held a very old-fashioned conception of the tsar as the stern father of his people. In any case the Decembrists in Siberia had various fates. Eight of the most "guilty" actually worked in an open-pit silver mine for several months, while others had lighter tasks. The labor sentences were lightened by the 1830s. A number of the Decembrists' wives were allowed to join them, and as the years passed the labor sentences were entirely commuted to simple prison and eventually exile (outside of prison). Many of the former rebels were given positions in the local administration. In Siberian towns the Decembrists and their wives provided the first glimpse of European culture, for they set up schools and orphanages, put on amateur theatricals, and became the centers of local society. What they were not allowed to do is publish anything or even to return to European Russia. A blanket of silence descended around them, to remain until the death of Nicholas thirty years later.

The new tsar could now turn to ruling the country, which he did with an iron hand. Nicholas was nearly twenty years younger than Alexander, for he was born in 1796. Thus he entirely missed the reign of his grandmother Catherine, and his formative years were those of the defeat of Napoleon. His upbringing was narrowly military and he was not educated as a future ruler. Personally he was convinced that only autocracy could prevent the spread of revolution, liberalism, and constitutional government, all of these essentially the same in the minds of European and Russian conservatives. He relied on the ministries to provide his government with a trained staff to execute the laws, but increasingly he centralized decision making and in particular directed any new initiatives from his personal chancellery using men, mostly with military backgrounds, who were personally close to the tsar himself.

One of his first acts was to add a "Third Section" to his personal chancellery, one that was to keep track of potential political opponents through the Corps of Gendarmes and their network of agents. The new organ removed political police from the Ministry of Internal Affairs and subordinated it directly to the tsar through its head, General Alexander Benckendorf. The Third Section reflected in its actions the conceptions of the tsar, for in addition to looking for "secret societies" of revolutionaries it was to track insults to the tsar and imperial family, counterfeiters, and religious sects, especially the Old Believers. It was also supposed to collect news of peasant discontent and rebellion, a new note from a government hitherto only concerned about liberal ideas among the nobility.

The Gendarmes who were its main agents were also to look out for corruption among government officials, especially in the provinces. In the mind of Nicholas, paternalism and the repression of revolution were two sides of the same coin. Though the actual agents of the Third Section were few and it continued to rely heavily on denunciations, it was large enough to become a major factor in the life of Russia's small political and cultural elite.

Nicholas was not in theory opposed to all reform, and he set up a series of committees to consider the needs of the country and even to wrestle with the issue of serfdom. None of the reform programs came to anything, for the tsar believed serfdom to be an evil, but also that any attempt to change the system would lead to a massive revolt like that led by Pugachev in the previous century. Perhaps the only important positive measure of the reign was the codification of Russian law, a massive task entrusted to the capable hands of Michael Speranskii. In 1835 his committee published a code of law derived from carefully collected Russian precedent. Speranskii and his staff also compiled codes of local law from Finland, the Baltic provinces, and the formerly Polish provinces in the western part of the empire. Speranskii's code remained the basis of Russian law until 1917. Nicholas was himself enthusiastic about the project, as it fitted his image of himself as the stern yet just monarch, careful of the law as well as of his own authority.

The utter stagnation of government was not matched by stagnation in Russian society, slow as it was to develop. The colonization of the southern steppe continued, and Odessa emerged as a major port, exporting the growing surplus of Russian grain to Europe. In the interior of Russia all was not stagnant either, for within and around the serf system industrial capitalism made its first appearance. In the villages of Ivanovo and Voznesenskoe, Sheremetev estates northeast of Moscow, textile factories powered by steam engines were built starting from the 1790s. The entrepreneurs who bought and imported English steam engines, however, were themselves serfs who only gradually bought themselves out in the course of the early nineteenth century. The workers were also mostly Sheremetev serfs, though they worked for the factory owners and only paid the count, their owner, a yearly rent. Peasant entrepreneurs, some of them serfs, and townsmen began to

Figure 9. A village council from John Augustus Atkinson, *A Picturesque View of the Manners, Customs, and Amusements of the Russians*, London, 1803–04.

start small enterprises in and around St. Petersburg, Moscow, and other towns and villages of the Russian interior. In St. Petersburg many of the businessmen were foreign or non-Russian citizens of the empire – Germans, Swedes, Finns, Englishmen. In Moscow many of the richest textile manufacturers came from Old Belief groups, and thus for religious reasons were treated with some suspicion by the authorities. By the standards of Western Europe all this activity was small, labor was expensive, and industry was usually techni- cally backward, but it was a beginning. The overall prosperity of the Russian Empire also benefited from the beginnings of industri- alization in Russian Poland, the Baltic provinces and Finland.

The attitude of the tsar and his government toward industri- alization was highly ambiguous. On the one hand he supported it, if modestly, establishing the first commercial high schools and maintaining a protective tariff. Nicholas played a major role in the construction of Russia's first railroad, the line from the capital to the Tsarskoe Selo (1837) and then in a much more important project, the line from St. Petersburg to Moscow that opened in 1851. Russia acquired its first engineering school in 1828 with the St. Petersburg Technological Institute, but the builder of the Moscow-Petersburg railroad was the American engineer, G. W. Whistler, the father of the famous painter. Russia simply did not have the trained specialists for the project. Nicholas supported the railroad, but at the same time he did not want Russia to acquire a large industrial base, as he saw that as the seedbed of revolution as well as fundamentally unnecessary. The most basic issue was, of course, serfdom, for as long as that lasted Russia was saddled with increasingly backward agriculture, a highly restricted labor market, and capital tied up in serfs and noble estates. Russia could not hope to move forward until that system was removed, but that act would entail fundamental change in society, the legal system and the state. Nicholas would not have that.

As Russian society slowly grew in complexity with some hallmarks of modernity and began to move away from state tutelage, the government began to sense the need for a newer conception of itself. Autocracy alone was not enough, as it implied only obedience by the public, including the upper classes, and society outside the peasantry was by now too sophisticated for simple obedience. In the early years Nicholas relied on the traditions of cosmopolitan monarchism inherited from his brother and the Holy Alliance. The main government spokesman in the press (and a major informer for the Third Section) was Faddei Bulgarin, journalist and author of moralizing novels of Russian life. Bulgarin, however, was actually the Pole Tadeusz Bułharyn, who had even fought against Russia in 1812. His support of Russia over his native country was the result of firmly anti-revolutionary views and loyalty to the idea of monarchy: Russia's greatness lay in its adherence to these ideas. Another note entered the chorus of conservative ideas with count S. S. Uvarov. Uvarov was also cosmopolitan in education, more comfortable in French than in Russian, and Nicholas appointed him Minister of Education. In 1832 he sent around a rescript to the ministry's institutions informing them that their task was to encourage "autocracy,

Orthodoxy, and nationality," and thus was born the doctrine of official nationality, as it came to be called. Autocracy was not new, and Alexander and others had believed religion was the natural prop to the throne, but Uvarov specified Orthodoxy and added nationality to the mix. For the time this notion remained mainly the ideology of his ministry; for Nicholas, whose ministers and entourage included generals Benckendorff and Dubelt in the police, Karl von Nesselrode as foreign minister, and whose court included numerous Baltic Germans, Finns, and even conservative Polish aristocrats, could hardly advocate a purely Russian state. Russian nationality was still more a vague idea than a strict ethnic principle. The result was a contradictory mix of ideas, a mix that remained until the death of Nicholas and to a large extent until the end of the old regime in 1917. The mix was perfectly incarnated in the architecture of Konstantin Toon, the builder of the Kremlin's Grand Palace and the Church of Christ the Savior – the two great projects of the later reign of Nicholas. To provide the tsar with a modern Moscow residence Toon, consulting the tsar at every step, produced an essentially classical building that, seen from a distance, was no different from dozens of St. Petersburg palaces. At the same time decorative details like the window frames and décor were adapted from the older Russian architecture still visible in the Kremlin. The Church of Christ the Savior was much more Russian looking, but Toon took the style of the much smaller twelfth-century churches and simply blew it up to colossal size and placed it on a high platform with classical (or at least non-Russian) decorative elements such as massive lions.

Not just the architecture of church buildings but the church itself became an integral part of the autocratic regime. Nicholas put a final end both to the mild enlightenment of the eighteenth-century church and the fascination with Biblical evangelicalism of Alexander's time. In 1836 he appointed to the post of ober-procurator the Most Holy Synod Count N. A. Protasov, a general of hussars. Protasov's task was to make the church more "Orthodox," to restore its doctrinal purity and eliminate practices and intellectual trends from the West. He continued to manage the affairs of the church until 1855, and in the process he succeeded in making the church into a consciously conservative and obedient instrument of autocracy. In his time the church also absorbed a large dose of nationalist ideology, a combination that endured to the end of the old regime. Protasov's church was not the whole of Orthodoxy. Paradoxically the secularization of monastic lands in the eighteenth century led to a revival of monasticism, the "elders" (*startsy*), becoming the most charismatic figures of Russian Orthodoxy in the nineteenth century. The elders were monks whose asceticism included a large element of spiritual service to the surrounding society. In the 1820s the most famous was Saint Seraphim of Sarov, and at mid-century Makarii and Amvrosii of the Optina Monastery in southern Russia. Famous writers and intellectuals as well as ordinary laymen of all classes came to visit the monks and seek their guidance, a practice that formed a new element alongside the more traditional pilgrimages to the shrines with the relics of the saints. In spite of all these efforts, however, some twenty-five percent of the Russian peasantry followed the various versions of Old Belief rather than the Orthodox Church.

Uvarov's ideological experiments and the commitment to autocracy that lay behind them probably reflected the sentiments of most of the gentry, but they did not have universal success, even in the government and the imperial family. Mildly liberal circles existed even at the pinnacle of Petersburg society. The salon of the tsar's sister-in-law Elena Pavlovna (1806–1873) was one such place. Born Princess Frederike Charlotte Marie of Württemberg, she came to Russia in 1824 to marry the younger brother of the tsar, Mikhail Pavlovich (1798–1849). Grand Duke Mikhail was mainly interested in his military duties, and Elena became one of St. Petersburg's most important figures. Her drawing room in the Michael Palace, still carefully preserved in the building that became the Russian Museum, was an important artistic salon, especially for music and art. In the 1840s the emphasis was artistic, but the Thursdays with the Grand Dutchess also saw discussion of issues that never appeared in the press and were frowned upon in other aristocratic houses.

In Russian society at large the absence of political discussion in the press or any public forum did not imply that everything was calm below the surface. By this time a whole generation of young men, mostly of gentry origin, had finished a university or one of the elite schools like the Tsarskoe Selo Lycée. This education was supposed to fit them for state service, and indeed most of them with such an education chose that path, if only as a livelihood rather than an avocation. If public political discussion did not exist, however, literature and philosophy flourished. To some extent they served as an outlet for otherwise frustrated reflection on Russian life, but the absorbing interest in art and thought was also a response to cultural trends in Western Europe, especially Germany.

Starting in the late 1820s more and more young Russians fell under the influence of the metaphysical idealism of Friedrich Schelling, whose popularity in Germany was then at its peak. Schelling's appeal was the result of his extensive writing on religion, art, and the philosophy of nature and his desire to find a single unifying spirit in them all. For the esthetically inclined Russians of this moment, Schelling, for all his murky abstraction, seemed a real guide to understanding the world of culture and thought. By the 1830s Schelling's thought seemed so restricted to that sphere that some of the students at Moscow University turned to the more all-embracing and more rigorous world of G. F. W. Hegel. Their leader was Nikolai Stankevich (1813–1840). From 1831 until his departure for Europe in a vain search for a cure for his tuberculosis, Stankevich included in his circle nearly everyone who would make a difference in Russian thought for the next generation.

Stankevich's patience, wide reading, and gentleness attracted widely disparate personalities, at that time all united by a fascination with German philosophy and literature. The future anarchist Michael Bakunin (1814–1876), the critic Vissarion Belinskii, and the future socialist Alexander Herzen (1812–1870) were all part of the circle. They would all in different ways form the Westernizer camp, which saw Russia's destiny as a belated variant of European socio-political development. Also part of the circle were the future Slavophile Konstantin Aksakov and the conservative publicist M. N. Katkov. For the moment their common effort was to master Kant, Fichte, Schelling, and their idol Hegel, writing long letters to one another describing their understanding of their reading, turgid abstractions in Hegelian jargon. Yet out of the Stankevich circle came the major trends in Russian thought, ideas with echoes that have outlived the moment of their creation.

For Belinskii the problem Hegel posed was that he saw the history of the world as the development of the idea of freedom, but also identified its outcome with the existing order of Europe in his time. Thus everything in the world had a place, leading to ultimate self-knowledge of the Idea. Belinskii at first concluded, as did many of his friends, that Russian conditions were therefore justified, they were part of the development of humanity. This was a very uncomfortable conclusion, and further reflection on Hegel's dialectic took them in another direction: Hegel was right about Europe, it was the ideal toward which humanity headed, but Russia needed to catch up. Thus Hegelian idealism provided an intellectual foundation for thinking Russia needed to imitate the West, and that imitation could take two forms. Either Russia needed to imitate the existing Western societies, which seemed to be moving toward industrial capitalism and constitutional states, or Russia needed to follow the new trend that had emerged in the West, socialism.

For Belinskii, Herzen, and Bakunin the choice of liberalism or socialism was not one that they yet had to make. Either was considered utopian by Russian standards, and it seemed more important to analyze the condition of Russia and form a theory for future action. Belinskii chose to analyze Russia on the basis of its literature, and became Russia's most famous literary critic in the 1840s. This choice fitted well with Hegelianism, for Hegel had seen art and literature as another manifestation of the development of the Idea, whose political incarnation was the idea of freedom. Literary criticism also gave Belinskii, as a provincial doctor's son and the most plebeian of the group, a modest means of livelihood. Herzen was a more complex story, as the illegitimate son of a Russian nobleman, part of the gentry and yet permanently an outsider. Arrested in 1834, he spent several years in exile, and back in Moscow he devoted himself to reading Hegel and writing novels. In 1847 he left Russia for Western Europe, wanting to see the society he had been so long praising. He never returned to Russia, constructing his own version of socialism in exile. Bakunin followed a similar trajectory. The son of wealthy nobles, he went directly from the Stankevich circle to the West in 1840, where he joined the left Hegelians. Bakunin moved quickly from an inchoate radicalism to anarchism, coining his famous slogan, "the passion for destruction is also a creative passion." By 1848 he had acquired a name in European radical circles. Other members of the Stankevich circle interpreted Hegel in a liberal light; V. P. Botkin and M. N. Katkov remained typical liberals in their views, opponents of serfdom and autocracy and advocates of a constitutional monarchy. Konstantin Aksakov was another story, for his reading of Hegel and the Germans ultimately led him to a complete rejection of it as irrelevant to Russia. In his mind, Russia was fundamentally different from the West, with a unique Slavic national culture. Thus Slavophilism was born.

The Slavophiles rejected the premise that Russia ought to follow Western models, for they believed that Russian civilization was fundamentally distinct from that of Europe. Europe was mired in egoism, whose results were evident in political strife and the impoverishment of the people in consequence of industrial capitalism. Religion offered the West no escape, for Protestantism only reinforced individualism and the Catholic Church strove mainly for political power and influence. Russia, with its traditions of the peasant community and the (supposed) harmony of noble and peasant, tsar and subject, had largely escaped from the evils that plagued the West. Peter's westernization of Russia threatened to draw Russia into the morass, but a return to Russian values would reverse the process. Orthodoxy would continue to provide the spiritual cement, as it maintained a Christian community but refused to strive with the state for secular power. This heady mix of Orthodoxy and nationalism produced a vivid ideology but in practice was less significant, if only because it remained something of a sect. Most of the intelligentsia and the upper classes, however patriotic and sometimes even religious, remained to a greater or lesser degree Westernizers. Slavophilism was also much less conservative in practice than in theory. For all their romantic visions of the autocratic tsars of the age before Peter, the Slavophiles actually wanted autocracy tempered by a consultative legislature, as did the more moderate Westernizers. It was a different culture more than a different politics that inspired the Slavophiles.

By the 1840s these cultural impulses, Official Nationality and Slavophilism, Westernizing liberalism and radicalism had crystallized into distinct ideologies with their more or less numerous followers. Most of them were centered in Moscow, while St. Petersburg remained rather quiet politically in the wake of the Decembrist defeat. Around the middle of the decade, however, new voices appeared, also small in number but which revealed some of the outlines of the future. These voices were heard in the St. Petersburg living room of a minor government official, Mikhail Butashevich-Petrashevskii.

Petrashevskii and his followers represented a different social type and a different ideology from the Decembrists or the Stankevich circle. None of them came from the aristocracy, and some were very recently noblemen. Petrashevskii himself was the son of a military doctor born into a family of Ukrainian priests. Only his father's military rank conferred nobility on Petrashevskii, and this background was virtually identical to that of his most famous listener, Russia's great writer Fyodor Dostoevskii. Yet the Petrashevskii group did not include marginal outsiders. Most of the members had attended the Lycée in Tsarskoe Selo, the same institution that had earlier produced many Decembrists, Pushkin and his aristocratic friends, and a large number of aristocrats and dignitaries of the empire. In the late 1840s they were young men serving at the beginning level in government offices, but rather than climbing the career ladder they were spending their time reading economic and political tracts under Petrashevskii's leadership. Very soon they turned to the works of the French utopian Charles Fourier, and declared themselves socialists. Fourier was not a revolutionary, as he believed that the foundation of utopian colonies without private property and based on joint labor would quickly spread to found a new social order. As many American followers proved, this idea was an illusion, but in 1845 that conclusion was still in the future. Petrashevskii's group was convinced it would work but they realized that in Russian conditions they could not operate, and they needed first to secure legal order and political freedom. Debates and divisions over tactics soon surfaced, with some of the group favoring a concentration on propaganda while others looked to organize a revolt. The European revolutions of 1848 provided a stimulus to the idea of revolt, but also to government surveillance. The Third Section planted three spies in the group and in April 1849, they were all arrested.

The government's treatment of the Petrashevskii group differed sharply from the general legality with which it had treated the Decembrists twenty-four years earlier. After months of interrogation, during which the accused were not informed of the charges against them until very late, they were placed before a military court though there were only a few officers among them. The court found them guilty of plotting against the life of the tsar, of organizing a secret society, and of planning a revolt. Only the last charge was substantiated in the evidence, and only for some of the accused. The point of the first charge, plotting to kill the tsar, was that it alone in Russian law carried the death penalty. Thus forty of the defendants were sentenced to death, including Petrashevskii and Dostoevskii. They were then taken to the place of execution, and the first three were tied to stakes before a firing squad. At that point, an officer appeared with the announcement that the death sentences had all been reduced to hard labor in Siberia, and the prisoners were taken on the spot to the road east. This gratuitous piece of cruelty had been part of the traditions of the monarchy – the clemency of the tsar instead of death – but by 1849 this was out of place with the culture of the times.

Thus Russia reached the middle of the century with autocracy and serfdom intact, but there was ever-growing ferment under the surface, both in society at large and among the ruling elite. Change was inevitable, but Nicholas was immoveable. The downfall of his system came from the area he considered his greatest success, foreign policy.

Russia's foreign policy was intimately bound up with its imperial structure and its overall imperial aims. Along the Western boundary, Russia was a status quo power; its only aim was to maintain control over what it already held. In Finland and the Baltic provinces, this aim was easily satisfied. Though Nicholas never called the Finnish diet, the rest of the autonomous Finnish government remained in place and built up the country, the new capital in Helsinki with its modern university and other institutions. The Baltic provinces were quiet as well, with a newly free peasantry and a combination of imperial central and local noble government. The problem in the west was Poland, for the 1815 Constitution provided for a diet, a

Polish army, and a local government only generally subject to Russian control. Increasing conflict between Warsaw and St. Petersburg and the impact of the July Revolution of 1830 in France led to an uprising in November 1830 and a full-scale war. The Russian army crushed the Polish revolt and Nicholas abolished the constitution, retaining only the Polish legal system under Russian administrators. Nicholas warned the Poles that they must give up the idea of separate statehood. Eighteen years later the revolution in Germany and Hungary brought the tsar back to the fray, for the Habsburgs, defeated by the Hungarian rebels, called on him to rescue them. Nicholas marched his army into Hungary, the first Russian military expedition in Europe since 1814, and the Hungarians had to surrender. Nicholas would pay dearly for this act of monarchical solidarity.

In the south, Russia confronted a situation infinitely more complicated if ultimately less dangerous. In Alexander's reign Russia had taken control of Georgia and then conquered Azerbaidzhan from Iran. An Iranian attempt at revenge in 1826 led to a short war that brought Russia a more defensible border that included the khanate of Erevan, an Iranian vassal state on part of the territory of medieval Armenia. After the end of the war in 1828 Russian policy varied in each of these areas. The most obvious partner was the numerous Georgian nobility, and the Russians set out to include them in the empire's elite. To do this, the new rulers first had to reorganize the Georgian nobility along more "European" lines, abolishing the various types of dependency and vassalage within the nobility, making all nobles equal. New schools appeared, with curricula the same as Russian gymnasia, and the higher Georgian aristocracy entered the elite schools in St. Petersburg. The viceroys of the Caucasus even set up operas and introduced other European entertainments and forms of sociability to Europeanize the "oriental" Georgians. Russian rule affected the Armenians of Georgia as well. The small Armenian nobility of Georgia acquired the same status as Russian and Georgian nobles, and Russian administrators freed the largely Armenian townspeople from serfdom. In the khanate of Erevan, as in the Azeri khanates, most land belonged to the khans and now came under the Russian state. Thus the peasantry continued on their lands, paying taxes to the tsar rather than the khans, while much of

Muslim elite left for Iran. The khanate of Erevan was unique in all
the lands once under the Armenian kings, for on its territory was
the great monastery at Echmiadzin and the residence of the Kato-
likos (head) of the Armenian Church. The Russian administration
granted the Armenian Church, in spite of its dogmatic disagreements with Orthodoxy, the right to maintain an extensive system
of schools under its own supervision, a privilege highly unusual
in the Russian empire. Even more important, the khanate in 1828
was only about twenty percent Armenian: most of the population
were Kurdish or Turkic nomads. Under Russian rule Armenians
from Ottoman and Iranian territories migrated to the Erevan area,
so that they formed a majority by the end of the century. In other
words, in Transcaucasia the Russian Empire once again relied on
the local nobility where it could find one, and in its absence on the
Armenian Church and the local notables of the Azeri towns.

Transcaucasia was fairly quiet once Russia established control.
The lands on the north slopes of the Caucasus range, however,
were another story. The North Caucasus was the domain of a series
of semi-nomadic mountain peoples, the most important of whom
were the Circassians and the many tribes of Dagestan. Starting
in 1817 the Russian army began to build new lines of forts and
move south toward the high mountains, encountering continuous
resistance from the Circassians. Around 1830 the center of warfare
shifted east to Dagestan, to the Murids, the "disciples" of a purified
Islam. In 1834 the Avar warrior Shamil became their leader, taking
the war against the Russians into Chechnia and the northern parts of
Dagestan while conflict with the Circassians still continued farther
west. By the outbreak of the Crimean War in 1853 the Russian
army had pushed Shamil into his stronghold in the high mountains
of Dagestan, but had subdued neither him nor the Circassians. This
was not a war of great engagements and Russia never had more than
60,000 troops in the entire area before 1856. It was a guerilla war of
raids and counter-raids, of kidnapping and the siege of small remote
forts and villages. In many ways its importance came not from local
events but from its proximity to the main front of Russian foreign
policy, the Ottoman Empire.

In the eighteenth and early nineteenth century the Ottoman
Empire had been the main direction of Russian expansion. By the

time of the Greek revolt of 1821, however, Russian policy faced a number of dilemmas. The new Russian boundaries in the West created the need to defend a vast expanse that had few roads and no natural defenses along the frontier. Russia had an army of 800,000 men – the largest army in Europe – but most of it was deployed on the western border and could not be easily moved south in case of war. Further territory in the Balkans would be very far away from Russia's home bases and even more difficult to control and defend. Prudence dictated a stationary policy and the maintenance of existing boundaries in the south. At the same time, the Christian subjects of the Turks were becoming increasingly restive, and all of them were Orthodox, potential allies in any imaginable conflict. Yet they were also influenced by the political events in Western Europe and the Greek rebels imagined their future under some type of constitutional monarchy, anathema to both Alexander and Nicholas. Russia could also not afford to let the Ottoman Empire collapse, for it was not the only power interested in the area. France had long possessed major commercial interests in the eastern Mediterranean and in 1830 began the conquest of Algeria. Even more serious was British rivalry, for Britain, completing the conquest of India, had become the first world superpower and considered itself privileged to dictate the shape of the world wherever it chose. The Anglo-Russian rivalry began to turn into a long-standing conflict, an early "cold war" that lasted until 1907. A collapse of the Ottomans could lead to British or French control of the Balkans, so Nicholas preferred to maintain a weak neighbor under Russian influence, rather like Catherine's policy toward Poland before 1788.

In this situation Russia tried to work with its potential rivals. Britain agreed to help the Greeks and an Anglo-Russian naval force sank the Turkish fleet at Navarino (1827). Turkey then declared war on Russia, and in 1828–29 the Russian army moved into the Balkans, going nearly to Constantinople. The resultant treaty forced Turkey to recognize Greek independence and autonomy for Serbia and the Rumanian principalities. Russian influence in Turkey now seemed predominant, a situation that was not to the liking of either France or Britain. For the time being the rise of Mohammed Ali in Ottoman Egypt and his establishment of a de facto independent state were more important as they threatened the collapse of the whole empire. Thus Russia supported Britain against France in 1840 to uphold the Ottoman Sultan against his subject in Egypt. For one last time Russian and British interests in the Ottoman Empire coincided. A new element entered the scene with the 1848 revolutions in Europe, for Louis Napoleon was elected president of the new French republic. He soon proclaimed himself emperor as Napoleon III, and set out to restore the grandeur of France as it had been under the rule of his great uncle. He also needed the support of Catholic conservatives in France who were loyal to the Bourbons and suspicious of the Bonapartes. Looking for areas to affirm French power, Napoleon III elevated an obscure dispute over the control of the holy places in Palestine between Catholics and Orthodox into a major international issue. Nicholas was contemptuous of Napoleon III and slow to recognize the seriousness of British interests in the Ottoman Empire. Thus he presented the Turks with an ultimatum early in 1853 that led to war.

The Crimean War was actually rather inglorious for most of the participants. Though the Russian Black Sea fleet destroyed the Turkish navy at Sinop right at the start, it was no match for the British and French navies. The Russian army did well against the Turks in Asia Minor, but in the Crimea it was pushed back and forced to defend the main base at Sevastopol. The Russian Black Sea fleet had to be sunk to close the harbor to enemy ships. Russia had massive forces in theory but could not get them to the Crimea quickly and could not release enough of them in any case with long frontiers to defend. Obsolete weapons further complicated their task.

In spite of these obstacles, the Russian army and navy managed to hold Sevastopol for 349 days under intense bombardment. The Anglo-French forces were able to beat off Russian attempts to relieve the siege albeit with numerous catastrophes of which the charge of the Light Brigade was only the most famous. Sanitation and medical care were appalling on both sides, relieved only by the English hospitals reorganized by Florence Nightingale and the surgical work of the great Russian surgeon Nikolai Pirogov. As the slaughter continued at Sevastopol, the British navy tried to penetrate Russian defenses in the Baltic, but, frustrated by the powerful Russian fortresses at Sveaborg and Kronstadt, all it could do was burn

Finnish coastal towns and capture the unfinished fort at Bomarsund in the Aland Islands. Other British ships attacked Russian monasteries in the White Sea and even tried to take Petropavlovsk in Kamchatka. A squad of Cossacks beat them off.

During the war Austria's open support of Russia's enemies surprised Nicholas in view of his actions in 1849 and contributed to Russia's diplomatic isolation. Normally friendly Prussia took an ambiguous position. Then in February, 1855, Nicholas I died. In September 1855, Sevastopol fell after the French army took the Malakhov kurgan, the heights overlooking the city, and in November the key Turkish fort of Kars in Asia Minor fell to the Russians. These events and the death of Nicholas set the stage for a peace conference in Paris, which ended the war.

As a military defeat, the outcome was hardly catastrophic for the Russians. Russia agreed to give up its claim of a legal right to protection of the Orthodox subjects of the Sultan, to give up its Black Sea fleet (in any case at the bottom of Sevastopol harbor), and to surrender a small strip of land on the Danube delta to Rumania. Only the second was a major concession, and naturally Russia made it its eventual aim to acquire the right to rebuild the fleet. For the time being there were more pressing issues, for the real defeat was in the revelation that the system of Nicholas I had failed to preserve Russia's position as supreme land power in Europe that seemed guaranteed in 1815. The huge army could not move, it was too expensive for the treasury and its cost meant that it could not be modernized. Serfdom prevented the army from going over to a reserve system, as no one wanted serfs with military training. Nicholas' army, his navy, and the state that maintained them had failed. This was the signal for reform, the most basic upheaval in Russian life between the time of Peter the Great and 1917.

10

Culture and Autocracy

One of the ironies of the reign of Nicholas I is that his unrelenting autocracy presided over the first great age of Russian culture. Nicholas realized to some extent the growing importance of Russian culture and the extremely high level it achieved in a short time, but he was more concerned to direct it in the proper conservative channels than to celebrate it. He abrogated the more tolerant censorship system of Alexander I in favor of one with the emphasis on combating subversion in religion and politics while retaining the paternalistic aspects of the older laws. The new structure remained under the Ministry of Education, but included a greater role for the bureaucracy and the more ominous Third Section. Its head, Alexander von Benckendorff, exercised erratic and arbitrary authority over publications while clumsily trying to encourage the appearance of pro-government material. Even with writers and artists well disposed toward the state, this policy was largely a failure, for Russian society was beginning to grow away from court and state tutelage, a process too fundamental for the actions of the tsar to stop. Some of the changes were even the result of state policy, particularly the support of the universities and the gymnasia, which produced a much larger and educated public, eager for the products of the new Russian culture. Another factor was the growth of commercial capitalism, which gradually brought into being a market for books and journals, concentrated in Petersburg and Moscow but slowly spreading to the provinces as well.

The cultural explosion took place in a number of areas. Painting and the visual arts remained largely bound to the Academy of Fine Arts in St. Petersburg and thus indirectly to the court and its network of patronage. The Academy continued to favor large historical, classical, and Biblical canvases over the increasingly popular landscape and genre painting. It continued to supply paintings for official building projects like St. Isaac's Cathedral in St. Petersburg, or the Church of Christ the Savior in Moscow. Nevertheless the Academy also offered for its students and graduates some possibility of travel and long residence in Italy, and many painters and sculptors took advantage of the opportunity. Karl Briullov, the best of the academy painters, returned from Italy and obtained many contracts for the decoration of churches and palaces as well as acquiring court and aristocratic patrons. Alexander Ivanov, in contrast stayed in Italy to avoid the halls of the Academy and fell under the influence of German romantic painting in its religious guise (the "Nazarenes"). The main result of his Italian years was an enormous painting, "Christ Appearing to the People," which showed Nazarene influence but rejected the pseudo-medievalism of the Germans to depict the people whom Christ saved rather than a hieratic portrait of the Savior. Ivanov's innovations seem minor today, but in the world of Nicholas I he had a great impact.

Music, especially opera and ballet, remained to a large extent within the court sphere. Catherine had built an opera theater in 1783 outside the palace to provide public access to the performances, and it quickly became the center of operatic and social life. The court did not let go of the opera, however, for the Ministry of the Court acquired control over all theaters in 1802. Thus the repertory of the Petersburg theaters was the result of the taste of the Ministry's officials and even of the tsar himself. Originally Alexander I had set up four opera companies – Italian, French, German, and Russian – according to the language of the libretto and the singers, more than the nationality of the composer. The Italian company soon faded out, leaving the French company dominant until 1811, when it was closed in the patriotic atmosphere leading up to the war with Napoleon. The German and Russian companies continued, performing Italian operas as well as German with translated librettos. The Russian opera company could present only a few original works and relied largely on the European repertory.

Instrumental music flourished outside of state sponsorship, as much of Russian musical culture in these years was the product of aristocratic amateurs and private societies. The court banker Alexander Rall helped found the St. Petersburg Philharmonic Society in 1801 and the aristocrat V. V. Engelhardt's concert hall on Nevskii Prospect provided much needed performance space for a generation. In the salon of the Russian-Polish Counts Mikhail and Matvei Wielhorski, Russian and foreign musicians met, played, and made the personal contacts that took Russian music forward. Count Matvei (1794–1866) was a superb cellist who earned praise from Hector Berlioz, and his brother Mikhail (1788–1856) was not only a gifted performer but a composer as well. Both brothers had studied with Luigi Cherubini in Paris in their youth, returned to Russia and eventually received high positions at the tsar's court. The Wielhorski house stood on the same square as the palace of Grand Duke Michael, where his wife Elena Pavlovna held her own musical and political salon. The Philharmonic Society and the salons brought most of European music to Russia – Mozart and Beethoven being particular favorites of the Wielhorskis. Count Mikhail even performed Beethoven's first seven symphonies at his wife's country estate with an orchestra composed of their own and their neighbors' serfs. Later on it was Count Matvei who introduced the young Anton Rubinstein to Elena Pavlovna, a meeting that was to bear fruit in later years.

With no professional conservatory yet in existence in Russia, musicians relied on private teachers and trips to Europe for their training. Out of this semi-amateur musical world came Russia's first major composer, Mikhail Glinka (1804–1857). After some training in Italy, Glinka wrote a patriotic and very monarchist opera, *A Life for the Tsar*, first performed in 1836. The story was the suggestion of the poet Zhukovskii, who also found a librettist in Baron G. F. Rosen, a Baltic German turned Russian writer who also tutored the heir to the throne, the future Alexander II. The Wielhorskis and other aristocratic patrons of the arts provided rehearsal space. There was some quibbling from the director of the imperial theaters, but the support of Zhukovskii and the Counts Wielhorski, given their positions at the court, meant that any objections were ultimately irrelevant. The opera's premiere enjoyed an authentic success. Glinka's success did not, however, inaugurate a new age for Russian opera, for in 1843 Nicholas I was entranced and delighted by a traveling Italian company. He immediately hired them as a permanent troupe and gave them the facilities of the Russian opera company, which moved to Moscow. The result was two decades of brilliant performances of Bellini, Rossini, Donizetti, and their lesser contemporaries in St. Petersburg while Russian opera languished.

If music and theater remained tied to the court, Russian literature began to emancipate itself with the spectacular brilliance of the first wave of Russian writers, Alexander Pushkin, Nikolai Gogol, Mikhail Lermontov, and the critic Vissarion Belinskii as well as numerous lesser but still highly skilled writers and critics. Emancipation from the court coincided with the emergence of Russian literature as a mature and original literature, the first contribution of Russia to the culture of the world. The emergence of Russian literature also brought to the fore the old issue of Russia and the West in a new form. This issue had lain dormant in the eighteenth century, when Russia's cultural products were heavily imitative of Western models in form and content. Now a vibrant and original Russian literature, even as it followed Western trends and used them, had created a peculiarly Russian culture, one that was part of Western literature but not identical with it. The old question of Russia and the West now had a major cultural component.

Such a spectacular debut could not have been easily predicted in 1820, so closely had Russian literature continued to follow its European models. It was competent, occasionally inspired, but ultimately modest in achievement. In the early years of the nineteenth century the leading figures were Nikolai Karamzin, who had turned his attention to Russian history after 1803, and Vasilii Zhukovskii. Zhukovskii had a marvelous way with language, and his poetry remains to this day part of the heritage of Russian verse, but his best works were translations of the German and English poetry popular in the Romantic era – Goethe and Gottfried Bürger, Sir Walter Scott and Thomas Campbell. Through Zhukovskii European Romanticism came to Russia. To be sure, Karamzin and Zhukovskii were creating an audience for Russian literature that began to spread beyond the court and the capital cities, but it was an uphill battle. The Russian nobility, especially after the founding of the universities and gymnasia under Alexander, was much better educated than before, but it also knew French even better than before and often better than Russian. The main reading matter of many gentry families was French novels, and the latest fashionable novel in Paris was widely read in St. Petersburg in a few weeks. The numbers of the educated public were still small, and thus Karamzin's and Zhukovskii's journals, with their selection of new Russian poetry and prose among articles on history or occasionally politics, were thin small-format volumes with a circulation that rarely went much beyond a thousand copies. In this situation writers needed the patronage of court and state to survive. Much verse circulated in aristocratic drawing rooms, in the notebooks of young men and women, and only in manuscript, even when it had no political content. Zhukovskii came to play a key role. Already the most prominent poet of the age, he took up a position at the court teaching Russian to Nicholas I's Prussian wife Alexandra and then in 1819 became the principal tutor to Nicholas's son Alexander, the future Tsar Alexander II. For the next two decades Zhukovskii continued to live in the Winter Palace and served as the main patron for Russian literature and art.

Zhukovskii spotted Pushkin's talents as early as 1815, when the young poet was still a pupil at the Tsarskoe Selo Lycée. On leaving the Lycée in 1817, Pushkin took a very junior position in the Ministry of Foreign Affairs. Though he came from an ancient noble family (his ancestors had served in the boyar duma of the Moscow princes in the fourteenth century), his fortune was limited and the tradition of government service meant that he, like other writers of his generation, started out as an official. He also spent much of his time carousing in the demi-monde of St. Petersburg with his old Lycée comrades, and participating in a number of literary societies (including Green Lamp and Arzamas). All of these groups included many future Decembrists, though none of them thought he was the type to be recruited for their revolutionary activities. To be sure Pushkin was sympathetic to many of the political goals of his friends, and occasionally wrote poems expressing these views, which circulated in manuscript. These came to the attention of the Special Section of the Ministry of the Interior early in 1820, and

Pushkin was sent into exile to the south, first to Kishinev and then to Odessa. A few weeks later his first major poem appeared in print, a fairy tale called "Ruslan and Liudmila".

In the next decade, one of the most remarkable in the history of Russian culture, Pushkin published poem and after poem: "The Prisoner of the Caucasus" from the events of the Caucasian Wars, "The Fountain of Bakhchisarai" with its Crimean background, "The Gypsies," "Poltava" from Ukrainian history in the time of Peter the Great, and others. From his reading of Shakespeare he was moved to write a verse drama, "Boris Godunov," a tragedy of ambition and power that served as the basis for Modest Mussorgskii's later opera. Pushkin's masterpiece was the novel in verse *Evgenii Onegin*. On the surface the story of a bored young nobleman's flirtation with Tatiana, a country girl brought up on French novels, it provided a portrait of Russian gentry society. Onegin emerges as a man with no purpose in life, neither a career nor an absorbing occupation, well educated in European culture but contributing nothing to the Russia around him. In contrast Tatiana, for all her girlish naivité, is the deeper and stronger character, the prototype of many of the women in Russian literature. The book had phenomenal success and later Tchaikovsky was to turn it into his own greatest opera. The echoes of European Romanticism were apparent in almost all these works, but Pushkin was no imitator, alongside the echoes from his reading was a powerful melody all his own.

Pushkin's astonishing creativity was not alone. The decade saw an explosion of Russian poetry and a gradual transformation of the audience. Normal commercial publication was still barely profitable, but innovative booksellers found a new genre, the almanach. Small format volumes with fancy bindings and paper, they were designed as New Year's presents, especially for young ladies. They normally included only Russian authors with few translations, all of them new. Poets competed to be published in them, and they were guaranteed an audience, for part of the appeal of the format was that they could be easily carried in a lady's purse. In aristocratic drawing rooms the French novel now had a competitor.

In 1824 Pushkin received permission to return to his estate near Pskov, south of St. Petersburg, but not to the capitals. The Decembrist revolt complicated his attempts to restore his position, and the newly founded Third Section sent agents to observe him. They were particularly concerned to discover if he talked to the peasantry, and about what. Their findings were meager: the worst they could discover was that he wore a straw hat and a Russian traditional shirt with a pink sash around it. The point was that his dress could be construed as an attempt to mix with the people to stir up revolution, but his neighbors reported that he never talked about politics or even went out much. Finally Pushkin, with encouragement from Zhukovskii, appealed directly to tsar Nicholas, who granted him an interview in Moscow in 1826. After a long conversation, Nicholas agreed to end the exile, to allow Pushkin back to St. Petersburg, and to help him with his problems with the censorship. Henceforth his censor would be the tsar himself.

Pushkin returned to the capital still closely observed by the authorities, but also with the court title of kammerjunker and a direct relationship to the tsar and to the head of the Third Section, Benckendorf himself. Pushkin chafed at Benckendorf's philistinism, but he admired Nicholas and remained loyal to the monarchy, if critical of its officials and many of its policies. He received an official appointment as historian and wrote a history of the Pugachev rebellion as well as a novella on the same subject, *The Captain's Daughter*. Pushkin even borrowed money through the Third Section, and eventually received permission to found a journal, *The Contemporary*. This was in part a commercial venture, for the economic circumstances of literature were rapidly changing. In 1834 the Polish conservative turned Russian writer Osip Senkovskii founded the *Library for Reading*, which quickly outsold any other Russian journal with its thick issues that contained a mixture of light fiction, serious literature, non-fiction, and much chitchat from the editor himself. Pushkin was hoping to move into this market while offering more sophisticated material for the reader when fate intervened.

Pushkin had married a woman of great beauty, limited intelligence and depth, and great social ambitions. Her life centered on the houses of the great aristocracy, the court and its entertainments, its balls and intimate gatherings, which she attended as lady-in-waiting to the empress. There she met Georges-Charles D'Anthès, a young Alsatian-French nobleman serving in the Russian guards, a monarchist refugee from the French revolution of 1830. Adopted as a son by the Dutch ambassador Baron van Heeckeren, he revolved in the highest society and was utterly unscrupulous. He began a flirtation with Natalia Pushkina (how serious it was remains unclear to this day), and in November 1836, Pushkin received an anonymous letter that asserted the flirtation to be a real affair. He challenged D'Anthès to a duel, but Zhukovskii and others managed to patch up the quarrel. It erupted again a few months later and on January 27, 1837, it ended in a duel. In the snow on the outskirts of St. Petersburg the two opponents faced each other and D'Anthès fired first. Fatally wounded and bleeding profusely, Pushkin raised himself on his elbow and fired, but only inflicted a slight wound. His second brought him home where Zhukovskii got the best doctors in the city, those who treated the tsar, but they could do nothing. Pushkin sent a message to Nicholas, asking him for forgiveness (dueling was a crime) and Nicholas granted it, but advised him to take the last rites like a Christian, and promised to take care of his family. Count Mikhail Wielhorski, the poet Prince Peter Viazemskii, and Zhukovskii visited and stayed with him until he died. D'Anthes was expelled from Russia, and went on to a long career in his native France. Nicholas paid Pushkin's debts and took care of his family and Natalia soon remarried.

Pushkin's death was a huge event in the history of Russian culture, soon mythologized into martyrdom at the hands of an unfeeling aristocracy and court, but his death was the result of his deep roots in precisely that milieu. Though most of the later Russian writers were still noblemen, none were as much part of the court circle as was Pushkin. The closest to Pushkin's social position was the poet Mikhail Lermontov, also a nobleman but without distinguished ancestors like Pushkin's. His political views were not really radical, but his poetic reaction to Pushkin's death earned him a transfer to the Caucasus, the scene of his greatest work, *A Hero of Our Time*. An interconnected series of stories, the book's hero Pechorin is a sort of Onegin, this time serving in the army in the Caucasus but again placed between European education and the limits of Russian reality. On Lermontov's return to St. Petersburg in 1838 he, too, frequented aristocratic salons if not the court, and as if repeating Pushkin's fate, got into a duel over a woman with the son of the French ambassador. The duel ended in reconciliation, but

Lermontov was sent back to the Caucasus. There he met his end in yet another duel in July 1841. Pushkin and Lermontov were typical of the writers of their age though far more talented. Both noblemen, with many friends and relatives in the court, the government, and the army, they lived as did the men of their social rank. They were present at the great social events of the capital and spent much of their time playing cards, drinking, hunting, and occasionally visiting their country estates. The next generation of writers, though also noblemen, lacked the connections at court and experienced St. Petersburg less as the home of the court than as a great modern city.

The first of this new generation to emerge was Nikolai Gogol'. Gogol' was the son of a provincial Ukrainian landowner, and on his father's side even the noble ancestry was rather recent. He attended the lycée in nearby Nezhin, an institution of the highest educational quality but lacking the connections with the court and the high aristocracy of Pushkin's school in Tsarskoe Selo. On graduation the young Gogol' found a position in St. Petersburg at a school for the daughters of military officers. His livelihood came from the school and soon from his writings after his first great success, a series of comic stories from Ukrainian life, *Evenings on a Farm near Dikan'ka*. Gogol' eventually met Pushkin, who published some of his stories, and Zhukovskii, who appreciated his talent but never played the role of patron with Gogol' that he had in other cases. Gogol' was something of a loner, and at first he did not need Zhukovskii's patronage. There was already enough variety of outlets for his work and they paid enough to keep him going. Nevertheless, the Russian market was still too narrow to provide more than a modest living and Gogol's poor health left him vulnerable. The solution found by Zhukovskii and others of his friends after 1840 was a series of direct grants from the tsar himself, one of the last examples of court patronage of literature. Nicholas I liked most of the work done by Gogol', and the grants came regularly until the writer's death.

Gogol' brought new themes into Russian literature. His stories of St. Petersburg, often fantastic and grotesque, introduced an urban theme into Russian literature that was previously absent. The capital was growing, both because of the expansion of the central bureaucracy and because of the city's role as a port and an industrial center. The St. Petersburg that Gogol' knew was the city of the impoverished clerk and the lonely wanderer in a vast and cold mass of huge buildings, not the city of glittering balls and brilliant salons. The heroes of these stories were such little people as the clerk in "The Overcoat," but St. Petersburg also inspired the fantastic strain in his writing, with stories such as "The Nose," in which the nose of a minor bureaucrat leaves his face and roams around the city in a carriage wearing an official uniform.

Gogol' remained all his life the product of the Ukrainian provinces, deeply religious, nationalistic, and conservative in his political views. He took the conservative ideal for Russia seriously and realized that the reality was different. His first play, "The Inspector General" of 1836, was a scathing satire of provincial life and official corruption. Poorly performed at first, it was not a success until much later, though it showed the direction in which he was heading. Nicholas I liked it, as he saw himself struggling with the corruption and incompetence of the Russian bureaucracy, and found an echo of that effort in the play. His greatest work, the novel *Dead Souls* (1842), was a picaresque account of the adventures of a swindler traveling through provincial Russia. Again Gogol' saw Russia's shortcomings from the point of view of a conservative ideal of autocracy and Orthodoxy, but it was a sign of the times that reaction to the novel divided very much along ideological lines. The pro-government conservatives Bulgarin and Senkovskii hated it. More independent conservatives, the Slavophiles, and the Westernizer Vissarion Belinskii loved it, but for different reasons. The Slavophiles saw it as an apotheosis of Russia and its mystical future, while Belinskii praised it for its unvarnished portrayal of Russia's present.

The debate over *Dead Souls* was a harbinger of the future: literature was fast becoming a battleground of political and cultural ideology. It was changing in other respects, for Zhukovskii left for Europe in 1842 in search of better health and never returned to Russia. He had no replacement at the court, and Russian literature no longer had a patron with the ear of the tsar himself. By the 1840s the "fat journals" pioneered by Senkovskii and Pushkin fought lively and vituperative battles over Gogol', Lermontov, Goethe, and Georges

Sand. The most powerful of the younger writers was Fyodor Dostoevskii, whose early works took up the thread of Gogol' in his Petersburg stories, with his own tales of impoverished seamstresses and other little people of the great metropolis. The commanding figure of the decade in criticism was the critic Vissarion Belinskii, the main spokesman of the Westernizers.

Belinskii came to be seen in Russia as the archetypical "committed" critic who judged works of art by largely utilitarian standards and by their significance for the reformation of Russian society. This judgment placed him in the straightjacket of the conceptions of a later generation, for Belinskii's view of art was essentially historical, a view derived from his Hegelian youth. Belinskii got from Hegel the idea that art was one of the many manifestations of the Idea in history, alongside philosophy or the development of the state. Art was, in his words, "thinking in images," and thus was the equivalent of political or social thought in another form. Since the development of the Idea in society was the progress of freedom, art in Russia should reflect the movement of the country toward that ideal. Art that did not was condemned to ultimate insignificance and was considered bad art to boot. This theoretical framework gave him a basis for his total rejection of older Russian culture, his qualified approval of the eighteenth century, and his enthusiastic approval of Pushkin, Lermontov and particularly Gogol'. In Gogol' he saw a relentless critic of the existing order of Russian society, the satirist of nobility and state alike. His appreciation of Gogol' was only partly correct, for Gogol's satire came from a conservative position with a religious basis, the idea that Russia was not yet living up to its potential to create a society profoundly different from the West. Here Belinskii parted company with Gogol' entirely, for the critic was a firm Westernizer. To him Russian society was only acceptable insofar as it approached the standard of an idealized West, a West that itself needed to be transformed by the French utopian socialism that became Belinskii's credo.

The discussion of literature was to a large extent a discussion of political and social issues that could not otherwise be aired in print. Eventually they broke out into the open, or partly so. Gogol's publication of his conservative manifesto, *Selections from Correspondence with Friends*, in 1847 created huge controversies, muffled by censorship, for he seemed to be not just supporting the existing state and church but losing faith in literature itself. Belinskii's response, the letter to Gogol' in 1847, became a classic example of liberal and radical thought in Russia for the next two generations. "The public... looks upon Russian writers as its only leaders, defenders, and saviors from the darkness of autocracy, Orthodoxy, and nationality." In Belinskii's mind, "Russia sees her salvation not in mysticism... but in the successes of civilization, enlightenment, and humanity." The Russia of his day needed to start with the abolition of serfdom and corporal punishment and the establishment of legal order. Belinskii's life was perhaps as important as his views, for he was the first important example of the Russian intelligentsia, the educated stratum of society that took Russian culture out of the hands of the nobility. Himself the grandson of a priest and the son of a military doctor, he was only technically a noble because of his father's promotion in the army. He survived, and survived very poorly on his income from his articles and editiorial work in the journals where he published, most importantly *The Contemporary*, originally Pushkin's journal and a publication that would have a remarkable future.

Belinskii's literary tastes and views pointed to the future in other ways. One of his early friendships was with Ivan Turgenev, again a writer of noble origins and some wealth. Turgenev had come to Moscow from his provincial estate and made acquaintance with the Stankevich circle that included Herzen and Bakunin, whom Turgenev came to know better when he studied in Berlin. On his return to Russia in 1841 Turgenev became close friends with Belinskii, a friendship that lasted until the critic's death in 1848. Turgenev shared Belinskii's support of Western culture and his critical view of Russia, if not the critic's radicalism. The great event of Turgenev's youth was his meeting with the Spanish opera singer Pauline Garcia-Viardot in 1843, who came to St. Petersburg as one of the stars of the Italian company that was to have a major effect on Russian opera. The passion seems to have been mainly on Turgenev's side, but it unlocked his creative powers. In his middle thirties he found his voice, first in his play "A Month in the Country," and then in his series of stories of rural life, *A Hunter's Sketches* (1847–1852). The *Sketches*, with their portraits of eccentric and domineering nobles and their very human (but unsentimentalized) serfs, caused a sensation. Turgenev's were the not the first attempts to describe the life of the peasantry, but they were both the most effective by far and under their mild surface they conveyed the poverty and humiliation in which the great mass of the Russian people, the peasants, lived. The son of a despotic and sadistic mother who mistreated her serfs as well as her children, Turgenev knew what it meant to live under arbitrary power. The publication of such work in the darkest period of the reign of Nicholas was a major act of civil courage, but ironically it was not the *Sketches* that earned him his first brush with the authorities.

In 1852, just as the publication of the *Hunter's Sketches* was proceeding, Gogol' died. Turgenev had been acquainted with Gogol' but was not a close friend. As a fellow writer, however, he admired him intensely, and was so moved by his death that he quickly wrote a short essay about Gogol' and his significance for Russia and its literature. In St. Petersburg the publisher was afraid it would not pass censorship for there were many conservative officials who did not share the tsar's approval of Gogol'. Turgenev sent the essay to Moscow, where it was approved and appeared in print. Turgenev was then arrested for violating the censorship rules, a charge that was legally dubious, but convincingly presented to Nicholas by the Third Section. The punishment was a month in prison followed by exile to his estate, time that he used to write another novella. The incident only confirmed Turgenev's oppositional attitude to the autocracy.

Turgenev was extremely sensitive to the trends of Russian society and thought and his stories of peasant life prefigured by only a few years the great debate over serfdom that erupted after the Crimean War. He was also aware of another trend in Russian culture, the turn away from philosophy, German or otherwise, toward a fascination with the natural sciences, a trend that would also come to the surface only after Crimea. This fascination did not grow in sterile soil, for the universities founded under Alexander I were fully equipped with faculties of the natural sciences. Until the middle of the nineteenth century they competently taught the achievements of European science adding nothing of importance to that body of learning, with one enormous exception: mathematics. In 1829–30, the same years as the publication of Pushkin's *Evgenii Onegin*, Nikolai Lobachevskii inaugurated a revolution in geometry in a series of articles in the official journal of the University of Kazan', where he taught and eventually became rector. Lobachevskii's idea was very simple: all geometry since the time of Euclid had included the assumption that two parallel lines do not meet. Suppose you reverse the assumption: what sort of geometry would you construct? This Lobachevskii proceeded to do, a discovery so bizarre that it earned him no recognition in his lifetime. Europeans with similar ideas, Christian Gauss and the young Hungarian Janos Bolyai, had never developed them, for Gauss thought them too odd to publish. He did not want to risk his own reputation and discouraged Bolyai from taking steps to make his suggestions better known. It was left to Lobachevskii, in the obscurity of provincial Russia, to work out the notion. Unknown to almost everyone, Russia had its first major scientific discovery, but Russian science would not come into its own until the 1860s, and it would be Turgenev who would bring science and its implications to the public for the first time. The new fascination with the natural sciences also brought a new current of thought into Russian radical politics.

I I

The Era of the Great Reforms

Russia's defeat in the Crimean War caused a tremendous political shock in the country. It was not the scale of the defeat but its revelation of the weakness of a political system that prized its unique conservatism on the European scene and its supposed military might above all. It was the autocracy that was defeated, all the more so because the long siege of Sevastopol demonstrated to many Russians that the army still had the spirit to fight, a spirit hampered by the backwardness of society and government. Russia's backwardness was not only the result of the slow evolution of economy and society under the tutelage of Tsar Nicholas. The greatest problem was that the world was changing very quickly in the middle years of the nineteenth century, and the most rapid changes were taking place in Great Britain, Russia's primary imperial rival. Railroads were transforming the landscape in all of Western Europe and the United States, building on and stimulating the rapid modernization of iron and steel production, thereby raising output to new heights. Besides railroads, all sorts of machines came into existence – improved steam engines, telegraph equipment, and huge metal-hulled ships. Britain and other powers imported increasing amounts of food and raw materials from colonies and distant countries in the Western hemisphere, sending out masses of cotton and wool cloth, machinery, and innumerable consumer goods. Society evolved to support all this growth, with high-speed presses to produce daily newspapers and rapidly expanding educational systems to produce engineers, lawyers, politicians, and an educated public to use the new products. In this new world, Russia was lagging behind. The reformers in the government realized all this and saw that Russia needed the new production techniques and a new economy simply to survive as a major power. They also realized that technology alone was not enough: Tsar Nicholas had built railroads, but had not succeeded in transforming the Russian economy. Russia would need a new legal system, a modernized and expanded educational system, and even some forms of public discussion of major issues. What Russia could not stand, the reformers believed, was a new political system. Most of them admired the emerging constitutional regimes in Europe, but believed that Russia was far too primitive with its illiterate peasantry, outmoded agriculture, and thin layer of educated people. Such a society could not sustain a free, constitutional government. For the foreseeable future, it would have to remain an autocracy.

With the death of Tsar Nicholas in February 1855, a new regime came to power with his son Alexander. Alexander II would preside over the greatest changes in Russia since the time of Peter the Great – changes that brought the country into the modern world, hesitantly and only partially, but nevertheless across the threshold toward industrial capitalism and the beginnings of a modern urban society. The new tsar was as often against as for these changes, and had to be pushed all the way, but nevertheless he did allow himself to be convinced and to make the decisive moves. Ultimately the tsar decreed the reforms, but like the reformers he intended to preserve autocracy intact and keep society, even upper-class society, out of political decisions. This was a difficult and ultimately impossible goal, for Russian educated society emerged now for the first time as a force in the political and social process, even if it was a force of limited power. Its emergence, even if modest, was a revolution in Russian politics and a revolution with wide implications.

At first the initiative for reform came from the government. During the Crimean War, however, Herzen and other émigré radicals had raised their voices, and inside the country even conservatives among the gentry and intelligentsia began to circulate memoranda proposing reforms of various kinds. None of this had any effect, as these groups were too small and had little echo even among the

educated sectors of the social elite. The situation changed with the
Peace of Paris in March 1856, which put an end to the war. The war
had revealed that the unreformed autocracy was no longer capable
of maintaining Russia's position in the world, and would have to
develop a more modern economy. Serfdom was the main obstacle.
Soon after the signing of the peace, Tsar Alexander spoke to the
assembled gentry of the province of Moscow (that is, to much of
the top aristocracy) in his first major public pronouncement. The
mere fact of such a pronouncement was unusual and the content
even more so. He warned the nobles that the peasant question now
had to be addressed. It was much better, he told them, that it be
resolved from above than from below. In other words, the state had
to reform the countryside or the nobles would face a peasant revolt.

The virtually simultaneous relaxation of censorship meant that
the issues raised in the tsar's speech as well as other pressing concerns could now be addressed, albeit cautiously. Debate appeared
in unexpected places such as the publications of the Ministry of the
Navy, headed by the tsar's more liberal brother, Grand Duke Konstantin Nikolaevich. While Alexander's government, or at least part
of it, was convinced of the need for reform, every step met opposition from conservatives within the corridors of power and also
from the gentry, who now could express their views publicly and
still had access to the court and the important ministries. The first
committee appointed by the tsar in January 1857, to deal with the
peasant questions was thus secret. The reformers in the government
showed their hand only at the end of the year, when the Ministry of
the Interior sent a memorandum to one of the provincial governors
ordering him to require the local gentry to form committees to provide suggestions on the emancipation of the serfs, its desirability,
and paths to achieve it. The Ministry published the memorandum
in its official printed register, and now the gentry and the educated
part of the population knew what was afoot.

Not surprisingly most noblemen were against the idea of emancipation, and hoped that if it did come, all the land would remain
in the hands of the gentry. This would be a landless emancipation
like that earlier in the Baltic provinces, and peasants would have to
rent their land from the gentry or go to work as day laborers. The
government reformers did not like this idea, for they feared that it

would produce a vast landless proletariat that would be the source of endless revolts and upheavals. Instead the committee, blandly called the "Editorial Committee," proposed that the peasants be freed with land, for which they would have to pay the landowners, and furthermore they would have to pass through a period of temporary obligation to the owners of the estates. The redemption payments would be spread over sixty years, the state giving the gentry a lump sum that the peasants were to repay to the treasury. This plan evoked intense hostility among the gentry, who thought it would undermine their livelihood and their place in Russian society. Throughout 1859–60 battles raged in the committee, in government ministries, and the court itself.

The reformers were a powerful and well-connected group. Much of the responsibility fell on the Ministry of the Interior, whose vice-minister was Nikolai Miliutin. Miliutin's brother Dmitrii, a professor at the General Staff Academy and adjutant to the Minister of War, had come to the attention of Grand Dutchess Elena Pavlovna, and in the 1850s attended her "Thursdays," the weekly gathering of her friends and allies. In the new atmosphere, the Grand Dutchess's salon added political reform to its agenda, and Nikolai Miliutin, a well-educated and progressive younger official, joined his brother in the Grand Dutchess's good graces. Both Miliutins had strong reformist views, and Nikolai was appointed to the Editorial Committee on its inception. In the committee Nikolai Miliutin could count on the support of its chairman, General Iakov Rostovtsev, an officer whose career had not been in the field but in the role of adjutant to Tsar Nicholas and who had been close to Alexander in his years as heir to the throne. During the Crimean War he rather unexpectedly became a strong reformer and exploited his access to the new tsar to the fullest. Grand Duchess Elena also monitored the progress of reform, and her network of informants at the palace insured that the reformers knew who was trying to influence the tsar and in what direction. Dmitrii Miliutin, after several years in the Caucasus, in 1860 went on to head the Ministry of War. With Grand Duke Konstantin Nikolaevich in charge of the Navy, both military ministries as well the Minstry of the Interior were in the reform camp. The reformers were a tightly interconnected group, well educated, highly placed, and ready for action.

Figure 10. Alexander II and his dog Milord.

At the beginning of 1860 General Rostovtsev died suddenly, but the committee continued its work moving on toward a reformist solution. Then in September the tsar appointed his brother Konstantin to chair the committee, and by that act ensured an outcome favorable to emancipation. The result was a swift conclusion to support the original idea of emancipation with land for the peasants on the basis of redemption payments, as the reformers had proposed two years before. The proposal went to the Council of State, the highest body of government, which debated the proposal for several weeks. On February 17, it voted against the proposal. The majority wanted more land for the gentry and the Council sent the two opinions on to the tsar, the majority against and the minority for emancipation with land for the peasants. The fate of twenty million serfs hung in the balance, for Russia was an autocracy, and the tsar had no obligation to accept the majority of the Council of State, or the minority for that matter. After two days of deliberation, Alexander II chose to accept the minority report and signed the decree of emancipation. In the tsar's mind, disaster loomed if he went with the majority: the peasants should not be made "homeless and harmful to the landowners as well as to the state." The government decided to wait until the beginning of Lent to announce the decree, and it was read in churches everywhere in the country beginning on March 5/17, 1861. The hope was that the Lenten atmosphere would encourage a quiet response to the decree among the people. Whatever the reason, there were only a few minor disturbances among the peasantry.

The balance of power inside the government was the only thing that really mattered, but the reformers also looked to societal support and in some sectors they found it. Early in 1856 the exiled radical Herzen realized that reform was coming in Russia and he decided to help it along. His first act was to use his base in London to begin publishing a series of essays, *Voices from Russia*, that provided background information and uncensored discussion of the current problems. Herzen understood that his own views were too extreme for most of his potential audience, so he found contributors who were liberals rather than radicals, even quite moderate liberals. In 1857 he began to publish a monthly newspaper, *Kolokol* (the Bell), which did reflect his own views, though in many cases he held his fire to avoid alienating the readers. Both the essays and *Kolokol* were smuggled into Russia and quickly became widely available. The Third Section acquired copies and circulated them to high officials and even to the tsar himself. Herzen's vivid prose and clear perspective gave him popularity with many readers who did not share his particular views, his peasant socialism, and his opposition to autocracy. His was not the only voice heard, for the (at first temporary) relaxation of censorship allowed newspapers and journals to appear in increasing numbers. This new phenomenon was not only a function of change in the censorship rules, for technological innovations in printing now made daily newspapers possible for the first time in Russia. They were, to a large extent, commercial enterprises, and many of the editors learned to combine sale-ability with liberal ideas. Newspapers whose editors were critical of the authorities from a conservative point of view began to appear as well. Many topics were beyond the pale, such as the personalities and views of the tsar himself and the imperial family, but the editors were able to find ways to discuss current issues and at the same time present a mass of information on Russian life and on the affairs of the world. In the conditions of wide debate over the reforms, even a bare account of village life or a criminal trial could take on relevance to the reform process. Detailed accounts of Western politics, of English parliaments, French foreign policy, or even American presidential elections offered Russian readers regular accounts of political systems different from their own. The reformers inside the state bureaucracy were not unhappy with these developments, as the press allowed them to assess the degree of support or lack of it for their actions, although they had no intention of following suggestions from anyone outside the government. Much of their effort went to keeping the gentry and the aristocrats from influencing opinion or the reform process, as they correctly believed the nobility, high and low, to be mainly against reform. Thus the government reformers kept the government's deliberations as secret as they could.

Until the actual emancipation decree of 1861 the government, however secretive, enjoyed the guarded support of emerging opinion among the educated classes. After that moment tensions began to arise between the government and the pro-reform wing of the educated classes, for many of the liberals felt that the reforms did not go far enough. At the same time the pro-reform elements of society began to divide into moderate and radical wings. Herzen was highly critical of the inadequacies of the emancipation, and his views contributed to the formation of a radical camp inside Russia. Most liberals, the intelligentsia, and the liberal minority of the nobility, continued to support the government and enthusiastically plunged into the reform process, the nobles serving on local committees to implement the reforms. Moreover, the government continued with additional reforms, the next steps being the reform of the judiciary, local government, and the army.

Other factors, however, complicated the politics of the reform. In January 1861, there were a series of disturbances in Warsaw, the first such manifestations of Polish discontent since the 1830 revolt. Tsar Alexander and the ministers sent Grand Duke Konstantin Nikolaevich to Warsaw as viceroy with the hope that he could manage a compromise that would introduce some reform into Russian Poland and defuse discontent. The attempt was a failure, and a new revolt broke out in 1863. This revolt undermined Grand Duke Konstantin's authority in St. Petersburg, and he never again played a major role. It also created a permanent split between Herzen and the liberals, for Herzen supported the Polish effort and the liberals came out for Russian national interest. *Kolokol* quickly declined into insignificance. Fortunately for Russia the revolt was largely a matter of small guerilla groups operating within the countryside, and in the western Ukrainian provinces the peasants even joined the government troops against the rebels. By the end of 1864 Russian authorities had restored order in Poland, and in the meantime they even managed to decree two important measures for the rest of the Empire, judicial reform and the establishment of a new form of local government.

The new decrees established a series of local administrative boards, the zemstvos, which were to take care of roads, bridges, public schooling, health, and other matters of local concern. The innovation was that the members of the boards were to be elected. Most delegates to the zemstvos were noblemen, but the newly emancipated peasantry was also regularly represented. Liberals correctly complained that the zemstvos were too closely supervised by the bureaucracy and lacked many of the powers needed to carry out even their modest tasks. The provincial governors and the Ministry of the Interior kept a close watch on the new institutions and had the power to override their decisions. At the same time the zemstvos took on an important role in Russian life, both for the practical problems they addressed and as elected institutions. Whether the government liked it or not, they became centers of modest political activity and provided the local nobility with an outlet for their energies and the experience of political and administrative activity. The zemstvos also employed large numbers of experts from the intelligentsia, teachers, doctors, and statisticians, and this group also became a force for the politicization of the zemstvos as time went on. Ultimately the zemstvos became centers for liberal political organization.

More radical were the judicial reforms. Nicholas I had codified the laws, but the judicial system remained largely as Catherine II had left it at the end of the eighteenth century. The judiciary was not completely separated from administration, the judges lacked independence and often legal training as well, and judicial procedure still depended on written testimony. Proceedings were not public, and the judges decided cases without a jury. The 1864 decree changed all that, paradoxically giving Russia one of the most progressive judicial systems in Europe. Trials were henceforth conducted in public as an adversarial trial with both a public prosecutor and a defense attorney. In the great majority of criminal cases the decisions on guilt or innocence were made by a jury. The Ministry of Justice appointed the judges, but they could not be removed except for misbehavior. Overnight, Russia acquired a legal system up to European standards and a legal profession. Trials, criminal and civil, became news and were reported in the newspapers, often at length. Unfortunately this brilliant judicial system had to enforce laws that were far from progressive in many areas from family law to commercial matters, but the many areas of ambiguity in the legislation allowed judges to reshape the law in a more modern direction. A more basic flaw in the system was the continued existence of laws allowing the state administration to issue various punishments outside the courts. The most notorious was the use of administrative exile, by which the provincial governors and the Minster of the Interior could sentence anyone they found problematic to exile (not prison) for a number of years merely by decree. Liberal publicists and zemstvo activists increasingly found themselves the target of this practice.

The other exception to the new system was the formation of a separate court system for the peasants, the township courts. These courts were to formalize the older informal village courts, with a panel of judges elected from among the peasants and a clerk (often the only literate person in the court) to record its actions. Peasants were to settle all civil cases and minor crimes in these courts, which worked not by the law of the state but by the customs of the villages orally transmitted, or simply on the basis of "conscience." Their decisions could not be appealed to state courts. The township courts often decided cases on the basis of the reputation of the plaintiff and defendant, and the main punishment was flogging. This system kept the peasantry separate from the rest of society, conserving the village community and its values.

In the zemstvos and the new courts some part of the public finally had a sphere of activity, even if it was not political activity. Even this modest public sphere could not function easily without the press. In April 1865, the government finally promulgated permanent censorship laws. The statute itself was an amalgam of two contradictory principles, both Western in origin. The new laws abolished prior censorship that had been largely rendered unworkable by high-speed presses and the new political situation, but retained penalties for undermining respect for the state, the family, and religion. How were these to be enforced? The statute provided for settling the main issues in the new courts, which meant that the state would have to bring a case to a trial open to the public. The attempts to control critical journalists by this method were a failure and soon abandoned, for the courts either found the defendants innocent or if guilty, imposed largely symbolic punishments. The state had recourse to other methods, however, for the statute had taken censorship from the Ministry of Education and placed it under the Ministry of the Interior, the principal body in charge of preserving public order. The statute had also borrowed from French legislation a whole series of administrative measures including fines and warnings to editors that allowed the authorities to bypass the court system. After the initial failures in the court, these administrative sanctions triumphed, including eventually the prohibition of specific works of radical literature. The new censorship rules suppressed much public debate, but were never intended to eliminate it entirely.

Perhaps the most complicated reform issue after the emancipation of the serfs was that of the army. Minister of War Dmitrii Miliutin made his first proposal in 1862, and though it was approved by the tsar, it took until 1874 to be fully implemented. The core of the proposal was the replacement of the twenty-five-year service of the soldiers with a reserve system based on a limited term that was ultimately determined at six years. The conservatives wanted to keep the army a caste, in which peasants were made into soldiers commanded by nobles, while Miliutin saw such an army as reactionary and slated to repeat the defeats of Crimea. He saw no reason why free peasants could not serve and then return to their villages to resume farming. It was his powerful will, and the tsar's determination to maintain an effective army, that kept the military reform on track through many political vicissitudes.

Vicissitudes there were. Almost immediately with the appearance of public discussion of reform in 1858–59 the debate went beyond the parameters of government-sponsored liberal reform and conservative resistance. Both liberals outside the bureaucracy and young radicals began to present ideas that went far beyond what the ministers pondered behind the closed doors of government committees. Much of the reason for the challenge lay in the transformation of educated society, the formation of an intelligentsia defined by education and profession – often of plebeian origin and unconnected to the nobility. The core of the intelligentsia were the professionals – teachers, doctors, scientists, and engineers – but the term came to include anyone with some sort of education beyond the basic level, and of course it included students. Young men and (for the first time) women, mostly in and around the universities rejected not only state leadership but were also part of a new culture, for this was the generation that abandoned the interest in German idealist philosophy that had inspired Herzen and Bakunin as well as many liberals, and turned instead to the natural sciences. Turgenev's 1862 novel *Fathers and Sons* gave the term "nihilists" to this new generation for their rejection of the pieties of the past. The accusation was that they believed in nothing (in Latin "nihil"). Ferment began among the university students who had been granted a great deal of freedom in the post-Crimean era. In the autumn of 1861 a number of rather minor disturbances at St. Petersburg University led the authorities to close the university and begin to look for radical activity there and at other universities and academies. Small groups of radicals, no more than a few dozen individuals, also began to spread revolutionary manifestoes, convincing the government that vast plots were afoot. In most Russian university cities communes of students with more or less radical ideas came into existence in these years, partly for purely economic reasons but also from conviction that a simple communal life was the path to the future. The students knew about Herzen and read widely in Western liberal and radical literature, but their hero was Nikolai Chernyshevsky, whose ideas continued to inspire radicals long after he was lost to Siberian exile.

From the time of his emergence as a leading journalist in 1853, in the pages of the *Contemporary*, still one of the leading journals, Chernyshevsky had become the dominant intellectual and cultural figure of the radical intelligentsia and remained so for nearly a generation. The son of a priest and the graduate of a seminary rather than a secular high school, Chernyshevsky managed to enter St. Petersburg University, and ultimately acquired a master's degree in literature. In the pages of the *Contemporary*, however, his writing covered far more than literature. He wrote on philosophy, economics, and politics when he could, especially West European politics, on which it was easier to publish than on Russian politics. He also devoted a great deal of space to the peasant question, the economic, administrative, and social issues involved in the emancipation. Contrary to the views of liberal economists in the government and in educated society, Chernyshevsky advocated the preservation of the Russian peasant community with its communal landownership and agriculture and village-level decision making. Chernyshevsky, in this respect close to Herzen, believed that Russia could construct a kind of agrarian socialism built around the village community and thus avoid the horrors of industrialization familiar from Victorian England and continental societies. Chernyshevsky was also a revolutionary, though he never created an actual revolutionary organization, but he did look forward to the overthrow of the tsarist regime and sympathized with those who tried to take an active role in the process.

Chernyshevsky's most powerful contributions to the emerging revolutionary movement were his articles in the *Contemporary*. The radicals around the journal were convinced that the natural sciences were the key to all knowledge, that the social sciences were simply a backward area that would soon catch up to biology and chemistry. Their view of man was ruthlessly biological: there were no spiritual entities, and indeed their objection to religion seems to have been founded more on disbelief in the soul than in God. Chernyshevsky and his colleagues also held an essentially utilitarian view of art, the task of which was to transform the consciousness of the readers with its arguments and its presentation of the images of reality as it actually was. By 1862 the government had become aware that he was the most important figure among the radicals, and decided to put an end to his activity. The Third Section had him arrested on suspicion of relations with Herzen and of agitating to arouse the people against the government, but they could find very little against him. Relations with Herzen could not be proven and Chernyshevsky's articles were not in themselves criminal. After some months they found a police agent among the radicals, already arrested on another charge, who claimed to have letters from Chernyshevsky's hand and a manifesto calling on the peasants to rise. Using these documents as evidence, the Third Section brought up a new charge, and Chernyshevsky was convicted of trying to inspire rebellion. The sentence was fourteen years labor in the mines (a sentence that was later commuted) and perpetual exile in Siberia. Chernyshevsky was allowed to leave Siberia only in 1883, six years before his death.

The most complete expression of the values of the new generation came in Chernyshevsky's novel, *What is to be Done?*, written in the prison of the fortress of St. Peter and Paul after his arrest in 1862. The novel managed to be published legally through an error of the censor, even though it presented a case for the complete reorganization of society and a plan of the future. The idea was to construct a series of communal production workshops and living arrangements that would liberate the individual from the constraints of poverty and the traditional family. Chernyshevsky's novel was as much a feminist as a socialist tract. The emancipation of women, even from the upper classes, was a central part of his platform, for Chernyshevsky saw himself as the advocate of individual liberation to a society of "rational egoism" as much as the advocate of peasant and worker emancipation. The book became the Bible of a whole generation and its characters, the devoted revolutionary, the emancipated husband, the new woman – all these provided the youth of the time not only with ideals but also specific models of behavior, which many followed to the letter. Long hair for men and short for women, contempt for upper class manners and dress to the point of rudeness and general sloppiness became the fashion among students and gave the tone to a whole generation. Chernyshevsky's arrest and exile deprived the radicals of a public voice, and also led to the emergence of a whole underground and émigré literature that circulated among students and youth throughout the empire.

The radicals would soon capture the center stage of Russian life and culture and even provoke a series of "anti-nihilist" novels designed to demonstrate their limitations and errors. The post-Crimean decade, however, was also the period of formation of Russian liberalism, which had much greater support than the radicals among the intelligentsia: the professors, doctors, and teachers who made up its core. The liberal generation was also deeply affected by the new scientism of the era, which seemed to find a European model in Darwin, Herbert Spencer, and French positivism. The first and primary leader of the liberals, however, remained true to the older Hegelianism of his youth, albeit in the liberal rather than radical interpretation. This was Boris Chicherin, a professor of law whose conception of Russian history neatly fit his political ideas and legal training. His idea was simply that early Russian history to Peter the Great, had been the history of the development of statehood. Autocracy was a primitive survival from the later phases of this era, necessary in its time but now becoming outdated. Peter's reign had signaled the beginning of the development of legality within the autocratic structure, a development that was reaching its maturity in his own times with the great reforms. The task of the reform generation was to move this process forward, so that the further development of society would raise Russia to the level of civilization suitable for a constitution. The constitution was for the future, the task of the present was to move along the process of reforming the state, not to blow it up.

Chicherin's ideas or some variant of them were easy to fit with the general fascination with progress in nineteenth-century Europe, and the liberals felt they were part of a worldwide process that sooner or later would triumph in Russia too. These ideas were the inspiration of the zemstvo activists, as well as the journalists and writers who gathered around the new newspapers and the more intellectual "thick journals." The latter were ideally suited for the age, as the censorship was much more interested in daily newspapers and popular literature than the thick journals. Long learned discussions of local government in England or economic problems of the Russian countryside were much easier to get through censorship (thus Karl Marx's *Capital* was legally published in Russia). The most popular of the thick journals was the *Messenger of Europe* (*Vestnik Evropy*), founded in 1866. Every month its subscribers received three or four hundred pages of high-level journalism and even scholarly articles on current topics, novels, and verse that included the future classics of Russian literature and usually a novel translated from some Western language. The journal was full of useful information, long articles in which the authors discussed not only the alleged subject at hand but also many excursions into various types of useful knowledge – scientific, social, economic, even medical. In the drawing rooms of the provincial gentry and the libraries of gymnasium teachers throughout the Empire, journals of this sort were a lifeline, a connecting link with the larger world in Russia and beyond, and an inspiration for dogged persistence in zemstvo work and other humble attempts to make a modern society of Russia.

Conservative thought, as well, radically changed after Crimea. Unlike the liberals – numerous and in general agreement with one another – the conservatives remained a series of small mutually hostile groups alongside several idiosyncratic thinkers who lacked a following. The most important group was still the Slavophiles, who found a constituency among the bankers and textile millionaires of Moscow. The millionaires subsidized their journals and allowed them to keep their ideas before the public even if their circulation never reached the same volume as the liberal publications. The Slavophiles were generally supportive of the reform process, but they thought that too much of it was the result of mechanical adoption of Western models. Nationalism was increasingly the dominant feature of Slavophile ideology. They also feared farther moves in certain areas, especially any liberal (government or outside) measures that might weaken the peasant community, for them the basis of Russia's unique harmony in a world of political and social strife. Their general support of the autocracy and its policy was by no means uncritical, and earned them considerable official suspicion and hostility.

A more powerful advocate of conservative ideas was Mikhail Katkov, who until the Polish revolt was a liberal spokesman. In the wake of the revolt Katkov and his *Moscow News* (*Moskovskie Vedomosti*), subsidized by the Russian government in spite of occasional clashes, became the principal public voice of Russian nationalism and the idea of autocracy. Katkov advocated a sort of "westernizing" conservatism, one where Russian would acquire an industrial social order but retain the authoritarian form of government of the past, modernized by modern administrative methods. In many ways Katkov admired Bismarck's Germany and hoped that Russia would imitate it, not least in its strident nationalism. Katkov's nationalism was nastier than the vague "nationality" principle of Uvarov and Nicholas I. Katkov was relentlessly anti-Polish and anti-Semitic, and for all of his admiration of Germany, he was relentlessly hostile to the Baltic German aristocracy still so prominent in Russia's government and army, as well as at court. He also favored an aggressive foreign policy and came to advocate a strongly anti-German policy. The government was not always happy with Katkov (the Baltic German issue was a constant irritant) as it did not admit the propriety of even friendly criticism, but it could not do without him. For the conservative gentry and officialdom, Katkov was an oracle. None of the other conservative voices, even Dostoevsky's, had his following.

The conservatives and the government were most of all afraid of the revolutionary movement, which they correctly perceived as a political, social, and cultural threat. Indeed the communes of radical students inspired by Chernyshevsky's novel were very far from the privileged world of the court or the liberal journalists and their readers. The students operated by strict equality, including that of men and women. Their communes were broader than the revolutionary movement, including many members with only vague political views, but they formed an ideal recruiting ground. The expansion of the universities meant that many of the students were much more plebeian than their predecessors – the children of priests, minor officials, and noblemen whose incomes, to say the least, did not match their status. After 1859 women gradually entered universities, and their presence, entirely in accord with radical ideology, led to a major role for women in the revolutionary movement and gave it a distinctive style.

The young revolutionaries operated entirely underground. The reform of Russian society had not led to the appearance of legal public politics, for the state retained all power in its hands and political parties were not permitted. Not only liberals and radicals, but even conservatives were prevented from forming any sort of political associations, even in support of the state. Among the principal victims of the censorship was the Slavophile leader Ivan Aksakov, who supported the autocracy and was highly conservative and openly anti-Semitic. Aksakov nevertheless believed that he should have the right to criticize the autocracy in the press. The government saw things differently, and Aksakov's publications eventually came to an end. The liberals enjoyed broad support among the intelligentsia, especially its core of professionals, and controlled a number of key newspapers and periodicals, but they had no organization. The closest to a liberal (or conservative) forum was the zemstvo, whose meetings sometimes took on a political air, but the police and administration made sure that these attempts came to nothing. The only political actors outside the government were the revolutionaries.

In the early years, the 1860s, the main radical groups were small, only a few dozen members at the most, and were short-lived. They were also conspiratorial and dominated by a few charismatic leaders, some of them young men of very questionable character and motives, the most famous being Sergei Nechaev. Nechaev convinced his followers that he represented a revolutionary "central committee" under whose orders he worked. In fact it existed only in his imagination. In late 1869 he told his small group that one of their number was an informer for the police and that they should murder him, which they did. The result was that the police, while investigating the murder, uncovered the organization. Nechaev fled abroad, leaving his followers to their fate – exile in Siberia. Even the anarchist Bakunin, who at first thought that Nechaev represented some sort of new wave in Russia, finally realized that he was mentally unbalanced and morally depraved.

The few small groups like Nechaev's were doomed to failure, but events also kept the incipient radical movement from taking off in the first decade of its existence. The occasion was the attempt to assassinate the tsar on April 4, 1866. The would-be assassin was one Dmitrii Karakozov, a minor nobleman from the Volga region who had been involved in various radical groups, mostly composed of students, for several years. His comrades, who were more serious personalities than the like of Nechaev, actually opposed the idea and tried hard to dissuade him. They failed, and Karakozov shot at Tsar Alexander as he was leaving the Summer Garden but he missed. He was immediately captured and the tsar spoke to him, asking him if he was a Pole. Karakozov replied that he was pure Russian, and the police now knew that they were dealing with terrorism, a new phenomenon in the Russian revolutionary movement. Karakozov believed that killing the tsar would inspire a popular revolt, or at worst weaken the government and thus force further reform. The opposite happened, for it produced a government shakeup and the appointment of several less liberal ministers and the reactionary count Petr Shuvalov to head the Third Section. The pace of reform notably slowed.

By 1870 enough experience had accumulated among the radicals to suggest that the conspiratorial methods were unsavory and ineffective. The issue in any case was to spread radical ideas among the people, primarily among the peasantry. The result was the formation of new organizations whose members decided that the young radicals should "go to the people." Thus in 1874 thousands of young men and women began to learn practical skills and move to rural areas to try to fit into peasant society. Concrete political goals were placed far in the future, and the radicals concentrated on spreading their ideas. The effort lasted for several years, and was a complete failure. The peasants were at best unreceptive, suspicious of outsiders, especially from higher social levels (no matter how plebeian the students were, they were still not peasants). Many of them turned the radicals (or "populists") over to the police.

By the summer of 1876 it was clear that going to the people had failed and the remains of the group in St. Petersburg created a formal organization called *Zemlia i Volia* ("Land and Freedom"). The authorities noticed the actions of the new group and arrested many of them, holding mass public trials in 1877 that featured the veterans of "going to the people" as well as newer detainees. The trials were a disaster for the government as prisoner after prisoner presented impassioned and well-reasoned explanations for the misery of Russia's people and their plans for the future. The government struggled against the movement with inadequate forces and antiquated methods, but it could not break its spirit. The conditions and practices of the Russian prisons were primitive and caused much suffering, something widely known in society as well as in revolutionary circles, and it gave the rebels a halo of martyrdom. Then in early 1878 one of the prisoners in St. Petersburg was ordered to be flogged by general Trepov, the governor-general. A few weeks later a young woman walked into his office during the period reserved for petitioners, and in revenge shot him several times with a revolver. The general survived his wounds, but the young woman, Vera Zasulich, became the object of yet another public trial. The jury failed to convict her, and she escaped abroad. From then on the government avoided the civilian court system and tried revolutionaries in military field courts.

Zasulich's act inaugurated three-and-a-half years of a fantastic duel between the revolutionaries and the police. Most of the populists were now convinced that the social revolution could not occur without the destruction of the Russian autocracy. Unless Russia became a federal and democratic republic, the radicals would never have the freedom of action to preach social renewal. Therefore they shifted their effort from preaching radical social ideas to propaganda for political revolution, and most important, for a program of terror against the state. They did not target random populations: the objects of terror were only the officials of the state, and among those, mainly the ones responsible for political control and repression, that is policemen, governors of provinces, the Minister of the

Interior, and the tsar himself. The terror campaign produced a split in the movement, with the majority in favor of terror forming a new organization, *Narodnaia Volia* ("People's Will") and the minority, which wanted to stick to the old policy of agitation and propaganda, keeping the old name, Land and Freedom. Most of the latter soon emigrated. The People's Will then began a coordinated campaign of terror that came increasingly to focus on the tsar himself. Alexander responded slowly to the campaign, believing that his fate was in God's hands and in any case the traditions of the court made strict security very difficult. As before, the tsar frequently rode about St. Petersburg with only a squad of Cossacks and resisted any greater measures for his protection. His attention was focused on government and his private life, for the death of the empress in 1880 allowed him to finally marry his longtime mistress, Princess Ekaterina Dolgorukaia, which legitimized their children. The attempts on his life continued and after several failures terror came even to the Winter Palace. Stepan Khalturin, one of the few revolutionaries actually of peasant origin, managed to disguise himself as a carpenter and get access to the palace, where he exploded a bomb early in 1880, killing many soldiers of the guards but missing the tsar. A small band of revolutionaries had caused a crisis in the state, too old-fashioned even after the reforms to operate effectively against the terrorists and too autocratic to command or even solicit universal support. This time, however, the government responded immediately. Alexander replaced the Third Section with a Department of Police under the Ministry of the Interior and established a Supreme Executive Commission under general Count Michael Loris-Melikov. Loris-Melikov, an Armenian who knew numerous European and Caucasian languages, had an excellent military record from the Caucasian wars, the Russo-Turkish War, and a recently successful administrative career. His plan was to fight the revolutionaries both by repression and a return to the reform process that had been stalled for nearly a decade. Thus liberal journalists dubbed his program "the dictatorship of the heart." Soon Loris-Melikov moved up to head the Ministry of the Interior, and began to circulate plans for greater reform. By February 1881, he had constructed a plan for a consultative legislature based on the zemstvos to be called together to provide support for the state and to show society that the government was truly committed to reform. Perhaps Russia would change, but fate determined otherwise.

Narodnaia Volia had paid no attention to Loris-Melikov and the rumors of reform. In any case the prospect of reform did not cheer them, for it might help the government survive and further economic reform might damage the peasant commune. *Narodnaia Volia*'s Executive Committee under Alexander Zheliabov and Sofia Perovskaia put all its resources into killing the tsar, and on March 1, 1881, they succeeded. As Alexander was returning to the Winter Palace along the Catherine Canal in Petersburg, one of the revolutionaries threw a bomb at his carriage. Several of his guards and a fourteen-year-old boy were killed, many were wounded, and the tsar got out of the carriage to see what had happened. A second terrorist in the crowd threw another bomb at him, fatally wounding the tsar and killing himself. Alexander was carried to the Winter Palace with his legs blown off and soon died. The last words of the tsar who had freed the peasants, and, however haltingly, transformed Russia were, "it is cold, it is cold . . . take me to the Palace . . . to die."

Now his son Alexander came to the throne as Alexander III, and after some initial discussion, any talk of reform or legislatures came to an end and Loris-Melikov lost his position. The assassins were publicly hanged. The educated classes were appalled that the revolutionaries had killed the tsar, while many of the peasants believed that it was a conspiracy of the nobles acting in revenge for the emancipation of the serfs. Another effect of the assassination was the first great wave of pogroms against the Jews in the Ukrainian provinces of southern Russia. It was a fitting beginning to more than a decade of conservative politics and attempts at counter-reform. Yet counter-reform ultimately achieved little. It was a tribute to the strength of the original reforms and their anchoring in law that most of them could not be undone. The zemstvos, for example, were continually harassed by the minions of the Ministry of the Interior, but they continued to exist and work. The new institutions had become part of the fabric of Russian society, whose increasing progress kept them alive. In spite of the use of censorship and forms of repression like administrative exile for liberals and radicals alike, the press flourished and expanded, providing a forum for the discussion of as much of the government's policies as it could get away with. Alexander III's autocracy could retard the development of Russian society, but could not stop it.

12

From Serfdom to Nascent Capitalism

The city of St. Petersburg exemplified the transformation of Russia in the decades after the emancipation of the serfs. As the nineteenth century progressed, it changed from an administrative capital of government buildings and aristocratic residences with a seaport into a major industrial center served by railroads as well as the ever-expanding port and the older canal system.

Though built as a seaport on the Baltic, the shape of the older St. Petersburg was created by the Winter Palace and the ring of military and government buildings around it. Most of these were classical in style, and three or four-stories high at most. Peter had wanted to concentrate the actual government on the north side of the Neva River, on Vasil'ev Island, but the site was too remote in the absence of permanent bridges, and in any case the government needed to be near the center of power, the tsar. Thus the Winter Palace, on the south side of the river and near the western end of Nevskii Prospekt, the main street, quickly became the center of the city. The General Staff of the army and the Ministry of Foreign Affairs were right across the Palace Square, the Ministry of Finance nearby, as well as the Senate, the Council of State, and other major offices. Only the expanded Ministry of the Interior came to occupy new buildings on the Fontanka River farther to the south. Trade and commerce, until mid-century, were concentrated along Nevskii Prospekt and on Vasil'ev Island, the latter home to the city's large German and foreign merchant population.

The transformation of the city began to speed up after the Crimean War, as railroad building and new industries began to change the landscape. In these years St. Petersburg's port was a great asset, for much of the equipment and raw materials for the new industries came from abroad. The great industrial boom of the 1890s changed all that, as Russia began to rely more on internal resources. Metallurgy and machine building became the city's biggest industries. Located primarily on the outskirts, the huge factories with smoking chimneys replaced the suburban villas, forests, and villages of former times. The port turned into a giant shipbuilding yard. Factories with newer technology, such as the electric industries, were built in the center of the town, so that the city never acquired the radical social segregation characteristic of Western cities at the time. The industrial boom also brought a tremendous expansion in banking and finance, centered still on Nevskii Prospekt and the adjoining streets.

The economic boom changed the city in other ways. The population doubled between the 1890s and 1914, from about a million to around two million. Most of these new residents were workmen, living in barracks near the main factories, often without their families who remained back in their native villages. At the other end of the social scale, the newly rich bankers and railroad kings bought or built grand mansions on the river near the center of town. Many of the great aristocrats were heavily invested in the new industries, and their increased wealth showed itself in ever more luxurious residences in and around the city. The boom also brought a new middle class into being, employees of the new businesses, engineers and technicians, and the many schoolteachers, doctors, and retailers who served them. The burgeoning population and its needs brought a boom in construction, especially along the central streets and on the northern edge of the city. The new buildings displayed the architectural fads of the time, neo-Renaissance, neo-Baroque, and often the Russian versions of art nouveau. The strictly classical St. Petersburg was becoming a much more eclectic city, but the classical core remained. Builders were not allowed to build higher than the Winter Palace, so there were limits to the scope of change. The result was also a city very much less densely built up than Paris or Berlin, even if much of it lacked formal public parks.

Daily life changed, especially after 1900. New department stores
sprang up around the city, one off Nevskii Prospekt even built as
an investment by the Imperial Corps of Guards Regiments. Farther
down the street were the new Singer Sewing Machine building and
the Eliseev Delicatessen, with its imported and domestic stocks for
the wealthy gourmet. The city sponsored or built telephone service,
and new sewer and water systems were financed through loans from
foreign banks. In 1907 Westinghouse and Russian investors opened
the city's first electric tram lines, which quickly came to cover most
of the city. Electric lights lit up the main streets in the center and
more and more gas lights in other parts of town illuminated the
winter dark and fog. New bridges across the Neva contributed to
the charm of the city's waterfront but also made communication
among its various parts easy for the first time.

The social life of the city was centered on the court. Until the
1890s the court balls and other grand events provided a glittering
backdrop to the dramas of life and politics in the capital. The great
aristocratic houses were not far behind. They too put on magnificent
entertainments, some of them in private theaters in their palaces, like
the one in the Yusupov palace, with professional artists. The great
imperial theaters, especially the Mariinskii, were another venue for
the display of wealth by the old aristocracy and the newly rich as
well. For the intelligentsia and the middle classes, the legitimate
stage, state financed and private, provided the more "advanced"
culture they craved. On the edges of the city where the working
people lived were popular theaters, many of them outdoors in the
summer, which provided cheap entertainment for the masses. A
whole range of restaurants, from the elite establishments off Nevskii
Prospekt to the lowest dives on the edge of town, filled the various
needs of a variegated population. St. Petersburg was very much
the artistic center of Russia. The imperial ballet at the Mariinskii
Theater was the darling of the aristocracy, but the opera and stage
flourished as well. Most of the new trends in Russian painting, from
World of Art to suprematism, came into being in St. Petersburg, and
the major writers from the 1890s onward were almost all based in
the city.

For all its artistic glory, St. Petersburg remained quintessentially
a center of political power. After 1905 the main newspapers of the

legal political parties were published in St. Petersburg, reporting on the government as well as the new Duma. The Duma occupied the old palace of Catherine's favorite Potemkin, to the east of the main center of power. Politics remained the principal concern of the tsar, and his presence in the city was essential to the functioning of the state. In actual fact Nicholas II spent relatively little time in the city itself, preferring a quieter life at nearby Tsarskoe Selo or Peterhof, or even his Crimean estates. He rarely attended the theater, restricting his social events to court balls and a few other crucial ceremonies, a practice that did not win the approval of the aristocracy. The tsar and his advisors were nervous about public appearances in the face of the persistent terror campaign waged by the populist revolutionaries, and Nicholas personally preferred a simple life with his family. These were understandable decisions, but they contributed to the drift and instability of power at a time of rapid social and political change. The state had been central to Russian development for centuries, and suddenly the ship seemed to have no pilot.

In no area did the policies of the Russian state have more unintended consequences than in economic and social development. The reformers of the 1860s, as well as count Sergei Witte a generation later, tried to encourage industrial capitalism while conserving as much of the existing social structure as possible. The government sponsored railroad building throughout the period, both private and state projects, helping to secure loans from abroad and awarding lucrative contracts to Russian businessmen. It constructed the tariff system to favor railroad building and then later in the century moved to a more protectionist system to encourage Russian industry. The maintenance of the landed gentry and the peasant community remained a basic goal, however, even at the expense of industrial development. The maintenance of the peasant community restricted the movement of peasants out of the village to join the industrial labor force, but it could not prevent it. The survival of gentry landholding, under siege from the new economic forces, was also a government goal. Even Prime Minister Stolypin's attempt to loosen up the village community after 1907 was a gradualist program designed to strengthen the gentry, not undermine it.

Ultimately, however, the state could only influence, not direct, the evolution of Russian society. Factories sprung up, banks and other financial and commercial institutions grew, even when government rules hindered them. State-sponsored development programs like railroad building created whole new towns and new industries that the increasingly archaic state administration could not direct in the ways that policy demanded. Modern cities with newspapers and tram lines, restaurants and amateur cultural institutions created forms of life unknown in the older Russia but essentially the same as those in Western Europe and America. Whatever the government did, Russia was becoming modern, slowly but relentlessly.

The driving force in the changes to Russian society was industrialization. At the end of the Crimean War Russia was not without industry, for the textile industry in Central Russia – in Moscow and surrounding towns – was flourishing and working with mostly modern equipment, steam-driven looms, and other machinery. At the head of that industry were a whole series of native businessmen, mostly of peasant origin and many of them Old Believers in religion. Some families from the Old Believer communities, including the Morozovs, Riabushinskiis, and Guchkovs, built factories in Moscow and other towns in the surrounding areas. Their faithful adherence to the inward-looking and occasionally xenophobic variants of Old Belief did not prevent them from buying English and German machinery and hiring foreigners to run it and teach their workmen. The founders of all these great business dynasties had moved from the peasantry or small-scale trading to owning factories and even banks by the 1840s, and they set their children – sons and daughters alike – to master foreign languages and learn about the modern world, including its new technology. If the Old Believers were perhaps the richest of the Moscow industrialists and bankers, Orthodox businessmen flourished as well, such as the Tretyakovs, who rose from the ranks of provincial shopkeepers to own textile factories in Moscow, Kostroma, and elsewhere. In Petersburg the businessmen were more cosmopolitan, for alongside Russians (mostly Orthodox) were Germans, Englishmen, Swedes like the Nobel family, and the Jewish banker Baron Horace Ginzburg. Businessmen in St. Petersburg concentrated less on textiles and more on metallurgy and new technology as well as finance and a flourishing import-export trade. Other centers quickly emerged in the south, the Baltic provinces, and Poland. In Poland most of the bankers and manufacturers were German or Jewish, while in southern Russia the Jewish Poliakov brothers, railroad kings and eventually bankers, made deals with Russian and Polish noblemen in the sugar beet business. In the south the Welshman John Hughes founded Iuzovka, the first major metallurgical center in the Don River Basin, the coal and iron area that came to be known as the Donbass. Today it is Donetsk in the Ukraine.

In the first years after emancipation, however, the textile industry was by far the most successful. The Moscow textile manufacturers were a colorful group, with Old Believers and Orthodox rubbing shoulders with noblemen-turned entrepreneurs. Many of them ran their factories with marked paternalism, building cheap housing, places for entertainment, and schools. Timofei Morozov was one of these, an Old Believer who ran his business largely on his own and with an iron hand. His factory was noted for the high quality of its products, made with English machinery and (until the end of the century) imported cotton. He also provided medical facilities and various forms of welfare for his workers, as well as the usual housing and entertainment. He struggled tirelessly with working class drinking habits, both from religious conviction and the realization that drunk or hung over workers could not perform high quality work for him. Morozov remained very much in the old world, for his cultural patronage went to the history and the culture of Russia before Peter. He also had many connections among the Slavophiles, whose publications were heavily subsidized by the Moscow businessmen. None of this did him any good when the market for textiles contracted suddenly early in the 1880s: he responded by cutting wages and demanding more from his workers. They responded with riot and destruction in January 1885 – one of the first major strikes in Russian history. The age of paternalism was passing, though his son Savva tried to keep it going for another twenty years. Eventually management of the firm, like so many others, passed to engineers and the middle level of management, replacing the personal style of the older businessmen.

Important as the textile industry was, it relied on imported equipment and did not solve the overall problem of Russian economic development. The results of the Crimean War made it abundantly clear to the government that something had to be done. As the state moved toward emancipation of the peasantry, it simultaneously moved to encourage a massive program of railroad building. Railroads were the crucial infrastructure of the nineteenth century, providing the freight services essential to industrialization. In a country with Russia's vast distances and natural resources spread over thousands of miles, they were even more necessary. Without railroads Russia could not enter the modern age. The center of the efforts to build railroads was the Ministry of Finance, especially in the tenure of Mikhail Reutern (1862–1877), a Baltic German nobleman who had worked under Grand Duke Konstantin Nikolaevich. Reutern had a difficult problem, for the Crimean War had left the treasury depleted, and the emancipation settlement demanded even more expenditures. Though a principled supporter of private industry, he realized that Russia lacked capital. Reutern and most of the progressives in the government were convinced that railroads were vital, and that they could be built by private initiative, given an adequate supply of capital. Reutern's predecessors had turned to the French Credit Mobilier bank, which formed a large company to build Russian railroads. This attempt proved an expensive failure, and only after 1866 did the real boom begin, this time with Russian financing at the center of the operations. The Russian treasury continued to provide guarantees and sometimes direct subsidies often kept secret from the public, but most of the initiative and capital was private.

The private investors not surprisingly came from the ranks of businessmen with good government contacts and often from the ranks of government officials. Some, like P. G. von Derviz and K. F. von Meck, were Russian-German officials who left government service to build railroads. Others had gotten their starts in farming the state vodka monopoly. The vodka monopoly had produced huge fortunes, and provided much of the private capital for investment, as well as the crucial government contacts.

The great "railroad king" of the era, Samuel Poliakov, had started out working in the vodka monopoly around his native town of Orsha in the Jewish Pale of Settlement. He came into contact through that activity with Count I. M. Tolstoi, briefly the Minister of the Post and the Telegraph. Poliakov quickly abandoned the vodka business to become a construction contractor, working on a variety of railroad projects with the patronage of Tolstoi. By the 1870s he was famous throughout Russia for the speed and efficiency (if not always the quality) of his work, landing lucrative contracts with the army during the Russo-Turkish War. The Jewish Poliakov had plenty of Christian rivals as well as business partners, and the partners were Moscow textile manufacturers and bankers and a variety of aristocratic grandees. Railroad building necessarily involved collaboration between business and government, and thus every railroad builder had his patrons and paid agents throughout the administration. As in other countries engaged in rapid railroad construction (France and the United States, for example) the age's greatest technical marvel was also the most powerful engine of corruption. To complicate matters, foreign capital remained crucial, and the treasury stepped in with guarantees to reassure the French, German, and Belgian investors. Though the state guaranteed and regulated virtually all of the rail companies, until the 1890s most Russian railroads remained in private hands.

Railroads required great amounts of iron, steel, and coal, and Russia had plenty of iron ore and coal, but few facilities to process them. The Urals iron industry was old-fashioned – technically backward – and just too small to supply Russian needs. The government thus adopted a tariff policy that allowed the importation of rails, rolling stock, and industrial materials like scrap metal at low tariffs. It encouraged Russian metal working plants, like the Putilov factory in St. Petersburg, to produce rails and other equipment with imported scrap metal and pig iron. By the 1890s Russia was moving toward an industrial society.

Engineering was an important part of that development. Russia, however, lacked modern engineering schools. The only institution of that sort was the Mining Institute that dated from the time of Catherine the Great. Such schools stood under the jurisdiction of the Ministry of Finance, the principal state agency behind economic development from the Crimean War onward, and it quickly moved to encourage engineering education. The St. Petersburg Technological Institute, founded in 1828 as a trade school and named for tsar Nicholas I, reorganized itself in the 1860s under rector Ilya Tchaikovskii (the composer's father) into a thoroughly modern engineering school. It was joined by similar schools in Riga (1862) and Khar'kov (1885). Older trade schools in Moscow were reorganized on the St. Petersburg model. The end of the century saw another new wave of foundations. The Warsaw and Kiev Polytechnical Institutes came in 1898, followed by another school in Siberian Tomsk in 1900. In St. Petersburg the Technological Institute had concentrated on mechanical and chemical engineering and did not address many emerging engineering specialties that had come to play increasing roles in the industrial age. The young Abram Ioffe, the future builder of Soviet physics, found its physics department small and antiquated. In 1899 the minister of finance Sergei Witte and the now world famous chemist Dmitrii Mendeleev organized yet another new institution, the St. Petersburg Polytechnic Institute. Here the students could specialize in electronics, shipbuilding, metallurgy, physics, or even economics. Ioffe, after more training in Germany, moved to the new institute, a move fraught with major significance in later years. Russia was beginning to train more and more engineers alongside the foreigners heretofore so prominent in building Russia's railroads, bridges, and factories.

Russian agriculture did not keep pace with industrialization. The Emancipation Statute burdened the peasantry with redemption payments, but also conserved the village structure that had existed under serfdom. The now free peasants did not own their land, which remained the property of the community. To leave the village, the peasant had to have the permission of that community, which in practice meant the village elders. The village was responsible for the redemption payments and taxes, not the individual peasant. Better-off peasants could and did own or rent land outside the village allotments, but the great mass of the peasantry survived on the village land alone, still occasionally redistributed as families grew or died out.

Russian peasant farms were much less productive than European and even less than American. Chemical fertilizer was unknown, natural fertilizer was inadequate, and machinery was a rarity confined to gentry estates. The peasantry was too poor and too burdened with the redemption payments and rent to accumulate the resources that would be necessary to modernize their farms, and

Figure 11. Russian Peasant Girls around 1900.

the nobility, except for the great aristocracy, also was unable to move beyond the traditional routine. Only in a few favored areas, like the Ukraine and the south, did the presence of commercial crops like sugar beets and nearby export ports for grain allow more modern agriculture to develop. There machinery appeared on a few great estates together with more modern methods of crop rotation. In most of Russia the village community encouraged the maintenance of routine agriculture, and most of the crops stayed in the village to feed the peasants. Still the growing towns and railroad network provided a much greater market than existed before. In central and northern Russia the peasants turned to dairy farming and more profitable grains like oats to supply the new and growing markets. The Transsiberian Railroad turned the Siberian peasantry toward massive exports of butter and other dairy products to

European Russia, and by 1914 the Siberian peasantry was so prosperous that American companies had opened dozens of stores in the region to sell agricultural machinery, something unimaginable west of the Urals. Market gardening spread around the big cities, and even remote regions eventually were pulled into the seemingly unlimited export market for grain. In these areas a thin layer of better-off peasants emerged with better ties to the market and slightly more modern practices, and were quickly dubbed *kulaks* (*kulak* meaning "fist") by their neighbors. The black earth regions of southern Russia, however, potentially the country's richest land, remained the domain of impoverished peasants working with ancient methods, consuming their own grain, and gazing longingly at the massive gentry estates that surrounded them.

Not surprisingly Russian villages, even the more prosperous ones, lived at a standard unknown for decades in Europe. Peasant houses were still small, usually one-room buildings without a chimney – the smoke went out a hole in the roof or the window – and the livestock shared the space in winter. Several generations shared the same house. Dirt, crowding, and simple ignorance were the basis of medieval levels of hygiene. Not surprisingly typhus, tuberculosis, dysentery, and in some areas even malaria flourished. In areas where many male peasants worked in the cities syphilis was endemic. Smallpox could not be eradicated because the number of trained vaccinators was tiny, and many peasants hid in the forest from the vaccinators, convinced that the vaccination was the mark of Antichrist. In the middle years of the nineteenth century child mortality was at forty percent, though it declined noticeably by 1914. Though homespun cloth increasingly gave way to industrially produced fabrics, clothing remained homemade and most peasants still wore the traditional shoes made of birch bark. Alcoholism and heavy drinking were the norm: on Sundays in many villages the township courts did not meet because the male population was too drunk for serious deliberations. Husbands routinely beat their wives. The traditional values, centering on religion and folk wisdom were unchallenged, and religion still meant only the Sunday liturgy, which was rarely supplemented by a brief homily from the priest. Little could change with the great majority of peasants being illiterate. Only around 1900 did the slow growth of rural education begin to have an effect, as the younger generation in the villages came to be literate in larger numbers. Small rural libraries came into existence, and soon acquired a noticeable readership. The zemstvos put scarce resources into health care as well as education, and by 1914 vaccination was beginning to make a modest dent in the high levels of disease and mortality.

The greatest change to peasant society was the enormous increase in migration out of the villages, both permanent and temporary. The factories of St. Petersburg and the Moscow region drew more and more workers, both men and women (many textile workers were women). The rapid expansion of the railroad and of the cities, large and small, meant a huge demand for construction workers and other seasonal laborers, and many areas of rural Russia by 1900 were virtual "women's kingdoms" for much of the year, as the men went north for the factories and construction and south to work on the great estates. Though grain production per capita rose slowly after 1861, it was not enough to prevent periodic famines, like the catastrophic events of 1891. Official encouragement of grain exports did not help. The peasantry remained poor and convinced that its poverty was the result of the unequal distribution of land. Though noble landholding fell slowly but relentlessly after emancipation, by 1913 roughly half of the land still remained in the hands of a few tens of thousands of noble families. The other half was the property – burdened by redemption payments – of some 120 million peasants.

THE LAST DECADES

The 1890s witnessed an economic boom that went far to transform Russian industry, if not the whole of Russia. For the first time heavy industry began to catch up to textiles and other light industries. The Donbass came into its own as a major coal and steel area, while St. Petersburg acquired more and more plants that serviced a modern economy. This was the great age of metal technology, not just in Russia but throughout the world, and the St. Petersburg metal working plants were able to produce most of the innumerable metal parts that made up railroad engines and bicycles, samovars, and wood stoves. Newer technologies were mainly represented by branches of European or American companies, like the

German Siemens-Halske electric plant that produced electric motors for the Russian market. The Nobel petroleum interests, producing kerosene from Baku oil, and the Nobel diesel engine factory in St. Petersburg, were other examples. In the traditional industries and banking, Russian entrepreneurs predominated, though the colorful pioneers of the 1860s were dying off and their replacements were more impersonal syndicates and trusts. Some of their sons continued in business, others became art patrons, and yet others gambled away their inheritance in Monte Carlo.

The boom of the 1890s was the product of the business cycle not government policy, but the Ministry of Finance under count Witte certainly helped it along. Witte was a commanding figure in the government, more far-sighted than his colleagues and energetic to a fault. He inherited a new protectionist tariff from his predecessor, and enforced it rigorously to the satisfaction of Russian businessmen. In 1897 he put Russia on the gold standard, a move that enormously strengthened its international economic position. At the same time Witte was not an advocate of unlimited free enterprise: in his tenure in office the government took over most of the private railroads, and indeed his greatest accomplishment was the state's construction of the Transsiberian railroad, already begun in 1891. Witte's contribution was to propose a comprehensive plan for the line, taking into account the whole region and the problems of supply and construction, with the result that the tsar quickly approved his plan. By 1905 it was largely complete, though with single track only on certain segments and one flaw that almost proved fatal: Witte ran the line through Manchuria rather than inside the Russian border and in doing so helped provoke Japan to attack in 1904.

In 1900 Russia experienced its first major recession after the industrial boom. Primarily a stock market crash and financial crisis, it affected the metal and coal complex more than any other, and the response of the industry (with government support) was to form syndicates and trusts to regulate production. The French investors who figured heavily in this sector of the Russian economy supported this syndication of the industry as well. Light industries, textiles, food and drink, and other consumer-oriented businesses were much less affected by the recession and continued to grow. The 1905

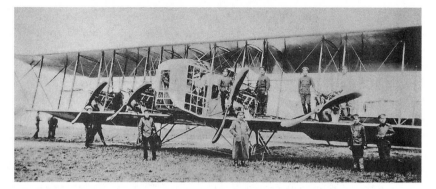

Figure 12. The *Ilya Muromets*, designed by Igor Sikorsky for the Russian air force in 1914, the first successful four-engine aircraft.

revolution naturally disrupted production as well as politics, but when the government reestablished its authority in 1907, economic prosperity returned, for the recession came to an end.

The last years before the outbreak of the First World War saw a return to prosperity, and the further modernization of Russian city life. Cities, including the small ones, now housed about fifteen percent of the population. Telephones, motorcars, electric trams, mass media, advertising, and even the beginnings of the cinema turned Russian cities into modern centers. Not just St. Petersburg, but also Moscow, Warsaw, Odessa, and Kiev became largely modern cities. Large apartment blocks arose in place of the older courtyard houses filled with trees that still predominated in smaller centers and the more traditional parts of Moscow. Luxurious and not so luxurious stores opened, with the latest fashions from Paris or Vienna. Restaurants, cafés, and hotels became major social centers, replacing the aristocratic clubs of the past. Automobiles appeared on the streets, and by 1914 there was intense public interest in air flight. Modern social organizations, like the Boy Scouts, took root in the major cities. St. Petersburg, Odessa, parts of Moscow, and some of the industrial cities differed only in degree from their European counterparts.

It was the Russian village, still largely unmodernized, if not unchanging, that made Russia backward by European, if not Asian, standards. After 1907 Prime Minister Stolypin pushed his famous plan to create independent farmers, on the model of European peasants, outside the village communities, and some peasants took advantage of the opportunity. Most of them, however, greeted the scheme with relentless hostility, and the numbers that did opt for independent farms were too small to have any substantial effect by the time that war broke out. A more promising change in rural life was the migration of the peasantry to Siberia and the Kazakh steppe of Central Asia. Here the peasants became more independent farmers on their own, without conflict with pre-existing village communities, though the native Kazakhs were not happy with the loss of some of their prime grazing lands. In Siberia the native population was much smaller and such conflicts were few, so that on the eve of the war, Siberia seemed to be coming into its own for the first time, not just as a place of mines and convict labor but as a land of rural settlement, growing industry, and booming towns. The Urals as well was growing rapidly, just beginning to overcome the legacy of the outdated local iron industry of the past. None of these regional shifts, however, were yet extensive enough to change the overall pattern of Russian society: a sea of backward agriculture dotted with larger or smaller islands of modern industry and society.

The large-scale economic changes of the decades between 1861 and 1914 had all sorts of unexpected or at least unplanned effects. The government stuck to the older system of classification by social estate – gentry, merchants, townspeople, and peasants – but social change rendered it increasingly irrelevant. Millions of peasants actually spent most of their lives as urban workers. Businessmen came from all sorts of backgrounds, not just urban families but noble and peasant families. The intelligentsia had representatives of virtually every social group, if townspeople and nobles (often only technically nobles) predominated. Economic development rearranged the ethnic pattern of the empire. St. Petersburg added a Jewish community to its many other ethnic groups, some 35,000 people (officially) in 1910, the largest community outside the Pale. Masses of peasants and townspeople poured into the new industrial cities in the Donbass – Russians, Ukrainians, Poles, Jews, and many others – producing a multi-ethnic but Russian-speaking area. The Baku oil fields brought thousands of Armenians and Georgians to the largest city in the Azeri provinces. The lives of women changed, if not to the same degree at all levels of society. For noblewomen, already with property rights greater than those typical of bourgeois Europe, life went on as before. Noblewomen either supported an aristocratic life and the government or military career of their husbands and fathers by an endless round of parties and social occasions, or they managed the estates for absent spouses. Many noblewomen, however, like their male counterparts, took advantage of the new educational opportunities that emerged in the reform era. For the men those opportunities were more places in universities or new sorts of institutions, like the engineering schools. For women the change was much more radical, because starting in 1858, the government began to radically expand the network of secondary schools for girls as part of the general expansion of education. By the 1880s there were already 50,000 girls in the new schools, and they continued to expand into the twentieth century. Even more radical was the appearance of university education for women. Earlier universities were closed to women, but in 1858–1863 there were experiments with opening them. Conservative fears, prompted in part by the nascent revolutionary movement's advocacy of women's liberation, led the government to shut the doors. Into the gap stepped the liberal intelligentsia, which started private university courses for young women in 1869. The lecturers were normally university professors who took on the extra duties, often for free, as part of a general commitment to the liberalization of society. The emancipation of women was a major cause to liberals as well as radicals, as both saw the patriarchal family as a mirror of the political autocracy that ruled the country. Finally in 1876 the government authorized "women's courses" that offered a university training but no degree, other than in certain professions such as teaching and midwifery, deemed suitable for women. Ever inconsistent, the government left open one loophole: foreign degrees were recognized in the Russian Empire, so a woman who received a degree in one of the few foreign institutions (mainly in Switzerland) that admitted women obtained a degree recognized officially in Russia. Ironically, the Russian women at Swiss universities found that there were no Swiss women in the universities, only Russians,

Poles, and some young women from Serbia and other Balkan countries.

The new educational opportunities attracted women from well beyond the nobility. The daughters of the intelligentsia, the clergy, and the middle classes joined them in the women's courses. The transformation of Russian urban society created new professions that women entered and even dominated. In addition to medical work and teaching at various levels in both town and country, office work on the soon-to-be ubiquitous typewriter created a whole new stratum of employed young women from the middle classes. The telephones of the time required manual connections and switchboards, and women found work here. These trends were particularly marked after about 1900 in the larger cities, and this meant that for the first time Russian women of the middle classes were working outside the home.

In the working classes, the proportion of women in the factories grew from about twenty percent in the 1880s to thirty percent on the eve of the war. Most of them worked in textile or other light industries. The rapid growth of the cities meant a huge demand for domestic labor in the form of cooks and maids, most of them inevitably women. Some of these women were already born in the cities, but like the men, most of them were migrants from the villages. In the villages the traditional family patterns persisted, and in areas where out-migration was not important, the lives of peasant women changed little over the course of time. In the cities women workers were more likely to be illiterate than men, were paid less than male counterparts, and endured the unwanted attentions of male supervisors and foremen. In the end, however, working class women had their revenge: it was the women in the bread lines in March 1917, who began the revolution that brought down the monarchy. Once their men joined, the Romanov dynasty came to an end.

Ultimately the most important social result of the increasing industrialization of Russia was the appearance of the factory working class. At the time of the emancipation there were a bit less than a million miners and factory workers, but by 1913 their number had grown to a bit over 3 million, with perhaps another half a million railroad and other transport workers. These 4 million formed the core of the working class, alongside many more seasonal workers in construction and agriculture and some 1.5 million domestic servants. In a country of some 180 million people these were a small minority, but they were strategically placed. They worked in industries that used increasingly modern equipment, and the elite of the working class, the skilled metal workers, performed tasks of considerable technical complexity, cutting precision parts following blueprints supplied by the engineers. For such skilled workers, some education was necessary, and for all the workers, a mental break with the village routine and adjustment to city life was essential.

City life was in itself a whole new world for young migrants from the countryside. Most of them male and living without families for years, they slept in barracks put up by the factory owners. The barracks were notorious, but the managers put them up precisely because they actually kept workers at the factory, since the fast pace of urbanization meant a permanent shortage of housing. Married workers and some single men who found places outside the barracks ended up renting "corners," parts of basements partitioned off by clotheslines. Sanitation was minimal, and the crowding in the poorer areas of St. Petersburg made it the tuberculosis capital of Europe. A city nevertheless afforded more than a village. Cheap theaters and musical halls provided entertainment, and in the summer were often outside. For those who wanted to better themselves, there were small popular libraries and reading rooms, and popular literature boomed – the first tabloid newspapers and cheap adventure stories appeared on the streets. Workers were increasingly literate. In 1897, 60 percent of male workers were literate, and 35 percent of women workers were literate, but in St. Petersburg the figures were 74 percent and 40 percent, respectively.[1] At the same time, the absence of mass education for workers beyond the most elementary meant

---

[1] In Russia as a whole, in the same year, only 29 percent of men and 13 percent of women were literate. In France, Germany, and northern Europe by the 1890s literacy was nearly universal for both men and women. The Russian figures were matched only in southern Italy, and even Spain was slightly ahead. By 1914 Russian literacy rates reached about 40 percent of the whole population, with great differences between women and men.

that many had little formal education but sharp intelligence and a thirst for knowledge.

While the work took them out of the village routine, it soon established another routine of its own. Ten and twelve hour days were normal, with only Sunday and a few hours on Saturday off. Pay was low, but the low skill level of most workers meant that Russian labor was expensive to the employer in spite of the low wages. Conditions were probably not radically worse than in the West, but labor unions and strikes were forbidden, so even the most elementary improvements were hard to come by. The 1885 strike at the Morozov textile works near Moscow brought new factory legislation, requiring managers to at least pay the workers on time. On the whole there was little government supervision of the workplace, and ironically the major result of the government's efforts was the Factory Inspectorate. It had little power to enforce proper conditions, but its voluminous reports and statistics left a treasure for historians.

Those historians would not have been much interested in the Factory Inspectorate's records had the Russian working class not become the recruiting ground and principal base of the revolutionary movement. The populists of the 1870s had already attempted to recruit workers, but their great hope was the peasantry, not the workers. The emergence of Marxism in the 1880s under the leadership of Georgii Plekhanov changed the focus. For Russia Marxism was an exotic import, a German ideology with entirely West European roots. In exile in the West, Plekhanov observed the growing strength of Marxist socialism in Germany and was deeply impressed. Armed with a new worldview, Plekhanov rejected the entire heritage of Chernyshevsky and populist ideology. The populists had believed that industrial capitalism in Russia was an artificial growth, the result of the economic policy of the autocracy. Once the autocracy was overthrown, they thought capitalism would disappear and the peasants would build socialism out of peasant communities and artisanal collectives. As a Marxist, Plekhanov believed that the growth of capitalism in Russia was inevitable. It might not grow swiftly, but it was growing and creating a working class – the proletariat, who, in Karl Marx's words was, "the class called to liberate humanity" and the class that would bring socialism. For the time being, however, Plekhanov and his tiny band of exiles remained in Switzerland translating Marx into Russian and smuggling pamphlets across the Russian border.

It was the industrial boom of the 1890s that gave the Marxists their chance, and from then on their influence and strength grew from year to year. Small Marxist groups appeared in the larger cities, led by young men and women from the intelligentsia like Vladimir Lenin and Iulii Martov, distributing leaflets and organizing reading groups to spread the new ideas. By 1898 they were able to form a party, the Russian Social Democratic Workers' Party. Alongside the Marxists the populist strain in the Russian revolutionary movement revived, producing a series of small groups committed to a peasant revolution but in practice recruiting among workers. They combined the older belief in the socialist potential of the village community with the Marxist notion that the workers would organize socialism in the industrial cities. Much of their activity went into terrorism (which the Marxists rejected), but ultimately the populists were able to form a party in 1901–02, the Party of the Socialists-Revolutionaries to rival the Marxist Social Democrats.

Thus the industrialization of Russia had brought forth new social classes, the businessmen who owned and ran the factories and the workers who toiled within them. It created new forms of urban life and new opportunities for women. Ultimately it also created the social forces that would blow Russian society apart.

13

The Golden Age of Russian Culture

The development of Russian society in the reform era profoundly affected Russian culture, both by changing the institutional environment of culture and by calling forth new intellectual and artistic impulses. For almost all spheres of thought and creation, the period was the first great age of Russian culture, and the first one to bring that culture an audience beyond its boundaries. By the 1880s Russia had become part of the world, not just as a major political power but as a major contributor to the arts and even to science.

SCIENCE IN THE AGE OF REFORM

Science had not flourished in the years of Nicholas I. While the universities did provide high-level instruction, the professors were often foreigners and facilities were small and inadequate. Lobachevskii's new geometry was the work of an isolated provincial professor whose calculations needed only his own genius and a pencil and paper. After the Crimean War, the government realized that the scientific level of the country needed to be raised, and the Ministry of Education provided for the expansion of science departments in the universities as part of a general upgrading of higher education. Equally or more important were the initiatives of the Ministry of Finance, especially its reorganization of the Technological Institute in St. Petersburg. A modern engineering school was crucial to the industrialization program, but the reformed curriculum had one unexpected result of worldwide significance. The young Dmitrii

Mendeleev set out to provide a new, up-to-date chemistry course, and in the process found the existing textbooks unsatisfactory. He started to create his own, and in the process of looking for a way to explain the relationships among the various elements in nature, realized that they fit a certain pattern. The idea of a regularity was not absolutely new, but Mendeleev went further: he saw that there were gaps in the pattern and in 1869 he predicted that new elements would be found to exist that filled in these gaps. Soon scientists abroad found his prediction to be correct, and Mendeleev became Russia's foremost scientist. His fame endured on the walls of science classrooms ever after in the form of charts of the periodic table of the elements that came from Mendeleev's discovery.

The very process of educational reform and the new role of the natural sciences in Russia had sparked a major discovery. Mendeleev went on to work extensively to promote not just chemistry but scientific education and Russian economic development, working closely with the government on these tasks. Another case of the intersection of social changes and science was the work of Vasilii Dokuchaev, the creator of modern soil science. Dokuchaev's insight was simply that soil could not be treated as just the top layer of rock mixed with decaying organic matter but as a distinct stratum of its own. Trained in geology and mineralogy, he came to this conclusion while working to survey the black earth districts of southern Russia for the Free Economic Society, a project explicitly designed to help Russian agriculture. The Ministry of Finance also helped sponsor other scientific and technological societies, in an effort to spark more public interest and channel it into directions that would contribute to industrialization.

In these years Russian science came into its own, not only because of the fame of Mendeleev but because dozens of lesser lights acquired solid if modest places in many new and old specialized fields of chemistry, physics, and biology. The other reason for the advances in science was its immense popularity with the intelligentsia of the reform era. For educated people the natural sciences seemed to be a model of rationality and progressive thought. They debated whether the experiments on the nervous system of frogs conducted by the physiologist Ivan Sechenov proved that the soul existed or not, a topic which Sechenov thought went way beyond the possible consequences of his modest work. Darwin was tremendously popular in Russia, though "social Darwinism" never caught on. Part of the popularity of Darwin came from the lack of interest on the part of the church in debating the details of biology or the biblical account of creation. Concerned about the spread of "materialism," the church nevertheless avoided direct polemics with scientists. In Russia, Darwin's works were approved by the Ministry of Education as soon as they appeared, even before Russian translations were available. The atmosphere of the time as well as government policy combined to rapidly raise the level of scientific activity in the country.

If government policy was crucial to the emergence of world-class natural sciences in Russia, its relationship to the arts was more complicated. For the writers, the relaxation of censorship was crucial, but an equally great change came from the end of court patronage and the rise of a market for books and journals. The painters also benefited from the new social environment, as the new millionaire businessmen became crucial patrons for the artists. Music was more complicated still, since the main opera and ballet theaters fell under the Ministry of the Court, while philharmonic societies and the conservatories worked with a combination of state and private funding and control.

The social and institutional environment of the arts was only one side of the story of Russia's Golden Age. Central to the period was also the attempt to grapple with Russia's history, its current politics and problems, and its place in the world of culture and ideas. Liberal intellectuals and later Soviet historians regularly portrayed almost all of the cultural figures of the era as either "democratic" or "critical," but this description fits only some of them. Tchaikovsky was an admirer of the autocracy, as was Dostoyevsky, and both of them had only amused contempt for liberal democracy. Perhaps the only internationally famous figure to fully fit the liberal model was Turgenev, but it is perhaps futile to explore the views of most of the great artists, as many of them were too idiosyncratic to classify. Tolstoy is perhaps the most striking example, and not only in his later Christian anarchist phase. What they all did was to create works that were permanent parts of Russian culture, and in the case of the writers and composers, of the whole of Western culture of the modern age.

MUSIC

The musicians had the weakest base to work from and yet produced in only a few decades an enormous amount of new music, much of it part of the international repertory to this day. Before the Crimean War Glinka had been virtually the only important composer, an amateur from the nobility who made his name with the help of the Wielhorski salon and Grand Duchess Elena Pavlovna. She was also to play a crucial role in taking Russia into the world of professional music education, for she was the patron of Anton Rubinstein. Rubinstein was the son of a Jewish businessman from the Ukraine who converted to Christianity and moved to Moscow in the 1830s. There his children's music teacher quickly noted Anton's immense talent at the piano and took the boy and his parents to Berlin, where he soon found fame as a child prodigy and acquired a solid musical education and the favor of Mendelson and Liszt. On the father's death young Anton had few resources and returned to St. Petersburg. There the Wielhorskis introduced him to Elena Pavlovna, and he became her personal pianist, an invented position designed to provide him with an income. By the late 1850s Rubinstein, now world famous, persuaded his patroness that Russia needed a real music school, and in 1861 the St. Petersburg Conservatory opened its doors, across the street from the Mariinskii Theater, where it still stands. Elena Pavlovna's support ensured state financing to the new institution. From the very beginning Rubinstein ruled it with an iron hand, demanding deep study and long hours, and during his tenure as director the Conservatory produced many prominent musicians. The most important would be Peter Tchaikovsky, one of Rubinstein's first students. Four years later, a similar conservatory came into existence in Moscow under the directorship of Anton's younger brother Nikolai, also a talented pianist and composer, though not in his brother's league. While Anton was in Berlin, Nikolai had stayed behind in Moscow, forming lifelong friendships with his neighbors, the future leaders of the Moscow industrialists, the Tretyakov brothers, and Nikolai Alekseev. The Moscow conservatory had no significant state financing and the businessmen had to periodically help it through crises, a new source of patronage for Russian art. The Moscow Conservatory was on a sound enough footing to hire Tchaikovsky as one of its professors (1867–1877) during the years of his maturation as a composer.

The Rubinstein brothers and Tchaikovsky constituted one of two musical circles active in Russia from the 1860s to the 1880s. The other major group, also centered in St. Petersburg, consisted of the five composers of the Balakirev circle: Milii Balakirev, Cesar Cui, Modest Mussorgsky, Nikolai Rimskii-Korsakov, and Alexander Borodin. These were a curious group – Balakirev was a gentleman amateur like Glinka, while Cui and Mussorgsky were military officers. Mussorgsky soon abandoned the army for music (but had to take positions in the civilian bureaucracy to support himself), while Cui continued in the army as a fortress engineer, rising to the rank of general before his death. Borodin was the illegitimate son of a Georgian prince and by profession a chemist, teaching at the Medical Academy and achieving some small discoveries in chemistry. Rimskii-Korsakov was a former naval officer and had even participated in the visit of the Russian fleet to New York in 1864, Tsar Alexander's gesture of support for the Union cause in the American Civil War.

None of the circle had formal musical training, and not surprisingly their relationship with Rubinstein and the Conservatory was hostile. The hostility was stoked by their foremost defender among the music critics of the time, Vladimir Stasov (1824–1906). Stasov was a librarian at the St. Petersburg Public Library, but quickly acquired a name for himself as a writer both on music and the visual arts. The son of a well-known architect, he had traveled in Europe and was extremely erudite in the music and painting of the time. In both cases his esthetic was simple. He hated any remnant of classicism, and thus condemned all painting since 1500 and most of the music of the eighteenth century. He despised Italian opera, even Verdi, for its adherence to the conventions of aria, duet, and chorus, as well as for the insubstantiality of the plots. Another mark against it was its immense popularity with the aristocratic public in Russia, from the 1830s onward – in Stasov's view a mark of the elite's ignorance and love for showmanship. He was for free forms, forms that would adequately express the true nature of human beings, their inner world and their place in society, and thus he believed that art had to be realistic and national. In music that meant a certain preference for program music, and his European heroes were Berlioz, Liszt, Chopin, and Schumann. He advanced his views with wit, rudeness, savage personal attacks, and name-calling when he could, but his intelligence could not be denied. His great enemies in music were Wagner, the European classic tradition that he identified with the heritage of Mendelson, Anton Rubinstein, and the Conservatory. The Conservatory was his particular bugbear, for he thought that it would conserve traditional classic form in music and establish the dominance of German music in Russia – not "true" German music like that of Beethoven or Schumann, but a German-based cosmopolitanism.

Fortunately the Balakirev circle, soon to be christened the "mighty handful" or "mighty five," originally a derisive epithet, was not as combative or as rigid as Stasov. They had their own views, developed under the leadership of Balakirev, the group's main mentor at first, and later in the writings of Cui and the other composers. They were not as exclusively enamored of Russian themes as was Stasov: Balakirev and Mussorgsky from the first wrote program music and songs to non-Russian themes. Cui in particular made a very odd "nationalist." The son of a Polish noblewoman and a French officer who stayed in Russia after 1812, he was born in Wilno and what training he had in music came from the Polish composer Stanisław Moniuszko. Among all of them, however, the atmosphere of the 1860s, as much as Stasov's hectoring, encouraged an interest in Russian folk music and operas and instrumental music on Russian themes.

The Russian themes they chose reflected in a general way the concerns of the 1860s. The use of folk music went along with the intense interest in the peasantry that was the hallmark of the emancipation era. In Russian history they turned to the pivotal moments and the eternal questions of the role of the tsars, their aims, and their effect on Russia. Even in opera, where the portrayal of figures from the Romanov dynasty was prohibited, they presented the Russian past in all its complexity. Rimskii-Korsakov's first successful opera, "The Maid of Pskov" (1873), addressed the paradoxes of the reign of Ivan the Terrible, while the greatest achievement of any of the five, Mussorgsky's "Boris Godunov" of 1868–1874, followed Pushkin's play to portray a tsar whose ambition and greed for power destroyed him and his country in the process. He took the events of the Musketeer revolt of 1682 to portray the end of the old Russia and the dawning of the new in his second opera "Khovanshchina." These were not political tracts, and Mussorgsky was no radical, but they did offer a reflection on the painful issues of the time, earning them later fame as "critical." Mussorgsky's innovations in harmony and other areas would also bring him great fame in the twentieth century, but in his lifetime the operas were only limited successes, and he died of alcoholism before he could finish "Khovanshchina."

Of the rest of the five the most successful was undoubtedly Rimskii-Korsakov, who eventually joined the Conservatory and taught himself counterpoint and orchestration, becoming one of its most distinguished professors. His series of operas based on stories from Russian history and folklore became a mainstay of the Russian operatic repertory. Borodin's opera "Prince Igor" and his music on Central Asian themes won him a permanent place in world repertory, and his symphonies and other music continue to be popular in Russia. Balakirev, a contentious if charismatic personality, went through a religious crisis in the 1870s and stopped writing, only to take up music again in the 1880s. His religious and conservative views earned him the patronage of Alexander III's court, and Balakirev received a position as director of the Imperial Chapel choir.

Cui, in contrast, wrote a great deal, including many articles on Russian music in French, but his extensive musical work has not retained an audience. As the move of Rimskii-Korsakov to the Conservatory shows, the five gradually moderated their hostility to the "cosmopolitans" over the decades, and musical life gradually became less contentious. Nikolai Rubinstein helped in this process, and even Stasov had to pull in his horns a bit, though he remained hostile to Tchaikovsky to the end.

The Balakirev circle made a great deal of noise as well as music in Russian musical life, but Tchaikovsky overshadowed them in popularity, especially outside of Russia. He whole-heartedly adopted Rubinstein's point of view that Russian composers needed to be

Figure 13. Peter Tchaikovsky as a young man.

trained properly and that meant in the Western manner, and he utterly lacked the hostility of Stasov and his followers to the formal conventions of Western music. Indeed Tchaikovsky's idol was Mozart, and he believed that much of his inspiration for a musical career came from an early acquaintance with Mozart's "Don Giovanni." Tchaikovsky's father was a well-educated official and mining engineer of noble origin but without estates or independent means to leave to his son. After the Conservatory, Tchaikovsky was unwilling to take non-musical employment, and thus his appointment to the Moscow Conservatory was crucial to his survival. There in the relatively relaxed atmosphere of Moscow he produced his first major works, the second, third, and fourth symphonies and the first and most famous piano concerto. He also began the work on the ballet "Swan Lake" and the opera "Evgenii Onegin," both of which brought him enduring fame.

Tchaikovsky moved to St. Petersburg in 1877, abandoning his position at the Moscow Conservatory. He then was in contact with the center of the Russian opera and ballet world, and the results were soon seen. He added "Sleeping Beauty" and "Nutcracker" to his ballets, and "Mazeppa" and the "Queen of Spades" to his list of operas, as well as a violin concerto and two more symphonies, the fifth and the sixth ("Pathetique") before his death in 1893.

Tchaikovsky's operas were not in the Italian tradition so despised by Stasov and others. He himself called "Evgenii Onegin" "lyric scenes" rather than an opera as it was a series of scenes strung together by the story, something Stasov should have liked but characteristically found reason to fault anyway. His operas used libretti based on Russian literature rather than folklore, and thus were "national" as well, but again in ways quite different from what Stasov advocated. They had none of the reflections on Russian history that prompted Mussorgsky and Rimskii-Korsakov to write, and by the late 1870s Tchaikovsky was politically quite conservative. In his correspondence he made fun of the idea of government without a strong tsar.

In some respects Tchaikovsky's ballets were even more important, for they were not only great pieces of music, but the first native compositions of importance for the St. Petersburg ballet under Marius Petipa (1818–1910). Petipa came to Russia in 1847 as a dancer and by 1862 had become the principal choreographer at the Imperial Theater, the Mariinskii. Himself a product of the French ballet of the first half of the nineteenth century, he was the creator of ballet in Russia as we know it. From Petipa come not only a whole series of ballets now still in repertory but many of the now standard Russian practices, including the strong male roles that were unusual in the mid-nineteenth century. The ballet, even more than the opera, retained its ties to the court and had a predominantly aristocratic audience: a number of the ballerinas were also mistresses of the Grand Dukes and great aristocrats. As the ballet was directly subordinate to the Ministry of the Court, it was provided with lavish subsidies for the productions and support for Petipa until nearly the end of his life. As George Balanchine later put it, "St. Petersburg was now the ballet capital of the world."

Russian music came to maturity in a relatively short period of time, the result of both state and private patronage. The continuation of the state theater system was a great boon to ballet, less so to opera, but by the 1890s operas could be staged by private companies subsidized by the Moscow industrialists. Rubinstein founded the Imperial Russian Music Society with court patronage to provide symphony concerts as early as the 1860s. Stasov and the Balakirev circle were particularly concerned to bring music to a larger public, founding a Free (not for payment) Music School and giving many semi-amateur concerts of choral music. At first the audiences were sparse, but by the 1890s St. Petersburg and Moscow boasted a number of concert series and private theaters and orchestras with growing and enthusiastic audiences. In the provinces small, mostly private music schools sprang up, creating music far from the capitals and producing many great musicians. The institutional basis of Russian music reflected the changing society of the time, combining as it did state subsidy and control, private patronage from the new class of industrialists, and intelligentsia activism. On this basis the composers and musicians were able to create and perform some of the world's greatest music.

THE VISUAL ARTS

For Russia's painters the most important event was the resignation of thirteen students from the Academy of Art in 1863. The students, led by the most talented of the group, Ivan Kramskoi, objected to the traditional conditions of the annual Gold Medal competition at the Academy. For these competitions the students were assigned a historical, mythological, or biblical subject for their painting, and the specific theme that year was "Odin in the Hall of Valhalla." The winner received not just a medal but also a trip to Europe and the right to sell the painting from the Academy but Kramskoi and his colleagues would not accept the assigned subject. Instead they chose to resign from the Academy, thus forfeiting their chances to win, and formed a "Free Association of Artists."

The Academy rebels were not alone in wanting to reject the academic models. Both the artistic conventions and the subject matter seemed to most younger artists to be old-fashioned and foreign, having nothing to do with the Russian reality changing so swiftly around them in the 1860s. Insofar as any of them had European models, they were Courbet and some of the German realist painters, but mostly the Russian painting that emerged in the decade had native roots in the genre painting of the 1850s and to some extent in Alexander Ivanov. The new painting was to be realist, and it was to depict the life of the Russian people in its fullest extent. Not surprisingly, the self-appointed spokesman of the new trend was once again Vladimir Stasov.

The association of the Academy rebels soon fell apart from internal squabbles, but in 1870 Kramskoi came up with the idea of the "Itinerant Association of Russian Artists," designed to put on exhibits of their work not just in the capitals but in a variety of Russian cities. The idea was an immediate success, and many artists joined. The new association came to encompass virtually all Russian artists other than the privileged academicians. It found a new public beyond the St. Petersburg elites, bringing the work of its members to provincial audiences, to the intelligentsia and also to the emerging middle class. The exhibitions also brought the artists in contact with wealthy businessmen, the most important being the Moscow textile millionaires. Pavel Tretyakov had been collecting since 1856 and made his private collection available to the public from early on. He thus was able to support the artists by buying their work and also making it better known. In 1881 he opened the collection to the general public. Petersburg had no equivalent, though Tsar Alexander III did purchase many paintings, including the work of the Itinerants. Supposedly it was one of Repin's religious paintings which Alexander bought at the Itinerant exhibition in 1889 that gave him the idea for establishing a museum of Russian art in St. Petersburg. It opened only in 1895, after Alexander's death, in the Michael palace, the old residence of Grand Duchess Elena Pavlovna.

The Itinerants chose as their subject matter Russian landscape, genre scenes of life in the countryside, and portraits of the writers and artists of the day, as well as of the businessmen who served as their patrons. The most important was Ilya Repin, who made a sensation in 1873 with a simple depiction of workmen hauling a barge on the Volga. Though Repin's sympathies were with the Itinerants, he was an Academy student and made use of its stipend to spend several years in Paris. Though he intensely admired the French painters of the time including Manet, and improved his technical skills, he remained true to the ideals of his Russian mentors and colleagues. His most famous paintings were the work of the 1880s, monumental canvasses depicting a religious procession in Kursk province, the return of a political prisoner to his family, and other subjects that implied mild criticism of the existing order. Repin also tried historical subjects, the most powerful being his painting of Ivan the Terrible in the moment after killing his son. Repin saw this work not as an unambiguous condemnation of despotism but as a tragedy of crime and repentance, though many among the public took it in a more political sense.

Repin was only the best known of many painters of the time. Vasilii Vereshchagin's horrifying pictures of the wars in Turkestan and the Balkans were a sensation for their realistic depictions of the aftermath of battle. The Siberian Vasilii Surikov's huge historical paintings, showing Peter the Great's execution of the musketeers, the imprisonment of the Old Believer martyr Morozova, and the conquest of Siberia, formed Russia's visual conception of its past for decades. The landscape painters, Ivan Shishkin with his forests and Isaak Levitan with his many elegiac rivers and fields with their churches conveyed the vastness and humble beauty of the Russian countryside. Most of these painters were pupils or friends of Repin, for St. Petersburg's artistic life changed rapidly. The Academy was less of a threat as salons and studios appeared, as did new patrons. Tsar Alexander III was deeply impressed by Repin, bought more and more of the Itinerant paintings, and eventually the Russian Museum in St. Petersburg provided the city with its first museum devoted exclusively to Russian art. The rebels had found a supporter where they least expected it.

Russian painting never acquired the fame abroad of Russian literature or music. Some of the painters (Vereshchagin, for example) had a brief vogue in Europe at the time, but were largely forgotten in the twentieth century. Russian art of the nineteenth century was too far in its esthetic from the dominant French school to have any impact. Indeed Russian painters other than Repin and a few others did not travel in the West and knew little of French art. Their work did not even resemble the European realist art that was dominant

outside of France, though they were aware of the Germans to some
extent. Impressionism left the Russian painters cold until the very
end of the century. What the painters of the period – the Itinerants
and others – did produce was a portrait of Russia, its people, its history, and its land, that still resonates with virtually every educated
Russian.

LITERATURE

The glory of Russian culture in the decades after the Crimean War
was in its literature, which not only was central to Russian society and culture but for the first time breached the barrier of language to enter into the common culture of the West. Within a
few years, Ivan Turgenev, Fyodor Dostoevsky, and Leo Tolstoy all
acquired enormous fame and popularity in Russia. The vehicle of
this new popularity was the press, particularly the half dozen or so
"thick journals" that published almost all of the new work. The
public for Russian literature, as opposed to Western Europe, was
not concentrated in the big cities. Even Petersburg was not yet a
huge metropolis like Paris or London, and much of its population
was barely literate. No large educated middle class yet existed to
provide readers for the new novels, whose place in Russia was
taken by the gentry and the intelligentsia. They were spread all over
the country as landowners on their estates, provincial doctors and
gymnasium teachers, and minor officials throughout the empire.
There were often no bookstores in the provinces, and the monthly
arrival by post of the "thick journal" was the main focus of cultural
life.

Ivan Turgenev had already made a name for himself with the
Sportsman's Sketches and several novels when he achieved real
notoriety with *Fathers and Sons* in 1862. In his later novels Turgenev's heroes and his very strong heroines, mostly from the gentry,
spent their time trying to puzzle out the meaning of the changes in
Russia and the world and their role in them. Turgenev presented
various possibilities, and in the process satisfied no political camp,
but earned for himself a large and appreciative public. His nearly
full-time residence abroad kept him aloof from much of the details

of ever-changing Russian life, but it also made him a link to European literature. His friendship with the leading lights of French literature, Emile Zola, the Goncourt brothers, and others, eased the way for translations and thus earned Russian literature a place in wider European culture for the first time.

Fyodor Mikhailovich Dostoevsky had made his literary debut, like Turgenev, in the 1840s. His involvement in the Petrashevskii circle had brought him four years in prison in Siberia, followed by another five years in the army in remote fortresses bordering the Kazakh steppe. In prison Dostoevsky's view of the world began to change, for he abandoned utopian socialism as too far away from the people and began to turn to Orthodoxy, in his mind the "people's" religion. In the army he was able to at least read and write, and finally returned to European Russia in 1859 with a bundle of manuscripts in his trunk. One of them was his *Notes from the House of the Dead* (1860–61), which brought him instant fame. Its harrowing account of prison life was in harmony with the public mood of the emancipation era, and many readers seemed to have missed the note of redemption by faith in the work. Unlike most of the Russian writers of his time, Dostoevsky did not come from the hereditary gentry. His father was a doctor who had acquired noble rank through service but little means of subexistence. Dostoevsky had to live by his pen, and that was not easy. In 1861–1865 he tried his hand at journalism, together with his brother putting out two journals that sold only moderately and quickly collapsed. In the journals he espoused a variant of Slavophilism, calling for the return to the soil and traditions of the Russian people. In his mind, this return meant Orthodoxy and respect for the tsar. A trip to Western Europe broadened his experience, but also confirmed in him an increasingly negative view of modern society as individualistic, irreligious, and mainly devoted to greed. The trip also introduced him to the casino, and added an addiction to gambling to his medical problems (epilepsy) and his chronic indebtedness.

Dostoevsky had already made a contribution to the literary debate of the time in his 1864 *Notes from the Underground*, a savage attack on the utopianism of Chernyshevsky's *What is to be Done?*, but this was not a work calculated to win popular acclaim, indeed its fame came only in the twentieth century. The collapse of his journals impelled him to furious work just to survive, and the results were spectacular in the literary sense, if not the financial. His first major success was *Crime and Punishment*, published in Katkov's conservative "thick journal" *Russian Messenger* in 1866. Eventually it would win him worldwide fame, but right from the start it was his greatest Russian success. The story of the student Raskol'nikov who murdered an elderly woman pawnbroker because he needed money and felt that he was above normal moral rules caught the imagination of his contemporaries, and has never ceased to fascinate. Over the next decade and a half he would produce more great novels as well as a host of shorter works. In them he showed himself a master of human psychology, though he disliked the term: he thought he was simply portraying the human soul as it was.

Crime and Punishment brought him enduring fame, but it did not solve his monetary problems. The Russian book market was developed enough to circulate new novels widely, but not enough to provide a living even for a now famous author. The second of the great novels, *The Idiot*, was an attempt to portray a positive character in Prince Myshkin, the main character, but it is perhaps for the mysterious Nastasia Fillipovna that it is best remembered. Soon after came *Demons* (1871–72), among other things an attack on the liberals and radicals of his time, whom he portrayed as ineffective dreamers playing with fire in the elder Verkhovenskii or amoral and power-hungry fanatics in the younger Verkhovenskii, a combined portrait of the revolutionary Nechaev and Dostoevsky's erstwhile leader Petrashevskii.

Demons cemented his reputation as a conservative spokesman and once again in financial straits, Dostoevsky turned back to journalism, but this time in different circumstances. In 1872 Dostoevsky began to visit the political salon of Prince V. P. Meshcherskii, the close friend of the heir to the throne, Alexander Alexandrovich. The heir was the center of the conservative opposition to his father's reforms, reinforced in his views by the conservative lawyer Konstantin Pobedonostev, who had served as one of his tutors. All of them espoused a monarch-centered statist conservatism, nationalist and Orthodox, but lacking the specific Slavophile doctrines about the village community and the spiritual unity of the nation.

Meshcherskii had just founded a newspaper called *The Citizen* and convinced Dostoevsky to become the editor. As an encouragement, Alexander Alexandrovich also paid Dostoevsky's debts, a fact not known until the 1990s. Part of Dostoevsky's contribution was the regular feature, *The Diary of a Writer*, which contained some of his most famous as well as his most notorious contributions. In the *Diary* and its later continuations he used the opportunity it provided to criticize the new reformed Russia. The new court system in particular aroused his wrath, as the idea of trial by jury seemed to him pernicious. In any case, he saw crime in a religious light, as an issue of sin and repentance, and mocked legal formulas and trial procedure. His journalism was intensely nationalistic, glorying in Russia's military achievements in the Russo-Turkish war and indeed in warfare itself. The Poles, Ukrainians, and Jews came in for his wrath, the latter in his mind the incarnation of the grasping, individualistic spirit of modern society. None of these ideological positions and national prejudices endeared Dostoevsky to the intelligentsia outside its small conservative contingent.

The last of Dostoevsky's novels, *The Brothers Karamazov*, again brought him success, with its family intrigue and philosophical ruminations, and finally established his position among Russian writers. His last important public appearance took place in 1880, as a speaker for the celebrations surrounding the erection of a statue of Pushkin in Moscow. Here he surprised his audience by praising Pushkin not as just a Russian writer, but one who embraced all of humanity. The speech went a long way to repairing his reputation with the intelligentsia, but did him little good with his conservative friends like Pobedonostsev. Pobedonostsev was by now the head of the Holy Synod, and as guardian of Orthodoxy he had begun to think Dostoevsky's view of Christ much too vague and not sufficiently in accord with church teaching. Dostoevsky's Christ had indeed come to resemble his Pushkin, a figure for humanity, not just for Russia. This was to be Dostoevsky's ultimate fate as well.

The religious theme that was central to Dostoevsky's work and thought also came to preoccupy the other of Russia's greatest writers, Tolstoy. Count Lev Nikolaevich Tolstoy was born in 1828 into a family of well-off landowners with lands in the rich provinces south of Moscow. Tolstoy was born in Iasnaia Poliana, the primary family estate, and it remained his principal home until his death. The family was not part of the great aristocracy that frequented the court and Petersburg salons, but was certainly of ancient date and with a distinguished record of service in the army and the civil service of the Russian empire. He grew up on the family estate under the guidance of various tutors and then spent some time as a student in the University of Kazan,' all described in unforgettable detail in his autobiographical trilogy, *Childhood, Boyhood, Youth*. At the university he also participated in the normal life of the young nobleman, drinking, playing cards, and pursuing women far removed from polite society. He never took a degree at the university and so, restless at home, he took off for the Caucasus where he enlisted as a volunteer in an artillery unit. The outbreak of the Crimean War brought him a commission, and he saw serious fighting, not least at the siege of Sevastopol. His stories of that siege were published while it was still continuing and brought him instant fame as a writer. At war's end he spent several years in Petersburg and Moscow, quarrelling with nearly all the important and unimportant literary figures of the time. Fundamentally he was not in sympathy with their ideas, neither with the progressivism and fascination with science and progress of the liberals nor the subservience to autocracy of the conservatives. The Slavophiles seemed to him nice people but hopelessly doctrinaire. Personally he remained a nobleman and country gentleman (not a courtier) and found most of the literati crude or self-serving or both.

In these years he made his first trip to Western Europe. Europe as a whole left him with much the same critical view as that of Dostoevsky, that Europe's vaunted progress was just materialism, greed, and spiritual emptiness. The difference was that Tolstoy lacked Dostoevsky's chauvinism, and had no great respect for Russian autocracy or Orthodoxy. He did not see any "Russian" answers to Europe's dilemmas. His next project was a school for the peasant children on his estate, which he determined to run on lines derived from Rousseau's pedagogical theories. That meant no compulsion, no punishments, work projects, and a determined attempt to engage the pupils in the subject matter. The school was eventually successful, though perhaps more due to Tolstoy's charisma than to the efficacy of his theories. Tolstoy founded a magazine to propagate his views, in the process annoying most of the educational establishment. The school gave him considerable notoriety, and also inspired a second trip to Europe to meet famous pedagogues and inspect schools. He found European schools, especially the famous Prussian schools, to be depressing, regimented, and heavily dependent on memorization, all of which merely substantiated his prejudices. Returning from abroad early in 1861, just after the emancipation of the serfs, he found himself with a new occupation: Intermediary of the Peace for one of the districts of his home province of Tula. These were the men the assembled gentry were supposed to elect to deal with disputes between peasants and landlords over the implementation of the emancipation. The Tula gentry rejected Tolstoy as too sympathetic to the peasants, but the provincial governor, a general, overruled them and appointed Tolstoy. He served for nearly a year, most of the time in battles with his fellow intermediaries. The rumors of his unusual views caused him even more trouble, for the spreading revolutionary movement in the spring of 1862 led to a police raid on the estate. The police were looking for underground printing presses and revolutionary manifestoes, and found nothing of the sort. Tolstoy wrote to the tsar to complain of the insult to his honor and reputation, and received assurances from the ministers that there would be no consequences. Neither his neighbors in the gentry nor the government knew quite what to make of him.

The same year he married Sofya Bers, the daughter of one of his neighbors, and for the next twenty years devoted himself to his family, his school, his duties as Intermediary of the Peace, and to writing. The fruit of those years would be *War and Peace*, which appeared in 1865–1869, like many of Dostoevsky's works, in Katkov's *Russian Messenger*.

Tolstoy's immense epic was devoted to Russia's wars with Napoleon, and mainly to the French invasion of 1812. Though certainly patriotic in a general sense, Tolstoy was no nationalist. He hated Napoleon, not the French, and his view of Russia was far from rosy. He portrayed the tsar, the court, and the government as inept and removed from the realities of life and warfare. The many Germans in Russian service came in for contemptuous treatment, and only his hero Kutuzov stands above the crowd of cold and formalistic commanders. Though the book concluded with long reflections

Figure 14. Lev Tolstoy Plowing a Field, drawing by Ilya Repin. Tretyakov Museum.

on the meaning of history (Tolstoy was particularly incensed by notions that "great men" determine the course of history), the book is not really about the events of 1812, it is about man and his fate, as Tolstoy understood it.

For Tolstoy the real issues of life were not political, they were moral. Pierre Bezukhov and his spiritual pilgrimage in particular incarnated the desire to act in a moral manner and to find what meaning might be hidden behind the rush of everyday life and the mindless acceptance of inherited values and institutions. Prince Andrei Bolkonskii is his opposite, the rational analyst of warfare, events, and human beings. Ultimately it is Pierre who finds happiness, first learning from the peasant Platon Karataev and his humility and faith in God, and then in family life with Natasha Rostova. Much of Tolstoy was in Pierre, not only his experiments with schemes to benefit the peasants on his estate but also in his spiritual search.

After the success of *War and Peace* Tolstoy turned again to pedagogy and several schemes for new novels. The outcome was *Anna Karenina* in 1875–1877. This was the story of the aristocratic Anna, her lover Vronskii and her bureaucrat husband, contrasted with Levin and his wife Kitty, again a portrait of Tolstoy, a happy family life contrasted with Anna's disastrous affair. While he was writing the book, however, Tolstoy went through the final and deepest spiritual crisis of his life.

Tolstoy's was a religious crisis. Haunted by death and the problem of the meaning of life, he turned to philosophy and religion, but could not make out which religion he should follow. He first turned to Orthodoxy, the religion in which he had been brought up, mainly on the grounds that it was the religion of the peasantry and he wanted to remain close to them and their wisdom. Orthodoxy, however, did not satisfy him. The liturgy left him cold, and he disliked the enthusiastic support of the church for the state and all its doings – warfare, oppression, and capital punishment – all already unacceptable in his mind.

Finally in 1879–80 he began to read the Bible intensively, particularly the Gospels, and came to the conclusion that the core of the teaching of Christ was non-resistance to evil. ("I say unto you, That ye resist not evil; but whosoever shall smite thee on thy right cheek, turn to him the other also." Matt. 5:39) In Tolstoy's mind, everything flowed from that principle. It meant that the state, in fighting crime or foreign enemies, was basically un-Christian, and that the only proper stance was radical pacifism and a sort of Christian anarchism. He developed these ideas in a series of long tracts, the *Confession* that recounted his inner development toward these views as well as accounts of what he saw as true Christianity. Needless to say, none of these works could be published in Russia though they circulated widely underground and attracted to him a small but devoted following.

Tolstoy did not abandon literature, in 1899 he published his last major novel, *Resurrection*, about a prostitute wrongly convicted of a murder and her spiritual rebirth (this book was banned in Russia) and he wrote *Khadji Murat*, a novella of the Caucasian Wars. Shorter works like *The Kreutzer Sonata* and *The Death of*

Ivan Ilich as well as innumerable articles on public issues gradually made him the most famous person in the country, and the most famous Russian in the world.

Tolstoy's views and his stubborn defense of them created problems with the church and the state and with his family as well. His wife thought that he was neglecting their welfare, though by the 1890s the changing book market in Russia meant that he, like other authors, began to realize more substantial returns on his many works. The Revolution of 1905 was a hard time for him as well, since he was opposed to the autocracy but did not believe in the violence used against it, much less the violence of the state against strikers, revolutionaries, and peasant rebels. Finally in 1910, at the age of eighty-two, he decided to leave everything and lead the life of a religious recluse. His trip on an unheated third class carriage in winter proved too much for him. He died in the house of the railroad stationmaster in a small town only a few hundred miles south of Iasnaia Poliana.

By the time of Tolstoy's death Russian literature and culture had passed into new phases, with which he had little sympathy. He was the last survivor of the greatest age of Russian literature, and perhaps of Russian culture in general. The arts as well as the sciences had put Russia on the map of world culture. For the first time the vast Russian empire was known for something other than size and military power.

14

Russia as an Empire

The Russian Empire's foreign wars over the centuries laid the foundation for its expansion to include the whole of northern Eurasia. Of course by British standards, the results were not impressive. Most of the Russian Empire lay in Siberia, the largest part of which was seemingly impenetrable forest and tundra. Russia's newest acquisitions in Central Asia were small in population and were poor – no equivalent to India or even Burma. The resultant state included extensive areas on its borders with non-Russian populations, effectively two empires, a traditional land empire in Europe and an attempted imitation of the British example in Central Asia. In both west and south internal and foreign politics were inextricably intertwined.

Nicholas I had understood that Russia's empire had very limited possibilities for expansion. After 1828 its main effort went into subduing the Caucasian mountain peoples already within Russia rather than the conquest of new territory. In Central Asia the army also concentrated on strengthening the existing frontier and control of the Kazakhs of the steppe while making no serious attempt at expansion. Even in the Balkans, Nicholas had pursued a status quo policy, preferring to maintain Russian influence in a unitary Ottoman state rather than run the risks of partition schemes. Even this modest policy had been too much for Britain and France, but it reflected the tsar's strategic prudence as well as his tactical blunders. The new situation after Crimea brought different possibilities.

The treaty of Paris not only ended the Crimean War but put an end to hopes of Russian influence on the Ottomans, leaving Russia with only the local nationalist movements in Serbia and Bulgaria as potential allies. Bands of insurgents with plans for democratic republics, the Balkan nationalists were unlikely allies for the Russian empire, and the international and military position of Russia, weakened by defeat and saddled with debts and an enormous deficit, rendered Russia's European policy essentially passive. The need for stability on the European border also arose from the feeling that the Russian Empire's boundary in the west was very difficult to defend, running an enormous length through territories poorly served by communications. The answer would be railroads, but they took a long time to build. Threatening noises from Britain and France during the Polish revolt in 1863–64 caused nightmares in St. Petersburg, but they came to nothing, in large part because of the firm Russian alliance with Prussia, now under its new chancellor, Otto von Bismarck. The Prussian alliance meant that the western boundary was largely secure, especially as Bismarck defeated Russia's rivals, Austria and then Napoleon III, establishing in the process a powerful new state in the unified imperial Germany, for the time being Russia's friend.

Preoccupation in Europe with Germany and Italy and the pacific policies of Russia's foreign minister, Prince Gorchakov, secured peace in the 1860s. Russia could gradually reform itself and also begin to rebuild its army on more modern lines, but crisis in the Balkans soon created a new dilemma. The Serbian and Bulgarian revolutionaries had repeatedly attempted insurgencies inside Ottoman territories, calling on the Slavic and Orthodox peoples to rise against their Turkish masters. The response was increasingly savage reprisals, until in 1875 the Serbs of Bosnia revolted again and were able to hold their own for several months before the Ottomans crushed the revolt, in the process perpetrating the largest genocide in modern European history up to World War I. The next year the Bulgarians rose as well, and Turkish irregular units exterminated entire villages, causing even English public opinion to waver in its support of the Turks. Here was a chance for Russia to reassert itself and secure influence in the Balkans, and in 1877 Russia proposed to the Turks an autonomous status for the rebel areas. The Ottomans refused, and Russia declared war. The war that ensued was bloody but relatively short. The Turks had first-class fortresses, were well supplied with European weapons, and fought with their usual courage and determination. The Russian army, though larger, was still in the process of reformation and hampered by old-fashioned and unimaginative generals. After a series of bloody assaults on the Turkish forts, the Russians finally pushed their way over the mountains and arrived near Istanbul in 1878. They then made a treaty with the Turks that established Bulgaria as the main Slavic state in the Balkans, one that would presumably become a Russian client. This alarmed Britain and Austria, and the result was the treaty of Berlin, which created a much smaller Bulgaria with a German monarch. Austria was allowed to take Bosnia as a protectorate. This was Bismarck's work, and it was a qualified defeat for Russia after all the sacrifices and heroism of the war.

The Russian Empire had become a conglomerate of two very different sorts of empire, each posing its own problems for St. Petersburg. At the same time as the failure in the Balkans, a new empire arose in Central Asia, where Russian generals overwhelmed the local khanates of Kokand, Bukhara, and Khiva. The first was entirely annexed to the empire, while the latter, much reduced in territory, became Russian protectorates. By the 1880s all of Central Asia was directly or indirectly under Russian rule. In explicit imitation of British India, Russia set out to build a modern colonial empire.

On the western border, the issues were mainly those of nationality, not colonialism. The Poles posed the chief national issue throughout the nineteenth century and, after mid-century, it was the Jews. For quite different reasons, neither Poles nor Jews fit well into the imperial structure. The Poles were seen in the government as a hostile element, and for many government officials the Jews were not able to assimilate and exploited the local peasantry. The Polish revolts and the pogroms directed against Jews added an element of violence absent in relations with the other European minorities of the empire. Finland, in contrast, was quiet and largely loyal to the tsar until the 1890s. Both Poland and Finland were important to a large extent for military reasons, as they both formed part of the crucial western frontier. The economies of both western borderlands contributed to the overall prosperity of the empire, but Russians had few investments there in either land or industry. In population together the Poles and Finns were less than ten percent of the total population of the empire. The largest non-Russian group in the European part of the empire was actually the Ukrainians (about seventeen percent), whose ambiguous ethnicity and national consciousness kept them on the margins of Russian politics until 1905.

The integration of the western borderlands of the Russian Empire had depended since the eighteenth century on the inclusion of local elites in the imperial power structure. The ruling circles of nineteenth-century St. Petersburg were very far from uniformly Russian. Prominent Germans included Nicholas' minister of finances Georg Kankrin, his foreign minister Karl von Nesselrode and the head of the Third Section, Alexander von Benckendorf. Among the Ukrainians in the imperial elite were minister of internal affairs Viktor Kochubei and the victorious field marshal Ivan Paskevich, the viceroy of Warsaw after 1830. Finlanders were important in the army and navy, and two of them (Arvid Adolf Etholén and Johan Hampus Furuhjelm) were governors of Alaska in its Russian period. The diplomatic core had several princes Lieven, Baron Nicolai, and a host of others, as did the court and the army. Only the Polish nobility, loyal to its traditions of Polish statehood, held back from Russian service, aside from a few prominent exceptions.

The reliance on noble supporters of the Romanov dynasty, so successful earlier on, had one shortcoming. In the course of the century the development of commercial and then industrial capitalism, however slow by European standards, changed the society of the empire. In the western borderlands the result was the declining economic fortunes of the nobility, the principal support of the empire. Businessmen, on the other hand, in Finland, Poland, and other western areas benefited considerably from the imperial market and were willing to cooperate (within limits), but the aristocratic conservatism of the court and most of the ruling elite made an arrangement with newer social groups difficult or impossible. The Russian empire could not fully abandon its alliance with the local nobilities, nor could they survive without the tsars, and they all went down to destruction together in 1917.

POLES IN THE RUSSIAN EMPIRE

The outcome of the Congress of Vienna meant that the historically Polish lands incorporated into the Russian Empire fell into two areas with quite different character and status, central Poland (Congress Poland) and Poland's former eastern territories. In both parts the Polish nobility did not cooperate in large numbers with the Russian Empire, and instead provided the social basis for nationalist revolt. The central Polish lands around Warsaw formed the Kingdom of Poland, an autonomous unit within Russia, with the tsar as king of Poland. Its population was overwhelmingly Polish, and until the 1830 revolt, the Kingdom of Poland had its own government, legislature, and army under the general aegis of the tsar and his viceroy in Warsaw. After the revolt was crushed, the Russian viceroy field marshal Paskevich ruled the area directly, with the assistance of appointed officials. Polish émigrés in France and Britain formed a series of revolutionary societies aimed at overthrowing Russian rule, but none of them had any success until after the Crimean War. The eastern territories of the old Poland, today's Lithuania, Belarus, and the western Ukraine, were quite different in their fate. There the Poles were primarily the nobility, owning serfs of different nationalities whose relationships to the Polish cause ranged from somewhat friendly in Lithuania to quite hostile in the Ukraine. As the townspeople were largely Jewish and thus not part of the Polish nation in the eyes of the revolutionaries, the potential base of the Polish cause in these areas was thin indeed. To make matters worse, these areas were never autonomous within the empire, though the Russian authorities continued to apply Polish law in civil and criminal matters until the 1830s.

To make things even more complicated, the Kingdom of Poland, where serfdom had been abolished by Napoleon, developed more rapidly than the Russian interior. Textile industries came into being in Warsaw, Lodz, and other cities, mostly the work of Jewish, German, and other immigrant entrepreneurs but attracting Polish and Jewish workers and gradually building more modern cities in place of the old centers with their noble palaces and impoverished artisans. Warsaw became the center of unrest in the area. The Russian authorities' reactions to the new revolt of 1863–64 was to further reduce the limited autonomy of Poland, the policy that came to be known as "Russification." Even the official name was changed from Kingdom of Poland to "Vistula Provinces" and the school system was henceforth required to teach in Russian. The Russian government enacted reforms of landholding more favorable to the peasantry, seen as a potential counterweight to the nobles. The Polish response to the defeat was a generation that avoided politics and turned toward smaller deeds, the building of civil society through education, even if in Russian, and taking advantage of the booming economy. The irony was that much of the prosperity of Poland's economy was the result of the huge market provided by the Russian Empire, where Polish goods, uncompetitive in Western Europe, found ready customers. The revival of Polish politics in the 1890s brought new groups into the underground, the National Democrats, a middle-class nationalist group and the various socialist parties, all of whom would play a major role in 1905.

THE BALTIC PROVINCES

In some ways the Baltic provinces, Estonia, Livonia, and Kurland (modern-day Estonia and Latvia) were more profoundly affected by the evolution of state and society in the Russian Empire than other non-Russian European areas.[1] Alexander I had abolished serfdom in the Baltic provinces in 1816–1819. The landless emancipation left the Estonian and Latvian peasants still the sharecroppers or tenants of the German nobility, and frequently still obligated to perform labor services, but the emancipation did begin the process of modernization. The role of the Baltic provinces as ports of entry to the Russian Empire made Riga a major commercial and eventually industrial center by the end of the nineteenth century. At the same time the restoration of Baltic noble privileges under Paul I meant that the provincial assemblies of nobles – all of them Germans – and the restoration of traditional forms of city government meant that

---

[1] In the eighteenth and nineteenth centuries the term "Baltic Provinces" did not include Lithuania, which was part of the former Polish political and cultural sphere. Latvia, Estonia, and Lithuania came to be called the "Baltic states" and seen as a group only after independence in 1918.

effective control of the area remained in the hands of the nobility and the German city patriciate. The noble assemblies were freely elected, and worked directly with the tsar, often bypassing the Russian governors, the only representatives of the central government in the area. These were free institutions of a type that did not exist in the rest of the empire (except Finland), but their existence perpetuated the rule of an ethnically distinct nobility over the rural population.

The persistence of the autonomous noble institutions and the freedom of the peasants meant that the effects of the reforms of the 1860s were different in the Baltic provinces from the rest of the empire. For the peasants the great issue was not their legal status but access to land ownership, granted only in the 1860s. The press flourished and was much less restricted than in the rest of the empire as a result of the local legal system. Latvian and Estonian journals and newspapers appeared beside the older German press, providing a forum for political debate as well as cultural and national polemics. There had always been minorities of Latvian and Estonian artisans and small traders in the towns, and the economic development of the area led to a rapid flow of population from the countryside into the city, so that by the end of the nineteenth century the Germans were a minority in the cities. At the same time the spread of education, as elsewhere in the empire, gave rise to an educated class among the Baltic peoples, and voluntary cultural societies carried national ideas to the Latvians and Estonians. For these emergent nationalities the Germans, not the Russian tsar or the Russian people, were still the enemy. Indeed Russian Slavophiles thought that the imperial government should encourage the Latvians and Estonians against the Germans, but the conservative pro-nobility policies of St. Petersburg, as well as the excellent court connections of the Baltic nobles, prevented the full emergence of such a tactic by the Russian authorities.

All of these changes led to conflict between St. Petersburg and the Baltic nobility, but the local noble assemblies continued to exist and function, and in the countryside the German nobility was still completely dominant. Most of them continued to serve in the Russian army and administration and particularly the aristocratic elite remained loyal to the Empire. The existence of the new united

Germany after 1870 provided an attraction for some, but on the whole the reliance on the nobility in the area was a largely success-ful policy in the Baltic provinces. The situation began to change only after 1900, when social changes and national movements brought the Latvian and Estonian majorities onto the front stage of society and politics. And they were not nobles.

Like the Baltic provinces, Finland retained autonomous institutions until the end of the empire, but these institutions and Finnish society were otherwise quite different from the Baltic provinces. Finland, in the words of Alexander I, had been "raised to the rank of nations" by the Russian annexation of 1809. No longer was it merely the eastern extension of Sweden with an exotic language spoken by peasants, but it was a country of its own under the Russian tsar. Alexander had also granted Finland the continuation of the laws and Lutheran religion from the Swedish time, a separate government in Helsinki, and a legislature modeled on the old Swedish diet. Unlike the situation in the Baltic provinces, Finnish peasants had never been serfs but were free tenants and freeholders, and the Finnish diet continued the Swedish practice of including peasant representatives.

Thus the Russian tsars at first could rely in Finland on the loyalty of the Swedish-speaking nobility for they found that the nobility lacked both the antagonism to Russian rule of the Polish nobles and the caste egotism of the Baltic Germans. Indeed for much of the century the Russian tsars looked favorably on Finnish economic development, state building, and emerging national consciousness. The generally peaceful relationship was not wholly untroubled, for Nicholas I never called the Finnish diet to meet. The local gov-ernment in Helsinki remained in power, carrying out numerous educational and economic projects with the support of the Russian governors-general and the Finnish State Secretariat in St. Peters-burg (usually headed by a Finn). The establishment of a university in Helsinki not only raised the cultural level of the country but also provided a center for an emerging national culture in both Swedish and Finnish that affirmed national dignity while maintaining loy-alty to the empire. Perhaps the most important result was Elias

Lönnrot's compilation of Finnish folkore, the *Kalevala*, most of it collected among the Finnish-speaking peasantry of northern Russia rather than in Finland itself. Finnish rapidly became a literary language alongside Swedish, though the latter remained the primary language of administration until the end of the Russian Empire. As the 1809 agreement added the Finnish territories taken by Peter the Great to the rest of Finland, the border ran almost to St. Petersburg itself. Thus only a few hours from his capital, the Russian tsar became a constitutional monarch. Finnish law remained separate from that of the rest of the empire, with the result that Russian revolutionaries could hide in Finland without legal obstacles to their activities.

The Crimean War brought some destruction to Finland, as the British navy shelled and burned a number of coastal towns, though no bombardment could knock out the great fort of Sveaborg in the Helsinki harbor. Finland repeatedly demonstrated its loyalty, and was rewarded in the reform era that followed. As in the rest of the empire, the end of the Crimean War meant a radical relaxation of censorship and a new economic policy oriented toward capitalist development. Economic development and reform brought newspapers and public opinion to Finland as well, and political groupings began to form. The decisive change came in 1863 when Tsar Alexander called the Finnish diet into session, an elected legislature that represented "estates" (nobility, townspeople, clergy, and peasants), not the country as a whole since the franchise was sharply restricted. The peasants were overwhelmingly Finnish speakers, and the tsar recognized their needs the same year, mandating that petitions and other documents to the administration could be presented in Finnish as well as Swedish (Russian was not contemplated). The Finnish peasant deputies, all firm supporters of the Finnish language, were the tsar's main allies in Finland, against the mostly Swedish-speaking liberals among the urban and noble deputies.

Inclusion in the Russian Empire created a new economic situation for Finland, as St. Petersburg was an enormous market for labor and goods. In the early nineteenth century more Finns lived in St. Petersburg than in any Finnish city, and the Finnish countryside provided an increasingly large proportion of the capital's food supply. The more rapid development of the Russian interior after the emancipation and the construction of railroads only speeded the integration of Finland into the empire's economy, as textile mills and metalworking plants provided products for the seemingly unlimited Russian market. Thus businessmen as well as nobles had an interest in preserving a stable autonomy within the empire. This success story only came to an end with the attempt at "Russification" by governor-general N. I. Bobrikov in 1896–1902. Bobrikov decided that Finland needed to be further integrated into the empire, a goal shared by Tsar Nicholas II. Bobrikov's actual measures were rather limited (use of Russian by high officials, a threat to draft Finns to the Russian army) and most of them remained on paper, but they were enough to create a crisis without actually advancing Russian rule in the country. The result was the emergence of radical nationalist groups and dissension among the nobility and business classes. Finland retained almost all its autonomous rights up to 1917, but Nicholas II and Bobrikov had succeeded in alienating large sections of the population, including the elites.

JEWS

The Jews constituted a substantial population – accounting for approximately five million in the Russian empire, about four percent of the whole. At first the social and legal structure of the Jewish community was inherited from Poland and only in the 1860s did the Russian state began to mark out a distinctive Jewish policy in keeping with the principles of the reform era.

Russia had no Jews among its population from the end of Kievan times until the First Partition of Poland in 1772. In the eighteenth century some Jewish merchants and artisans settled in the Ukraine and in Riga, but this was technically illegal and the groups were small. When Russia acquired its first substantial Jewish community, the reaction of the Russian government was to preserve the status quo. The kahal organization of the Jewish community remained as it had been in Polish times, with the chief rabbis of each town collecting the taxes for the state and administering justice. Further, the Jews were restricted to the former Polish provinces (the "Pale of Settlement"), so that they could not move into the Russian interior, though the Pale did come to include the Black Sea coast provinces with the new city of Odessa. Nicholas I's attitude toward the Jews was essentially hostile, but his only measures of consequence were to draft them into the army (at a higher rate than Christians!) and to formally abolish the kahals in 1844. Virtually all Jews remained inside the Pale until the 1850s.

The reforming governments of the 1860s took a different direction, one of selective integration. (Assimilation or "Russification" was not contemplated.) The idea was that the Jews needed to become more useful to the state and to Russian society, and therefore were to be encouraged through education to form elites that could both render that service and provide modern leadership for the Jewish community. To that end the Russian government listened to the petitions of the Jewish commercial and banking elite, and in 1859 permitted individuals of that elite to take up residence outside the Pale. In 1865 similar permission was granted to the wealthiest artisans. The result was the formation of an important Jewish commercial and intellectual elite in St. Petersburg, whose leaders were the Ginzburg banking dynasty. The Ginzburgs' ties to the government and court ensured them a voice on Jewish affairs until the 1880s.

The other side of the reform policy was the opening of Russian universities to Jews beginning in the 1850s. Crucial to the fate of Jewish students was the November 1861 decree permitting all Jewish university graduates the same rights to private occupations and residence granted to Christians upon completion of the university degree. Though state service, however, remained closed to them, these measures speeded the transformation of Jewish society, especially since they more or less coincided with the first wave of the Haskalah, the Jewish enlightenment that rejected the traditional Jewish religious world for the adoption of European education and norms. By 1886 some fourteen percent of all university students in the empire were Jews, and some ten percent of gymnasium students.

The assassination of Alexander II proved to be a disaster for the Jews of the Russian Empire. In wake of his death a wave of pogroms swept the southwestern provinces (mainly the Ukraine) and continued on and off for two years. The mob blamed the Jews for the tsar's death, looted their houses, and assaulted and raped thousands of people, though only two died in the violence. Alexander III's government blamed Jewish exploitation of the peasantry for the riots and began to rescind some of the existing legislation. The most important measure was the introduction in 1887 of quotas in the universities, to be only three percent for Jews in St. Petersburg and Moscow, five to ten percent elsewhere. Outside the two capitals, however, the quotas were not strictly enforced. Petitions for exceptions presented to the Minister of Education and other means led to the actual growth in percentage of Jewish students to twenty-seven percent (Kharkov University) and twenty-four percent (Odessa). Thousands of Jews also went abroad for education, especially to universities in Germany and Austria. There they confronted a paradox. Though legally equal in all respects to native students, Russian Jews confronted a student culture that was, by the end of the century, nationalistic and militantly anti-semitic. In Russian universities, where the students mostly supported the liberal opposition to the state or even the revolutionaries, the student culture was largely favorable to the Jews.

Thus the government had gone back on the spirit of selective integration, but most of the legal structure remained and the modernization of Jewish society continued, if slowly. The lack of more general progress inspired various responses, one being massive emigration to Western Europe and the United States, but this option also was not universally available or desired. Another response was the appearance of a Jewish press that was liberal in its politics and oriented toward the reform of the empire. Baron Ginzburg and the St. Petersburg Jewish elite lobbied unceasingly, but with less and less success after 1881. More radical options, especially among students and young people generally were the various revolutionary movements. Many Jews joined the Russian populists, including the terrorist groups, and later the Marxists who preached international solidarity. Others formed specifically Jewish socialist groups, the Jewish Workers' League (the Bund), and finally the growing Zionist movement encouraged Jews to opt out entirely and move to Palestine. As the Russian government after the 1880s tried more and more to present itself as "Russian," anti-Semitism became more or less an official policy. Pogroms like the Kishinev pogrom of 1903, in which nearly fifty Jews died, further poisoned the atmosphere. In response, Russian liberal and radical groups underlined their opposition to legal and social discrimination against the Jews, and Jewish parties grew more radical as well.

In spite of the restrictions, the evolution of Russian society meant that more and more Jews entered the business classes, the professions, the intelligentsia, and more of them found ways, legal or otherwise, to evade their confinement to the Pale. By 1897 six percent of Jews lived officially outside the Pale – many unofficially. Jewish communities emerged in St. Petersburg and Moscow, and even in towns on the Volga far from the legally permitted areas. Jews were entering Russian society, and the emergence of mass politics in 1905 would bring them to center stage in many ways, some of them highly explosive.

UKRAINIANS

Though the largest non-Russian group in the empire, the Ukrainians played little role in imperial affairs until 1905, except as a potential opposition to the Polish national movement and its claims. Their minor role was the result of the ambiguities of Ukrainian national consciousness, only slowly and incompletely changing among some parts of the local intelligentsia from a Russian regional identity into a national Ukrainian one.

Before the Crimean War the Ukrainian territories were Ukrainian only in the nationality of the peasantry, with the exception of the Left Bank, the former Hetmanate, and the Kharkov province. In these latter regions the local nobility was descended from Khmelnyts'kyi's officers and maintained local traditions of history and a modest regionalist literature in Russian and occasionally Ukrainian. In the 1830s and 1840s, Ukrainian cultural activities of that local nobility were looked upon with favor from St. Petersburg as a counterweight to Polish political movements and a regional example of Russian uniqueness. The dominant figure in Ukrainian culture, however, came from a wholly different milieu. He was Taras Shevchenko, a serf whose talents at drawing led him to an education at the St. Petersburg Academy of Arts and liberation from serfdom. A lottery organized by Russian noblemen, with the prize being a portrait of the poet Vasilii Zhukovskii, raised enough money to buy him out of serfdom. His first volumes of poetry attracted more attention than his art, and back in Kiev he soon joined the historian Nikolai Kostomarov and other local intelligentsia who were dreaming of Slavic federalism. These dreams came to the attention of the authorities on the eve of 1848, and earned the poet a decade of exile on the shores of the Caspian Sea.

After Crimea the changes in Russian society and government policy had a sharp effect on the tiny Ukrainian intelligentsia. They began to publish a journal in St. Petersburg and involved themselves in the many activities of Russian radicals and liberals, including trying to educate the peasantry. Shevchenko returned from exile and resumed his central place in Ukrainian culture. The cultural efforts of the nascent Ukrainian intelligentsia came to a sharp stop in 1864 and 1867, when most publishing in Ukrainian became forbidden out of fear that Polish nationalists would penetrate the Ukrainian movement. In the Ukrainian cities small groups of intellectuals with a Ukrainian cultural orientation emerged, but they had little impact as yet. The cities remained firmly Russian speaking up to 1917 and after. Most university students in Kiev or Kharkov, Ukrainian or otherwise, ignored the Ukrainian movement and joined Russian radical groups or entered careers in the Russian administration or other institutions. The zemstvos, the elected local councils, were introduced into the Left Bank provinces, but their occasional forays into politics were oriented to the empire as a whole, not to specifically Ukrainian problems. Disagreements among the various layers of Russian bureaucracy over the language issue meant that some Ukrainian language books did appear, and local history and traditions were cultivated in the Russian language. Ironically the chief venue for Ukrainian history was the Archeographical Society in Kiev, which subsisted on funds from the Russian imperial military governors-general of the southwestern provinces. The main area of concern to the Russian empire was the Ukrainian movement across the border in Austrian Galicia, where electoral politics made possible a variety of Ukrainian parties, most of them not friendly to the Russian tsars. In the Russian Empire, however, the Ukrainian movement would not spread beyond the small Ukrainian intelligentsia to a larger population until the eve of the 1905 Revolution.

THE ASIATIC EMPIRE

If the European side of the empire was largely the result of territorial and strategic ambitions, the Asiatic Empire combined those same goals with a largely chimerical desire to imitate the economic success of the European colonial empires. Within that general framework, the Asiatic possessions of Russia fell into two areas, the Caucasus acquired by 1828 and Central Asia, where Russian conquest began in earnest only in the 1860s. To make matters more complex, the Crimean and Volga Tatars and the Bashkirs, conquered earlier and largely surrounded by Russian settlers, played a role both in Russian imperial rule and in the formation of native nationalism in Central Asia and elsewhere. Altogether the various Asian parts of the empire constituted about twenty-five percent of its population.

In the Caucasus Russia began to move beyond the sixteenth century boundary only at the end of the eighteenth century, annexing (rather theoretically) the North Caucasus and then Transcaucasia. Formal control was largely complete by 1828. South of the mountains the Russians established an administration based on Russian officials and the cooperation of the local Georgian and Armenian nobility. These Christian elites were integrated into the imperial nobility rather like the Baltic Germans or the Finns, and many of them played major roles in the Russian state and especially in the army up until 1917. The Azeris and other Muslims were a different story, though the Russian government was to a large extent able to coopt the Muslim clergy and other local elites after the end of the Caucasian wars.

The conquest of the Caucasus had been carried out to secure the eastern flank against the Ottomans. Commercial motives played some role in the planning, for trade with and through Iran was assumed to be a viable path to enormous profits. That idea proved to be an illusion, since Russia lacked the commercial infrastructure to make use of what was available, but that result did not become clear until the 1830s. In any case, the strategic value of the Caucasus and Transcaucasia as a southern frontier against Turkey was immense, and the Russians were not going to leave just because trade with Iran did not prove to be a bonanza. The mountain peoples of the north slopes of the Caucasus were not impressed by Russian strategic interests and liked even less the gradual penetration of Russian settlers in the adjacent lowlands. The result was war.

The Caucasian Wars of the nineteenth century fell into two fronts and two phases. One front was in the western end of the mountain range and its foothills, and the principal opponents were the Circassians, while the other front was far to the east, in Dagestan and parts of Chechnia. The wars began with the Russian attempt to build a solid line of forts to control the area in 1817, which met furious resistance both in east and west. Dagestan emerged as the main center of resistance in 1830, with Islam as its banner. The leaders were part of the Naqshbandi sufi order, which acted as the leadership group for the rebellion. The mountaineers proclaimed Shamil their imam in 1834 and for the next twenty-five years he led the struggle in Dagestan and Chechnia from his stronghold in the southern Dagestani mountains where he was born. This was a war of small units, night raids, guerilla tactics, and occasional massacres, which irritated the Russians but did not defeat them. The Russian army's attempts to send expeditions into the mountains to defeat the insurgents were equally fruitless until the 1840s. Then they realized that the solution to their problem was not more troops or battles but the construction of roads in the mountains and particularly the cutting of pathways and cleared areas in the dense Caucasian forests. It was the axe more than the gun that gave the Russians an advantage in the Caucasian wars – new "American" axes wielded by thousands of Russian soldiers. Finally, with the end of the Crimean War, Prince Alexander Bariatinskii, the viceroy of the Caucasus, decided to put an end to it and introduced large Russian forces. Shamil had to surrender in 1859, the effective end of resistance. On the northwest slopes of the Caucasus the war with the Circassians continued intermittently until the 1860s, when the Russian government began to encourage them to migrate to Ottoman domains, leaving large areas on the western slopes of the Caucasus for Russian settlers. From then until 1917 the north Caucasus was largely quiet. Even the Sufis turned to purely religious concerns and rejected holy war, and in 1914 Russia fielded an entire cavalry division consisting of Dagestanis, Chechens, and other Caucasian mountaineers with Russian and Georgian officers and commanded by a Grand Duke. There were ten Muslim generals and 186 Muslim colonels in the Russian army in 1914, mostly Caucasians, though Muslims did not join the imperial elite in St. Petersburg. Most of the North Caucasus remained under military rule, with Russian (and often Georgian or Armenian) officers appointed to supervise the local communities where the village elders remained in power.

On the southern side of the mountains society evolved in response to Russian rule and the social changes that it brought. The great reforms brought an end to serfdom in Georgia, creating a crisis for much of the Georgian nobility. At the same time the slow spread of education led to the formation of a Georgian intelligentsia, liberal in politics and determined to preserve and continue the national culture. A few of the younger generation were already attracted to Russian populism, and in the 1890s the first Georgian Marxist groups appeared in Tiblisi and Baku. Similarly the Armenians formed a local business class and intelligentsia, both with centers in Tiblisi and Baku rather than Erevan, still a sleepy provincial town. For Russian Armenians the great issues were the condition of the Armenians across the border in the Ottoman territories and increasing Russian pressure on the Armenian Church. The increasing nationalist radicalism of the Armenian intelligentsia led to the formation of the Armenian Revolutionary Federation (Dashnaktsutiun) party in Tbilisi in 1890, a nationalist party with a mildly socialist program. Though its main opponent was the Ottomans, the Dashnaks quickly attracted the enmity of the Russian authorities.

In spite of slow economic growth, development in Trancaucasia remained on the level of peasant agriculture, artisan production and trade with one major exception: Baku. The great irony of Russian Transcaucasia was that it did eventually provide a great economic benefit to the empire in the form of the Baku oil fields. Local producers, mostly Armenians, already exploited the oil in a small way for lighting and other purposes, but by mid century more modern drilling technology appeared, some in local or Russian hands, but the Russian branch of the Swedish Nobel family became the main producer, selling kerosene as fuel for lamps all over Russia. The American Rockefellers joined them, but Nobel remained dominant until the revolution. The result was to produce a modern, European type city on the shores of the Caspian, populated mainly by Georgians, Armenians, Russians, and Azeris. Until 1905, the Azeris themselves showed little interest in secular politics or new ideas, but beneath the surface they too were influenced by the changes emanating from Baku.

CENTRAL ASIA

Russia had started to move south into Kazakhstan in the eighteenth century, but until the Crimean War its main activity was the building of border stations and trying to maintain influence among the various tribal rulers of Kazakhstan. Attempts to make a more permanent penetration were failures. Only in 1853 did the Russians manage to seize the small fort of Ak Mechet on the Syr Darya near the Aral Sea, on the south side of the Kazakh steppe. Nothing further happened until 1860. The driving force behind the expansion of Russia into Central Asia was the army and Ministry of War, operating partly out of the need to control the frontier in Kazakhstan and partly out of fear of British expansion into and beyond Afghanistan. The immediate context was the decision to maintain a fortress line south of the Kazakh steppe, on the northern borders of Central Asia proper. This meant seizure of the forts built by the khans of Kokand to control the southern Kazakhs, and put Russia into conflict with both Kokand and Bukhara. In 1860–1864 the Russians took control of the Kokand forts on the southern fringe of the Kazakh steppe, and then moved south to the Central Asia cities. Acting on his own initiative but with the general approval of the Ministry of War, General Mikhail Cherniaev took Tashkent in 1865, giving Russia a stronghold in the rich and well-watered Ferghana valley, Kokand's base. The largely Uzbek Central Asian khanates of Khiva, Bukhara and Kokand were old-fashioned and weak even by the standards of the Near East in the nineteenth century and soon fell to Russian arms. The khanates' attempts to fend off the Russians only led to more defeats for them and in 1876 the whole of Kokand fell under Russian rule. Bukhara and Khiva were reduced to Russian protectorates on the model of the native states of British India, and in 1881 general Mikhail Skobelev eliminated the last resistance among the Turkmens. The Russian Empire now stretched to the borders of Iran and Afghanistan. The conquest was achieved at a low cost to Russia, only a few hundred soldiers died over the years of fighting. The soldiers of the Khanates were not used to European warfare and though numerous and brave, could not stand up to disciplined troops. Thus the largest problems for the Russians were logistic: learning to transport men and equipment over arid steppes and actual deserts, coping with intense heat in the summer and cold in unsheltered steppe in the winter. Fortunately, for all the British concern about Russian expansion, Central Asia was just too far away for the authorities in Delhi and London to try to counter the Russian moves. Iran and Afghanistan separated the Russian possessions from the British and the Ottomans as well. That is not to say that Britain was not concerned by Russian policy, obsessed as it was by the specter of losing India. The result was the continuation of the long "cold war" between the two empires – a situation that caused immense problems for Prince Gorchakov at the Russian foreign ministry, for his focus was stability in Europe. Thus the army often acted without informing him of its moves until it was too late for him to object.

The Russian colonial administrators, with general Konstantin von Kaufman at their head, were determined to avoid the mistakes of the Caucasus, which they saw as a narrowly military approach to empire. Instead they were going to imitate the master imperialists, their English rivals, and build a modern empire. Central Asia was to be slowly modernized by building European infrastructure, giving modern education to the natives, and encouraging or directly setting up investments that would benefit the empire. The great idea was the development of cotton growing, already a major crop, to supply the Russian textile industry. This project enjoyed modest success, but only by the early twentieth century. All these plans brought a small measure of modern society to Central Asia, one of the poorest and most backward parts of the Muslim world. Those modern elements, however, had other effects, for they called into being a small local intelligentsia with some modern ideas.

The development of the local intelligentsia was a response not just to Russian rule and its consequences but also to developments among other Muslim peoples of the Russian Empire and beyond. One current was pan-Turkism, the idea that all Turkic speaking people were really one nation, propounded by the Crimean Tatar aristocrat Ismail Bey Gasprinskii. Gasprinskii advocated a modernized

Figure 15. Nomadic Kirghiz (Kazakhs) around 1900.

state and modernized Islam, but his views on the unity of the Turkic peoples raised the suspicion in St. Petersburg that he was essentially furthering Ottoman foreign policy aims against Russia. Another trend, influential also in Central Asia was jadidism, from the Arabic work jadid ("new"). Jadidism began in the late nineteenth century among the Muslims of British India, who believed that a modernized Islam would be closer to the original inspiration of Mohammed, stripped of the accretions of centuries in between. Like Gasprinskii, the jadidists wanted a modern education system that went beyond rote memorization of the Koran in Arabic and the study of classic Islamic texts. They also wanted many of the features of modern society, which they did not see as contradictory to the Islamic spirit, if not to the Islamic practice of their time. These ideas soon spread among the Volga Tatars, living as they did among Russians who had already achieved a more modern society than that of the Tatars. The Volga Tatar merchants had been for centuries the intermediaries in trade between Bukhara, Khiva, and Russia, and now many came to settle in Central Asia under the aegis of the Russian Empire. They found an audience among the local intelligentsia, which began to try to put their ideas into practice. In the Central Asian cities the only result was the creation of a few small cultural circles, but it was the beginning of modern nation building.

For the Russian Empire, Central Asia, once conquered, was not a serious problem until nearly the end of the empire. Aside from a small Islamic revolt in 1898 in Andijan, the interior of Central Asia was quiet. In the Kazakh steppe matters were more complicated. Russian cities appeared on the northern fringes of the steppe and in them a small Kazakh intelligentsia emerged, dependent on Russian institutions and loyal to the empire. At the same time the economic integration of the Kazakhs into the emerging Russian industrial economy brought demand for cattle and other products that disrupted the traditional nomadic society. Even worse, large numbers of Russian peasants settled among them with the encouragement of the state. Before 1905, however, open conflict was largely absent.

THE MANCHURIAN GAMBLE

Russia's last attempt at empire on the Western model was its expansion into Manchuria. Witte's Transsiberian Railroad went right through Chinese territory to Vladivostok, and Russia carved out a sphere of influence like those of the other Western powers in China. The railroad was under Russian control, and the Ministry of Finance had its own police force to guard it. The Russian fort at Port Arthur provided a base for the Russian navy and also anchored the Russian military presence in Manchuria. The center of Russian administration and business, however, was Harbin, a modern city built from scratch by the Russians, with a Russian administration and a progressive urban order unknown in the rest of the empire. Most restrictions on Jews, for example, did not apply in Harbin. Witte was building a modern Russia on Chinese soil. All these plans came to an end, however, with the Russo-Japanese war. The final peace gave the Russian naval base at Port Arthur to Japan, and

Japan proceeded on the path of development and control that led to its further expansion in China. Russia retained control of the railroad, but never achieved dominance in northern China. Manchuria was too far away from the Russian heartland, and too close to Japan.

The Russian Empire, conglomerate as it was, functioned successfully only as long as it could remain a coalition of nobilities united by loyalty to the Romanov dynasty and rewarded appropriately for faithful service. Clearly this model of the empire mainly applied to the European areas and the Christian Caucasus, but there it did work until the strains of modernization undermined the domination of the nobility. The Russian state also tried to increase administrative uniformity and centralization, the policy known as Russification, but its efforts were half-hearted. There were too many obstacles, lack of financial resources, the influence of local elites, and the general backwardness of the country. The state could not abolish the variety of legal status and local administration in favor of a single unified state that might strive to assimilate all minorities to Russian language and culture, and indeed almost no one in the government had any such aim. Outside government policy, there were, of course, other more modern forces of integration – the power of the huge Russian market, the modernization of Russian culture, modern transportation and media, as in other countries, but they were all weaker than in Western Europe. The result was an unstable equilibrium in an empire too modern to remain an empire of nobilities around the tsar but too backward to fully unleash the social forces that integrated minorities in Western Europe. The Russians could not hope to imitate the ruthless and highly successful Germanization schemes in the German parts of Poland, for those depended on the combination of state resources, enthusiastic public support from a populace mobilized around nationalism, and the economic pull of German society. Russia had little of this, and its policies, especially in Poland, antagonized the people without being effective. Such integration of non-Russian minorities that did occur, and it was not small, came about simply by the ordinary motion of social change, not from state policy.

As time progressed, traditional loyalties eroded. Nationalist movements among the minorities emerged during the 1890s, but did not yet set the tone among non-Russian peoples. Few, save the Poles and the more radical of the Finns, actually anticipated or sought independence: their aim was greater autonomy within Russia. Many of the minorities were more concerned about one another than about Russians or the imperial state. The Baltic peoples saw their main antagonists in the Germans, the Finns fought over the Swedish-Finnish language issue, the nationalist movements of the Poles and Ukrainians feared each other and the Jews. Politicized Jews increasingly turned to Jewish socialist movements (the Bund) or to Zionism. At the same time, the great cities, especially St. Petersburg, Moscow, and the Donbass mining and manufacturing towns, were powerful integrating forces, attracting thousands of migrants from among the Baltic peoples, Finns, Poles, and Jews. The main concern of the state remained the politics of the Russian core, the maturing liberal opposition and the revolutionary socialists. The autocracy saw them, not local nationalists, as their main threat, and it was right.

15

Autocracy in Decline

The quarter of a century from the assassination of Alexander II until the 1905 Revolution was one of political stagnation. The response of the new government to the assassination was to stop the process of reform, to publicly affirm the necessity of autocracy, and to formulate plans for counter-reforms. The latter came to little, but the government took advantage of every possibility to block criticism, political discussion, and organization among the public. Though it returned to sponsoring economic development in the 1890s under Minister of Finance Sergei Witte, it refused to recognize the implications of the further modernization of society that resulted in part from its own measures. The increasing isolation of the government and its own internal lack of coordination led to the botched attempt at modern imperialism in Manchuria, an attempt resulting in a failed war with Japan that nearly brought down the monarchy.

Alexander III had become the heir to the throne in 1865 on the death of his older brother. Alexander was already twenty at the time and the product of a rather narrow military education unlike that provided for his brother. In 1866 he married Princess Dagmar of Denmark (Mariia Fedorovna after her conversion to Orthodoxy), leading to a stable marriage with a woman of intelligence and extremely conservative views. The young heir was no intellectual, but he did come in contact with Slavophile ideas at court and through his tutor in jurisprudence, Konstantin Pobedonostev. Through the guards and other aristocrats he became friends with the conservative publicist (and the most prominent gay in the St. Petersburg aristocracy), Prince V. M. Meshcherskii. These were highly principled radical conservatives, with nothing but contempt for freedom of speech, democracy, and representative government, all of which they saw as shams and likely to lead to revolution. In their view what was needed was the unity of society and the monarch, which they saw as the essence of autocracy. By the 1870s they formed a powerful opposition to the more liberal ministers around Alexander II, powerful largely because of their association with the heir. As part of his attempt at balanced government, Tsar Alexander II appointed Pobedonostsev head of the Synod, a position he held for the next twenty-four years. After Alexander III came to the throne, Pobedonostsev used his position at the Synod to retain constant access to the tsar, offering him advice on all sorts of subjects well beyond the ecclesiastical issues under his purview. In the eyes of liberal society and many government officials, he had far too much power and influence, all of it in a conservative direction. "Prince of Darkness" was one of his milder nicknames.

In reality Alexander listened to Pobedonostsev and Meshcherskii, but in his decisions usually went along with the ministers, conservative to be sure but unwilling to tear down the structure so carefully built up by the previous reign. Those structures still left many areas where the ministers and local administrators could act on their own discretion – in relations with the zemstvos, cases of administrative exile of liberals and socialists, and others. Here the tsar and his officials almost always chose the harsher and more authoritarian line. The 1881 "Temporary Regulations" were directed against the revolutionaries and allowed provincial governors to declare states of "reinforced security," which allowed them to imprison subversives without trial, transfer security cases to military courts, and shut down universities and businesses. The regulations lasted until 1917. At the same time, few "counter-reforms" were actually enacted. University autonomy was further restricted, and the tsar issued a decree establishing noblemen as appointed "land captains" to monitor law enforcement in the villages. The decree did, as intended, reinforce the power of the gentry in the countryside, and other regulations tinkering with local administration strengthened the bureaucracy against the zemstvo, but none of these measures was a major change. In the cities the government eventually raised the property qualification for elections to the city Dumas and prohibited Jews from sitting in the Dumas but left the basic structure intact. The reactionary character of the reign of Alexander III lay in the absence of response to ongoing social and economic change rather than any concerted attempt to return to a previous era.

Part of the new reign was also increasingly shrill official nationalism, including official anti-semitism. Again this was more a change in tone than substance, for little in the way of new measures or policies appeared, but a more rigorous enforcement of discriminatory legislation against Jews, such as the restrictions on settlement beyond the confines of the Pale did appear. In 1887 the government introduced the formal quota for Jews at universities in addition to the new laws on city government. There were other occasional forays into Russification. The latter was often more declaratory than real, for the Russian empire lacked the resources to form a firm policy in this area. Proposals to substitute Russian-language for German-language schools in the Baltic provinces, a particular campaign of Russian nationalists at the time, failed because the Ministry of Education pointed out that it lacked the resources for either teachers or school buildings. Thus the schools in the Baltic provinces remained in local, that is to say German, hands. The continued prominence of German and other non-Russian aristocrats at the court, in the army, and diplomatic corps also put a very sharp limit to the amount of "Russianness" the government could claim or try to enforce.

It was in foreign and economic policy that the years of Alexander III brought the most changes. In the years after Crimea Prince Gorchakov had kept the country firmly in the traditional camp of friendship with Prussia, at the same time trying to ease the tension with Britain and France. In the latter he was only partially successful, and the ambiguous position of Bismarck's Germany at the end of the Russo-Turkish war in 1878 undermined the old alliance of Berlin and St. Petersburg. As Germany grew closer to Austria in the course of the 1880s, the relationship fell under even greater strain, for both Russia and Austria had designs on the Balkans. The competition between Russia and the two German powers led to the end of Russian influence in Bulgaria in 1886. The resultant cooling in Russo-German relations left Russia effectively isolated in Europe. The new Germany, however, had been built on victory in the Franco-Prussian War and the annexation of Alsace-Lorraine, and thus had in France an implacable enemy. Both Russia and France quickly recognized a common interest, and in 1893 the great republic and the autocracy of the east signed a treaty that made them allies against Germany. The political constellation that had lasted on the European continent since 1815 came to an end, and the first seed was sown that would lead to war in 1914. To this day the Alexander III Bridge in the center of Paris serves as a reminder of that fatal alliance.

The alliance was not yet, however, a trigger of war, for none of the potential enemies wanted it as yet. The dynastic ties between Berlin and St. Petersburg remained, and allowed both sides to retain the illusion that things might eventually work out. The respective armies, however, thought differently, for the Russian army had begun to rethink its western defenses starting in the 1870s, when Germany and Russia were still allies, and the German army also moved quickly to plan for a two-front war. For the time being, however, the attention of governments and societies was more focused on the Far East. Here two quite separate issues came together, Sergei Witte's economic plans and the rise of Japan.

Sergei Witte was perhaps the last really dynamic and thoughtful statesman in the Russian Empire, a man with great plans and abilities as well as a giant ego, who never easily worked with others on an equal basis. Contemptuous of the other ministers of state – in large part justifiably – he formulated his plans with his staff and worked directly with the tsar. How he came to this position is a story in itself. Witte always claimed that his ancestors were Dutch and came to Russia through the Baltic provinces. In fact his grandfather was simply a middle-class Baltic German (perhaps with Dutch ancestry) who served as a tutor in Russian noble families. The young Witte finished Odessa University in natural science, not administrative law like most future officials. He also seems to have participated in a shadowy right-wing society called the "Union of St. Michael the Archangel," but then went to work for the South Western Railway, a private railroad running between Odessa and Kiev. This gave him a sense of the workings of capitalist enterprise that few high Russian officials could duplicate. Alexander III first appointed him to the government's railroad department and his rise was swift: by 1892 he was Minster of Finance at the age of forty-three, a notable achievement in an increasingly elderly government. Like earlier favorites of the tsar, his power rested entirely on the trust of the monarch, for Witte was too arrogant, too uncouth, and too unused to the subtleties of Petersburg politics to find allies among the ministers. He regarded most of them as timid incompetents, but failed to realize that without them he had only the tsar on whom to rely. With Alexander III on the throne, this attitude seemed sensible.

Witte's great project was the Transsiberian Railroad, begun already in 1891. This enormous line of track, stretching across the whole of northern Asia, was to become in many ways his monument. Against many skeptics he pushed the project through, first with the support of Alexander III and then with that of his son Nicholas II. Witte's plans were not merely to improve communications with the farthest point of the empire. A radical change was needed to be sure, for the only ways to get from European Russia to the Pacific were to go by horse and riverboat over several months, or to take a steamer from Odessa through the Suez Canal around India and China. Witte intended to develop Siberia, both for its natural resources and its potential as a settlement area to relieve the peasants' hunger for land. At the same time he was aware that the European powers were carving up China into spheres of influence and he did not want Russia to miss acquiring its share. Thus the last leg of the new railroad's route was to run from Lake Baikal through Manchuria to Vladivostok, leaving a line inside Russian territory for later. The aim was to take Manchuria as Russia's share of China and a space for a new, more modern style of colonialism. Witte's aim had been "peaceful penetration" of China for economic reasons, but the Russian military wanted a naval base, and in 1896 managed to lease Port Arthur, on the south coast of Manchuria, from China. Russia seemed to have a firm position in the Far East.

The only problem with this brilliant plan was Japan. Exactly in the 1890s Japan was making its own first steps toward empire in Asia, with its defeat of China and increasing informal power in Korea. The presence of a Russian railroad, Harbin, and a naval base

Figure 16. Count Sergei Witte, probably in New Hampshire for the Portsmouth Treaty in 1905.

at Port Arthur was a serious irritant to the Japanese and a direct consequence of Witte's policies. For the time being, however, peace remained, and Russia, Japan, and the European powers worked together to suppress the Boxer Rebellion in China (1900).

In 1894 Alexander III died. Though his policies kept Russia from moving forward in almost all areas but industrialization and empire building, he was at least a firm leader capable of making difficult decisions, as Witte recognized. His son, Nicholas II, was a man of very different character. He utterly lacked his father's ability to

Figure 17. Tsar Nicholas II on the imperial yacht *Shtandart*.

take charge and make use of his ministers. Alexander had gone along with them on most occasions but had also been willing to accept a minority view and support it. Nicholas often simply agreed with whoever spoke to him last, and then changed his mind again. He shared his father's views of the worthlessness of legislatures, freedom of speech, and human rights and tended to see the hidden hand of the Jews in liberalism and socialism. Had he not been the tsar, he would have made an ideal conservative country gentleman, for he was also gracious, kind, and a good family man. His wife Alexandra, the German princess Alix of Hesse-Darmstadt, encouraged all these characteristics, as she was equally conservative and equally devoted to her family.

Unfortunately Alexandra's devotion to her family and her limited horizons were not helpful in dealing with the hemophilia that her son, the heir to the throne Alexei, had from birth. Her response was to turn to a series of faith healers, each one more influential than the last. To top it off, the fully justified fear of terrorists increased the isolation of Nicholas and his family, in turn making it even harder for them to understand what was happening around them. The endless round of trips to the Crimea and elsewhere, the occasional court entertainments and family excursions on the imperial yacht did not leave much space for contact with the people. The only public appearances were carefully staged, often as part of religious ceremonies, which gave both tsar and people an utterly false sense of the country's needs and public opinion.

At first, however, everything went well. Nicholas was a great enthusiast for the Far East and its development and supported Witte to the hilt. He even supported the Minister's controversial placing of Russia on the gold standard in 1897, a measure designed to encourage investment and industrialization but a decision that was not necessarily good for the agrarian interests that the nobility defended. After 1900 the tsar's support for Witte began to erode. The appointment of Viacheslav Plehve, a career official and powerful personality, to head the Ministry of the Interior gave Witte a strong rival, and by the middle of 1903 Nicholas had removed the Minister of Finance from office. Plehve's only solution to Russia's problems was more repression, both of revolutionaries and middle and upper class liberals.

All of these opposition groups rapidly grew and consolidated in the 1890s. The first to organize were the Marxists, who rejected terror in favor of organizing workers to strike and fight employers and the state in collective action. The Marxists who managed to meet and adopt a general program in 1898 were then immediately arrested and the various Marxist groups did not come together again until 1903. When they met in London that year a new figure came to the fore, a graduate of the law faculty of St. Petersburg University with experience in the underground and exile. This was Vladimir Il'ich Ul'ianov, whose revolutionary pseudonym was Lenin. The son of a high school science teacher and inspector of public schools in Simbirsk on the Volga, Lenin had gone from

Siberian exile to Western Europe to edit a socialist journal, *Iskra* (*Spark*), through which he and Marxism acquired a following among the students and few workers who were the seedbed of the revolutionary movement. At the congress in London the party was refounded with a more elaborate program and structure, and the first disagreements broke out. The aim of the Marxists was to overthrow the tsar and establish a democratic republic (a "bourgeois revolution"). That is to say, they believed that until this task was completed, they should not try for the dictatorship of the proletariat and the introduction of socialism. The enemy for now was the tsar. Thus they would be operating under the autocracy, continuously at war with the police, and Lenin believed that the party should be primarily an underground movement of professional revolutionaries. His opponents, with their most accomplished leader Iulii Martov, thought that Lenin was exaggerating the need to concentrate on the underground struggle and wanted a looser party. In the vote on the question Lenin won by a narrow majority, and his followers thus acquired the name Bolsheviks (*bol'she* meaning "more") and Martov's followers Mensheviks (*men'she* meaning "less"). This dispute did not yet engage the few worker activists, and remained the province of the party's intelligentsia. For that is what the leaders were in these early years. Martov's father was a prosperous Jewish businessman and journalist in the Russian-language Jewish press, and he himself attended the gymnasia in St. Petersburg and had a year at the university before he was arrested for revolutionary activity. Trotsky came from a family of Jewish farmers, the descendents of settlers in New Russia from the time of Alexander I. The graduate of an elite Lutheran high school in Odessa, Leon Trotsky, like Lenin and Martov, was typical of the early revolutionary leaders.

The Marxists were not the only political group to form. In 1901 the revolutionary groups who looked back to the old populist tradition of the 1870s came together to form the Party of Socialists-Revolutionaries. They continued to believe that capitalism was an artificial transplant on peasant Russia, and in theory would concentrate their efforts on the villages. In practice they found the peasants hard to organize, and most of their followers were in the urban factories. The SRs, as they were called, also absorbed some

Marxist ideas to produce an eclectic ideology no less appealing for its lack of consistency. They also continued to believe that terror against government officials was a useful tool, and alongside the SR party agitators in the factories the Fighting Organization waged a relentless war against the government with a series of spectacular assassinations. The police naturally concentrated most of its attention on this group, and from 1903 to 1908 the head of the Fighting Organization was a police agent named Evno Azef.

The last to form an organization, not surprisingly, were the liberals. Their appearance on the political scene was part of the larger ferment in middle and upper class Russia that grew rapidly toward the end of the century. Since the 1860s innumerable professional groups and societies had come into existence, organizations of chemists and engineers, doctors and agronomists. The businessmen were particularly active in forming lobby groups to pressure for favorable economic policies, protective tariffs, and a more modern (and friendly to business) legal framework for their activity. The business groups were not merely groups of manufacturers or bankers dealing privately with the government, they met in conventions, using the great Nizhnii Novgorod fair and the many exhibitions as fora for public discussion of their needs. The newspapers reported extensively on these meetings, which addressed Russia's many needs but studiously avoided constitutional issues. Many of these organizations were initially supported or even created by the Ministry of Finance as a measure to encourage progress, and the members were mostly intensely loyal in their politics. In the course of time, however, business and other organizations broadened the discussion of social and economic issues, expressing the frustration of these levels of society with a government that they increasingly perceived as too conservative and too slow to respond to the needs of a changing society.

Some of the liberal leaders in the intelligentsia and the gentry began to think that time had come to organize in a more political fashion. For decades they had hoped that the zemstvos would evolve into a system of representation of the public or that new, more liberal measures would come from the government that would replace arbitrariness with basic rights and consultation of the people in some form. None of this transpired, but the zemstvos did provide a forum in which many liberal noblemen and others learned to deal with the innumerable local issues that gave them experience with public life and with the government's unwillingness to share power to any large extent. By 1901 they had given up, for the government refused to budge, and a small group of liberal activists formed an underground group, the Union of Liberation. Opposed to terror and revolutionary methods, they decided that only an illegal group could get beyond specific issues and conduct the needed discussion and supplement publications smuggled in from abroad.

By 1904 networks of activists of varying persuasions covered the Russian interior's major cities, and on the western and southern fringes nationalist and socialist groups among the Poles, Jews, Georgians, Armenians, and others added another dimension of instability. Then on January 27 (February 9), 1904, the Japanese navy attacked the Russian base at Port Arthur and sank most of the Russian squadron. Russia was now at war with Japan on the other side of the globe from St. Petersburg. The only line of communication was the Transsiberian Railroad, much of it still a single track and not all of it completed. The Russian army, far from its bases and lumbered with elderly generals, suffered a series of further defeats through the year. In July an SR terrorist assassinated Plehve, and Nicholas appointed the more tolerant Prince Petr Sviatopolk-Mirskii in his place. The appointment came unexpectedly and in large part was owed to the efforts of Nicholas's mother, the dowager Empress Maria. At the same time as Sviatopolk-Mirskii seemed to move toward some mildly liberal measures, another crisis was brewing in St. Petersburg.

The police in the capitals had long been frustrated by the success of the Social Democrats and the SRs among the workers of the city. In spite of continuous arrests they seemed to be making modest progress and alarmed the authorities by their dogged persistence and the readiness of workers to listen to them. Then the head of the political police for Moscow, Sergei Zubatov, had the idea of building a labor union controlled by the police. It would provide some modest social services to the workers to alleviate their conditions while inculcating in them loyalty to the Orthodox Church and the tsar. In St. Petersburg the leader of the union was father Georgii Gapon, who quickly came to enjoy the enthusiastic support of the workers and pose a serious threat to the revolutionaries. Thus when a spontaneous strike broke out at the huge Putilov machine works on the southern fringe of the city, Gapon was in a dilemma. The policy of the police unions was to oppose strikes (seen simply as violations of public order in Russian law), but if he chose that path he knew he would lose the support of the workers to the radicals. He chose to go along with the strike but conceived the idea that the workers should present their grievances to the tsar himself. Gapon assumed that the tsar would listen and do something, which would appease the workers and settle the strike. As the workers approached the Winter Palace in the snow on January 9/22, 1905, the response of the government, nervous about the unrest in the city, was to line up soldiers in front of the palace and order them to open fire on the unarmed crowd. Over a hundred were killed and many more wounded.

Within a few days workers all over the country, from Poland to Siberia, went out on strike by the hundreds of thousands. These were spontaneous movements with no unions, no strike pay, and virtually no leadership. The police union was immediately discredited, and the revolutionary parties were swamped, as they had only a few thousand activists in the whole country.

The Revolution of 1905 that ensued was an extraordinarily complex event. The urban strike movement was enormous, especially considering the lack of experience at such actions on the part of almost all workers, and the inadequacy of organizational structures. In the villages for the first time peasant unrest became widespread enough to provoke massive campaigns of military repression, even if SRs and others still found it extremely difficult to actually organize the peasants. Most of the non-Russian areas experienced the same upheavals as the interior of the country, with nationalist or socialist forces predominant in different areas at different times. The liberal middle classes generally supported all these upheavals, if only passively, and solidly blamed the government for the bloodshed. The government found itself extremely isolated, though Tsar Nicholas tried to hold on to the fantasy of the loyal peasantry corrupted by the intelligentsia and the Jews.

To complicate everything, the war with Japan continued and went from bad to worse. In the spring the Japanese inflicted a major defeat on the Russian army at Mukden. To replace the lost Far Eastern squadron, the navy sent the Baltic Fleet on an epic voyage around Africa and Southern Asia to the theater of operations. There it encountered the Japanese navy at Tsushima in May 1905, and was almost entirely destroyed. At this point, Nicholas and his government realized that they had no option but to make peace, and with Theodore Roosevelt as intermediary, the peace was signed at Portsmouth, New Hampshire, on August 23 (September 2), 1905. Russia lost the base at Port Arthur and the southern half of Sakhalin Island, but kept its Manchurian railroad and its buildings in Harbin.

These events took place against a background of rapidly growing unrest. In the spring nearly a million workers struck for greater or lesser times in St. Petersburg alone. Some of these were political strikes, but most were about wages and particularly about condescending and rude treatment at the hands of the factory administrations. Peasant seizure of land and attacks on the houses of the nobility reached a peak over the summer and spread throughout central Russia, the Ukraine, Poland, the Baltic provinces, and Caucasus. In Georgia whole areas were out of control of the government, and bandits flourished alongside peasant rebels. Starting in Baku, Armenians and Azeris attacked one another, killing thousands. In the Baltics the ethnic antagonism of German landlords and Latvian and Estonian peasants added extra viciousness to the violence, and Russian Cossacks were put in the position of defending Baltic German nobles. The high point of the summer of 1905 was the mutiny of the sailors on the battleship Potemkin, later immortalized in Sergei Eisenstein's film. The sailors demanded better conditions and an end to autocracy, supporting strikers in Odessa before they sailed off to internment in Rumania. This and other military mutinies, continuing into 1906, kept the government at bay.

In August Nicholas, under pressure from his government and his mother, issued a manifesto conceding a representative legislature, but with very limited powers. The manifesto had no effect, and in the autumn the strike movement in the cities resumed with even greater force. In October the strikes turned into a general strike, now a political strike directed against autocracy with calls for a democratic republic. In the absence of other organizations, the St. Petersburg workers began to form councils (in Russian, *soviets*) at the factory level and then came together to form a city soviet. The Social Democrats were dubious about the soviets at first, but the Mensheviks realized their potential. The most vigorous leader in the St. Petersburg soviet of workers' deputies was Leon Trotsky, a vivid and powerful orator and one of the main leaders of the Mensheviks. Lenin and his followers quickly jumped on the bandwagon. Finally on October 17/30 the tsar conceded that Russia would have to have a representative legislature, to be called the Duma, and some sort of constitution. The general strike came to an end, but Lenin and the Bolsheviks wanted to keep pushing the revolution farther. The result was an insurrection in the factory districts in the west of Moscow in December 1905, suppressed with considerable force by the army and police.

The October Manifesto changed Russian politics completely, perhaps more so than Nicholas had intended. Witte now came back to power in the new office of Prime Minister. Liberal and conservative groups began to form parties, and some of the revolutionaries came at least partially out of the underground. The new parties founded newspapers and enrolled members, preparing for the elections. The beginnings of mass politics brought more sinister forces as well in the form of the Union of the Russian People and many lesser groups of the same type. These were the "Black Hundreds," devoted to autocracy and Orthodoxy and proclaiming the Jews the source of all of Russia's problems. Intensely nationalistic, they opposed equality for all the national minorities, but singled out the Jews for bloody pogroms which they believed would put an end to revolution, in their mind the work of the Poles and the intelligentsia, but most of all the Jews. Two Jewish deputies to the Duma fell victim to their terror as well as hundreds in the pogroms. At least four hundred Jews died in the Odessa pogrom alone. While ineffective at combating revolution, the Black Hundreds added another element of violence and chaos to Russian politics.

The government had promised Russia a constitution, and Witte and the ministers produced one that the tsar would agree to. This was Russia's first constitution, the Fundamental Laws, written by Witte and other government officials and proclaimed on the opening day of the new Duma – April 27, 1906. In the new structure, the Duma was to pass laws, and if the Council of State agreed, they were sent to the tsar for his approval, without which they were not valid. The Council of State became an upper house, appointed by the tsar mainly from the great dignitaries of the state but with some representatives of the nobility, businessmen, and the universities. Rather inconsistently the document proclaimed the tsar an autocrat, but he now had to make laws through the Duma. His power remained predominant, for the Fundamental Laws reserved to the tsar foreign policy, the power to make war and peace, command of the army, and all administrative appointments. For the first time the tsar had something like a cabinet with a prime minister (Witte at first), but the ministers were all responsible to the tsar, not to the Duma.

This was a highly conservative constitution, though not as odd in the Europe of 1906 as it later seemed. The concentration of military and foreign policy power in the hands of the monarch was also a feature of the German and Austrian constitutions, and even in Sweden the ministers were still responsible to the king, not the parliament. What made the Russian system more distinctive was the failure of the cabinet to emerge as a united force (results depended on personalities) and the complex system of electoral franchise for the Duma. The Duma was elected not simply from regions or with property qualifications for voting, but by a complex of regional districts, indirect voting, and the curial system. For each social group (peasants, townspeople, workers, nobles) there was a curia, and the voters cast their ballots within a curia. Still believing in the loyalty of the peasantry and its social conservatism, the elections to the first Duma that took place in winter 1905–06 were based on a distribution of seats that favored the peasantry. Nicholas was convinced that only the upper and middle classes opposed autocracy, but the peasants were on his side.

The outcome of the elections presented the government with a Duma that was impossible to work with. Boycotts by the revolutionary parties meant that the liberals, the Kadets (Constitutional Democrats, officially the Party of Popular Freedom), were the largest party in the Duma, while the peasants, only slowly moving into parties, were the largest group. For the Kadets, the government's concessions to constitutionalism were far too small, and the peasant deputies surprised everyone by voting for any measure that would give them land. Many did express loyalty to the tsar, but they also wanted the land, something Nicholas and Witte had not bargained on. Nicholas dissolved the Duma in July, hoping new elections would prove more favorable. Witte resigned, and his replacement was Petr Stolypin, a former provincial governor with a reputation for crushing rebellion but also for an interest in reform. The first sign of the latter was the law he sponsored in the fall of 1906 allowing peasants to leave the village community and set up independent farms.

The strike movement and the rural disturbances gradually died down in the course of late 1906. Stolypin sent out punitive battalions into the countryside to repress peasant rebels, with executions carried out on the spot. The elections to the second Duma, however, did not produce the results that Stolypin and the government hoped for. If anything, the new Duma was even more radical than the first. The peasant deputies were now organized into the "Labor Group" that demanded all land for the peasantry. Finally on June 3, 1907, Stolypin dissolved the Duma, and there was virtually no reaction from the public. The revolution had spent its force.

The 1905 Revolution had been a bloody affair, with some fifteen thousand killed, most of them peasants executed or simply killed during government reprisals in the countryside. Several thousand revolutionaries were also executed, and many workers perished in conflicts over strikes or in the various insurrections. Some landowners in the countryside suffered as well, and much property was destroyed. In late 1905 an "All-Russian Peasant Union" had come into existence, which enrolled several hundred thousand members and demanded the surrender of all the land to the peasantry. The Union tried to avoid violent tactics, but its members grew increasingly radical into 1906 and allied with the Labor Group in the Duma. The Peasant Union too was suppressed. The most important outcome was the radical change in Russian politics. The virtual disappearance of censorship and the elections to the Duma and its debates took politics from the halls of the court and the offices of the bureaucracy into the public, even into the streets for the duration of the revolution. Whole social classes began to think differently: the nobility stopped flirting with liberalism and quickly united behind slogans of autocracy, nationalism, and preservation of the social order. The urban middle and working classes lost their passivity and began to participate in political action and to support some of the more radical parties. The businessmen formed small parties of their own and lobby groups, the peasantry heard the speeches of the Peasant Union activists and the SRs, and learned to vote for its interests in the land issue. The various national minorities now had active political parties: in Georgia the Mensheviks combined socialism with nationalism to become the far and away strongest force. In Latvia the Social Democrats allied with the Bolsheviks and dominated the labor movement. In Poland all the political parties came out into the open, and the National Democrats competed with some success against socialist groups for the allegiance of the workers. Among the Muslim peoples of the empire, the progressive intelligentsia put up candidates for the Duma and won, going on to form a Muslim Duma group that united Tatars, Bashkirs, Crimeans, Azeris, and North Caucasus mountaineers to press for equal status. Like many of the autonomist groups, they allied with the Russian Kadets and participated actively in Duma debates.

However much power the tsar and his ministers retained – and it was considerable – they now had to contend with a wholly new political situation, and few of them, Nicholas least of all, were prepared for it.

The next seven years after the dissolution of the second Duma were Russia's only peacetime experiment in constitutional government with an open press and active public organizations. The fate of the country depended on the ability of Stolypin and others to deal with this new reality. Stolypin's repression of the revolution met with apparent success: hundreds of activists were executed, especially from the SR terrorist group, and all radical parties lost members in droves to prison, exile, disillusionment, and simple exhaustion. The dissolution of the Duma in 1907 went along with a new, even more indirect and undemocratic electoral system. Some fifty percent of the seats in the new Duma went to the nobility, while the representation of peasants was radically cut, as were the number of seats assigned to the national minority areas in the south and west. The new Duma was overwhelmingly noble, Russian, and very conservative.

Most nobles and many businessmen supported the Octobrist party (so-called in their support of the tsar's October Manifesto), but there was also an extreme right, mostly noblemen, that included leaders of the Black Hundreds. Stolypin seemed to have a perfect situation in which to carry out his modest reforms, maintain the power of tsar and government, and move toward a more Russian nationalistic policy in the empire. In fact he accomplished little beyond his agrarian program, which proved to be of limited effect. The result of the endless bargaining of Prime Minister and Duma was only to drive a wedge between him and the upper classes. His reforms were too radical for the nobles and yet not strong enough to placate society and the liberals in the Duma. The climax was his 1911 plan to introduce the zemstvo into the western provinces, areas where nobles were predominantly Polish. In order to stack the zemstvo boards against the Poles, Stolypin proposed to increase the number of peasant deputies, Ukrainians and Belorussians whom Stolypin saw as more loyal to the tsar than Polish nobles. At the same time, the zemstvo would relieve the administrative burden on the state and hopefully placate the liberals. In the event, the scheme was too clever to succeed. He managed to get it through the Duma only to have it fail in the Council of State. Stolypin resigned in protest, knowing that Nicholas thought him indispensable. The tsar begged him to return, but Stolypin would not agree unless Nicholas removed some of the extreme conservatives from the government, prorogued the Duma, and enacted the western zemstvo bill by his emergency powers. The tsar agreed, but the incident confirmed his growing suspicion that Stolypin's plans were too far reaching, and he was too powerful and not trustworthy. Before their disagreements reached a crisis, an SR terrorist assassinated Stolypin in September at a performance in the Kiev opera house.

With Stolypin gone, the tsar turned to lesser figures to run the government. He particularly disliked the institution of a prime minister, and appointed to the office men who would not dominate the cabinet. The result was drift. None of the problems facing Russian society were addressed, and the government was increasingly isolated. In educated society the perception grew, even among conservatives, that the tsar and government did not understand the country and lived in a world of their own. No major issues were addressed, and government measures achieved neither reform nor successful repression. Attempts to use nationalism and anti-semitism to garner popular support backfired. In 1911 the investigation of a murder in Kiev led to accusations of ritual murder against Mendel Beiliss, a Jewish supervisor in a brick factory. The Ministry of Justice in Petersburg and the police "organized" a trial and pamphlets appeared about ritual murder and other supposed crimes of the Jews. Russia, however, now had a relatively free press and the liberal dailies mounted a furious counter campaign. Passions were so inflamed among the intelligentsia that the performance of a play based on the works of Dostoyevsky was shut down in St. Petersburg, on the grounds that the great writer's anti-semitic nationalism gave support to the prosecution. The trial took place in the fall of 1913 in a regular criminal court in Kiev. The jury remained unconvinced by the prosecution's evidence and acquitted Beiliss. The result was a major humiliation for the government.

To top it all off, the presence of Grigorii Rasputin at the court added an element of the grotesque to an already bad atmosphere. Rasputin was a wandering monk from Siberia who was introduced into the court at the end of 1905. Empress Alexandra had always been interested in faith healing and hoped that he could help her son, the heir Aleksei. She soon came to believe that Rasputin alone could stop the bleeding. Rasputin thus had unlimited access to the imperial family, in spite of his heterodox religious views and stories (largely true) of drinking bouts and womanizing. The security police set up a whole detachment to watch the monk with the purpose of stopping the rumors as they discredited the tsar and his wife. Rasputin was a real concern to the monarchists and conservatives in the government and Duma and they managed to bring the issue to the floor of the assembly, in the process enraging the tsar. He never realized that they were trying to save the prestige of the throne and instead interpreted their acts as disloyalty. Rasputin, rumors aside, had no political effect that can be traced, but his presence and the real and exaggerated stories further undermined the monarchy.

If the liberals and conservatives in the Duma, for all their frustrations, found in the new order a vast arena for political activity, the revolutionary parties were demoralized, losing thousands of members, especially from the intelligentsia. The leadership went into exile in the West, spending their time trying to keep the movement alive. The movements fissured: Trotsky abandoned the main Menshevik movement and founded his own newspaper in Vienna, commenting from cafés on world politics. The Bolsheviks were particularly contentious, torn by philosophical disputes as well as party tactics and organization. Lenin wrote an entire book denouncing the attempt of some Bolshevik intellectuals to integrate the epistemology of the German physicist Ernst Mach into Marxism. Only around 1912 did the various factions coalesce into organized parties and reestablish a network in Russia. For the Bolshevik party the moment came that year at a conference in Prague that finally consolidated the Bolshevik structure and program, reaffirming Lenin's belief in the need for an underground party. The Prague conference also marked the beginnings of a generational shift among the Bolsheviks, for the intelligentsia leadership of Lenin's youth gradually gave way to a younger group that was more plebeian (if not exactly proletarian). They usually lacked university education but were experienced in the ways of the underground and used to making contact with the workers in continuous struggle with the police. One of these was a Georgian Bolshevik, Soso Djugashvili, known as Koba – a shoemaker's son from the Caucasus. As he made his mark on the movement throughout Russia, he took a new revolutionary pseudonym, Stalin. As Joseph Stalin he would be known to history.

During the time that Stolypin was struggling to control the Duma, the formation of political blocs in Europe continued. Nicholas and the Kaiser repeatedly tried for a rapprochement, but the attempts came to nothing. In 1907 Russia and Britain signed a treaty dividing up spheres of influence in Iran, thus eliminating a major object of their imperial rivalry. The result was not exactly an alliance, but it did put an end to the decades old "Cold War," and in the presence of an Anglo-French agreement, meant that Russia, with Britain and France, now faced Germany and Austria-Hungary. There were plenty of areas of conflict, the most important being the Balkans. Russia had allied with Serbia, which stood right in the path of any Austrian or German expansion in that area, and both had great ambitions focused on the Ottoman Empire. Germany hoped to make the Turks semi-allies and semi-dependents in their larger rivalry with Great Britain. In 1909 Austria, with German backing, humiliated Russia by annexing Bosnia-Herzegovina, since 1878 an Austrian protectorate. A series of local wars in the Balkans added to the growing tension. Then in June 1914, the heir to the Austrian throne, Archduke Franz Ferdinand, made a tour of the new Bosnian province. As his motorcade proceeded along the narrow street by the river at Sarajevo, a young Serb nationalist, Gavrilo Princip, stepped out from the crowd with a revolver and shot him dead. For Russia as for the rest of Europe, it was a fatal shot.

16

War and Revolution

The Russian revolution of 1917 was one of the many consequences of the First World War. The war placed strains on the Russian state and society that neither could withstand. The result was six years of war and upheaval that created the Soviet Union.

WAR

Russia's participation in the First World War was not an accident. After the Russo-Japanese War Russia's foreign policy turned west. In 1907 Russia concluded the treaty with its long time rival, Great Britain, to establish a condominium over Iran. The Russians took control of the northern part of the country down to Teheran, and the British the south. This compromise put an end to Anglo-Russian imperial competition in Asia, and meant that Russia was now effectively allied with Britain as well as France. The only imaginable enemies were Germany and Austria. The agreement over Persia set the stage for 1914, but it was imperial rivalries in the Balkans that provided the spark for the explosion. There, Russia faced a resurgent Ottoman Empire allied with Germany and Austria and Bulgaria tagging along. At this point Russia's only ally was tiny Serbia, which stood right in the way of Austro-German expansion in the south. A series of Balkan crises in these years repeatedly showed Russia's weakness in the area: it had no formal allies other than Serbia and none of the informal power that came from business ties established by the Germans and Austrians as well as the French and

British. When Gavrilo Princip assassinated the Austrian archduke in Sarajevo in 1914, Vienna issued an ultimatum to Serbia and Russia had to back up Serbian resistance. Russia's basic credibility was at stake, and the result was war. It had not sought the war, but had drifted into the crisis as it was doing in so many other areas.

If the government of the Russian Empire after the death of Stolypin merely drifted on the current of events, neither Russian society nor the revolutionary movement demonstrated such passivity. The years just before the First World War were years of dynamic economic growth for the islands of modern industry in the sea of rural backwardness. Industrial development meant growth in the size and to some extent in the sophistication of the working class, and the revolutionary parties were poised to make use of it. In some places the workers turned to strikes again. In 1912 on the Lena River in Siberia, several hundred workers perished when soldiers and police suppressed a strike at the English-owned gold fields. About this time the revolutionary parties had recovered from defeat in 1905–1907. Bolsheviks, Mensheviks, and SRs were all reasonably well organized, and the labor movement recovered. In the spring of 1914 a wave of strikes swept St. Petersburg, one where the Bolsheviks for the first time seemed to be in the lead, not the Mensheviks or SRs. The rest of the country was relatively quiet, however, and the news of war hit Russia like a thunderbolt. Russia had actually devoted much effort to rebuilding its army and navy since the war with Japan, and one of the many factors encouraging the German General Staff and the Kaiser to push for immediate war was the fear that Russia would be much harder to defeat in only a few years. That being said, both planning and equipment were still deficient. At the insistence of the tsar huge sums had gone to rebuilding the Baltic Fleet, which in the event was far too small to challenge the German navy and never left port. Russia's armaments industry was still inadequate to supply a modern army and its transport network, adequate for peacetime, was too small for rapid mobilization and supply of the army on the western frontier. To make matters worse, the rapid advance of the German army through Belgium and France created a crisis at the front. Under heavy French pressure the Russians dealt with the crisis by sending an unprepared army into East

Prussia, an expedition that ended in defeat at Tannenberg in August 1914. Thus, Russia began the war with a defeat.

At home the war produced an orgy of patriotism at first. To universal acclaim the government changed the German name St. Petersburg to Petrograd, a Russian translation, more or less, of the same. Liberals and reactionaries in the Duma united on a war platform and the intelligentsia, like their counterparts farther west, poured out a flood of anti-enemy propaganda and nationalist ravings. The workers as well were swept up in the fever and the strike movement in the capital evaporated. The police came down hard on the revolutionary parties, particularly on the Bolsheviks, and within days their leaders inside Russia disappeared into prison and Siberian exile. Stalin was among them. The Bolsheviks were the particular object of the government's wrath because of their position on the war, a position that transformed an obscure Marxist group into a world movement that fundamentally reordered the twentieth century. For it was out of Lenin's reaction to the war, not as a response to the later Russian Revolution, that Communism was born.

Before 1914 the European Socialist parties had repeatedly pledged at their international meetings to oppose all wars among the European states as inimical to the interests of the working class. These were large powerful parties with mass membership, control of major labor unions, and elaborate social and cultural services, utterly unlike Lenin's little band of underground fighters. As the declarations of war came thundering out of the governments in July and August 1914, the expectation was that the socialists would likely oppose the war, and even go on strike, as they had threatened earlier, in order to stop it. Nothing of the kind happened. Instead, almost to a man the socialist leaders came out for the war, and joined the chorus of patriotism and hate in their respective countries. The few that dissented felt bound by party discipline to keep silent and follow the leadership. Among the Russians, the elderly founder of Russian Marxism, Plekhanov, came out in support of the war, and the Mensheviks adopted a compromise position, not calling for Russian victory but not opposing the war. Alone among the European Socialists, Lenin's Bolsheviks and a handful of dissident Mensheviks like Trotsky opposed the war from the first day.

Lenin was no pacifist, and his program on the war was not just to oppose it. He proclaimed that the defeat of the Russian Empire would be the best outcome for Russia and called for all socialists, in Russia and elsewhere, to turn the international war into a civil war. In other words, he was calling for armed insurrection in wartime. This position seemed to him the only correct Marxist attitude, but why did so few of the European Socialists agree? They had, he thought, betrayed the working class they were supposed to lead, but why? In despair at the future, Lenin turned to Marxist theory to try to understand what had happened. He reread Aristotle's *Metaphysics* (in Greek; he was a product of the Russian gymnasium) and Hegel's *Science of Logic* to try to recapture the original sense of dialectics as Hegel and Marx understood it. He also made a long study of recent economic developments. His aim was to understand the support for the war by the European Socialists. His conclusion was that the answer lay in imperialism, in the superwealth generated by the European empires in Africa and Asia, fuelled by the ever-growing concentration of capital. Empire was the real aim of the warring powers, concealed under a deceptive jargon about freedom or national honor. Wealth from empire also produced a labor aristocracy, happy with the status quo and thus unwilling to cause trouble in wartime. In the short term, it would benefit from imperialism. Both conclusions would have enormous effects after the Russian Revolution, but for the moment the reading did little more than keep Lenin busy while the world slipped deeper into the bloody swamp of war.

As the casualties piled up in the millions, opposition to the war began to surface among the socialists in Western Europe. The first to break ranks were the left wing of the German Social-Democrats, Rosa Luxemburg, Karl Liebknecht, and their followers, who voted against the war credits in the Reichstag in December 1914. Soon the anti-war socialists held small meetings in Switzerland to call for an end to the war and discuss tactics, and even here Lenin, with his uncompromising call for revolution, was in the minority. The Russian Bolsheviks for the first time came to the attention of the world, as a tiny band of revolutionaries who stuck to their position even though it seemed to doom them to isolation and defeat. Their position began to attract support among Western socialists, and out of these small groups meeting in Switzerland came a world movement with decisive consequences for Russia as well as for China, Vietnam, and other countries as well. The consequences of these obscure meetings lay in the distant future. Back in Russia, the situation gradually deteriorated and offered no comfort to either the tsar and his government or the Bolsheviks. At the start of the war Nicholas suspended the Duma, hoping to rule alone. The initial defeat in East Prussia was followed in spring, 1915, by a general Russian retreat from Poland, and this retreat finally led to a government crisis. The Duma was recalled over the summer, and the Kadets and moderate conservatives managed to put together a "Progressive Bloc" that offered to cooperate in the war effort with the government. Ultimately the government did have to call on the zemstvos and various committees of businessmen to resolve the crises in supply, but only reluctantly and too late. New agencies appeared to regulate the economy for the war, as in Germany and other warring powers, but Russia lacked the infrastructure to make them work. The government regulated grain prices to supply the army and cities with cheap food, but the result was that the peasants began to cut back on their sowing, and food production began to fall, worsening the situation.

In late 1915 Nicholas himself took over command of the army, moving from Petrograd to the Stavka, the army headquarters near Mogilev. His move did the army no good and only further disorganized government in the capital, for he remained the sole authority and now it was even harder to get his attention. His repeated consultation with Empress Alexandra and Rasputin probably did not have much impact on policy but served to further alienate the public. The Russian army had mixed successes, for it could do little against the Germans but scored a major victory against Austria in 1916 (the "Brusilov Offensive" led by General Aleksei Brusilov) and against the Turks. Erzerum in eastern Anatolia fell to General Nikolai Yudenich the same year. These successes could not change the general stagnation in the war nor stop the bloodshed. Russia's casualties mounted toward some two million dead, two-and-a-half million wounded, and five million prisoners of war. In the Duma the Kadet leader Pavel Miliukov spoke of treason in high places (a reference to the Empress Alexandra, among others) and then in

December 1916, a group of young aristocrats fearful of the fate of the monarchy assassinated Rasputin. Inviting him to dinner, they first fed him heavily poisoned food and wine, and then when that had no effect on his massive frame, they shot him and put him under the ice of the St. Petersburg canals. Rasputin was gone, and the monarchy soon followed.

In many respects the fall of the Romanov dynasty was almost an anticlimax. In late February 1917, the worsening food situation in St. Petersburg led to long lines at bakeries and other food stores in working class parts of the city. On International Women's Day (February 23/March 8; a socialist holiday) many women workers, exhausted by standing in the food lines on top of long work days, went out on strike. In a few hours the men in the factories heard the news and they went out on strike as well, soon shutting down the entire city. Students and the middle classes joined them. The government called out troops, who fired on the demonstrators, killing several dozen. The next day, however, the very same soldiers who had fired refused to fight and mutinied, taking other regiments with them, even the Cossacks. The ministers and the Duma sent increasingly desperate telegrams to the tsar, and Nicholas hurried back from the Stavka. Before he got to the capital he was met by representatives of the government who convinced him to abdicate. This he did, on March 2/15, and the monarchy abruptly came to an end.

REVOLUTION

Even before the tsar's abdication two new governments were forming in Petrograd. As the tsar's government collapsed, the Duma leaders formed a Provisional Government led by Prince Georgii Lvov, the head of the Union of Zemstvos, a liberal country gentleman with a law degree and a record of service in the local councils and the Duma. His foreign minister was the leader of the Kadet party, the historian Pavel Miliukov. The only more or less radical voice was that of Aleksandr Kerenskii, a lawyer known for defense work in political trials and a member of the Duma's "Labor Group," agrarian socialists close to the right wing of the SRs. His father had been the principal of the high school in Simbirsk when Lenin was one of the pupils. These men were the flower of liberal

Russia, broadly conceived, but as a group had no idea how to lead the masses and spent much of their time worrying about the reactions of Russia's wartime allies, Britain, France, and soon the United States. Their preferred solution to all problems facing Russia was to call a Constituent Assembly to write a constitution for a democratic republic that would address the peasants' desire for the land and the grievances of the workers. In the meantime they would pursue the war, hopefully to an allied victory over Germany.

The other "government" was the Petrograd Soviet. On Menshevik urging, the workers at nearly every factory in the city elected delegates to the city Soviet, which numbered nearly a thousand members. Its first act was "Order no. 1" that specified that the army was to be run by elected soviets of the soldiers, the officers having command only during operations. As the revolutionary parties came out into the open for the first time in Russian history, the Mensheviks and SRs, not the Bolsheviks, quickly asserted dominance in the Soviet in Petrograd and most other towns. The Menshevik tactic was to refuse support to the Provisional Government and simultaneously push it toward a more radical direction, a hopeless compromise position. Right at the start, the war had to be faced as an issue. While the Russian Mensheviks differed from most European socialists by arguing that the war should be ended without victory for either side, they had no workable plan to stop it, nor did they advocate an immediate socialist revolution. Their position did reflect real popular hostility to the war, and in May Miliukov and others had to leave the Provisional Government, for they wanted to push the war to a victorious end and the Soviet would not have that. Lvov organized a new government with several moderate socialists, including Kerenskii who was in charge of the army and navy, and started a new offensive at the front. Soviets were also formed in Moscow and other cities, in the army, and even in some parts of the countryside. They represented workers, soldiers, and peasants only, not the middle or upper classes. Reelected every few weeks, the local soviets reflected the popular mood very closely.

In all these deliberations during the first months of the revolution the Bolsheviks remained a minority in the soviets. Lenin heard of the fall of the tsar in Switzerland and managed to return to Russia through Germany, having convinced the German government that he was more of a threat to Russia's war effort than to their own. He traveled in a train whose doors were sealed until he reached neutral Sweden, reaching Petrograd via Finland on April 3/16, 1917, to the tumultuous welcome of his followers. He found that the Bolshevik leaders, including Stalin, had returned from exile and were beginning to organize themselves. They all lacked, however, a clear idea of what their platform ought to be. Lenin's was absolutely clear, as expressed in the "April Theses." The fall of the tsar, he wrote, meant that the bourgeois revolution, the one the party had aimed for in 1905, had ended. In the country there was now dual power, the soviets alongside the Provisional Government. The aim should now be the seizure of power by the proletariat with the aim of transforming Russia into a socialist society. The instrument of that seizure was to be the soviets, primarily the workers' and soldiers' soviets. The immediate aim of the Bolsheviks was thus to secure a majority in the Petrograd and other soviets.

The story of the next few months is the story of the fulfillment of that goal. It was the situation of Russia that made it possible, for the whole country entered a major crisis. The collapse of the old government left little effective authority in its place, and much of that was cowed by the revolutionary crowd. In the villages the peasants simply took the land during the summer. In many places there was violence, but often they simply ignored the noble landowner and began to plow up his fields for their own. Sometimes they came to the mansions of the aristocrats and politely told them to leave. However it occurred, the peasant seizure of the land was a cataclysmic change in Russian society, in a few months putting an end to a social order that had lasted for centuries. Most nobles were no longer the masters of the land but impoverished refugees in the big cities. In the cities the workers used their new freedom to demand an eight-hour day, higher wages, and to form factory committees that tried to take control of the work place.

The left parties all came out into the open and tried to become mass organizations. The time of the revolutionary underground was over. At first the most successful were the SRs, with their traditions of direct action and appeal to the peasantry. For the first time they actually managed to organize significant numbers of peasants into their party, and their working class following was very large. They had one deep problem, however – the war. Even before 1917 some of the SRs had come out against the war, with a position very close to Lenin's, but remained part of the larger party. As the crisis deepened over the summer of 1917, the split widened. The Mensheviks, always hoping to build a mass party in freer conditions, benefited enormously from the new freedom. When the soviets held their first congress of delegates from all of Russia in June, the SR's and Mensheviks had nearly three hundred deputies each, and the Bolsheviks only a little more than a hundred. Moderation seemed to triumph, but the mood changed very fast.

The Bolsheviks for the first time were becoming a mass party, too. In place of the few thousand professional revolutionaries the party grew rapidly to over two hundred thousand, with the largest concentration in the large cities and in Petrograd in particular. These new members were overwhelmingly young factory workers, most under twenty-five. As more and more revolutionaries returned from abroad, the Bolsheviks also began to attract dissidents from the Mensheviks, the most important being Trotsky, whose opposition to the war brought him to join Lenin for the first time. Trotsky was a powerful orator, and his speeches were a major weapon in winning the masses to Bolshevism. The new members transformed the Bolshevik party, especially at the level of the rank and file, whose radicalism came to the fore in early July. The Petrograd Bolsheviks staged an armed demonstration that seemed to be turning into a bid for power. The Provisional Government, with support from the city soviet, was able to put it down and arrest many Bolshevik leaders. Lenin went into hiding in Finland and Trotsky landed in jail. In reaction to the events Kerenskii replaced Prince Lvov as prime minister. For a few weeks the revolutionary wave seemed to subside, but that was not to be. The war ground on, discontent in the army multiplied into a gradual collapse of discipline and Kerenskii replaced Brusilov with general Lavr Kornilov as commander in chief, hoping that Kornilov could restore order in the army. The task was beyond his powers. The transport net of the country, already weakened by the war, began to collapse, as did many essential industries and services. In the cities the soviets organized Red Guards, who contributed as much to disorder as to order. Revolutionary organizations and groups "expropriated" buildings for their own use, the most famous example being the Petrograd Soviet's seizure of the buildings of the Smolnyi Institute in Petrograd, the aristocratic girls' school founded by Empress Elizabeth. Thus it came to serve as the Bolshevik headquarters. For the middle and upper classes, it was the beginning of anarchy; for the workers, it was the dawn of a new world, chaotic, but their own. Endless discussion and meetings further disrupted factory work but also built a constituency for ever more radical demands. Life in Petrograd was feverish, and in the provinces only a bit calmer. Moscow and all towns and settlements with any industry boiled with meetings, speeches, and demonstrations. On the fringes of the country nationalist movements appeared with demands for autonomy. In Kiev groups of nationalist intellectuals and party activists proclaimed themselves the Ukrainian Rada (council) alongside the Provisional Government and the local soviets. Other groups formed in the Baltics and the Caucasus, though none of them advocated actual independence as yet.

The July days had put a crimp in the Bolshevik organization and its rise to dominance among the workers. Then at the end of August general Kornilov advanced on the capital with the Mountaineer Cavalry Corps consisting of the Muslim peoples of the North Caucasus – Chechens and Circassians – to restore discipline and order in the country. In the face of this challenge Kerenskii had to turn to the Petrograd Soviet, which armed the workers. The Bolsheviks had grown in strength since the July Days. They were now crucial for the defeat of Kornilov, and their leaders emerged from jail into the open again. The inability of Kerenskii to defend the revolution on his own was the last blow to his power, and from the time of the defeat of Kornilov on September 1/14, the Provisional Government essentially drifted. The locus of action had shifted to the soviets. During and right after the Kornilov episode the Bolsheviks finally secured a majority in the Petrograd and Moscow soviets. As the weeks advanced and the economic and military crisis continued to worsen, another Congress of Soviets met, again with delegates from all over the country. Here the divisions in the SR party were to play a decisive role, for the Bolsheviks had clearly won the majority of the city workers, but in the villages they had no organization at all. The left wing of the SR party, increasingly radicalized by the revolution and demanding an immediate end to the war, was prepared to join the Bolsheviks. On October 10/23, Lenin returned from hiding in Finland and assembled the Bolshevik leaders. With the support of Trotsky and Stalin, he overcame the pessimists in the leadership, Zinoviev and Kamenev, and the Bolshevik Central Committee voted to seize power. With the votes of the Left SRs the Bolsheviks captured the leadership of the Congress of Soviets, and on October 25/November 7, 1917, the Red Guards moved on the Winter Palace to eject the Provisional Government. Only a few hundred defenders were left in the palace, officer cadets and the "Women's Batallion of Death," a unit formed of mostly middle-class women to fight in the war. On a signal from the naval cruiser Aurora, anchored in the Neva River, several thousand Red Guards in a fast walk through the autumn chill took the palace with minimal firing and casualties. Attempts at looting the wine cellar and the many treasures of the palace were quickly suppressed, and the ministers of the Provisional Government were escorted to prison in the St. Peter and Paul Fortress. Kerenskii escaped south in a US embassy car in a fruitless attempt to rally support at the front.

Relying on their majority in the Congress of Soviets, the Bolsheviks and the Left SRs now took power, proclaiming Russia a Soviet and Socialist Republic. The Mensheviks and Right SRs walked out of the Congress in protest as Trotsky consigned them to the "garbage heap of history." The first actions of the Reds were to organize the new government. The Congress of Soviets elected a government of People's Commissars with Lenin at the head and Trotsky as People's Commissar of Foreign Affairs. The other positions went to prominent Bolsheviks and Left SRs, the most significant among the former being Joseph Stalin as Commissar of Nationalities. Trotsky went to the Ministry of Foreign Affairs at the Choristers' Bridge near the Winter Palace, turned off the lights, and told everyone to go home. For the next few months, he ran foreign policy from a small office in the Smolny Institute.

The new Soviet government came into power with great support from the workers and intense opposition from the old upper classes, the middle classes, and the intelligentsia. These divisions were reflected in the Constituent Assembly that convened on January 5/18, 1918. Called by the Provisional Government, the Assembly elections had proceeded through the autumn, before and after the Bolshevik seizure of power. In the cities the Bolsheviks routed the moderate socialists (SRs and Mensheviks) leaving the increasingly more conservative and nationalistic Kadets as the second urban party. In the countryside, however, the SRs emerged with the most votes, though most candidates had not declared whether they supported the left or right, muddying the result. The Assembly met for some thirteen hours, after which the Bolshevik guard of Red sailors from the navy simply told the deputies to leave and go home. They obeyed. A few days later another Congress of Soviet Deputies proclaimed the new state, the Russian Soviet Federative Socialist Republic, with ringing declarations of the rights of the workers, peasants, and national minorities.

CIVIL WAR AND SOVIET POWER

By this time civil war had already begun, as groups of military officers in southern Russia came together to organize resistance to the new government and discontent grew among the Don Cossacks. The Cossack leader Kaledin formed a Cossack government of sorts on the Don, and the Reds quickly moved against him. Through the Civil War the Cossacks were to be the foundation of resistance to Soviet power. Living on the southern and eastern fringes of Russia, they were no longer the rebels of the eighteenth century. They combined peasant farming with service in the army, and secure in possession of their land, they had been the tsar's most loyal servants since the 1790s. The largest and most prosperous of the Cossack hosts was on the Don, and there was the fiercest resistance to the new order. At the same time the nationalist intellectuals in the Kiev Rada declared themselves to be the supreme power in the Ukraine. A Cossack-Ukrainian front seemed to be forming against the Reds in the south. A motley collection of red guards and sailors were enough to defeat both the Don Cossacks and the Rada by January 1918. At the same time chaos spread through the country, along with episodes of resistance elsewhere. At the end of December 1917, to meet these threats, Soviet authorities also formed the Cheka, the Extraordinary Commission for the Struggle with Banditism and Counterrevolution, an organization that combined security police functions with a sort of political army. Its first head was a Polish Communist, Felix Dzerzhinskii, incorruptible and ruthless.

The quick defeat of opposition to the Bolsheviks did not mean that order returned. The war had ruined the Russian economy. Inflation was out of control and the transport networks and the distribution of food were breaking down. Heat and light disappeared in Petrograd and other big cities, and workers began to return to their native villages, if they could. In the former capital of the Russian Empire the lights went out in the great palaces, the nobility fled to the south to warmth and food, along with much of the intelligentsia and the middle classes. As the army disintegrated, millions of soldiers clogged the trains going home, taking with them rifles and hand grenades. Criminal gangs terrorized many cities. The first measures of the Bolsheviks only increased the disintegration, for the new government set out to build a new socialist state in the midst of chaos. The workers frequently interpreted socialism to mean that they should physically eject the factory owners and managers and elect committees of workers to run the plants. These committees had no way to procure supplies or distribute the goods, and in the general social chaos labor discipline collapsed. It was a vicious circle. The Bolsheviks went along with this for several months, as part of the need to dissolve the old order, but by spring of 1918, the collapsing economy and the needs of civil war caused them to reverse themselves and begin to appoint single managers, former workers or party activists, to run the factories. In theory these Red managers were accountable to the newly established Supreme Economic Council and the various People's Commissariats (Industry, Trade, Agriculture, Labor, Food Supplies). Here was the embryo of the later Soviet state.

For the moment the Bolshevik priority was simple survival. The first order of business in November 1917 was the war, and immediately after the Bolshevik revolution the new government proclaimed a truce with Germany and its allies and opened negotiations. Trotsky went to Brest-Litovsk on the Polish border, now under German occupation, to try to make peace. The German demands were exorbitant, and Trotsky dithered, proclaiming that the right policy was "neither war nor peace." The Germans responded with a massive offensive, occupying all of the Ukraine, Belorussia, and the Baltic provinces. Local nationalists proclaimed their independence of Red Petrograd, but the Kaiser's armies paid them no attention. The Germans set up a puppet regime in Kiev with the Russian general Pavel Skoropadskii, a former adjutant of the tsar who had suddenly discovered his Ukrainian roots, as their instrument. Red Guards were too amateurish a force, and the Bolsheviks now formed a real army, the Workers' and Peasants' Red Army, in response, but the new army could not stop the Germans. The government moved to Moscow, farther from the German lines. Even so some of the Communist leaders, Nikolai Bukharin especially, and the Left SRs wanted to continue to fight a "revolutionary war." Lenin realized that this was madness, and convinced the leadership to sign on to the German conditions. Peace came in March, with the loss of all the western territories to Germany and Austria, but it was peace and the Kaiser recognized the red republic. The Left SRs resigned in protest, leaving the Bolsheviks entirely in charge of the new state.

The fiasco at Brest-Litovsk encouraged opposition to the Reds in the south. The southern Cossack areas rose in revolt again, this time allied with the Volunteer Army of General Mikhail Alekseev formed from officers of the old army. On the Don the new Red Army managed to suppress the Whites, who fled south to the Kuban River area, but other troubles soon arose. Serious fighting began in May 1918, in a wholly different part of the country, after the actions of the Czechoslovak Corps. The Czechoslovak Corps had been formed under the tsar from prisoners of war, former Austro-Hungarian soldiers of Czech and Slovak nationality, to assist the Allies against Austria and Germany. After the Soviet peace with Germany, they wanted to continue to fight and the new government allowed them to exit the country through Siberia to Japan and the United States so as to be able to continue the war in France. A series of clashes with local Soviet authorities led them to seize control of the rail lines from European Russia all the way to the Pacific Ocean. In Samara in June, guarded by the Czechs, some SR deputies of the dispersed Constituent Assembly formed a government that attempted to continue the practices of parliamentary democracy. It also managed to get together a "People's Army" that moved toward Moscow against the Reds.

Figure 18. Trotsky, Lenin, and Lev Kamenev 1918–1920.

For Lenin and the Bolsheviks, this was a real crisis, aggravated by the revolt of their recent allies, the Left SRs. Enraged by the peace with Germany and out of power the Left SRs attempted a revolt in Moscow, assassinating the German ambassador in the process. Similar revolts took place in other Russian towns, all quickly suppressed but indicative of serious opposition to the new government. The main threat, however, was the Czechoslovak Corps and its Russian allies moving from the east, and the ramshackle Red Army, formed of poorly trained militias with inexperienced officers, fell back in retreat. This was the moment that Trotsky first showed his mettle as a military commander, as well as his ruthlessness in imposing order and discipline. He made full use of officers from the old army of the tsar, holding their families hostage to guarantee their loyalty. In addition the political commissars assigned to each military unit were to maintain and inspire its reliability. He had officers who failed, commissars, and simple soldiers shot in the hundreds. With this new organization, the Red Army recaptured the Volga towns and pushed the rapidly disintegrating People's Army back to the Urals.

These crises sealed the fate of the former Tsar Nicholas and his family. Their presence in Siberian Tobolsk, where the Provisional Government had sent them, was too close to the emerging centers of resistance, and so the Reds brought them to Ekaterinburg in the Urals. In July 1918, as the Whites approached, the Soviets ordered the imperial family executed, the final end of the Romanov dynasty that had ruled Russia for three centuries. The house where they lived and where they were killed remained unnoticed for decades until 1977, when an overzealous Communist party boss, Boris Yeltsin, had it razed to the ground. Back in Moscow, Lenin himself was the target of an assassin's bullet at the end of August. The response of the Cheka was to declare Red Terror, arresting thousands from the middle and upper classes. Some were executed immediately, others kept as hostages against future attempts.

By the autumn of 1918, the new Red Army had retaken most of the Volga and the Urals, and the People's Army melted away. Farther east in Siberian Omsk another White army had come into being, Siberian Cossacks and units formed by ex-imperial officers determined to fight the Reds. In November, Admiral Alexander Kolchak seized power as Supreme Ruler of Russia, and dissolved the remnants of the SR leadership from the Constituent Assembly. Kolchak also shot many of the SRs as well as any other Bolshevik or left-wing activists whom he could find. Kolchak was a military dictator, and there were to be no more games with democracy. In addition there was a new element coming into play, for the First World War ended on November 11, and allied commissioners, British, French, American, and Japanese, arrived in Omsk. The allies, too, were for dictatorship, and quickly moved to support Kolchak as the leader of the opposition to Bolshevism.

If Kolchak was the titular supreme leader, his was not the only White army in the field. After the Reds had retaken the Don early in 1918, the Volunteer Army had moved south through the winter to establish themselves on the Kuban. The death of Alekseev and his replacement Kornilov (of the 1917 putsch attempt) in rapid succession led to the emergence of General Anton Denikin as the supreme commander of the Volunteer Army in the south. While

Trotsky was preoccupied on the Volga, Denikin had held on, and on the Don the Cossacks rose again later in 1918. With covert German support, they tried to move north and east. As yet they were too weak to break the Red resistance, though they did cut off much of the crucial grain producing areas, and if they crossed the Volga, they had a distant chance of linking with Kolchak. On the Volga at Tsaritsyn, the Cossacks and the Whites confronted Joseph Stalin, sent originally just to organize grain deliveries, but Stalin quickly moved to take control of the military apparatus and shore up resistance. His ally among the soldiers was Kliment Voroshilov, who had fled east with a ragtag workers' militia from the Donbass ahead of the advancing Germans. Stalin and Voroshilov were also unhappy with Trotsky's policy of extensive use of professional officers from the tsar's army, but Lenin supported Trotsky on this issue and they had to back down. Red units commanded by professional officers were decisive in holding the line, but at Tsaritsyn the Commissar of Nationalities had his first taste of warfare. The Cossacks did not cross the river, and Kolchak was thousands of miles to the east, unable to join them.

Behind all these front lines the Reds proceeded to build utopia. While Marxism provided a detailed analysis of capitalism and the projected path to proletarian revolution, it provided almost nothing beyond generalities about socialism. The worsening crisis in food supplies caused by increasing chaos and the German seizure of the Ukraine had led to the proclamation of the "food dictatorship" in May 1918. Under the People's Commissariat of Food Supplies armed detachments went out into the countryside to seize "surplus" grain at fixed, pre-revolutionary prices or simply to confiscate it. The idea was to get at grain allegedly held back by kulaks and traders with the help of the poor peasants organized in committees, but in fact the distinctions among the peasants were hard to make, and the measures affected all of rural society. Continued hyperinflation and the disappearance of money worsened the ongoing economic collapse, and the Reds instituted rationing and a system of cooperatives to distribute food and consumer goods.

Early in 1919 the Soviet authorities formalized the system of obligatory grain deliveries, to be accompanied by a centralized allocation of consumer goods to the peasants. Some sixty thousand men were now mobilized into a "food army" to extract grain from the countryside. The peasants responded by reducing the size of their crops, further plunging the cities into crisis. These new measures, in part the product of ideology and in part the necessity of war, lasted throughout the civil war. The Bolsheviks had always been hostile to markets, and the collapse of transport and general chaos broke down normal market ties. This situation gave them an opportunity to institute utopian schemes of distribution through the central allocation of goods. Virtually all factories and all trade were nationalized. Small retail shops disappeared, while the Soviet municipalities tried to set up large city-owned bread factories instead of small neighborhood bakeries, worsening the food situation. This was the system that came to be known as "War Communism." Reality soon intervened, for local Soviet authorities regularly violated the rules, and the impossibility of full central control led the major factories and even the Red Army to set up their own procurement systems for food, including substantial numbers of farms operated by the factories and the army. The only remaining markets were the flea markets and the black market, both of which made simple survival easier for much of the urban population. The new central economic institutions were incapable of implementing their schemes, for they were not grand bureaucratic structures, but rather small offices staffed by former revolutionary activists with no relevant experience, assisted by a few engineers or economists and the more qualified workers.

The emerging Soviet state was also a party-state, for the Bolshevik party expanded in size, to over three hundred thousand in early 1919. These men and women were the cadre for the new state. The remaining Mensheviks and SRs were pushed out of political life by the end of 1918 and the new institutions required loyal officials to run them. The party itself became more centralized, especially with the establishment of the Politburo (Political Bureau) over the Central Committee in 1919. The new Politburo included only Lenin, Kamenev, Trotsky, Stalin, and Nikolai Krestinskii as full members; Zinoviev, Bukharin, and Mikhail Kalinin were included as candidates. Here was the core of the Bolshevik leadership. Zinoviev was the son of Jewish dairy farmers in the Ukraine and had been close to Lenin during his years of European exile. After the government moved to Moscow in 1918, Zinoviev headed the Petrograd party organization, effectively running the city until 1926, at the same time leading the new Communist International. Lev Kamenev was the son of a Jewish railroad worker, but had acquired some university education and was married to Trotsky's sister. After 1917, he functioned as Lenin's deputy and ran the Moscow party organization. Bukharin, the best educated of the Bolsheviks after Lenin, was something of a Marxist theorist and had spent time both in Western Europe and briefly in the United States. He was a bit younger than the others, and personally popular in the party. Like Lenin he was also actually Russian, as were Krestinskii and Kalinin, both minor figures. Krestinskii served as Commissar of Finance, while Kalinin, the only worker in the group and even born into a peasant family, headed the Central Executive Committee of the Soviets – in other words, he was the technical head of government. All of them shared, with Stalin, solid credentials of unwavering Bolshevism. Trotsky, in contrast, was a flamboyant ex-Menshevik who fit poorly into the group.

The crucial person in the whole party and government was Lenin. Until 1917 he had spent his life as a revolutionary organizer and journalist, turning out masses of articles explaining his position and denouncing his opponents. He was also more intellectual than the others, as his writings on philosophy and the economics of imperialism demonstrated. In such matters only Bukharin came close to him. As an orator he was clear and capable of moving an audience, but not on the level of Trotsky or Zinoviev. On taking power in 1917, he proved to have political and administrative skills far in excess of most of his comrades, as well as a powerful will and the ability to make decisions. He rapidly absorbed himself in the details of government, including the myriad economic problems that arose when the Bolsheviks nationalized the economy. He tried and largely succeeded in imposing a spirit of teamwork on the party leadership, getting contentious and often arrogant comrades to work together. When he argued his position in person, he could convince his opponents without belittling them (although his published polemics were another matter). Even if all of the other leaders disagreed with him on occasion, he remained the unchallenged leader of the party and hence of the state.

This highly effective leadership controlled a very imperfect state apparatus, but it had, besides the party, other instruments of power. The Red Army was five million strong by the end of the Civil War but "labor armies" made up much of its theoretical strength and it took on many economic functions, providing horses for plowing and restoring railroad service. The Cheka provided internal security, eliminated active and potential opponents, and tried to suppress the growing number of criminal bands in the cities. There were some twenty-five thousand people in the Cheka by the end of the Civil War, but it also controlled over a hundred thousand internal security troops, infantry, and cavalry. The party, the army, and the Cheka made possible the Red victory, but they could not stop the deepening economic crisis and accompanying anarchy. The near collapse of rail transport meant that the northern cities could be supplied only with great difficulty. Petrograd suffered in particular, losing some three quarters of its population by 1920. With the move of the government to Moscow the Reds evacuated a number of key factories with their workers and equipment, and hundreds of thousands of workers came to work in Moscow, joined the party apparatus, the Cheka, or the Red Army. Many simply went home to their native villages in search of food, heat, and work. As order collapsed, disease began to spread. Typhus, influenza, and other diseases were epidemic.

The spring of 1919 brought new life to the White movements. The end of the war in Europe in November 1918 meant the withdrawal of German troops from the western territories. In the Baltic provinces and the Ukraine, local nationalists declared independence from the Bolsheviks, but the Red Army quickly returned power to the Soviets. The Reds drove out the nationalist Ukrainian Directory in Kiev. At the approach of the Red forces, the Directory's peasant army simply melted away. Under their military leader Semyon Petliura the Ukrainian nationalists moved west, carrying out a ferocious massacre of the Jews in Proskurov on the way. Kolchak held Siberia and the Urals and Denikin moved north through the spring, taking the Donbass, most of the Ukraine and southern Russia. Denikin was able to advance as far as Orel, raiding far behind the Red lines with substantial groups of cavalry. The mobility of the Civil War put a premium on cavalry, and the Cossacks and the cavalry officers of the old army were a formidable challenge. The Reds answered with Semen Budennyi's First Cavalry Army, formed in the middle of the battles against Denikin, at first a ragtag band of poorly disciplined men whipped into shape by Budennyi's charisma. In July mass mobilization by the Reds allowed them to send substantial armies against Denikin and stopped him. Behind his lines in the southern Ukraine a new army appeared seemingly out of nothing, the anarchist army of Nestor Makhno, an ex-sergeant of the Russian Imperial Army and an instinctive guerilla leader. Makhno shredded Denikin's communications, and with the Reds driving him from the north, he had to retreat.

Denikin was an accomplished general but this was a political war. The White governments were military dictatorships with civilian ministers recruited from former liberals to give them some minimal credibility. Their social policy was bound to antagonize the masses, as they opposed not only the Reds but also anything the workers saw as conquests of the revolution. In the cities, only the middle and upper classes supported them. Massacres of Jews were frequent. In the countryside their policy inevitably supported the noble landowners against the peasants and could not exploit rural antagonism to Bolshevik measures. To make matters worse, the White governments financed their operations by printing money and the peasants were reluctant to sell grain for worthless currency. Like the Reds, the Whites turned to confiscation of grain. As in the Red-held areas, the peasants reduced their farming to subsistence, creating food shortages in the richest agricultural areas in the country, western Siberia and the south. As resistance to them grew, the Whites could only answer with repression, and the cities that the Whites occupied saw mass executions. Behind the White lines in Siberia and the Ukraine the peasants formed armed bands to confront the Whites. Not only Makhno but also hundreds of peasant bands bent only on preserving their own territory kept the Whites from effective control of the countryside.

Even foreign intervention could not save the Whites. With the end of the First World War the Allies had free access to Russia through the Black Sea and elsewhere, but the exhaustion of war meant that they could offer little in the way of actual troops. Japan sent some sixty thousand to Siberia as part of a scheme to take control of

Russian territory (thereby antagonizing the United States), but the other powers sent fewer troops. A brief intervention in Odessa and other southern cities in 1919 ended after only a few months, although Britain, France, and the United States continued to send weapons. They were not of much use, for transportation bottlenecks (especially in Siberia) held up the supplies in the ports and massive corruption meant that arms and ammunition often ended up in the hands of the Reds. To make matters worse, the officers who formed the core of the White movement were intensely patriotic and many were offended by the need to rely on foreign armies. The intervention weakened morale as much as it strengthened it.

In the fall of 1919 the Reds pushed Kolchak's forces back into Siberia, the first victories of the later Soviet marshal M. N. Tukhachevskii, an aristocratic guards officer turned revolutionary enthusiast. The Red Army finally defeated Kolchak, capturing and executing him in Siberian Irkutsk. There was another try at a White victory: General Iudenich, the victor of Erzerum in 1916, led an expedition from Estonia toward Petrograd. Zinoviev thought the city defenseless, and Lenin agreed with him. Trotsky and Stalin vehemently objected, and convinced Lenin to let them defend the city. They raced north to Petrograd, Trotsky personally jumping on a horse to rally the troops. In October of 1919, Iudenich began the retreat back to Estonia. In the south, Denikin gave up command early in 1920 and went into exile. The remains of the White Army retreated to the Crimea and set up a new army and government under Baron Peter Wrangel. At that point the new Polish state invaded the Ukraine. The aim of the Poles was to conquer the lands held by Poland before the partitions of the eighteenth century, and to do so they allied with Petliura, who thus further discredited himself with the Ukrainian peasantry for whom the Poles were only noble landlords, and as such, their enemies. The Red Army redeployed west to meet the new threat, mobilizing some half a million soldiers. Lenin was convinced that the Reds should go all the way to Warsaw, an attempt to help the spread of revolution in Europe as well as to defeat the Poles. Trotsky was skeptical. The Red Army, led before Warsaw by the brilliant but erratic Tukhachevskii, moved too far to the west in an attempt to encircle the city. A huge gap opened in the Red lines, but the Red troops farther south under Budennyi, with

Stalin as political commander, delayed moving north to help close the gap. The Poles, with French advice and weapons, swept north in a maneuver of brilliant simplicity to encircle Tukhachevskii's troops. The Reds retreated far to the east, their major defeat in the Civil War, and made peace with Poland. The treaty established a boundary that gave Poland large parts of western Belorussia and the Ukraine, but not the main cities, Kiev, Odessa, and Minsk.

At the critical moment of the Polish war Baron Wrangel had moved into the Red rear from Crimea. Now his was the only hostile force left in the field against the Bolsheviks. At the end of 1920 the Red Army stormed across the isthmus into Crimea with the help of Makhno's irregulars, and the White cause was finished. The last refugees, soldiers and civilians evacuated the southern cities under the guns of the British navy, in a chaotic scene that marked the final end of the old Russia.

The revolution and civil war was largely a Russian event but it had profound effects for the various nationalities that made up the periphery of the Russian Empire. In Poland nationalism trumped class and socialism, and the transition to an independent government was (internally) fairly smooth. In Finland a vicious civil war in 1918 between the local Social Democrats and the Whites led to a White victory after the Kaiser sent an expeditionary force to aid Baron Gustav Mannerheim, a former Imperial Russian general. In the Baltic provinces the collapse of the German occupation led to civil war as well, for Riga especially had a large and very radical working class. Britain, however, saw the Baltic as its sphere of influence and landed Freikorps soldiers, German right-wing nationalist paramilitaries, in 1919 to push out the Reds. The British then set up a nationalist government in their place, evicting the Freikorps as well. The Baltic Reds went into exile in Soviet Russia, providing in particular a major component in the Cheka and Red Army. In the Ukraine the task of the Reds was made easier by the fact that all of the cities were Russian-speaking. The largest urban minority was Jewish, not Ukrainian, and the local nationalist movement was a small layer of intellectuals trying to lead the peasantry. Their armies were totally disorganized, and in addition they were reluctant to be clear on the land question, the crucial issue to the peasants. The Reds easily swept them away.

In the Caucasus the Reds were also victorious. The Brest-Litovsk treaty had led to the German-Turkish occupation of the Caucasus, and the end of the war meant their withdrawal. The Reds tried to make a revolution in their wake, but local nationalist parties took power with British help. As Britain was busily occupying the nearby Middle East, it had few resources to spare, and the local governments were left to their own devices. In 1920 the Red Army came south under the command of Stalin's fellow Georgian and close friend Sergo Ordzhonikidze and took Baku. The small Azeri army was largely led by Turkish officers, by now supporters of Kemal Ataturk's resistance to the western powers in Anatolia, and greeted the Reds as allies. Furthermore, Baku itself was a city in its majority not Azeri but Russian, Georgian, and Armenian, a population drawn by oil to what was largely a European city. The Reds had plenty of allies. The Reds moved on quickly to eject the Armenian nationalists, and a few months later it was the turn of the Georgian Mensheviks. A new Soviet republic, the Transcaucasian Federation, came into existence, combining all of the area under one government. In Central Asia resistance to the Reds ended by 1922, and the Japanese were eventually persuaded to withdraw from eastern Siberia, so that everywhere but in the West the old boundaries were reestablished.

The new, Soviet, Russia that came into being was devastated by years of war and revolution, with its economy in pieces. Perhaps a million men had died on the many fronts of the Civil War and (estimates vary) five or six million civilians – the greatest number of these from typhus and other epidemic diseases, followed by hunger. Executions and massive reprisals by all sides made up the rest of the death toll. Some million or two Russians, including much of the old upper classes and the intelligentsia, left the country, never to return. Transport and production were at a standstill. For the time being, the Soviets continued the policy of War Communism and mobilized the Labor Armies under Trotsky to rebuild the damage. This was not a viable policy and resistance to the new order grew throughout the country. Lenin realized that some sort of compromise was needed, an economic policy that provided enough room for the population, particularly the peasantry, to work without state direction. This compromise would be named the New Economic Policy and it inaugurated a whole new era in the history of Soviet Russia and the other Soviet states under the rule of the Communist Party.

17

Compromise and Preparation

The end of the Civil War presented the Soviet leadership with a whole series of new issues, some immediate and some more long term. If the White armies were defeated, internal discontent was growing rapidly, fueled by the catastrophic economic situation and resentment of the party dictatorship. In 1920 in the Tambov province in central Russia a major revolt of the peasantry broke out, largely unpolitical but no less fervent. It required major army forces under Tukhachevskii to suppress it. As the army moved into Tambov province, the sailors of Kronstadt rose in revolt. The revolt at the naval base in the harbor of Petrograd was much more visible and more political. The sailors had been crucial supporters of the Bolsheviks in 1917, and now they were calling for Soviets to be elected without Communists, a direct challenge to the emerging Soviet system. At the end of March, 1921, Trotsky sent troops across the ice to retake the fort with much loss of life, the whole event illustrating the fragility of Soviet power. The revolts and the obvious failure of War Communism led to a sharp turn in economic policy. As the fighting raged in Kronstadt, Lenin and the party abolished the system of compulsory grain deliveries, substituting a tax in kind and permitting the peasantry to trade freely in the products left after the payment of the new tax. This step was the foundation of the New Economic Policy, known as NEP. A return to a money economy soon followed, and with it came permission from the state, even encouragement, for private individuals to trade and set up businesses to supply a population starved of the most basic consumer goods. Socialism was no longer on the immediate agenda. Industrial recovery would eventually provide a basis for further development, and at an indefinite point in the future peasant agriculture would be drawn somehow into the socialist system (a process called "collectivization").

The next immediate issue was the famine that appeared in 1922, the result of years of devastation, neglect of equipment and infrastructure, the absence of peasants from the fields while fighting in the various armies during the Civil War, the Soviet grain requisitions that discouraged farming, and general death and destruction. The Soviets took up the offer of the American Relief Administration under Herbert Hoover, fresh from relief operations in Belgium, to provide food to stricken areas in the south and the Volga region. Relief and the return of peace could contain the famine, but longer-term issues remained. The outcome of the revolution and civil war was that the peasantry finally controlled virtually all arable land in Russia. With the urban economy devastated, however, they at first had little incentive to sell their grain to the cities. Yet NEP depended precisely on the peasant sale of grain for consumer goods, and eventually it worked. The peasants now had cloth, industrially manufactured consumer goods, and some farm equipment to buy in return for their grain. At this point, the party did little to advance any sort of socialist agriculture. It abandoned the experiments with the "communes" of the Civil War era, and settled for modest cooperatives among the peasants while trying to build a basic party network among them, especially from younger peasants who had served in the Red Army.

The result was a certain return to normalcy on the part of urban society, but that was very much a matter of the surface of things. In reality, all had changed. The old state, upper classes, and much of the intelligentsia were gone, dead, marginalized, or abroad. In their place was the new party-state, the core of which was the Communist Party. In the old palaces of the nobility the Party set up museums and kindergartens, party offices and schools, and Cheka headquarters and administrative offices. Interspersed among drab new institutions were the more garish shops and restaurants of the Nepmen (as the new businessmen were called) with their hints of luxury and hedonism. Bright lights reappeared and private restaurants featured jazz bands and European cabaret acts. Advertisements for privately manufactured rubber boots and champagne hung alongside banners calling for world revolution. Prostitutes and smugglers rubbed shoulders with German Comintern agents and Latvian Cheka officers. Workers were enrolled in instant higher education projects (the "Workers' Faculties") and peasants came to the cities looking for unskilled work as before.

The Soviet Union of the 1920s was a colorful place, but there was more than an easier daily life in the cities. The economy revived from the catastrophic situation of 1920; indeed it revived much faster than the party leadership expected. Instead of decades of rebuilding, production in almost all areas had rebounded by 1926 to pre-war levels, in some areas exceeding them. Of course this was merely a revival, and in the years since 1914 the world had not stood still. Especially in the United States and Germany, new technologies were changing the landscape, and the Soviet Union had merely rebuilt the pre-war world. Automobiles, new chemical industries, aircraft, and radio technology were all new and growing rapidly in the West. The USSR would have to move very fast just to catch up. Unfortunately one crucial area lagged behind: agriculture. The problem was not total production, for the country produced almost exactly the same amount of grain – the crucial commodity – as in 1914, but now much less came to market. On average the peasants marketed only a bit more than half of the amount of grain marketed before the war. Explanations for this phenomenon vary, but it seems that it was the result of land seizures in the summer of 1917. Large estates, which had been market-oriented, disappeared, and the distribution of land among the peasants was radically equalized. Well-off peasants (the kulaks) did remain in the villages, but most land went to middling producers who consumed more of their harvest than before the war. Soviet pricing policies increased the problem, as the peasants thought the state purchase prices were too low. Here was the dilemma: if the country was to continue to industrialize, and to keep up with the West, it would need vast new industries and new cities, and their workers would need food. How to get it? Agriculture would have to become more productive, but how and how fast? Thus the rather technical questions of balancing industrial growth rates and modernizing agriculture became the object of increasingly acrimonious debate and vicious internal struggles inside the leadership of the Communist Party. The outcome of these debates and struggle was the supreme power of Joseph Stalin. The Civil War had further centralized an already centralized party and also imbued it with a civil war mentality. All disagreements became necessarily matters of life and death – all opponents were covert enemies of the entire revolutionary idea. Lenin and Trotsky defended and practiced terror against the Whites and other enemies. The remaining moderate socialist parties, the Mensheviks and Left SRs as well as the anarchists were suppressed. Not surprisingly, the end of the Civil War had no effect on the Bolshevik mentality, and the demands for ideological unity, if anything, became sharper. Personality clashes and differences in strategy, however, militated against unity. Lenin, in his last writings, was critical of all of the major figures – Stalin, Trotsky, Bukharin, and others – but offered no clear choice among the leadership. The first major dispute broke out in 1923, as Lenin's health deteriorated after several strokes. Trotsky and a number of his allies from the Civil War began to criticize the "bureaucratic tendencies" in the party. Then in January 1924, Lenin died. The mantle of leadership was not passed on to any one man: Stalin, Zinoviev, and Kamenev were the dominant figures. In 1922 the Party Congress had appointed Stalin General Secretary of the party, a position he held until his death. It gave him control or at least knowledge of all appointments in the party to any positions of significance. Bukharin, as editor of *Pravda*, the party newspaper, was their most important ally. Trotsky still possessed great power and prestige but the others did not trust him. As the Commissar of War for many years, he seemed the most likely to become the Bonaparte of the Russian Revolution. If not as well educated as Bukharin, he was sophisticated, cosmopolitan, and arrogant – too aloof to form powerful allies. Trotsky's Menshevik past continued to haunt him. He also seriously underestimated Stalin, thinking him a provincial boor who was only good at bureaucratic maneuvers. Stalin, as a Georgian with a heavy accent, was in some ways even more of an outsider than Trotsky, but he had to his credit long years of faithful service to the party and an unflinching loyalty to Bolshevism. He had not spent long years abroad before 1917, and in that sense was more part of the Russian scene and more familiar to the party rank and file than the other leaders. Unlike Trotsky, he did not read French novels when bored at party meetings.

These biographical details would be only curiosities of the time if they did not come into play when real and basic issues arose in the party leadership over the future of the country. The most important of these was the controversy over "socialism in one country," both for its own sake and for the implications it had for decisions in so many areas. The struggle began in the last years of Lenin's life, the first major one being Trotsky's 1923 opposition platform. Trotsky's main point was that the party was becoming less democratic and more bureaucratic through the practice of appointing its officials through Stalin's secretariat rather than by election. His letter to the party leadership on this issue sparked an intense discussion that eventually came out into the open just on the eve of Lenin's death on January 21, 1924. His opponents were Stalin, Zinoviev, and Kamenev on this issue, the three forming a triumvirate that ruled the party and the country after Lenin's death. Trotsky's opposition for the moment produced some concessions, but the triumvirate remained in control. In any case the dispute was not as radical as it might seem, as Trotsky was a principled supporter of a centralized and authoritarian party. All he wanted was a little room for maneuver. More basic disagreements quickly emerged. Trotsky believed that the revolution could not survive, and socialism could not be built in the Soviet Union unless there were revolutions in the advanced countries of the West. Only fraternal socialist aid could overcome Russia's backwardness. In the meantime, the USSR needed to pursue a policy of super-accelerated industrialization. The economist Evgenii Preobrazhenskii supported Trotsky on the issue of party structure, but also propounded a more detailed economic platform. His idea was simply to strip resources from the countryside by confiscations and other methods reminiscent of War Communism and use them for extremely rapid industrialization. The dilemma, as Preobrazhenskii saw it, was that the existence of private, small-scale peasant farming would lead to the strengthening of capitalism within the Soviet Union. He shared with Trotsky the idea that the Soviet Union could never survive as a socialist society encircled by capitalism: revolution in the advanced countries was essential to the building of socialism in the USSR, but in the short run extreme measures were necessary to ensure that the country would still be around when the revolution came in the West. This was the platform of the Left Opposition, as it came to be known.

This perspective met furious rejection from Bukharin, whose position as editor of *Pravda* meant that his views would receive wide circulation. Bukharin's platform was a strident defense of NEP. He ridiculed the super-industrialization schemes of the opposition and explained that the crucial issue was the recovery of agriculture and the gradual enrichment of the peasants. As long as the party controlled the state and industry remained in state hands, there was nothing to fear from the peasants and the country would move rapidly toward a socialist industrial society. Stalin allied with Bukharin and himself began to formulate the notion of "socialism in one country," the idea that the USSR alone could totally transform its society, including its agriculture, before the ultimate triumph of socialism in the West. For Stalin did not reject the prospect of world revolution, as he was convinced that the capitalist powers would eventually unleash a new world war and that revolution would come out of it if not earlier. Where he differed from Trotsky was in the belief that the Soviet Union could manage to build a socialist society on its own while waiting for revolution abroad.

The effect of the struggle was first to marginalize Trotsky, who lost his position as head of the War Commissariat and other offices in 1925. In that same year Zinoviev and Kamenev switched their allegiance, coming out in opposition to Stalin and Bukharin. For Zinoviev and Kamenev the main issue before had been fear of Trotsky: now they feared Stalin more. The now united opposition failed to win much support in the party and in 1926 Stalin had Zinoviev removed from his position as head of the party in Leningrad (Petrograd had acquired another new name on Lenin's death). Thus the opposition had no longer any substantial base in the organization of the party. Stalin and Bukharin triumphed at the end of 1927. The NEP policy triumphed, it seemed, if with an increased push toward industrialization. Trotsky, Zinoviev, and Kamenev were expelled from the party along with their followers. Zinoviev and Kamenev soon recanted their errors and were readmitted, but Trotsky went first into exile in Alma-ata, and then was expelled from the country in 1929. Stalin had utterly defeated the opposition, and it seemed that NEP might continue.

Stalin's victory went along with increasing prohibitions on dissent in the party and particularly on the formation of factions and oppositional platforms. Before the principle of absolute ideological unity could triumph, one last major dispute shook up the party leadership. Starting early in 1928, Stalin and his supporters changed their plans entirely. The cause was a drop in grain procured by the state agencies to feed the cities at the end of 1927. Stalin believed that the peasantry, mainly the kulaks, were simply holding grain back in the hopes of better prices or even to harm the Soviet state. His response was to organize an expedition of party officials led by himself into the Urals and Siberia early in 1928 to seize the grain. His expedition returned with freight cars loaded with grain, and he proclaimed it a success. Stalin and his allies now moved toward a policy of rapid industrialization and the collectivization of agriculture, effectively the end of NEP. The new policy provoked opposition from Bukharin as well as from Mikhail Tomskii, the head of the trade unions, and Aleksei Rykov, the Soviet Prime Minister. Basically their platform was simply that NEP was working out well, in spite of occasional problems, and that there was no need to force the pace, either in industry or the countryside. The Right Opposition was less of a defined group than the Left and had much more support in the party than the small group of Trotskyists and followers of Zinoviev and Kamenev. Nevertheless, Stalin fought it to extinction, expelling the Rights from the leadership and from the party by the end of 1929. Their many followers, especially in the party organization in Moscow, followed them into defeat. Stalin now had complete control over the central leadership of the party.

NEP, for all the concessions to the peasantry, implied a centralized, state-owned, and managed industry, and that implied a new kind of state. The Soviet state did not just regulate industry, it also directly managed it at every level. The overall structure was a refined form of the one established in 1918, the Supreme Economic Council placed at the center over a series of units for each branch of industry, one for iron and steel, another for coal, yet another for machine-building, grouped along regional lines. These units made the decisions that in capitalist economies are made by businessmen, and the decisions were subject to a single overall plan. That plan was the work of the State Planning Committee, or Gosplan. For most of the time from its foundation in 1921 to 1930 Gosplan worked under the leadership of Gleb Krzhizhanovskii. An exception to the norm among Bolshevik leaders, he was both a trained electrical engineer (from the St. Petersburg Technological Institute) and an Old Bolshevik. The original Gosplan was primarily an advisory office for the Supreme Economic Council, but it soon worked out an electrification plan for the whole country. By 1925 it was compiling "control figures," a sort of crude general economic plan, and by the late twenties it moved to writing the first five-year plan adopted in 1929.

The state's management apparatus for the economy, however, did not match these ambitious goals. In the 1920s most of the state officials were not Communist Party members. Even in the Supreme Economic Council and Gosplan, most were economists or engineers who neither belonged to the party nor were particularly sympathetic to its goals. Many had been active as Mensheviks, SRs, or even liberals before 1917, but they did have the technical skills the Bolsheviks needed. Lenin had always maintained that they would grow to accept the new order, but it was far from clear that this was the case. The party's instrument in all these offices was a small number of People's Commissars and chairmen of committees appointed by the party from its own leadership ranks – men with political rather than technical experience. The same was true at the factory level: the director was usually a party official, but the engineers and clerical workers were not. Thus the party gave orders to the economic managers and factories, but did not have full control. Even so, the party's Politburo and Central Committee spent long hours on the technicalities of economic administration, the timber industry or the acreage sown of sugar beets as well as arcane issues of monetary circulation and foreign trade. Some of these issues also had a political side and were involved in the factional battles of Trotsky, Stalin, and the "Rightists," so that economic decisions were frequently decided on political grounds. Indeed Stalin and the other leaders thought that politics should go ahead of "narrowly" economic concerns.

The other side of the new state was its federal structure based on a hierarchy of national units. Soviet federalism was about ethnicity, not just territory, and it grew out of the experiences of 1917–1920. The Bolshevik party had always maintained that the Russian Empire was a "prison of peoples" that combined the worst of European colonialism with the old military despotism of the tsars. Therefore they advanced the slogan of self-determination for the non-Russian peoples (including full independent statehood if desired) well before the First World War. During the revolution most of the national groups of the empire formed nationalist parties, if they did not have them before (as in Finland and Poland), parties that advocated some sort of national autonomy. Before most of them had time to formulate a clear platform and build a base, the Bolsheviks had seized power in Petrograd. With most cities speaking Russian and following the Reds, more or less, the nationalists had as their constituency only the local intelligentsia and, potentially, the peasantry. As most of the periphery was occupied by the Whites or interventionist troops until 1920, the Reds dealt only with the Ukraine and Belorussia in the west and the Muslim peoples of the Volga, the North Caucasus, and Central Asia. In each case the situation differed.

Belorussia was a largely artificial creation mandated by the party authorities in 1919–20 to counter Polish designs on the area. Most of the population was indifferent to the issue and the local Communists were flatly opposed to a local ethnic republic. Lenin (and Stalin, as Commissar of Nationalities) overruled them. The Ukraine was quite different. Here the nationalist movement was quite well established among the minority of the intelligentsia that considered itself Ukrainian and was initially able to mobilize wide support among the peasantry. They faced, however an insurmountable obstacle in the cities, largely Russian and Jewish in population. The working class was absolutely uninterested in the Ukrainian cause and most intellectuals were Russian or identified with Russia (meaning the White cause). Jews followed one or another of the Russian or Jewish parties (Zionists, the Bund), not the Ukrainians. Nevertheless the Bolsheviks in Moscow realized that they had to provide some sort of Ukrainian framework if only to neutralize the nationalists and thus they forced local Communists to form a Ukrainian

Communist Party and proclaim (in 1919) a Ukrainian Soviet Republic. Both the Belorussian and the Ukrainian republics were de jure independent of Moscow, but their Communist Parties were not. They were explicitly subject to the orders of the Central Committee in Moscow.

The Muslim peoples were a wholly different issue. In the North Caucasus nationalism was very weak and the predominant identity was Islamic and very local. Some groups had allied with the Cossacks against the Reds and supported the White armies, but the hostility of the latter toward any sort of local autonomy made allies for the Reds, especially in Daghestan, and this led to a multi-sided struggle of extraordinary complexity. The outcome was decided by the victories of the Red Army, and in 1920 the Soviet government began to set up a series of local autonomous republics in the mountains. Each of the local peoples acquired its political unit (some of the smallest combined).

The other main Muslim groups with whom the Reds had to deal were the Tatars and Bashkirs of the Volga and Urals. These were substantial minorities, several million each, living in relatively prosperous areas and largely surrounded by Russians and in mainly Russian cities. Under the Provisional Government the Muslim Duma deputies and other political figures had formed local parties in favor of national culture and autonomy but supported the Provisional Government. In the course of the Civil War the nationalist groups had started out on the side of the Whites but some of them switched to the Reds, unable to stomach Admiral Kolchak's nationalist orientation. In March 1919 the Bolsheviks set up a Bashkir Soviet republic as an autonomous unit within Russia and a year later a Tatar republic. Central Asia had provided yet another challenge, as fighting lasted until 1922, but the establishment of Soviet rule did bring a single Turkestan Soviet republic within Soviet Russia in 1918. Here nationality was an especially problematic issue that was not addressed until 1924.

In one way the most important of the Muslim peoples in 1920 was in the Caucasus. These were the Azeris, for the simple reason that their largest city, Baku, was also the principal center of oil production in the previous Russian Empire. The rapid conquest of the area led to the formation of a united Transcaucasian Federal

Soviet Republic in 1921. The idea came at the insistence of Stalin and Ordzhonikidze over the objections of other Georgian Communists, for Stalin did not want to encourage the aspirations of the larger nationalities. The brief years of independence had seen Georgian Mensheviks refuse to grant national rights to Abkhazia and Southern Ossetia as well as repeated Azeri-Armenian clashes. The solution was a federation that gave some sort of autonomy to all of the many ethnic groups of Transcaucasia, and in that way provided an obstacle, it seemed, to nationalism among the larger groups.

By 1922 Moscow was the center of several Soviet republics, technically independent but ruled by Communist Parties subordinate to the Russian Central Committee. Stalin decided to change this clumsy arrangement. His plan was to simply incorporate the other republics into Russia as autonomous units rather like Bashkiria but with somewhat more autonomy. His plan met opposition from Lenin, who believed that the greatest danger to party rule was Russian chauvinism. He did not want to provoke nationalist resistance on the periphery, and of course Russian nationalism had been the ideology of the Whites. Lenin's objections led to a new scheme, in which all the Soviet republics, including Russia, formed the Union of Soviet Socialist Republics. In this scheme the larger non-Russian units entered the union on an equal legal status with Russia. In the 1920s only some functions were formally centralized in Moscow. There was no Commissariat of Agriculture or Education for the whole union, only in the republics. At the same time the Communist Party was centralized in the Politburo and Central Committee and gave orders to all the republican party organizations. In addition, the management of most of the industrial economy from Moscow was a powerful centralizing element.

The new union now had to face a series of unresolved issues throughout the country. The basic presumption of the Soviet leadership was that nationality was a matter of language. Though both Lenin and Stalin added common history and culture to this definition, in practice it meant language was the deciding factor. This criterion that worked fairly well in the European part of the country did not fit other areas so well. It committed the Soviets to forming autonomous units wherever there were language differences, and thus they began to set up autonomous units among small Siberian peoples without any political or national consciousness in the modern sense. Even among peoples of European Russia there were problems. The small Volga people who spoke a Finno-ugric language that Russian scholars called Mordovian had a common language but no common word for both of the two Mordovian subgroups. The Soviet authorities simply declared them all Mordovians and introduced the Russian word for their nationality into their language. In the Ukraine large cities with few Ukrainian speakers such as Odessa soon had no newspapers in Russian, only in Ukrainian. Multi-national cities like Baku were a particular problem.

The language issues in the western parts of the country paled compared to the situation in Central Asia. The Kazakh population of the northern steppes was a relatively coherent group and received the status of an autonomous republic within Russia in 1924 (and a union republic in 1936). Farther south, the population of the Syr-Darya and Amu-Darya river basins presented tremendous difficulties. Identity in these areas did not fall along linguistic lines. Most of the people thought of themselves first as Muslims, and then only as parts of one or another group. The urban and much of the settled village population fell under the category of Sarts, whether they spoke a Turkic or Iranian language. "Uzbek" usually meant Turkic-speaking nomads around and among the settled areas. The great cities, Bukhara, Khiva, and Samarkand had been the centers of Uzbek dynasties but their traditional culture was both Turkic and Persian. The area more or less compactly settled by Iranian speakers had no large urban center. The most prosperous agricultural area, the Ferghana valley, was also one of the most ethinically diverse. While the Turkmens, Kazakhs, and Kirgiz formed relatively coherent units, they were also divided along tribal lines. The Soviets took all of this as merely backwardness and feudalism and proceeded to create republics along linguistic lines, though in the Ferghana Valley this meant leaving large minorities on all sides of the new borders. The outcome was five republics: Kazakhstan, Kirgizia, Turkmenia, Uzbekistan (the most populous) and Tadjikistan (the Iranian-speaking area).

In the 1920s the conditions of NEP meant that there were few grand plans to transform the new republics. Starting in 1924–25 the party pursued a policy of "nativization" of the party and state apparatus outside the Russian republic. The main thrust was the promotion of non-Russian cadre at all levels, though the key positions were usually exempt from this policy, being reserved by Moscow for its most trusted workers. These party leaders were not necessarily Russians, however: Georgians, Armenians, Latvians (especially in the political police), and Jews were prominent in the leadership of the non-Russian republics, far from their presumed home territories. Both culture and the peasantry were to a large extent left to the republics during the 1920s, not surprisingly as in Bolshevik ideology the peasants were the reserve of nationalism and the intelligentsia were the carriers of the local national cultures. In the NEP years, both were to be conciliated and indeed local cultures could not be advanced or created without the native intelligentsia.

The cultural autonomy of the new republics went along with a largely centralized political and economic system. While the republican Communist parties managed their own day-to-day affairs, the guidelines and top personnel were firmly in the hands of the leadership in Moscow. Economic management was split between the Supreme Economic Council of the USSR in Moscow and analogous offices in the republics. The most important centers of production, such the Donbass and the huge metal industry of the Ukrainian republic, were under the authority of the center. This situation led to complaints from all the republican governments, including even the Russian republic.

The Soviet Union came into existence at the end of years of war and during upheaval around the world. Lenin and the Bolsheviks believed that their revolution was only the first of a series that would soon come, and not even the most important. The whole Bolshevik leadership believed that a revolution was imminent in Germany, and the overthrow of the Kaiser in 1918 seemed to be the beginning, the German version of Russia's February Revolution. For the next few years it seemed that the German October was just around the corner. The brief establishment of a Hungarian Communist government in 1919 and upheavals around the rest of Europe seemed to confirm the prognosis, but the anticipated revolution never came. In 1923 the German Communists made a last failed attempt, and Lenin and the Soviet leadership recognized that the revolutionary wave had ebbed.

The Soviet Union was now isolated in a world of hostile capitalist powers. It needed to survive, and its leaders, including Stalin, also believed that the world revolution would come sooner or later. This was the basic contradiction of Soviet foreign policy, and it remained until the final end of the Soviet state. The revolutionary side of Soviet relations with the world in the 1920s was the province of the Communist International (the Comintern). Founded in 1919 as the Communist answer to the Socialist International of moderate (and mostly formerly pro-war) socialists, it aimed to organize and promote revolution throughout the world. It boasted an international leadership and staff, but its headquarters in Moscow was firmly under Soviet control, in the person of Grigorii Zinoviev until 1925. It brought together under its leadership all the many groups of socialists who had opposed the First World War and then had gone on to espouse revolution in its aftermath, forming Communist Parties in nearly every country in the world. These were fractious parties, most of them with tactics far more militant than Moscow approved, but the Soviet leadership soon brought them into line.

The Soviet government also realized that it needed to break out of its isolation. Early in 1921 Britain had made a trade agreement, the first breach in the economic blockade imposed by Western powers in 1918. Then in 1922 the Soviets made an agreement with Weimar Germany, an agreement that included recognition, mutual trade, and a secret military protocol that allowed German military officers to train on Soviet territory and other forms of military cooperation. Weimar Germany, as the main victim of the peace settlement of Versailles, wanted maneuver room, and Lenin accommodated them. For the next decade relations with Germany warmed and then cooled, but the military agreement remained intact and trade expanded. In contrast, relations with Britain took a sharp downward turn, in large part the result of Soviet and Comintern policies in the East.

The policies of the Soviet leadership in Asia formed a historic turning point, both in Russian history and in world history, generally. Their impact has far outlasted the particular goals of Lenin and the Comintern in 1919–20. Lenin's conception of imperialism implied that the European colonial empires provided crucial resources for the dominance of capitalism in the world and over the European working classes in particular. The oppressed people of the colonies were therefore crucial allies of the proletariat in the battle for socialism. The first meetings of the Comintern proclaimed this principle loud and clear, and its agents and supporters around the world spread the news. In Paris a young Vietnamese working at painting pseudo-asian pottery in a French factory read that the Comintern wanted to support the colonized peoples, and he decided to join the Communists. His name was Ho Chi Minh. At the time, however, it was the events in China that took most of the attention of the Comintern's Asian sections and the Soviet government. In 1911 nationalists led by Sun Yat-sen had overthrown the Ching dynasty and established a republic, but the struggle raged to make the republic work and to expel, or at least radically weaken, the treaty regime that held China in bondage to the Western powers and Japan. The Comintern and the infant Chinese Communist Party supported the Nationalists, only to have Chiang-kai Shek turn on them and virtually exterminate the Communists in 1927. The Chinese Communists would recover, but for the time being Soviet policy in China was one of the major reasons Britain broke off diplomatic relations with the USSR in 1927, provoking a war scare in Moscow that lasted for several months. The small groups of Communists in the various Asian colonies continued to exist, largely ignored by all but the colonial administrations, but their actions would eventually have enormous consequences that the modest growth of Communism in Europe could not match.

In spite of the failure in China the Soviet leadership was convinced that the setbacks were only temporary. Stalin, as well as his opponents in the party, was convinced that a new war was inevitable sooner or later – a war between the western powers, for the "contradictions", in Marxist terminology, between Britain, France, and Germany were too serious to be resolved in any other way. War would lead to another social crisis like that after World War I. In 1928 the Comintern made a sharp turn to the left, proclaiming that a new era of instability and revolution was coming soon, a notion that the depression beginning in 1929 seemed to confirm. Stalin was entirely behind the new Comintern line, especially as it urged the Communists to focus their attack on Social Democrats in the hopes of weaning the working class away from moderate leaders. At the same time he did not want to provoke a war with the great powers, and the policy of the Soviet state was much more conciliatory than the Comintern's proclamations. Stalin needed peace on his frontiers, as he was about to launch a giant upheaval.

18

Revolutions in Russian Culture

Unlike Russia's state and society, its culture did not experience such a sharp break in 1917. The period from about 1890 to the middle of the 1920s was full of artistic revolutions, happening simultaneously and in entirely different directions. These revolutions shared many characteristics with artistic movements in the rest of the world, but paradoxically the Russian culture of the Silver Age, as it is known (by comparison to the Golden Age in the nineteenth century) has never acquired an audience outside of Russia comparable to that which the writers and musicians of the earlier period secured. Perhaps one of the main reasons is that most of the truly talented writers of the Silver Age were poets, masters of that most untranslatable of art forms. The natural scientists, in contrast, began to acquire an international audience, in large part because of the efforts of the Soviet regime to encourage and use the sciences to build a new society.

LITERATURE, MUSIC, AND ART

The writers and artists who came to maturity in the 1890s were a mixed lot: symbolists and realists in literature, the "World of Art" group in the visual arts. In about 1910 new waves, or often wavelets, came on to the scene. A whole series of new movements in poetry, futurism, acmeism, and other groups contended for the attention of readers and critics, while the Ballets Russes introduced both new forms of dance and the radical (it seemed) new music of

Igor Stravinskii. The speed of innovation only increased. Working in Germany, Wassily Kandinsky produced entirely abstract work by 1911, and in St. Petersburg Kazimir Malevich painted his "Black Square" in 1915. The revolution and civil war split Russian culture in two, with many of the great names of the time staying abroad or emigrating, and others remaining behind with varying degrees of sympathy for the Bolsheviks. The émigrés largely continued their earlier styles, while in Soviet Russia the situation was more complex. Some saw the new order as of the same essence as their artistic revolution, while others espoused even more radical notions and still others tried to combine modernism with socialist content. By the end of the twenties, with the aging of the émigrés and the new Soviet order in art, a new phase began.

The generation of the 1890s confronted not just new ideas but also new conditions of work. The Russian publishing industry had expanded enormously since the Emancipation, and by 1900, prominent writers could actually live and even prosper on the earnings from their writing alone. Maxim Gorky was the first to be able to do so and in a spectacular fashion. As recounted in his autobiography, he came from a family of minor traders and earned his living by casual labor until he started writing. Virtually a tramp, he followed the course of the Volga working on the boats and taking factory jobs for short periods. By 1905 he was the best-paid author in Russia with a worldwide reputation and he spent his time mostly in Capri or Paris. Gorky was also typical of the artistic currents of the time, a fact muffled by later Soviet attempts to cast him as the father of "socialist realism." Gorky's prose was "realist" only by comparison to that of his contemporaries, for it also reflected his worldview, a kind of anarchistic rebelliousness and admiration for strong individuals. European critics immediately branded him a follower of Nietzsche, which was incorrect (Gorky read Nietzsche for the first time long after he formed his ideas and style) but it was an understandable mistake. His other great fascination was with religion, though not with official Orthodoxy but with what he saw as the semi-pagan and mystical religion of the people. It was the latter fascination that drew him to the Bolsheviks, for he saw in Marxism a kind of religion of the future that could lead the people to salvation.

Equally famous in the 1890s were the plays of Anton Chekhov. Chekhov's great fame was preceded by over a decade of writing short stories for newspapers, and in some ways he was aesthetically closer to the generation of Tolstoy and Turgenev. In his theatrical practice, however, he was in the Russian vanguard, for the most famous stage for his plays was the Moscow Art Theater. The Moscow Art Theater was the first major Russian dramatic theater that was not an Imperial Theater, for the court had abandoned its monopoly in 1882. The Moscow Art Theater was strictly a private enterprise operation with the sponsorship of local businessmen such as Savva Morozov, the heir to the family textile fortune. It was also the first major laboratory for the work of Konstantin Stanislavsky, who reformulated theatrical performance in Russia and much of the world in the first half of the twentieth century. Stanislavsky's demand that the actor live his role from the inside was a new departure over the (as he saw it) declamatory styles of the nineteenth century.

If Gorky, Chekhov, and Stanislavsky remained influential or at least revered for decades afterward, they were not entirely typical of an era dominated by Symbolism and other new trends. Dmitrii Merezhkovskii was the most prominent of the symbolists, beginning his career with a series of critical articles attacking the utilitarianism of the liberal and radical artistic theories of the previous generation. His call was for a sort of pure art, but in fact his own works were suffused with the philosophical and religious ideas of his generation. His subject matter was far from that of the earlier Russian classics – his first great success being a trilogy of novels set in ancient Rome (*Julian the Apostate*), the Renaissance, with Leonardo Da Vinci as its hero, and the Russia of Peter the Great. The idea was the eternal struggle of paganism and Christianity, with Peter as a sort of neo-pagan in the tradition of the emperor Julian and Da Vinci. Now largely forgotten, Merezhkovskii was a dominant figure for a generation. A more vital legacy was in the poetry of the younger symbolists, especially Alexander Blok.

Music and art also changed rapidly at the end of the century. For the St. Petersburg musicians the appearance of a patron, the timber merchant Mitrofan Beliaev, opened new possibilities in the 1880s. Beliaev not only sponsored concerts, but he also ran a

Friday evening salon that featured regular performances of new music, and even more important, he founded a music publishing firm in Leipzig to publish Russian music and paid generous honoraria. The core of Beliaev's circle comprised the survivors of the Five, though Balakirev rarely attended the salon. The Beliaev circle was also broader in its tastes than the original Five: to their admiration of Berlioz and Liszt they added Wagner, and grew more friendly to Tchaikovsky. Rimskii-Korsakov was the strongest artistic influence, though Stasov continued to command deep respect. As time passed, a younger generation such as Alexander Skriabin and Sergei Rakhmaninov benefitted from the circle's attention. The end of the monopoly of the Imperial theaters also allowed the formation of a private opera company in Moscow sponsored by the millionaire businessman Savva Mamontov, whose company attracted Russia's greatest singer, Fyodor Shaliapin. Mamontov also was the patron for a whole series of innovative painters, especially Valentin Serov. For Serov the light in his paintings was as important as the subject, as in the case of the Impressionists in France. This sort of art was a sharp break with the Itinerants and their fascination with the Russian landscape and the Russian people and its dilemmas.

In St. Petersburg the Russian artistic scene was transformed under the leadership of Sergei Diagilev, the main force behind a new magazine devoted to the visual arts named *Mir Iskusstva* (World of Art). The journal gave its name to a whole movement, a revolution in subject matter if not in technique. Though World of Art painters had a definite look that differed from the older painters of the Itinerant school, their greatest innovation was the turn from peasant life, landscape, and portraits of the intelligentsia toward more decorative depictions of interiors, retrospective pictures of eighteenth-century France or Russia, and portraits that stressed appearance and style as much or more than the sitter's inner life. The World of Art was also notable in that its impulses came to a large part from European painting, but there was no direct European prototype. Impressionism, Art Nouveau/Jugendstil, and other European trends played a role. The World of Art group also valued European styles from the past, the Renaissance and the eighteenth century, which the Itinerants despised. The same was the case with Russian art: Diagilev was perhaps the first to discover the value of eighteenth-century Russian portraiture. He organized regular exhibits of contemporary European art, starting with that of Finland and Scandinavia, to educate the Russian public. The goal was to promote painting that was not concerned with social issues and only rarely sought to affirm Russian nationality. Yet the artists like the writers of these years were not yet in pursuit of pure art. Almost all of them were looking for some reality behind the world of appearances, and found it in mysticism, theosophy, encounters with mediums, or occasionally even Orthodox Christianity. They also revealed a great deal of cultural pessimism, and a profound sense of ending. The World of Art painter Alexander Benois published a history of Russian art in 1898 that ended with the statement that art was now coming to an end, and would either cease to exist among humanity or be replaced by an art that served a religious idea.

Into this artistic ferment came the Revolution of 1905. The artistic world reacted variously to the events, but most of the artists were not sympathetic to the tsarist regime. In 1905 the issues were not only the general ones of political representation of the people and the social state of the workers and peasants, because the artists also chafed under the various hindrances and monopolies imposed by the state. Writers were doing well economically, but still had to deal with state censorship. Tolstoy's last major novel *Resurrection* could not be published in Russia and was passed around by students in mimeographed copies. The great theaters were under the Ministry of the Court, and their capacities and repertoire were far behind the expectations of the audience in the big cities. In St. Petersburg the only state-financed orchestra, the ancestor of the later Petrograd/Leningrad/St. Petersburg Philharmonic Orchestra was still technically the private orchestra of the tsar, and was founded only in 1882. The imperial patronage of music and the arts that made much of Russian artistic life possible in earlier decades was no longer necessary and felt as a burden.

Thus the establishment of the state Duma in 1906 and the accompanying relaxation of censorship found great approval among writers and artists, who quickly moved to exploit the opportunities. Whole new subject matter appeared in literature: the first novels to make sexuality an explicit theme and books with all sorts of heterodox religious conceptions that the Orthodox Church could no longer keep out. Alongside the more traditional locations of cultural activity, St. Petersburg and Moscow quickly developed a café and cabaret culture that attracted the leading lights of literature and art alongside the general public. A bohemian style of life was increasingly fashionable, including various experiments in sexuality and dress. Some writers acquired signature appearances, dandified clothing and hairstyles, or a studied artistic look. Sergei Diagilev had pioneered all this with his elegant suits and a lock of hair died silver to make him look more distinguished.

Private patronage became easier and more abundant as Russian businessmen prospered. After 1909 Sergei Kussevitskii was the conductor of a private orchestra in Moscow, the first in Russia to be successful. (After emigration in 1920 he became the long-time conductor of the Boston Symphony Orchestra and the founder of the Tanglewood Festival.) The most famous example of a private dance company was Diagilev's Ballets Russes, which made its debut in Paris in 1909 as well. In the following year the company presented the premiere of Igor Stravinskii's ballet, the *Firebird* and in 1913 his even more revolutionary *Rite of Spring*. The latter caused an uproar with its dissonances and apparent celebration of pagan sexuality and vigor, brilliantly interpreted by the lead dancer Vatslav Nijinskii. Stravinskii was the vanguard of Russian music, but not the whole of it. Of the older generation, Rimskii-Korsakov was active until his death in 1910 and among the younger musicians Sergei Rakhmaninov and Sergei Prokofiev took different paths to fame, Rakhmaninov with his rich neo-romanticism and Prokofiev already heading toward the irony and precision of neo-classicism. Not only Diagilev but also many of the musicians began to gravitate to Paris and Berlin, for the St. Petersburg theaters and orchestras with the necessary resources were usually too conservative for the new music and performance styles.

The painters also moved very rapidly. Kandinsky in Munich had a limited impact on his Russian colleagues, but in Russia painting evolved very quickly. Especially in Moscow a group of young painters in several informal groups ("Jack of Diamonds" and "Donkey's Tail") under the influence of Cubism and Russian folk art began to move sharply away from realist technique. One of the most talented among them, Kazimir Malevich began to turn toward full abstractionism, painting his famous "Black Square" and other fully non-representational works. Malevich evolved the notion of Suprematism, in which the artist should work with geometric forms, in their turn the key to hidden reality behind the appearance of the world. Few of his associates followed him all this way, but it was this world that produced such painters as Marc Chagall.

For writers the years after 1905 were equally frenetic with change. The most important of the new prose writers, Andrey Belyi, published his phantasmagoria of St. Petersburg in the revolution, the novel *Petersburg*, in 1913. Belyi was emblematic of the period in other ways, as he was an adept of the "anthroposophy" of Rudolf Steiner, at whose center in Switzerland he spent much of his time. The poets were even more active and contentious, with new groups, each with a manifesto, forming every year. The Acmeists in St. Petersburg met in the Stray Dog café and proclaimed Apollonian clarity against the "Dionysian" symbolists. Mostly very young, their most striking work came long afterward, as in the case of their greatest writer, the poet Anna Akhmatova. The futurists appeared a bit later with their manifesto, appropriately titled "A Slap in the Face of Public Taste." The futurists were as apocalyptic as the Symbolist generation in their evaluation of the world, but saw the approaching upheavals in a more positive light. They were fascinated with technology and saw the end of the older forms of art as liberating. The principal writer of the futurists was the poet Vladimir Mayakovskii, who was not only an artistic revolutionary but also a revolutionary in real life. Earlier on he had worked in the Bolshevik party and later he was to become the most famous poetic spokesman for the Reds after 1917.

Mayakovskii's attraction to Marxism was as unusual among the writers and artists as it was among the intelligentsia as a whole. The intelligentsia, however, outside the artistic avant-guard in Petersburg and Moscow, remained committed to the older ideals of the nineteenth century, liberalism in politics, occasional populist socialism, and its artistic canons as well. They preferred Turgenev to Merezhkovskii or Belyi, and only some of the poets managed to break out of the rarified atmosphere of the St. Petersburg cafés to reach the provincial reader. When the war came, most of the writers followed the general reaction of the country and the intelligentsia and supported the war effort. The revolution was another matter. By 1917 most realized that the war effort had largely failed, and they were happy with the fall of the tsar but were not heavily engaged in politics or at first even distracted by it. While Mayakovskii enthusiastically worked for the Bolsheviks, the composer Prokofiev was more typical: 1917 was one of his most productive years as he composed major works having nothing to do with the cataclysm around him. Most of the artists and writers, like the rest of the intelligentsia, greeted the Bolshevik revolution with hostility, but it was the outbreak of the Civil War and the economic collapse of Petrograd that forced them to make decisions.

To the writers and artists, whatever their reaction to the Bolsheviks, the Russian Revolution was not so much the seizure of power by Lenin and his comrades as a fundamental and total upheaval, a descent into chaos and anarchy. It seemed to them that Russia had returned to the Time of Troubles, that all the veneer of civilization that the country had acquired since Peter the Great had been blown apart by a massive upsurge of popular anger and violence. For many it was the reign of Antichrist.

A small number of the writers, however, were sympathetic to the revolution, if not to the specific Bolshevik platform. Alexander Blok's most famous poem, "The Twelve" (1918), depicts the anarchy and violence of Petrograd in the dark of the winter, but the twelve working-class Red Guards marching through the half-deserted streets are following a leader who is Jesus Christ. In contrast Vladimir Mayakovskii was entirely in the Bolshevik camp, and spent the years of the Civil War writing not only poetry but also agitational verse and drawing pictures for political posters. He changed his elegant futurist suits for a proletarian look in dress and a shaved head. In his poetry he tried to make the masses the heroes, most famously in "150,000,000" that began

150,000,000 is the name of the creator of this poem.
Its rhythms – bullets,
Its rhymes – fires from building to building.
150,000,000 speak with my lips . . . [trans. E. J. Brown]

Some of the painters and artists worked for the Reds as well, making huge modernist decorations for the May Day parades and other Bolshevik rituals. Most writers and artists, however, waited on the sidelines or hoped for White victory. Many moved south to the White-occupied territories. As the Reds drove the White armies out of the country, large parts of the intelligentsia followed them, producing a Russian culture in exile in Berlin and Paris.

For the musicians, dancers, and some of the painters, the move to Western Europe or America was the start of another career. Rakhmaninov made so much money from concerts that he was able to support other Russian émigrés, contributing to Igor Sikorsky's aircraft company in Connecticut. Prokofiev, the great singer Fyodor Shaliapin, and the dancers of the Ballet Russes worked throughout the world. Though the Ballets Russes fell apart after Diagilev's death in 1929, it left a legacy to the world of ballet in its many active dancers and in the work of George Balanchine in America. For the writers, however, the emigration was largely a disaster. Dependent on a Russian audience, they were cut off from Russia where their works could not be published and ceased to circulate legally after the early twenties. Russian émigrés did set up publishing companies, journals, and newspapers in Paris and elsewhere, but their readership was necessarily small, limited to the Russian and Russian-speaking exile communities in the West. Nevertheless, some were able to create remarkable works, especially in the early years. The poet Marina Tsetaeva wrote through the revolution, and when she came to Paris in 1921 continued to publish her verse in large quantity until about 1925. Even the older writers were able to produce a great deal at first, but the lack of audience soon began to tell. Western publishers were not interested in translations of any other than a select few, and even Ivan Bunin's 1933 Nobel Prize could not awaken much interest in the latest émigré literature.

In the emigration new intellectual currents arose, like Eurasianism, the idea that Russia was not really European, but part of a separate "Eurasian" civilization exemplified by the Mongol Empire. Other small groups elaborated new philosophies of religion, or drifted toward fascism. Some made their peace with the Soviets and returned home, such as the writer (Count) Alexei Tolstoy, a distant relative of Lev Tolstoy. Prokofiev returned in 1935. Maxim Gorky, who had maintained his distance from both the Soviets and emigration after 1920, returned in 1932 to become a major figure in the Soviet literary world. Others were not so lucky: Tsvetaeva, after returning, committed suicide in 1941.

CULTURE AND NEP

In the years of NEP the fate of the émigré writers and artists abroad seemed to be increasingly irrelevant, as the cultural world of the new USSR burgeoned with new artistic trends and new names. In the early years the Bolsheviks had no definite position on the arts. During the Civil War some of the radicals in the party formed the Proletarian Cultural-Educational Organizations, known as Proletkult, which combined schools to teach workers to write poetry and paint with radical esthetic notions. Lenin and Trotsky were skeptical of Proletkult, believing its claims to represent the correct proletarian line in art to be spurious. The Bolshevik leadership was also generally skeptical of much modernist art: Lenin reproached the Commissar of Education Anatolii Lunacharskii for printing so many copies of the works of Mayakovskii. Whatever their content, the verses failed to impress Lenin with their quality and he thought the money better spent elsewhere.

The Civil War had a catastrophic effect on music and the theater, for the simple reason that there was no money to keep the theaters going at any but the most minimal level. The Imperial Ballet School closed, and the ballet and opera theaters closed for various periods until the early 1920s. Orchestras suffered similar fates. With NEP and the revival of the Soviet economy, the Soviet government gradually reestablished the old theaters and orchestras under different names, and at the same time the NEP economy and the absence of a defined party line on the arts meant that many smaller ballet companies and theaters of various types came into existence. Instrumental music did better, for the conservatories continued to function with many of the old staff, and produced a whole generation of new composers. By the end of the 1920s Dmitrii Shostakovich already had a name, both for his "serious" compositions and for film music. Perhaps the most innovative theater was established under the leadership of Vsevolod Meyerhold in Moscow in 1922. Meyerhold had begun under Stanislavskii in the Moscow Art Theater, but by 1917 had rejected the master's ideas to develop his own theory and style of acting which he called "biomechanical." The idea was that the actor should not strive for naturalism but use his body and his voice for the most expressive possible performance, making his point by an "unnatural" style that would strike the audience more powerfully. Meyerhold in turn had a powerful effect on another art form that was just coming into its own at the time, the cinema. Sergei Eisenstein was just starting on his career as a director in the 1920s with his historical masterpieces such as *Battleship Potemkin*. The actors in the film reflected Meyerhold's theories, while the overall structure was the product of Eisenstein's technique of montage, using a series of discontinuous images to hammer home his esthetic and political points. This was a radical break with the normal technique of Hollywood and other films of the time, which stuck to visual continuity to tell the story. Eisenstein's innovations seem to have bothered no one among the Soviet authorities, for whom film was in some ways the perfect art form: it spoke to the masses, was based on the latest technology, was easy to reproduce, and was cheaper and more portable than the stage. It was also much more adaptable for political messages, as Eisenstein and other directors proved. As Lenin had said, in a comment endlessly repeated, "of all the arts, cinema is the most important to us." The Soviet authorities funded movies through their cultural offices, but resources were inadequate to produce films in large numbers. The great majority of the movies shown in the NEP era were actually imported Hollywood films.

With the end of the Civil War, publishing also revived, and in the NEP years a number of private publishers supplemented the products of the state publishers. The rich artistic world of the past could not be recreated. The NEP cafés lacked the elegance and panache of their pre-revolutionary prototypes, and the state publishers did not pay very well. The young Shostakovich survived by playing the piano in movie theaters to accompany silent films. The economy of artistic life was only one issue, as artists had to deal with the ambiguities of Soviet policy toward the intelligentsia, a policy based on an attitude of suspicion combined with an awareness of its value. The party also had very little to say about art. Certainly openly anti-Soviet works could not be published and the émigré writers gradually disappeared from the bookstores. Yet the party did not even publish a statement on literature until 1925, and that one contained little in the way of positive recommendations. The gist was that the party should help and promote "proletarian" writers as well as writers from the peasantry, but should also show tolerance of the "fellow travelers" (originally Trotsky's phrase), writers from the intelligentsia to a greater or lesser degree sympathetic or at least neutral toward the new order. Party critics should not expect the "fellow travelers" to have and express a complete Bolshevik world-view. In a sense, the party's position on the writers was similar to its position on engineers or government officials from the old intelligentsia. Until the end of the decade, the party relied on their skills and seemed to be willing to let them gradually move toward a friendlier attitude to the party and its aims.

The result of all these different elements was a great deal of varied writing, much of it innovative in language, style, and narrative technique. Even the "proletarian" writers wrote in a language that was full of slang, local dialects, and obscenities, a language that was later edited out of reprints of their work after the 1930s. While some of the proletarians wrote stories of Civil War sacrifice and heroism, pulling few punches to describe the horrors of the war, others tried to write about the working class in their factories, accounts of the rebuilding of Soviet industry and the new forms of life emerging around them. There were not very many of the actual proletarian writers, however, and most literature of the time presented a wide variety of daily life – often the semi-criminal margins of Soviet urban life, the complexities of the personal and private life of the intelligentsia and party officials. While many of the writers also spent much time in acrimonious debate among the various groupings, others managed to produce work of more enduring significance. In 1921 Boris Pasternak published a collection of poetry, "My Sister Life," which instantly established him as a leading poet. In 1926 Isaak Babel's *Red Cavalry* with its brutal honesty placed it at the head of all descriptions of the Civil War. The stories of NEP-era marginal characters culminated in 1928 with Ilf and Petrov's *Twelve Chairs*, whose con man hero Ostap Bender passed into Soviet and Russian folklore. Other writers found it impossible to publish: Anna Akhmatova was not published from 1925 to 1940, and Mikhail Bulgakov began to have difficulties from the mid-twenties. Though his Civil War–era play "Day of the Turbins" was scarcely a flattering portrait of the White cause, it was also not crudely hostile, and the play was repeatedly banned and then allowed again until it finally disappeared from the repertory to return only in the 1960s. His other works were simply forbidden entirely. Some writers were allowed to emigrate, such as Yuri Zamiatin whose novel of an anti-utopian society *We* would come to influence Aldous Huxley and George Orwell.

In literature and art, the 1920s were in many ways a continuation of the Silver Age under new conditions. Many of the most important voices of the twenties, Mayakovskii or Pasternak, Meyerhold or Prokofiev, were already accomplished artists by 1917, and the younger generation that came to maturity after 1920 was profoundly influenced by the culture of the pre-revolutionary decades. Even some of the young "proletarian" writers with their new themes wrote with Belyi or Blok in the back of their heads. The numerous literary or artistic platforms and groups maintained some of the organizational forms of artistic life of the Silver Age until the end of the NEP era.

THE NATURAL SCIENCES

For the natural sciences, in contrast, the revolution marked a more fundamental break, not so much intellectually but institutionally. The years before the revolution had been a period of change for Russian science. Perhaps the most important innovation had been the foundation of the new engineering schools under the Ministry of Finance. These technical schools not only produced sorely needed engineers but also were less conservative in their curricula than the universities under the Ministry of Education. Thus they were open to rapidly changing and growing disciplines like physics, while the universities tended to keep chemistry at the center of scientific education. The technical institutes were more open to society. They maintained ties with business, and were less restrictive about their admissions. Thus Jewish students like Abram Ioffe finished the St. Petersburg Technological Institute, studied in Germany, and received his first position in physics at the new St. Petersburg Polytechnic Institute, which was Witte's creation. His years there from 1906 to the Revolution were to be the incubation period of the later Soviet physics, for Ioffe quickly revealed his talent for organization and intellectual leadership. Yet the conditions of science as a whole left much to be desired. Physics had suffered a major blow in 1911 when much of the science faculty of Moscow University and the Kiev Polytechnic Institute resigned over Minister of Education Kasso's illegal repression of student meetings (a meeting in honor of Tolstoy's death was at issue). There were few other institutions where the scientists could move, though some managed to find a home in the Academy of Sciences in St. Petersburg. Among the successful few among the protestors was the geochemist Vladimir Vernadskii, one of the founders of the science of ecology, who managed to find a place in the Academy.

For the scientists, laboratory equipment and space was a crucial issue, and unfortunately most government offices did not see it as a priority. Pre-revolutionary Russian scientific laboratories and research stations were mostly small divisions within ministries or government offices like the Division of Agriculture within the Ministry of Finance or the small research laboratories of the Ministry of War, devoted to such problems as the production of optical sights for artillery. Most science took place in university departments, and there were scarcely any privately financed laboratories. Science was already dependent on government support throughout the world, but Russia was still too poor and backward to provide facilities similar to those of Germany or France. There were exceptions, like the physiologist Ivan Pavlov's laboratory at the Imperial Institute of Experimental Physiology in St. Petersburg which had state funding and aristocratic donors and patrons, primarily Prince A. P. Oldenburgskii, a relative of the tsar and a general. It produced medicines while Pavlov conducted experiments on conditioned reflexes. Most scientists lacked such facilities, and all these problems came to a head during the First World War, in which Russia's technological backwardness played a crucial role in its defeats. The scientific community was patriotic if not monarchist and in 1915 the Academy of Sciences founded a Commission for the Study of Natural Productive Forces, that was designed to survey the Russian Empire for natural resources that would be useful in war and industry. The result was a massive accumulation of data that came to be used by an entirely new regime after 1917.

The new Bolshevik government inaugurated a revolution in Russian science. For the Bolsheviks, the natural sciences were central to their utopian project. Their own ideology, Marxism, was in their minds a science, not just a political viewpoint. To them it was an objectively true account of the character and laws of development of human society. They believed that knowledge of the natural sciences would help convince people of the truth of Marxism, as it would impart knowledge of scientific methodology. There were other more practical benefits. The spread of scientific knowledge would combat religion, a high Bolshevik priority in the early years. Most important, however, they believed that science held the key to technology, and that the new Soviet Union needed technology to become a modern state and society.

Right from the beginning, the Bolshevik regime treated science and scientists very differently from other sectors of the old intelligentsia. The Soviets preferred large-scale, state-financed institutions mostly detached from university teaching, and the scientists were mostly in favor of the same structure, frustrated by the conservatism and limited resources of the pre-1917 Ministry of Education. Thus as early as 1918, as the Civil War was beginning, the Soviet government set up what became the Leningrad Physico-Technical Institute under Abram Ioffe. As the Civil War ended, Ioffe's institute was given a series of buildings and money to build new laboratories at a time when the state had almost no resources and famine swept the interior of Russia. Similarly, the Section of Applied Botany and Selection, a small laboratory of the old Agriculture Department, became the All-Union Institute of Plant-Breeding under the botanist and geneticist Nikolai Vavilov.

These were highly sophisticated institutions, and the Soviet government did not spare expense. Vavilov's institute moved into the former mansion of the tsarist Minister of State Properties off St. Isaak's Square in the center of Leningrad, with greenhouses and research facilities in Tsarskoe Selo (renamed Detskoe Selo in the 1920s and later Pushkin) in confiscated properties from the old regime. Even more important, Vavilov was sent abroad to Europe and to the United States to acquire scientific literature, equipment, and seeds for research. In the United States he traveled widely, met Luther Burbank, and spoke at American universities – all of this at

Soviet government expense. Ioffe and the physicists fared as well or better. Ioffe made a similar journey to Europe in 1920–21, and the students at the physics institute were not only allowed but even officially encouraged to spend years abroad working at Cambridge, England, with Ernest Rutherford or in Germany with the leading physicists of the time. In the rapidly changing world of physics in the early twentieth century, these contacts were crucial and established international reputations for many Soviet physicists. They published their works in the German *Annalen der Physik*, until 1933 the leading outlet for physics research in the world. Vladimir Vernadskii, in spite of his participation in the Kadet party before the Revolution, spent several years working in Paris in the 1920s with the full approval of the Soviet authorities. The Soviet government created a system that supplied scientists with better housing and favored access to consumer goods even in the 1920s, when the NEP market could have supplied many of their needs and wants. Pavlov, who was openly anti-Soviet, was appointed the head of the new Institute of Physiology of the Academy of Sciences in 1925.

Standing over and financing the scientific institutes in the 1920s were a variety of government offices. Some institutes were supported by the Russian republic Commissariat of Education, but the physical sciences increasingly came under the industrial commissariats or the Supreme Economic Council. Biology was mainly the purview of the Commissariats of Health or the Russian Commissariat of Agriculture. The idea was to unite theory and practice, an idea central to Marxism but also popular with many scientists on the eve of the Revolution who thought that Russia needed their expertise to overcome its backwardness. Thus the Leningrad Physical-Technical Institute had contracts with many industrial agencies, including a long-lasting and ultimately unsuccessful study of insulation for long-distance power cables. Successful or not, these contracts provided supplementary financing and demonstrated to the party leadership the usefulness of scientific research. The party authorities were perfectly aware that the scientists were not Bolsheviks. Many of them did believe that they should help the new state to modernize the country, whatever its leadership, but they were not Marxists. For the time being, this divergence of aims was not a problem.

The end of NEP meant, however, a radical upheaval in society launched by Stalin and the party leadership and a radical upheaval in art, literature, the humanistic disciplines, and the natural sciences. No area was spared this "cultural revolution," as it was called at the time, an upheaval in culture that matched that in the villages and the factories of the Soviet Union. This cultural revolution itself was short-lived but it was the beginning of a fundamental transformation of Soviet culture.

19

Building Utopia

Starting in 1929, the Soviet leadership began to transform the society of the USSR, to build an industrialized modern state, but not a capitalist state. The new society was to realize the old dream of socialism, a place without private property where the state ran and managed production of goods and services for the benefit of everyone. This was the idea. The reality that emerged after more than a decade of upheaval served as the framework of the Soviet Union until its demise two generations later.

The basic outlines were in place at the end of 1927 with the first five-year plan and the course toward collectivization of agriculture. The plan was to last from the beginning of 1928 to the end of 1932, and called for a twenty percent annual increase in industrial production, a rate of growth that was unheard of at the time. Such a growth rate implied a huge increase in urban population, and that required much more food than the country produced with its backward peasant agriculture. To complicate matters, grain exports were the Soviet Union's main source of hard currency to buy the new industrial equipment abroad that was essential for rapid industrialization. The solution was to be the collectivization of agriculture, which would increase per acre yield and free millions of hands to work in the new industry. The original plan for the pace of collectivization was moderate, with about a fifth of peasant households to be collectivized by the end of 1932.

The first thing that went wrong was the crisis in grain procurements early in 1928. The response of Stalin and the leadership was to return to grain requisitioning such as they had practiced in the Civil War. In 1929 the food supply situation was so serious that local authorities began to introduce rationing, soon established throughout the country. The crisis also stimulated Stalin and his supporters toward faster industrialization, for they felt that it showed that the kulak was getting stronger and could eventually make socialism impossible. The solution was to change the first five-year plan in 1929, with vastly increased production targets for state industries and huge construction schemes. These were the decisions that led to the opposition of Bukharin and the "rights," so that the plan was also political. To fulfill the targets and discredit the "rights," Stalin also had to make the speeded up plans work at whatever cost. The result of the speedups was that the plan ceased to work: managers in the targeted areas took supplies and workers wherever they could get them at whatever cost, wrecking the balances in the plan. The quality of production suffered as the physical output target consumed all attention. As food supplies decreased, the factories began to find their own sources, making semi-legal deals with farms to supply the factory dining rooms, which quickly became the main sources of food for their workers.

The plan called not just for more production but also for a total modernization of the key industrial sectors. The Soviet engineers and planners wanted to follow American industrial models such as Henry Ford's River Rouge auto plant, which relied on a moving production line rather than on many highly skilled workmen as was the case in Europe. To the Soviets, with millions of unskilled workers, this seemed to be the solution and the great Soviet tractor (and tank) factories were set up on these lines. The tractor factories were crucial to the collectivization plan, but for them as for everything else the country needed far more iron and steel for machines. Throughout the world this was the great age of metal and machines, and if the USSR was to have them, it would have to build huge new complexes. A giant dam on the Dniepr River was built to provide electricity for Ukrainian industry. In the Urals a great industrial base began to grow with whole new cities like Magnitogorsk built from scratch in order to mine iron ore. These were what were called "shock construction" sites, and resources were pulled from everywhere to supply them. The party mobilized youth to work there – the youth lived in tents and mud huts – as a grand campaign to continue the work of the revolution. The press plastered their achievements all over the country, and the most successful "shock workers" saw their pictures in *Pravda* and on billboards.

The first five-year plan was to be the great turning point in the building of socialism, the decisive break with the past, and Stalin and his allies saw it as a class war. The organs of the state and party under the Georgian Bolshevik Sergo Ordzhonikidze turned their fire first on industrial management, enlisting former Trotskyists to ferret out alleged bureaucratism. Workers and local party committees were encouraged to inform on their bosses, accusing them of incompetence, or even worse, "wrecking." Anyone responsible for a factory where production flagged or accidents were frequent could be accused of consciously trying to stop the building of socialism by sabotage. Local activists and the GPU (Main Political Administration, successor to the Cheka) also went after Communist managers with enthusiasm, but anyone from the old order was a particular target. During these years the GPU staged show trials of "enemies," engineers and managers from the pre-revolutionary elites, Menshevik economists, agrarian experts who had supported the SRs or liberals before 1917, and other "former people." The attack on the old intelligentsia went far beyond the economic sphere: historians and literary scholars, even some natural scientists were arrested and tried. In the non-Russian republics the authorities went after the local intelligentsia as well, accusing them of links with foreign states and various separatist schemes. Most of the managers and engineers were accused of "wrecking"; that is, intentionally causing accidents and slowing down production, usually on the orders of émigré organizations and foreign intelligence agencies. By 1930 these methods had discredited much of the existing administrative units, and Stalin placed Ordzhonikidze in charge of the Supreme Economic Council, where he brought his staff, many former Trotskyists among them, to manage the speedup of the plan.

The ever-increasing plan targets and the chaos that resulted from collectivization meant that millions of people were displaced, roaming the country from one construction site to another. Housing became an acute problem, especially in Moscow and other big or new cities. Most of the urban population came to live in communal apartments, usually older apartments cut up into several rooms with a common kitchen and bathrooms. Whole families lived in one room or two small rooms. In many places workers lived in barracks or "temporary" housing. Initially the plan had called for rapid expansion of at least basic consumer goods, but the increasing targets for heavy industry gutted the production of textiles and other basic commodities. To make things worse, the series of war scares in the late 1920s encouraged massive investment in the military industry until 1934, and this investment reached levels not seen again until the eve of World War II. The standard of living of the population began to fall precipitously. In a few places strikes even broke out over the shortages of food supplies. The managers in the crucial industries could not maintain their workforces without radical measures, and they went beyond supplying food in the factory cafeterias to building apartment houses and schools, tram lines, and clinics for their workers. A whole new type of hierarchy appeared in Soviet society, which put not just the party elite but also entire factories and industries above the rest. Workers in priority industries like the auto and tractor factories or the defense complex managed to get through these years with at least the basic needs of life supplied, while at textile factories or other light industries, many of them with predominantly female work forces, the workers had too little food even to work a full day.

City life meant intense privation, even for the youthful enthusiasts at shock construction sites. These hardships were nothing compared to the disasters of collectivization. At the beginning the party was not even clear what the new collective farm was to look like: was it to be some sort of association of peasant households for common planting and harvesting, or was it to be a total commune with farmers living in communal housing and eating together, as well as farming all the land together? And how fast was it to proceed, and how? In any case, it was in the autumn of 1929 when Stalin decided to go for as much collectivization as he could get. To prepare the ground the leadership decided on the "liquidation of the kulaks as a class" and the GPU set out to round up and deport the kulaks. Several thousand were executed, but nearly two million were deported to the north, the Urals and Siberia, where they were put in "special settlements" to cut timber or sometimes to work in the mines or on construction. They arrived in remote areas where they had to build their own houses, often in the dead of winter without any facilities, medical care, or established food supplies. Thousands escaped and thousands died, until in 1931 the GPU took over the special settlements, the first large group to come under the auspices of the GULAG. For the time being, the special settlers vastly outnumbered the prisoners in actual concentration camps.

With the kulaks out of the way, collectivization went on at top speed. Under intense pressure from rural party officials as well as emissaries sent from the cities, the peasants were convinced to abandon their strips of land and combine them, in theory at least, into one huge farm to be worked together. To make matters worse, the authorities in some areas tried to push the peasants not just into collective farms but even into communes, the super-collectivized units with communal living and eating arrangements. By early 1930, almost half of the peasants had agreed to join a collective, but they also slaughtered their livestock, not wanting to waste them in the new order. There was as yet no equipment to work the farms beyond the old plows and horses, whose numbers were rapidly decreasing. Opposition was rife, with thousands of "incidents," ranging from real rebellions to minor objections blown up into anti-Soviet demonstrations by the GPU. Early in 1930 Stalin realized that he had to pull back. The economic results of forcing the peasants into collective farms were becoming serious, and he published an article in *Pravda* under the title, "Dizzy with Success." Local party members were getting too enthusiastic, he wrote, and were pursuing target numbers for their own sake, not paying enough attention to local circumstances and the mood of the peasantry. After the article, the number of collective farms fell rapidly and the communes were abandoned, but the process did not stop, it only paused and then resumed at a slower pace. In the meantime, disaster struck.

As collectivization continued, with all the disruptions that it caused, the weather played a cruel trick. In 1931 and 1932 bad weather struck – cold in some areas and drought in others – in the Ukraine and southern Russia, the main grain producing areas. By the summer of 1932 this meant famine that spanned a wide belt running from the Polish border into Siberia. The authorities reacted slowly, keeping up their collections of grains at the amount fixed in better years. Only toward the end of the year did they begin to ease off, but it was already too late, and famine had spread taking with it some five to seven million peasants throughout the southern regions of the USSR, about half of these in the Ukraine. The casualties of the famine, not the kulaks, turned out to be the principal victims of collectivization. The drought hit the peasants when the numbers of livestock had fallen, on average, by half and they had no reserves of grain; all of this was the result of the chaos of collectivization and the relentless collection of grain for the cities. The famine disturbed the authorities, but they did very little about it. Stalin did not take any extraordinary methods against the famine, which crushed opposition to collectivization. Not until better weather in 1933 produced a better harvest did the famine come to an end.

By the middle of the 1930s the basic outlines of the Soviet collective farm, the kolhoz, were in place, for the notion of setting up communes had been abandoned. The Russian village had always been a community, with houses clustered in the village surrounded by the fields. What was new was that the fields were now under the control of the kolhoz (actual property rights were still vested in the state). The kolhoz had a chairman and a governing board that set the farming tasks, which the peasants carried out together, plowing and sowing, harvesting and taking care of the livestock. For their work on the farm the peasants received payment, not in money but in the form of part of the harvest calculated by a system known as "labor-days." The bulk of the harvest went to the state at a fixed price, one that favored the state and the cities over the kolhoz.

The kolhoz rarely owned its own machinery. As the new tractor factories came on line, the tractors went to a new institution, the Machine-Tractor Station, some eight thousand of them by the end of the decade. These were state operations, and they rented out the tractors and other machinery with the drivers and workers, providing the essential equipment for the kolhoz as well as assuring state control over the collective farms. If the machinery put the state into farming directly, the market did not disappear entirely in the countryside. Unlike the cities, where all retail trade was in state hands by the early 1930s, the peasantry was explicitly granted the right to farm small private plots alongside their houses. They used them primarily for vegetables and smaller livestock and took the produce to the peasant markets that reappeared in all Soviet cities. Though the private plots were only about four percent of the kolhoz land, they produced forty percent of vegetables and potatoes and over sixty-six percent of the meat coming from the collective farms. Their products were sold at prices much above those fixed in the stories and factory cafeterias, but at least they were available.

From 1933 to about 1936 the tension and upheaval in Soviet society lessened considerably. The rightists in the party had capitulated and publicly recanted their errors as had the Trotskyists, and Bukharin became the editor of *Izvestiia*. In 1932 the government abolished the Supreme Economic Council, replacing it with a series of People's Commissariats for different branches of industry. The most important was the People's Commissariat of Heavy Industry, headed by Ordzhonikidze. It seemed that a more rational style of economic management had triumphed, for Ordzhonikidze took with him to the new organization many of the former Left Oppositionists and even many "bourgeois specialists" like those whom he had harassed in 1926–1929. New methods of increasing productivity in the work force emerged. In 1935 the Donbass miner Aleksei Stakhanov managed to produce fourteen times his norm of coal and was proclaimed a national hero. Other workers tried to imitate the simple reorganization of work methods that he used to achieve the goal, and were rewarded as Stakhanovites. Work gangs and shops within factories announced "socialist competition" contests to over fulfill the plan, earning brief fame as well as more concrete benefits. In themselves these campaigns, heavily sponsored by the party, achieved little, but labor productivity managed to grow anyway. The extreme shortages of food and consumer goods began to abate and in 1935 the rationing of food and other consumer goods ended. Nevertheless, many basic commodities would be periodically or permanently in deficit. Elaborate systems of informal supply among the population formed to deal with these shortages, ranging from crude black market operations (strictly illegal and widely punished) to relatively harmless exchanges of goods among families and friends. The population was learning to cope. Unemployment had disappeared, to be replaced with a permanent labor shortage, though real wages were well below those of the late 1920s for the great majority of workers.

In these somewhat brighter years, the seeds of destruction were already sown. On December 1, 1934, an assassin killed the leader of the party in Leningrad, Sergei Kirov. The authorities proclaimed the murder to be the work of unrepentant Trotskyists, though the most likely theory is that it was the result of Kirov's romantic entanglements. In public the uproar died down quickly, but in the ensuing months the NKVD (in place of the GPU from 1934) began to search for enemy agents, particularly among the former oppositionists working in Soviet institutions. By 1936 they were ready to bring Zinoviev and Kamenev together with other old Bolsheviks, mostly former oppositionists, to trial. The charges were the murder of Kirov, a conspiracy to kill Stalin, and treasonous arrangements with fascist agents. The defendants all "confessed" in a carefully staged public trial and were mostly sentenced to death. In January of 1937, another trial followed, and this time the main defendants were Karl Radek, a journalist and Comintern official, and Georgii Piatakov. Both were former Trotskyists, and Piatakov had in recent years been the right-hand man of Ordzhonikidze in the People's Commissariat of Heavy Industry. Ordzhonikidze seems to have been the only one in the leadership to resist the coming terror – at least as it applied to the institutions he headed at the time. On February 17, after a long conversation with Stalin, Ordzhnokidze committed suicide. His death was announced as the result of sudden illness, and he received a grandiose state funeral.

In late February 1937, the Central Committee of the Party met in plenary session, its agenda being to discuss the new constitution about to be promulgated for the country. The new constitution replaced the formal institutions formed in the Civil War with ones that looked more like those of a normal state, though it had no impact on the actual relations of power, dominated as they were by the party. A rather dull meeting seemed to be in prospect. Early in the proceedings Molotov and other confidants of Stalin arose to add to the deliberations the need to "unmask the Trotskyist agents of fascism" whom they asserted to be hiding in large numbers in the party and state apparatus. By the end of the meeting the unmasking of traitors had become the main task proclaimed by the Central Committee. In the ensuing months the NKVD, under its new head Nikolai Ezhov, began to arrest tens of thousands of people as enemies of the people. In May the NKVD ordered the arrest of nearly the whole of the high command of the Red Army. Marshal Tukhachevsky and seven others, almost all Red Army heroes of the Civil War, were accused of treason and confessions were extracted by torture. They were tried in secret, and quickly executed. Some forty thousand officers perished or went to prison in the wake of the Tukhachevsky trial. At the ranks of brigade commander and above nearly ninety percent were executed, altogether some eight hundred men. The terror was not confined to such elite groups, for other and larger classes of victims accompanied them to the camps and the firing squads. In July the Politburo issued order 00447 (the 00 signified top secret) providing each regional unit of the NKVD with a quota for arrests and executions. The total for the country in this order alone was to be seventy-two thousand. The victims were to be, in principle, all known former kulaks, White officers, Mensheviks or SRs, and a multitude of lesser and vaguer categories. Each office of the NKVD began frantically to search through its card files for anyone ever arrested or under suspicion in any of the relevant categories. Regional NKVD units wrote to Moscow begging to be allowed to over fulfill the plan for executions and arrests. Their requests were granted, and similar orders followed. These orders at least targeted (mostly) real potential enemies of the Soviet order.

Stalin also struck at the party apparatus with the NKVD, again by torture extracting confessions from party members that they were wreckers and Japanese or German spies. To enforce the terror, Stalin sent trusted deputies, Kaganovich, Georgii Malenkov, and others, to republican and provincial capitals to "unmask" the enemies in the party hierarchy and order their arrest. Ezhov presented Stalin with long lists of enemies and wreckers, some forty-four thousand in all, and Stalin personally checked off the names, presenting them to Molotov and others in his inner circle for confirmation. Molotov and Stalin even added comments in the margins of the list: "Give the dog a dog's death," or "Hit them and hit them." Most of the members of the central party leadership, including the Central Committee of the Party, People's Commissars, and other high government officials perished. The same occurred at the republican level, and even reached down to provincial and city party and government circles. Thus most of the party apparatus perished. The names of the dead and imprisoned simply disappeared from public documents, and they were erased along with Trotsky from the history books.

The last of the show trials took place in March 1938, and featured the former rightists, Bukharin, Rykov, and others, as well as Ezhov's predecessor as head of the NKVD, Genrikh Yagoda. The usual confessions and violent denunciations from the prosecutor, Andrei Vyshinskii (himself an ex-Menshevik), were the highlights. This lurid spectacle was the last of the show trials, and though it and its predecessors attracted world attention, it served mainly as a background to the real killing. In the course of 1937–38, the NKVD executed some three quarters of a million people, including the bulk of the military and political elite, all former oppositionists from within the party, but the majority of the victims, however, were people in all walks of life who fit into the prescribed categories of enemies such as former nobles or Mensheviks. To top all this off, the NKVD also decided to deport the entire population of the so-called "western national minorities": the Poles, Latvians, Germans, Finns, and others who lived near the western boundary of the USSR. Hundreds of thousands perished in transit. When the NKVD ran out of people in the assigned categories, they rounded up common criminals, executed them, and listed them as political. In the two years, the total who were executed or died of privations in transit came out to a million people. Finally, the blood came to an end. Through 1938 Stalin gave increasingly frequent signals that "excesses" had been committed, putting the blame on the NKVD, and Ezhov himself was soon executed. By 1939, the wave had passed. A semblance of peace descended on a terrorized society.

After the end of the terror, the subject passed entirely from Soviet public discourse. Stalin soon ordered the composition and extensive publication of the *Short Course of the History of Communist Party* and ordered all members of the party to study it thoroughly. It became a compendium of the official line, and offered a wholly falsified history of Bolshevism and the 1917 revolution, with Trotsky and other leaders omitted except to vilify them for their opposition in the 1920s and their alleged later roles as spies and traitors. Its centerpiece was a simplified sketch of Marxism authored by Stalin himself though not publicly acknowledged as such. The book offered no explanation of the events of 1937–38 other than to describe the results of the show trials. The actual terror never received any public explanation then or later in Stalin's lifetime. Though the specific charges at the show trials and in secret arrests normally had been manufactured, Stalin, Molotov, and the others around them seem to have seriously thought that they were fighting and destroying real and dangerous enemies. Such, at least, is the language of their surviving private correspondence with one another. Their public statements in 1937 asserted that the successful building of socialism only "sharpened the class struggle," which seems to have meant that Stalin's policies, especially collectivization, produced more and more doubters, whom Stalin and his circle interpreted as conscious enemies suborned by foreign intelligence services. In addition they feared that such internal enemies might try to strike when the inevitable war in Europe broke out and involved the Soviet Union. The mentality of Soviet leaders, and particularly the NKVD, encouraged such conclusions. NKVD officials during collectivization regularly interpreted objections by the peasants to minor aspects of the new order as conscious political opposition to the Soviet system. In their minds and in Stalin's, if someone disagreed with some details of the plan targets for the aluminum industry, that person must be a secret opponent of the regime, and as the *Short Course* taught, all enemies of socialism are ultimately in league with one another.

Not everyone who was arrested was shot, and as a result, the population of the prison camps boomed. In the 1920s the prison camps had been relatively small and organized around the main camp on the Solovki Islands in the White Sea. In those years just over one hundred thousand people languished in Solovki and various other prisons, in cold, insect-infested cells, required to work cutting peat or felling trees. In 1929 Stalin and the security police decided to turn the prison system into a network of labor camps on the Solovki model, and common criminals were placed in the same camps. The great expansion came with the collectivization of agriculture, for those kulaks considered especially dangerous were sent to camps rather than to the special settlements. By 1934, when the GULAG, or the Chief Administration of Camps, under the OGPU/NKVD came into being, there were half a million prisoners. By 1939 a million-and-a-half prisoners lived in camps and "labor colonies," which had a somewhat less strict regime. Though plenty of people died in Soviet camps, they were not death camps, but labor camps, and the GULAG took the labor component quite seriously. At first they even advertised their "successes," such as the building of the White Sea Canal in 1931–32, touted as an example of labor successfully re-educating class enemies. From 1937, however, the camps were in principle secret. The system was a complex hierarchy, ranging from "special settlements," where the prisoners lived in fairly normal housing or minimally livable barracks, to horrific mining settlements like Vorkuta or the Kolyma gold fields on the east coast of Siberia, reachable only by ship. Most prisoners were assigned labor in forests, cutting trees for the timber industry with primitive tools, or were assigned to mine, or work in construction. Death was the result of disease, accidents, and general privation, for the GULAG needed labor to meet its own plans. Most deaths occurred during the shipment out to the camps in 1937–38 when hundreds of thousands were shipped east and north in unheated boxcars to places where facilities for the prisoners were almost non-existent. In the Stalin years, failure to meet the plan could be fatal, so the camp commandants engaged in a complex juggling game to keep the prisoners well-enough fed and housed to be able to work while not expending too much on them. With the special settlements, some four million people lived "under the jurisdiction of the NKVD" by 1941. Of these most were not political prisoners in the usual sense. In the camps and colonies, only about twenty percent had been convicted of "counter-revolutionary actions" or other political offenses, and the rest were a mixture of common criminals and those who fell afoul of increasingly strict laws on labor discipline, hooliganism, or "theft of state property," a particularly murky area given the realities of Soviet life. Many were imprisoned for passport violations after the introduction of internal passports in 1932. Even the "political" prisoners included many classified as political only in the super-politicized categories of Stalin and the NKVD. The camp system under Stalin was primarily a system of convict labor into which political prisoners were added.

At the end of the 1930s the Soviet Union was even more a land of paradox than before. State centralization had continued to increase. The defeat of the Right Opposition had put Stalin's allies in all the key positions of state: Molotov became the chair of the Council of People's Commissars, the head of state and government. Along with Molotov and Stalin the inner circle now consisted of Lazar Kaganovich, Sergo Ordzhonikidze, Kliment Voroshilov, Anastas Mikoyan, and, until his death Valerian Kuibyshev. While Ordzhonikidze and Kuibyshev oversaw industry, Kaganovich took care of transport and Mikoyan of the crucial area of food supplies and trade. Voroshilov was in charge of the armed forces. All of them had other duties as well, and they regularly met to discuss even minute issues of economic management as well as political questions. Around this inner group until 1937–38 was a large number of managers and party officials who had mostly come out of the Civil War and come into power under Stalin. This was the core Soviet elite at the time, and most of them did not survive the terror of 1937–38. The result of the terror was to further concentrate power in the inner circle and even more so on Stalin himself, but to also bring new men into the leadership. Foremost among them was Lavrentii Beriia, another Georgian who replaced Ezhov as head of the security police. Others of the younger men were Andrei Zhdanov, Georgii Malenkov, and Nikita Khrushchev, all of whom would play major roles in the coming war and post-war years. Zhdanov was the son of a school inspector and worked his way up through provincial party leadership to take over Leningrad's party after the assassination of Kirov. Malenkov, also from the Urals, and with a pre-revolutionary gymnasium education, made his career in the central party apparatus in Moscow. Khrushchev, by contrast, was actually a worker in the Donbass who rose through the party ranks when Kaganovich was running the Ukrainian party in the 1920s, and then moved on to Moscow. All three had served in the Civil War. Along with these new men came a shift in the structure of power at the center, with all of the leaders taking more direct roles in managing the state, not merely supervising it from the Politburo.

Figure 19. The funeral of the writer Maxim Gorky in 1936. From right to left: Genrikh Iagoda, chief of the political police, Stalin,Viacheslav Molotov, Bulgarian Communist and Comintern leader Georgii Dimitrov, (in white) Andrei Zhdanov, Lazar Kaganovich.

The centralization of power was formalized in May 1941 when Stalin replaced Molotov as Chairman of the Council of People's Commissars. Stalin now formally and actually headed both party and state.

Alongside the centralization of power in the Politburo and then with Stalin alone a whole cult of the leader appeared, managed from the center. It was already normal in the early 1920s to display portraits of Lenin, Trotsky, and the current leadership at major celebrations like November 7 and May 1. By the end of the 1920s Stalin was the central figure in these displays and by the end of the 1930s almost the only figure. Statues of Stalin sprouted in addition to the ubiquitous statues of Lenin, and cities and institutions were named in his honor. At party meetings it was the ritual to stand when his name was mentioned and acclaim him.

Stalin was not a dynamic public speaker, in part because of his pronounced Georgian accent, and he never seems to have desired the unceasing public display and admiration that Hitler and Mussolini craved and staged over and over. He rarely appeared in public and his actual personality remained private, but the standard epithets – "great leader of peoples"– were obligatory. His writings were the required textbooks of Marxism and his image and his name were everywhere and became basic components of Soviet political culture.

The centralization of power also affected the complex federal structure of the USSR. Starting in 1929–30 all-union Commissariats of Agriculture, Education, and Culture and other organs had been created that stood over the analogous republican agencies. The policies and structures of the NEP era had meant a sort of de facto alliance of the party with intellectuals in the non-Russian republics to build and in some cases create local cultures. This arrangement in many ways paralleled the role of the pre-revolutionary Russian engineers and economists in Soviet industry, and it met the same fate beginning in 1929–30. Show trials of local nationalists signaled the end of collaboration, as did the appearance of an all-union Commissariat of Culture and Education. In 1932–33 the party carried out a campaign against Ukrainian nationalism, including show trials of Ukrainian intellectuals accused of nationalism and ties with foreign powers. The Ukrainian party leaders who preferred the older policy committed suicide and others were arrested or demoted. Similar campaigns took place in other republics, all of them part of the "cultural revolution" of 1929–1932.

Even more important for the fate of the Soviet republics was the tremendous growth in centralization of the economy. Republican plans for economic development were swamped by new central authorities' grandiose schemes for regional development based on economic, not ethnic, criteria. In the northern autonomous republics of Russia, no local authority could compete with the sheer economic power of the GULAG, even when the political arm of the NKVD was not involved. Ukrainian and Siberian economic development followed the dictates of the all-union industrial Commissariats, Gosplan, and other agencies. The result in many areas was massive economic development but also ultimate erosion of the authority of local party committees and republican governments. The republican authorities (including the Russian republic) were largely left with agricultural issues, by their nature requiring more local control. The hierarchy that emerged from industrialization was not based on the federal state structure, but on the economic structure. The hierarchy was not ethnic or political: a district or a republic with many factories under a high priority commissariat such as heavy industry or defense was favored both with investment and consumer goods. A district with light industry was not. This system favored the Ukrainian Donbass and neglected central Russian towns where the predominant industries were textile factories.

In some respects the central authorities continued to pay attention to local issues. For all the centralization, the formal federal structure remained. The 1936, "Stalin" constitution perpetuated the federal structure of the USSR, by now including twelve union republics and many autonomous republics under them. The end of the "indigenization" policy in the party came with the assault on local nationalism, but Stalin did not replace the local minorities in the party leadership with Russians. Local nationality party members came to be the majority in almost all union and autonomous republics, including the leadership groups, though Stalin continued to bring in occasional trusted outsiders at the top, like Nikita Khrushchev in the Ukraine in the wake of the 1937–38 terror. The Soviet Union's central leadership was multi-national. Stalin himself was Georgian as was Orzdzhonikidze and the post-1938 head of the NKVD, Lavrentii Beriia. Molotov and Voroshilov were both Russian, while Kaganovich and the foreign minister in the 1930s, Maxim Litvinov, were Jewish. Mikoyan was Armenian. The campaign against local nationalism did not imply cultural Russification. Stalin and the leadership were perfectly happy for the non-Russians to speak and write native languages, as long as Moscow retained political control and Moscow ran most of the economy. In Russian-speaking Ukrainian cities the newspapers were still mostly in Ukrainian until 1939. After about 1932 the Soviet authorities began to heavily promote the celebration of non-Russian writers and artists in the central press, organizing meetings with Stalin and other leaders in Moscow to great press coverage. Pre-revolutionary

Russian culture received a similar positive re-evaluation, culminating in the Pushkin anniversary celebrations of 1937. In the same years in the Ukraine new statues of the poet Taras Shevchenko appeared, to great organized festivity, and similar figures were glorified or occasionally invented in the other republics. This was not merely a cultural campaign, for it formed one of the foundations of "friendship of peoples," the Soviet attempt to bond the various nations of the Soviet Union by downplaying conflicts of the past and emphasizing the supposedly harmonious present and future. In a predominantly centralized economy and state, the promotion of local culture alongside Russian provided a way to build a multinational society that would move toward a unified socialist state.

Soviet policy was not uniform in all the non-Russian republics in these years. In the Muslim areas Soviet leadership moved very cautiously against Islam. In Central Asia the main issue in the 1920s had been the abolition of the veil for Muslim women, an issue on which the small local intelligentsia was in general agreement. Most of the southern Islamic areas were also not yet the object of massive industrialization drives, though collectivization, when it came, was normally as harsh as in Russia and the Ukraine. The one great disaster in Central Asia was in Kazakhstan. Kazakhstan was still to a large extent nomadic in 1930 and collectivization implied "sedentarization," that is, nomadic herders were to settle down and raise their stock in one area. This policy set off internal struggles inside the clans that combined with intense party pressure and produced a massive crisis. The nomadic Kazakhs responded by slaughtering their animals or fleeing across the border to other Soviet republics and even to China. Over a million became refugees and over a million, some twenty percent of the Kazakh population, died of hunger or disease. In the succeeding years, the Kazakh authorities managed to resettle most of the refugees in Kazakhstan, and stock-raising slowly recovered, but the demographic catastrophe's effects lasted for decades.

Another series of paradoxes grew from the outcome of the transformation of Soviet society. Though terrorized by the events of 1937–38, the population at the end of the 1930s was much better educated, more urban, and in most ways more "modern" than in 1928.

Some thirty-one percent of the population lived in urban areas, double the pre-1917 figure, and almost all of the population had at least basic literacy. Ties with older traditions disappeared. The Orthodox Church and other religions were essentially smashed by the anti-religious campaigns: only a few hundred churches remained open in the entire country, and the great majority of the clergy were dead or in camps. The traditional rhythm of the Russian year, with Shrovetide, Lent, and Easter simply evaporated without churches to support it, and the Communist festivals, November 7 and May 1 replaced them, with a secular New Year celebration in between. The huge expansion in urban population meant that millions left the world of the peasantry. People who had never seen a complex machine before now ran tram lines and built airplanes. Basic consumer goods were scarce, but movies, popular music, and the radio provided mass entertainment of a more or less modern sort. Mass education, especially in technical subjects, was a priority and tens of thousands of students received the basics of modern science, while surviving crowded, unheated dormitories and wretched and erratic food. This sort of speeded-up education allowed Stalin to fill the positions left empty by the arrests of the great terror with people from peasant and working class backgrounds but who were more or less able to do their jobs.

The five-year plans were a qualified success. The Soviet leadership regularly used deceptive statistical methods to make the results look better, but the actual results in industry were impressive enough by 1940. The USSR was now the world's third industrial power, after the United States and Germany. The new industrial plants had modern equipment, and many of them were located in the Urals and Siberia, places of yet untapped wealth that were also far from the increasingly threatened frontier. Small villages had turned into cities, and entirely new industrial areas came into being. Some of the promises of socialism were beginning to be realized. The People's Commissariat of Health doubled the number of doctors and medical personnel between 1932 and 1940, and vaccination and hygiene programs markedly decreased the death rates from disease. At the same time, years of famine, deprivations, and crowded and unsanitary housing provided immense obstacles to the new and mostly female medical personnel. The Communists had always promoted the equality of women, and by the 1930s the work force was almost half female. Some women began to appear even as tractor drivers on the collective farms and workers in heavy industry. Some professions, such as medicine, were rapidly becoming primarily the domain of women. The successes of women pilots and workers were the subject of huge propaganda campaigns in the media. The large gap in education between women and men virtually closed, at least in the cities. As in all cases, the reality of daily life provided major obstacles: in light industry, where most workers were women, there was never enough daycare for children. Though women were paid the same as men for the same work, the predominantly female light industries were lower in priority and hence the wages were lower and fewer, and worse consumer goods were available through the workplace. The burden of family continued to fall on women even when daycare centers and kindergartens appeared. It was women who bore the brunt of standing in lines for scarce commodities and forming informal networks to obtain them.

In the late 1930s consumer goods continued to trickle back into the stores and the lives of women as well as men eased. The weak point of the Soviet economy was and remained in agriculture. The collective farms were just barely able to supply the burgeoning cities with grain, but pre-1940 meat production never reached the levels found in the late 1920s. Meat and milk came overwhelmingly not from the kolhoz but from the private plots the state had allowed the peasants to retain after collectivization. The population continued to rely heavily on the peasant market, more expensive than state stores, and on workplace distribution centers for anything beyond the most basic foodstuffs. Nevertheless, the country was able to vastly increase military production again at the end of the 1930s, in the face of the danger of war, without completely wrecking the plan and the supply of consumer goods. This was not nearly the promised utopia, but it did provide the basis of the Soviet version of a modern society. It was just barely enough.

For Stalin's new industrial giant of a country was about to face a threat greater than any kulaks or imaginary Japanese spies. By 1938 the heart of Europe was under the power of Adolf Hitler, who had made it clear in *Mein Kampf* that Germany must conquer "living space" to survive, and that Germany's living space was to be found in the Soviet Union. In 1931, Stalin had told a conference of industrial managers that Russia "was fifty to a hundred years behind the advanced countries. Either we catch up in ten years or they crush us." Perhaps his evaluation of the state of the Soviet economy had been too pessimistic at the time, but his prediction of the time they had at their disposal was right on the mark. They had exactly ten years.

20

War

From the very beginning the Soviet leadership expected an invasion sooner or later. This conviction grew from the actual situation of the Soviet Union since the revolution, the experience of intervention and hostility of almost all other states, and also from their analysis of the world. For they expected not just an attack on their own country but a war among the western powers as well, and thought it likely that the war in the West would come first. Their analysis of the world came from Lenin's view of the most recent stage of capitalism, which he understood to be the period of imperialism. He believed that the First World War was the result of the increasing concentration of capital in the hands of a small number of massive semi-monopolistic corporations and banks, which in turn led to a speeded up competition for markets and resources. The result was the division of the world among great empires, and the desire of the late-comers in that process, Germany in particular, to re-divide the world. Thus, even without the existence of the USSR, another war was inevitable. Stalin and the Soviet elite accepted this conception of the world without any doubts, and their own historic experience in the First World War, as well as their observation of the various rivalries in the world after 1918, only strengthened their conviction. At the same time they realized that the differences ("contradictions") among the capitalist powers might be temporarily shelved in an anti-Communist alliance or that one or more of the western powers might be strong enough to attack them on its own. Until 1933 the principle threat seemed to come from the British Empire, the apparently hegemonic power of the time. The Red Army constructed its war plans on the assumption that an attack would come from Poland and Rumania with British (and perhaps French) backing or even participation. The de facto military arrangements with Weimar Germany were designed in part to obstruct such an eventuality. When Adolf Hitler came to power in Germany in January of 1933, the Soviets confronted an entirely new situation.

At first the Soviets were not excessively concerned. Since 1928 the Comintern had predicted a new crisis of capitalism, and the Depression seemed to bear out that prediction. The Soviet leadership, like many other observers, was not convinced that the Nazis were really much different from other reactionary German groups that had supported restoration of the Kaiser and suppression of the left parties. Anti-Semitism, the parades, and the uniforms, all seemed to be just trappings to deceive the naïve, not symptoms of a more serious and sinister purpose. Though Hitler eliminated the German Communist Party (and the Socialists) in a matter of months, the Soviets were still convinced that Hitler's support was limited and his regime unstable. The 1934 purge of the Storm Troopers seemed to confirm this picture, and Soviet propaganda as well as internal discussion stressed the alleged unpopularity of Hitler's economic and other programs with the German working class. At the same time, the Soviets noted the rearmament of Germany and its increasingly aggressive tone in international affairs. Late in 1934 the Soviet Union joined the League of Nations, a step both symbolic and practical, especially as Hitler had taken Germany out of the League the year before. Soviet Commissar of Foreign Affairs Maxim Litvinov used the League as one of his principle stages on which to proclaim the need for the Western powers to make an agreement with the USSR to oppose Hitler.

Talk of opposing Hitler from the Soviets was not merely a gesture, for the Soviet Union now possessed a new army, much more powerful than the old-fashioned Red Army of the 1920s. Two factors were crucial in the transformation of the army. One was the pre-1933 cooperation with the army of the Weimar republic, which provided the Red Army with a complete picture of the most recent developments in military technology and organization. The turn of Western armies toward motorized units, tanks, and aircraft was perfectly clear, yet in 1928 the Red Army still relied on cavalry and infantry armed with rifles and machine guns. Even artillery was inadequate. The second factor was the first five-year plan. The five-year plan originally called for quite considerable increases in military production, but the highly charged atmosphere of world politics (the Japanese seizure of Manchuria in 1931) impelled Stalin to raise the targets for military production even higher. In the next year, the Soviet Union produced four thousand tanks, an immense number by the standards of the time, and they reflected sophisticated designs, both foreign and Soviet. The same enormous effort was put into aircraft production, particularly of heavy bombers. These modern weapons reflected the military doctrine of the Soviet army staff, particularly that of Tukhachevskii, who believed that modern wars would be decided by fast mechanized and armored units as well as long-range aerial bombing. By 1935 the USSR had one of the most advanced armies in the world. Its only limitation was size, for budgetary constraints kept the standing army relatively small.

With this new army in the background, Stalin and the Soviet leaders still had to confront an increasingly dangerous world situation. The most important consequences of the new situation created by Hitler and his allies were the new policies enunciated at Geneva by Litvinov and also a sharp turn in the strategy of the Comintern. At the Seventh Comintern Conference in 1935 the Bulgarian Communist leader Georgii Dimitrov announced the new policy: the Popular Front. The new policy abandoned the attacks on the Socialists as agents of the ruling class and the orientation toward revolution, putting in its place the demand for Communists to make an alliance with the Socialists and indeed any group opposed to fascism for the purpose of preventing the extension of fascist power. At the same time the Soviet state began to try to form alliances with Western powers, signing mutual aid pacts with France and Czechoslovakia in May of 1935. Soviet relations with Britain, however, remained poor, and Hitler was on the march: in 1936 he remilitarized the Rhineland to thundering silence from London and Paris. A few months later the Civil War broke out in Spain with General Francisco Franco's revolt against the Republic, now governed by a popular front elected by the people. Soviet reaction was initially cautious, as they feared that overt aid to the Republic would provoke intervention by the Western powers on the side of the monarchist-fascist rebels. Hitler and Mussolini soon solved that problem, for their supplies of troops and munitions gave the Soviets an opening. Stalin also sent tanks, aircraft, and many officers to Spain through the dangerous waters of the Mediterranean. In Spain, Stalin and the Comintern followed the popular front strategy, the Spanish Communists being instructed that they were not to make revolution but to continue to ally with the Socialists and Liberals to support the Republic. The Spanish situation revealed the limits of that strategy, for Stalin also wanted the Communists to control things as much as possible and insisted on eliminating the Trotskyists and Anarchists, powerful especially in Barcelona. In the long run, neither the Popular Front strategy nor Soviet aid and interference made much difference. The Spanish Republic succumbed to brute force and was extinguished by the end of 1938.

The defeat of the Republic only increased the danger for the USSR. The lack of enthusiasm on the part of Western powers for the Spanish Republic only revealed – in Stalin's mind – the increasing chances of his nightmare scenario, a four-power pact that included Britain, France, Germany, and Italy, which would be directed against the Soviet Union. And Hitler continued to move. In 1936–37 Germany, Japan, and Italy signed the "Anti-Comintern Pact," forming the alliance that came to known as the Axis. In 1938, Hitler annexed Austria, again causing no reaction from Britain and France, and soon began to make demands on Czechoslovakia, the only power in Eastern Europe with a substantial and modern armed force. For the Soviets as well as Europe as a whole, this was a crisis.

Soviet actions were stymied by two factors. One was the generally pro-German policy of Poland, which controlled the corridors through which any Soviet aid to Czechoslovakia had to pass. The other factor was the suspicion on the part of the Western powers, especially Britain – both of the Soviet Union in general and the capacities of the Red Army in particular. The Soviet mutual assistance pacts with France and Czechoslovakia hinged on cooperation, which was not forthcoming from Paris. In the days leading up to the final crisis at Munich, the Soviets did actually begin to mobilize the Red Army in secret, but all was in vain. Chamberlain surrendered the Czechs to Hitler in what from the Soviet point of view was a four-power pact. Such a pact, in their view, must be directed against the Soviet Union.

In this situation the Soviet leadership, convinced that war was coming, moved to its other possible strategy, making a deal with Hitler. Off and on since 1933 the Soviets had put out feelers to Berlin, but nothing had come of them. Early in 1939 discussions with the Nazis suddenly became serious, and the attitudes in London and Paris propelled them forward. Though Chamberlain began to realize that Hitler was a threat, he was not willing to discuss a serious agreement with Stalin. In the summer of 1939 a British mission to Moscow explored the possibilities of cooperation, but when Commissar of Defense Voroshilov asked for specifics on military cooperation, the British could reply only that they had no instructions. The result was the German-Soviet pact of August 23, 1939, signed in Moscow by Ribbentrop and Molotov, now Litvinov's replacement as Commissar of Foreign Affairs.

The pact unleashed Hitler to attack Poland, which brought declarations of war against Germany from Britain and France. The German invasion of Poland was so successful and so quick that Stalin was caught off-guard. He was also preoccupied with the Japanese probing attack on Mongolia at the end of August, thrown back at Khalkhin Gol by some hundred thousand Soviet troops. Though the pact implied a partition of Poland, it had not included any delimitation of frontiers. The Red Army hurriedly marched into the eastern territories of the Polish state inhabited mainly by Belorussians and Ukrainians, annexing the new territories to the respective Soviet republics. The Communists quickly established Soviet institutions and deported the Poles in the area. Most went to camps or as "special settlers" to Siberia and Kazakhstan, but the army officers, police, and other officials were executed in the camp at Katyn forest and elsewhere early in 1940.

The pact also put the Baltic states into the Soviet sphere of influence. Stalin moved quickly to assert control over the area, in the process awarding the city of Vilnius to Lithuania, a city then almost entirely Polish and Jewish in population. By 1940, control was sufficient that the three states were incorporated into the USSR as Soviet republics, after "popular assemblies" went through the ceremony of "requesting" incorporation. Stalin thought his western border was now secure except for one area: Finland.

The Finnish-Soviet border was the result of the internationalization of an internal border of the Russian empire. When Russia annexed Finland in 1809, the Karelian isthmus to the west of St. Petersburg had been part of the Russian Empire for a hundred years, but in a concession to the Finns, was reunited with the rest of Finland. By 1918, at the time of Finnish independence, this meant that the border was only a short tram ride away from the center of Petrograd. The border had been a problem for Soviet military planners ever since, and Stalin decide to fix it. He proposed to the Finnish government a deal, giving the USSR control of strategic islands near the coast and moving the border some kilometers west in return for territory in the far north. The Finns decided that this was a ploy to take control of the country and refused. Thus began the Winter War, in which the small but well-trained and enthusiastic Finnish army held off the Soviets for several months, eliciting support from Britain and other Western powers that allowed them to draw public attention from the "phony war" along Germany's western boundary. After many setbacks and heavy casualties, the Soviets finally got their army together and defeated the Finns, leaving an impression of incompetence that only encouraged their future enemies in Berlin. In the wake of the war, Stalin replaced the Commissar of Defense, his old Civil War crony Voroshilov, with S. T. Timoshenko, a professional military officer who quickly proceeded to reform the army and speed up its re-equipment.

Thus by 1940 the Soviet western frontier had moved hundreds of miles west, and Stalin and Timoshenko had bought some time to put the armed forces in order. This was a huge task, one that had many complications. In 1935 the Soviets had realized that they had the ability and need to finally turn the Red Army into a mass army with a peacetime strength of one-and-a-half million men; in 1939, Stalin ordered an increase in the size of the army to three million. The expansion followed in short order, but the inevitable result was that the soldiers, and particularly the officers, were poorly trained and inexperienced. Hundreds of thousands of soldiers and junior officers were only a step away from the villages. For many soldiers, their rifle was the first really modern piece of equipment that they had ever seen. The army purge of 1937–38 only made things worse, especially at the level of high command. Here lay the explanation of the army's poor performance in the Winter War. Furthermore, the army's equipment was no longer up-to-date. After the great push in the early 1930s, Soviet military production had stagnated and new designs were not forthcoming. Thus the appearance of the German Messerschmidt fighter over Spain in 1937 was a great shock to the Red Air Force, for their best planes were no match for it. German tank technology was moving quickly as well, and all this came at just the moment when the Soviet design bureaus and the armed forces were paralyzed by the purges. Starting in 1938, new designs came into being, but they had to be tested and then put into mass production. Thus by the summer of 1941, the USSR had the first of its modern weapons, the Ilushin-2 ground attack fighter, the T-34 and KV tanks, and the Katiusha rocket artillery. The tanks and rockets were way ahead of the German equivalents, but there were not nearly enough of them or of any modern aircraft.

As the Soviet factories furiously put the new weapons into production and the army struggled with the problems created by rapid expansion and new borders, Hitler was planning his assault. In 1940 he had overrun France and the Balkans. He had failed in the Battle of Britain to bring the English to their knees, but the British Empire, dangerously overstretched by the need to defend the Far East and the Mediterranean as well as the home islands, seemed to the Führer doomed. He would turn his attention to Russia.

All through the winter Wehrmacht units moved east into Rumania, Finland, and what had been Poland. Hitler's tactical intelligence was excellent, for he knew exactly where the Soviet units were stationed, their strength, and their defensive positions. What he did not know, or even care about, was the economic and military potential of the USSR. To Hitler, the Soviet state was simply a Jewish-Mongol horde that would fly apart at the first blows. His generals, who thought in terms of the Russia of 1914, were only slightly less contemptuous of the enemy. Stalin was perfectly aware of the German moves, for his spy network was just as good as Hitler's. His interpretation of the German moves, however, was completely wrong. Stalin never fully grasped the radicalism of the Nazi regime, still seeing it in the light of older German rightist movements, or perhaps as a German version of Mussolini's fascism. He also was convinced that Hitler would not invade the Soviet Union until he had defeated Britain, for Stalin could not imagine that Hitler would be stupid enough to repeat the Kaiser's mistake and fight a war on two fronts at the same time. Thus Stalin interpreted the troop movements as a bluff: he expected that Hitler would hold off for a year or two, and in the meantime perhaps try to bluff the Soviets into delivering much needed raw materials to the Reich. His worst fear was that Soviet troops along the border might provoke Hitler too soon; hence he ordered them to ignore German overflights and other suspicious actions. Soviet military intelligence believed differently, but when their reports reached their top commanders, they were shelved as not consistent with the policy and analysis that emanated from the Kremlin. Nevertheless, in April 1941, Stalin ordered nearly a million additional men mobilized under the cover of large-scale maneuvers and he moved more troops west. The Red Army now had a theoretical strength of some five million men. Only in the last days before the war were orders issued to put some of the troops into a state of greater readiness: the night before the invasion Timoshenko ordered the air force to disperse the planes on the air strips so that they would not make an easy target. Only the Odessa military district obeyed the orders, for even in Stalin's Russia, commands from the center did not necessarily get through in time or call forth instant obedience.

On Sunday, June 22, 1941, at first light – 3:30 in the morning – Hitler launched the invasion of the Soviet Union, Operation Barbarossa, named after the medieval German warrior emperor. Some three million German soldiers crossed the border, together with nearly a million allies, Finns, Rumanians, Slovaks, Hungarians, Italians, and small volunteer and collaborationist units from nearly every country in Europe, including neutral ones like Sweden (SS Nordland). Hitler's army was fresh from victory all over the continent, from Norway to Greece, backed by an economic machine greater than that of the USSR (if not by much) and the resources of occupied Europe. Facing them were the five million men in the Soviet armed forces, but almost half of them were either deployed far in the rear or were still only in the process of formation and training. In addition to being caught in the middle of mobilization and learning to use new equipment, the Soviet forces were placed too close to the border and were easy targets for the Luftwaffe and the German armor. The placement was a relic of the long-standing offensive orientation of the Soviet army, which assumed that soon after an attack the Soviet forces would move to make a series of deep incursions into enemy territory to spoil the attack as the Red Army moved to full mobilization. To make things worse, the Soviets erred in predicting the main direction of the German attack. Until 1940 all Soviet war plans had assumed that the German army would attack directly east through Belorussia toward Moscow, as indeed turned out to be the case. In 1940, however, Timoshenko, the new chief of staff general Georgii Zhukov, and Stalin had decided that Hitler would more likely strike south into the Ukraine. Along the central axis there were only farms and large forests, while the Ukraine was still the most important industrial area of the USSR and a major agricultural region to boot. Surely Hitler would go for needed resources. Thousands of troops were moved south into the Ukraine.

Instead the main blow came directly forward the east. German armor repeated its tactics from France and slashed through Soviet defenses along the main roads and rail lines, pushing deep into the country. Lithuania and much of western Belorussia fell in days. The Luftwaffe destroyed most of the Soviet air force on the ground in the first few days, leaving the army with no air cover and no ability to move without German knowledge. With the weight of the German advance directed toward the center, the Soviet front was overrun within weeks and nearly a million and a half Soviet soldiers found themselves in captivity. Almost none of them survived, for the Germans, as part of their racial policies, chose not to feed them and simply let them die. To the north and south, the Germans advanced almost as swiftly, and by the end of the summer they were at Kiev and the gates of Leningrad.

Conditions on the Soviet side of the front were chaotic as poorly designed communications collapsed under the onslaught, command posts were destroyed, and large bodies of Soviet troops desperately tried to retreat east. The Soviet commander in Belorussia was out of communication with his men as well as with Moscow for days. The orders from Moscow at first followed the old and now utterly irrelevant scheme of counterattack against the invaders. Local commanders were lucky if they never got the orders and just followed their instincts. Some units fought to the end, others until food and ammunition ran out. The next orders from Moscow were to hold on long after the situation was hopeless, and commanders who led their troops out of entrapment found themselves under suspicion or worse for retreating without orders. In July Stalin ordered the trial and execution of a number of the generals whose armies had been destroyed in the first weeks of the war.

Fortunately Stalin and army leadership did more than look for scapegoats. On the second day of the war Stalin set up a State Defense Committee headed by himself, soon replacing Timoshenko with himself also as People's Commissar of Defense, and additionally he became the head of the High Command and formal supreme commander of the armed forces. Zhukov remained as chief of staff. Stalin thus took personal responsibility for the whole conduct of the war. He learned to work with Zhukov and the other generals, but his was the final decision in all matters. Sometimes his orders led to more defeats, but ultimately they led to victory. He had, more than ever, supreme power. The mobilization of the army continued, and became even more essential with the loss of millions of men over the first summer of war. As the situation at the front deteriorated, the government began to evacuate industry from the Ukraine and Leningrad and other areas threatened by the advancing Nazis. In the short run this meant a fall in military production just as the Wehrmacht was capturing and destroying masses of Soviet equipment. Ultimately it was a crucial and a heroic effort, for tens of thousands of men and machines and their families had to move thousands of miles east to the Urals and Siberia, and then build factory buildings to house the equipment, build housing for themselves, and start production on vital goods as quickly as possible. Not just factories were evacuated: the kolhoz and state farms were ordered to move their cattle and other larger animals to the east as well. Huge herds of thousands of cattle moved through the cities, prodded along by women from the villages heading toward the east.

In September the Germans began the final advance toward Moscow, sure of victory. Hitler even considered that he could soon send troops to help Mussolini in the Mediterranean. As the Nazis advanced, Soviet armies to the west of Moscow were ordered to hold on and hundreds of thousands were encircled and perished, but their deaths bought time. Time was of the essence, for the Germans had no conception of Soviet resources. Their pre-invasion intelligence had underestimated the size of the Red Army at the moment of the attack by nearly a third, by one hundred divisions. Even in the first weeks German commanders in the field were surprised to find that new Soviet units suddenly appeared where they thought that resistance had been smashed. Yet as the autumn advanced, German victory seemed assured: in October the foreign embassies and most of the Soviet government evacuated east to Kuibyshev (Samara) on the Volga. Only the announcement that Stalin was still in Moscow and did not intend to leave staved off panic in the capital. On November 7, he appeared on the Lenin Mauseoleum on Red Square as in previous years to review the parade in honor of the October Revolution, a major Soviet ritual. This time the soldiers marched past in the snow straight to the front. German reconnaissance units began to appear on the outskirts of the city, around and inside the ring highways that encircle it today. The government formed volunteer units of students, older office and factory workers, and sent them to the front to fill the gaps torn by the attackers. Yet the situation was better than it appeared. As the Germans plowed on toward Moscow, the Soviets had formed a substantial strategic reserve, part of which now moved west of the city to meet the Nazis. Now for the first time the Germans were halted, for the apparently seamless advance to the east had in fact cost the Wehrmacht dearly. German casualties were greater than the German losses for all campaigns of the war until the invasion of the USSR. German armor had lost thousands of tanks to enemy fire, and many were inoperable from the wear and tear of Russian conditions or out of ammunition. German engines and automatic weapons froze in the cold. Unlike the Russians they had not thought how to keep them working at night temperatures of forty below freezing. Even the Luftwaffe, which had ruled the skies in the first months, was taking rapidly mounting losses as newly built Soviet aircraft with newly trained pilots filled the gaps left by the massive losses of the summer. In early December, the Red Army counterattacked, pushing the Germans away from Moscow and far to the west, inflicting (and taking) massive casualties. By the end of January 1942, the Nazis had lost nearly a million men and four thousand tanks, half of them in the final battle for Moscow. The Soviets had stopped the Wehrmacht, the first time any army had done so since 1939. While the Red Army's losses were horrific, the German losses were ultimately crippling. Germany lacked the population of the Soviet Union, and its superbly functioning industry had not been used to prepare supplies for a war on this scale. The German army at Moscow lacked winter clothes not just because Hitler had assumed a rapid victory but also because he had not counted on the massive expenditure of supplies and the need to fully mobilize to counter Soviet industry. He had no idea that the Soviets could produce far more tanks and aircraft than Germany from a smaller industrial base. By early 1942 the evacuated Soviet industries had come back into production and began to turn out equipment in numbers Germany could not match. This equipment was also superior to the German, especially the tanks, the rocket artillery and many of the aircraft. Now the Soviets had to learn how to use it properly, but they had already inflicted a major strategic defeat from which Germany did not have the resources to recover. Germany could no longer defeat the Soviet Union, although Hitler had no intention of stopping.

The German invasion was not only a military conflict but also a political conflict as well. Stalin saw the war in political terms, as he did everything else, and as in the case of the conduct of war, it took him some time to understand what he was dealing with. He made no statement at first, ordering Molotov to make the formal announcement of war on June 22, several hours after the invasion. Stalin's first speech came on July 3 and reflected his determination to fight, for he ordered a scorched earth policy in the path of the German invaders and called on Soviet citizens to form partisan units. The old illusions still remained, for he asserted that the Nazis were coming to restore tsarism and the rule of the landed gentry. Though he also stated that the Germans wanted to destroy the culture and statehood of the Soviet peoples, his description of the Nazi aims missed the essential truth. The Wehrmacht and its European allies were paving the way for the extermination of the great majority of the Russian and other Slavic peoples and the colonization of the territory by Germans, the famous "Lebensraum" that Hitler had wanted from the beginning. Yet Stalin concluded with a ringing declaration that the German people, enslaved by the Nazi leaders, would be an ally. Nothing could have been further from the truth. The extermination began in the first days. The orders to the German troops had been that all "representatives of the Soviet way of life" were to be eliminated, and that no food was to be given to soldiers or civilians out of any misguided sense of humanity. These orders applied to Russians, Ukrainians, and other Soviet citizens and were behind the destruction of Soviet prisoners of war. The extermination of the Jews also followed the first German victories, for Einsatzgruppen began to round up Jews in occupied territory, the first large-scale massacre taking place in Kaunas on June 25, 1941, with the enthusiastic participation of the local Lithuanian population. Ultimately two million of the five million European Jews who perished in the holocaust were Soviet citizens. Contrary to Stalin's expectations, Hitler did not restore the pre-soviet order, keeping the collective farms since they made it easy for the Germans to extract grain and meat from the population. The remaining factories went to German businessmen, though sabotage by the workers meant that few really went back into production. Any remaining Russians, elite or otherwise, were to become the slaves of the Reich and were to be prepared for that role. Most schools closed and the Germans frequently hanged the teachers as "representatives of the Soviet way of life."

The thousands of soldiers who had been surrounded by the Germans but escaped captivity formed a new menace to the invaders. In the huge forests of Belorussia, the northern parts of the Ukraine, and western Russia they took refuge, collected food and weapons, and formed partisan units. The partisans began to attract local peasants as well, and to attack German communications and transport. By the fall of 1941, the disruption to the rail network was considerable, seriously reducing the output of the already desperately overstretched German supply routes. By the end of the next year there were nearly a half million partisans under arms, and they controlled substantial areas where the Nazis could not move. The Soviet command established a central partisan staff to supply them

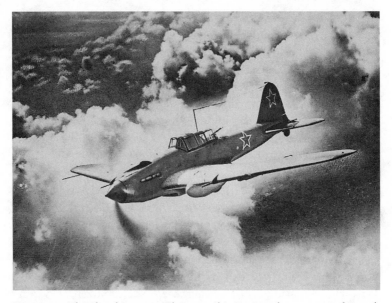

Figure 20. The Ilyushin 2m3 (Shturmovik). Designed as a ground attack aircraft, the two-seater bomber was the Soviet Union's most effective warplane.

by air, sending over old and slow but sturdy and hard to detect biplanes that could land on a dime in forest clearings. Hitler's army reacted to the partisan attacks with vicious brutality, exterminating village after village – men, women, and children – where they suspected contact with partisan units. Collaborationist units from all over Europe and the western territories of the USSR were often more savage than the Germans in dealing with the population of the partisan areas.

Still in Soviet hands but gripped by the vice of the German and Finnish armies was Leningrad. The Germans and their allies had reached the outskirts of the city in September, and from then on the only road was over Lake Ladoga. Around the city were substantial numbers of Soviet troops, but the Germans lacked the resources to take it by assault, so they hoped instead to starve it out. Hitler planned to have it destroyed when he won, as a place of no use to the new Reich. Without effective means of replacement and further reduced by German bombing, food supplies dropped rapidly and starvation began. By mid-winter ten to twenty thousand people were dying every month. Heat and electricity virtually disappeared, all with continuing German shelling and bombing to make things worse. Only workers in the few remaining factories – almost all now devoted to weapons and other war production – had anything close to adequate rations. Fortunately the lake froze, and some supplies could come in over the "Ice Road." The authorities had to improvise, opening stations in food stores that served only hot water or tea substitutes just to keep people a bit warmer. During the next summer the improvised transportation across the lake improved, but by the time the Red Army raised the siege in January, 1944, some eight hundred thousand people had starved to death.

In Leningrad many of the factories had been evacuated before the Germans came, and more were evacuated in 1942. They were part of the massive move of Soviet industry to the east, and the population went as well, in the tens of millions all across the country. The Soviets evacuated ordinary people and groups of children as well as officials. Indeed officials were often required to stay behind to form resistance groups, and those who tried to get out ahead of the Germans, as in the Moscow panic of October 1941, found themselves stopped by the NKVD and even the local populace. Virtually everything and everyone in the country was part of the war effort, a degree of mobilization unknown even in Germany. Women not only staffed the hospitals and took care of orphan children, but they also fought in the army. Anti-aircraft regiments were mostly female, pitting young women just out of high school against the Luftwaffe. In the army, radio operators were women as were other auxiliary positions, and women also made up a fighter regiment and two bomber regiments, including a night bomber unit. Altogether over half a million women served in the armed forces. The intelligentsia went to war as well, not only scientists and engineers. The Soviets evacuated the universities, research institutes, and theaters. Artists and writers who had lived in fear through the 1930s found themselves on transport planes coming out of Leningrad with fighter escorts. Moved east to Siberia and Central Asia, they continued to work, producing major works like Eisenstein's epic movie *Ivan the Terrible*, filmed in Kakazhstan, or Shostakovich's Seventh ("Leningrad") Symphony, finished at Kuibyshev on the Volga. Their work contributed immensely to the morale of the population, not only by their content but also by the simple fact that something normal was still taking place. In the rear food was spartan if generally unfailing, and housing often meant several families crammed into a school classroom. Workers who had come east with their factories lived in tents in the Siberian winter while they built buildings and barracks in which to live, sometimes starting work in new buildings before the roofs were built. Yet most who remembered the war remembered it as a time of privation and sorrow mixed with enthusiasm and the warmth of solidarity. Stalin had greatly overestimated the extent of discontent among the population, and while his agents read mail and listened in on telephone conversations in search of German sympathizers, most people just went to work to help the army, whatever their views of the ultimate value of the Soviet system.

The victory at Moscow encouraged Stalin and the generals to try to exploit their success, and early in 1942 they mounted a series of attacks from Khar'kov in the south to well north of Moscow. All of these offensives were costly failures. The Germans were pushed back here and there, but with heavy Soviet losses. Again several large units were surrounded and ground to pieces. When the spring ended and the mud season with it, Hitler decided not to move against Moscow again, as Zhukov and Stalin expected, but to go south. His aim was the Caucasus with the oil supplies in Grozny and Baku. The Third Reich was short of oil, and this seemed the way to solve the problem. The Nazis smashed through Soviet defenses, getting all the way to the line of the Caucasus Mountains, but also directly east toward the Volga. To protect his flank and cut off the Russians from Baku, he needed to cut the rail lines at Stalingrad and cross the river itself. Stalingrad was the old Tsaritsyn, where Stalin had first encountered warfare in 1918 and was now the site of an immense tractor factory that was also producing tanks, but its main importance was its location.

By the end of August the Germans were on the edge of the city, sending wave after wave of armor and mechanized infantry against the defenders dug into the ruins of the city. It seemed that the war hung in the balance. Yet the German advance had brought many problems with it. The rail lines back to Germany were now so long that transport was jammed up almost to the German border. Hitler no longer had enough German troops to secure his flanks, so the sides of the German wedge pointed at the city were held by Italian and Rumanian troops. Most important, the defenders just kept fighting. By the end of the year the Russian salients were down to just a few acres, their artillery support coming from batteries on the eastern side of the river. In one place sergeant Iakov Pavlov held out for months with just a few dozen men in the basement of a shattered apartment block. The fighting went from house to house, and many Soviet soldiers decided that the most effective weapons were sharpened trenching shovels and grenades. The Nazis could not cross the river.

Around the burning wreckage of the city the Red Army was preparing its trap. Huge armored forces moved up to the north and south, facing the hapless Italians and Rumanians across the frozen steppe. Then on November 19 they attacked with massive artillery and air support and in four days came together to encircle the six hundred thousand German soldiers in Stalingrad. German attempts to supply the trapped army were futile, and in February the Wehrmacht's Sixth Army surrendered. Berlin radio played Siegfried's Funeral March from Wagner's opera over and over again. Nearly a half a million men had died at Stalingrad on each side, but Soviet victory was now assured.

The German invasion had immense consequences for Soviet foreign policy and for the position of the USSR in the world. The day after the invasion the Soviet leadership was surprised to learn not only that Great Britain wanted an alliance but also that Winston Churchill had spoken on the radio to explain the new alliance. "No one has been a more consistent opponent of Communism than I have for the last twenty-five years, and I will unsay no word that I have spoken about it. But all this fades away before the spectacle that is now unfolding... I see the Russian soldiers standing on the threshold of their native land, guarding the fields which their fathers have tilled from time immemorial... I see advancing upon all this in hideous onslaught the Nazi war machine... " Churchill's conclusion was that "Any man or state who fights on against Nazidom will have our aid.*"* Until the rise of Hitler the Soviets had always assumed Britain to be their main enemy, and the rapprochement with France and Czechoslovakia in 1935 never extended to the British Empire. The day of the invasion many Russians, including some in the leadership, assumed that Hitler must have made a secret treaty ending the war with Britain, so Churchill's announcement came as a great relief. In August, Franklin D. Roosevelt declared that the Lend-Lease program designed to help England and any other power fighting Hitler would be extended to the Soviet Union, and after Pearl Harbor the United States joined the USSR and Britain to fight Germany and Italy as well as Japan. The Soviet Union and Japan, however, did not declare war on each other: both were far too preoccupied elsewhere to risk another front in Eastern Siberia or Manchuria.

Lend-Lease provided significant support to the Soviet war effort, both in equipment and food supplies. The Studebaker trucks went to make up the shortfall in Soviet truck production, crucial to the support of mechanized warfare, and many of them served as launching platforms for the Katyusha rockets. The American Airocobra fighter covered gaps in Soviet aircraft supply in 1942, and Spam filled out the meager wartime diet for millions of Russians. If the scale of American efforts was not decisive, the contribution was real as was the morale effect. The Allied convoys around the North Cape of Norway through winter seas infested with U-Boats and under continuous bombardment from German aircraft were a difficult and dangerous operation, giving the Russians concrete proof that they were not alone against Hitler.

For Stalin and the generals, however, the real issue was not Lend-Lease but the possibility of a second front. After much discussion Roosevelt and Churchill decided to make their first move in the Mediterranean, in North Africa, and then in the 1943 landings in Italy. These moves led to the overthrow of Mussolini and knocked Italy out of the war, though fighting continued against the Germans. Stalin was deeply disappointed that the moves came in the south rather than in France and were limited in scale; he complained bitterly, but to no effect. He never realized the extent of the US commitment in the Pacific theater. Finally he met with Churchill and Roosevelt in Teheran at the end of 1943, where the three allies agreed that they would demand unconditional surrender from Germany, that the USSR would declare war on Japan as soon as Germany was defeated, and that the second front would consist of an allied invasion of northern France in the early summer of 1944. Stalin promised to coordinate a major offensive with the Anglo-American landing. Issues also arose at Teheran about the future of Europe, as Britain and America recognized by now that the Red Army would be the one to liberate Eastern Europe from the Nazis and reach Germany first. In October 1944, Churchill came to Moscow and proposed to Stalin a "percentage agreement" on the Balkans: Britain was to have predominant influence (ninety percent) in Greece, while the Soviet Union was to have the same in Rumania. Bulgaria was to be seventy-five percent under Soviet influence, while the two powers would have equal shares in Yugoslavia and Hungary. Stalin agreed, but Eastern Europe was a major issue again at the Yalta conference in February 1945. There the three powers generally agreed on the joint occupation of Germany (for an undefined period), the destruction of the legacy of Nazism, and reparations to the Soviet Union. Stalin agreed to Roosevelt's proposal to set up the United Nations. Some greater agreement was achieved on the status of Eastern Europe, such as the future Polish-Soviet boundary, and an agreement that the future Polish government would represent both Stalin's Polish allies and the conservatives. Stalin promised elections after the war. Most of the other issues involving Eastern Europe were not settled. Roosevelt and Churchill did not want simply to cede control of Eastern Europe to the Soviet Union, but with the Red Army in possession of most of the territory and accounting for three quarters of the Wehrmacht's losses, there was little that they could do.

The fate of Eastern Europe and Germany were not just issues of Soviet foreign policy. Since 1939 the Comintern had experience dizzying shifts in policy. The pact with Germany implied that fascism was no longer the main enemy: the war was a new "imperialist war" and the Communists were to oppose both Hitler and the Allies equally. The German invasion of the Soviet Union prompted yet another abrupt change in revolutionary strategy, a return to a variant of the Popular Front idea of 1935–1939. Stalin dissolved the Comintern in 1943, but most Communist parties of the world remained oriented toward Moscow. The Communists were ordered once again to make a coalition with anyone who opposed the Nazis, from conservative and aristocratic army officers like the French Gaullists to the Social Democrats. In most of occupied Europe resistance movements acquired this make-up, and even in France many aristocratic Russian émigrés joined the resistance, fighting and dying alongside working-class French Communists. As the Soviet army passed its western borders and came into the lands allied with Hitler or occupied by his troops, decisions had to be made. What sort of government should the Soviets put in place? Many local Communists believed that the time had come to seize power, to make up for the defeats of the interwar era. The Soviet tactic, however, was different. The new slogan was "people's democracy," meant to indicate a continuation of the wartime coalition. Land reform and limited nationalization of industry were to be central features of the new order, not "dictatorship of the proletariat," and the Communists were to rule together with Socialists and even anti-fascist liberals and conservatives.

At the moment of the German surrender at Stalingrad, all these issues were barely on the horizon. The task was to begin to drive the Nazis out of the country, and the Red Army moved to the west, pushing the Germans back to their starting points from the previous summer. In the spring of 1943, as the snow melted and the mud dried, Hitler tried for the last time to reverse the tide of defeat. The Wehrmacht planned a massive counter attack into the Soviet salient around Kursk, in the middle of the steppe, ideal ground for armored warfare. It was the German armor, the giant Ferdinand assault guns and the new Tiger tanks that were to carry the weight of the attack. The Red Army, however, fully reequipped and with new skill and confidence, planned its countermeasures without flaw. Though Stalin at first wanted a swift counter-offensive, Zhukov and the generals persuaded him to stay in defense until the Nazis were worn down. The German armor confronted massive fire from artillery, rockets and anti-tank guns as well as the Soviet air force. In a matter of days the offensive stalled and then the Soviet armor pushed the Germans back. The Red Army went on through the rest of the year to take back the eastern parts of the Ukraine, Kiev itself in November, as well as most of Russia proper. Soviet troops lifted the siege of Leningrad in January 1944. In the next months the Red Army surrounded and destroyed some fifty thousand German troops in one battle at Korsun, southwest of Kiev, pounding them to pieces in the snow with artillery and air strikes.

Hitler had now lost the war. All that he could do was feed more men and equipment into the meat grinder in the hope of staving off the inevitable defeat. By the early summer of 1944 the Soviets were ready to launch a huge offensive through Belorussia; the offensive was timed to coincide with the landings at Normandy. In this one operation the Red Army encircled the whole of the German army group Center, hundreds of thousands of German soldiers, and moved into Poland. There they faced an unpleasant surprise. Without informing the Soviet command, the Polish Home Army, the main underground resistance group, staged an uprising against the Germans in Warsaw. The Soviet army was at the end of its operational line, on the other bank of the Vistula, with little capacity to help the Poles quickly. Molotov wanted to push on, not to help the Poles but just to exploit the victory. Zhukov was against any new offensive, for the army was exhausted and needed to rest and reequip. In any case, Stalin decided that it was not necessary; he was not going to help his opponents in the Polish Home Army and the Poles were left to fight on alone. In the same summer the Soviets moved south into Rumania, and the pro-German governments in Rumania and Bulgaria collapsed. In Yugoslavia the Red Army linked up with Tito's partisans and went north toward Hungary. In Budapest the Germans put up furious resistance, but the Soviets were able to crush the resistance and move on to Vienna. Hitler's coalition continued to collapse. In Finland, Baron Mannerheim, the commander in chief of the army, became the president of the country and immediately took Finland out of the war, signing an armistice in September.

The Red Army was now pounding at the gates of Hitler's Germany. The Nazi command placed the bulk of their army in Poland and Eastern Germany facing the Soviets, even with the Americans and British moving rapidly to the German western border. The last year of the war brought incredible slaughter, as the now desperate Wehrmacht faced a well-equipped and huge Red Army. The Soviet

command had learned how to fight and now had the equipment
to do it, and Stalin had learned to work with his generals. The
Russians fought their way through Poland, in the process liberating
those prisoners of Auschwitz and other Nazi death camps who were
still alive. Soviet soldiers, many of whom had spent time in Soviet
labor camps, had a glimpse of something even more sinister in the
gas chambers and crematoria. As they moved into Germany, they
found a country in ruins but still showing the signs of pre-war prosperity. As one Soviet soldier said to a Western journalist, "if they
had all this, why did they attack us?" As the Soviets approached
Berlin, Hitler threw everything he had into battle. Northeast of the
Nazi capital stood SS Charlemagne, the French SS brigade, and high
school boys were mobilized to fight Soviet tanks with hand-held
anti-tank weapons. None such desperate measures nor the persistence of the German army could stand up to the huge barrages by
152-millimeter self-propelled guns, rockets, and masses of heavy
Stalin tanks. Even with such overwhelming force, the encirclement
of Hitler's capital and the final assault through the flaming ruins of
the city cost the Red Army hundreds of thousands of men. By early
May of 1945, they had fought their way into the city and raised the
Soviet flag over the Reichstag. The Red Army had pounded a stake
into the heart of the Third Reich.

21

Growth, Consolidation, and Stagnation

The Soviet Union emerged from the war victorious but with tremendous population losses and economic damage. The number of dead was at least twenty million, twenty-seven million by some estimates, including three million prisoners of war, some seven million soldiers killed in battle, two million Soviet Jews, and at least fifteen million Russian, Ukrainian, and Belorussian civilians. All areas occupied by the Germans were devastated, including the USSR's richest agricultural land and the whole Ukrainian industrial complex, which had supplied the country with almost half of its products on the eve of the war. Housing stock and city services were smashed, and even in unoccupied areas the strain of the war showed everywhere. To make things worse, a bad harvest in 1946 led to famine conditions in much of the country. Soviet reparations from Germany and Eastern European countries helped somewhat, but the scale of loss and destruction was so great that even such measures provided only small recompense for the losses.

At the same time, the victory brought with it a new order in the Kremlin. Soon after the war, Stalin ordered the People's Commissariats to be called Ministries, for he announced (in private) that such names had been appropriate to a revolutionary state, but that the Soviet Union had now consolidated itself enough to operate with more permanent institutions. For the first time Stalin and his inner circle began to delegate power to a series of state committees, usually headed by the principal ministers who managed the main areas of the economy. In principle, Stalin was no longer going to monitor all the details of government and economic activity, and some new faces joined the pre-war leadership. Beria and Zhdanov (until his death in 1948) continued on in Stalin's inner circle, while Molotov, Mikoyan, Kaganovich, and Voroshilov remained from the pre-war years but were less powerful, especially Voroshilov, disgraced by his military failures. New faces in the top leadership were Malenkov (vice-chairman of the Council of Minsters under Stalin's chairmanship), Nikolai Bulganin (minister of defense and a longtime economic manager), and Khrushchev, until 1949 head of the Ukrainian party organization and then of the Moscow city party. To a large extent the system did work in a more regular fashion for the last eight years of Stalin's life, but at the same time he did not refrain from scolding and bullying his closest collaborators and from directing a series of political "cases" with murderous results. The cult of Stalin reached its apogee in the post-war years. Besides the ubiquitous portraits and statues an official adulatory biography appeared on his seventieth birthday. The press produced endless accolades to the "great leader of peoples," the great Marxist, and the genius military commander Stalin. As much as he may have realized that the USSR needed a more normal mode of government, Stalin could not let go of the reins of power, and continued to behave like a revolutionary commissar of the civil war era, jumping into the middle of the fray with a firing squad ready.

The main task before the Soviet leadership was first of all reconstruction of the war damage, and then the continuation of "socialist construction," including the progressive technical modernization of industry.

In some ways reconstruction was the easy part, for it meant the rebuilding of previously existing plants and infrastructure, and it was largely completed by 1950. The expansion and modernization of industry was more complicated. It is the case that the growth rates of the post-war era were some of the highest (actual) growth rates in Soviet history. In those years many of the pre-war investments began to pay off, with huge growth in the Urals-Western Siberian metallurgical and mining areas. To a large extent the crucial Soviet industries came up to world standards, and an enormous nuclear industry came into being, at this time largely for military purposes but with planning for power generation and other civilian uses in the future. What did not happen was proportionate investment in consumer goods or agriculture, the latter still hampered by the leadership's fascination with agronomic fantasies such as the "grass-field" system of crop rotation. Reconstruction brought housing only to the pre-war level, with most people living (at best) in communal apartments. A rare improvement of the post-war years was in medicine, for the number of doctors grew again by seventy-five percent, and the 1946 famine did not lead to massive epidemics, as had occurred in 1932–33.

Stalin's insistence on centralized discipline and his assumption that all disagreement masked political subversion created a series of incidents among the leadership that terrified even Stalin's allies. The first sign was Marshal Zhukov's demotion in 1946 to commander of a local military district. This and later incidents fell in a period of intense ideological campaigning that affected more than just cultural life. The party issued reproofs to composers, poets, and biologists, but it also launched campaigns to celebrate Russian culture and its importance (as well as selected aspects of the non-Russian cultures) as part of a closing-off of Western influence wherever possible. After the creation of the state of Israel in 1948, the Soviet authorities suddenly launched a campaign against "cosmopolitanism" that was in fact directed against the many Jews prominent in Soviet culture as well as the state and party apparatus. The campaign soon died down, but not without casualties. The wartime Jewish Anti-Fascist Committee was dissolved and its leading members – Yiddish poets, Jewish scientists, and party officials – were arrested and shot. On Stalin's orders the security forces killed the famous actor and director of the Moscow Yiddish theater, Solomon Mikhoels, in a faked auto accident in Minsk. It is in these years that travel and correspondence abroad became essentially impossible for almost all Soviet citizens. The irony of these campaigns and repressive measures was that the war had for the first time given the Soviet Union legitimacy in the eyes of millions of its people, but rather than relying on that new found legitimacy, the party simply tightened the screws.

Potentially even more serious was the Leningrad affair of 1949. Arising from an arcane dispute over a trade fair held in Leningrad, it soon turned into the dismissal of several thousand party members in the city and the secret trial of nine local party leaders, charged with treasonable offenses. Six were executed and three sent to camps, their real crimes apparently being the creation (in Stalin's mind) of a sort of local fiefdom that did not consult the central leadership. Another victim was Nikolai Voznesenskii, who had headed Soviet planning since 1938. Peripherally involved in the Leningrad affair, his actual crime seems to have been conceal- ing information from Stalin about the 1949 plan, something the aging dictator would not leave unpunished. Voznesenskii also per- ished. In 1952 Stalin called a Congress of the Party, the first since 1939, where Georgii Malenkov presented the main report on Soviet achievements, including a wildly inaccurate account of the supposed progress of agriculture. This sort of public spectacle gave an appear- ance of unity in the party leadership, but in reality Stalin's behavior was beginning to worry his comrades. In 1951 the Ministry of State Security forces arrested more than a dozen Georgian party officials, charging them with nationalism and spying for the West (the "Min- grelian affair"), resulting in the exile of over ten thousand people from Georgia. Late in 1952 a new "conspiracy" surfaced, in which a supposed plot of Kremlin doctors, most of whom were Jewish, planned to murder Stalin. The horizon was darkening.

    In the background of these lurid and sinister events, the party leadership was beginning to realize that some changes were needed. Malenkov and other leaders knew perfectly well that agriculture was not prospering. The collective farms managed to produce enough to feed the people at a sufficient but low level. Every harvest was still a gamble, and meat and dairy products came overwhelmingly from the collective farmers' private plots. Another area of crisis was the GULAG. By 1950 the special settlements had two and a half million people, most of them from various national minorities deported for unreliability: Germans, North Caucasian peoples, Crimean Tatars, as well as some remaining kulaks. The camp system had about the same number, in this case heavily Russian, including political pris- oners from the 1930s, Nazi collaborators real and mythical, and a great majority of people convicted of non-political crimes and common murderers and thieves. For the GULAG administration the problem was that prison labor was no longer economically effective. Though prisoners made up some ten percent of the work force in logging and construction and were used in projects where ordinary labor seemed too expensive, the costs of the GULAG were too great. The expenditures on administration and hundreds of thousands of guards were just too high, and to make matters worse, the prison labor system rested on unskilled labor. Even in logging, mechanization was beginning to penetrate Soviet industry, and prison laborers lacked the skills and motivation to use the new equipment. By 1952 the GULAG officials and Beria himself were considering some sort of changes in the system.

Then Stalin died at his dacha on March 5, 1953. The response of Stalin's inner circle was to declare collective leadership, with Khrushchev (now made first secretary of the party) and Malenkov (now made chair of the Council of Ministers) as the main figures. The immediate problem they faced was Beria. Since 1946 Beria had not headed the security police, the Ministry of State Security or the Ministry of Internal Affairs, but he did have Stalin's ear. He was also head of the Special Committee within the defense network that ran the increasingly important nuclear industry, at that time still almost entirely working for military production. In the new division of power after Stalin's death Beria obtained the united Ministry of Internal Affairs and State Security. Once again, as in 1938, he was in charge of all police functions. The first political crisis of the new regime came at the end of June, when Malenkov raised the issue of Beria at the Presidium of the party (the new name for the Politburo). The meeting on June 26 was actually a conspiracy, for Beria was not told that his fate was on the agenda. Right in the meeting Marshal Zhukov and a group of officers arrested him. A week later Malenkov and Khrushchev explained their actions to the Central Committee, claiming that Beria was trying to control the party through the security police and was aiming for absolute power. He was an intriguer who had poisoned Stalin's mind against the other leaders and ultimately was an agent of Western imperialism. He was presenting himself as a reformer to create a political base in the party. After a closed trial, Beria was executed in a military bunker by the Moscow River.

The removal of Beria solved only one problem. Even before his arrest the new leadership knew that some changes had to take place. Agriculture was in poor shape, the camp system was in crisis, and ferment in eastern Germany was creating a problem in Eastern Europe. Khrushchev sponsored a series of agricultural reforms, higher purchase prices for kolhoz products and lower taxes on the peasants' private plots. After Stalin's death Khrushchev had acquired the position of first secretary of the Communist Party, but Malenkov was the prime minister and Molotov still a powerful minister of foreign affairs. Both sat on the Presidium of the party and all of its members, with Khrushchev leading the chorus, proclaimed that the party and country now had collective leadership. To carry out his plans, however, Khrushchev needed to eliminate potential rivals. First he managed to convince his colleagues to demote Malenkov from the position of prime minister to minister of electrification and replace him with Bulganin. He then moved to sideline Molotov, though the latter remained foreign minister. By the time of the 1955 Geneva Conference it was clear that Khrushchev was the most powerful, not Bulganin or Molotov.

While these maneuvers in the Kremlin were bringing Khrushchev to the top, the leader was carrying on in secret a complete revision of the Stalin era policies of repression. The news of Stalin's death and the first reforms provoked revolts in the GULAG in 1953 and 1954 that were put down by the military, but the process of release began, from the camps and labor colonies as well as from the special settlements. Almost a million were released by the beginning of 1955. Equally important were the various investigations that the authorities launched under the aegis of the USSR Supreme Court to examine the more egregious cases of execution and imprisonment back to the 1930s. Their findings were overwhelmingly that in the cases of these victims they found "an absence of the components of a crime" (*otsutstvie sostava prestupleniia*), leading to their release and the posthumous rehabilitation of the dead. Rehabilitation was not merely symbolic, for it meant that the families of those who perished were no longer enemies of the state, and if they had languished in the camps, they were released. All over the Soviet Union hundreds of thousands of people found themselves with a ticket home and papers allowing them to live normal lives, returning to families some had not seen for fifteen or more years, and whose families did not even know if they were alive. For the time being, the release and rehabilitation of the prisoners and the dead took place in silence. Nothing appeared in the newspapers.

At the end of 1955 Khrushchev convinced his colleagues, even those who had been Stalin's closest associates like Molotov and Kaganovich, to establish a party commission to look into Stalin's "violations of socialist legality," particularly the extermination of most of the party elite in 1937–38. The head of the commission was P. N. Pospelov, a former editor of *Pravda* and to all appearances a fervent Stalinist. His commission's report became the basis of Khrushchev's famous "secret speech" at the Twentieth Congress of the Communist Party in February 1956. Khrushchev's speech, with additions from himself and editorial work by another party ideologist, M. M. Suslov, came at the end of the Congress. As everyone was packing to go home, the announcement came to the Soviet and foreign Communists that there would an additional session. There, Khrushchev read his speech for four hours (with a short break) to a stunned and silent audience. In it he blamed all the crimes of the 1930s and after on Stalin personally, with some room for Beria. He focused primarily on the destruction of the Central Committee in 1937–38, seventy percent of whose members had perished, and on Stalin's conduct of the war. Neither of his accounts was fully honest, for in blaming Stalin for the terror he omitted the role of Molotov and other leaders, including himself, to say nothing of the thousands of enthusiastic denouncers of wreckers and spies from among the population. Khrushchev's account of Stalin's role in the war was simply wrong, giving rise to numerous legends that came to be refuted only after 1991. He said almost nothing about collectivization, which ultimately involved more people and more deaths than the terror. The point, however, was to shift the blame onto Stalin for all the crimes of the past and to underscore the importance of the collective leadership of the party, to avoid "the cult of personality" that surrounded Stalin in his lifetime. To prevent a recurrence of such horrors, the need was for collective leadership and the preservation of "socialist legality."

The leadership had debated how much to publicize the speech, and the result was a compromise. It was not published in the Soviet Union (it appeared only in 1989) but was circulated among party organizations where it was read in its entirety to party members, some seven million people, and the whole of the Komsomol, more than eighteen million. As it was also circulated to foreign Communists, the speech got to the West through Poland and was quickly printed in many translations. Khrushchev's lurid depictions of torture and execution (taken directly from Pospelov's report) were a tremendous shock to foreign leftists, especially in the West, but elsewhere reaction was mixed. In China Mao Tse-tung never really approved of it, and Stalin's works remained canonical in the Chinese party. In the Soviet Union itself the report produced pro-Stalin riots by thousands of students in Tbilisi and Gori in Stalin's native Georgia, and it caused outbursts of violent criticism of the regime among Moscow intellectuals. Mostly, however, the population was more concerned with meat prices and accepted the new policies, even if many harbored more positive views of the Soviet past than those now propagated by Khrushchev.

The main effects of the secret speech were in Eastern Europe, leading to riots in Poland and the Hungarian revolution in the fall of 1956. Khrushchev survived these threats with his power intact, and moved on with more reform projects. In the late 1950s the release of prisoners and special settlers grew to a flood. The deported nationalities from the North Caucasus returned home, their autonomous republics restored. (Crimean Tatars, Volga Germans, and some other groups, however, did not return, though their personal legal statuses were restored.) By 1960 the GULAG had come to an end. More change was in the works. Soviet industry was doing much better than agriculture, but the pressure to build a fully modern society, now in competition with the United States, mandated greater progress in both manufacturing and agriculture. Khrushchev publicly called on Soviet agriculture to surpass US production in meat and milk products. For industry the solution he adopted early in 1957 was to decentralize the economy, creating "Councils of the National Economy" on the regional level instead of the central industrial ministries that had managed the economy since the 1930s.

Before this plan could be implemented, a new crisis arose, this time in the central leadership of the party. Molotov, Malenkov, and Kaganovich had been discontented with Khrushchev for some time. Molotov was unhappy with the partial reconciliation with

Tito, the increasing talk of peaceful coexistence with the West, and with the increased priority given to agriculture and consumer goods. His allies shared these doubts, and also opposed the growing personal power of Khrushchev. Behind these particular concerns was the looming issue of de-Stalinization: how far would Khrushchev go? The lesson of Hungary was that the process could get out of hand, and even without that, as the main survivors of Stalin's old guard they were themselves acutely vulnerable. In the early months of 1957 they lobbied the members of the Presidium, gaining seven votes – themselves, the aging Voroshilov, Bulganin, and two important economic managers – out of eleven for ousting Khrushchev from power. The plotters then told Khrushchev that they needed to meet to discuss a joint appearance in Leningrad for its anniversary, but when he arrived on June 18, he learned that they wanted to replace him as the leader of the party. Furious debate raged and Mikoyan, alone of the Stalin old guard in support of Khrushchev, left the room briefly and went to Leonid Brezhnev and Elena Furtseva (the only woman ever to play a role in Soviet leadership), both candidate members of the Presidium. He told them to contact the Minister of Defense and a candidate member of the Presidium, Marshal Zhukov, who was absent because the plotters had sent him off on maneuvers. Brezhnev raced to the telephone and summoned the Marshal, who arrived in the Kremlin while the debate still raged. Molotov had his seven votes, but all but one of the candidate members stuck by Khrushchev. Mikoyan and others had also contacted the Central Committee members resident in and near Moscow, and by the party statute the ultimate arbiter of such decisions was the Central Committee (CC). Molotov and the others at first refused to meet with the CC members, but soon realized that they had no choice, especially with Zhukov unwavering in opposition to their plans. He had been the man who had arrested Beria and had the loyalty of the armed forces. The full Central Committee convened on June 22, 1957, the sixteenth anniversary of Hitler's invasion.

These events had taken place in secret, and only a very few were aware that something was up. For a week the CC, some two hundred strong, lambasted Molotov and his allies, accusing them of mistaken policies, splitting the party, trying to seize power, ignoring the Central Committee, and bringing up the behavior of Molotov and Kaganovich in the great terror. The party elite did not want a return to the fear and despotism of the Stalin era. One of the most outspoken was Brezhnev, a provincial party leader from the Ukraine who had only recently entered the ranks of the party's central elite. Finally Khrushchev and his supporters denounced the three main plotters as an "anti-party group" and expelled them from the Presidium, replacing them with Brezhnev and Furtseva. In Stalin's time the plotters could have expected only death: instead they received minor appointments, Molotov going as ambassador to Mongolia. He and his allies had grossly underestimated the new party elite that had come into power since the 1930s – people with a great deal of experience in wartime and economic management and who were appalled at the prospect of a return to the Stalin era. These younger people were Khrushchev's base in the party, and they would remain in power until the 1980s.

Molotov had criticized Khrushchev for trying to create a new "cult of personality" and run everything himself, but the Central Committee had taken that charge as mere demagoguery. They were to be proved to a large extent wrong in the coming years. Only a few months later Khrushchev arranged the demotion of Marshal Zhukov, accusing him of ignoring party control of the armed forces and despotic behavior. These charges had some truth to them, but his removal from the Ministry of Defense and the Presidium meant that Khrushchev now had no rivals at the top. He was not a dictator like Stalin, but he alone was at the pinnacle of power in the USSR.

Khrushchev used his power to conduct a foreign policy that increasingly involved bluffing his way through crises, alternating cautious diplomacy with wild risks, the most famous being the Cuban missile crisis of 1962. He also faced the increasing disintegration of the Soviet bloc, as Albania and Rumania gradually turned into independent Stalinist states, and most important, China moved inexorably away from the USSR toward the Cultural Revolution. Mao and his allies in the Communist movement saw Khrushchev as the embodiment of "revisionism," of a turn away from the true revolutionary path. Khrushchev's colleagues in the Kremlin most certainly did not share Mao's views, though they did think that Khrushchev had frequently exacerbated the conflict by his clumsy personal style. All of these events undermined his standing with the party elite, but equally problematic were the economic policies he pursued.

The problem here was not Khrushchev's goals. The party elite clearly agreed that the country needed a radical improvement in agriculture. In the late 1950s the urban population still lived largely on black bread, sausage when it was available, and whatever could be afforded from the peasant market. Consumer goods were far more available than earlier but hard to actually obtain. Hence Khrushchev's desire to put more resources into agriculture, consumer goods, and even housing, was extremely popular not just with the people but with the party leaders. They realized that they could not maintain stability if living standards did not improve radically.

The biggest problem was agriculture. One of his first acts was to abolish the machine–tractor stations set up in the 1930s and transfer their machinery to the kolhozes, a move that meant much greater autonomy for the farms. More was to come. On his 1959 trip to the United States he caused a considerable stir by his visits to American farms in Iowa and his meetings with American farmers. From this experience he seems to have been confirmed in his belief in large-scale, higher-technology farming, for American agriculture was already turning from family farms toward agribusiness. He realized that the USSR was way behind in the production and use of chemical fertilizer. The Stalinist industrialization model had consciously favored metallurgy and coal over chemicals and oil, as they were more suited to the then level of economic development as well as more important for defense production. This decision meant that increases in agricultural production, which did occur after the mid-1930s, came from mechanization, hybridization of plants, and more systematic crop rotation, rather than from the use of fertilizer or pesticides. None of these methods did more than keep pace with rapidly increasing urbanization, and to make matters worse Stalin and his agricultural bosses had accepted various crank schemes in agronomy like the notorious "grass-field" system. This was the notion, accepted by the authorities from the late 1930s, that food grains should be rotated with grasses rather than clover or other plants that aid nitrogen fixation. The system became a major bugbear for Khrushchev, who demanded that Soviet agriculture follow the rotation patterns accepted in American and other agricultural systems, and in 1963 he got his way.

Unfortunately Khrushchev's programs combined solid planning with dubious schemes like the virgin lands project. Khrushchev, who considered himself something of an agricultural expert because of his years in the Ukraine, was aware that there was a great deal of uncultivated land in Western Siberia and Kazakhstan. To him the solution was obvious: the Soviet Union's low yield in grain could be solved by sending thousands of settlers to these areas to put the steppe under the plow. The result was a 1930s-style mobilization, with the Komsomol in the lead, sending young people out to live in tents while they sowed grain and built houses. The overall size of the Soviet harvest did increase rapidly as a result, but the program also took resources from modernizing the collective farms and it turned out that much of the land was indeed fertile but too arid for continuous cultivation. Environmental degradation was the inevitable result, with falling output. The Kazakh leadership had warned Khrushchev that there was not much suitable new land, but he simply replaced these naysayers with his cronies from Kiev and Moscow.

Besides the virgin lands, his other agricultural obsession was corn. Khrushchev knew even before he went to America that corn was a major component of animal feed throughout the world, and he decided that the Soviet Union should produce corn. Most agronomists thought that it was not a suitable crop outside of some small areas in the far south of the country, but Khrushchev would not agree, even trying to force the authorities in the Baltic republics to grow corn in place of the more traditional crops. Much time and money was expended trying to find a hybrid that would grow well under various conditions, but the project just turned into another centrally sponsored campaign with no major results. Khrushchev, however, would not give up.

Khrushchev's record in industry was mixed. The 1950s were a period of very high growth rates, even after the end of post-war reconstruction. Soviet achievements in technology, such as the building of a nuclear industry and rockets that could go into space were visible symbols of a modern state. Most of the nuclear development was still secret, but the Sputnik launch in 1957 was a worldwide event. Even more spectacular was Iurii Gagarin's flight into space in 1961, followed by a whole series of space flights. Until the American moon landing in 1969, the Soviets seemed to be way ahead in the space race. Along with these very real achievements there were persistent problems. The new decentralized management system was no better than the old one, and in many areas it simply added a new layer of bureaucracy. More promising was the decision, which Khrushchev enthusiastically supported if he did not originate, of turning massive resources toward the chemical industry and the production of oil and natural gas. The two were related, as much of the raw material for the chemical industry would be petroleum byproducts. The Soviet Union would have plastic. For Khrushchev, the chemical industry was also to be a panacea for agriculture, as he did realize that corn and the virgin lands were not enough.

Unfortunately none of these plans addressed immediate problems. The decisions made in 1959–1960 did lay the basis for subsequent massive developments that shifted the energy base from coal to oil and gas by the 1970s and created a huge chemical industry, but there was little to show for it in the short run. Perhaps his most successful program for the average person was the first attempts at mass housing, the five story (with no elevator) small apartment houses that mushroomed around Moscow and other large cities. These were no longer communal apartments and although they were small they had the usual modern conveniences.

Khrushchev kept tinkering with agriculture and proclaiming grand goals. In 1961 he held another party congress in which he announced that the Soviet Union was going to "build communism," Marx's second stage beyond socialism in which the state would wither away among a universal abundance of all possible goods and services. For a population that was still struggling with deficit goods, long lines at stores, and high prices at the peasant market, this program tasted of megalomania. In the next year the authorities even faced a riot in the southern town of Novocherkassk – a riot entirely with economic causes that was harshly repressed.

Coming on top of the Cuban missile crisis, the economic problems were increasingly disturbing. To top it off, Khrushchev did seem to be constructing a "cult of personality." Movies appeared chronicling his trips abroad in loving detail with titles like *Our Nikita Sergeevich*. With his son-in-law Aleksei Adzhubei controlling *Izvestiia*, one of the two main newspapers, his doings were spread all over the country. He appeared at various meetings with writers and artists, lecturing them about politics and art, the most famous being his performance at an exhibit of mildly modernist art in 1962, where he told the artists that their work looked like a donkey's tail had painted it. The party leadership did not necessarily disagree, but disliked his practice of dealing with these issues off the cuff and without consultation. It was too much like Stalin's incursions into economics and linguistics. Khrushchev also antagonized large numbers of people by a new campaign against religion. After Stalin's recognition of the Orthodox Church and most other religions at the end of the war, the churches gradually began to acquire a modest position in Soviet society. Khrushchev decided to change that, and embarked on another massive wave of persecution. Fortunately it lacked the murderous results of the 1930s, but it did result in the closing of many churches, arrests, and the virtual proscription of religion from Soviet life. The party elite was certainly not in favor of religion, but like Stalin, they no longer thought it was a major issue and preferred simply to control it. Khrushchev's campaign was unnecessary and was the result of his personal quirks imposed on the country.

Ironically the straw that broke the camel's back for Brezhnev and the other party leaders came from the intersection of agriculture and science, for a long time one of the chief sore points of the Soviet system. Khrushchev, for all his anti-Stalinism, remained a convinced supporter of Trofim Lysenko and his officially sponsored 1949 condemnation of modern genetics. Lysenko had his own fiefdom in the network of agricultural research institutes, but the Academy of Sciences kept most of his cronies out. Early in 1964 Khrushchev tried to get a number of these cronies elected to the Academy of Sciences, but the physicists, led by Andrei Sakharov and Igor Tamm, mobilized so much opposition that the prospects were voted down. Khrushchev was furious, though his own scientist daughter tried to persuade him that Lysenko's work was simply wrong. At a full meeting of the Central Committee in July, after a long rambling speech about agriculture, Khrushchev suddenly announced that part of the problem was with the scientists, with Sakharov's and the Academy's meddling in politics, as he saw it, to reject the Lysenkoites. Then he announced that they should just abolish the Academy as a relic of the nineteenth century. Brezhnev and his colleagues decided that the time had come. The Academy issue was only one of many, but it was just too much. As they were struggling to modernize Soviet society, here was their leader trying to wreck the principal source of innovation, their only hope of catching up to the West. In October 1964, the Central Committee met again, presenting a whole list of charges against Khruschev, including the Academy affair. He did recognize his "rudeness" about Sakharov and the Academy and his obsession with corn, but he continued to defend this behavior in the Cuban missile crisis ("the risk was inevitable") and in the various Berlin crises. The Committee voted him out, placing Brezhnev in the position of head of the party and Aleksei Kosygin, an economic manager, in the position of Prime Minister.

The new regime largely continued Khrushchev's policies without his erratic style. The regional Economic Councils were quickly abolished, and the more exotic agricultural campaigns ceased. There was no return to Stalinist methods of rule. Stalin remained unmentionable in most contexts, though some of the World War II generals did describe aspects of his wartime leadership in memoirs, mostly rather negatively. In history textbooks and public statements the achievements of the Stalin era were attributed to "the party and people," and accounts of his crimes remained as they stood in 1964. Further revelations ceased. The new policy produced some disquiet in the intelligentsia, but for most of the population Stalin was no longer an issue. If anything, popular estimation of the former "great leader of peoples" was more positive than the official line. In two important respects the Brezhnev era actually brought further liberalization. The campaign against religion came to an end, establishing a modus vivendi with the Soviet Union's various religions that lasted until the 1980s: religion was discouraged, but not prohibited, and the artistic heritage of Orthodoxy in icon-painting and architecture became the object of extensive study for the first time. In science the new regime totally abandoned Lysenko and restored genetics to Soviet biology. The last remnant of Stalinist science disappeared.

The first decade or so of the Brezhnev era was a period of enormous economic growth. Plans laid under Khrushchev came to fruition, as vast new fields of natural gas went into production. In only twenty years gas production increased tenfold, with about half coming from Siberia and a quarter from Turkmenistan and Uzbekistan. Whole new cities sprang up, like Navoi in Uzbekistan, named in typical Soviet fashion for a medieval Central Asian poet. New oil fields opened up, mainly in Western Siberia, and production nearly doubled by the 1980s. The Soviet Union launched a huge program in nuclear power, starting with the Beloiarsk station in the Urals. Beloiarsk followed a largely experimental reactor built near Moscow in the 1950s. It employed a slow-neutron reactor, a design not later used in the Soviet Union, and it produced its first electricity in 1964. Eventually the Soviet Union built nearly fifty nuclear power plants with pressurized water or graphite moderated designs, the latter being the version that failed at Chernobyl. By the 1980s nuclear reactors produced around a quarter of the country's electricity.

The huge growth in the energy sector signaled a shift from coal to petroleum-based energy sources and nuclear power. It also changed the distribution of energy among the republics, for coal had been mined mainly in the Ukraine until World War II, then increasingly in the Russian republic and Kazakhstan, although the Ukraine still produced almost half of Soviet coal. Oil, by contrast was ninety percent the product of the Russian republic and gas was nearly eighty percent. To some extent nuclear power reset the balance, for the policy was to build nuclear power stations where other resources were absent or in decline. Thus the Chernobyl graphite moderated reactor began to produce electricity in 1977, and the Ukraine came to depend on nuclear power for half its electricity, in contrast to only twenty percent for the USSR as a whole. The southern Ukrainian city of Zaporozhe received the largest nuclear power facility in Europe, whose reactors came on line starting in 1985, fortunately with the safer pressurized light water reactors. The other effect of the massive increase in the energy base was that the Soviet Union began to export oil and gas to Eastern Europe and the world in general. Trade with the West as well as Asia began to increase rapidly in the 1950s, but oil and gas exports were in a whole different league. In Eastern Europe, the new exports sped up the transition inaugurated under Khrushchev from one in which Soviet satellites subsidized the USSR with low resource prices to the reverse. In the 1960s Soviet gas and oil went to "fraternal" socialist countries at considerably below market price. The export of oil to the West compensated for these subsidies by bringing in large amounts of hard currency that allowed the Soviets to make much needed purchases of technology and grain abroad.

As elsewhere, the nuclear industry was also tied into military production, which allowed the Soviet Union to reach rough parity with the United States in the late 1960s, for the first time. The foundation of this parity was the development of nuclear submarines and of Intercontinental Ballistic Missiles (ICBMs), which now could actually strike the United States from the USSR in the event of war. Long-range bombers were no longer necessary. The result was an increasingly expensive arms race that absorbed huge amounts of capital and trained personnel, which the USSR could not afford as easily as its American rival. The arms race was only part of the social and ecological cost of the final decades of Soviet industrialization. Rivers and forests were polluted with nuclear waste, leading to serious health problems in the affected areas. The oil and gas fields disturbed the fragile sub-arctic ecology, and hydropower meant the flooding of large areas, removing the inhabitants and causing all sorts of changes in the environment, many of them totally unanticipated. This was not merely the story of arrogant party officials pushing scientists and engineers to construct shoddy plants in pristine nature: the scientists were convinced that their designs were perfectly safe and the ecological effects were minor. Indeed it was the physicists who most consistently pushed for more nuclear power plants, convincing party officials who worried about the massive costs.

The early Brezhnev years also saw a radical transformation of Soviet agriculture, at least of its technology. The same collective farms that had operated for decades without enough fertilizer and pesticides were using three to five times as much as American farms by the late 1970s. In 1966 the authorities abolished the labor-day system, and collective farmers received their share of the proceeds in money. Agricultural production expanded rapidly, freeing up millions of peasants for industrial work. The migration to the cities in the last thirty years of Soviet power was so great that large areas, especially in central and northern Russia, began to empty out, leaving thousands of abandoned villages dotting the landscape. For the first time in Russian history, the city population outnumbered the country residents, rising to more than two thirds of the total in the USSR by 1990.

These massive increases in production, the creation of a nuclear industry and a more or less modern chemical industry, also brought a wave of consumer goods for the first time in Soviet history. Food stores began to display some variety, both of Soviet products and canned goods imported from Bulgaria and elsewhere. Dairy products appeared in modest variety. To make up the needs in grain and fodder, the Soviet Union imported grain from Canada and the United States regularly. The result was a massive improvement, but not universal prosperity. Supplies were irregular, and one or another food item was in deficit every year. Carrots disappeared in one area for several months, and returned while beets disappeared from the stores. Workplace distribution continued, if on a lesser scale, to supply hard-to-find items like chickens. Consumer electronics became nearly universal in cities and television even appeared in the villages. At the same time actually buying a television set was a major operation. Telephones came mostly from Poland in exchange for cheap Soviet gas and were notoriously unreliable. The housing crisis eased as thick rings of pre-fabricated high-rise housing surrounded Soviet cities. Finally, most urban residents left the communal apartments for new apartments with their own kitchens and bathrooms. Unfortunately, the other necessary facilities, such as schools and stores, often failed to appear in the new neighborhoods for decades. Production boomed, but distribution remained in a state of permanent disorder. With all the problems, however, the first decade or so of the Brezhnev years was in many ways the high point of the Soviet Union. Not only had it achieved superpower status but the population also finally acquired the basic elements of a modern standard of living. There were two problems with that standard of living. One was the post-war boom in Europe and America that created a whole new world standard of living, and news about that seeped across the border. The USSR was chasing a moving target. The other problem was that the rise in Soviet living standards stalled after the middle of the 1970s. More housing appeared, but virtually all consumer goods gradually entered a permanent state of deficit, which meant that they were available but increasingly difficult to actually find. The struggle of daily life was the background to the malaise that settled over Soviet society.

This malaise was not explicitly political, outside of small dissident groups in the intelligentsia. The first dissidents had appeared in the 1960s, when it was finally clear that openly opposing the Soviet system would lead to harassment and even prison in some cases, but not death or long incarceration. The KGB under Yurii Andropov changed its mode of operation. It no longer looked for organized opposition groups tied to émigrés in the West and instead tried to police society with a combination of persuasion and selective force. For most people who fell afoul of the system, the KGB brought them in for a "conversation" and reminded them of the possible consequences of persistent action, and then left it at that. A very small minority of intellectuals continued to protest and went to prison or to psychiatric hospitals. The dissidents mostly came from highly privileged positions in Soviet society. Intellectuals continued to have apartments, privileged access to goods, and a select few maintained opportunities for foreign travel. Writers lived in dachas in the Peredelkino and other writers' colonies, while ordinary citizens struggled with long lines and mass-construction housing. Scientists, especially those in strategic areas like physics, lived in similar places, and also had contact with power on the basis of their utility to the military and the civilian nuclear industry. Not surprisingly some began to chafe at this privileged but ultimately powerless role. In 1968 Andrei Sakharov moved from criticism of nuclear weapons testing and Lysenko's biology to criticizing the whole system and formulating notions of convergence that would produce a society more like the West than the Soviet Union. Alexander Solzhenitsyn moved from fictional and non-fiction accounts of the Stalinist GULAG to a Russian nationalist position that criticized equally Western and Soviet society in favor of an authoritarian religious state based only on the Slavic peoples of the USSR. The phenomenon closest to widespread dissent was the emigration of almost a million Soviet Jews, some forty percent of the Jewish population, between 1970 and 1990. The first wave consisted of more or less committed Zionists who moved to Israel, but the by the 1980s that stream had dried to a trickle, and most Jewish emigrants had moved to the United States and Germany in search of better economic conditions.

The dissidents attracted enormous attention in the West during the Cold War, and their ideas and writings were well known in the Soviet intelligentsia. Some other intellectuals supported them but the dissidents had no popular following. Nevertheless the authorities saw them as a threat to their utopian conception of a unified society, exiling Solzhenitsyn to the West in 1974 and Sakharov eventually to Gorkii (Nizhnii Novgorod), east of Moscow. Needless to say their works were published only underground or in the West, and they were never mentioned in public. More serious was the general sense that the country was somehow on the wrong track, a feeling that crystallized with the Soviet invasion of Afghanistan in 1980. The most common reaction to the invasion was neither patriotism nor indignation, but the sense that the leadership had made a serious mistake. For most people the Soviet Union remained a legitimate state, but one that was most definitely in the hands of incompetent and short-sighted leaders.

In 1982 Leonid Brezhnev died. The generation that he represented, the young party leaders promoted in the late 1930s, was now a group of elderly men who simply could not understand why things had not come out as they had expected or even how bad the situation remained for the mass of the people. The world had also changed outside the USSR and they failed to grasp the challenge created by mass prosperity not only in the United States but also in post-war Europe and Japan. On Brezhnev's death the Central Committee put in his place Yurii Andropov, the head of the KGB since 1967. Nearly seventy and in poor health, Andropov never had time to formulate a new policy, but he did bring to Moscow Alexander Iakovlev, Mikhail Gorbachev, and other future reformers. On Andropov's death in 1984, the CC appointed the seventy-two year old Konstantin Chernenko to succeed him. Chernenko had been Brezhnev's director of personnel for decades and the appointment allegedly came against Andropov's wishes. If Andropov really did prefer Gorbachev, his wishes were fulfilled in 1985 when Chernenko died in turn, and Gorbachev became the General Secretary of the Communist Party. He was to preside over its demise.

22

Soviet Culture

With the end of NEP and well before the war, the Soviet Union
entered a new period of its history, with profound cultural implications. The first phase of that new period, from about 1928 to
1932, saw major upheavals in every area of culture, science, art,
literature, and the humanistic disciplines. It was a "cultural revolution" in the phrase of the time, though one neither so deep or
thorough as the much later Chinese events that borrowed the name.
For the people involved, it was certainly traumatic, for it was not
merely a new ideological campaign. In those years the party authorities carried out a systematic attack on the leaders of virtually every
field of culture, accusing them of failure to live up to the demands
of "socialist construction" and of harboring old-regime views and
hostility to the new order. These attacks came in the press and in
meetings held in various institutions and workplaces, where mostly
young and enthusiastic Communists were encouraged to attack their
elders and teachers in the name of the revolution. In addition, the
OGPU carried out systematic arrests of leading intellectuals – historians, engineers, writers, and some scientists. Most were accused of
participation in various, presumably mythical, underground organizations aimed at undermining or overthrowing Soviet power. Compared to later times, the treatment was relatively mild: some were
executed, more went to prison camps, but many were simply exiled
to provincial towns to teach or work in local institutions. Some
professions suffered more than others: the scientists were less com-
monly victims, but even for them there were consequences. At the

413

same time as the old authorities were removed, all sorts of radical super-Marxist notions achieved brief fame and dominance, along with the ideas of various cranks who presented themselves as new proletarian voices.

For the writers this period meant the virtual monopoly of the Proletarians connected with the Russian Association of Proletarian Writers (RAPP in Russian) and their leader, the critic Leopold Averbakh. The Proletarians assailed nearly all of the major writers of the 1920s as counter-revolutionary, particularly those from the pre-revolutionary intelligentsia and the "fellow travelers." Many major writers, including Evgenii Zamiatin and Mikhail Bulgakov, were the objects of furious attacks. Zamiatin was allowed to leave the country, but Bulgakov was not and for a while had almost no possibility to work. Other writers like the poets Akhmatova and Pasternak, escaped attacks because they published little or nothing during those years. The Proletarians were almost as savage with Communist writers who did not toe Averbakh's line. What the Proletarians wanted was a literature that engaged itself in the struggle for the building of socialism, and in this sense some of their productions were quite critical of bureaucratism and passivity in the party and the state. Their ideal novel featured heroic workers overcoming tremendous obstacles to construct a new town or collectivize a village, changing themselves in the process. In reality, these stories were rarely successful, and the only readable works to come out of the movement were about the Civil War and were mostly written before 1929. The best by far was Mikhail Sholokhov's *Quiet Don*, and the RAPP leaders were uncomfortable with this volume.

Music as well had its proletarian radicals, who attacked the young Shostakovich and virtually every other composer, whatever the aesthetic. For the Russian Association of Proletarian Music, the only "proletarian" musical culture had to be "mass songs," performed by semi-amateur choruses, preferably made up of workers. The proletarian musicians relied on the network of factory clubs and other amateur organizations to spread their work and doctrines, but most of their songs found little favor with the workers, who preferred a more traditional repertory. The Proletarians were allowed briefly to rule the conservatories, but in 1932 the party ended their monopoly as it did for the proletarian writers.

Even in the sciences meetings took place in research institutes, meetings that would have ominous consequences later on. In Nikolai Vavilov's botanical institute radical graduate students criticized his leadership, political views, and scientific work. In the sciences these attacks were not yet primarily ideological, the chief charge being that the scientists were "cut off from life" and paid insufficient attention to the implications of their work for technology and thus "socialist construction." It was at this time that Trofim Lysenko, a Ukrainian plant breeder, first came to the attention of the public and the authorities with his theories about breeding strains of wheat that were resistant to cold. Lacking the proper scientific training needed to develop his occasional practical insights, Lysenko was more of a crank at first, but he quickly learned to drape his claims in references to his plebeian origins and assertions that his was "proletarian" biology. The party authorities listened to him because his discoveries, real and imagined, seemed to promise much greater harvests very quickly, something the Soviet Union desperately needed.

After several years of chaos in many fields, the campaign came to a swift end in 1932. The exiled scientists and historians returned to their jobs, some returned from the camps, and generalized public attacks on the intelligentsia gradually ended. Thus began a new phase, one in which the party leadership, which increasingly meant Stalin alone, constructed the framework for what they considered a Soviet culture. In literature the Proletarians had alienated the party leaders, and in 1932 all literary groups were banned, a move mainly directed at Averbakh and his Proletarians. The pressure on non-party writers like Bulgakov and Pasternak eased. Bulgakov went to work for the Moscow Art Theater, writing original plays and adaptations that provided him with a livelihood even though they were often banned. He continued working on his masterpiece *The Master and Margarita* in private. Pasternak published prose and poetry in those years, becoming one of the country's best-known poets, in spite of being out of step with Soviet ideology. In the new situation Stalin set up a single Writers' Union, which met for the first time in a Congress of Soviet Writers in 1934. It was to include writers of all types, non-party member writers and Communists in one group, again a move in large part directed at taming the Proletarians. The Writers' Union was the prototype for a series of unions of creative intellectuals, for composers, painters, architects, and others, that dominated the daily life of Soviet literary and artistic culture until the end, in many ways parallel to the structure for the natural and social sciences and the humanities found at the Academy of Sciences. The Writers' Union had two functions. One was to provide ideological and artistic direction to the writers. At the head of the union was a committee whose membership was chosen by the Central Committee cultural apparatus and cleared with Stalin himself. These were the men who were to declare the party line in art and enforce it. The other function was to take care of the needs of writers in daily life. The Writers' Union controlled apartments and dachas in the countryside, had a privileged distribution center for scarce consumer goods, and the best restaurant in Moscow. Its headquarters was a nineteenth century Moscow palace supposedly the prototype of the Rostov house in Tolstoy's *War and Peace*. Similar unions of artists and composers were formed and took on similar functions.

The party now intended to give literature and art firm direction. Stalin told the writers that they were the "engineers of human souls," but he did not give them the blueprint. That was to come from the method of "socialist realism," and at the first Writers' Congress in 1934 A. A. Zhdanov and Maksim Gorkii, assisted by the former oppositionists Bukharin and Radek, tried to define what that was. The idea was to "reflect reality in its revolutionary development." The implication was that the writer needed to show the great changes in Soviet life, but avoid concentrating on mistakes or shortcomings, and indicate how society was moving forward. The result was to demand a kind of official optimism that was very hard to provide in practice, as it would lead to flattened characters and unconvincing conflicts. The other side of socialist realism was that it was to become the art of the people and as such had to be accessible. This issue peaked in 1936, not over literature, but as a result of the staging of Dmitrii Shostakovich's opera, *Lady Macbeth of the Mtsensk District*. The composer thought that he had made a good Soviet opera, based on a story by Nikolai Leskov that showed the dark, oppressive world of pre-revolutionary Russia. Instead he met savage criticism for his adoption of modernist musical language similar to that found in Western music of the time. In the minds of his critics, the opera was cacophonic and incomprehensible. It was "formalist," a term that immediately became one of the most serious charges an artist could face. The writers as well understood the implications of the attack on Shostakovich, and realized that their styles would have to change. Many of them, even the most loyal supporters of the revolution, had employed style and narrative techniques that were innovative and modern in the 1920s, but now they were supposed to construct a novel much as Turgenev had done in the nineteenth century.

Besides mandating the correct direction in the arts, the party leadership in the later 1930s moved to expand and subsidize artistic institutions, and indeed the intelligentsia as a whole. The great theaters, the Bolshoi in Moscow and the Mariinskii (Kirov) in Leningrad, no longer scraped by on small budgets. The opera and ballet became central parts of Soviet culture, and although they were concentrated in the two main cities, they were not restricted to those places. Older cities such as Kiev and Tbilisi, now serving as republican capitals, also found their theaters with more solid budgets. In provincial cities and new republican capitals large theaters for musical performances and concerts sprang up. The great companies were encouraged to do provincial tours. Budgets for dramatic theaters also increased, as did the number of theaters in provincial and republican capitals. The theaters and orchestras supported a great many actors and musicians and in a style that became increasingly removed from that of the Soviet population. The Writers' Union actually spent most of its effort in the 1930s not on ideological issues but on securing control of superior housing in the cities and the dacha districts, and even building them when it could. Pasternak was able to acquire a two-story house in Peredelkino – a dacha village for writers near Moscow – to use as his home for the rest of his life. Writers had access to the Union's closed food and consumer goods distribution service. By the war, Shostakovich had a multiroom apartment, servants, and a car with driver. Thus the artistic elite came to match the scientists in standards of living, remaining only slightly less well off than the party elite itself.

Perhaps the central art form of the 1930s was film. During NEP, the necessary resources were simply unavailable for mass production and circulation of movies, and Hollywood productions filled the theaters. The cultural revolution tried to change this situation, but the works of that era were as shallow and short-lived as they were in other art forms and they came under heavy criticism, to boot. In the course of the 1930s the Soviet film industry changed radically. The state devoted increasing sums to the production of film stock and studio facilities, and bought expensive equipment abroad, including the entire technology for sound films acquired from the United States. Unlike all the other arts, cinema was a state industry under the state film committee, which answered directly to the central government, not a branch industrial unit. In keeping with its central status, it also received personal attention from Stalin himself. Most of the new films were shown in the Kremlin in the presence of the heads of the film industry, who received extensive comments from the leader. Stalin's views of cinema were surprisingly sophisticated: he found most of the early films on revolutionary or other political subjects boring, and told the filmmakers that the country needed more comedies. That was a tall order, since the scriptwriters and directors were mostly afraid to satirize Soviet institutions, even mildly, though Stalin told them directly that they should do so. Ultimately the result was a series of authentically popular musical comedies, many of them starring Liubov' Orlova, who became the leader's favorite actress.

The expanded institutional base in film and theater came with much greater ideological demands on the arts. All forms of art were to be accessible as well as politically correct. The 1936 attack on formalism led to particular kinds of productions. In the ballet the many small experimental studios of the 1920s closed, and in their place came the large ballet companies that presented a basically classical choreography but with new sorts of ballets. There were attempts at "revolutionary" content, but very quickly Soviet dance moved toward story ballets, which were often based on literary classics and performed with undistinguished music – Boris Asaf'ev's *Fountain of Bakhchisarai* (based on Pushkin) became the most popular of all. Shostakovich turned to more accessible musical styles, and Sergei Prokofiev, back in the Soviet Union since 1935, did the same. His music for *Romeo and Juliet* gave the repertory at least one ballet that fit the required esthetic but provided great music, as did his film music for Eisenstein's two masterpieces, *Alexander Nevsky* and *Ivan the Terrible*. No one escaped criticism: Eisenstein had two movies banned in the 1930s and returned to favor only in 1938 with *Alexander Nevsky*. In this situation the scientists were – most of them, at least – in a better position. Their institutes also received improved funding, which was even more generous than for the arts. The new situation came at a price, for starting in the early 1930s the scientific institutes were required to come up with five-year plans like those in the economy. In part, this move was to increase their usefulness to industry, but for that aim the ultimate means was the creation of a large network of specialized institutes for different branches of technology, while basic research remained in the hands of the older institutes. Gradually all basic research was centralized under the Academy of Sciences during the cultural revolution, was brought under party control, and then subordinated directly to the central government, bypassing the various People's Commissariats. The Academy also had to leave its Leningrad headquarters for Moscow, which now acquired a new battery of scientific institutes to rival those of Leningrad. Thus in 1934 the Soviet government took advantage of the visit of the physicist Piotr Kapitsa from England to force him to remain in the country, and then set up the Moscow Institute of Problems of Physics under his leadership. The Soviet Union now had two world-class research institutes in physics. The scientists were also less often than writers and artists the object of ideological campaigns after the end of the cultural revolution. Abram Ioffe was the object of heavy criticism in 1935, but the charges were only that his Leningrad Physical-Technical Institute did not do enough to provide industry with new technology. The decade was in many ways the great age of Soviet physics. Some six Nobel prizes eventually went to Soviet physicists and chemists, all of them for discoveries made in the Leningrad and Moscow institutes during the 1930s. Biology was a different story. Throughout the decade Lysenko maintained a continuous assault on his opponents, spearheaded by his ideological spokesman, Isaak Prezent. The campaign culminated with Lysenko's promotion to the leadership of the Agricultural Academy, but the party did not proclaim his doctrines to be the sole truth, and classical genetics survived, if under something of a cloud, until 1948.

The terror of 1937–38 hit the arts hard but not evenly. Musicians and composers seem to have suffered relatively little. Among the critics connected with the party, like Leopold Averbakh and his Proletarians, almost all perished. Surprisingly the writers from that group did much better, though many of them, even Sholokhov, lived those years in daily fear. Stalin did not carry out a mass purge of writers, but he and his agents did arrest and imprison many of them. For whatever reason, many of the most famous victims were arrested at the very end of the terror, Osip Mandelstam in 1938, followed by Isaac Babel, and later Meyerhold. Mandelstam died in prison, while Babel and Meyerhold were shot. At the same time, Pasternak spent the years of the terror working on translations from Shakespeare in his Peredelkino dacha, and Bulgakov continued at the Moscow Art Theater, dying of kidney failure in 1940. The sciences endured similar trials. On the whole the physicists escaped lightly: the few party members among them perished, and a few non-party scientists were arrested, Lev Landau among them. He spent months in prison only to be released without explanation. Kapitsa had interceded for him and Kapitsa's institute survived intact. Biology was a different story. A denunciation from Lysenko's spokesman Prezent led to the arrest of Nikolai Vavilov, the Soviet Union's greatest biologist. He died in prison, as did several other important geneticists. The eve of the war was a dark time, both in the USSR and Europe. Stalin had decided by 1938 that the Soviet Union needed a fundamental ideological schooling, the beginning of a new and even more intrusive policy in culture. The basis of the new ideological campaign was to be the *Short Course of the History the Communist Party*, with its chapter on Marxism from the pen of Stalin himself. Yet the approaching war overshadowed even ideological efforts. The Soviet film industry's annual plans stressed the "defense theme" and epics from the history of the revolution and Civil War. Movies on "socialist construction" and "friendship of peoples" were few in number and did not have big budgets.

When the war actually came, it created an entirely new situation, and Stalin had to quickly adjust. The preservation of cultural institutions was a priority. As the Germans advanced, orders came to evacuate cultural institutions as well as factories. Science research institutes, ballet companies, and writers were evacuated to the east.

Eisenstein went to Alma-ata, and Shostakovich went to Kuibyshev on the Volga. The purpose was both to conserve the personnel of Soviet culture and to preserve some sense of normalcy during the war. Intellectuals joined the war effort with famous results such as the Leningrad symphony of Shostakovich, first performed in the besieged city. The physicists lobbied Stalin on behalf of an atomic bomb, as well as devoting their energies to more conventional weapons in factories and research institutes. For many engineers their war work took place as prisoners in NKVD laboratories, the most famous prisoners being the aircraft designer Andrei Tupolev and the later rocket designer Sergei Korolev. The war also created ideological problems for the party leadership. To mobilize as many people as possible meant including sectors of the population whom the official ideology had not reached or had even repelled. The answer was nationalism. After Stalin's early pronouncements about the virtues of the German working class ceased, the official line began to stress Russian heroes and Russian accomplishments. Historians dusted off manuscripts on Peter the Great or Kutuzov, hitherto unpublishable. Eisenstein made one of his classic films on the life of tsar *Ivan the Terrible*, a film designed to glorify the tsar's conquests and portray him as fighting for the unity of the land. Even Marxism had to be rethought: in 1943 the leading party journals declared that formerly there had been far too much emphasis on Hegel as the background to Marxism and he needed to be deemphasized. The result was an inaccurate history of the thought of Marx, but it made Marxism seem less German. For much of the intelligentsia, the new line on culture meant more breathing space, and many of them hoped that it would continue after the war. They were to be disappointed. Even as the fighting raged there were incidents: Mikhail Zoshchenko, a popular satirical writer, found his introspective autobiographical novel *Before Sunrise* banned after the first chapters were published in a leading literary magazine.

The return to orthodoxy came swiftly after the war, and the years from the victory until Stalin's death were the darkest and dreariest in the history of Soviet culture. The first signal was the attack mounted in 1946 by Andrei Zhdanov, one of Stalin's closest collaborators, on Zoshchenko and the poet Anna Akhmatova. Stalin himself regularly read the literary journals, and the judgments were ultimately his. Zoshchenko's work was trite and lacking in ideas, Zhdanov said, and the novella written during the war was "disgusting" and had no relationship to the conflict with Hitler. Akhmatova's poetry was pessimistic, oriented toward the past, and was a relic of a decadent aristocratic salon culture. Soviet literature was supposed to educate the reader and make the reader a fully conscious member of a socialist society who did not dwell on problems and shortcomings or on the details of individual psychology. It was also not to imitate Western literature, and indeed Stalin did not want too much Western literature translated: "Why do this?" he asked at one of the dressings-down for the writers. "It gives the impression that we Soviet people are second class, and the foreigners are the only first class people." The result was a long series of dull chronicles of Soviet life, fantastic in their sanitized depiction of everyday life. Even Stalin realized that they were dull, but continued to blame the writers for their lack of talent and mastery of their art.

In 1948 it was the turn of the composers Prokofiev and Shostakovich, attacked for supposedly dissonant music that was too far removed from folk music and inaccessible to the masses. In many ways a repeat of the 1936 attack on formalism, this new campaign had behind it both the rivals of the serious composers among the writers of popular songs and the party authorities. In the same year Lysenko was able to crown his long fight for power in biology by his appearance at a "discussion" on genetics, where he declared genetics to be a reactionary and "idealist" science and his own ideas progressive and "materialist." Stalin took a direct hand in this affair as well. Lysenko sent him his speech for criticism, and the General Secretary read it carefully. Lysenko originally wanted to contrast his own "proletarian" biology to the "bourgeois" biology of the geneticists and make a general pronouncement that scientific thought reflected class interests. Stalin crossed out that passage, writing in the margins, "Ha ha! What about mathematics?" He required Lysenko to drop the class terminology and substitute "progressive" and "reactionary." The result, however, was to destroy genetics for nearly twenty years and do enormous harm to Soviet biology. There were plans to hold a similar "discussion" to provide an ideological framework for physics, but for whatever reason, it never materialized.

In the last years of Stalin's life the official Soviet ideology was a strange mixture of dogmatic Marxism and nationalism. There were campaigns to prove Russian priorities in science, the most famous being the claim that the Russian engineer Alexander Popov had invented the radio in 1900 (Popov was in fact one of several pioneers in this area.) Pre-revolutionary Russian writers, composers, and artists became the object of mini-cults, with endless statues, films, and publications made in their honor. The promotion of Russian culture was largely aimed at the West, to show Russia to be equal to Western culture, if not superior. At the same time the party leadership continued the promotion of culture heroes from the other Soviet nationalities. The Politburo ordered celebrations of the work of medieval Muslim poets claimed as ancestors of Soviet nationalities, Alisher Navoi in Uzbekistan and Nizami of Gandzha in Azerbaidzhan. Russian poets were paid to translate their works and they were the objects of fulsome official praise in the central press. In these years, Shevchenko or the medieval Georgian poet Shota Rustaveli loomed larger than Shakespeare or Goethe. In every Soviet republic the authorities assigned composers, usually Russians or Caucasians, to help local talent produce "national" ballets and operas to provide repertory and prestige for the newly opened theaters. At the same time as the activity on the periphery, in Moscow and Leningrad the ballet struggled with the restrictions of Soviet esthetics. The sheer genius of the dancers like Galina Ulanova kept it alive. The anti-cosmopolitan campaign directed against Jews in 1948 only further poisoned the cultural atmosphere since so many musicians, writers, and artists were Jewish. The main Yiddish writers were imprisoned or shot. The intelligentsia remembered the 1930s and the various ideological campaigns seemed to be leading to another mass terror. That never materialized, and the number of actual arrests among the intelligentsia in those years was small, but for Shostakovich or Akhmatova, the fear in those years was real.

The death of Stalin changed the whole atmosphere. Within a few months prisoners began to return from the camps, and the intelligentsia sensed the possibilities. Ilya Ehrenburg, mainly known as a war correspondent and author of mildly modernist novels of the 1920s set in Western Europe, quickly produced a short novel called *The Thaw*, which gave its name to the whole period. The villain of the story is a factory director, a classic Stalinist boss. Attacked at first, the story set the tone for a whole series of writings that tried to deal with the past, if within definite limits. Khrushchev's secret speech gave another great impulse to this sort of literature, as well as relaxing the demands for orthodoxy in music and art. By the early 1960s a number of works had appeared describing the camp system that had just come to an end, the most famous being *One Day in the Life of Ivan Denisovich* by Alexander Solzhenitsyn. The novella appeared in the literary journal *Novyi Mir*, which gained huge popularity for its publication of many works in sympathy with the program of destalinization. Some writers, especially young poets like Evgenii Yevtushenko, acquired enormous popularity at this time, even reading his poetry in sports stadiums that filled to capacity. Shostakovich used Yevtushenko's poem "Babii Yar," about the wartime massacre of Jews in Kiev by the Nazis, in his Thirteenth Symphony. The ending of the post-war cultural policies and the rehabilitation of imprisoned and executed writers meant a sudden boom in the republication of the literature of the 1920s with its frequently modernist styles. Soviet publishers began to put out a wave of translations of Western authors: William Faulkner, John Updike, and many European writers. Soviet opera and ballet moved away from the Stalinist canon toward styles that were less narrative and more innovative, a compromise style that still required elaborate sets and more "acting" than was then popular in the West, then at the height of fascination with abstractionism in all the arts. The Khrushchev era was not all liberalism, however. The renewed campaign against religion affected many areas of culture indirectly, making impossible the republication of nineteenth century classics like certain works of Dostoyevsky or the expression of religious themes. The great event of the decade was the scandal around the award of the 1958 Nobel Prize to Pasternak for his novel *Doctor Zhivago*, a clearly anti-Soviet account of the revolution and Civil War. A huge propaganda success for the West, the book was prohibited in the USSR and Pasternak became the object of press attacks and official condemnation. This was not Stalin's time, however, and Pasternak continued to live quietly in his dacha in Peredelkino.

Perhaps the most striking relic of the Stalin era in Khrushchev's time was his refusal to accept modern genetics. Lysenko remained king in biology, primarily because of Khrushchev's support of him. At the same time science expanded enormously during these years. By the 1960s only the United States outranked the USSR in the number of publications in the natural sciences, and by the 1980s the Soviet Union had the largest number of natural scientists per capita in the world. The sciences had whole complexes at their disposal, like Akademgorodok ("Academy Town") near Novosibirsk in Western Siberia. Started in 1958 at the inspiration of Academy scientists, this entirely new town came to have some fifty thousand scientists and their families, with new and comfortable (by Soviet standards) housing and privileged access to a whole range of consumer goods. For the party leadership, science was not only the basis of a "scientific" worldview but also the key to economic growth, the path to victory in the rivalry with the capitalist world. The ability to concentrate resources on crucial areas had brought spectacular successes in rocketry and the nuclear industry, both military and civilian, and the idea was to broaden the base so as to ensure a more thorough modernization of industry and agriculture.

With the removal of Khrushchev the new leadership quickly moved to end the anti-religious campaign and allowed the churches to continue a modest and heavily supervised existence that lasted until the 1980s. Lysenko finally lost his monopoly of power in biology, his work was repudiated and genetics reappeared as a recognized discipline. Until the end of the Soviet Union the relationship of the authorities to the science community was polite and collaborative, though not without tensions under the surface. For the writers, however, the new regime was less positive. The young poet Joseph Brodsky had been sent into northern exile for "parasitism" in the last months of Khrushchev's leadership, and in 1972 the KGB threw him out of the country for publishing his work abroad. Brezhnev never repudiated the condemnation of Stalin, but he put an end to the toleration and encouragement of writing, historical or literary, that exposed the repressions of that era. Thus Solzhenitsyn's work could no longer be published, and appeared only in the West, leading to his expulsion from the Soviet Union. Cultural policy was essentially frozen in time, for the works of many writers repressed under Stalin continued to appear, but Bulgakov's unpublished writings or *Doctor Zhivago* could not. Large numbers of translations of Western literature appeared in translation, but major writers like

Marcel Proust (published in the Soviet Union in the 1930s) or James Joyce could not. Soviet writers began to write in a mildly modernist vein, and avoided the classic subjects of socialist realism. Some, Vasilii Belov and others, began to turn in different directions, influenced by Solzhenitsyn. They wrote romanticized accounts of village life with a strong nationalist undertone, the idea being that the peasantry had once had true Russian values, patriarchal and religious, which the Soviet order had destroyed. They were highly critical of the kolhoz, and their historical stories described a harmonic village destroyed by urban outsiders, often Jewish, in the 1930s. The critical edge and the nationalist tone gave them wide popularity among the intelligentsia in the later Brezhnev years. The village writers and their ideology shaded off into the dissident movement, which was heavily nationalistic in its outlook, though a minority of dissidents shared the more westernizing approach of Andrei Sakharov. Both tendencies were actually well known among the elite intelligentsia from underground manuscripts, but more than the dissidents it was some of the "bards," the singers like Bulat Okudzhava and Vladimir Vysotskii, who performed their songs on the guitar and who most accurately reflected the mood among educated people. Vysotskii rarely gave public concerts, for no state agency could permit that, but his songs performed in small gatherings or Moscow apartments quickly spread all over the country in tape recordings and amateur performances, again behind closed doors. Not quite political enough to be overtly anti-Soviet, the songs and their lyrics reflected a kind of introspective alienation characteristic of the time. Above-ground recordings of Okudzhava's songs appeared in the Soviet Union only in the later 1970s, and one recording of Vysotskii's surfaced only shortly after his death in 1980.

Soviet filmmakers followed similar trends. The breakthrough of Christianity and Russian nationalism in film was Andrei Tarkovsky's *Andrei Rublev* of 1966. Rarely shown in the Soviet Union, the film depicted the fifteenth century icon painter Rublev as a man who survives the disasters of his time by faith and art. Tarkovsky later moved on to more psychologically introspective themes, usually with religious overtones, in his later works such as *Stalker* (1979), more or less science fiction. Though the film was seen in the Soviet Union, its showings were extremely limited.

Tarkovsky had had enough and moved to the West, dying in Paris in 1986. Other film directors also divided their time between historical epics (*Siberiade*, also made in 1979 by director Andrei Konchalovsky) and mildly modernist films from the private life of the Soviet intelligentsia.

One of the most striking features of Soviet life from the 1960s onward was the emergence of popular culture. The beginnings lay in the Stalin era, and to a limited extent were there even before the revolution. In those years, however, the audience of popular culture was mainly the thin middle layer of urban society, with some extensions into the working classes. The main examples were the musical stages (estrada in Russian), which featured Soviet jazz bands and comedy routines, and film. The boundaries with the culture of the intelligentsia were fluid: Prokofiev and Shostakovich wrote film music, and major writers produced scripts as well. Some writers produced science fiction and detective stories, though both were under a cloud after the middle 1930s. The more liberal atmosphere of the Khrushchev era brought about a revival of popular fiction, especially science fiction, and jazz came back onto the radio and into musical theaters. What really changed Soviet popular culture, however, were television and the availability of Western popular music, not just jazz but eventually some forms of rock and roll. Television took popular music out of the theaters and into everyone's apartment. While Soviet television put on some culture programs, it was the popular entertainment that made a mass audience, like Iulian Semenov's World War II spy story, *Seventeen Minutes of Spring*, the hit miniseries of 1973 that so impressed the young Vladimir Putin.

Popular music had a complex history. As elsewhere, the jazz audience was increasingly elite after the 1960s, and American rock took its place. Soviet youth heard rock music on foreign radio stations, but also massive amounts of tape recordings began to circulate, many homemade, as tape recorders and players became widely available. The Brezhnev regime did not prohibit rock music. It tried to restrict what it saw as the more erotic and wild versions, but much rock music circulated openly, and the state began to sponsor rock bands and popular singers with eclectic styles. Some of them, like Alla Pugacheva, became wildly popular. Parallel to these more official versions of popular music were underground bands like Aquarium in Leningrad that also relied for a long time on taped recordings but by 1980 had acquired some state recognition. All late Soviet popular music was derived from Western models, even if modified with a local twist, and it also imitated Western music in creating a series of rapidly changing generational subcultures. Each new moment, from jazz to the disco craze of the late 1970s, had its own audience that often did not extend to listeners even a few years younger. Soviet popular culture, at least the musical variants, now had very little to do with "Soviet reality." It also had little to do with the culture of the intelligentsia, official, critical, or dissident culture, though it did share in the sense of alienation of much of the intelligentsia. It also shared a social background as many of the popular musicians, even rockers, came from privileged backgrounds in the intelligentsia or even the party elite.

By the 1980s most of the great writers and artists of the early Soviet days were gone: Pasternak died in 1960, Shostakovich in 1975, and Sholokhov in 1984. Almost all of the first wave of film directors and actors of the 1920s were gone. The newer generation of writers and artists was not in the league of their predecessors, no more than their counterparts in the West were in the league of Proust or Joyce. Soviet writers and artists had the additional burden of an ossified but obligatory cultural policy, one that no longer attracted the new generations among the intelligentsia. Even if the dissidents seemed to many educated people shrill and unconvincing, their own views of the Soviet system were scarcely enthusiastic. The official cultural line and its products became more and more a fantasy world that ignored what the public actually read or watched. For the intelligentsia, Gorbachev's Perestroika was an earthquake – a welcome earthquake, as they were sure that political freedom and a market economy would produce a great flowering of culture. They were sure that the time for the intelligentsia had finally come. They would find out otherwise.

23

The Cold War

The Cold War lasted for the whole of the last forty-six years of Soviet history. It was an epic contest, ranging over the whole world, from Berlin and Peking to the most distant parts of Africa and Latin America. For much of the time the Soviet Union seemed to have a good chance of "winning" in some form, and indeed the more hysterical of its opponents were convinced that it was immensely powerful. In reality, the Soviet Union came from behind in the struggle and was never close to defeating its new enemy, the United States. For most of the time, it struggled just to keep up and survive with its newfound power more or less intact.

At the end of the Second World War the two new powers seemed relatively evenly matched, for both were industrial powers and similar in population, the United States at 151 million and the Soviet Union at 182 million. The population figures were an illusion, however, for the Soviet figure was the result of concealment of war losses and may have been as low as 167 million. Soviet industry, however, had been only third in 1940 behind the United States and Germany and much of it was now in ruins. The devastation of the country was unparalleled, even in Germany, and the United States had suffered no war damage at all, outside of Pearl Harbor and the Aleutian Islands. The war had restored American prosperity after the Depression and was a huge boost to American technology and industry, as the rapid success of the atomic project demonstrated. At the time Stalin was convinced that after the war the "contradictions" between the United States and other Western powers would

429

grow, especially as he anticipated a rapid recovery and rearmament of Germany and Japan. Eventually there could be another war among the Western powers. Some in the Soviet hierarchy questioned this view, pointing out that England, for all its differences with the United States, was fundamentally dependent on American money and power, and so would be Germany and Japan. Stalin simply suppressed such dissent.

In spite of his optimistic assessment of the world, Stalin took no chances. During the war he had paid little attention to the construction of an atomic bomb at first, in spite of repeated warnings from Soviet scientists, who were concerned both about Germany and the United States. Soviet intelligence had actually acquired some very valuable information early in the war from Britain, but it sat in Beria's files unused. As always, he was afraid it might be just clever disinformation. Soviet physicists wrote to Stalin lobbying for action, for they realized that the Americans were working on a bomb (all publications by the relevant physicists in the United States had disappeared from science journals) and were fearful that the Germans might make a bomb first. Finally in 1943 Stalin decided to establish a research unit to build a reactor and put Igor Kurchatov in charge, one of the talented physicists to come out of Ioffe's Leningrad Physical-Technical Institute. Starting in a small building in the south of Moscow, Kurchatov and his group were able to make the reactor, but only with the news of Hiroshima did Stalin put the bomb project into full gear, establishing a laboratory south of Moscow called Arzamas-16 in the buildings of the famous nineteenth-century Sarov monastery. Beria was in charge of the bomb project, as well as the whole nuclear industry that was extracting and processing uranium in the USSR, eastern Germany, and Czechoslovakia. There remained the problem of the exact design of the bomb, and this time intelligence from Klaus Fuchs at Los Alamos and the mere fact of American success helped Soviet scientists to gain at least a year in time. In 1949 they exploded their first atomic bomb in secret. The US government learned of it only from analyzing atmospheric fallout.

The construction of the bomb was an immense technological feat for a relatively backward country, one that came at equally immense cost in capital investments. The mere existence of the bomb did not solve all Soviet military problems. No Soviet bomber then existing could fly from the Soviet Union to strike the United States, and bombers were the only delivery vehicles then available. To make things worse, the Soviets did not have aircraft engines big enough to power a large bomber. The United States maintained a network of bases in Western Europe and Turkey from which aircraft could strike virtually any important target in the USSR, but the only reply or preventive action would have to target those bases, not the United States itself. The Soviet air force had been primarily a ground support weapon, having abandoned strategic bombing before the war to build smaller bombers to support the infantry. Thus Stalin had to order the construction of long-range bombers and a massive air defense network to defend the main Soviet target cities, all at colossal expense. By the time of his death the foundations of these forces were in place.

Military power was all very well, but Stalin and his circle realized that their greatest advantage was in the political sphere, in the prestige of the Soviet victory over Hitler and of the Communist movement in the world generally. Spreading Communist rule and the socialist system, they assumed, would also spread Soviet power. The first arena in which they saw possibilities was quite naturally in Eastern Europe, which had been liberated from the Nazis and was now under Soviet occupation.

The Soviets hosted many exiled Communists in Moscow during the war, and came into contact with the underground as they advanced into Eastern Europe. The strategy that Stalin developed and required the local Communists to follow was the establishment of a regime of "people's democracy." The Communist party was to make a coalition in each country with other leftist and agrarian groups rather than seize power in its own name. New constitutions were to be worked out with new elected governments (a change from pre-war dictatorships) and in the one previously democratic country, Czechoslovakia, the old constitution was restored. Stalin, however, was by no means relinquishing the opportunity for control provided by the victory in the war. In all of the liberated countries the Communists were to be a major partner in the government, and if they could not do that honestly, then by manipulation of the elections. The local Communists everywhere took charge of the ministries of the interior that controlled the various police forces, and those ministries were effectively controlled by the Soviet security forces. Further, the local Communists consulted the Soviet authorities, either the Soviet ambassador or Moscow directly on virtually every issue of importance.

This situation was not stable in the long run. It had the same problems that the Popular Front did in the Spanish Civil War, the incompatibility of the Communist parties with their coalition "partners" in methods and aims. The disastrous economic situation of most East European countries added more instability, and the war had left a residue of violence and hatred that further complicated matters. Even the Soviet ambassadors were shocked at the amount of anti-Semitism in post-war Czechoslovakia and other countries, and were nervous at its exploitation by local Communists. As they came to realize, nationalism was just under the surface even in the Communist parties, for all East European countries had a modern history where nationalist movements predominated, not liberalism or socialism, and the war had only exacerbated the situation. The non-Communist coalition parties were determined not to surrender complete control to the Communists, something they found increasingly difficult. Finally, the Soviets were not popular everywhere, even if they had defeated Hitler. If the Yugoslavs and the populations of Czechoslovakia and Bulgaria greeted the Red Army as liberators, Hungary and Rumania were a different matter. The nationalist dictatorships had been popular until Hitler began to lose the war, and both were stridently anti-Soviet and anti-Russian. In Poland the Communists were a minority in a mass resistance movement that was also anti-Communist and anti-Russian, and the Warsaw uprising remained a bone of contention. Germany was especially difficult, as support for Hitler had been nearly universal and the victorious Red Army had behaved as conquerors toward Germans civilians, not as liberators, looting houses and raping women.

The turning points came late in 1947, when Stalin created the Communist Information Bureau as a smaller successor to the Comintern, signaling his intention to maintain formal control over his comrades. In February 1948, a government crisis in Czechoslovakia led the Communists under Klement Gottwald to form "action committees" and with some Soviet prompting, to seize power. The constitutional president Edvard Beneš soon resigned and the Communists were now in complete control. By various devices the Communists took power in all the other East European countries. The new governments then moved way beyond the original slogans of "people's democracies" (though officially the term remained) toward full nationalization and collectivization of agriculture. The new Communist governments also deployed the full arsenal of terror against their opponents, executions and imprisonment for hundreds of thousands. Show trials of allegedly dissident Communist leaders, like that of Rudolf Slansky in Czechoslovakia, imitated earlier Soviet show trials. With opposition cowed, the East European states began huge construction projects on the Soviet model, relying on very real enthusiasm for socialism, especially among youth, but nowhere did they approach a level of support large enough to maintain themselves without the threat of force and Soviet backing.

The one exception to many of these rules was Yugoslavia, which provided Stalin with a challenge from within the Communist movement that he never succeeded in crushing. Unlike his neighbors, Josip Broz Tito had come to power with considerable mass support, the fruit of his years leading the partisans against German and Italian occupation. In the postwar years Tito was more Stalinist than Stalin, and also had tactical disagreements over post-war Balkan structures and over the Greek Civil War, where Stalin ended his support of the Communists and thus enraged Tito. Finally in 1948 Stalin condemned Tito's "deviations" and tried to isolate Yugoslavia, without much success given tacit Western support. Later Tito came up with the idea that his socialist industries would be "self-managed" to differentiate them from Soviet practice, but fundamentally the issue was simply that Tito was not dependent on the Soviets for survival and did not see any reason to follow orders.

The other area in which Stalin was at least partially stymied was Germany. The four-power occupation gave the Soviets control over the eastern part of the new Germany and the eastern part of Berlin. As in Eastern Europe, the Soviets set up a people's democracy in the eastern zone with the Communists at the center. Otherwise the situation was somewhat different from East Europe. Germany was an industrialized country with much of that industry in the Soviet zone. The German Communists before Hitler had been a major political force and the tiny anti-Nazi resistance in Germany was heavily Communist. At the same time almost all of the Communists' pre-1933 supporters had enthusiastically embraced Hitler. The new German Communist leader Walter Ulbricht and his comrades were generals without an army. Furthermore, Stalin wanted to solve the German problem as a whole, not just set up a rump Communist state, so that all the decisions about the eastern zone were in effect temporary measures. He seems to have hoped for a united neutral Germany with major Soviet influence. Part of his reasoning was that such a policy would be a successful propaganda ploy, but he also seems to have believed that a neutral Germany would necessarily differ in its interests from the United States and Britain and even come into conflict with them. Molotov would stick to this policy well after Stalin's death. It was not until western Germany began to coalesce, starting in 1947 with the Marshall Plan, then the establishment of a common west zone currency, the failure of the Berlin blockade (1948–49), and finally the foundation of the Federal Republic in the West that Stalin accepted the inevitable. He allowed Ulbricht to form the German Democratic Republic in 1949, though even then it remained somewhat provisional into the 1950s.

Thus Europe was divided by 1949. Stalin had already abandoned the Greek Communists just as the West abandoned its allies in Eastern Europe, for both sides realized that Soviet and Western power were unshakeable in their respective spheres of influence. Stalin discouraged any adventures by Italian or other Communist hotheads in Western Europe, telling them instead that their goal was to maintain their structures intact and fight for peace against the possibility of a Western attack on the Soviet Union. As it turned out, events were unfolding in Asia that would come to put European affairs in the shadow.

Stalin had not paid much attention to Mao Tse-tung and the Chinese Communist party for years. After the Communist defeat in 1927 the party had spent years forming a guerilla base around Yenan, remote from the centers of the country. The Japanese invasion had led to a sort of Popular Front with Chiang Kai-shek's nationalists and in the course of the war the Communists grew immensely in numbers and strength. With the defeat of Japan,

Chiang's troops moved into northern China and Manchuria, where the Communists had strong bases in the countryside. Initially Stalin assumed that the Communists would not be able to match Chiang's professional army and were too weak politically to matter, but by 1947 Mao had proved his ability to hold off the apparently superior forces of the enemy. The Soviets upgraded their support, and Stalin began to send the Chinese telegram after telegram with advice on how to organize power as well as answers to questions of Marxist ideology. By the summer of 1948, the Communists were clearly winning, but even Mao thought victory might come in only three to five years. Even he did not expect the decisive Communist victories ending with the rout of Chiang's troops at the giant battle of Huaihai at the end of the year. The battle smashed the corrupt and incompetent Nationalist regime and the People's Liberation Army entered Peking in January 1949, sweeping on into southern China. Mao proclaimed the People's Republic of China on October 1. The Communist world had more than doubled in size.

One of the first international consequences of Mao's victory was in Indochina. Since 1940 the Vietnamese Communists under Ho Chi Minh had been battling first the Japanese occupation and then France, which was trying to rebuild its colonial empire. The Vietnamese Communists followed a variant of the people's democracy strategy, stressing opposition to colonial rule and land reform rather than an immediate transition to socialism. Ho's bases were in the north, and with the Chinese Communist victory he turned to link up with China, a ready source of supplies. The French fought on, but in 1954 made a fatal error in establishing a base in the mountainous northwest of the country to cut off Ho's links with Laos. The Communist army, no longer just a guerilla force and now equipped with heavy guns, surrounded the French and forced the garrison to capitulate after a siege of several months. The Geneva settlement divided the country at the seventeenth parallel, and the Democratic Republic of Vietnam now held the north. Vietnam would come to play a crucial role in the Cold War, but the most important immediate consequence of the Chinese Communist victory was in Korea.

In Korea events had moved very much as in China and Vietnam. Soviet troops had briefly occupied the north, giving a boost to the Communists under Kim Il Sung. Kim too followed the line of people's democracy rather than proletarian dictatorship but found himself stopped in the south, occupied by American troops. In 1948 American-sponsored elections led to the formation of the Republic of Korea under the despotic Syngman Rhee. From 1949 Kim began to press Stalin to allow him to invade the south, where Communist guerillas were active and victory seemed within grasp. Stalin was initially very skeptical, but in 1949 changed his mind, in part because of the Chinese revolution and in part as a response to the formation of NATO in that year. Mao had similar doubts, but both approved the plan. The Soviet Union provided North Korea with massive military aid and in June 1950, Kim's troops invaded South Korea, quickly defeating both American and South Korean troops. Soviet confidence in victory was such that they continued to boycott the UN Security Council over American policy toward Taiwan, allowing the United States to fight an American war under the UN flag. Stalin monitored the war's progress in detail, sending regular advice and instructions until the American landing at Inchon in September 1950, which turned the tide against the Communists. It seemed that Kim would go down to defeat, for Stalin had no intention of sending in Soviet troops. A request for Chinese troops met with refusal, to the surprise of both Stalin and Kim, and Stalin ordered the Korean leader to prepare for guerilla warfare and evacuate to the Soviet Union. Then the Chinese changed their minds, apparently in response to General Douglas MacArthur's bellicose talk of "rollback" and its implied threat to China. Chinese "volunteers" poured across the border, pushing the Americans and their allies back to the thirty-eighth parallel, more or less the starting point. By 1951 the war was at a stalemate, to be resolved only by the truce concluded a few months after Stalin's death. Kim had failed to conquer the south, but the Chinese and North Korean armies, barely out of their own revolutions and with only backward economies (and some Soviet aid) had held off the United States for three years.

At the time of Stalin's death in 1953 the Soviet Union had a great deal to show on the international stage for the years since the Second World War. There was now a "socialist camp" that included China and the northern parts of Korea and Vietnam as well as most of Eastern Europe. The Soviet Union did have an atomic bomb and was about to acquire a hydrogen bomb. These successes were also the reasons that galvanized Western opposition, in the process negating Stalin's belief in the inevitability of conflict among Western powers. The United States was now completely committed to prevent any more Communist successes, and it possessed resources that the Soviet Union could not match. Furthermore, Eastern Europe was a mixed blessing. None of the new regimes except (ironically) Yugoslavia had enough popular support to stay in power without Soviet backing, and the German problem remained unresolved. The German Democratic Republic had not been able to produce a stable economy and the open border with the West meant that thousands of people, mostly highly trained professionals, left every year. The emerging Cold War prevented the final resolution of the many problems created by the post war four-power occupation, the most explosive being the status of Berlin.

Behind the back and forth of Cold War diplomacy, with its periodic crises, loomed the larger issue of Soviet military power. The mere possession of an atomic bomb did not render the country invulnerable, much less equal to the United States. By 1953 the Soviets had gone a long way toward fending off the potential threat of US strategic bombers, but the world was not standing still. The United States realized that the next stage would be the construction of missiles and as such was working on them. Soviet scientists and military planners had come to the same conclusions, and thus missile construction proceeded, if slowly. The launching of the world's first satellite, Sputnik, in 1957 created the impression that the Soviets might be way ahead in missile design and construction, and set off a frantic search by the CIA for information about Soviet capabilities. In reality, the rocket that launched Sputnik was highly successful but useless for military purposes. It required a huge launching pad and several days' preparation time, besides being too expensive to manufacture in large numbers. The Soviets would not have even twenty or thirty ICBMs until the early 1960s, and rough parity with the United States did not come until after the fall of Khrushchev. The United States did not know this until relatively late, however. The notorious U-2 flight of 1960 was an attempt to find out just what the Soviets had, but it was, of course a failure though it did demonstrate the abilities of Soviet air defense. It was not until 1961, after the United States deployed its first spy satellites that the American government was able to determine just how weak the Soviet missile program was. Thus, for most of the 1950s Khrushchev could continue to bluff his way through a series of crises.

The absence of the ability to strike the continental United States during those years did not remove the problem created by nuclear weapons. The Soviets most certainly could destroy Western Europe in any nuclear exchange, and Washington could not be sure that some sort of weapons could reach farther. Fortunately in both the Soviet Union and the United States, political leaders, generals, and scientists were becoming increasingly concerned that the weapons were too destructive to be easily or even usefully deployed. Stalin had resisted this conclusion, but once he was gone, even his inner circle began to have doubts. When Eisenhower remarked in a speech at the end of 1953 that atomic weapons could end civilization, even Malenkov echoed the idea, though Khrushchev initially rejected it. Nevertheless they also began to move toward the idea of international cooperation in developing peaceful uses for atomic energy. For the scientists, led by Kurchatov, the 1955 Soviet hydrogen bomb test was a turning point. Still the scientific head of the Soviet nuclear project, Kurchatov began to speak in favor of peaceful coexistence and warning of the dangers of nuclear war. He and the other physicists also pushed for more contact with Western colleagues, and Soviet and Western physicists began to meet fairly regularly. This was important for science, and in addition the involvement of so many scientists east and west in weapons programs meant that an informal channel existed on nuclear issues. Even before the hydrogen bomb test, Khrushchev had Marshal Zhukov mention the possibility of peaceful coexistence in his May Day speech of 1955, in spite of Molotov's objections. Thus by the Geneva conference of 1955 the limitation of nuclear weapons became a major part of Soviet diplomacy, a concern shared by Eisenhower and most other Western leaders. Khrushchev's further proclamation at the Twentieth Congress in 1956 that war was not inevitable and peaceful coexistence between capitalism and socialism was possible had many dimensions, but one of them was to justify the need and possibility for talks on weapons limitations and disarmament. The continuous crises of the Cold War played out against powerful counter-currents in both the United States and the USSR, pushing both sides toward some sort of agreement on nuclear weapons. Fortunately these countercurrents were at least to some extent present in the minds of most of the political leaders on both sides. Ultimately they would lead to the 1963 Nuclear Test Ban treaty, which eliminated atmospheric and undersea testing of nuclear weapons. The treaty did nothing to stop the arms race, but it did sharply curtail the damage to the environment and public health caused by the testing of nuclear weapons.

With the knowledge that their nuclear arsenal was inferior to that of the United States and that American military doctrine in the 1950s included the first use of atomic weapons, Khrushchev was in a difficult position. The issues that mattered to him the most, at least at first, were the European issues that centered on Germany. For the Soviets there were three basic problems. First were the economic problems in East Germany and the resultant series of political crises, starting with the June 17, 1953, disorders in East Berlin that were put down by force. Second was the status of West Berlin, a thorn in the side of both the Soviets and the GDR, even if also a major inconvenience to NATO. Finally there was the problem of West Germany. After Stalin's death the Soviet leadership realized that the Federal Republic was not going to turn against the United States, and indeed early in 1955 it joined NATO and began to build an army. The Soviet response was to establish the Warsaw Pact with its East European allies and put an end to any ideas of a neutral Germany. Though Molotov stuck to older policy, he had no support in the Politburo and from this moment on the Soviet leadership was committed to the division of Germany and full support of the GDR.

The particular fear of Germany was largely a relic of World War II and the inability of Khrushchev and many others of his generation to realize how much Europe, including Germany, had changed after 1945. West Germany's chancellor of those years, Konrad Adenauer, while violently anti-communist, was also not interested in provoking conflicts and wanted much better trade relations with the Soviet Union than his American allies would permit. The immediate irritation for the Soviets was West Berlin, mainly because it created a threat to the GDR, where most of the Soviet Union's troops facing NATO were stationed. To make matters worse, no final resolution of the outstanding issues of the occupation or any other matter concerning Germany was possible without including Berlin, an issue on which Soviet and American views were completely incompatible. A solution of sorts came in 1961, as East Germany's Walter Ulbricht urgently requested Khrushchev for help in yet another economic crisis that led to a big increase in emigration from the east. Ulbricht suggested that somehow they close the border and Khrushchev responded with the idea of building a wall around West Berlin. The result was the Berlin Wall, put up in the early hours of August 13, 1961. Khrushchev was careful to make it clear that the access of the soldiers of the Western powers would not be affected, thus eliminating the incentive for Kennedy to respond with anything other than condemnation and more aid. Though it was a huge blow to the prestige of the socialist bloc, the wall defused the Berlin problem for the next decade.

European affairs had been at the center of Soviet attention for most of the time since 1945, but as the years passed China and what became known as the Third World came to take a larger place. The Third World meant the vast majority of the globe that in 1945 was still part of one or another European empire or (in the Western hemisphere) dominated by the United States. It was here that the Soviet Union was gradually able to challenge the West with increasing success until the 1970s. From the outset the Soviet leadership had assumed that sooner or later they would find allies in the colonial world, and their own policies in Central Asia were, in their minds, an anti-colonial revolution. The first Comintern Congress in 1919 had proclaimed the alliance of Communists and anti-imperialist nationalists, but the policy had little impact outside of China, and there it seemed a failure after 1927. The Second World War changed all that, and not only in China but also with its neighbors. In most other colonized countries the Communists were not strong, but virtually everywhere nationalist movements grew much more powerful than they had been before the war, which so weakened Britain and France that neither could put up much resistance. In 1948 the centerpiece of the British Empire, India, became independent, and by the 1950s it was clear that Britain would have to give up its empire sooner or later. France fought on in Indochina until 1954 and then in Algeria, but there too it went down to defeat. A whole host of new states came into being. Stalin had been skeptical of these new states, but his successors were not so wary.

The first Third World country that came into the good graces of the Soviet Union was Nasser's Egypt in 1955. After some debate among the leadership Khrushchev agreed to supply Nasser with tanks and planes, marking the USSR's first major entrance into the Middle East. When Nasser nationalized the Suez Canal, Khrushchev supported him during the ensuing crisis, though he had little real leverage over the area. In any case, the week that the Suez crisis peaked, the Soviet leadership was absorbed with a far more serious issue in Eastern Europe. The beginnings of de-Stalinization in the USSR had a prompt echo in Poland, where riots led to the installation of Wladyslaw Gomulka as party leader. Gomulka had been a victim of Stalinist purges in Poland and now steered the country on a course that was loyal to Moscow but differed in its social and other policies: most notably, Polish farmers received land on the breakup of the collectives and remained owners until the fall of communism. More serious was the challenge in Hungary. Here the local Stalinists tried to hang on, provoking the collapse of the regime, and the emergence of a new leader in Imre Nagy. Nagy announced that Hungary would have multi-party elections and leave the Warsaw Pact. The Soviet leaders, including Khrushchev, hesitated. They had moved troops near Budapest, but only after days of indecision did they finally move in and suppress the revolt, installing Janos Kadar as the new party leader. Nagy was taken to Rumania and executed.

After 1956, relations with all the socialist brothers became increasingly complicated. Kadar retained collective farms but permitted and even encouraged small businesses. Both Poland and Hungary (after initial repression) permitted oppositional opinion to express itself in ways that were generally modest but not seen in the USSR or other Communist ruled countries. Other East European countries began to exert much more independence, though not necessarily accompanied by more liberal policies. Albania's Enver Hoxha had opposed de-Stalinization from the first, and gradually built a Stalinist mini-state featuring crank economic schemes. Rumania became increasingly critical of Khrushchev and Soviet leadership generally, but also moved in a much more authoritarian direction than the USSR, and accompanied this course with super-industrialization schemes that impoverished the country by the 1980s. None of these changes in East Europe, however, were as significant as the growing break with China. Mao Tse-tung was not happy with Khrushchev's secret speech, claiming later that Stalin was seventy percent good and only thirty percent bad. With some ambiguity, Mao backed the Soviets in Hungary, but relations deteriorated in subsequent years. Mao's Great Leap Forward (1958–1961) reflected the growing radicalization of Chinese policy, establishing gigantic communes in the place of Soviet-style collective farms and promoting back yard blast furnaces to make steel. Mao was also increasingly unhappy with Khrushchev's attempts at peaceful coexistence with the United States, in his mind a fundamental impossibility. Khrushchev, as elsewhere, exacerbated the tension with his clumsy diplomacy, but totally different visions of socialism were at the heart of the dispute. The Soviet Union had spent a great deal of money in aid to China, especially after 1953, and sent many advisers on technical matters. Then in July 1960, Khrushchev ordered them all home. The final split came with the Cuban missile crisis in 1962, for Mao saw the resolution of the crisis as a surrender to the United States. Open polemics in the Chinese press calling Soviet policies "revisionist" made the split obvious for all to see, and continued until the beginning of the Cultural Revolution in China (1967). Now the Chinese leadership was claiming capitalist restoration in the USSR, and entered into a mad world all of its own. Border clashes only made things worse, but China was too absorbed in its own upheaval to make problems for the Russians. Nevertheless, the only major ally of the USSR in the Cold War was now gone, right at the time when Moscow had finally achieved strategic parity with the United States.

The rivalry with America moved more and more to the center of Cold War politics. Khrushchev continued to make attempts at promoting understanding, symbolized by his trip to the United States in 1959. The Soviet leader saw more than farms, for he toured the country extensively, meeting with Hollywood stars (though he was prevented from seeing Disneyland) and speaking with Eisenhower and other American officials. In spite of the ongoing Berlin problem, there seemed to be some progress, and more meetings were scheduled in Europe. Then in 1960 the Soviet air defense tracked a U-2 spy plane over Sverdlovsk and shot it down, ending any hope of talks on arms control or easing of tensions for the time being. The construction of the Berlin Wall the next year did not help either, but Khrushchev had much riskier plans in mind.

The Cuban revolution of 1959 had found a lukewarm reception in Moscow. Fidel Castro was not a member of the Cuban Communist Party, which had in fact opposed his movement until the last minute. Castro's orientation was nevertheless both against American dominance and toward socialism. The many US moves against Cuba, the 1961 Bay of Pigs invasion, covert operations, and threatening talk in the US Congress, convinced the Soviets that they should support him. Khrushchev thought that he could solve two problems at once by placing Soviet missiles in Cuba. One was that he had only a half dozen ICBMs, and the rest of his missiles were not yet big enough to reach the United States from the Soviet Union, leaving his country at a serious disadvantage. The other aim was to provide Castro with a serious defense against a possible invasion. Khrushchev made the decision largely on his own, with little consultation with the Soviet elite. Once the United States detected the missiles by U-2 overflights, Kennedy decided that they had to be removed. The outcome was inevitable, given that the USSR lacked a nuclear arsenal with the size and range of US equipment. Khrushchev had to withdraw, and to make matters worse the one US concession (removing US missiles from Turkey) remained secret. The humiliation was complete, and the internal repercussions were the beginning of Khrushchev's ultimate fall.

With the arrival of Leonid Brezhnev as Soviet leader, the bluff and risk-taking came to an end, and the USSR concentrated on building up its military so that the Cuban debacle could never be repeated. Its foreign relations with the United States remained central, but as the Americans were increasingly preoccupied with Vietnam, Brezhnev had a bit of breathing room. He certainly needed it, for the descent of China into the Cultural Revolution was followed in 1968 by crisis in Czechoslovakia. In many ways the "Prague Spring" was a repeat of Hungary with the same outcome: Soviet troops restored the rule of the Communist party in a spirit in accord with Soviet conceptions of socialism. Ultimately it was not Eastern Europe but Vietnam that became the main focus of the Cold War for a decade.

The Soviet leadership had never seen Vietnam as an important front of the Cold War, and regarded the United States as too powerful in Southeast Asia to challenge. To make things worse, the Vietnamese Communists generally supported China after 1956, in part because the policy of peaceful coexistence undermined their desires for a war in the south to reunify their country. Khrushchev largely ignored them. He scarcely had the time to react to the Tonkin Gulf incident of 1964, for he was soon out of office, but Brezhnev quickly decided to respond to American escalation of the war by sending large quantities of Soviet aid, including anti-aircraft missiles capable of hitting American bombers, even B-52s, over North Vietnam. Unlike Khrushchev's quixotic pursuit of Third World nationalist leaders like Nasser or Patrice Lumumba to almost universal failure, the support of North Vietnam led to the biggest defeat for the United States in the Cold War. By 1975, the last Americans had fled from the roof of the US embassy and the Vietnamese Communists ruled in the whole country, even if one devastated by war with a million and a half dead.

The victory of the Vietnamese Communists and the continued alliance with Cuba were certainly successes, even if neither country was large enough to make much difference in the geopolitical balance. In Europe the Soviet position seemed stable. The increasing economic problems in Poland were balanced by the restoration of normal relations with West Germany, the result of Willy Brandt's Ostpolitik in the early 1970s. This rapprochement defused the European Cold War's most serious conflict – the German problem. Brandt's new turn was possible because Communism was no longer an issue in Western Europe. The post-war economic boom combined with a solid welfare system produced a generation of satisfied consumers, so far from the desperate masses of the first half of the twentieth century. The West European Communist parties ceased to grow, and the smaller ones faded into obscurity and the larger ones, such as the Italian Communist Party, grew increasingly critical of the Soviets, if more so of China.

Though no one knew it then, the Vietnamese victory was the last Communist success. No Communist revolution materialized from Che Guevara's attempts in Latin America, and the mildly reformist Salvador Allende was overthrown in a coup most contemporaries believed to have been masterminded by the CIA. In Africa, the radical regime of Colonel Mengistu of Ethiopa (1974–1991) was a Soviet ally, but its land reform hardly made it a socialist country in the Soviet sense, and in any case was too poor and small to make much of a difference. Africa, like most of the Third World, evolved in various ways, some countries becoming relatively prosperous capitalist economies, others moving toward even more desperate poverty, but none of them toward socialism as Moscow understood it. The rhetoric of people's liberation that came from the Soviets rang increasingly hollow.

The first American response to its defeat in Vietnam was to move toward some sort of accommodation, the policy that was known as détente. The Nixon administration, knowing that the Soviets had rough parity in nuclear weapons and weakened by the war in Vietnam, decided to respond to Soviet overtures on arms limitations, the result being the 1972 Strategic Arms Limitation Treaty (SALT) limiting strategic weapons. The next stage was the 1975 Helsinki accord that recognized the post-World War II boundaries for the first time and also included generalities about mutual consultations and human rights, the latter soon to become a bone of contention. Discussions continued through the decade, ending finally with SALT II in 1979, limiting the number of delivery vehicles for nuclear weapons.

While limiting the hitherto frenetic pace of construction of nuclear arsenals and thus reducing the risks of annihilation, these moves did not end the Cold War, nor were they intended to. In many ways the more important move was the rapprochement with China that Nixon and Henry Kissinger inaugurated in 1971. With Nixon's visit to China the next year the Soviet Union found itself facing both China and the United States as rivals. China, of course, was still in the throes of the Cultural Revolution, with all its murderous effects and political and economic chaos. The US-Chinese arrangement coincided with the rise of the Gang of Four, who ruled China with terror until Mao's death in 1976. Only then was Deng Xiaoping able to restore some sort of normalcy, so that China was able to provide the United States with important support. During these years the United States and China traded intelligence on the Soviet Union. In public, the United States denounced the exile of Soviet dissidents and restrictions on Jewish emigration in the USSR while remaining silent about the thousands of people who perished in China during the last phases of the Cultural Revolution. The Soviets lambasted US imperialism while allying with Third World countries whose socialism or even nationalism was strictly nominal. Once the United

States had played its "China card," the US-Soviet contest gradually ceased to be a struggle for socialism or democratic capitalism and turned into yet another superpower rivalry.

The aging leadership around Brezhnev did not perceive these deeper shifts in society and politics in the world. It still lived in the world of revolutionary struggles and the building of socialism, even if their tactical orientation meant that revolutions abroad were rarely a priority. Their last move in that struggle was to be fatal, the involvement in Afganistan. The USSR had always had relations with its Afghan neighbor and occasionally provided aid and considered various schemes of meddling in Afghan politics, but the country was too poor, too traditional, and too marginal to the great power conflicts, especially after the end of British India. Then in 1973 a military coup overthrew the monarchy, and five years later it, in turn, fell to another group of army officers with more or less Marxist views. The new rulers passed various measures to destroy "feudalism," the many traditional customs which they viewed as oppressive, provoking massive discontent. The Soviet leadership took the Afghan government seriously, as Communists moving toward a society on the Soviet model, and the challenge to the regime as another US-sponsored revolt. The latter belief was correct, as the CIA had started to aid the rebels by mid-1979, in part in the hope that the Soviets would be forced to intervene. To make matters worse, the Soviets feared that the Afghan leaders at the moment might go over to the United States or China. Thus on December 27, 1979, Soviet troops seized Kabul, placed a more loyal government in charge, and the invasion began. The United States provided aid for the rebels through Pakistan, thus laying a foundation for the rise of Islamic extremism. This fighting led to massive destruction and casualties in Afghanistan, and the death of some fourteen thousand Soviet soldiers. For the next six years, until the rise of Mikhail Gorbachev, the Afghan war was the main issue of the Cold War as well as being an enormous drain on the resources and morale of the USSR. It also speeded up the collapse of the Soviet order.

EPILOGUE
The End of the USSR

The collapse of the Soviet Union and the reappearance of Russia were momentous events, but events that are difficult to describe in any depth. The main outlines are clear, as much of its fall took place in public under intense scrutiny by the Soviet population, Russian and foreign journalists, and the governments of the world. Yet many of the crucial decisions took place behind closed doors and are too recent to be the object of study by historians. Many of the major events of the time have already fallen from memory, and others have been probably exaggerated in popular accounts as well as in the few academic attempts at analysis. Real sources scarcely exist, and sensational memoirs and fragments of information do not make good history. To complicate matters, perceptions of the events outside Russia and among the Russian and most former Soviet populations differ profoundly. All that is possible is a sketch of the events and of some of the more obvious social, political, and economic trends of a quarter of a century of upheaval, with some attention to the understanding of these events and trends by the Russians who lived through them.

Mikhail Gorbachev became the General Secretary of the Communist Party in March of 1985, just a few hours after the death of Chernenko. He brought with him a new team – among others, Aleksandr Iakovlev as an adviser and Boris Yeltsin, whom he put in charge of the Moscow party organization. Gorbachev belonged to a new generation: born in 1931, he graduated from Moscow University in law in 1955. The last Soviet leader with a university education had been Lenin. After university Gorbachev soon became the party boss of his native Stavropol', an agricultural district in the plains north of the Caucasus. In 1979 he entered the Politburo. Iakovlev was older, born in 1923, and had risen through the party propaganda network in the 1950s. He spent 1958 at Columbia University in New York on an exchange, and was ambassador to Canada from 1973 to 1983. These two men would lead the attempt to reform the Soviet order. Their nemesis was another party boss from the provinces, Boris Yeltsin. Yeltsin, born the same year as Gorbachev, graduated from the Technical University in Sverdlovsk, also in 1955, and went on to become the party boss of the Sverdlovsk region, one of the USSR's key industrial regions. He remained at that post from 1976 until Gorbachev brought him to Moscow.

The first year or so after the appearance of Gorbachev brought little change on the surface. Indeed the most spectacular event of his first year in office was the explosion of the nuclear reactor at Chernobyl in April 1986. The country that had sent the first man into space could not maintain the safety of its reactors. Gorbachev called for a radical improvement in the economy at the 1986 party conference, but got nowhere. Andrei Sakharov was allowed to return to Moscow late in the year, but most of the policy discussion still remained behind the closed doors of party meetings. In 1987 Gorbachev began to call for "restructuring" (*perestroika* in Russian), publishing a whole book to promote his vision. He soon added to this *glasnost'*, which meant something like "openness" or perhaps even "transparency." The idea was simply that major issues should be part of public debate, not just discussion behind closed doors within the party elite. At the same time a whole series of measures began to open the economic structure to non-governmental enterprise. The first important example was the law that permitted "cooperatives" to function, which were, in fact, small private businesses such as restaurants. Largely unnoticed at the time, the leadership also took steps to speed up the economy by making use of the Komsomol, the Communist League of Youth. Founded in the Civil War as a means of mobilizing the young behind the party's goals, it had become an essentially bureaucratic organization, a lifeless adjunct to the party. Now it was encouraged to set up "Youth Scientific-Technical Groups," which were allowed to engage in tax-free entrepreneurial activities, mainly with electronics and automobiles. In these groups the later oligarchs took their first steps.

Just as important as these changes in attitude and policy was the Soviet withdrawal from Afghanistan. Gorbachev seems to have decided on this move almost immediately, but he did not announce the withdrawal until 1988. Within a year, the Soviets were out of Afghanistan, which then fell into civil war. The ensuing years of Perestroika were politically exciting, as new publications sprang up in Moscow and Leningrad and many other parts of the country. Issues from the Stalin era and other dark parts of Soviet history were the objects of intense discussion. Former dissidents like Sakharov for a moment were national heroes. Not all of this ferment was the result of newly found freedom: the first article to appear critical of Lenin was written on command from the authorities, and historians who questioned its nationalistic conclusions were told it was not for discussion. In parts of the country, such as the Ukraine or Central Asia, the press continued in the Soviet mode. Nevertheless in most of the central press, in film, in literature, at the theater, and at the dinner tables of ordinary people, intense arguments raged and no one any longer took account of what the authorities thought or did. The excitement of political debate, the first such debate in seventy years, went along with a rapidly deteriorating economy. Gorbachev's first economic reforms removed many of the mechanisms of the Soviet economy but put nothing in their place. A real market did not yet exist. The supply of consumer goods, already very poor in the early 1980s, fell catastrophically. The state also began to lose control of the periphery. In 1988 Armenia began to make claims to Nagorno-Karabakh, an Armenian enclave in neighboring Azerbaidzhan. Moscow was unable to resolve the dispute, and Armenia began to reject the authority of the Soviet state.

The pace of change quickened. Behind the scenes, the Komsomol entrepreneurs had accumulated vast sums, and were soon joined by Soviet banks and industrial ministries, which converted themselves into "firms" oriented toward the growing market. In 1989 the Ministry of Natural Gas Industry became Gazprom, and it was only one of many such organizations. Essentially, a kind of privatization was taking place behind closed doors. Other changes were public. Everywhere in the country Gorbachev's policy was to replace the hierarchy of party offices with "Soviet," that is to say, government, offices. In many cases the local party boss simply moved across the street to head the local government, but the change meant that the party suddenly was becoming irrelevant. Inside the party opposition to Perestroika was growing. Then Gorbachev announced that the old Supreme Soviet, the nominal legislature of the USSR, would be replaced with a "Congress of People's Deputies." Elections to the new Congress would be real and open: there was to be more than one candidate for each seat. The result was a more or less free election, the first since 1917, but the results were mixed. Gorbachev wanted the new Congress as a vehicle to move ahead the process of economic liberalization as well as "democratization," newly included in the agenda of reform. Unfortunately the composition of the new Congress meant a stalemate. Moscow and Leningrad predictably elected strongly reformist deputies, most of them from the intelligentsia, as did many Russian provincial cities and districts. The Ukraine, however, still firmly under party boss Leonid Kravchuk, and the Central Asian republics elected conservative deputies opposed to reform. The Baltic republics, swept by a wave of nationalism, were more interested in separation than reform, and the Transcaucasian republics were focused on their mutual quarrels. The elections also brought Boris Yeltsin into the public eye. In 1987 he had fallen afoul of Gorbachev, who had then removed him from his Moscow post. Now as a deputy to the Congress, he used the platform to criticize the pace and scope of reform. He also began to affirm the need for the Russian republic to look after its own rights and needs, and not defer to the central, or Soviet, authorities. The year 1989 also saw the collapse of Communist power everywhere in Eastern Europe, climaxed by the fall of the Berlin Wall in November. Even anti-Soviet Communists in Rumania were overthrown. Gorbachev accepted all this, apparently hoping it would lead to better relations with the West.

The next year Gorbachev formally became the head of state of the USSR, completing the transfer of formal power from party to state institutions. It did not help him. In the ensuing months growing nationalism in the Baltic republics and Georgia created a whole new series of problems. In Georgia the colorful dissident writer Zviad Gamsakhurdia was elected president in 1990, leading to an immediate conflict with Abkhazia and South Ossetia. The Georgian government tried to impose Georgian language on the two minorities, banned local parties, and then shortly after abolished their local autonomy. Soviet troops had to come and separate the contending parties. Thus all three Transcaucasian republics were now in turmoil. Gorbachev was losing control over the country. Nationalist ferment in Lithuania led to a violent confrontation with Soviet troops and many deaths in January 1991. In June, Yeltsin won election to the leadership of the Russian republic by a big majority, in large part because there was no real opposition in the field against him.

By 1991 the economy seemed to be reaching a nadir, and the authority of the state was at an all-time low. Yet public politics still revolved around the battle of reform versus retention of the Soviet system. The public advocates of reform were mostly from the intelligentsia, and were increasingly impatient with Gorbachev, whom they saw as too slow and inclined to compromise. Advocates of the old system seemed to come mainly from the ranks of the party elite, increasingly under threat from Gorbachev's reforms, economic as well as political. In the background and unnoticed by all, new groups were forming and waiting in the wings, political clans and a few new entrepreneurs working largely within the Soviet structure, but using it to form de facto businesses. The Communists intent on preserving the system then unwittingly provided the opportunity to destroy it.

In August of 1991, while Gorbachev was taking a brief vacation in the Crimea, the vice-president, the Ministers of Internal Affairs and of Defense, and several other high officials decided to declare an emergency and take power to reverse the entire process of reform. They brought several regiments of troops into the city, but found little support. Most local governments either rejected their appeals or like the Ukrainian leadership, sat on the fence. The people of Moscow were clearly against them, and Yeltsin as head of the Russian republic government led the opposition, famously standing on a tank to rally the people. The coup leaders kept Gorbachev isolated in the Crimea in his dacha, hoping to hang on, but it was no use. After a few days of almost bloodless confrontation, they surrendered.

The outcome was the collapse of the Soviet Union. Gorbachev returned to Moscow, but the country was in chaos. As he struggled to hold on, Yeltsin met with the leaders of Belorussia and the Ukraine in a hunting lodge in the Belovezha forest in Belorussia. The three of them abolished the Soviet Union. Other republics were not asked: the Baltics and Georgia had already declared independence, but the Central Asian republic leadership groups were aghast at the prospect. The public was not asked either: early in 1991 there had been referenda on the status of the union, and most people, including in the Ukraine, had voted for more autonomy but to also preserve the union. This, of course, had been the desire of the local leadership in Kiev and elsewhere. Now Yeltsin was in power and the leaders had changed their minds. After seventy-four years of existence, the Soviet Union came to an end.

The first result, visible already in the weeks after the coup, was a transformation of the economy unlike anything earlier discussed in public by the main reformist groups. One part of this policy of privatization was already largely complete: the transformation of state production units and banks into private firms. Many or most of these had an effective monopoly over one or another area of the economy, and they constituted the cream of the financial system and the "real" economy. The other part of the policy was "voucher privatization." In theory everyone would get vouchers for property in the new system, but the vouchers were largely worthless. Some people papered their bathroom walls with them. In fact the state simply turned over its remaining resources to freshly baked "businessmen" at fire sale prices. Real private businesses existed only at the level of small businesses, which were heavily taxed and consequently conducted business to a large extent outside the law.

The central role of the state and connections of the new owners with important figures in the government did not mean that the transformation of power into property was an orderly process. Rival clans of businessmen intrigued with powerful political clans for favor. Gangsters became a regular feature of Russian business, and fought one another other with armed bands. Every week expensive cars turned up in Moscow parks with the cars and their occupants riddled with machine gun bullets. Chechen and other Caucasian gangs controlled the peasant markets and other lucrative sources of profit.

While a new elite of oligarchs came into being, the standard of living of the population collapsed. Hyperinflation wiped out the savings of ordinary people. Doctors, teachers, coal miners, and factory workers were not paid for months or even years at a time. Many people lived on a barter economy, and the formerly better off grew potatoes in the yards of their dachas. An overvalued ruble meant that Russia suddenly became a dumping ground for the world's goods. Cheap vodka poured into the country from Belgium and Germany with labels picturing Rasputin, and the American Snickers candy bar became so ubiquitous that economists used its price as a benchmark of inflation. The infrastructure, already frail from years of neglect, began to collapse. Culture disappeared. The great theaters and orchestras lived on the proceeds of foreign tours. Few films were made, and movie theaters showed American "action films." Scientists moved abroad or tried to find foreign grants. The intelligentsia, for the first time since the middle nineteenth century, ceased to play a major role in Russian life. Emigration boomed, not only Jewish emigration but also the departure of other ethnic and religious minorities and many ordinary Russians. Only Moscow and a few other areas maintained a limited prosperity, fuelled by the new businesses and the rapidly expanding state bureaucracy. While the Yeltsin years seemed to the West an era of "democratization" and the transition to a market economy, they seemed to most Russians a dark night of anarchy, poverty, and total unpredictability.

The ongoing collapse of the economy was paralleled by a collapse of state power. National republics like Tatarstan began to assert "sovereign" rights, though no one knew exactly what that meant. In purely Russian regions provincial governors, mostly from the old Communist apparatus, got themselves elected and challenged the central powers. Yeltsin responded in many cases by driving them out of office and appointing governors himself, but local legislatures were harder to control. Yeltsin's largest political problem, however, was the Russian parliament, the Supreme Soviet of the Congress of People's Deputies, in Moscow. The new president was never able to translate his own electoral victories into a secure majority in the Supreme Soviet, mainly because he was never able to create a political party to serve his aims. The result was a series of deadlocks, and increasing opposition to Yeltsin. Popular despair over the consequences of economic reform created a political vacuum and gave the Supreme Soviet a chance to try to block further privatization measures. Yeltsin's vice-president, Alexander Rutskoi, elected with him in 1991, joined his opponents as did the speaker of the Supreme Soviet, Ruslan Khasbulatov, a Chechen by birth. When Yeltsin ordered the Supreme Soviet dissolved, contrary to the constitution, the Supreme Soviet impeached Yeltsin and proclaimed Rutskoi president. In response demonstrators supporting Rutskoi and Khasbulatov barricaded the parliament building, the "Russian White House," seized the mayor's office and then the television tower on October 3, 1993. The next day Yeltsin brought in tanks that shelled the Russian White House, a moment shown live on television throughout the world. Yeltsin inaccurately portrayed his opponents and their leaders – both his former allies – as attempting to restore Communism, a fantasy noticed by a few Western journalists. Most Russians thought the conflict an unprincipled struggle for power and the levers of privatization. US President Clinton spoke in favor of Yeltsin's actions and accepting his description of the events, sending Russian opinion of America into a decline from which it never recovered. Yeltsin rewrote the constitution to give more power to the president, and renamed Russia's legislature the Duma to recall tsarist times.

Even worse was to come. In the North Caucasus, Chechen president Dzhokhar Dudaev proved completely intractable to Yeltsin's attempts to make a deal. As Chechnya was a major center of oil production, much was at stake. In October 1994, Yeltsin sent troops to take Grozny, the Chechen capital. The result was an ignominious failure, and government bombing killed thousands of civilians, many of them Russians living within the city. Fighting continued until 1996, when the Russian air force managed to track down Dudaev and kill him with a missile strike. Grozny was in ruins.

The Yeltsin years were also the time of the emergence of some dozen oligarchs, many of them from the Komsomol networks of 1987–88, who came to head huge personal business empires, usually centered on banks and controlling vast production units and all the important electronic and print media. All of them had close connections with the government, but acted largely on their own and in ruthless competition with one another. For the mass of the population, the standard of living continued to fall. The mortality rate skyrocketed, much of it the result of massive vodka consumption – the product of despair and cheap imported liquor. The birth rate fell well below the rate needed to reproduce the population. In spite of all this, Yeltsin managed to achieve his re-election in 1996. Crucial to his victory was the work of Anatolii Chubais, the head of the privatization program, who was well connected with Russian oligarchs and foreign sources of support. Another crucial factor was the absence of any other candidate than Gennadii Ziuganov, the head of the Russian Communist party. Ziuganov preached a strange mixture of Soviet ideology, Russian nationalism, and sheer eccentricity, and found support among the elderly and provincial workers, as well as masses of protest votes. Yeltsin entered his second term, sick from heart attacks and heavy drinking, which he displayed in public on several occasions. Western governments and companies moved into the former Soviet republics in Transcaucasia and Central Asia in search of new oil and gas supplies. Although there was a respite in Chechnya, Russia was at its nadir.

The turning point came as a consequence of the Asian financial crisis of 1997–98. This crisis had repercussions in Russia, and in August 1998, the State Bank let the ruble fall sharply. The results were immediate: Russian goods began to replace imports in Russian stores in a matter of weeks. The rickety financial structure that was the centerpiece of the oligarchic business empires collapsed. Russian industry began to revive. The few remaining financial oligarchs of the 1990s now were joined by an increasing number of new oligarchs, whose fortunes rested on industry and the extraction of resources. Rising revenues from the sale of oil and natural gas, mainly to the European Union, made Russian finances healthy again. The war in Chechnya revived in 1999, but this time to Russia's favor. After a series of bombings of apartment houses in Moscow and other Russian cities that were attributed to Chechen militants, the Russian army moved in on Chechnya, this time slowly but deliberately. By the spring they had retaken Grozny and most of the area, and established a new government led by Ahmad Kadyrov, a Muslim cleric and erstwhile supporter of Dudaev.

Yeltsin, evidently exhausted by the years of upheaval, heavy drinking, and bad health suddenly resigned and appointed his prime minister, Vladimir Putin, as his successor on the last day of 1999. No one knew why Yeltsin chose Putin, nor even if Yeltsin's was the deciding voice. Putin had served twenty-five years in the KGB, five of them in East Germany, but then joined the political team of St. Petersburg's reformist mayor Anatolii Sobchak. In 1996 he went to Moscow, at some point attracting Yeltsin's attention. Much younger, ascetic by contrast to Yeltsin, and a colorful personality, he attracted world attention and very quickly acquired popularity among the overwhelming majority of Russians. He remained president through two elections until 2008.

Putin very quickly put together a new order. He inherited a constitutionally strong presidency from Yeltsin's 1993 rewrite of the constitution, but more important, his team managed to create a pro-government political party that supported the president in the Duma. He regularized the practice of appointing provincial governors, and appointed military officers and some of his former comrades from KGB to important offices. President Putin was much more powerful than his predecessor, though most Russians still saw the state as the instrument not of the president, but of the now ever more numerous oligarchs. The Chechen war gradually died down, though terrorist acts continued sporadically, like the assassination of Ahmad Kadyrov and the seizure of school children in Beslan, both in 2004. If foreign journalists saw all these changes as creeping dictatorship, the Russian population felt that order was coming back. A new prosperity was as important as order and relative stability. Moscow and other large cities went into an orgy of home improvements, as a new middle class emerged and began to replace aging Soviet appliances with Siemens and Bosch washing machines and dishwashers. Huge traffic jams appeared every day as millions bought cars for the first time: ancient used Volkswagens and gleaming new Japanese SUVs. Hundreds of thousands began to take vacations abroad to Europe and the Middle East in search of the sun. The Turkish coast at Antalya was packed with Russians all year around. The birth rate inched up, nearing the replacement rate for the first time in decades. Culture revived, with massive expenditures on projects like the reconstruction of the Bolshoi Theater in Moscow. Publishing boomed, spurred by the new mass market in detective stories and romance novels, many of them translated or imitated from Western models. Serious journalists and scribblers turned out endless biographies and "exposés" of current politics as well as pseudo-historical accounts of Russian history. Historians continued to publish ever more massive series of documents from Soviet history, concentrating on the Stalin era but eventually reaching into the 1950s. After a few years it was fairly clear that the new prosperity was not just the result of oil revenues from sales to the European Union: the internal market had begun to grow and increasing trade with China began to revive old Soviet-era factories. Prosperity began to spread outside Moscow and the oil-producing areas to St. Petersburg and provincial cities. Small business increasingly became a normal part of the economy as the Putin government removed the punitive taxes of the Yeltsin era. Verbally, Russia began to challenge American hegemony in the world. Though still isolated from most world economic organizations, and with only a de facto ally in China, Russia reentered world politics after a decade of absence.

The end of the Soviet Union left the new Russia with many dilemmas. One of them was very basic: What is Russia? And what is to be the political ideal to cement the state? In the Yeltsin years the government struggled with this issue largely by itself, for society was essentially flattened, desperate merely to survive. In theory, the ideology of the new regime was democracy, but for most Russians that simply meant the public pronouncements of the people in power. When the Russian air force bombed Grozny in 1994, one of the older Russian residents told Western reporters, "I survived the Nazis, now I have survived the democrats." A variety of intellectuals and political groupings tried to come up with new ideologies to replace Marxism, most attempts being a Russian nationalism similar to that propagated by Ziuganov and Vladimir Zhirinovsky. The Yeltsin government realized that "democracy" meant to ordinary Russians nothing more than kleptocracy and anarchy and tried to fill the vacuum, often to comic effects. The television stations, then entirely in the hands of pro-government oligarchs, ran endless programs about the Romanov dynasty and often imaginary pre-1917 traditions. Yeltsin not only renamed the parliament the Duma, in recognition of the 1906–1917 institution, he also restored the double-headed eagle as the state symbol of Russia, a dynastic emblem of autocracy, not democracy. The government decided that Russia needed a "state ideology" and appointed a committee headed by a nationalist mathematician to come up with one. After a year the committee dissolved itself because it could not come up with anything reasonable.

The Putin presidency inherited a state that had little legitimacy with the population. The Soviet Union after the war had been legitimate to most people; that is, they may have thought all the policies were wrong but it was still their state. The new Russia was nobody's state, even if most people approved of Putin. Many Russians believed that the new elite was even further from the population than the Communists had been. Ordinary people said of the new elite, "they don't ask us" about what they were doing. As the years passed, the population began to look back more positively on the Soviet era, and the Putin government responded by memorializing Soviet heroes from the war or the space race, and suggesting that history textbooks should be less negative about that part of the Russian past. Increasing segments of the population were better off after 2000, but in what country did they live? What was Russia? The boundaries that collapsed in 1991 were not created by the Soviets, but the Russian Empire centuries before. These were not abstract questions. Millions of people had personal ties with the Ukraine, Georgia, Armenia, Kazakhstan, and even more remote areas. They still lived in terms of the former Soviet space, not just Russia. Narrow Russian nationalism turned out to be a failure with no wide echo in the population, young or old. The new Russia moreover did not reflect the social values of substantial parts of the population. At least the new state did not become an ethno-state, like most other ex-Soviet republics. At Putin's 2000 inauguration the Russian Orthodox clergy were seated in the audience alongside the rabbis and imams, an arrangement that in a strange way retained the traditions both of the Russian Empire and the Soviet Union.

If the Caucasus remained a problem, official terminology included all citizens of Russia as "rossiane" (roughly, people of Russia), not just "russkie" (Russians in an ethnic sense), a terminology impossible to translate but highly significant for its attempt at inclusiveness.

In the Perestroika era, a popular joke was that the Soviet Union was the only country in the world with an unpredictable past – a comment on Soviet historical ideology and the speed and superficiality of its replacement. Indeed Russia had been a land of thinly populated northern forests for the first eight or nine centuries of its existence, but it turned into one of the world's most populous countries and is still the world's largest in area. It was the world's fifth industrial power in 1914 while still overwhelmingly rural. Then it embarked, or the Bolsheviks embarked it, on a utopian scheme to realize a new socialist order of society, one without classes or exploitation. At the same time they sought to become a fully industrialized modern state. In the latter goal it largely succeeded, if at colossal cost. For a short time, the Soviet Union was a superpower, or was almost one. For most of the twentieth century Russia was even a major player in world science and in literature, even if these never reached the heights achieved in the era of the tsars. The fate of the socialist dream is more a matter of irony than tragedy: the ruling party that was to create the new order, after seventy years of effort, effectively decided that wealth was better than power, that inequality was better than equality and it privatized itself. The result was a hybrid society, with private businesses that are not quite private and government institutions not quite governmental. The smaller and less powerful but (for many) richer state that succeeded the Soviet Union appeared on the scene mimicking the old Russia, with an ambiguous place in the world and in the eyes of its people. Whether or not it can realize the potential created by the previous millennium of Russian (and Soviet) history remains to be seen.

FURTHER READING

Russian history has never been blessed with an abundance of accessible works on its history and culture in English. Much of the existing literature is now seriously out of date and is not being replaced quickly. Hence the following is by no means an exhaustive list; rather it attempts to provide the general reader with accessible literature where possible though it occasionally includes academic studies. Reference works such as the *Cambridge History of Russia*, 3 vols. (2006) provide full bibliography.

RUS AND EARLY RUSSIA

For the earliest centuries of Russian history, to the time of Peter the Great, the situation is particularly bad. The best overall introduction to the earlier centuries is Janet Martin, *Medieval Russia 980–1584* (1995). John Fennell's *History of the Russian Church to 1448* (1995) covers the medieval period. Translations of the devotional and other literature of medieval Russia are Serge Zenkovsky, ed., and trans., *Medieval Russia's Epics, Chronicles, and Tales* (1974) and Michael Klimenko, ed., *Vita of St. Sergii of Radonezh* (1980). Medieval Novgorod has never inspired the works in English that it deserves, especially after the decades of archeological excavation. An introduction is Henrik Birnbaum, *Lord Novgorod the Great* (1981). For the Mongol invasion and rule the foundation is Charles Halperin, *Russia and the Golden Horde* (1985).

For the politics of the sixteenth and seventeenth centuries see J. L. I. Fennell, *Ivan the Great of Moscow* (1963), Andrei Pavlov and Maureen Perrie, *Ivan the Terrible* (2003), the old but still useful S. P. Platonov, *The Time of Troubles* (1970), Philip Longworth, *Alexis, Tsar of All the Russias* (1984), and Lindsey Hughes, *Sophia: Regent of Russia 1657–1704* (1990). Isolde Thyret, *Between God and Tsar: Religious Symbolism and the Royal Women of Muscovite Russia* (2001) provides a new perspective on the ruling dynasty. The evolution of the church and religion is covered mainly in scholarly monographs such as Paul Bushkovitch, *Religion and Society in Russia: the Sixteenth and Seventeenth Centuries* (1992) and Paul Meyendorff, *Russia, Ritual and Reform: the Liturgical Reforms of Nikon in the Seventeenth Century* (1991). Ioann Shusherin's seventeenth century account of Patriarch Nikon's life has been translated as *From Peasant to Patriarch*, Kevin Kain and Katia Levintova, translators (2007) and see *Archpriest Avvakum, the Life Written by Himself*, trans. Kenneth Brostrom (1979).

THE EIGHTEENTH CENTURY

The political and cultural history of the era of Peter the Great and the eighteenth century are well covered. For Peter the best all around study remains Reinhard Wittram, *Peter der Grosse, Czar und Kaiser* (1964). More modern treatments are Lindsey Hughes, *Russia in the Age of Peter the Great* (1998) and Paul Bushkovitch, *Peter the Great 1671–1725: the Struggle for Power* (2001). A shorter version exists for both: Hughes' *Peter the Great: a Biography* (2002) and Bushkovitch, *Peter the Great* (2001). The empresses between Peter and Catherine have not attracted much attention, but see Evgenii Anisimov, *Empress Elizabeth: Her Reign and Her Russia 1741–1761*, trans. John T. Alexander (1995); and *Five Empresses*, trans. Kathleen Carol (2004). Isabel de Madariaga's *Russia in the Age of Catherine the Great* (1981) and John T. Alexander, *Catherine the Great: Life and Legend* (1989) are lively accounts of the empress and her court while Simon Sebag Montefiore's massive *Prince of Princes: the Life of Potemkin* (2000) describes a crucial figure. The correspondence of Catherine and Potemkin has been translated as *Love and Conquest: Personal Correspondence of Catherine the*

Great and Grigory Potemkin, trans. Douglas Smith (2004). For court politics and other events see David L. Ransel, *The Politics of Catherinian Russia: the Panin Party* (1975) and John T. Alexander, *Emperor of the Cossacks; Pugachev and the Frontier Jacquerie of 1773–1775* (1973). Influential attempts to analyze the Russian state are Marc Raeff, *The Well-Ordered Police State: Social and Institutional Change through Law in the Germanies and Russa 1600–1800* (1983) and John P. LeDonne, *Absolutism and Ruling Class: the Formation of the Russian Political Order 1700–1825* (1991). Social history is less well represented in English but see Michelle Marrese, *A Woman's Kingdom: Noblewomen and the Control of Property in Russia 1700–1861* (2002) and David Ransel, *A Russian Merchant's Tale: the Life and Adventures of Ivan Alekseevich Tolchenov, Based on His Diary* (2009). Important studies of foreign policy and empire include Jerzy Lukowski, *The Partitions of Poland 1772, 1793, 1795* (1999); Alan W Fisher, *The Russian Annexation of Crimea 1772–1783* (1970); and Michael Khodarkovsky, *Where Two Worlds Meet: The Russian State and the Kalmyk Nomads 1600–1772* (1992).

In the eighteenth century Russia entered the world of European culture and the Enlightenment. James Cracraft chronicles Peter's time in *The Petrine Revolution in Russian Architecture* (1988), *The Petrine Revolution in Russian Imagery* (1997), and *The Petrine Revolution in Russian Culture* (2004). The best introductions to Russian culture from Peter to 1800 are Marina Ritzarev, *Eighteenth Century Russian Music* (2006); W Gareth Jones, *Nikolay Novikov: Enlightener of Russia* (1984); Denis Fonvizin, *Dramatic Works,* trans. Marvin Kantor (1974) and *Political and Legal Writings,* trans. Walter Gleason (1985); and Alexander Radishchev, *Journey from St. Petersburg to Moscow,* trans. Leo Wiener (1966).

For the time of Paul and Alexander I Roderick E. McGrew, *Paul I of Russia 1754–1801* (1992) attempts to defend Paul's reputation, while Janet M. Hartley, *Alexander I* (1994) is briefer and more balanced. Russia's wars are well handled in Norman E Saul, *Russia and the Mediterranean 1797–1807* (1970) and Dominic Lieven's magisterial *Russia against Napoleon: the Battle for Europe 1807 to 1814* (2009). For the internal politics of the empire in the first half of the nineteenth century see Marc Raeff, *Michael Speransky:*

Statesman of Imperial Russia 1772–1839 (2d ed., 1969); W. Bruce Lincoln, *Nicholas I: Emperor and Autocrat of All the Russias* (1989). On the Decembrist revolt a now rather old introduction is Anatole G. Mazour, *First Russian Revolution, 1825: the Decembrist Movement: its Origins, Development, and Significance* (1967), while more modern treatments of the main figures include Patrick O'Meara, *K F Ryleev: a Political Biography of the Decembrist Poet* (1984); Glynn Barratt, *Rebel on the Bridge: a Life of the Decembrist Baron Andrey Rozen 1800–1884* (1975); and Christine Sutherland, *Princess of Siberia: the Story of Maria Volkonsky and the Decembrist Exiles* (1984). The debates inside the Russian intelligentsia from 1825 to the Crimean War are reflected in Andrzej Walicki, *The Slavophile Controversy: the History of a Conservative Utopia in Nineteenth Century Russian Thought*, trans. Hilda Andrews-Rusiecka (1975) and E. H. Carr, *The Romantic Exiles* (1933). The best portrait of the era is Alexander Herzen's autobiography, *My Past and Thoughts*, trans. Constance Garnett, 4 vols. (1968). The evolution of thought in government circles is the theme of Cynthia Whittaker, *The Origins of Modern Russian Education: an Intellectual Biography of Count Sergei Uvarov 1786–1855* (1984) and W Bruce Lincoln, *In the Vanguard of Reform: Russia's Enlightened Bureaucrats 1825–1861* (1986).

FROM THE GREAT REFORMS TO 1917

For the reform era W. Bruce Lincoln, *The Great Reforms: Autocracy, Bureaucracy and the Politics of Change in Imperial Russia* (1990) provides an introduction. Unfortunately there is no full biography of Alexander II or any other major figure of the government during his reign. The revolutionary movement during the same period has attracted more attention. Nikolai Chernyshevsky's *What is To Be Done?*, trans. Michael R. Katz (1989) influenced a whole generation, for which see Irina Paperno, *Chernyshevsky and the Age of Realism: A Study in the Semiotics of Behavior* (1988). Another important influence was Herzen, whose writings in translation are Alexander Herzen, *From the Other Shore and The Russian People and Socialism*, trans. Moura Budberg and Richard Wollheim (1979). A brilliant portrait of the age is Ivan Turgenev's novel

Fathers and Sons. The fullest account of the movement is Franco Venturi, *Roots of Revolution: A History of the Populist and Socialist Movements in Nineteenth Century Russia*, trans. Francis Haskell (1960).

Sidney Harcave, *Count Sergei Witte and the Twilight of Imperial Russia : a Biography* (2004); Terrence Emmons, *The Formation of Political Parties and the First National Elections in Russia* (1983); Abraham Ascher, *The Revolution of 1905*, 2 vols. (1998–1992); and the same author's *P A Stolypin, The Search for Stability in Late Imperial Russia* (2001) cover the politics of the last generation before 1917. Sergei U. Witte's *Memoirs of Count Witte*, trans. Sidney Harcave (1990) provide a vivid if scarcely objective picture of the government.

Russia's First World War is a neglected subject. For the background see D. C. B. Lieven, *Russia and the Origins of the First World War* (1983) and for war itself Norman Stone, *The Eastern Front 1914–1917* (1975) is still the only overview. See also Peter Gatrell, *Russia's First World War: a Social and Economic History* (2005). Allan K. Wildman, *The End of the Russian Imperial Army*, 2 vols. (1980–1987) provides a transition to the revolution. The revolution itself was fully portrayed in William Henry Chamberlin, *The Russian Revolution*, 2 vols. (1987, originally 1935). The best brief account is Steven Anthony Smith, *The Russian Revolution: a Very Short Introduction* (2002). John Reed's *Ten Days that Shook the World* (originally 1919) is the classic picture of October by a sympathetic American. For the February Revolution Tsuyoshi Hasegawa, *The February Revolution: Petrograd 1917* (1981) is unsurpassed, and on October there is Alexander Rabinowitch, *The Bolsheviks Come to Power: Petrograd 1917* (1976). For the Civil War see Evan Mawdsley, *The Russian Civil War* (1987) and Jonathan D. Smele, *The Civil War in Siberia: the Anti-Bolshevik Government of Admiral Kolchak 1918–1920* (1996).

ECONOMIC, SOCIAL, AND RELIGIOUS HISTORY

Work on the economic history of Russia is mostly old and not numerous. An exception is Peter Gatrell, *The Tsarist Economy 1850–1917* (1986). The largest group in Russian society, the peasantry has not found many students in the English speaking world, but to be recommended are David Moon, *The Russian Peasantry 1600–1930: the World the Peasants Made* (1999); Steven L. Hoch, *Serfdom and Social Control in Russia: Petrovskoe, a Village in Tambov* (1986); and Christine Worobec, *Peasant Russia: Family and Community in the Post-Emancipation Period* (1991). The merchants becoming modern businessmen have found their historians in Alfred Rieber, *Merchants and Entrepreneurs in Imperial Russia* (1982) and T. C. Owen, *Capitalism and Politics in Russia: a Social History of the Moscow Merchants 1855–1905* (1981). The working class and its early strike and political activity was once a subject of great interest. Reginal Zelnik, *Labor and Society in Tsarist Russia: the Factory Workers of St. Petersburg 1855–1870* (1971) and Walter Sablinsky, *The Road to Bloody Sunday: Father Gapon and the St. Petersburg Massacre of 1905* (1976) were pioneers. Women, the family and sexuality are the subject of Barbara Engel, *Between the Fields and City: Women, Work and the Family in Russia 1861–1914* (1994), the same author's *Mothers and Daughters: Women of the Intelligentsia in Nineteenth Century Russia* (1983); Richard Stites, *The Women's Liberation Movement in Russia: Feminism, Nihilism, and Bolshevism 1860–1930* (1978); and Laura Engelstein, *The Keys to Happiness: Sex and the Search for Modernity in Fin-de-siècle Russia* (1992). There is no overview of the history of religion in modern Russia for any period, but useful monographs include Vera Shevzov, *Russian Orthodoxy on the Eve of the Revolution* (2004); Nadieszda Kizenko, *A Prodigal Saint: Father John of Kronstadt and the Russian People* (2000); and for the theologically inclined Paul Valliere, *Modern Russian Theology: Bukharev, Soloviev, Bulgakov – Orthodox Theology in a New Key* (2000).

FOREIGN POLICY AND EMPIRE

The study of Russia as an empire has flourished in recent years. Older studies looked at Russia as a conglomerate of national minorities: Andreas Kappeler, *The Russian Empire: a Multiethnic History*, trans. Alfred Clayton (2001); Ronald Suny, *The Making of the Georgian Nation* (2d ed. 1994); Mikhailo Hrushevskyi, *History of*

Ukraine (1941); M. B. Olcott, *The Kazakhs* (2d ed., 1995); and Edward C. Thaden, ed., *Russification in the Baltic Provinces and Finland* (1981). On the Jews in Russia Hans Rogger, *Jewish Policies and Right-Wing Politics in Imperial Russia* (1986) and Benjamin Nathans, *Beyond the Pale: the Jewish Encounter with Late Imperial Russia* (2002) offer some new perspectives. More recent work takes the perspective of empire: Robert Crews, *For Prophet and Tsar: Islam and Empire in Russia and Central Asia* (2006); Daniel R. Brower, *Turkestan and the Fate of the Russian Empire* (2003); Mark Bassin, *Imperial Visions: Nationalist Imagination and Geographical Expansion in the Russian Far East 1840–1865* (1999); and David Wolff, *To the Harbin Station: the Liberal Alternative in Russian Manchuria 1898–1914* (1999). Some historians combine foreign policy with the imperial perspective, such as David Schimmelpenninck, *Toward the Rising Sun: Russian Ideologies of Empire and the Path to War with Japan* (2001). The crux of Russian foreign policy in the nineteenth century was its involvement in the Balkans with the Ottoman Empire and the Slavs. See Barbara Jelavich, *Russia's Balkan Entanglements 1806–1914* (1991); and David Goldfrank, *The Origins of the Crimean War* (1994).

THE SOVIET ERA

For the Soviet era, the most accessible are probably the recent biographies of Soviet leaders. Robert Service's trilogy *Lenin* (2000), *Stalin* (2004), and *Trotsky* (2009) make a good beginning. William Taubman's *Khrushchev: the Man and his Era* (2003) covers his subject's early years in the Stalin era as well as his years of power. Ronald Suny's *The Soviet Experiment: Russia, the USSR, and the Successor States* (2d ed., 2011) is more comprehensive and provides extensive bibliography.

The 1920's and 1930's are the subject of many recent monographs. Some of the more useful are Jeremy Smith, *The Bolsheviks and the National Question 1917–1923* (1999); Lewis Siegelbaum, *Soviet State and Society between Revolutions 1918–1929* (1992); Moshe Lewin, *Russian Peasants and Soviet Power: a Study of Collectivization* (1968); Sheila Fitzpatrick, *Everyday Stalinism: Ordinary Life in Extraordinary Times – Soviet Russia in the 1930's*

(1999) and her *Stalin's Peasants: Resistance and Survival in the Russian Village after Collectivization* (1996); and Wendy Goldman, *Women, the State, and Revolution: Soviet Family Policy and Socialt Life 1917–1936* (1993); Terry Martin, *The Affirmative Action Empire: Nations and Nationalism in the Soviet Union 1923–1939* (2001); Oleg V. Khlevniuk, *Master of the House: Stalin and His Inner Circle*, trans. Nora Seligman Fvorov (2009).

DOCUMENTARY COLLECTIONS

The Soviet Union was not just another dictatorship. It also was an attempt to remake the whole of society, and even the best historians often have difficulty conveying a sense of what life was about in those years. Since 1991 Russian historians have produced a vast and continuing flood of documents from that era, many of which have been translated into English. A dip into the volumes of the Yale University Press series, Annals of Communism, will reward the general reader. The most useful are: J. Arch Getty and Oleg Naumov, eds., *The Road to Terror: Stalin and the Self-Destruction of the Bolsheviks 1932–1939* (1999); *History of the Gulag: from Collectivization to the Great Terror*, Oleg V. Khlevniuk et al. ed., trans. Vadim A. Staklo (2004); *The Stalin-Kaganovich Correspondence 1931–1936*, ed., R.W. Davies et al., trans. Steven Shabad (2003); *Stalin's Letters to Molotov 1925–1936*, eds. Lars T. Lih, Oleg V. Naumov, and Oleg V. Khlevniuk, trans. Catherine A. Fitzpatrick (1995); *War against the Peasantry 1927–1930*, ed. Lynne Viola et al., trans., Steven Shabad (2005).

THE WAR

The Soviet war against Nazi Germany has given rise to a gigantic and ever-expanding literature, complicated by new understanding of both sides. The best overall history is that of Evan Mawdsley, *Thunder in the East: the Nazi-Soviet War, 1941–1945* (2005). A portrait of Moscow in the terrible days of 1941 is Rodric Braithwaite, *Moscow 1941: a City and its People at War* (2006). For those with greater interest in detailed military history the many works of David Glantz, such as *When Titans Clashed: How the Red Army Stopped Hitler* (1995) will be satisfying. For understanding the

German side of the war the turning point was the appropriately titled work of General Klaus Reinhardt, *Moscow – the Turning Point: the Failure of Hitler's Strategy in the Winter of 1941–42*, translated by Karl B. Keenan (1992, German original 1972). Reinhardt was the first to point out that the casualties and material losses of the Wehrmacht were so great by the end of 1941 that the German effort was essentially doomed. Greater background on this issue is provided by Adam Tooze, *The Wages of Destruction: the Making and Remaking of the Nazi Economy* (2006). On German extermination and exploitation policies see Geoffrey P. Megargee, *War of Annihilation: Combat and Genocide on the Eastern Front, 1941* (2006). The vast literature on the Holocaust also provides insight into German policies in the occupied territories of the Soviet Union.

THE COLD WAR AND THE END OF THE USSR

Stalin's last years are only now beginning to be studied. Fundamental is Yoram Gorlitzki and Oleg V. Khlevniuk, *The Cold Peace: Stalin and the Soviet Ruling Circle 1945–1953* (2004). For the Cold War itself, David Holloway, *Stalin and the Bomb: the Soviet Union and Atomic Energy 1939–56* (1994), makes compelling reading. Aleksandr Fursenko and Timothy Naftali recount the Soviet side of the Cold War in *Khrushchev's Cold War* (2006), with many revelations, especially for those who lived through it. William Taubman's *Khrushchev: the Man and His Era* (2003) is fundamental. For the last years of the Soviet Union and post-Soviet Russia reliable studies are hard to find. A fascinating introduction to life in the provinces, popular culture, and the origins of the post-1991 oligarchy is provided by Sergei I. Zhuk, *Rock and Roll in the Rocket City: the West, Identity and Ideology in Dniepropetrovsk, 1960–1995* (2010). The best all around account remains Steven Kotkin, *Armageddon Averted: the Soviet Collapse 1970–2000* (2d. ed. 2008). On the origins of the post-Cold War order new perspectives are in Mary Elise Sarotte, *1989: the Struggle to Create Post-Cold War Europe* (2009). Typical Western views of Russian leaders are provided in Archie Brown, *The Gorbachev Factor* (1996); Timothy J. Colton, *Yeltsin: a Life* (2008); and Richard Sakwa, *Putin: Russia's Choice* (2d ed. 2008).

CULTURE

An excellent introduction to a major component in Russian culture is William Brumfield, *History of Russian Architecture* (1993). For music, Richard Taruskin's studies of Mussorgsky and Stravinsky are fundamental but daunting for the non-musician. For other composers see Roland John Wiley, *Tchaikovsky* (2009); Stephen Walsh, *Stravinsky: a Creative Spring, Russia and France 1882–1934* (1999); Harlow Robinson, *Prokofiev* (2002); and Laurel E. Fay, *Shostakovich: a Life* (2000). Russian art has only recently come to the attention of English speaking scholars. Pioneers are Camilla Gray, *The Russian Experiment in Art 1863–1922* (1986) and Elizabeth Valkenier, *Russian Realist Art: the State and Society: the Peredvizhniki and their Tradition* (1989) as well her *Ilya Repin and the World of Russian Art* (1990) and *Valentin Serov: Portraits of Russia's Silver Age* (2001). Another source is David Jackson, The *Russian Vision: the Art of Ilya Repin* (2006). For the emergence of modernism see John Bowlt, *Moscow and Saint Petersburg 1900–1920: Art Life and Culture of the Russian Silver Age* (2008). On Sergei Diaghilev and the Ballets Russes see Sjeng Scheijen, *Diaghilev: a Life* (2010). The best introduction to Russian literature is to read it. Otherwise see Joseph Frank, *Dostoyevsky* (2010), and Ernest J. Simmons, *Leo Tolstoy* (1946).

On the culture of the Soviet era a good place to start is Richard Stites, *Revolutionary Dreams: Utopian Vision and Experimental Life in the Russian Revolution* (1989) and *Russian Popular Culture: Entertainment and Society Since 1900* (1992). The best attempt to understand Socialist Realism is Katerina Clark, *The Soviet Novel: History as Ritual* (2000), and for visual arts there is Matthew Cullerne Bown, *Socialist Realist Painting* (1998). Film was one of the USSR's main cultural efforts. The classic study remains Jay Leyda, *Kino: a History of the Russian and Soviet Film* (last edition 1983). For Eisenstein see David Bordwell, *The Cinema of Eisenstein*, 2nd ed. (2005). Much of the drama of the history of Soviet culture is found in *Soviet Culture and Power: a History in Documents: 1917–1953* (2007) edited by Katerina Clark and Evgeny Dobrenko with Andrei Atizov and Oleg Naumov. On Soviet physics see Paul R Josephson, *Physics and Politics in*

Revolutionary Russia (1991); Alexei B. Kojevnikov, *Stalin's Great Science: the Times and Adventures of Soviet Physicists* (2004); and for biology and the Lysenko affair David Joravsky, *The Lysenko Affair* (1970) and Nils Roll-Hansen, *The Lysenko Effect: the Politics of Science* (2005). The connection of science and technology is treated in Paul R Josephson, *Red Atom: Russia's Nuclear Power Program from Stalin to Today* (2000).

INDEX

Page numbers in *italics* refer to illustrations.

Abkhazia, 328, 451
Adams, John Quincy, 147
Adashev, Aleksei, 50, 51
Adenauer, Konrad, 439
Adzhubei, Aleksei, 406
Afghanistan, 266–67
Soviet war in, 412, 446, 449
Akhmatova, Anna, 340, 345, 414,
421–23
Aksakov, Ivan, 202
Aksakov, Konstantin, 162, 164
Alaska, 153, 252
Albania, 402, 441
Alekseev, Mikhail, 306, 308
Alekseev, Nikolai, 231
Aleksei, Saint, Metropolitan of Kiev,
29, 31, 35
Aleksei I, Tsar, 64–74, 108
Aleksei Alekseevich, Tsarevich (son
of Aleksei I), 71, 73
Aleksei Petrovich, Tsarevich (son
of Peter the Great), 79, 82,
90–92
Alembert, Jean d', 125
Alexander I, Tsar, 130, 141–54, 160,
173, 176, 232, 254, 256–57
Alexander II, Tsar, 174, 176, 187–96,
190, 203, 205–6, 257, 259,
272–73

Alexander III, Tsar, 206–7, 234,
238–39, 242–43, 259–60, 272–77
Alexander Nevsky, Saint, Grand Prince
of Vladimir and Novgorod, 22, 27,
31, 95, 418–19
Alexandra, Tsaritsa (wife of Nicholas
I), 176
Alexandra, Tsaritsa (wife of Nicholas
II), 278–79, 290, 297
Alexei, Tsarevich (son of Nicholas II)
279, 290
Algirdas, Grand Prince of Lithuania, 28
Allende, Salvador, 444
All-Russian Peasant Union, 287–88
All-Union Institute of Plant-Breeding,
348
Amvrosii, elder, 161
Anastasiia, Tsaritsa (wife of Ivan the
Terrible), 48, 51, 53, 55
Andrei Bogoliubsky, Grand Prince of
Vladimir and Kiev, 12
Andropov, Yurii, 411–12
Anna, Empress, 99–102, 104
Anna, Duchess of
Brunswick-Bevern-Lüneburg, 102
Anna Petrovna, Duchess of
Holstein-Gottorp, 113
Anthès, Georges-Charles d', 178–79
Anti-Comintern Pact (1936–37), 374

Antonii, Saint, 8, 16
Apraksin, Fyodor and Petr, 75, 87
Arakcheev, A.A., 151, 153–54
Araya, Francesco, 104–5, 126
Argunov, Ivan, 131
Aristotle, 5, 10, 72, 296
Armenia, 167, 449, 458
Armenian Church, 16, 168, 265
Armenian Revolutionary Federation
    (Dashnaktsutiun), 265
Armenians, 62, 167–68, 223, 263, 265,
    282, 284, 316, 330, 366
arms race, 409, 429–31, 437–39, 443,
    445
Asaf'ev, Boris, 418
Assembly of the Land, 55, 58, 64
Astrakhan', 37–38, 49, 66
Atatürk, Mustafa Kemal, 316
Atkinson, John Augustus, 124, 144,
    158
Augustus of Saxony, King of Poland,
    83–84
Austerlitz, Battle of, 146, 148
Austria (Austria-Hungary), 77, 81–82,
    91, 104, 113, 114, 118, 137, 171,
    250–51, 262, 274, 286
    Napoleonic wars and, 140–41, 146,
    149–52
    partitions of Poland and, 121, 135
    WW I and, 291–94, 297, 306
    WW II and, 374, 391
Averbakh, Leopold, 414–15, 420
Avvakum, Archpriest, 68–70
Azef, Evno, 281
Azerbaidzhan, 21, 167, 449
Azeris, 167, 223, 263, 265–66, 284,
    288, 316, 327–28
Azov, 80–81, 83–84, 102

Babel, Isaak, 345, 420
Baku, 220, 222–23, 265–66, 284, 316,
    327–29, 386
Bakunin, Michael, 162–64, 183, 203
Balakirev, Milii, 232–34, 337
Balanchine, George, 236, 342
Balkans, 5, 46, 152, 274–75, 291–94,
    377, 389
Balkan Wars (pre-1914), 121, 133,
    169, 239, 249–51

Ballets Russes, 334, 339, 342
Baltic provinces (republics), 1, 83, 85,
    87, 93, 111, 120, 139, 254–56,
    271, 274, 284, 302, 306, 312, 315,
    375–76
    collapse of USSR and, 450–52
    defined, 254n
    emancipation of serfs in, 150, 166,
    188, 254
Barclay de Tolly, Michael, 147–48
Bariatinskii, Prince Alexander, 264
Bashkirs, 62, 67, 111, 123–24, 124,
    263, 288, 327
Batu, Mongol ruler, 20–21
Bayle, Henri, 114
Beccaria, Cesare, 119
Beiliss, Mendel, 290
Bekbulatovich, Semen, 52
Belarus (Belorussia), 28, 29, 121, 135,
    253, 289, 306, 315, 326–27, 379,
    383, 391, 452
Beliaev, Mitrofan, 336–37
Belinski, Vissarion, 162–63, 175,
    181–83
Belov, Vasilii, 426
Belyi, Andrey, 340, 346
Benckendorf, Alexander von, 156, 160,
    172, 178, 252
Beneš, Edvard, 433
Benois, Alexander, 338
Beria, Lavrentii, 363, 366, 394, 397,
    399, 401, 430
Berlin, 392, 434, 437, 439–40
    Wall, 440, 442, 450
Berlin, Treaty of (1878), 251
Berlioz, Hector, 174, 233, 337
Bessarabia, 146, 148
Bestuzhev-Riumin, Aleksei, 103,
    114–15
Bielfeld, Baron J.F. von, 119
birch bark letters, 25–26, 25
Birger, Earl of Sweden, 27
Biron, Ernst-Johann, 101–2
Bismarck, Otto von, 201, 250–51,
    274
Black Hundreds, 285, 289
Blok, Alexander, 336, 341,
    346
Bobrikov, N.I., 258

Bolsheviks, xviii, 280, 285, 288, 291, 294–97, 299–315, 321, 326, 330–31, 335, 340–45, 348–50, 360–61. *See also* Communist Party
Bolshoi Theater, 417, 457
Bolyai, Janos, 185
Boris, Saint, 11, 16, 31
Borodin, Alexander, 232, 234
Borodino, Battle of, 148
Borovikovskii, Vladimir, 131
Bortnyanskii, Dmitrii, 130
Bosnia, 250–51, 292
Botkin, V.P., 164
Brahe, Tycho, 72
Brandt, Willy, 444
Brest-Litovsk, Treaty of, 305–6, 316
Brezhnev, Leonid, 401–2, 406–10, 412, 425–26, 443–44, 446
Briullov, Karl, 173
Brodsky, Joseph, 425
Brusilov, Aleksei, 297, 301
Budennyi, Semen, 313–14
Bukhara, 251, 266, 269, 329
Bukharin, Nikolai, 306, 310–11, 321, 323–24, 352, 357, 360, 416
Bulgakov, Mikhail, 345–46, 414–15, 420, 425
Bulganin, Nikolai, 394, 398, 401
Bulgaria, 121, 250–51, 274–75, 293, 373, 389, 391, 432
Bulgarin, Faddei, 159, 181
Bunin, Ivan, 342
Bürger, Gottfried, 175
Byzantine Christianity, 8–10, 13–16, 18, 26
Byzantine Empire, 4–9, 35–36

Cadet Corps, 104–5, 107, 125–26
Campbell, Thomas, 175
Caresano, Aloisio da, 43
Casimir the Great, King of Poland, 28
Castro, Fidel, 443
Catherine I, Empress, 80, 88–92, 99
Catherine II, the Great, Empress, 89, 113–37, 127, 143, 148, 152, 194
Catherine, Duchess of Mecklenberg, 102

Caucasian Wars, 177, 263–65
Caucasus, 6, 49, 249, 284, 302, 316, 327–28, 386, 459
Central Asia, 20–21, 249, 251, 263, 266–69, 316, 327, 329, 367, 385, 450, 452, 455
Central Committee of the Communist Party, 310, 325, 327–28, 358–60, 397, 401–2, 406–7, 416
Central Executive Committee of the Soviets, 311
Chagall, Marc, 340
Chamberlain, Neville, 374–75
Chancellor, Richard, 42
Charles XII, King of Sweden, 84–87
Charter of the Nobility, 132–33, 139
Charter of the Townspeople, 132–33
Chateaubriand, François-René de, 152
Chechens (Chechnia), 49, 168, 264, 302, 453–56
Cheka (*later* GPU), 304–5, 308, 312, 315, 319–20
Chekhov, Anton, 336
Cherkasskii, Prince Mikhail, 76
Chernenko, Konstantin, 412, 447
Cherniaev, Mikhail, 266
Chernobyl disaster, 408, 448
Chernyshevsky, Nikolai, 197–99, 201, 226, 241
Cherubini, Luigi, 174
Chesme, Battle of, 121
Chiang Kai-shek, 332, 434–35
Chicherin, Boris, 199–200
China, 2, 19–20, 61, 82, 270, 276–77, 332
  Communist, xviii, 400, 402, 434–36, 440–43, 445–46
Chubais, Anatolii, 455
Churchill, Winston, xviii, 387–89
Church Slavic, 8, 26, 68, 106
Chuvash, 49, 67, 111
Circassians, 49, 62, 67, 168, 264, 302
Civil War (1918–20), 304–10, 312–14, 319, 326–28, 341–44
Clinton, Bill, 454
Cold War, xvi, xvii, 412, 429–46
collective farms (kolhoz), 324, 351–57, 361, 369, 383, 396, 398–99, 403, 409–10

Commission for the Study of Natural Productive Forces, 347
"communes" of 1930s, 355
Communist International (Comintern), 311, 320, 331–33, 372–74, 389–90, 440
Communist Party. *See also* Bolsheviks; Central Committee of the Communist Party; Politburo
  centralization of, 317, 319–25, 328
  Gorbachev reforms and, 450
  terror of 1936–38, 358–60
Communist Party Congresses
  of 1922, 321
  of 1952, 396
  of 1956 (Twentieth), 399, 438
Congress of People's Deputies, 450, 453–54
Congress of Soviets, 302–4
Congress of Soviet Writers, 415–16
Constant, Benjamin, 152
Constantine XI, Emperor of Rome, 35
Constantinople, 6–9, 35–36, 38, 140
Constituent Assembly, 299, 303–4, 306, 308
constitutional monarchy, 144–45, 150, 152–54, 163–64, 187, 199–200, 257
  Nicholas II and, 285–92
copper revolt, 66
Cossacks, 55–61, 65–68, 74, 86, 110–11, 149
  Civil War and, 306, 308–9, 312–13, 327
  revolts of, 56–60, 66–67, 65–66, 123–25
  Revolution of 1905 and, 284
Council of Ministers, 394
Council of People's Commissars, 363, 364
Council of State, 138, 144, 191, 208, 286, 289
Councils of the National Economy, 400
Crimea, 6, 21, 34, 37–38, 48, 67, 73, 77–78, 121–22, 133, 288, 314–15, 400
Crimean War, 168, 170–71, 184, 186–89, 196, 212–14, 244, 249–50, 253, 257, 261–64

Crusaders, 26–27
Cuban missile crisis, 402, 407, 443
Cui, Cesar, 232–34
Czartoryski, Prince Adam, 143
Czechoslovak Corps, 306–7
Czechoslovakia, 432–33, 373–75, 388
  Prague Spring of 1968, 443

Dagestan, 168, 264, 327
Daniil, Prince of Moscow, 22
Darwin, Charles, 199, 230
Dashkova, Princess Elizabeth, 115, 116, 129
Decembrist revolt, 152–56, 165–66, 176–78
Deng Xiaoping, 445
Denikin, Anton, 308–9, 312–14
Denmark, 4, 39
  war of 1700 and, 83
  war of 1762 and, 115
Depression, 332, 372
Derviz, P.G. von, 214
Derzhavin, Gavriil, 129–30
de-Stalinization, 401, 424, 441
détente, 445
Diaghilev, Sergei, 337–39, 342
Diderot, Denis, 125
Dimitrov, Georgii, 364, 373
dissidents, Soviet, 411–12, 426, 428, 445, 449
Dmitrii, Tsarevich (son of Ivan the Terrible), 53–54. *See also* False Dmitrii
Dmitrii Donskoi, Grand Prince of Moscow and Vladimir, 23, 31
Dokuchaev, Vasilii, 229
Dolgorukii, Prince Iakov, 74, 77, 87
Dolgorukii, Prince Vasilii, 87, 91–92, 99
Donbass (Don River basin), 213, 219, 222, 271, 312, 330, 357, 363, 366
Don Cossacks, 304, 308–9
Dostoyevsky, Fyodor, 165–66, 182, 201, 230, 240–43, 290, 424
Dubelt, General, 160
Dudaev, Dzhokhar, 454
dumas. *See also* Russian Duma
  boyar, 40, 53, 55, 60, 83, 176
  city, 274

Dutch East India Company, 42
Dzerzhinskii, Felix, 305

Eastern Europe, 389–90, 398, 400,
    409, 431–34, 437, 441, 444
  collapse of Communism in, 450
Eastern Slavs, 1, 3, 7
East Slavic language, 1, 28
Editorial Committee, 189
Egypt, 140, 169–70, 441
Ehrenburg, Ilya, 423–24
Eisenhower, Dwight, 438, 442
Eisenstein, Sergei, 27, 51, 284, 344,
    385, 418–19, 421
Ekaterina, Tsaritsa (wife of Alexander
    II), 205
Ekaterina Pavlovna, Grand Duchess
    (sister of Alexander I), 145
elections
  of 1906–17 286–89
  of 1996, 455
  Gorbachev reforms and, 450
Elena Glinskaia, Grand Princess of
    Moscow (wife of Vasilii III), 47, 48
Elena Pavlovna, Grand Duchess, 161,
    174, 189, 231
Elizabeth, Empress, 89, 99, 102–6,
    113–15, 122, 126, 131, 302
Elizabeth I, Queen of England, 50
Elphinstone, John, 121
Emancipation Statute, 216, 233
Engelhardt, V.V., 174
English Bible Society, 150
English Muscovy Company, 42
Erevan, 167–68, 265
Estonia, 26–27, 51, 84, 150, 254–56,
    284, 314
Ethiopia, 444
Etholén, Arvid Adolf, 252
Evdokiia, Tsaritsa (wife of Peter the
    Great), 79, 82
Ezhov, Nikolai, 358–60, 363

Factory Inspectorate, 226
Falconet, Etienne-Maurice, 89, 131
False Dmitrii, first (Grishka Otrep'ev),
    55–58
False Dmitrii, second (thief of Tushino),
    57

Faulkner, William, 424
feminism, 198–99
Feodosii, Saint, 8, 16–17
Fichte, Johann G., 162
Fick, Heinrich, 90
Fighting Organization, 281
Filaret, Patriarch of Russia (Fyodor
    Romanov, father of Michael I), 55,
    58, 60
Filipp, Metropolitan of Moscow, 52
Finland, 1, 27, 39, 87
  annexation and autonomy of,
    144–46, 150, 153, 158, 166,
    251–52, 256–58, 271, 376
  Civil War and, 315, 376
  Winter War and, 376
  WW II and, 376–77, 384, 391
Finns, 26, 67, 360
Fioravanti, Aristotele, of Bologna, 43
First Cavalry Army, 313
five-year plans, 325, 351–53, 368–69,
    373
Florence, Council of (1439), 35, 36
Fonvizin, Denis, 129
Ford, Henry, 352
Fourier, Charles, 165
France, 4, 102, 118, 250, 274, 275,
    291, 332
  Crimean War and, 169–70
  culture of, 105, 107–8, 125, 152,
    176, 199
  Holy Alliance and, 151–53
  Indochina and, 435, 440
  July Revolution of 1830, 167, 178
  Napoleonic, 140–41, 143–50
  Revolution of 1789, xviii, 134–40,
    143
  Russian Revolution and, 299, 308,
    314
  Seven Years War and, 114–15
  WW I and, 293–94, 306
  WW II and, 372–75, 377, 388–91
Franco, Francisco, 373
Franco-Prussian War, 275
Franklin, Benjamin, 129
Franz Ferdinand, Archduke of Austria,
    292, 294
Frederick the Great, King of Prussia,
    104, 113, 115, 121

Free Association of Artists, 237
Free Economic Society, 125–26,
    229
Freemasons, 128, 135, 153
Free Music School, 237
French language, 107–8
Friedland, Battle of, 146
Fuchs, Klaus, 430
Furtseva, Elena, 401–2
Furuhjelm, Hampus, 252
Fyodor Ivanovich, Tsar, 53–55
Fyodor Alekseevich, Tsar, 72–76

Gagarin, Iurii, 405
Galich, 12, 14, 33
Galicia, 28
Galuppi, Baldassare, 126
Gamsakhurdia, Zviad, 451
Gapon, Georgii, 282–83
Garcia-Viardot, Pauline, 183
Gasprinskii, Ismail Bey, 267–68
Gauss, Christian, 185
Gazprom, 449
Gediminas, Grand Prince of Lithuania,
    27–28
Gendarmes, 151, 156–57
Geneva Conference (1955), 398, 438
Genghis Khan, 19–20
Georgia, 62, 223, 263, 265, 282, 284,
    288, 291, 316, 328, 330, 366,
    396
  annexation of, 146, 167
  collapse of USSR and, 450–52, 458
German Communists, 330–31, 372,
    433
German Crusaders, 26–27
Germans, Russian society and
  nobility, in Baltic provinces, 254–56,
    274, 284
  pre-1917, 72, 80, 208, 212, 252, 274
  terror of 1936–38 and, 360
German Social-Democrats, 296
German-Soviet pact (1939), 375, 389
Germany, 4, 13, 20, 38, 147, 162, 201,
    250, 274–75, 286, 320
  post-WW II, 389, 392, 430, 433–34
  Revolution of 1848, 167
  Russian Revolution and, 299–300,
    305–7, 309, 312, 316
  socialism and, 226, 330

Weimar, 331–32, 372
WW I and, 291–96
WW II and Nazi, 24, 369–70, 372,
    375–92
WW II invasion of USSR, 378–88
Germany, Democratic Republic of
    (East), 434, 437, 439–40
Germany, Federal Republic (West),
    434, 439–40, 444
Ginzburg, Baron Horace, 212, 260
Gleb, Saint, 11, 16, 31
Glinka, Mikhail, 174–75, 231
Godunov, Boris, Tsar, 53–56, 58–59,
    234
Godunov, Irina, Tsaritsa, 53, 54
Goethe, J.W. von, 152, 175, 181
Gogol, Nikolai, 2, 175, 180–84
Golden Horde, 20–24, 34–35, 37,
    48
  end of Russian dependency on,
    42–43
gold standard, 220, 279
Golitsyn, Prince Alexander, 150–51
Golitsyn, Prince Boris, 76–78, 99
Golitsyn, Prince V.V., 75, 76
Golovin, Fyodor, 81–82, 84, 87
Gomulka, Wladyslaw, 441
Gorbachev, Mikhail, 412, 428, 446–52
Gorchakov, Prince, 250, 267, 274
Gordon, Patrick, 80, 82
Gorky, Maxim, 335, 342–43, 364, 416
Gosplan (State Planning Committee),
    325, 365
Gottwald, Klement, 432
GPU (Main Political Administration),
    353–55
Great Britain (England), 42, 53, 81,
    107, 134, 152, 186–87, 274,
    291–93
  Central Asia and, 266–67, 291, 293
  Cold War and, 430, 440
  Crimean War and, 170–71, 257
  early USSR and, 331–32
  Napoleonic wars and, 140–41,
    145–46, 149–50
  Ottoman Turks and, 169–70,
    249–51
  Russian Revolution and, 299, 308,
    314–16
  Seven Years War and, 114–15

WW I and, 293, 294
WW II and, 371–78, 387–88
Great Horde, 34, 37, 42–43
Greece, 169, 389, 433–34
  antiquity, 5, 8
  revolt of 1821, 152, 169
Greeks, 8, 12, 17, 40, 62, 72–73, 133
Green Lamp society, 153, 176
Gregory, Johann, 72
Grimm, Baron Friedrich M., 125
Grozny, Battle for, 454, 456–57
GULAG (Chief Administration of
  Camps), 362–63, 365, 396–98,
  400, 411
Gustavus III, King of Sweden, 133, 134

Hansa League, 13, 24, 27
Haskalah, 259
Heeckeren, Baron van, 179
Hegel, G.W.F., xvii, 162–64, 182, 199,
  296
Herzen, Alexander, 162–63, 183, 187,
  191–93, 197–98
Hitler, Adolf, 369–70, 372–75, 377–79,
  382–84, 386–88, 390, 392, 434
Ho Chi Minh, 332, 435
Holy Alliance, 151–52, 159
Holy League, 77
Holy Roman Empire, 9, 38, 48
Holy Synod, 92, 107, 150, 160, 243,
  273
Homer, 5
Hoover, Herbert, 319
Hoxha, Enver, 441
Hughes, John, 213
Hungary, 1, 20, 38, 167, 330, 389,
  391, 432
  Revolution of 1956, 400–401,
  441–42
Huxley, Aldous, 346

Iagoda, Genrikh, 360, 364
Iakovlev, Alexander, 412, 448
Iaroslav "The Wise," Grand Prince of
  Kiev Rus, 11, 17
Iavorskii, Metropolitan Stefan, 83,
  90–91
ICBMs, 409, 437, 443
icons, 18, 26, 31–33, 407
Igor, Prince of Kiev, 3

Ilarion, Metropolitan of Kiev, 12
Ilf, Ilya, 345
imperialism, 296, 331–32, 371
India, 92, 114, 169, 251, 266–68,
  440
Indonesia, 42
Ingrians, 27, 67
Ioakim, Patriarch of Moscow, 72
Ioffe, Abram, 216, 346–49, 419, 430
Iona of Riazan, Metropolitan of
  Moscow, 36
Iosif, Patriarch of Russia, 69
Iran (Persia), 20, 38, 92, 146, 167, 263,
  266–67, 329
  British Treaty on (1907), 291, 293
  war of 1826–28, 167–68
Iraq, 20
Irina, Tsarevna (aunt of Fyodor
  Alekseevich), 74–75
Isidoros, Metropolitan of Kiev, 35, 36
Islamic revolt (1898), 269
Islam (Muslims), 4–5, 21, 49, 67, 168,
  264–65, 267–69
  Elizabeth and, 111
  Russian Revolution and, 288, 302
  Soviet federalism and, 326–29, 367
Israel, 395, 411
  ancient, Russia as "new," 45
Italy, 4, 43–44, 96, 104, 151, 155, 173,
  175, 250
  Napoleonic wars and, 140, 147
  post-WW II, 434–44
  WW II and, 374, 388
Itinerant Association of Russian Artists,
  238–40, 337
Iudenich, General Nikolai, 314
Iurii Danilovich, Prince of Moscow, 22
Iurii (uncle of Vasilii II), 33
Ivan III, Grand Prince of Moscow,
  36–45
Ivan IV, the Terrible, Grand Prince of
  Moscow, 42, 46–53, 84, 234, 239
Ivan V, Tsar (co-ruler with Peter the
  Great), 73–76
Ivan VI, Tsar, 102–3, 122
Ivan Ivanovich (heir of Ivan the
  Terrible), 52
Ivan "Kalita," The Moneybag, Prince
  of Vladimir, 22–23
Ivanov, Alexander, 173, 238

Iziaslav I, Prince of Kiev, 17

jadidism, 268
Jadwiga, "King" of Poland, 28–29
Jan III Sobieski, King of Poland, 77
Japan, 275–77, 308, 313–14, 316, 332,
    430, 434–35
    war of 1904–5, 220, 269–70, 272,
    283–84
    WW II and, 374–75, 388–89
Jesuits, 68, 72, 82
Jewish Anti-Fascist Committee, 395
Jewish Pale of Settlement, 214, 258–59,
    261, 274
Jewish Workers' League (Bund), 260
Jews, 121, 212–15, 222, 243, 251, 253,
    258–61, 269, 271, 274, 278, 280
    emigration of Soviet, 411–12, 445,
    453
    pogroms and, 206, 251, 259–60,
    285, 290, 312–13
    Russian Revolution and, 282, 283,
    315
    Soviet, 326, 330, 346, 366, 395–96,
    423
    WW II and, 375, 377, 383, 393, 424
Jochi, 20
Jogailo, King of Poland, 28–29
Jones, John Paul, 134
Joseph II, Emperor of Austria, 133, 137
Joseph of Volokolamsk, Saint, 45–46
Judaism, 5, 7, 16
Judaizers, 45
judicial system, 63–64, 132
    reform of 1864, 193–95
Justinian, Emperor of Rome, 7, 17

Kadar, Janos, 441
Kadets (Constitutional Democrats),
    286–88, 297–98, 304, 349
Kadyrov, Ahmad, 456
Kaganovich, Lazar, 359, 363, 364, 366,
    394, 399–400, 402
Kaledin, Alexei, 304
Kalinin, Mikhail, 310–11
Kamenev, Lev, 303, 307, 310–11,
    321–23, 358
Kandinsky, Wassily, 335, 339
Kankrin, Georg, 252

Kant, Immanuel, 152, 162
Kapitsa, Piotr, 419–20
Karakozov, Dmitrii, 203
Karamzin, Nikolai, 142, 145, 175–76
Karl VI, Holy Roman Emperor, 90,
    91
Kasso, Lev, 347
Katkov, Mikhail N., 162, 164, 201,
    242, 245
Katyn massacre, 375
Kaufman, Konstantin von, 267
Kaunas massacre, 383
Kaunitz, Count Wenzel Anton, 114
Kazakhs, 222, 249, 329, 408
Kazakhstan, 2, 21, 266, 269, 329, 367,
    404, 458
Kazan', 34, 37–38, 43, 48, 49, 124
Kazan' University, 142
Kennedy, John F., 440
Kerenskii, Aleksandr, 298–99, 301–3
KGB, 411–12, 425, 456
Khalkhin Gol, Battle of, 375
Khalturin, Stepan, 205
Khar'kov, 261–62, 386
Khar'kov Technological Institute, 216
Khar'kov University, 142, 260, 262
Khasbulatov, Ruslan, 454
Khazars, 5, 6
Khitrovo, Bodgan, 74
Khiva, 251, 266, 269, 329
Khmel'nyts'kyi, Bohdan, Hetman of the
    Ukraine, 65–66, 261
Khovanskii, Prince Ivan, 76
Khrushchev, Nikita, 363, 366, 394,
    397–407, 424–25, 438–44
    "secret speech" on Stalin, 399, 424,
    442
Khwarezm, 20, 21
Kiev, 60, 68, 73, 221, 262, 302, 304,
    306, 315, 379, 390–91
Kiev Academy, 68–69
Kiev Archeographical Society, 262
Kiev Polytechnical Institute, 216, 347
Kiev Rada, 304
Kiev Rus (principality), *xix*, 1–22,
    28–29, 135
    Mongol invasion, 18, 20–23
Kim Il Sung, 435–36
Kipchaks (Polovtsy), 5–6, 15, 18, 20–21

Kiprian, Metropolitan of Kiev, 35
Kirghiz, 268, 329
Kirill of Belozero, Saint, 30, 31
Kirov, Sergei, 358, 363
Kishinev pogrom, 260
Kissinger, Henry, 445
Knights of Malta, 140
Kochubei, Viktor, 252
Kokand khanate, 251, 266
Kolchak, Alexander, 308–9, 312, 314, 327
kolhoz. *See* collective farms
Komsomol (Communist League of Youth), 400, 404, 448–50, 454
Konstantin Nikolaevich, Grand Duke (brother of Alexander II), 188–91, 19, 214
Konstantin Pavlovich, Grand Duke (brother of Alexander I), 154
Korean War, 435–36
Kornilov, Lavr, 301–2, 308
Korolev, Sergei, 421
Korsun, Battle of, 391
Kosciuszko, Tadeusz, 135, 139
Kostomarov, Nikolai, 262
Kosygin, Aleksei, 407
Kramskoi, Ivan, 237–38
Kravchuk, Leonid, 450
Krestinskii, Nikolai, 310–11
Kronstadt, 88, 170
   revolt, 318
Krüdener, Baroness Julie von, 150
Krzhizhanovskii, Gleb, 325
Kuchuk Kainardzha, Treaty of (1774), 121
Kuibyshev, Valerian, 363
kulaks, 218, 354–55, 362
Kulikovo, Battle of, 23
Kurbskii, Prince Andrei, 51
Kurchatov, Igor, 430, 438
Kursk, Battle of, 390
Kussevitskii, Sergei, 339
Kutuzov, Mikhail, 146, 148–49, 245

labor movement, 226, 282–83, 288, 294
LaHarpe, Frederic, 143
Land and Freedom, 204
Landau, Lev, 420

Latin language, 68–69, 71, 82
Latvia, 26–27, 150, 254–56, 284, 288, 330, 360
LeFort, Francois, 80, 81, 82
Leibniz, Gottfried, 107
Leipzig, Battle of, 149
Lend-Lease, 388
Lenin, Vladimir Il'ich Ul'ianov, 227, 291, 341, 364, 371, 448–49
   "April Theses," 300
   background of, 279–80
   culture and, 341, 343–44
   Civil War and early Soviet state, 307–12, 307, 314, 321, 321–22, 325–26, 328
   death of, 321
   foreign policy and, 330–32
   NEP and, 316–19
   Revolution of 1905 and, 285
   Revolution of 1917 and, 299–303
   WW I and, 295–96, 306
Leningrad. *See* St. Petersburg
Leningrad Affair, 395–96
Lermontov, Mikhail, 175, 179–82
Lesnaia, Battle of, 86
Levitan, Isaak, 239
Levitskii, Dmitrii, 131
Liebknecht, Karl, 296
Lithuania, 19, 23, 26–29, 33, 38–39, 42, 253, 254n, 451
   partition of Poland and, 135
   WW II and, 375, 379, 383
Litvinov, Maxim, 366, 372–73, 375
Livonia, 93, 254
   war of 1558–80, 50–54
Livonian Order, 27–28, 39, 50
Lobachevskii, Nikolai, 185, 228
Lomonosov, Mikhail, 106–7
Lönnrot, Elias, 256–57
Loris-Melikov, Count Michael, 205–6
Louis XVI, King of France, 135
Lunacharskii, Anatolii, 343
Lutheran church, 92–93, 256
Luxemburg, Rosa, 296
Lvov, Prince Georgii, 298–99, 301
Lysenko, Trofim, 406, 407, 415, 419–20, 422, 424–25

MacArthur, Douglas, 436

Mach, Ernst, 291
Machine-Tractor Stations, 356, 403
Maistre, Joseph de, 152
Makarii, elder, 161
Makarii, Metropolitan of Moscow, 48, 51
Makhno, Nestor, 313, 315
Maksim the Greek, 46–47
Malenkov, Georgii, 359, 363, 394, 396–98, 400, 438
Malevich, Kazimir, 335, 339–40
Mamai, Emir, 23
Mamontov, Savva, 337
Manchuria, 220, 269–70, 272, 276, 284
Mandelstam, Osip, 420
Mannerheim, Baron Gustav, 315, 391
Mao Tse-tung, 400, 402, 434–35, 441–42, 445
Marfa (regent and mother of Michael I), 58
Marfa Apraksina, Tsaritsa (wife of Fyodor III), 75
Mariia, Tsaritsa (second wife of Ivan the Terrible), 51
Mariia, Tsaritsa (wife of Aleksei I), 64, 73
Mariia Fedorovna, Empress (wife of Alexander III, mother of Nicholas II), 272, 282, 284
Mariia Nagaia, Tsaritsa (fourth wife of Ivan the Terrible), 53
Marshall Plan, 434
Martov, Iulii, 227, 280
Marx, Karl, 200, 226–27, 296
Marxism, xvii, 226–27, 260, 265, 279–80, 291, 296, 309, 340–41, 348–49, 361, 421
Matveev, Artamon, 72–77
Maximos, Metropolitan of Kiev, 23
Mayakovskii, Vladimir, 340–41, 343, 346
Mazepa, Ivan, Hetman of Ukraine, 77, 86, 93
Meck, K.F. von, 214
Mehmed the Conqueror, 36, 38
Mendeleev, Dmitrii, 216, 228–29
Mengistu Haile Mariam, 444

Mensheviks, 280, 285, 288, 291, 294–95, 299, 301, 303–4, 310, 321, 325, 353, 358–60
Menshikov, Alexander, 82, 84, 87–91, 99, 116
Merezhkovskii, Dmitrii, 336, 340
Meshcherskii, Prince V.P., 242–43, 273
Metternich, Klemens von, 151–52
Meyerhold, Vsevolod, 343–44, 346, 420
Michael, Saint, Prince of Tver, 22, 31
Michael I, Tsar, 58, 60–61, 64, 65, 68
Mikhail Pavlovich, Grand Duke (brother of Nicholas I), 161, 174
Mikhoels, Solomon, 395
Mikoyan, Anastas, 363, 366, 394, 401
Miliukov, Pavel, 297–99
Miliutin, Dmitrii, 189, 196
Miliutin, Nikolai, 189
Miloslavskii, Ilya, 64, 73–74
Minin, Kuzma, 58
Mirovich, Vasilii, 103, 122–23
Mniszech, Jerzy, 55
Mniszech, Marina, 55, 57–58
Mohammed Ali, Khedive of Egypt, 169–70
Molotov, Viacheslav, 358–59, 361, 363–64, 364, 366, 375, 382, 391, 394, 398–402, 434, 438–39
monasteries, 8, 10, 29–33, 41, 46, 161
    lands secularized, 161
    Peter the Great and, 83, 95, 96
    serfs and, 108, 109
Monastery of the Caves (Kiev), 8, 12, 16, 29
Monastery of the Dormition of the Mother of God (Kirillo-Belozerskii), 30
Monastery of the Miracle of Saint Michael the Archangel, 46
Monastery of the New Jerusalem, 69–70
Mongol invasion, 18–20. See also Golden Horde
Mongolia, 2, 375
Moniuszko, Stanislaw, 233
Mons, Anna, 80, 89

Montesquieu, Charles-Louis de, 114,
117, 119, 136, 152
Morozov, Boris, 64, 73
Morozov, Savva, 336
Morozov, Timofei, 213
Morozova, Feodosia, 239
Moscow Art Theater, 336, 343, 415,
420
Moscow (city), 158–59, 212–14, 216,
219, 221, 231–32, 237–38, 261,
271
culture and, 237, 339
early building and growth, 41–46,
44, 61–63
industrialization, 158–59, 212–14,
216, 219, 221, 231–32, 237–38
Kremlin, 22, 40–41, 160
Napoleon invades, 148–49
Polish occupation of, 57–58
Revolution of 1905 and, 285
Revolution of 1917 and, 299, 302
riots of 17th century, 64–66
Soviet capital moved to, 306, 312
Soviet centralization of government
in, 328, 330
textile strike of 1885, 213
WW II Battle for, 380–82, 386
Moscow Conservatory, 231–32,
235–36
Moscow Institute of Problems of
Physics, 419
Moscow (principality), 22–23, 29–36
annexes Novgorod and becomes
Russia (1478), 37
Horde burns (1382), 23
Isodorios and, 35–36
monastic revival in, 29–33
Moscow show trials, 358–61
Moscow University, 105–7, 125–26,
128–29, 148, 162, 260, 347
Moscow Yiddish theater, 395
Mstislav, Grand Prince of Kiev Rus, 12
Mukden, Battle of, 284
Münnich, Count Burkhard, 101–2
Murav'ev, Nikita, 153
musketeers, 62, 78
revolts of, 60, 75–76, 82, 234, 239
Mussolini, Benito, 374, 378, 380, 388
Mussorgsky, Modest, 56, 177, 232–34,
236

Nagorno-Karabakh, 449
Nagy, Imre, 441
Napoleon Bonaparte, 140–42, 144–49,
152, 173, 245, 253
Napoleon III, Emperor of France, 170,
250
Narva, siege of, 84–85
Nasser, Gamal, 441
Natalia Naryshkina, Tsaritsa (wife of
Aleksei I), 74–76, 78–80
NATO, 439
Navoi, Alisher, 423
Nechaev, Sergei, 202–3, 242
Nerchinsk, Treaty of, 82
Nesselrode, Karl von, 160, 252
Nestor, Monk, 16–17
Netherlands (Dutch), 42, 53, 81, 96,
147
New Economic Policy (NEP), 317–20,
323–25, 329–30, 343–46, 349–50,
365
Nicholas I, Tsar, 154–76, 178–81, 184,
186–87, 201, 215, 228, 249, 252,
256, 259
Nicholas II, Tsar, 211, 258, 276–92,
278, 297–98, 308
constitutional government of
1907–14, 288–92
execution of, 308
Nicolai, Baron, 252
Nietzsche, Friedrich, 335
Nifont, Bishop of Novgorod, 15
Nightingale, Florence, 170
nihilists, 196–99
Nijinskii, Vatslav, 339
Nikon, Patriarch, 64, 66, 68–70,
73
Nil Sorskii, 46
Nixon, Richard, 445
Nizami of Gandzha, 423
Nizhnii Novgorod (Gorkii), 58, 109,
281, 412
NKVD (*formerly* GPU), 358–63, 365,
366, 385, 421
Nobel family, 212, 220, 265
Nogai Horde, 37, 38
North Caucasus, 168, 263–65, 288,
302, 327, 400, 454
Nöteborg (Schlüsselburg), siege of,
85

Novgorod, 1–4, 6, 12–13, 19, 21, 23–28, 33, 45, 52, 58
archeological excavations of, 24–26, 25
Moscow annexes, 37, 41–42
pagan revolt of 1071, 15
Novikov, Nikolai, 128–29, 135, 139
Novosil'tsev, Nikolai, 143, 150
nuclear industry, 397, 408–10, 425, 430
Nuclear Test Ban Treaty, 439
nuclear weapons, 421, 430–31, 436–39, 445
Nystad, Treaty of (1721), 95–96

October Manifesto, 285, 289
Octobrist party, 289
Odessa, 134, 157, 221, 259, 284, 314–15, 329
pogrom of 1905, 285
Odessa University, 260
Ogedei, Khan, 20
OGPU, 362, 413
oil and gas industry, 220, 222–23, 265, 316, 327–28, 386, 403, 405, 408–9, 454, 455
Okudzhava, Bulat, 426
Old Believers, 71–72, 111, 123, 156, 161, 212–13, 239
Oldenburgskii, Prince A.P., 347
Oleg, Grand Prince of Kiev, 3, 6, 15
Olga, Grand Princess of Kiev, 6
oligarchs, 449, 453–58
Oprichnina, 52–53
Order 00447, 359
Order no. 1, 299
Ordin-Nashchokin, Afanasii, 73
Ordzhonikidze, Sergo, 316, 328, 353, 357–58, 363, 366
Orenburg, seige of, 123–24
Orlov, Aleksei, 116, 121
Orlov, Grigorii, 115–16
Orlova, Liubov', 418
Orthodox Church, xvii, 7–10, 14–17, 21, 28, 60, 65, 107, 111, 118, 130, 151, 160–61, 230, 241, 243, 247, 338–39, 368, 406–7
adopted by Vladimir, 7–8

autocephaly, 45, 54
Council of 1666–67, 70–72
Council of Florence and, 35–36
Judaizers and, 45
lands secularized, 117, 126
monastic controversy of 16th century, 46–47
monastic revival of 14th century, 29–32
Nikon reforms of, and Old Believers, 64, 68–72
Ottoman Empire and, 169, 171
Peter the Great and, 83, 90, 92, 95–96
Slavophiles and, 164
schism of 1054 and, 9–10, 16
Orwell, George, 346
Ostermann, Count Andrei, 101–2
Ottoman Empire (Turks), 38, 39, 48, 73, 77, 263
Alexander I's war vs., 146, 148, 152
Anna's war vs., 102
Crimean War and, 170–71
Greek revolt of 1821 and, 152
Peter the Great's war vs., 80–83
war of 1769–74 and, 118–19, 121–22, 148
war of 1787–91 and, 133–34
war of 1827–29, 168–70
war of 1877–78, 249–51
WW I and, 291–93, 297

paganism, 6, 15, 16, 26, 28
Pahlen, Count Peter von der, 141
Pakistan, 446
Panin, Count Nikita, 115, 117, 123, 129
Panin, Count N.P. (nephew), 141
Paris, Peace of (1856), 171, 188, 250
Paskevich, Ivan, 252–53
Pasternak, Boris, 345–46, 414–15, 417, 420, 424–25, 428
Paul, Tsar, 114, 123, 128–29, 138–42, 145, 151–52, 254–55
Pavlov, Ivan, 347, 349
Pechenegs, 5–7, 12
Pereiaslav Treaty (1654), 66–68
Perestroika, 428, 448–51, 459

Perovskaia, Sofia, 206
Pestel', Pavel, 153, 155
Peter, Saint, Metropolitan of Kiev, 23,
  31
Peter I, the Great, Emperor, xvii, *xxi*,
  60, 74–100, 89, 106, 131, 164,
  199, 208, 239, 257, 336
  culture and state transformed by, 79,
  82–83, 92–99, 106
  death of, 99–100
  navy and, 80–81
  Orthodox church and, 90, 95–96
  personality and travels by, 77,
  79–82, 84–85, 88–90
  regency of Sofia and, 76–78
  son Aleksei attempts to overthrow,
  90–92
  St. Petersburg built by, 85, 87–88, 90
  war vs. Sweden and, 82–87
Peter II, Tsar, 99, 102
Peter III, Tsar, 113–16, 122–23, 138
Petipa, Marius, 236
Petliura, Semyon, 312, 314
Petrashevski, Mikhail, 165–66,
  241–42
Petrov, Yevgeni, 345
Photios, Metropolitan of Kiev, 35
Piatakov, Georgii, 358
Pirogov, Nikolai, 170
Plato, 5
Platon Levshin, Metropolitan of
  Moscow, 126
Plehve, Viacheslav, 279, 282
Plekhanov, Georgii, 226–27, 295
Pobedonostev, Konstantin, 242–43,
  272–73
Poland, 1, 28–29, 50, 73, 77, 117–18,
  158, 166, 213, 251–55, 258, 270,
  288
  Anna's war vs., 102
  constitution of 1791, 134–35, 153
  constitution of 1815, 166–67
  Napoleonic wars and, 147, 149–50
  partition of 1772, 121, 258
  partition of 1791, 134–35
  partition of 1794, 135
  Peter the Great and, 83–84
  post-WW II, 389, 400, 432, 441,
  444

revolt of 1768–72, 118, 121
revolt of 1787, 133–34
revolt of 1830 and, 167
revolt of 1863–64, 193, 201, 250,
  253–54
Revolution of 1905 and, 284, 288
Revolution of 1917 and, 314–15,
  326
serfdom and, 137, 152, 253
treaty of 1667, 66, 73
war of 1632 vs., 60
Warsaw riots of 1861, 193
WW I and, 297
WW II and, 372, 374–75, 377, 389,
  391–92
Poland, Kingdom of, 150, 253–54
Poland-Lithuania, 28–29, 38–39, 47,
  50–51, 57–58, 65–66
Poliakov, Samuel, 214–15
Poliane/Rus tribe, 6
Polish Home Army, 391
Polish National Democrats, 254, 288
Politburo (*later* Presidium), 310, 325,
  328, 359, 364–66, 423, 448
Polotskii, Simeon, 71–72
Poltava, Battle of, 86
Poniatowski, Stanislaw, King of
  Poland, 114, 118, 121, 133–35
Popov, Alexander, 423
Portsmouth Treaty (1905), 277, 284
Pospelov, P.N., 399, 400
Potemkin, Grigorii, 122–24, 130, 133,
  134, 211
Potemkin mutiny, 284
Pozharski, Prince Dmitrii, 58
Prague conference (1912), 291
Preobrazhenskii, Evgenii, 322
Presidium (*formerly* Politburo),
  397–98, 401, 402
Prezent, Isaak, 419–20
Primary Chronicle, 3–4, 8–9, 15, 29
Princip, Gavrilo, 292, 294
Prokofiev, Sergei, 27, 339, 341–42,
  346, 418, 422, 427
Prokopovich, Bishop Feofan, 90, 92
Proskurov massacre, 312
Protasov, Count N.A., 160–61
Protestantism, 69, 72, 118, 150, 151,
  164

provincial administration, 63–64
  Alexander II and, 193–94
  Alexander III and, 273–74
  Catherine II and, 126, 131–33
  Paul I and, 139
  Peter the Great and, 83, 87, 93–94,
    98
Provincial Assembly of Nobility, 132
Provisional Government, 298–303,
  308, 327
Prussia, 26–27, 113, 118, 121, 133,
  135, 137, 151, 152, 250, 274
  Crimean War and, 171
  Napoleonic Wars and, 146–47,
    149–50
  Seven Years War and, 104, 108,
    114–15
Puffendorf, Samuel, 94–95, 136
Pugachev, Emelian, 123–25, 130, 157,
  178
Pugacheva, Alla, 427
Pushkin, Alexander, 56, 106, 112, 165,
  175–82, 185, 234, 243, 367
Pushkina, Natalia, 178–79
Putin, Vladimir, 427, 456–58

Radek, Karl, 358, 416
Radishchev, Alexander, 135–36,
  139
Rakhmaninov, Sergei, 337, 339,
  342
Rall, Alexander, 174
Rasputin, Grigorii, 290, 297–98
Rastrelli, Bartolomeo, 104, 131
Razin, Stenka, 59–60, 66–67
Razumovskii, Aleksei, 103, 111
Razumovskii, Kirill, Hetman of
  Ukraine, 111
Red Army, 306–8, 310, 312–16, 327,
  372–82, 385, 387, 389–92
  Air Force, 377–79, 384
  purge of 1937–38, 359, 377
Red Guards, 301, 303–4, 306
Red Terror of 1918, 308
Repin, Ilya, 238–39
Reutern, Mikhail, 214
Rhee, Syngman, 436
Rhineland, 140, 150, 373
Ribbentrop, Joachim von, xvi,
  375

Rimskii-Korsakov, Nikolai, 232–34,
  236, 337, 339
Rokotov, Fyodor, 131
Roman Catholic Church, 7, 9–10,
  28–29, 69, 97, 72, 107, 111, 118,
  164
Romanov, Fyodor Nikitich. *See* Filaret
Romanov-Koshkin, Iurii, 48
Roosevelt, Franklin D., 388–89
Roosevelt, Theodore, 284
Rosen, Baron G.F., 174
Rostovtsev, Iakov, 189–90
Rousseau, Jean-Jacques, 136, 152
Rubinstein, Anton, 174, 231–33
Rubinstein, Nikolai, 231–32, 234,
  237
Rublev, Andrei, 32–33, 426
Ruffo, Marco, 43
Rumania, 21, 169, 171, 372, 377, 389,
  391, 402, 432, 441, 450
Rurik, ruler of Novgorod, 3–4
Rurikovichi dynasty, 3–4, 6–7, 13
Rus, origin of, xvi, 3–4. *See also* Kiev
  Rus
Rus Justice, 11–12
Russia
  idea of, xviii
  formation of state, with rise of
    Moscow, 22–25
  maps of, *xx–xxiii*
  post-Soviet (*see* Russian Federation)
  Soviet (*see* Union of Soviet Socialist
    Republics)
Russian Academy of Sciences, 94, 105,
  107, 125–26, 135, 347, 349,
  406–7, 416, 419
Russian Association of Proletarian
  Music, 414
Russian Association of Proletarian
  Writers (RAPP), 414
Russian Constitution
  (Fundamental Laws) of 1906,
    285–86
  of 1993, 456
Russian Duma
  1905–17, 211, 285–88, 290, 295,
    297–98, 327, 338
  post-Soviet, 454, 456, 458
Russian Federation (post-Soviet),
  xvi–xvii, 457–59

Russian language, 19, 35
  first dictionary, 129
  grammar codified, 106
Russian Ministry of Education, 142,
  150–51, 159–60, 172, 228, 230,
  260, 274
Russian Ministry of Finance, 208, 214,
  215, 220, 228, 229, 269, 276, 281
Russian Ministry of Foreign Affairs,
  176, 208, 267, 303
Russian Ministry of Internal Affairs,
  156
Russian Ministry of Justice, 144
Russian Ministry of the Court, 173,
  230, 236, 338
Russian Ministry of the Interior,
  188–89, 193–95, 205–6, 208, 279
  Special Department, 151, 176–77
Russian Ministry of the Navy, 188–89
Russian Ministry of War, 147, 151,
  189, 196, 266
Russian Navy, 80–81, 102, 121, 170,
  252, 284, 294
Russian Revolution of 1905, 221, 248,
  272, 283–88, 294, 338
Russian Revolution of 1917, xviii, 293,
  296, 298–304, 335, 341–42,
  346–47, 360–61
Russian Senate (Tsarist), 87, 90–91,
  101–3, 138, 144, 208
  Secret Department of, 136
Russification, 258, 270, 274
Russo-Japanese War (1904–5), 269–70,
  282–84, 293–94
Russo-Turkish War (1877–78), 215,
  243, 251
Rustaveli, Shota, 423
Rutherford, Ernest, 349
Rutskoi, Alexander, 454
Rykov, Aleksei, 324, 360
Ryleev, Kondratii, 153, 155

Sakharov, Andrei, 406–7, 411–12, 426,
  448–49
salt trade, 42, 64, 110
Saltykov, Sergei, 114
Samoilovych, Ivan, Hetman of the
  Ukraine, 77
Sand, Georges, 181–82
Sarai, 20–22

Savvatii, Saint, 30–31
Schelling, Friedrich, 162
Scott, Sir Walter, 175
Scythians, 2, 147
Sechenov, Ivan, 229–30
Secret Chancellery, 102
Semenov, Iulian, 427
Senkovskii, Osip, 178, 181
Seraphim of Sarov, Saint, 161
Serbia, 169, 250, 291, 293–94
serfs and serfdom, 67, 139–40, 145,
  152–53, 157, 159, 164, 166, 171,
  183–84, 253, 261–62
  Catherine II and, 117, 120–21,
    123–26, 136–37
  emancipation of, 188–93, 197
  emancipation of, in Baltic provinces,
    150, 254
  emancipation of, in Georgia, 167
  ended on church lands, 117
  established, 27, 54–56, 59, 61–62,
    108–12, 120
Sergii of Radonezh, Saint, 29–31, 46
Serov, Valentin, 337
Sevastopol, siege of, 170–71, 186,
  244
Seven Years War, 104, 114–15, 117
Shaliapin, Fyodor, 337, 342
Shamil, Imam, 168, 264
Shemiaka, Dmitrii, 33–34
Sherwood, John, 154
Shevchenko, Taras, 261–62, 367, 423
Shishkin, Ivan, 239
Sholokhov, Mikhail, 414, 420, 428
Shostakovich, Dmitrii, 343–44, 385,
  414, 416–18, 421–24, 427–28
Shuiskii, Prince Vasilii, 57
Shulalov, Alexander, 103
Shulalov, Peter, 103
Shuvalov, Count Ivan, 104–6
Shuvalov, Count Petr, 203
Siberia, 1, 37–38, 42, 53, 59, 70–71,
  110, 155–56, 216–18, 222, 249
  border of, 61
  Civil War and, 308, 312–14, 316
  railroad and, 276–77
  USSR and, 329, 365–66, 368, 394,
    408
  WW II and, 380, 385, 386
Sigismund, King of Poland, 57

Sikorsky, Igor, 221, 342
Silvestr, Priest, 50–51
Skobelev, Mikhail, 266
Skoropadskii, Ivan, 93
Skoropadskii, Pavel, 306
Skriabin, Alexander, 337
Slansky, Rudolf, 433
Slavophiles, 95, 162, 164, 181,
    200–202, 213, 241–42, 244, 255,
    272
Smolensk, 14, 28, 47, 58, 60, 66
Smol'nyi Institute, 126, 302–3
Sobchak, Anatolii, 456
Social Democratic Workers' Party, 227
Social Democrats, 282, 285, 288
"socialism in one country," 322–23
socialist realism, 335, 416
Socialists-Revolutionaries, Party of
    (SRs), 227, 280–83, 288, 294,
    299–304, 306–8, 310, 321, 325
Sofia, Tsarevna (regent, sister of Peter
    the Great and Ivan V), 76–79, 82
Solari, Pietro Antonio, 43
Solomoniia Saburova, Grand Princess
    of Moscow (wife of Vasilii III), 47
Solzhenitsyn, Alexander, 411–12,
    424–26
Sophia Paleologue, Grand Princess of
    Moscow (wife of Ivan III), 47
South Ossetia, 328, 451
South Western Railway, 275
Soviet Union. *See* Union of Soviet
    Socialist Republics
Soviet Ministry of Defense, 402
Soviet Ministry of Education, 347
Soviet Ministry of Finance, 346, 347
Soviet Ministry of Internal Affairs and
    State Security, 397
Soviet Ministry of Natural Gas
    Industry, 449
Soviet Ministry of State Security, 396
Soviet People's Army (1918–20), 306,
    308. *See also* Red Army
Soviet People's Commissariat of Food
    Supplies, 309
Soviet People's Commissariat of
    Health, 368
Soviet People's Commissariat of Heavy
    Industry, 357, 358

Soviet People's Commissariats, 305,
    325, 359
soviets, 285, 299–303
Spain, 4–5, 45, 147, 151, 155
    Civil War, 373–74, 377
special settlements, 354–55, 362, 375,
    396, 400
Spencer, Herbert, 199
Speranskii, Michael, 144–45, 155, 157
Sputnik, 437
Stael, Germaine de, 152
Stakhanov, Aleksei, 357
Stalin, Joseph, xvi, 291, 295, 364, 403,
    407, 415–16, 418, 420–23,
    429–36, 440
    Civil War and, 309–11, 314–15
    centralized power under, 363–66
    collectivization and industrialization
        and, 350–57, 367–69
    Comintern and, 331–33
    death of, 397–99
    Eastern Europe and, 432–34
    federalism and, 326, 328, 366–67
    Hitler and WW II and, 369–78,
        380–83, 386–92, 399
    Khrushchev's secret speech of on,
        399–400
    post-WW II repression by, 393–97
    purges and GULAG under, 353,
        358–65, 399–400
    Revolution of 1917 and, 300, 303
    struggle for control of Party and,
        321–26
Stalingrad, Battle of (1942–43),
    386–87, 390
Stanislavsky, Konstantin, 336, 343
Stankevich, Nikolai, 162–65, 183
Stasov, Vladimir, 232–38, 337
Stefan Bathory, King of Poland, 52
Steiner, Rudolf, 340
Stendhal, 149
Stolypin, Peter A., 211, 221–22,
    287–89, 291, 294
St. Petersburg (Petrograd, Leningrad),
    131, 142, 144, 153, 158–59, 161,
    165, 172–81, 208–13, 219–20,
    225–26, 236–40, 252, 257–61,
    271, 323, 339, 341
    Anna moves capital to, 102, 104–5

Finnish border and, 257, 376
renamed Petrograd, 295
Peter the Great builds, 84–85, 87–90, 95, 98
Revolution of 1905–6 and, 282–85
Revolution of 1917 and Civil War and, 298, 300–302, 305, 311–12, 314, 341
WW I and, 294, 298
WW II and, siege of (1941–44), 379–80, 384–86, 391
St. Petersburg Academy of Arts, 105, 130–31, 173, 237–39, 261
St. Petersburg Conservatory, 231, 233–34
St. Petersburg Philharmonic Society, 174, 338
St. Petersburg Polytechnic Institute, 216, 346
St. Petersburg Technological Institute, 159, 215–16, 228–29
St. Petersburg University, 197
Strategic Arms Limitation Treaties (SALT, 1972, 1979), 445
Stravinskii, Igor, 335, 339
strikes, 213, 226, 283–85, 294
Stroganov, Pavel, 143
Sumarokov, Alexander, 105, 126, 128
Sun Yat-sen, 332
Supreme Economic Council, 305, 324–25, 330, 349, 353, 357
Supreme Executive Commission, 205
Supreme Privy Council, 99, 102
Supreme Soviet, 450, 453–54
Surikov, Vasilii, 239
Suvorov, Alexander, 134–35, 140
Sviatopolk-Mirskii, Prince Petr, 282
Sviatopolk "the Cursed," Grand Prince of Kiev Rus, 16
Sviatoslav I, Grand Prince of Kiev Rus, 7
Sviatoslav II, Grand Prince of Kiev, 17
Sweden, 39, 58, 67, 90, 93, 98, 146, 286
early wars vs., 27, 51, 54
treaty of 1609 and, 57
war of 1700–21, 82–87, 92, 95–96
war of 1741–43, 102–3

war of 1787, 133
WW II and, 378
Swordbearers, 26–27

Table of Ranks, 92
Tacitus, 114
Tadjikistan, 329
Tadzhiks, 63
Tambov revolt, 318
Tamerlane, 23–24, 34
Tamm, Igor, 406
Tarkovsky, Andre, 426–27
Tatars, 21, 37–39, 42–43, 47, 49, 61–63, 67, 77, 111, 123, 263, 288, 327, 400
Tatarstan, 1, 453
taxes and tariffs, 63, 64, 83, 93, 98, 110, 158, 211, 215, 220
Tchaikovsky, Ilya, 215, 235
Tchaikovsky, Peter, xvii, 177, 230–32, 234–37, 235, 337
Teheran Conference, 388–89
Temporary Regulations of 1881, 273
Temriuk, Prince of Circassia, 51
terrorism (pre-1917), 203–5, 211, 227, 260, 279, 281
Terror of 1936–38, 358–63, 366–68, 399, 402, 420
Teutonic Knights, 26–29, 38
Theodore, Saint, 18
Theognostos, Metropolitan of Kiev, 23
Theophanes the Greek, 26, 32
Third Section, 156–57, 159, 165, 172, 178, 184, 191, 198, 203, 205, 252
Thucydides, 5
Time of Troubles, 56–58, 60, 84
Timmerman, Frans, 77
Timoshenko, Marshal Semyon, 376, 378–80
Tito, Josip Broz, 391, 401, 433
Tokhtamysh, Khan, 23–24
Tolstoi, Count I.M., 214–15
Tolstoi, Peter, 91
Tolstoy, Alexei, 342
Tolstoy, Lev Nikolaevich (Leo), xvii, 106, 148, 230, 240, 243–48, 246, 338, 416
Tolstoy, Sofya Bers, 245
Tomskii, Mikhail, 324

Tomsk Polytechnical Institute, 216
Toon, Konstantin, 160
township courts, 195
Transcaucasia, 146, 167–68, 263,
    265–66, 450, 455
Transcaucasian Federation, 316,
    327–28
Transsiberian Railroad, 217, 220, 269,
    276–77, 282, 284, 306
Trepov, General Fyodor, 204
Tretyakov, Pavel, 238
Trivolis, Michael, 46–47
Trotsky, Leon, 280, 285, 291, 295,
    301, 303, 305–11, 307, 314, 316,
    318, 321–25, 343, 345, 358–60,
    364
Tsaritsyn, Battle of (1918), 309. See
    also Stalingrad, Battle of
Tsarskoe Selo (Detskoe Selo, Pushkin),
    159, 348
Tsarskoe Selo Lycée, 161, 165, 176
Tsvetaeva, Marina, 342–43
Tukhachevskii, Marshal M.N., 314–15,
    318, 359, 373
Tupolev, Andrei, 421
Turgenev, Ivan, 112, 183–85, 196, 230,
    240–41, 340, 417
Turkestan, 239, 327
Turkey, 316. See also Ottoman Empire
Turkic people, 2, 5–6, 168, 266, 329
Turkmenistan, 408
Tver, 22, 33, 42, 67

U-2 flight, 437, 442
Ukraine, 1, 29, 135, 139, 243, 252–53,
    258, 261–62, 271
    Civil War and, 312–16, 326–27
    collapse of USSR and, 450, 452, 458
    Cossacks revolt (1648), 65, 66
    Hetmanate, 67–68, 73–74, 77, 86,
        93, 111
    Revolution of 1905 and, 284, 289
    USSR and, 326–27, 329, 352,
        365–67, 408
    WW I and, 306, 309
    WW II and, 379, 380, 383, 390–91,
        393
Ukrainian Church, 29, 68–70, 126
Ukrainian language, 262, 329

Ukrainian Rada, 302, 304, 312
Ulanova, Galina, 423
Ulbricht, Walter, 434, 440
Uniates, 65
Union of Liberation, 282
Union of Salvation, 153
Union of Soviet Socialist Republics
    (Soviet Union, USSR)
    boundaries of, at end of Civil War,
        315–17
    collapse of, xv, xviii, 447, 452–53
    Constitution of 1936, 366
    creation of, 310–12, 319–20, 324,
        328–31
    federal structure of, 326, 365–67
    map of, in WW II, *xxiv*
Union of St. Michael the Archangel,
    275
Union of the Russian People, 285
Union of Welfare, 153
Union of Zemstvos, 298
United Nations, 389, 436
United States, 152, 186, 232, 260, 319,
    320, 348–49
    Cold War and, 409, 429–30, 437,
        442–46
    Russian Civil War and, 308, 314
    WW I and, 306
    WW II and, 388
Urals, 1, 53, 70, 110, 111, 123–24,
    215, 222, 312, 327, 352, 368, 380,
    394
Uvarov, Count S.S., 159–61, 201
Uzbek, Khan, 21–22
Uzbekistan, 329, 408
Uzbek khanates, 266

Vasilii I, Grand Prince of Moscow, 33
Vasilii II, Grand Prince of Moscow,
    33–34, 36
Vasilii III, Grand Prince of Moscow,
    37, 47–48
Vasilii IV (Shuiskii), Tsar, 57
Vasilii Iur'evich "the Squint-eyed," 33
Vavilov, Nikolai, 348–49, 415, 420
veche (popular assembly), 11, 13
Vereshchagin, Vasilii, 239
Vernadskii, Vladimir, 347, 349
Viazemskii, Prince Peter, 179

Vienna
  siege of 1529, 38
  siege of 1683, 77
Vienna, Congress of, 150, 253
Vietnam, 20, 435–36, 443–45
Vikings, 3–4, 12
Vladimir I, Saint, Grand Prince of Kiev
  Rus, 7–8, 16, 45
Vladimir II Monomakh, Grand Prince
  of Kiev Rus, 12
Vladimir, Principality of, 12, 14, *14*,
  20–24
Volga Bulgaria, 1, 7, 20–21
Volga Tatars, 263, 268–69
Voltaire, 105, 107–8, 114, 125
Volunteer Army, 306, 308
Volynskii, Artemii, 102–3
Vonifat'ev, Stefan, 68
Voroshilov, Kliment, 309, 363, 366,
  375, 394, 401
Voznesenskii, Nikolai, 396
Vsevolod, Grand Prince of Kiev, 12, 17
Vyshinskii, Andrei, 360
Vysotskii, Vladimir, 426

Wagner, Richard, 233, 337
War Communism, 310, 316–18
Warsaw Pact, 439
Warsaw Polytechnical Institute, 216
Warsaw uprising (1944), 391
Westernizers, 95, 162, 164, 181–83
Whistler, G.W., 159
White armies, 306, 308–9, 312–15,
  326–28, 342, 346
Wielhorski, Count Matvei, 174–75
Wielhorski, Count Mikhail, 174–75,
  179, 231
Winter Palace, 88, 104–5, 144, 176,
  208, 283, 303
Winter War, 376–77
Witte, Count Sergei, 211, 216, 220,
  269, 272, 275–77, 277, 279,
  285–87, 346

Wladyslaw, Prince of Poland, 57
Wolff, Georg Christian, 107
Women's Battalion of Death,
  303
World of Art, 210, 334, 337–38
Wrangel, Baron Peter, 314–15
Writers' Union, 415–17

Yalta Conference, 389
yasak (tribute), 49, 67, 111
Yedigei, Emir, 47
Yeltsin, Boris, 308, 447–48, 450–58
Yermak the Cossack, 53
Yevtushenko, Evgenii, 424
Youth Scientific-Technical Groups,
  449
Yudenich, Nikolai, 297
Yugoslavia, 389, 391, 432–33,
  437

Zamiatin, Evgenii, 346, 414
Zarutskii, Ivan, 58
Zasulich, Vera, 204
zemstvos, 193–95, 200, 202, 206, 219,
  262, 273, 281–82, 289, 297
Zhdanov, Andrei, 363–64, 394, 416,
  421–22
Zheliabov, Alexander, 206
Zhirinovsky, Vladimir, 457
Zhukov, Georgii, 379–80, 386,
  390–91, 395, 397, 401–2, 438
Zhukovskii, Vasilii, 174–76, 178–81,
  261–62
Zinoviev, Grigorii, 303, 310–11, 314,
  321–23, 331, 358
Zionists, 260, 271, 411
Ziuganov, Gennadii, 455, 457
Zoe Paleologue, Grand Princess of
  Moscow (wife of Ivan III), 43
Zola, Emile, 241
Zoshchenko, Mikhail, 421–22
Zosima, Saint, 30
Zubatov, Sergei, 282

Other Titles in the Series (continued from page iii)

A Concise History of Greece, 2nd Edition
RICHARD CLOGG

A Concise History of Hungary
MIKLÓS MOLNÁR, TRANSLATED BY ANNA MAGYAR

A Concise History of Modern India, 2nd Edition
BARBARA D. METCALF AND THOMAS R. METCALF

A Concise History of Italy
CHRISTOPHER DUGGAN

A Concise History of Mexico, 2nd Edition
BRIAN R. HAMNETT

A Concise History of New Zealand
PHILIPPA MEIN SMITH

A Concise History of Poland, 2nd Edition
JERZY LUKOWSKI AND HUBERT ZAWADZKI

A Concise History of Portugal, 2nd Edition
DAVID BIRMINGHAM

A Concise History of South Africa, 2nd Edition
ROBERT ROSS

A Concise History of Spain
WILLIAM D. PHILLIPS JR. AND CARLA RAHN PHILLIPS

A Concise History of Sweden
NEIL KENT

A Concise History of Wales
GERAINT H. JENKINS